FOREIGN TONGUES

FOREIGN TONGUES

VICTORIAN LANGUAGE LEARNING
AND THE SHAPING OF MODERN IRELAND

Phyllis Gaffney

UNIVERSITY COLLEGE DUBLIN PRESS
PREAS CHOLÁISTE OLLSCOILE BHAILE ÁTHA CLIATH
2024

First published 2024
by University College Dublin Press
UCD Humanities Institute, Room H103,
Belfield,
Dublin 4

www.ucdpress.ie

ISBN 978-17-3-90863-12

CIP data available from the British Library

The right of the author to be identified as the author of her work has been asserted by her

Typeset in Dublin by Gough Typesetting Limited
Text design by Lyn Davies
Printed in England on acid-free paper by
CPI Antony Rowe, Chippenham, Wiltshire

For Cormac

Contents

List of Tables   ix

List of Illustrations   xi

Preface   xiii

Acknowledgements   xvii

PART ONE: CONTEXT

1   Irish Universities: Why all the Languages?   3
    Language Study, The Victorians and Ireland   3
    Catholic University of Ireland, University College Dublin (UCD)   7
    Why Study Modern Languages?   10
    Polarities: Pen/Tongue, Monastery/Marketplace   12
    Language Study in England and Scotland: A Slow Tilt to the Modern   15
    Languages in Ireland's Universities: A Different Perspective   18

2   Language, Creed, Identity   24
    Ireland's Shifting Languages: Irish, English, Latin   24
    Continental Irish Colleges: A Loquacious Diaspora   27
    French in Early Nineteenth-Century Seminaries   33
    Catholic Missionary Colleges: Euntes Ergo Docete Omnes Gentes [Going Forth
       Therefore Teach Ye All Peoples]   35
    Linguistically Agile Clergy   36
    Translation: Church Triumphant, Nation Resurgent   39

PART TWO: LAYING THE FOUNDATIONS

3   Varieties and Milestones of Language Education   47
    Diverse Models of Schooling   48
    Language in Post-Primary Schools: French Connections   51
    The French College and University College, Blackrock   55
    Recognition, Regulations and Repercussions   59
    Modern Languages Versus Classics in Irish and English Schools   62
    Matriculation, Gender, Class and Language Study   69
    Women Outside the Walls: Erasmus-Cum-TEFL Ante Diem   74

4   Ancient Celtic: Respectable Roots   82
    Irish in Victorian Universities: A Catalogue of Challenges   83
    Celtic Philology   89
    Rationales for the Study of Irish: Sectarian Contests   94
    Antiquarian Rationales: Some Pre-Famine Irish Grammars   96

5   The Modern Irish Battleground   102
    The Gaelic League and Identity Politics   102
    The Gaelic League and Other Modern Languages   109
    The Gaelic League and the Language Classroom   113

PART THREE: WITHIN THE GROVES OF ACADEME

6   Profiles and Patterns: Modern Language Professors   123
     Early Appointments at the CUI (UCD)   124
     What patterns emerge from these and other such profiles?   130

7   Home-Grown Language Professors   156
     Irish-born modern linguists   156
     Irish professors in the Gaelic Revival   159
     Pioneering Women Professors of Modern Languages   170
     Political allegiances in a changing university landscape   185

PART FOUR: BEYOND THE VICTORIANS

8   Shifting Language Perspectives   193
     Regulatory Frameworks (1922–1970s)   194
     North and South: Divergent Policies, Divergent Cultures   205
     Shifting Contexts of Language Learning Since the 1970s   209

9   CODA   222

     Notes   228

     Appendix 1: Timeline of Events, Institutions, Policies   303

     Appendix 2: Tables   311

     List of Works Consulted   319

     Index   347

List of Tables

Table 1   Professors of Modern Languages in Ireland's Universities (1776–1921)   311

Table 2   Professors of Celtic/Irish in Ireland's Universities (1800–1921)   314

Table 3   NUI's First Women Professors (Modern Languages, including Irish)   316

Table 4   Numbers of candidates taking classics at Leaving Certificate (1980–2022)   317

Table 5   Numbers of candidates taking Languages at Leaving Certificate (2022)   318

List of Illustrations

1.1   Trinity College, Dublin (DU/TCD)
1.2   St Patrick's College, Maynooth
1.3   Catholic University of Ireland, Dublin (CUI) (1943)
1.4   Queen's College, Belfast (QCB)
1.5   Queen's College, Cork (QCC)
1.6   Queen's College, Galway (QCG)
1.7   Royal University, Dublin (pre-1910)
2.1   Queen Elizabeth I
2.2   Cardinal Paul Cullen, archbishop of Dublin
2.3   John Henry Newman, 1844
3.1   Ballinaboy School (1850s)
3.2   Nano Nagle with Pupils, 1809
3.3   Ad for Portarlington Educational Institution, 1848
3.4   Two school ads (Pas-de-Calais and Laurel Hill, Limerick, 1845)
3.5   Ad for Convent of St Louis Boarding School, Monaghan, 1866
3.6   French College prospectus, 1860
3.7   French College, Blackrock, 1866: 'Boney Boys'
3.8   Sacred Heart Convent, Leeson Street, garden with cow, 1886–7
3.9   Ad for Alberta School, Antrim Road, Belfast, 1888
3.10 French College, Blackrock: Castle students, 1892
3.11 Letter from Agnes Ryan (Ursuline boarding school, Antwerp), 1907
4.1   O'Donovan and O'Curry
4.2   William Neilson
5.1   Douglas Hyde in his prime
5.2   John Pentland Mahaffy, classicist, ancient historian, Provost, TCD 1914–19
5.3   Douglas Hyde, Professor of Modern Irish, UCD, & first President of Ireland
6.1   Peter le Page Renouf, CUI
6.2   Abbé Félix Schürr, CUI
6.3   Édouard Cadic, RUI Dublin, in Iveagh Gardens, 1902
6.4   Tombstone of Édouard Cadic (d.1914)
6.4a Tombstone medallion of Édouard Cadic
6.5   Evasio Radice, Italian and Spanish, TCD
6.6   Testimonials of Basilio Angeli, Italian and Spanish, TCD (1857)
6.7   Augustus Bensbach, QCG
6.8   Tombstone of Augustus Bensbach, QCG (d.1868)
6.9   Tombstone of Raymond de Véricour, QCC (d.1879)
6.10 Charles Geisler, QCG and RUI Galway
6.11 Valentine Steinberger, RUI Galway
7.1   Michael O'Hickey, Maynooth
7.2   Tomás Ó Máille, UCG
7.3   Frederick William O'Connell, QUB

7.4   The 'Nine Graces': First women graduates, RUI, 1884
7.5   Early woman graduate, RUI Cork, c.1890
7.6   Mary Ryan, UCC: First woman professor in Ireland
7.7   Mary Macken, UCD
7.8   Professor Emily Anderson as a child, with mother, sister, governess, c.1901
7.9   Mary Kate Ryan, UCD 1902
7.10   Agnes O'Farrelly [Úna Ní Fhaircheallaigh], UCD 1904
7.11   Max Freund, QUB, 1979 (aged 100)
7.12   Gilbert Waterhouse, TCD and QUB
7.13   Roger Chauviré, UCD
8.1   Ten Graces of Belfast

Preface

Ireland's engagement with language study, a centuries-old pursuit on the island, crystallised in a peculiar way during the second half of the nineteenth century, with enormous consequences for Irish people's sense of identity. The fortunes of language learning in Victorian times may sound like a specific topic but, when placed in context, it will illuminate social, economic and cultural developments spanning several centuries. Victorian universities witnessed significant changes as modern languages began to take their place beside the classics; access to learning was extended to new groups – including women – and cultural nationalism peaked. The pace, impact and scale of these combined changes helped to change the face of Ireland.

This book was prompted by a casual question from my colleague Síofra Pierse, during the pandemic winter of 2020: 'Since when has French been taught at UCD?' The short answer seemed obvious. When John Henry Newman's fledgling Catholic University (later to become University College Dublin) opened in 1854, lectures in French were on the curriculum, along with Italian and Spanish; German was added in the following year. The long answer – which considers contextual questions ('Why?', 'Under what circumstances?', 'Taught by whom?') – unearthed some half-forgotten curiosities of Victorian Ireland as well as highlighting the country's all-too-familiar fault-lines. Consistent patterns emerged: the Catholic University was not alone in hiring professors of modern languages. They all did. Things were very different in the universities of mid-nineteenth-century England.

Clearly, the long answer had to explain Ireland's education culture, including the place of languages in schools and the position of the native vernacular at all levels. Broadening the scope meant that language learning became, to borrow a phrase from Berkeley sociologist Arlie Russell Hochschild, a 'keyhole issue'[1] highlighting certain aspects of societal change in the past and prompting reflections on Irish self-perception today, as the rabbit-hole of Brexit yawns.

The notion of peering at Irish history *through the language glass* may conjure up an echo of an English Victorian literary masterpiece. And the words 'Victorian' and 'Ireland' sit awkwardly together now that we have moved so far from that era. How far? Ireland has a long, fascinating, convoluted cultural history, but the structures of modern life in the Republic and in Northern Ireland, characterised by coherent political, administrative and educational institutions, were largely solidified during the late nineteenth century. As a result, Victorian Ireland's assumptions about languages, reflecting the values of its time, still retain some relevance.

Paying particular attention to living European languages and contrasting features of Ireland's education history with the English experience,[2] the narrative addresses several questions. Why were Ireland's elite schools providing classes in French, German and other modern languages long before they hired any teachers of Irish? Why did Irish universities prioritise modern languages decades before their English and Scottish counterparts? Why were classical Latin and Greek regarded as more valuable? How did Indian Civil Service language examinations affect ambitious Victorian Irishmen?

The main thrust of the narrative concentrates on Queen Victoria's reign (1837–1901), a crucial time for language-related decisions and developments. It also takes account of factors both upstream and downstream of this chosen period. Cultural history can never be strictly date-bound. While parts of the story will already be familiar, the assembly of parts, placing continental-language study alongside the special position of Irish-language study, may throw a different light on Ireland's cultures, vernaculars and identities.

Scholarly language study interacts with vernacular essentialist forces. Language history cuts across large familiar themes – politics and religion, class and gender, Reformation and Counter-Reformation, empire and philology. The history of language learning shows how institutional and regulatory changes can create opportunities for powerful cultural forces to flourish. While Trinity College Dublin is justly proud of setting up the world's first chairs of modern languages (French and German, Italian and Spanish) in 1776, the story told in these pages reframes the picture. It explores how European languages were promoted by Ireland's mid-century university foundations (the 1849 Queen's Colleges in Belfast, Cork and Galway, and Newman's 1854 Catholic University in Dublin), and how those four colleges, during their later incarnation as the Royal University of Ireland (1880–1908), went still further in embedding continental language study as mandatory for access to higher learning.

Smaller-scale phenomena, emblematic of general trends, will also be considered: professorial profiles, petty rivalries, controversies. The book foregrounds modern-language professors in Victorian and Edwardian Ireland because individuals can drive cultural change. How did three of these appointments – a (Tuscan) professor of Italian and Spanish in Trinity, a (Huguenot) professor of French and German in Cork, and a (clerical) Maynooth professor of Irish – lead to legal dismissal, or attempted dismissal? Why was it impossible to graduate from the Queens' Colleges without taking a course in French or German? Why did so many of the NUI's earliest language professors happen to be women? Why, in the same period, were Trinity and Queen's University Belfast less inclined to appoint women to such chairs?

When I started this project in 2020, Brexit was still headline news. The book's many comparisons with English educational culture, an inevitable consequence of the entangled histories of Britain and Ireland, showed up deep-seated linguistic and cultural divisions between Ireland and her nearest neighbour. At the same time, enduring cultural affinities between Ireland and continental Europe, through linguistic and religious connections, also emerge as major strands in the story. Anything but isolationist, the most ardent proponents of Irish as a national project enjoyed it as a language among other languages. Douglas Hyde and Frederick O'Connell excelled in many languages, ancient and modern. Patrick Pearse observed innovative language-teaching methods in Belgian classrooms. Liam Ó Briain was a republican jailbird and professor of French who translated foreign plays into Irish.

Centuries ago, when English was 'a practically unknown (and wholly unprestigious) vernacular',[3] it was not much use beyond Dover. Today, the traffic in language learning flows in the opposite direction: English is the world's *lingua franca*. The book concludes by discussing how the language-heavy legacy of Victorian Ireland has fared since 1922, and why Irish Anglophones might still bother to learn foreign languages in the twenty-first century.

The subtitle consciously echoes two collections of essays with the same title.[4] *The*

Shaping of Modern Ireland, edited by Conor Cruise O'Brien in 1960, focussed on influential individuals who exemplified the formative and vibrant period of Irish history between 1891 and 1916. Deliberately using the same title, the second volume, edited by Eugenio Biagini and Daniel Mulhall, appeared in 2016. The reprise showcased some shifting perspectives in Irish historiography. It aimed to compensate for the gender imbalance in the first volume (where all of the essays concerned influential males and all but one of the contributing authors were men) and to identify other enduring phenomena from the same period such as the political and social role of the Gaelic Athletic Association or the success of the Guinness family business. Several contributions re-assessed the same individuals from the 1960 book. New generations of historians use new sources to frame the past in new ways. *Foreign Tongues: Victorian Language Learning and the Shaping of Modern Ireland* offers the reader a less prominent cast of characters and a slightly different frame for reading the cultural influence of late Victorian Ireland.

Acknowledgements

This book owes its genesis to the isolating circumstances of late 2020, when Ireland was sheltering under its first winter lockdown. Confinement at home allowed hours of unfettered time to absorb myself in the search for answers to the myriad questions that were forming in my head. As the Covid-19 pandemic dragged on, with library access closed for months, the hunting of source materials from home through other channels became part of daily life. Zoom lectures and seminars brought priceless information to the kitchen; couriers and postmen delivered books to the door; volumes long stored on top shelves became essential reading. On daily walks within the permitted radius, I listened to recordings of Victorian novels. I came to appreciate in a new way the growing numbers of scholars who generously share the fruits of their research on the web, allowing more and more sources, primary as well as secondary, to be digitally accessible. In our Victorian drawing-room, I could summon up not only scores of online entries in biographical dictionaries and scholarly articles, but also a wealth of Victorian voices: letters from Irish missionaries in far-flung corners of the globe; the thoughts on language teaching of Oxbridge dons; the poetic feats (in French and Latin) of senior students at the French College, Blackrock. Without the work of the scholars and technicians who make such primary sources available, the research would have been less enthralling and its findings less vivid.

I am indebted to the authors of institutional histories that have been constant guides, including McDowell and Webb for Trinity, Corish for Maynooth, Moody and Beckett for Belfast, McCartney for Dublin, Murphy for Cork, and Tadhg Foley's edited volume for Galway. In the latter volume, Rosaleen O'Neill's chapter on modern languages has been particularly illuminating. Biographies of individual professors, such as Stanford and McDowell on J. P. Mahaffy, or Nic Congáil for Agnes O'Farrelly, have also been invaluable. The work of Nicola McLelland has been a reliable source for the history of language learning and teaching in other jurisdictions.

With colleagues, friends and family members tolerant enough to lend me an ear, I shared enthusiastic bulletins about my latest discoveries. I am grateful to every one of them for humouring my obsession, particularly to those who took the trouble to drop by to the hall door, masked and socially distanced, extending a gloved hand with volumes that I had or had not solicited: Derval Conroy, Anna Farmar, Michael Gaffney, Áine Hyland, Corinna Salvadori Lonergan, Nóirín Ní Nuadháin and Julia Tomkin. As lockdown restrictions gradually eased, and it was possible to socialise again, conversations and chance suggestions sent me down fruitful tracks. I compared notes with Jackie Uí Chionna about her latest book exploring the double life of Emily Anderson, Galway's first professor of German. Among those who answered emails, sent material or lent books to sate my curiosity, during and since the pandemic, my warmest thanks go to: Joe Brady, Věra Čapková, John Curran, Gerry Dawe, John Dillon, Jennifer FitzGerald, Attracta Halpin, Eric Haywood, Gisela Holfter, Iseult and Patrick Honohan, Margaret Kelleher, Gabrielle McCann, Des MacHale, Liam MacMathúna, Nicola McLelland, Gerry Murphy, Grace Neville, Eiléan Ní Chuilleanáin, Léan Ní Chuilleanáin, Órla Ní Chuilleanáin, Meidhbhín

Ní Úrdail, Catherine O'Brien, Brian Ó Catháin, Daragh O'Connell, Anne O'Connor, Eunan O'Halpin, Fran O'Rourke.

After university libraries re-opened, it was possible to bridge the gaps needed to support or nuance the argument. I discovered a raft of first-rate monographs and edited volumes published in modern Irish history since my first degree, half a century ago. I am indebted to scholars whose detailed studies have enabled the present synthesis, which will hopefully display some connections and wider resonances that can be derived from their work. My dual focus, the history of continental language study alongside the history of Irish-language study, charts its way through their territory, trespassing on their fields while at the same time foregrounding the perennial concerns of the history of language learning. These include rationales for learning foreign languages, styles of teaching and assessing, tensions between the spoken and the written word, languages and power, language learning and gender.

The peculiar conditions under which the research was undertaken also shape its outcome, its quirks and oddities. It incorporates some findings from my previous work on the teaching of French in the early 1900s at UCD, where one of my grandaunts, Mary Kate O'Kelly (*née* Ryan), had run the department during the First World War. Over 20 years ago I helped to digitise (with Meliosa O'Malley and other family members) the Edwardian correspondence of Mary Kate and her seven sisters, who had all been engaged in modern language study. Other sources, happened on by chance, led to further revelations.

For me, the lockdown became an opening-up of Ireland's past, particularly the history of the Irish language. The central place of the seventeenth century in that language history brought back memories of a course on Irish cultural history in the 1600s, that I had taken as an undergraduate at UCD, with the late Margaret MacCurtain. My interest was sharpened when I heard she had written her doctoral thesis on an influential Counter-Reformation Dominican from a bardic family in County Kerry, who was a diplomat for the Portuguese Crown and who, like countless other Irish Roman Catholic clerics, had been ordained in Europe.

The research clarified other features of my own education, such as the traditional manner in which I had been taught six different languages at school, before Latin was abandoned by the NUI as a matriculation requirement, and even my doctoral research in medieval French literature. Thus, I came to discover how much my own training in languages and language teaching, and the debates on methodology that persisted throughout my career in third-level education, had been influenced by the long reach of the nineteenth century. Such epiphanies kept me absorbed.

The book's use of primary sources was greatly facilitated by archival staff, who were unfailingly helpful, going out of their way to accommodate my requests – even during the pandemic. For detailed answers to emails and specific queries, I am obliged to Clare Foley (Blackrock College Archives), Catriona Mulcahy and John Rooney (University College Cork Special Collections and Archives), and Noelle Dowling (Dublin Diocesan archives). Once access to their holdings resumed, I was kindly assisted by Jessica Cunningham (Blackrock College Archives), by Maura Tierney and Darren Fallon (National University of Ireland archives), and by the numerous staff members who facilitated me on my various visits to the Reading Room of the National Archives in Bishop Street. Further afield, Markus Enzenauer kindly delved into Mannheim's municipal archives on my behalf. The librarians in Trinity College Dublin's Libraries and Reading Room have been extremely helpful, as have those in University College Dublin's Special Collections and Archives; the National Library of Ireland's Main Reading Room and Manuscripts Reading Room; University College Cork's Boole Library Special Collections and Archives; and the Special Collections and Archives Room of the James Hardiman Library at the University of Galway. Lynn Brady, genealogist at Dublin Cemeteries, was prompt to answer my queries; and Conor Dodd, historian to Glasnevin Cemetery, sent precious information regarding the memorial to UCD's Professor Édouard Cadic; Maryann O'Connor, at the IBVM (Loreto) Irish Province Archives, confirmed a biographical detail for Nell Ryan.

Colleagues, friends and relatives commented on chapters and generously took the trouble to read a draft complete manuscript in the midst of other demands on their time. In particular, I thank Joe Farrell for his encouraging and incisive comments from Glasgow; John and Eithne FitzGerald for their wise suggestions and statistical wizardry; and Áine Hyland, to whom I turned on more than one occasion, for insights drawn from her expertise in education history. Nearer home, family members have been enthusiastic and constructive in their reactions to the draft: I am very grateful to my daughters, Léan and Órla Ní Chuilleanáin, their aunt Eiléan Ní Chuilleanáin, and my husband and constant research assistant, Cormac Ó Cuilleanáin.

For their kind advice and assistance when sourcing and clearing illustrations and reproductions, I thank the following: Marie Boran, Geraldine Curtin, Kieran Hoare and Jackie Uí Chionna (University of Galway); Liam Brady, Selina Collard, Evelyn Flanagan and Judith Harford (UCD); Elizabeth Bray (British Museum); Marco Cazzulo (Genoa); Damien Corridan, Ciaran Higgins and Ursula Mitchel (QUB); Patricia Dunlop (granddaughter of Professor Gilbert Waterhouse); Glenn Dunne and Berni Metcalfe (NLI); Barbara Ennis and John O'Farrell (Alexandra College, Dublin); Marcus Enzenauer (Mannheim); Stephen Ferguson (An Post); Rachel Granville and John Rooney (UCC); Emily Green (National Portrait Gallery, London); Melissa Kean (Houston); Sr Rosarie Lordan (Nano Nagle Place, Cork); Pat McSweeney (St Finbarr's Cemetery, Cork); Linda Murphy (Gill Books Ireland); Emma Stewart (Mount Anville, Dublin).

My thanks, finally, are due to UCD Press for agreeing to take on the publication, and to Noelle Moran and Órla Carr for their most valuable editorial support, and the Press team more generally. Thank you to Shane Gough and Jane Rogers also from UCD Press. I am beholden to my eagle-eyed daughter, Léan, for helping me to navigate an ocean of footnotes for formatting. Last but by no means least, I am indebted to the external reviewers, Professors Gisela Holfter and Nicola McLelland, who endorsed the submitted draft of the book and sent many constructive comments and suggestions.

A special thanks to UCD's School of Languages, Cultures and Linguistics, to UCD's College of Arts and Humanities, and to the NUI Publications Grant Committee, who have all contributed most generously to the cost of publication.

Specialist readers of occasional details in the book may find some of its claims to be redundant or even outrageous. That is a risk I'm running, as a modern language practitioner with a background in medieval cultural history. Errors, omissions and misrepresentations are my own.

Phyllis Gaffney
Dublin, February 2024

PART ONE: CONTEXT

CHAPTER I

Irish Universities: Why all the Languages?

When Latin and Greek were almost the only written languages of civilized man, it is manifest that they must have furnished the subjects of all liberal education. The question therefore is wholly changed, since the growth of a complete literature in other languages. [Thomas Arnold, 1834][1]

The status of foreign languages in Ireland was in some ways and at some times very different to that in England. [Nicola McLelland, 2014][2]

LANGUAGE STUDY, THE VICTORIANS AND IRELAND

During the second half of the nineteenth century, further education in the United Kingdom of Great Britain and Ireland experienced important changes, but these changes were not the same everywhere. It was a period of lengthy and intensive scrutiny, at all levels of education, by Royal Commissions, in England, Wales, Scotland and Ireland. Historians have charted a development from the older model of liberal universities as bastions of privilege, serving to perpetuate established elites by means of a narrow range of disciplines, towards the drivers of social mobility, offering professional or vocational training to a more diverse student intake, that they were gradually to become.[3] Within that slow shift, one unmistakable change was the increasing attention paid to the study of modern languages, most obviously in the upper echelons of society. The pressures that had favoured modern-language education were formulated, 50 years into Queen Victoria's reign, by Charles Colbeck, Assistant Master at Harrow, when he delivered a lecture in Cambridge in 1887:[4]

Sixty years ago, I do not believe that any public school taught French except as an extra, like drawing and dancing, and I do not believe that any taught German at all. A liberal education was an education for a class born into a world of already secured positions, a world of sinecurists and courtiers, of place-holders and pluralists, of broad acres and fat livings [...]. But the world outside the schools was widening. Science was already knocking at their doors. Commerce and industry, travel and geography, the inclusion in the public school system of the middle classes, the increase of population, the reform of the public services, competitive examinations, the Napoleonic wars, the writings of Goethe and Schiller, a German Prince Consort, international exhibitions, international trade, the struggle for existence and survival of the fittest, these and all that they implied combined to raise the study of modern languages from the status of an accomplishment, or a commercial art, on a level let us say with book-keeping, to rank as an integral portion of a liberal education.

Things were different across the Irish Sea. Unsurprisingly, for a lecture delivered to a Cambridge audience in 1887, Colbeck omits another significant pressure for change: expanding educational opportunities for women. Cambridge's women students had to wait until 1948 for the privilege of being allowed to graduate, whereas the Royal University of Ireland (RUI) had been conferring degrees on its female students since 1884. The RUI – a somewhat neglected chapter in the complicated history of Ireland's education structures – emerges as the route to university education for most of the educated elite in late Victorian Ireland. This will be an important part of our narrative because, as we shall see, modern-language study was one of the young disciplines where Irish women did particularly well, as students and as academics.[5]

The gender difference may be particularly striking to the modern reader, but it is not the only distinctive strand in the story of language study in Victorian Ireland. Other strands also reveal disparities between Ireland and its neighbour even when we find similarities on the surface. For example, we shall note differences in the appreciation of classical languages, and how the balance of ancient and modern languages played out in a different way at post-primary level. While in both jurisdictions social class is a determinant of who studies foreign languages, there are other significant nuances to be noted between the two islands. Changes in government policy had an undeniable impact on language study, but – partly due to different demographics and distinct education traditions – these changes affected the countries in different ways.

Although it was part of the same United Kingdom, then, the pace and impact of change in Ireland were quite dissimilar to what emerged in Britain. More fundamentally, there were crucial features separating the cultures of the two islands, each of which reposed on a rich subsoil of attitudes, existing knowledge and practices. Thus, for historical and cultural reasons, modern-language study was given prominence in all of Ireland's universities some decades before it became the norm for universities on the larger island. This chronological lead partly reflects a different pattern of language diversity.

We shall be exploring why there was less resistance, in Victorian Ireland, to encroachment on the dominant educational position held by ancient languages, and less anxiety than in England's liberal education establishment about the risk of this pre-eminence being eroded by the arrival of modern languages. Traditional linguistic ties with Counter-Reformation Europe, forged in continental Irish colleges during penal times, persisted. As we shall see, influential Catholic clerics and utilitarian educationalists alike believed in the value of teaching foreign languages to a steadily growing middle class population, while cultural nationalism encouraged openness to languages, cultures and ideas beyond Britain. All of these factors helped to make space for modern-language learning to prosper.

Cultural divergences were inevitably compounded by divergent political histories, and the period ended with the extraordinary and dramatic inclusion, in Ireland, of another modern language for study: the island's native vernacular. No account of Victorian Ireland's embrace of modern European languages could omit the late-Victorian Irish revival. The book will discuss how early Victorian rationales for learning Irish, whether antiquarian or confessional, morphed into the study of the contemporary vernacular for its own sake. The early professors of Celtic Studies in the Queen's Colleges give way to the Gaelic League champions of the turn of the century, who were in tune with the latest developments in modern-language teaching in Europe and elsewhere. In effect, the story will chronicle another time-lag: how modern European languages and literatures were embedded in Ireland's educational fabric before the study of Irish was admitted.

The first two parts of this book chart these social, cultural and historical strands that made the setting fertile for language study. Part Three ('In the groves of academe') takes the reader into the world of the Victorian Irish university itself, and considers the first modern-languages professors, who were mostly continental Europeans. While some of them are shadowy figures, others have left their mark as individual scholars or as litigants in cases of employment dismissal. Their profiles reveal patterns of provenance, religious allegiance, research and teaching approaches that are indicative of contemporary trends elsewhere, and of the prevailing interest in comparative philology that characterised the height of European imperialism. The following chapter, Chapter Seven, discusses the specifically Irish turn taken by the professoriate during the closing decades of Queen Victoria's reign, considering a new generation of Irish-born language professors, in continental languages and in Irish, as well as the cluster of women appointed to chairs in modern languages in the early years of the National University of Ireland, established in 1908. This gender turn is a distinguishing feature of Victorian Ireland's legacy. The university education landscape, on the eve of independence, had evolved considerably.

Whereas the book's focus is the Victorian period and its immediate aftermath, Part Four ranges beyond that. Cultural history cannot confine itself to a particular span of calendar years and it has to cover upstream and downstream of the changes it is charting. Chapter 8, 'Beyond the Victorians', looks at how the language-heavy education agenda, born of the Victorian era, played out in the hundred years since independence, and at how insular and continental languages fared over the period. This broad survey will end by discussing some of the challenges now facing Irish people who engage in foreign-language study, and their rationales for doing so, given the hegemony of English in the globalised world of today.

It goes without saying that education in the nineteenth century was a far cry from today's standardised State-driven system where access for all citizens is regarded as a normal aspiration. Post-primary schooling in Ireland was characterised by minimal government control and filled with a plethora of small schools in private hands of varying quality, many of them short-lived and long faded from local memory.[6] Other post-primary schools, founded and run by religious foundations, still form part of the landscape in Irish education today. In the largely deregulated environment of Victorian Ireland, age cohort boundaries were fluid,[7] half-hearted measures to make school attendance compulsory for children aged six to fourteen were limited in their effect,[8] and foreign languages remained an elite pursuit involving a very small proportion of the island's total population.[9] Throughout this book, the reader will be reminded of these and other contrasts with today's assumptions.

Another characteristic mark of the Victorian educational world is the degree to which confessional allegiances were a matter of serious concern, at all levels. In both Britain and Ireland, deeply ingrained anxieties about religious observance were keenly felt in higher education, as creeds of all persuasions considered university life to be a risky period for vulnerable youth, exposed to new ideas that might shake the foundations of their faith.[10] In 1836, a year before Victoria's accession to the throne, the University of London was given its foundation Charter. This institution, modelled as an alternative to the deeply Anglican universities of Oxford and Cambridge,[11] consisted of two very different colleges. University

College London, the 'godless institution' on Gower Street, was established in 1826 as the first secular university of the UK. However, UCL was followed, a few years later, by the founding of King's College London, firmly under Anglican control.

1.1 Trinity College, Dublin (DU / TCD) West front (Lawrence Collection, 1870–1910. *Courtesy of the National Library of Ireland.*)

Ireland's Victorian universities, too, owed much of their early history and structures to sensitive religious divisions. While there had previously been one university college founded in 1592 by Queen Elizabeth I for the education of Protestants – Dublin University (at Trinity College)[12] – by 1854 there were five (or six, if we include the national seminary for Roman Catholics at Maynooth, set up in 1795). Following the Act of Union of Great Britain and Ireland (1801), the need for tertiary education to accommodate the country's non-Anglican majority became more pressing. The multidenominational Queen's Colleges were established by Sir Robert Peel in 1845[13] and opened in Belfast, Cork and Galway in 1849–50. The arrival of those institutions prompted the setting up of the Catholic University of Ireland, which opened in Dublin in 1854.

1.2 St Patrick's College, Maynooth Maynooth College and Church. (Eason Photographic Collection, 1900–1939. *Courtesy of the National Library of Ireland.*)

As will be abundantly clear from the pages that follow, there was nothing new about denominational structures informing higher education. In the nineteenth century anxieties over 'mixed education' referred, not to the mixing of males and females, but of students from different religious denominations. What *was* novel about Ireland's four Victorian universities was the weight they ascribed to modern languages. We shall later discuss how this came about in the three Queen's Colleges, but first it may be worth turning to the other university, set up by the Catholic hierarchy as it hardened in its opposition to the 'godless' Queen's Colleges established by the Westminster administration. The complicated early history and evolving status of this, the most singular of the new foundations, will inform our account of how modern languages took hold in the new university sector on the island.

CATHOLIC UNIVERSITY OF IRELAND, UNIVERSITY COLLEGE DUBLIN (UCD)

The question of how long French and other modern languages had been taught at UCD was the pebble whose ripples have shaped this book. First, let us briefly recall the complicated, not to say funambulatory, fortunes of UCD's Victorian progenitor.[14]

Today's UCD, the largest of Ireland's universities, is a slightly remote descendant of the Catholic University (CU) that opened in 1854, with the future Cardinal John Henry Newman as its rector. Its governing structure altered considerably over the early decades. After 1880, when the CU became a constituent college of the newly established Royal University of Ireland (RUI), it became known as University College. Under Jesuit management from 1883, University College remained part of the RUI until forming a constituent college of the National University of Ireland (NUI), set up in 1908.

1.3 Catholic University of Ireland, Dublin (CUI) (1943)
Newman House. Reproduced from an album of photographs of 85 and 86 St Stephen's Green, Dublin. Taken and printed by Rev. F.M. Browne, produced by the Three Candles press. (*Courtesy of UCD Special Collections.*)

Newman's Catholic University (1854–79) was the sixth university college to open in Ireland. As noted above, all six were founded on strictly confessional principles. Trinity College Dublin (1592) was Anglican from its origins;[15] Maynooth's Royal College of St Patrick (1795) was established as a Roman Catholic seminary;[16] the Queen's Colleges in Belfast, Cork and Galway (1849), intended for the higher education of Catholics and Nonconformists, were multidenominational.[17] Three decades later, the Queen's Colleges were dissolved, and absorbed along with the Catholic University into a new institution, the Royal University of Ireland. This in turn gave way to the National University of Ireland (1908), at which point the Belfast college sundered its southern links to become Queen's University Belfast.

The university associated with Newman, established in the elegant Georgian surroundings of Dublin's St Stephen's Green, had emerged on foot of a campaign partly spearheaded by some of the Catholic hierarchy. At the plenary synod of Thurles in 1850, the bishops[18] denounced the 'godless' Queen's Colleges and moved to set up a separate university that reflected the aspirations and beliefs of the majority of the population. Catholic in name and in practice,[19] the Catholic University was licensed to award pontifical degrees but, lacking a charter from the Crown, was neither recognised nor funded by the State. Despite the aura of its illustrious founding rector, historians of the institution marvel at how it survived for the quarter century of its existence.[20] By all accounts, it clung on to life despite the odds, with one shining exception: its Medical Faculty at Cecelia Street (an older and well-established body) did prosper and expand, producing graduates accredited by the Royal College of Surgeons in Ireland.[21] Universities everywhere during this period catered for tiny elite groups of the population, but the numbers of day students in the CU's Arts and Philosophy Faculties were abysmally low even by nineteenth-century standards. In its first four years until 1858, when Newman left Dublin, student enrolment – outside of Medicine – had followed a downward trend and failed to pick up thereafter. In 1879 just three new students registered.[22] The place was

> unendowed, unchartered, reduced to a mere handful of students and a few tired and discouraged professors, with tight clerical control and a disappearance of all the hopes and most of the ideals associated with Newman's period as Rector.[23]

After the Royal University of Ireland (RUI) Act of 1879 established the new university structure and the Jesuits took over the management of University College (the successor to Newman's CU), things improved a little. Student numbers grew, so that by 1901–02, for example, there were well over one hundred attending lectures in arts.[24] The RUI was a degree-awarding and examining institution, modelled on the University of London. As well as the CU and the Queen's Colleges at Belfast, Cork and Galway, it absorbed a number of other constituent colleges, some of which were very successful. The Jesuits in St Stephen's Green attracted some brilliant students despite the college's poor material conditions. The latter were lamented by the Catholic hierarchy's spokesman, Bishop Edward O'Dwyer, in his testimony to the 1901 Robertson Commission on University Education in Ireland:

> As a university institution it is simply a burlesque. It is a house on the side of the street. It is number something in St Stephen's Green, but there are neither libraries, laboratories,

museums, nor any of the apparatus of a university college connected with it [...] I think it is a scandal it should be recognised as a University College.[25]

In similar vein, the Provincial of the Jesuits in 1883 described the premises as

a dingy old barrack that would require vast outlay, the floors are all rotten [...] the woodwork, window sashes, crumbling with powder.[26]

1.4 Queen's College, Belfast (QCB) Lanyon Building (Lawrence Collection, 1870–1910. *Courtesy of the National Library of Ireland.*)

In its early decades, then, the CUI was something of a Cinderella, its material deprivation contrasting vividly with the ample public resources poured into the Queen's Colleges campuses at Belfast, Cork and Galway, whose handsome Victorian neo-gothic quadrangles are still in use today.[27] In contrast, the CUI was funded by contributions partly from abroad and partly from 'pennies collected from the poor of Ireland'.[28] With its dilapidated buildings, its inability to attract students, no prospects of State recognition and (in respect of language professors, as we shall see) its own idiosyncratic protocols for hiring staff, the Dublin college differed egregiously from the three securely resourced and State-run provincial colleges.

1.5 Queen's College, Cork (QCC) Botanical Gardens, c.1890. (Lawrence Collection, 1870–1910. *Courtesy of the National Library of Ireland.*)

Yet, notwithstanding such difficulties, Newman's English-speaking Catholic University did survive, and was committed to modern languages from its inception. Why did its founding rector, himself an Oxford-educated classicist convinced of the primordial value of a liberal classical education, make space for teaching French and German, and for teaching Italian and Spanish, when the CU opened in 1854?

1.6 Queen's College, Galway (QCG)
(Lawrence Collection, 1870–1910. *Courtesy of the National Library of Ireland.*)

When we look at the tenor of a Victorian classical education, and at the status of modern languages in English universities of the same period, the fact is all the more remarkable.

WHY STUDY MODERN LANGUAGES?

Generally speaking, in the Victorian era, rationales for learning 'modern' (as opposed to ancient) languages at university ranged from the dilettantish to the professional. Traditionally, foreign languages had been seen as a polite embellishment to a young gentleman's education. 'A modern professor of Spanish would probably resent being put into the same category as a fencing instructor, but in the eighteenth century such a classification seemed entirely natural.'[29] At best, language study helped to prepare a gentleman for undertaking the grand tour or contributed to the accomplishments of cultured ladies. Thus, in the Regency fictions of Jane Austen, Caroline Bingley in *Pride and Prejudice* includes modern languages – along with music, singing, drawing and dancing – in her list of such accomplishments; Anne Eliott, heroine of *Persuasion*, is modest about her impromptu translation of Italian arias.[30] Learning languages promoted female character formation and discipline, as suggested in a rule for pupils at the French Protestant School for Girls, set up in Bray, County Wicklow, in 1864: 'I must not neglect to speak French or German with all the zeal required of me.'[31] At the University of St Andrews, French, German and Italian were offered to women students (denied matriculation on grounds of their sex), as part of the Ladies Literate in Arts Certificate, set up in 1877, fifteen years before St Andrews established its Modern Languages degree.[32] Although personal or private motivations persisted, they tended, over the course of the nineteenth century, to be supplemented by more professional or utilitarian arguments, even for those concerned with male education.

As already mentioned, one overarching strand in the present book charts the shift from ancient to modern in the sphere of language study. In Great Britain, the pace of change was glacially slow, and the merits of studying classical Greek and Latin were passionately clung to, they being considered the pillars of civilisation. For William Gladstone, writing in 1861, there was something almost sacred about a classical education, which he saw as complementing Christianity itself, in the formation of a human being 'for this world and for the world to come'. In his view, new-fangled school subjects, such as science, modern languages or history, had no 'right to a parallel or equal position; their true position is ancillary' to the 'old classical training'.[33]

This debate between ancients and moderns will crop up in different guises in the course of our story. It is tied up with wider social debates about broadening participation in education. In today's world, most of us have not experienced a classical education and may need reminding of the central, pre-eminent place it occupied in the minds of Victorian educationalists. In an apologia (1834) for the study of Greek and Latin, 'Rugby School – Use of the Classics', Rugby's headmaster Thomas Arnold gives us a sense that it involved much more than the mere study of ancient languages.[34] In the 1830s, his pupils were given a total immersion, at a tender age, in the experiences, minds and values of ancient writers, at every level:[35]

> There are exercises in composition, in Greek and Latin prose, Greek and Latin verse, and English prose, as in other large classical schools. In the subjects given for original composition in the higher forms, there is a considerable variety. Historical descriptions of any remarkable events, geographical descriptions of countries, imaginary speeches and letters, supposed to be spoken or written on some great question or under some memorable circumstances; etymological accounts of words in different languages, and criticisms on different books, are found to offer an advantageous variety to the essays on moral subjects to which boys' prose composition has sometimes been confined.

Classical study was so lengthy, intensive and painstaking that it offered a mental and moral training designed to steep the schoolboy in every aspect of ancient culture, bringing that culture vividly to life. For Arnold, ancient authors are honorary Victorians:[36]

> Aristotle, and Plato, and Thucydides, and Cicero, and Tacitus, are most untruly called ancient writers; they are virtually our own countrymen and contemporaries.

At its best, a classical training was a fine preparation for the life of a gentleman scholar, statesman or imperial administrator. It encouraged the imagination and the mind to enter into the ancient world and to appraise the behaviour of fellow human beings, long dead, who belong to a remote foreign culture. Its rigorous language training, via grammatical analysis and translation, developed accuracy and – crucially – served to deepen the learner's command and understanding of his own mother tongue. Knowing the grammar of Latin or Greek led, through the regular exercise of translation, to an appreciation of the limitations and possibilities of English structure, syntax and idiom. 'Every lesson in Greek or Latin,' declares Arnold, 'may and ought to be made a lesson in English.'[37] In some respects, these maxims still apply today.[38]

Arnold was well aware of the winds of change around him: indeed, that is the climate prompting his essay in defence of the study of classics. He even concedes that modern national languages have spawned civilisations comparable to those of the ancients:[39]

> France, and Italy, and Germany, and England, have each produced their philosophers, their poets, and their historians, worthy to be placed on the same level with those of Greece and Rome.

Nevertheless, for Arnold, the loss, at school or university, of the study of classical languages and culture would be incalculable, and he and other men of his ilk were prepared to defend that terrain against encroachment.

I use the term 'men' deliberately because in the early decades of our period, universities were of course still citadels not made for women, and a classical education was the preserve of a male elite. The classics-versus-modern languages debate formed the mood music to momentous social changes that occurred in education during the nineteenth century, the closing decades of which widened access to post-elementary education to include a socially broader constituency of learners; the period also saw the opening of higher education as an option for women. These issues were interconnected. The inclusion of the other sex and other social classes gave rise to assumptions based on established notions of power and societal roles. Thus, girls tended to be offered more modern languages to study than their brothers; the more elite the school, the more classical the education it offered; manual labourers and girls did not 'need' Latin or Greek; females were regarded as better at the spoken word than males, who were considered naturally superior at learning the written language.[40]

POLARITIES: PEN/TONGUE, MONASTERY/MARKETPLACE

Broadly speaking, the two goals of foreign-language acquisition can be seen in terms of a spectrum running between two polarities: written and oral competence.[41] Historically, the practice of modern-language teaching has always been caught between two complementary goals, doing and knowing, or between the learner's performance and reflection. There is a perennial tension between the need to impart spoken fluency in the target language and to convey an accurate knowledge of its grammatical structures and forms. In practice, language teachers pay attention to both approaches but sometimes, in different learning contexts, pedagogic theory and practice have concentrated more on one end of the spectrum than the other.[42]

Giuseppe Baretti, an eighteenth-century Piedmontese grammarian and Italian language teacher who worked in England, distinguished between the written and the 'colloquial' (or spoken) in terms of the pen and the tongue. Particularly in cultures with a stable written tradition, the gap between the two can be wide enough to generate two language systems:[43]

> Of every learned and elegant people the language is divided into two parts: the one lax and cursory, used on slight occasions with extemporary negligence; the other rigorous and solemn, the effect of deliberate choice and grammatical accuracy. When books are multiplied and style

is cultivated, the colloquial and written diction separate by degrees, till there is one language of the tongue, and another of the pen.

The divergence between the two – a unified written language for cultured elites versus a plethora of local dialects reserved for everyday oral communication – was the bilingual norm in most parts of Europe before nineteenth-century schools legislation began to tip the scales in favour of written national languages.[44] The written/colloquial polarity, as we shall see, is very pertinent to the case of Irish.

Another way of thinking about the two ends of the language-teaching spectrum, more in tune with nineteenth-century schooling, is to borrow Sabine Doff's evocative categorisation of the 'monastery' versus the 'marketplace'.[45] These broad tags are useful for what they connote: on the one hand, years of assiduous silent study of written texts, in a scholarly academic environment that is cut off from the world and, on the other, language study of a more practical and immediate kind, motivated by the need to communicate in order to effect a specific exchange in a foreign language, be it of goods, services, information or ideas.

The term 'monastic' designates the work of medieval monks and scribes, involving skills acquired over time with painstaking effort and silent concentration on a written text. The task of experienced monks in a scriptorium was to penetrate and gloss the mysteries of a manuscript, decoding and transmitting the truths it expressed. As well as writing skills, this painstaking work of copying texts required tools of analysis and understanding (grammar and figures of speech), and knowledge of a tongue that no longer matched the everyday spoken ('colloquial') language of ordinary people. Hence the growing social importance, in the later middle ages, of a literate or learned class, clerical and lay, whose educational priority was a knowledge of Latin grammar in order to read and write written texts. Education, first and foremost, entailed an induction into a foreign tongue: the primary function of grammar schools, or Latin schools, was to teach Latin grammar to the young.

As they emerged in the later middle ages, European universities, which grew out of the older monasteries and cathedral schools, have been concerned with transmitting belief systems, expressed in ancient languages, mainly Latin. The ideological load inherent in this model of language study intensified during the Reformation. While renaissance humanists revived the grammar and style of classical languages in order to access the texts of antiquity, Reformation scholars needed to return to the source languages of the early Christian era, in order to prepare vernacular versions of scripture. Translators in both camps – Protestant and Catholic – had to know the original languages of the sacred texts in order to interpret and convey their truths according to their own lights. The double impetus for the study of classical languages, on the part of humanists and religious reformers, served to enhance and reinforce the status of ancient languages in the education traditions of European lands. Thus, from the sixteenth to the eighteenth centuries, educated Europeans required a knowledge of Latin grammar[46] not just to penetrate the mysteries of theology or dogma, but also to master learning in all fields, from anatomy to law, botany to metaphysics, mathematics to natural philosophy.

Deriving its authority from that era when Latin and Greek had served as universal tools of knowledge, the 'monastic' model denotes how classical languages had been taught by humanists since the renaissance, and it was the method for teaching modern languages that was still favoured by nineteenth-century universities and their feeder schools, like the public school in England or the *Gymnasium* in Germany. With a heavy bias towards accurate knowledge of the written language, textbooks included an outline of grammar, with some vocabulary lists and sets of dialogues intended to be learned by rote, illustrated by exemplary excerpts in prose or verse from the target language, and sometimes adding translation exercises.[47] For learning the classics, this approach made sense. To interpret or construe an ancient text, it was important to recognise grammatical forms in order to decode the written words. The need to understand and perform *spoken* Latin, however, was dwindling.[48] Although university lectures and examinations had traditionally been performed entirely through Latin, this changed in Britain over the course of the century. In academic assessment, the shift from group oral disputation to solitary written examination was well underway by the 1830s.[49]

In contrast with the 'monastic' model, the 'marketplace' model for teaching and learning languages foregrounds the transactional performance of immediate communication, regardless of its ideological content. It concentrates on spoken proficiency and mutual understanding and is less intent on learners reaching deep structural accuracy in reading or writing the target tongue. As Michael Pye has recently shown, foreign languages were central for the exchange of goods and services in the large printing and trading centre of sixteenth-century Antwerp, a city that can claim to have published a significant proportion of all new language books in Western Europe. 'Antwerp women were famous for speaking six languages or more, even if they had never left Brabant. Language became another of the city's trades.'[50] The 'marketplace' model was useful for merchants and travellers and, in educational settings, it tended to be relegated to the status of an accomplishment for young ladies.[51] Girls should be allowed to indulge in unreflective chatter, but their properly *Gymnasium*-educated brothers must confront the language of foreigners at a loftier level and in a more substantial way. As one German educationalist pronounced in 1868:[52]

> Ich schätze es gering, einen Menschen perfekt Englisch sprechen zu hören, das kann jeder brauchbare Kellner, er muss es können; das französische Institutsgeplapper der Mädchen ist nicht viel werth, denn sie wissen schliesslich doch nicht, warum nach dieser und jener Conjunction der Conjunctiv steht, ob sie auch die Regel wissen, dass er steht. [...] Lassen wir Mädchen parliren vom Wetter und Spaziergängen, dem Gebildeten ist es um etwas anderes zu thun. Er will – er soll – eindringen in den Genius der Sprachen, er soll die Gedanken der Nationen, die Ideen der Fremden, nicht ihre Wörter beherrschen, er solle stehen auf sprachhistorischem Boden und die Art Sprachen zu studiren, diese Methode soll und muss vom Gymnasium ausgehen.

> [I do not greatly value hearing a man speak perfect English – any skilled waiter can and must be able to do that; the babbling of schoolgirls in French is of little worth, because they do not actually know why a subjunctive comes after this or that conjunction, even if they know the rule. [...] Let girls chat about the weather and aimless walks, the educated man has something else to do. He wants – he ought – to penetrate the genius of languages, his task is to master the thoughts of nations, the ideas of foreigners, not their words, he should be grounded in language history and should study language types; this method should and must come from the *Gymnasium* [grammar school].]

A scene from George Eliot's novel *The Mill on the Floss* suggests a more nuanced perspective on the gendering of language study. The author characterises a brother and sister by contrasting young Tom Tulliver's efforts at school Latin with the quick linguistic intelligence of his sister, Maggie, who (as a female) is not studying it at all. Her intuitive grasp that languages have arbitrary signs that can change semantically according to context shows up his failure to apply his grammatical knowledge to real situations. Her offer to assist Tom with his homework provokes the following exchange:[53]

> '*You* help me, you silly little thing!' said Tom, in such high spirits at this announcement that he quite enjoyed the idea of confounding Maggie by showing her a page of Euclid. 'I should like to see you doing one of *my* lessons! Why, I learn Latin too! Girls never learn such things. They're too silly.'
> 'I know what Latin is very well,' said Maggie, confidently. 'Latin's a language. There are Latin words in the Dictionary. There's *bonus*, a gift.'
> 'Now, you're just wrong there, Miss Maggie!' said Tom, secretly astonished. 'You think you're very wise! But "bonus" means "good", as it happens – *bonus, bona, bonum.*'
> 'Well, that's no reason why it shouldn't mean "gift"', said Maggie, stoutly. 'It may mean several things – almost every word does. There's "lawn" – it means the grass-plot, as well as the stuff pocket-handkerchiefs are made of.'

The nexus linking gender, spoken proficiency and modern languages is a feature of the history of language study in Ireland too. It is one of a range of cultural markers emerging across Europe in the late nineteenth century, which were played out differently in different lands.

LANGUAGE STUDY IN ENGLAND AND SCOTLAND: A SLOW TILT TO THE MODERN

Polarities between different uses of language, different user groups, different historical and social connotations of languages, even different genders, could impinge on which languages were taught, by whom and to whom, and when. Another distinction in this regard is the dates when modern-language study arrived in the universities of Britain and Ireland.

In English and Scottish universities, the ancient languages of the Mediterranean and Middle East had long been seen as essential tools for scriptural and patristic studies, and the study of classical authors was considered of primordial value for intellectual and moral formation. In keeping with Doff's 'monastery' model (which fits particularly well with classical languages), Latin, for centuries synonymous with university life, was 'the basic tool of scholarly discourse'.[54] And for some, even the key to school life: at Eton and other public schools, Latin was taught through Latin, and grammars of both Greek and Latin were written in Latin.[55]

During the second half of the nineteenth century, there were portents of change. At Oxford, in 1867, Matthew Arnold 'broke all traditions by lecturing in English instead of in Latin'.[56] Modern languages and literatures gradually began to acquire respectable status and to be seen as worthy of academic study in their own right, offering intrinsic mental and moral value on a par with the more prestigious and traditional study of ancient languages.[57] Great Britain was not alone in this trend: the 1880s and 1890s saw the appearance of a plethora of academic journals specialising in modern-language philology. Mostly emanating from Germany, these point to a community of scholars and teachers already large enough to sustain the kind of forum that such journals offered for the transnational exchange of new ideas.[58]

School teaching of modern languages also became professionalised. French and German were recognised as subjects for assessment in 1858 when Cambridge and Oxford started administering local examinations for school leavers; over three decades later, the Modern Language Teachers' Association was founded in England in 1892.[59] Modern languages provided access to secondary literature;[60] and they were gradually recognised as being useful, just as Latin and Greek already were, for careers in the army, diplomacy, commerce, science and teaching. Likewise, English literature began to be separated from History, its traditional academic home, to become an independent discipline.[61]

Coincidentally, the coming of the railways helped to promote public awareness of foreign languages. The connection is foregrounded at the opening of *Tom Brown's School Days*, the quintessential Victorian school story set in Rugby in the 1830s. Addressing the youths of England 'born into these racing railroad times', the author imagines them during their long vacations taking trains around Ireland, or 'dropping [their] copies of Tennyson on the tops of Swiss mountains; or pulling down the Danube in Oxford racing boats', and trying out their modern languages along the way. 'You all patter French more or less; and perhaps German.'[62]

However, the establishment of modern languages in schools did not lead to their immediate acceptability as university disciplines. That was a slow and uneven process. By the end of the century in Britain, French and German 'had become institutionalized in schools, though they were still finding their feet in universities.'[63] Charles Colbeck, in 1887, famously summed up the conventional wisdom: 'The living languages, we have been told, are too trivial to be scholarly, too easy to be learned, too useful to be dignified.'[64]

Of the oldest universities in the realm,[65] only two claim to have been teaching modern languages from before 1850: Oxford and King's College London. King's College London's online prospectus boasts: 'French, German and Spanish have been taught at King's since 1831 and Portuguese since the 1860s, making us one of the oldest modern-languages programmes in the country.'[66] In Oxford, in the mid-1840s, thanks to a handsome bequest from the architect Sir Robert Taylor, modern-language lectureships in European languages appeared within the University, and 1848 saw its first Professor of Modern European Languages. The post lapsed ten years later, but Taylorian teachers continued to offer optional classes. The Faculty of Medieval and Modern Languages was approved in 1903, and further recognition came with the Taylor Chair of German (1907) and Romance Languages chair (1909).[67]

The more typical pattern is for chairs to be established towards the turn of the century in languages that had already been taught for a short time beforehand. Cambridge's organisation of modern language studies dates from 1879, and it held its first modern-languages tripos in 1886, having appointed University Lecturers in French and German in 1884. Its endowed modern-languages professorships, however, date from later: the Schröder Professorship of German was endowed in 1907 and the Drapers Professorship of French in 1919.[68]

In St Andrews, the Modern Languages degree dates from 1892.[69] Ancient Greek is the only language listed among the six founding chairs of Edinburgh's Faculty of Arts, established in 1708. Sanskrit and Celtic were to follow in 1862 and 1882 respectively, but the chairs of French (1918) and of German (1919) had to wait until after the First World War.[70] At Durham, although a Modern Languages lectureship dated from as far back as 1833, it was intended for engineering students who were required to take a course in French and German, while Arts students were directed towards classical languages. Modern Languages only came to form part of the BA syllabus in the 1870s.[71]

This information, gleaned from current UK university websites, is a rough yardstick. A subject can be taught in a university without having a chair attached, and modern languages had been (unsuccessfully) introduced at Oxford and Cambridge, as far back as the 1720s, as ancillary to the study of modern history.[72] Contexts evolve, and terminology can mislead. Our understanding of what distinguishes a 'professor' today does not always correspond with what the term denoted in the past.[73] However, dates when chairs are founded may tell us something about official university priorities. Recognition can confer status and permanence on a subject that is already present. It can also signal protection if a subject is perceived to be vulnerable. Cambridge's apparent neglect of Latin – the staple of university life – is intriguing in this regard. While its Regius Chairs of Greek and Hebrew date from 1540, its endowed Chair of Latin was only created in 1869, partly in response to curriculum changes in the 1850s, and partly to acknowledge the importance of the language of Rome, overshadowed by 'the cultural prestige of Greek'.[74] Is it perhaps also conceivable that those who endowed the new Latin Chair partly feared that Latin was the ancient language most threatened by the emerging modern languages disciplines?[75]

Throughout Britain, the term 'modern languages' meant, essentially, two continental European languages: French and German.[76] Why these two? French had held and maintained an unassailable position as the first foreign language, at post-elementary and university levels, for historical reasons. It had been one of the vernaculars in medieval England and Normanised regions of Ireland, and was also the *lingua franca* of diplomatic and aristocratic circles since the seventeenth century.[77] A particular prestige was enjoyed by German universities, which were among the earliest to value the furthering of knowledge through research, so it was essential to know some German in order to keep abreast of new ideas and scholarship. German was perceived from a relatively early stage as a key to both philosophy and science.[78] This is what lies behind a remark in George Eliot's novel *Middlemarch*, made by the Revd Edward Casaubon's indolent young relative, Will Ladislaw, in a conversation with Dorothea, the clergyman's earnest and naïve young wife. Ladislaw opines that his relative's years of erudite research towards a never-to-be-published definitive scholarly study on comparative world mythologies are doomed from the start, because its author is ignorant of German:[79]

> '[...] If Mr Casaubon read German he would save himself a great deal of trouble.'
> 'I do not understand you,' said Dorothea, startled and anxious.
> 'I merely mean,' said Will, in an offhand way, 'that the Germans have taken the lead in historical inquiries, and they laugh at results which are got by groping around in woods with a pocket-compass while they have made good roads. [...]'

The Germans were already ahead, not just in science and engineering, but also in the humanities, including the new discipline of comparative philology. As we shall see, the new 'science of language' was the common currency of Victorian language professors.

French and German, then, the *sine qua non* among modern languages, were gradually being endowed with chairs at the turn of the twentieth century and later. Chairs in other modern languages derived from individual endowments: the four Serena Professorships in Italian (at Cambridge, Oxford, Manchester and Birmingham) were founded just after the Great War by a shipbroker who was the son of an exiled Venetian patriot settled in London.[80] While Italian had been studied since the days of the grand tour as a rich source of cultural capital, Spanish has tended to be perceived as useful for trade, and its chairs were founded by companies with commercial interests in Latin America: for example, the Gilmour Chair at the University of Liverpool (1908) or the Cowdray Chair at Leeds (1918).[81]

The First World War pointed to a need for mutual understanding between countries. In August 1916, Mr Stanley Leathes was appointed to chair a parliamentary committee, to enquire into the position and needs of modern-language study in Great Britain. The Leathes Report, printed in April 1918, highlighted the continuing neglect and relatively low status of modern-language teaching in Britain's schools and universities, and made several recommendations for reforms in staffing, conditions and curriculum. An appended letter, signed by 31 professors and readers, gives a flavour of the perceived shortcomings at university level:[82]

> In Scotland there are no Chairs in any of the modern foreign languages; in neither Oxford nor Cambridge is there a Chair of French language *or* literature, though both Oxford and Cambridge are provided with a Chair of German and Oxford with a Chair of Romance Languages. Russian, as is well known, has been till recently almost completely neglected, Italian has fared very little better, and Spanish has made its way into only a few of our Universities. In English University Colleges two modern languages, though unrelated, are still sometimes taught by the same man or are under the same head. Generally the professors of modern languages are on the lowest level of salaries paid and are provided with the worst equipped staffs and the meanest apparatus.

LANGUAGES IN IRELAND'S UNIVERSITIES: A DIFFERENT PERSPECTIVE

If it was exceptional for an English university to provide modern languages before the middle of the nineteenth century, for Ireland's university sector it was the general rule. By 1850, *all* Irish universities officially offered modern languages. Trinity College Dublin had been a pioneer: since 1776, it could claim two modern-language chairs set up by Provost John Hely-Hutchinson, one in French and German, the other in Italian and Spanish. Although these were to remain marginal as degree subjects for almost a century, a formal modern-language qualification was required for a degree in Music already in 1863,[83] and some notable scholarship and solid language teaching can be claimed among Trinity's early appointments. Trinity's first professor of Italian and Spanish, the Portuguese lexicographer and philologist Antonio Vieyra (1712–97), is a case in point. A refugee from the Inquisition and convert to Protestantism, Vieyra was an important early grammarian of Portuguese as a foreign language.[84] The College's first appointment in French and German, Antoine D'Esca (*c*.1732–84), was 'an avid collector of books, especially in French', and edited a collection of Voltaire's letters.[85]

In the late 1840s, a professorship of modern languages was built into the founding structure of the so-called 'godless' Queen's Colleges at Belfast, Cork and Galway. Each of the Queen's Colleges obliged arts students to study a modern European language, meaning French or German, for a year.[86] Making a utilitarian case for placing modern languages in their proposed core curriculum, the Board of presidents and vice-presidents of the Queen's Colleges, in their Resolutions of 1846, were unanimous in their view of the relative position of modern and ancient languages:[87]

> It was felt by every member [...] that although the ancient languages are certainly of the highest value in a liberal education, yet for the practical wants of the middle classes too much has been hitherto sacrificed to their exclusive study, and that for a community busily occupied with practical science, with commerce, with agriculture and with manufactures, the study of modern languages should hold an important place.

In their proposal modern languages were deemed pedagogically equal in value to ancient Greek:[88]

> the Board considers that a knowledge of the tongues of the two most important modern continental nations may be considered equivalent in education to an acquaintance with the language of ancient Greece.

The Board was aware of how unorthodox their proposal was. Its draft programme of studies for the Queen's Colleges allows us as good a glimpse as we can get of a blue-skies design for a university arts course in mid-nineteenth-century Ireland. Following broad guidelines from the Home Secretary, Sir James Graham, who had asked them to devise a general liberal course of undergraduate instruction that would precede professional degree study, the group of learned men came up with a scheme that (in their view) would fit local conditions and circumstances. Out of their proposed six language chairs, three were in continental European languages: French, German and Italian;[89] and their proposed matriculation examination prescribed a choice between French *or* ancient Greek authors, depending on whether candidates wished to specialise in modern or ancient languages.

This was a daring proposal for matriculation to a mid-nineteenth-century university. In the same year of 1846, the only languages required for the entrance examinations at both Dublin University (Trinity) and the University of London were Greek and Latin. For graduation purposes, classics were the only compulsory languages prescribed by the Scottish universities.

One of the models which the Queen's University scheme consciously followed was the University of London where, as we have seen, King's College was the only British university to offer modern languages since 1831. It was also unique in requiring a modern language as an obligatory component in an arts degree.[90] The Queens' proposed 'elevation of modern languages' at the expense of ancient Greek, however, was something even more radical than the London model, as Moody and Beckett note:[91] 'the optional status assigned to Greek in this scheme was a departure from the practice not only of the older universities of the United Kingdom but also of the University of London.'

Following scrutiny at the Home Office in London, the structure eventually adopted for each of the Queen's Colleges dramatically pruned the Board's initial blueprint, reducing modern languages to just one professorship (in French and German) out of 20, and also proposing a professorship in Celtic languages. For matriculation purposes, it restored Greek to obligatory status instead of leaving it optional against French. The compulsory status of a modern language as a component of the degree was, however, retained.

A few years later, the four archbishops (chaired by Paul Cullen) to whom John Henry Newman reported as rector of the Catholic University from June 1854, voiced no objection in principle to his inclusion of modern languages in his broad liberal arts curriculum.[92] Although Newman advocated the supreme value of a liberal classical education over a vocational model, and (unlike Cullen) was not himself skilled in modern languages, he was prepared to make allowances for circumstances on the ground.[93] Indeed, a range of language disciplines, both ancient and modern, was regarded as essential to the new university's arts faculty from the very design stage, as drawn up in 1851 by the university subcommittee reporting to the Catholic hierarchy: the list covered Greek, Latin, Semitic and modern languages.[94] The new Dublin institution was marching in step with the emerging consensus view elsewhere in Ireland.

1.7 Royal University, Dublin (pre-1910) Earlsfort Terrace (Lawrence Collection, 1870–1910. *Courtesy of the National Library of Ireland.*)

The march continued. In 1880, after the Queen's Colleges were restructured to form part of the new Royal University of Ireland along with University College Dublin, the RUI's matriculation language requirements included English, Latin and 'any one of Greek, French, German, Italian, Spanish, Celtic, Sanskrit, Hebrew, Arabic'.[95] This measure considerably altered the prescribed balance in the first Queen's University matriculation menu,[96] in effect replacing compulsory Greek with a compulsory modern language, and relegating the study of ancient Greek to a dwindling minority of candidates.

Why was the rapidly expanding Irish university sector of the mid-nineteenth century so ready to embrace arguments for including modern languages as core disciplines, which were slower to take root in Britain? Bearing in mind that these same years coincided with the Great Famine (1845–52) – a cataclysm prompting, *inter alia*, unprecedented emigration to North America – one may well wonder at the motivation for requiring modern foreign languages at this particular juncture in Irish history.

In more venerable British foundations, the weight of tradition inhibited change. There was stout resistance from those who feared that the study of living languages would lead to deteriorating standards in classics. Ann Frost notes that in Oxford, the oldest university in the English-speaking world,[97]

> the study of Classics was firmly entrenched, and repeated attempts to introduce a modern language met with anything from indifference to outright opposition. The feeling among the old guard was not only that classical languages were superior, but that they would be endangered by the introduction of their modern counterparts, since both resources and students would be diverted.

It was not accidental that Cambridge and Oxford's Language Faculties, when they were set up in the 1900s, coupled 'Medieval' with the term 'Modern'. The labels are still in use. The study of a language's ancient forms, along with comparative philology and textual history, lent academic credibility to the new enterprise.

Yet even in a less venerable university like Owens College Manchester (later the Victoria University of Manchester), which opened in 1851, three years before Dublin's Catholic University opened, professorships of modern languages were installed relatively late. The slow pace of language development may perhaps be explained by the fact that Owens College merged with a medical school in 1874 and concentrated on Medicine and Sciences. Perhaps partly to cater for medical and science students requiring practical skills, the College, northern England's first civic university, did have foundation teaching posts in German and French, and was offering optional classes in other languages by the 1880s, but its *chairs* of German and French date from 1895 and 1896 respectively. There were positive factors also at play in favour of language study: Manchester's leading professors were inspired by the research ethos of German universities, and German culture was well regarded in the great manufacturing city, host to a large and highly educated community of German immigrants who contributed to the city's cultural life in the nineteenth century.[98] Manchester Grammar School built a strong reputation for the teaching of German.[99] Local circumstances matter.

Ireland's new university sector was uninhibited by the reservations of an old guard. While at Trinity College Dublin there was resistance to expanding the role of modern languages, the Queen's Colleges were set up to cater for a more diverse student body than Trinity's.[100] London's recently established colleges were partly shaping the new ethos, as they too sought an alternative model, moving away from Oxbridge's narrow, classical and elitist education for clergymen, scholars and gentlemen. University College London (1826), open to all social ranks and religious denominations, was the first to present English as a degree subject and (later) the first to admit women students; King's College London (1829) also offered a practical education, in a new manner, to a broader range of middle-class students. In striving to offer a different model of university training, both UCL and King's College 'built their reputations upon their professorial teaching, their wide range of studies, which included modern languages and natural sciences as well as law and medicine, and the emphasis they placed on written examinations'.[101]

★ ★ ★

When it decided to give greater prominence to modern-language study, the Irish Queen's Colleges Board was building on ground that had already been prepared, at least where local demand for the study of French is concerned. As Máire Kennedy demonstrated in her comprehensive study, *French Books in Eighteenth-Century Ireland*, a large and varied quantity of French-language books, both printed in Ireland and imported from the continent, was circulating in the country in the 1700s. This vigorous French book trade was initially connected with Huguenot refugees who had settled in Ireland after the revocation of the Edict of Nantes in the late seventeenth century. 'From their ranks emerged teachers of French, booksellers and book importers, and authors whose original works were published in French in Dublin up to 1750.'[102] The small town of Portarlington, County Offaly, where many of them had settled, took on a distinct French flavour in its educational establishments.[103] Over the course of the century, the market for French-language reading material widened to embrace a growing urban middle class not only in the capital (the second city of the Empire), but in provincial towns throughout the country. Kennedy points out that a significant proportion of general foreign trade in eighteenth-century Dublin was in the hands of upwardly mobile Catholics, who were barred on religious grounds from the purchase or lease of land before 1778–82. Modern languages, especially French, were a major asset for this commercial sector.[104] Many of the French-language books in question were locally produced school textbooks;[105] and the trade in French-language schoolbooks was matched, in turn, by a stream of private academies and schools offering French as part of their curriculum.[106] Some of these establishments were short lived, but Kennedy's evidence shows that they remained widely spaced geographically, and provided a steadily growing level of urban demand for French-language books, in Dublin and provincial Irish towns, throughout the eighteenth century.

Indeed, Ireland was receptive ground for progressive education theorists who advocated the study of foreign languages in general. As Kennedy observes, John Locke's *Some Thoughts Concerning Education* (1693), was reprinted a number of times in Dublin; it was in favour of teaching spoken French to young children before introducing them to Latin.[107] There were readers for the very practical *Essays on Professional Education* (1809) of Richard Lovell Edgeworth (father of Maria, the novelist). He too recommends accustoming the young to the sounds of foreign tongues as early as possible, 'as soon as the child can articulate':[108]

> These should be learned during his earlier education; even from the nursery he should have been in the habit of speaking them. At the university, he should make himself acquainted with the principal works in these languages.

For political and military careers, Edgeworth considers French, German and Italian to be as essential as Latin. 'Modern languages are absolutely necessary to a statesman, not only as the keys of books, but of minds. He should speak French, Italian, and German.'[109] 'The youth destined for the army or the navy' does not need to be 'critically skilled in the dead languages';[110] rather,

> instead of Greek and a critical knowledge of Latin, he should learn all those modern languages, which may be of use to him in that intercourse with foreigners, to which his profession leads.

Such utilitarian reasons for foreign-language study struck a chord in Ireland. Máire Kennedy concludes that, in the eighteenth century, Irish links with France and French culture were not confined to members of the ascendancy like Lady Emily FitzGerald at Carton and her sister, Lady Louisa Conolly, at Castletown, both of whom spoke fluent French thanks to childhood governesses, and maintained a faultless correspondence with aristocratic European friends in that language. As well as signifying an accomplishment for polite society or a boon on a gentleman's grand tour, mastery of spoken and written French was also pursued by individuals from lower down the social scale, and increasingly valued by an urban middle class who had a utilitarian rationale for knowing a foreign language useful for business and scientific purposes. For the upwardly mobile among them, it offered the added value of gentility.

In opting for a curriculum that included modern languages to meet 'the practical wants of the middle classes', the Queen's Colleges Board was, therefore, acknowledging an existing strand in Irish culture.

There were other local continuities at play. Specific historical circumstances – linguistic, religious and political – obtaining in Ireland can further help us to explain the ready adoption in the 1850s of modern-language study at Ireland's Victorian universities. Complementing the arguments of the Queen's Colleges Board, and in addition to the eighteenth-century evidence of a steady French-language readership, the ground was well prepared by a number of other cultural and historical forces, deep-rooted and intrinsic to Irish people's experience of languages, past and present, native and foreign. These forces include the complex linguistic landscape of Ireland; diverse historical links with continental languages forged by influential sections of Irish society; the allegiance of the vast majority of the population to the Catholic Church; and the influence of French teaching congregations who set up secondary schools in Ireland in the nineteenth century. In the closing decades of the Victorian era, additional complexity is added to our chronicle by a rising tide of cultural nationalism and the inclusion of modern Irish in educational curricula.

It is to these historical circumstances and forces that we shall turn in the following chapters.

CHAPTER 2

Language, Creed, Identity

When a society is conquered, and apparently absorbed by its conquerors, it often retains its identity by insisting on a religious difference. [...] Even today the Scots and the Irish show a deplorable indifference to the self-evident truths of the Anglican Church. [Hugh Trevor-Roper, 1960][1]

HUGH: 'Wordsworth? ... no. I'm afraid we're not familiar with your literature, Lieutenant. We feel closer to the warm Mediterranean. We tend to overlook your island.' [Brian Friel, 1980][2]

IRELAND'S SHIFTING LANGUAGES: IRISH, ENGLISH, LATIN

Irish people did not come to the study of modern languages from a strictly monolingual culture. The island's linguistic atlas had grown increasingly complex over the centuries, due to the twin pressures of political conquest and religious reform.

Outside the Pale, the long cultural revolution that was the Protestant Reformation took root in scattered patches, and the Tudor and Stuart 'civilising' project to anglicise the country had been only partly successful. English had steadily gained ground, however, so that by the mid-nineteenth century two overlapping vernaculars co-existed, asymmetrically positioned. Irish speakers needed to use English for certain kinds of employment and trade, indeed, to perform any commercial or legal transaction. English was indispensable, for example, when disposing of property or making a will,[3] and it was the only language admitted for the administration of justice. Court interpreters were used in criminal cases involving monoglot Irish litigants.[4] English, then, was the language used for dealing with practical realities in the public sphere; Irish was confined to domestic matters. Monoglot Anglophones, for their part, lacked any strong incentive to learn Irish, so their ignorance of that language helped to ensure its relative loss of scope.

The Irish vernacular had been inextricably bound up with Catholicism since the sixteenth century. Revealingly, the native language had no word for 'Reformation' until the 1820s.[5] As Kevin Whelan argues, the Reformation had never been a ground-up project in Ireland.[6] Throughout the island, the language and its culture had become a repository for the folk beliefs and aspirations of a people who clung tenaciously to the 'dogma, rituals and institutional practices' of their Roman Catholic faith.[7] Vernacular folk culture also intensified a particular association with the landscape, which it loaded with sacred significance. While in other dissenting jurisdictions, recusant families retreated indoors for clandestine worship, Irish recusants saw in the holy wells, wayside shrines and desecrated abbeys around them the venerable reminders of past times and deeds.[8]

By the Victorian period, the mapping of religion and language was less straightforward and 'Irishness' and 'Englishness' were more complex signifiers, but traditional perspectives endured within the Irish language. Over the course of the nineteenth century, as English continued to spread and thrive, Irish came under increasing pressure, accelerating a process of decline in usage that was already well under way by the second half of the previous century, if not even earlier.[9] In 1800, Irish speakers made up about one half of the island's population; by 1851, that percentage had dropped to 23 per cent, of whom under one third were monoglot Irish speakers.[10] The island's population was inexorably moving from being predominantly Irish-speaking towards becoming predominantly English-speaking by the early twentieth century. A number of factors contributed to this radical language shift. Irish-language regions were disproportionately affected by population loss during the Great Famine (1845–52). Other reasons include the absence of a stable, viable Irish-language print culture and a reading public to sustain it; the failure of the Reformed Church's sporadic efforts to evangelise through the medium of the Irish vernacular; the spread of anglicisation through national schools, established in 1831; and the inadequate or inconsistent priorities of the institutional Catholic Church regarding the perceived need for an Irish-speaking clergy. Roman Catholic liturgy was performed through Latin. The decline of Irish was addressed only at the end of the century, by the activities of the Gaelic League.

Benedict Anderson has discussed how some vernaculars, through 'print-capitalism', became harnessed as part of the administrative machinery of political powers, especially during the nineteenth century. Since the sixteenth century, print-capitalism had facilitated the dissemination of standardised written forms which, in their turn, were reinforced by diverse means such as cartography and national education systems.[11] Ireland's vernacular-speaking townlands were measured by the Royal Engineers of the Ordnance Survey, and veiled in a cloak of foreign names, during the 1830s.[12] The same decade also saw national schools established. When children from remote Irish-speaking communities attended elementary school, they learned to count, read and write through English, the language of imperial officialdom. An analogous sense of the foreign often applies to peripheral peoples being assimilated by a dominant language. The experience can in some respects be perceived as an enrichment: for example, in *Le Cheval D'Orgueil*, Pierre-Jakez Hélias's memoir of his Breton childhood in the 1920s, the author-protagonist recounts how he grew to love the language of *la République* which he had first learned at school.[13]

The educational position of the Irish vernacular is intrinsic to our tale, and we shall return to discuss it more fully in later chapters. Another language now claims our attention: Latin, which for centuries had co-existed with Irish.[14] Although the Romans did not conquer Ireland, there had been extensive trading contacts with the Roman world even in pre-Christian times, before the heyday of the early medieval church, when Irish grammarians had helped to preserve the teaching of Latin, in monasteries at home and abroad.[15] Keith Busby, in his recent study of Ireland's place in medieval Francophonia, discusses how, in multilingual Cistercian communities of thirteenth-century Ireland, Latin, as the mother-tongue of nobody, was the required common language for everybody, along with the language of the colonists.[16] For centuries, Irish people could resort to the *lingua franca* of

Latin to speak with travellers landed on their shores – be they agents of the Crown, sailors and captains, or merchants.[17] As elsewhere in the nineteenth century, Latin remained the essential repository of traditional learning, and was the requisite for all higher education, both clerical and lay. Some rudiments of the classics were standard parts of the school curriculum, whether in great houses with private tutors, in formal school settings or even, as anecdotal evidence suggests, in informal private 'pay' or 'hedge'-schools, depending on the accomplishments of the schoolmaster in a given locality. Vestiges of fluency in Latin persisted in unlikely places. Thus, a traveller reported (1806) on the number of people he met in Kerry, who were 'all good Latin scholars, yet [did] not speak a word of English'.[18]

In Victorian times, Latin was arguably apprehended in distinct ways by the two main religious communities. If, for members of the reformed churches, it was the language of Caesar, experienced primarily in the schoolroom, for the vast majority of the population it had a recurring afterlife at Sunday worship. One can only speculate on the sociolinguistic effect of the pervasive presence of ecclesiastical Latin, in the practice of Catholicism, on people exposed to the weekly – at times daily – performance of the Roman liturgy. For most of the congregation, who had no access to formal Latin lessons, the words intoned or sung were presumably as arcane as the sacred truths they veiled. Catholic practice offered a portal to foreignness and to universality, as indeed it must have done in all parts of the world where the spoken vernacular was far removed from Latin. (A congregation in Italy or Spain would have found the Latin liturgy linguistically more semi-transparent.) The ritual mystique of church Latin made Irish Catholics accustomed to hearing foreign sounds, however unintelligible. In Irish-speaking regions, foreignness could be amplified: 'The Mass was Latin, and the sermon was English, and the congregation only understood Irish.'[19] Anglican worship, performed in the solemn registers of Lutheran-English hymns and the cadences of the King James Bible or Book of Common Prayer, was by comparison sonorous and engaging, but monoglot.

Ireland's fluid language atlas was neither monoglot nor stable and touched all sectors of the population and all ages, from schoolchildren onwards. Interlingual contacts between English and Irish were a matter of course as people wove their way through their intersecting lives. Latin played a key role for Roman Catholics in the weekly liturgy, and, for all denominations, it was a core subject in the schoolroom, as it was essential for further education.

For some, the study of Latin had also led to contacts with other foreign languages and cultures. As Sir James Caldwell, sheriff of County Fermanagh, pointed out in 1764:[20]

> The Papists are not only connected by the general Tie of the Religion that acknowledges the Pope for its common Father and Head, with the courts of *France* and *Spain*, but there is not a Family in the Island that has not a Relation in the Church, in the Army, or in Trade in those Countries, and in order to qualify the Children for Foreign Service, they are all taught *Latin* in Schools kept in poor Huts, in many Places in the Southern Part of the Kingdom.

It is principally the cultural and linguistic effect on the Catholic diaspora who experienced such foreign education – for so long a feature of Irish history – that will concern us in the next section.

Continental Irish Colleges: A Loquacious Diaspora

For Catholics, the traditional model of higher learning had necessarily involved a foreign dimension. As a consequence of the consolidation of Tudor power and the ensuing religious wars and plantations, generations of Irish Catholic men had travelled overseas to continental Europe for professional training and further study. Although Queen Elizabeth I had founded Trinity College Dublin in 1592 in a bid to save her Irish subjects from being infected by continental popery, her college, within a few decades, had become entrenched in confessional positions that brought about the opposite result as, until the last of the penal restrictions were lifted in 1793, papists could not attend Trinity without compromising their faith. Thus alienated, they travelled instead to Counter-Reformation centres in Catholic Europe that welcomed them. In compliance with the Council of Trent's injunction (1564) that seminaries be set up in order to equip the priesthood with the means to refute heresy, over 30 Irish colleges were founded in Spain, France, Rome, Portugal, the Spanish

2.1 Portrait of Queen Elizabeth I, founder of TCD. (*Frontispiece, The Book of Trinity College Dublin, 1892*).

Netherlands and Central Europe. Between the late sixteenth century and the last decade of the eighteenth, these Colleges had accommodated thousands of Irish students, mostly clerical, fleeing the discriminatory laws of the Crown. Some of them, already secretly ordained in Ireland, travelled to complete their studies, enrolling in courses in theology and philosophy at local universities and centres of higher learning. It was an enterprise fraught with hardship, hazard and prolonged absence from home. The younger among them, who left as adolescents, returned to Ireland years later, as priests destined to work in an underground church.

The continental colleges amounted, in effect, to a university network for a Catholic intelligentsia deprived of an alma mater at home that would accept them unconditionally. Some Irish colleges became renowned centres of scholarship, notably in Irish history, language and culture, disseminated with the help of the Irish Franciscans at Louvain, who had a printing press with Irish characters from 1611.[21] Many were closely in tune with continental thought. Ailbhe Ó Corráin has shown, for example, the familiarity with contemporary intellectual tradition of a sophisticated poet like Giolla Brighde Ó hEódhasa, who entered the Franciscans at Louvain in 1607.[22] Some scholars had multifaceted careers in Catholic Europe. Daniel O'Daly OP (1595–1662), member of a dispossessed bardic family in County Kerry, was educated in Lugo, Burgos and Bordeaux, became rector of the Dominicans in Louvain, before founding their Irish college in Lisbon and a convent for Irish women at Belém. As confessor to the Portuguese crown in the 1640s and 1650s, he was sent on several diplomatic missions and moved with ease among princes of church and state. He died as bishop-elect of Coimbra.[23]

The continental sojourns of early modern Irish scholars deepened their contacts with European Counter-Reformation thought, which informed their writings in all fields of knowledge, particularly church history. During this polemical period, both Catholic and Protestant scholars framed their narratives in distinct ways, each in order to claim an unbroken link with the origins of the true church. For Irish Catholics, living in Europe was also fundamental in forging an embryonic sense of national identity. The period witnessed 'a panoply of humanist apologetics for Ireland [...] in the scholarly networks of continental Europe'.[24] The disruption and trauma of leaving home were compounded by being faced with traditional negative stereotypes of the Irish as uncouth barbarians.[25] Irish men of letters reacted by writing their own accounts of Irish history, asserting the civilised nature of their culture, and how closely the island had always adhered to European civilisation, Christian and pre-Christian.[26] Thus, the need to defend Ireland's reputation incited Clonmel Jesuit Stephen White (1574–1646/7) to study Irish history, having lived for over 20 years on the continent, teaching and researching, and attracting the adulation of scholars for the extent of his erudition.[27] His *Apologia pro Hibernia Adversus Cambri Calumnias* (*c*.1611) refuted the arguments of Giraldus Cambrensis [Gerald of Wales], the medieval Welshman who had justified the conquest of Ireland.[28]

Along with several of his confrères, Stephen White was a descendant of the early Norman settlers who by this stage were well assimilated into native Irish families. One paradoxical effect of the Reformation in Ireland was to force recusant Old English families to re-draw their allegiances and send their sons to be educated in Europe rather than England. While White, O'Daly and others wrote in the *lingua franca* of Latin, some of them communicated in Irish. One of the most influential of these intellectuals was another son of an Old English family, the diocesan priest Seathrún Céitinn [Geoffrey Keating] (*c*.1580–*c*.1644), who had studied at Bordeaux and taken a doctorate of divinity in Rheims before returning to Ireland in 1610. In *c*.1634 he finished his *Foras Feasa ar Éirinn* [*Foundation of Knowledge about Ireland*], a history of Ireland from the creation of the world to the arrival of the Normans. Keating's seventeenth-century origin-myth was to be of lasting influence on Irish cultural self-perception and Catholic identity, and his linguistic style was to be heralded as a model of classical Irish during the late nineteenth-century Gaelic Revival.[29] Around the same time, a similar perspective on the Irish past was to emanate from the collaborative compilation known as the *Annálacha Ríoghachta Éireann* [*Annals of the Four Masters*], whose chief editor was the learned Franciscan, Mícheál Ó Cléirigh, from the Irish College of St Anthony at Louvain.[30] Keating's *Foras Feasa* was translated into Latin within a couple of decades and circulated among his continental contemporaries. Exile that brings a sharpened sense of identity forms an enduring strand in Irish cultural history; it takes many forms (some of them mordant), and makes its presence keenly felt right down to Wilde, Shaw, Joyce and Beckett.

Commenting on the remarkable flourishing of Latin learning among the Irish, at home and in Europe, during the period 1550 to 1700, Benignus Millett observes that this was particularly true of the Counter-Reformation Irish:[31]

> More remarkable even than the great influx of Irish pupils and teachers to continental universities and colleges was the flowering of scholarship among them at a high level of literary

productivity, and also the large proportion of such men who were of a high intellectual calibre, as witnessed by their writings, mostly in Latin, and their contemporary reputation.

He adds that, by comparison, Irish Protestants, apart from two distinguished exceptions, James Ussher and James Ware, 'produced relatively few serious scholars writing in Latin'.

Prolonged contact with the foreign works in both directions. As well as helping the expatriate to understand and articulate his own culture at crucial inflection points in its history, it could also lead to less benign consequences. Historians have identified the problem of diminished Irish-language proficiency among clergy trained in a continental environment. This was most acute among those students who, having spent their formative years abroad, risked losing their fluency in Irish, or indeed forgetting the language altogether. The waning of their Irish-language competence considerably weakened their ability to minister, preach and catechise on their return to Ireland. The issue had been perceived by their superiors in the seventeenth and eighteenth centuries, and in some continental Irish colleges deliberate measures – language classes, scholarships and prizes – had been taken to address it.[32] The Franciscans' Irish College in Prague, established in 1629, included the study of Irish.[33] A knowledge of Irish was important for the head of a college. There were objections in Lille in 1764 when a rector who did not speak Irish was appointed. He was replaced by a man who did.[34]

If proficiency in Irish was perceived as problematical, to what extent did the Irish seminarians gain proficiency in their host country's vernacular? In the case of the Jesuit order, one element of the novitiate involved a period of catechetical instruction in a poor parish near the seminary; this presumably impelled foreign novices to gain at least a rudimentary knowledge of the local vernacular.[35] More generally, it seems reasonable to suppose that a heightened sensitivity to language study, and hence to the language environments around them, was an inescapable part of the educational experience of this Catholic diaspora. For these cadet soldiers of the Counter-Reformation, the need to counter heresy inevitably required some training in verbal jousting. In addition to philosophy and theology, their studies included linguistic disciplines intended to develop their skills in preaching, persuading and debating: grammar, rhetoric and logic.[36] The *disputatio*, or formalised public debate to defend a thesis, *viva voce* [orally] in Latin, was part of their everyday curriculum.

Their counterparts from England and Scotland, the recusants who fetched up at the Tridentine English College, Douai (then within the Spanish Netherlands) and elsewhere,[37] were also being trained as 'theological gladiators for public disputation' – although, in practice, none of these *émigrés* were given much chance to profess their faith publicly on being smuggled home to increasingly hostile political climates.[38] The first generation of English Roman Catholic clerics, exiled from Oxford because they refused the oath of supremacy, saw the need for a vernacular English translation of the bible as a key weapon in the battle against heresy. The Douai New Testament was published in 1582, followed by the Old Testament in 1609–10. The volumes carried heavily polemical annotations as to the supremacy of the Roman interpretation of scripture over its rivals: as Eamon Duffy pithily asserts, 'this was holy scripture conceived as a fighting manual rather than an aid to devotion.'[39] Trawling through the Protestant texts, the New Testament translator Gregory Martin was motivated 'by a desire to document the wickedness of heretical translators in perverting the true meaning of holy scripture.'[40] The Reformation and Counter-Reformation, replete with unspeakably bloody deeds perpetrated by Christians upon Christians, were also fought on a linguistic battlefield. Creeds have to be expressed, or renounced, through language. *In the beginning was the Word*. And the word became an end in itself.

Irish clerics settled their theological controversies in public, if we are to believe eighteenth-century French pen portraits that depict them arguing volubly in the street. For example, in the satirical lines of Claude Carloman de Rulhière:[41]

> De pauvres Hibernois complaisants disputeurs,
> Qui, fuyant leur pays pour les saintes promesses,
> Viennent vivre à Paris d'arguments et de messes.
> Et l'honnête public qui, même écoutant bien,
> À la saine raison de n'y comprendre rien.

> [Penniless Hibernians, not loath to debate,
> Fleeing their land for the sake of holy vows,
> Come to live in Paris off disputation and Masses.
> And decent folk who listen with care as they pass,
> Of intelligible reason not a whit can they grasp.]

Rulhière does not specify the language used by these argumentative Irish expatriates. As the setting is the Sorbonne's Theology Faculty, are we to imagine them practising for their examinations in theology, contested *viva voce* in public? Was it their Latin pronunciation that their Parisian audiences found incomprehensible? Or could they have been arguing in their own tongue, like the Irish students portrayed by Montesquieu, who were wont to mill around the *Quartier Latin* and engage noisily in their illogical philosophical disputes in a 'langue barbare qui semble ajouter quelque chose à la fureur et à l'opiniâtreté des combattants' [barbaric tongue that seems to ramp up the fury and obstinacy of the brawlers]?[42]

Although Latin was the *lingua franca* for their formal learning and assessment, the same expatriates must have had occasion to talk to Parisians not versed in Latin, Irish or English. Indeed, the worries about students forgetting their Irish derived precisely from a perceived over exposure to the foreign vernacular, and not to a surfeit of Latin. A source from Paris in 1738 describes younger Irish students acquiring a perfect command of French but losing their native tongue. As they depended for their daily bread on local charity, this was perhaps understandable.[43] Irish *seminaristas* in Alcalà de Henares conversed with fellow students in Castilian; in Santiago de Compostela, they complained when prevented from mixing with Spaniards as this compromised their ability to perfect their fluency in Spanish.[44] In some cases, the sojourn among foreigners may have heightened their awareness of language divisions in Ireland: internal disputes occasionally broke out between Irish-speaking students from Ulster and Connacht and anglophone Old English students from Leinster and Munster.[45]

Many displaced scholars extended their stay abroad; a significant number never returned to Ireland, preferring to carry out their ministry in Catholic Europe.[46] Following over 20 years in Rome, Oliver Plunkett (1625–81) 'never really reconciled himself to being back in Ireland' and corresponded much more in Italian than in English.[47] Some clerics, regarded as too valuable to be sent back to the Irish mission, were asked to remain. Men like Peadar Ó Neachtain, SJ (1709–56), who sailed for Santiago at the age of 19, entered the Jesuits and spent the rest of his life teaching in their seminaries in Spain, presumably attained more than rudimentary linguistic competence.[48] Judging by a moving verse farewell on his departure written by Peadar's father, the renowned Dublin poet Tadhg Ó Neachtain, we can assume that this youth was academically well equipped for his career by the time he left Ireland, never to return, in 1728. The poem gives a precious glimpse of the kind of liberal arts education available to the son of a learned Gaelic-speaking household in early eighteenth-century Dublin.[49] The poet reminisces on his son's instruction in humanities, poetry and logic with the Jesuits, in their classical school:[50]

> Daondhacht d'fhoghluim is filigheacht fós
> Ó dhaltadh Dé d'órd Íosa
> Maolradh Ó Bruin,'t-uan gan mheang,
> Is ó Aodh eagnach ua Conaill.
>
> Tús a loighic lean gan locht
> Ag bláth na heagnadh 's na hollamhnacht
> Eóin Harald, an cáirneach caomh,
> Lóchrann an chreideamh 'sa chathaoir.
>
> [He learned humanities and poetry as well
> From God's student of the Order of Jesus
> Maolra Ó Bruin, the lamb without guile,
> And from wise Aodh Ó Conaill.
>
> The foundation of logic he followed without fault
> With the flower of wisdom and professorship
> John Harold, the gentle friar,
> The torch of the faith and its seat.]

As a small child at home, he had been initiated into the rudiments of grammar, as well as music, Irish writing and mathematics:[51]

> Tús a litreach do lean mo ghrádh
> Agus tús fós a ghramada
> Ag mo athair dil, Seán, mo shearc
> Ag deargadh aidhinne a inntleacht.
>
> Fós tús a cheoil do char mo chuid
> Uaim féin (fíor; ní fáth a dhearmad)
> 'S riaghalúgh a mhéir (gan bhríathar gó)
> A scríobhadh gaoiseach na Gaoidhiolgodh.
>
> Raoimh-eadhluighean lean mo leanabh dil
> Ag Gearóid gaoiseach ua Réadhmuin;
> Sin na saothaibh bhus oidígh do
> A n-íath aerach Éireann algodh.
>
> [The start of his letters my love followed
> And the start of his grammar as well

With my dear father, Seán, my love
Kindling the lighting of his intellect.

The beginning of his music too which my darling loved
From me myself (true: that is no reason to forget it)
And the directing of his finger (without word of a lie)
In the wise writing of Irish.

My dear child learned the art of enumeration
From wise Gearóid Ó Réamoinn;
Those are the wise men who were his teachers
In the pleasant land of noble Ireland.]

In their Irish province, the Jesuits ensured a supply of students sufficiently qualified for entry to the continental colleges.[52] Some cases of language competence among the early clerical exiles were outstanding. Salamanca, where Peadair Ó Neachtain stayed during his first year abroad, had become quite a centre for linguistic study. In the early 1640s, Paul Sherlock SJ, rector of Salamanca, left an account of his own life, written in Spanish.[53] An earlier Irish émigré there, William Bathe, SJ (1564–1614), was the main author (along with other faculty members of the Irish College) of the *Ianua Linguarum* [*Door to Languages*] (1611), a pioneering bilingual language-teaching method. Of prominent Old English stock and brought up in Drumcondra Castle, near Dublin, Bathe had studied in Oxford and London, before going to Louvain to study theology and join the Jesuits three years later, in 1595.[54] Juxtaposing simple sentences in Latin and Spanish, the *Ianua* sought to 'facilitate the speedy acquisition of fluent and accurate Latin in the case of native Spanish students and to help Irish students who had no competence in Spanish when they first arrived in Salamanca'.[55] Viewed as useful for the rapid acquisition of all languages, it was widely circulated, spawning 30 adapted, extended and translated editions in various parts of Europe before the end of the seventeenth century.[56]

Some of the priests who returned to Ireland became classical schoolmasters. The poet-scribe Seán Ó Coileáin (1754–1817), for example, returned from Coimbra in Portugal without completing his clerical training, and opened a school in the Myross peninsula, near Skibbereen.[57] Some returned clerics also taught French.[58] Jesuits, active in Ireland since the 1500s, were all trained in Europe, often for protracted periods of time.[59] This pattern recurs in the lives of the three Jesuits who are the focus of Thomas Morrissey's recent account of the order's work in semi-clandestine conditions in Dublin during penal times.[60] John Austin, SJ (1717–84), spent 15 years studying and teaching in France before coming home in 1750 to open a classical school in Saul's Court, near Christchurch Cathedral. James Philip Mulcaile, SJ (1727–1801), after living and teaching for almost 30 years in France, from the age of eight, likewise returned to join the staff as a classical teacher. He also helped to open a free school in St Michan's parish for the education of girls from poor families, who were taught basic literacy and catechism, needlework and household skills. Thomas Betagh, SJ (1738–1811), lived for 15 years in Lorraine and Paris, working as a professor of languages, before returning to teach at Saul's Court, and to open schools for the city's poor. He became a renowned preacher. All three of these men were highly competent linguists, as were many of their confrères. Betagh's friend, future bishop of

Meath Patrick Joseph Plunkett, SJ (*d.*1827), had spent 27 years in France. The two men corresponded on political matters in French during the period of total suppression of the Jesuit order.[61]

Given such instances of close engagement with foreign languages among Irish clerics abroad, it is no surprise to hear of evidence that priests returning to Ireland had foreign-language reading knowledge. Archived catalogues of auctioneers, as well as records of books confiscated at Irish ports during penal times, reveal glimpses of the kind of personal libraries that accompanied them home. One sample of such holdings found that their books tended to contain a preponderant amount of works in 'Latin and French, Italian, Spanish, or Portuguese, depending on which Irish College they attended'.[62]

In sum, it is probably safe to assume that study in continental Europe led, by and large, to a considerable degree of proficiency in the foreign vernacular, and even to linguistic assimilation.

FRENCH IN EARLY NINETEENTH-CENTURY SEMINARIES

Until the late eighteenth century, then – as penal laws were relaxed and seminaries opened on Irish soil during the turbulent aftermath of the French Revolution – continental Europe had been the locus of higher education for most Irish Catholics, or at least for the small cohort of the Catholic population who could aspire to such learning, for over 200 years.

Not all Irish Catholics who studied in Europe were clerical, of course.[63] We have been deliberately highlighting the clerical students, because of the clergy's direct influence in the education sphere. The Medical Faculty at Prague's Carolinum (Charles University) was a refuge for dozens of Irish émigrés between the late seventeenth and late eighteenth centuries, many of whom qualified as doctors while serving at the Imperial Hapsburg Court of Bohemia. Dr Jacobus Smith [MacGowan], descendant of a hereditary medical family, became professor of physiology, and died as rector (1744) there.[64] French-educated doctors and scientists also returned home; several of them left libraries containing French-language books.[65] Galway-born Richard Kirwan (1733–1812), who had been educated by the Jesuits at Poitiers and taught Humanities in St Omer, returned to Ireland after nine years abroad. As a chemist and natural philosopher, he was one of the founder members of the Royal Irish Academy, serving as its second president, from 1799 to his death in 1812.[66] Kirwan had no difficulty in corresponding in French with leading French scientists.[67]

French was the most useful language for trade, along Europe's western seaboard and as far as the West Indies. In the early nineteenth century, the thriving port of Cork had its own French Consulate. Catholic merchants often learned their trade abroad, like the prominent Corkman James Roche (1770–1853), who at 15 was sent to school for two years in Saintes before working in the wine trade in Bordeaux. After his return to Cork in 1797 he became involved in banking. 'It was said of him that "The purity of his pronunciation and his idiomatic precision in conversing in French were so perfect that he was frequently mistaken for a native of France".'[68] These cases illustrate how an ear for the spoken language was important for the marketplace, while scholars and scientists needed to take a more monastic approach to acquiring the foreign language, in order to read, write and translate it correctly.

Isolated cases of linguistic skills among the lay professions pale into insignificance, however, in terms of scale, and educational influence, beside the numbers of clerics with foreign-language fluency returned from sojourns abroad. Thomas O'Connor observes that the decline of the Irish Colleges as training centres for Ireland's priests 'deprived the nineteenth-century Irish church of an enriching continental influence'.[69] While this statement is no doubt true, the traditional model of educating the Catholic clergy overseas left resonances in Irish culture well beyond 1800. Where ecclesiastics were concerned, one of those resonances was foreign-language acquisition. During the early nineteenth century, most clerics of influence had studied in Europe. John MacHale, consecrated titular bishop of Maronia in 1825 and resident archbishop of Tuam in 1834, was 'the first Irish archbishop since the Reformation to receive his education entirely in Ireland'.[70]

After the demise of the penal laws, the newly established Irish seminaries maintained close contacts with Europe. The first of these to open was St Patrick's College, Carlow (1793). Most of its founding staff had spent their formative years being educated on the continent. Some were competent linguists. Its first president, Henry Staunton, had studied in Paris; its second, Andrew Fitzgerald OP, had spent 13 years at Louvain and then Lisbon; one of its early professors of theology and rhetoric, the Augustinian James Doyle, had studied in Portugal. Three of Carlow's earliest staff members, Abbés Noget, Chabout and Labruné, were French refugees following the 1789 Revolution.[71]

All of the initial staff at Maynooth's Royal College of St Patrick, founded in 1795, had studied on the continent, and four of its founding fathers, too, were émigrés from France. Two of these, François Anglade and Louis-Gilles Delahogue, remained there permanently and were laid to rest in the college cemetery, aged 76 and 88 respectively.[72] In Maynooth's early decades, French was spoken at the professors' dining-table (apart from one end reserved for Irish speakers), and French influence was, to quote Patrick Corish, 'pervasive, producing a kind of afternoon of the Catholic Enlightenment, a rustic Sorbonne in north Kildare.'[73] That influence was especially strong, albeit indirectly, in the core curricula of dogmatic and moral theology, courses that were devised and taught respectively by Frs Delahogue and Anglade practically since the college's foundation. These 'men from the Sorbonne were its intellectual fathers', authors of student textbooks in their respective disciplines;[74] moreover, the French professors' pronunciation of Latin (in which they lectured) was a daily reminder to every clerical student of linguistic diversity in a wider world. The French language has been continually on Maynooth's curriculum of studies since its foundation.[75] Some of those who taught it had spent time abroad. Matthew Kelly, for instance, Maynooth's professor of 'Belles-Lettres and French' from 1841 to 1867, had taught at the Irish College in Paris for three years before his appointment.[76]

Like the teaching of Irish and English, French language teaching was pushed to the margins in the seminary's overcrowded curriculum.[77] Although subordinate to the immediate needs of Irish diocesan clerical training, the fact that French was on the curriculum at all is nevertheless significant. And Maynooth was not alone. A trawl through *Battersby's Catholic Directory* for 1860[78] shows several diocesan colleges and seminaries advertising French as part of their curriculum: this was the case, that year, in St Augustine's Cavan, St John's Waterford, St Patrick's Thurles, St Peter's Wexford, and St Colman's Fermoy.

CATHOLIC MISSIONARY COLLEGES: *EUNTES ERGO DOCETE OMNES GENTES [GOING FORTH THEREFORE TEACH YE ALL PEOPLES]*[79]

It seems clear that ecclesiastical educators in pre- and early-Victorian Ireland valued the study of modern languages, and there were plenty of teachers available to put this value into practice. The advantages of language skills were well appreciated at the Missionary College of All Hallows in Drumcondra, founded in 1842 to train Irish seminarians destined for foreign missions. Unlike Maynooth's Mission to India, intended to meet the shortage of anglophone priests to serve Catholics in the colonies, the alumni of All Hallows were destined for wider global service.[80] The College's early *Annual Reports* testify to the endeavours of its graduate missionaries, whose letters from far-flung corners of the world frequently allude to the multilingual environment of their daily lives and the need to communicate in other tongues with both parishioners and ecclesiastics from other Catholic jurisdictions.[81] Thus, Fr Denis Spellissy, recently landed in Mauritius, on 3 March 1849:[82]

> I have not much more to add, unless to beg that you would impress on the minds of the young men destined for this mission the necessity of knowing French. Everyone here, even the British officials, know that language. If a priest know French, this is, I think, one of the finest missions in the world.

Eight years later, on 5 May 1857, the same priest writes from Rivière Sèche, Flacq, with a more nuanced language awareness, albeit equating Creole with 'broken French':[83]

> The priest here must know two languages – French and broken French. The whites would be displeased were we to speak in *patois* on Sundays, and the poor people do not sufficiently understand any other. We endeavour to instruct them during the week in Creole.

Writing from Agra, in India, on 28 January 1848, Fr Nicholas Barry is impressed by the linguistic skills of his bishop on Sundays, who 'has all the neighbouring priests that day to dine with him, and he talks to them all in their several languages with fluency – the French, Italian, and English; he is also acquainted with the Hindoostan, Persian, and Russian languages.'[84] Reporting from Buenos Aires, five years later, Fr Anthony Fahy makes a case for Spanish:[85]

> I wish our young men would study the Spanish language, particularly as they will be able hereafter to take charge of large parishes in the country, where there will be a large mixture of English and Spaniards. [...] I will also forward some good Spanish books for the use of the students.

In North American missions, too, there was an awareness of the need for priests with linguistic proficiency. Already in the eighteenth century, a Capuchin from Offaly, Charles Whelan ('Maurice' Whelan in religious life) (*d.*1806), was the first Catholic pastor to serve in the city of New York. He entered the order in 1770 at Bar-sur-Aube in Champagne, where he was trained, ordained and worked for ten years, after which he left Europe in 1781, as a chaplain to the French fleet that took part in the American War of Independence.[86] Upon his arrival in New York some months later, his command of French and of Gaelic were reportedly better than his English. Father Whelan wrote, in Italian, to the Papal Nuncio in France on 28 January 1785:[87]

> I would have written to you in Latin, if I were not persuaded that Your Eminence understands all the European languages. It is necessary for a priest in this place to know at least Irish, English, French and Dutch, since the congregation is composed of people of these nationalities, as also of Portuguese and Spaniards.

A few decades later, All Hallows alumni working in other parts of North America also remark on multilingual groups around them, whether fellow priests or parishioners.[88]

Such testimonies did not go unnoticed. Italian classes were offered at All Hallows;[89] and a professor of French and German, Revd Abbé Schürr, appears on staff lists in the *Annual Reports* for All Hallows during the mid-1850s. We shall return to l'Abbé Schürr in Chapter Six, as this missionary priest was to move to the staff of Newman's Catholic University.

These alumni reports remind us of what foreign travel meant before today's global position of English. In the nineteenth century, English was just one language among a myriad of others, and educated European travellers were assumed to be competent in at least understanding a couple beyond their mother tongue. Missionaries travelled with a clear professional rationale for language learning. The All Hallows reports illustrate the global and multilingual reach of Roman Catholicism.[90] An appendix to the College's *Annual Report* printed in 1855 compares the Eternal City, not without a touch of irony, to a supreme plurilingual empire:[91]

> Unless, perhaps, in the tens of thousands of various tongues, costumes, and lineaments, which one sees with uncovered heads when, like a messenger from Heaven the Holy Father raises his hand to bless the world, from St Peter's or St John Lateran's, nothing can give such an idea of the universality of the Church as the Feast of Tongues of the Propaganda College at Rome. Forty-four different languages, in song, address, and dialogue, announce the presence of the children 'of every place under Heaven', the subjects of the only empire which is 'from the rising to the setting of the sun'.

LINGUISTICALLY AGILE CLERGY

Within this universal empire, Irish churchmen were capable of communicating with their Catholic confrères in other realms of Europe, and not just in Latin. The historian Revd John Lanigan (1758–1828) used his multilingual skills outside the strictly ecclesiastical sphere. Having lived in Italy for two decades, training in Rome before teaching Hebrew and scripture at Pavia, he spoke Italian, French, German and Spanish along with English and Irish, as well as knowing classical languages. After his return to Ireland in 1794, he worked as assistant librarian at the Royal Dublin Society and sometimes taught languages in the homes of wealthy Dubliners.[92] When in Portugal preparing his doctorate in the 1800s, the future bishop of Kildare and Leighlin, James Warren Doyle (1786–1834), found his studies in Coimbra interrupted by the French invasion; he travelled to Lisbon working as an interpreter between English and Portuguese for Wellington's forces. Some 20 years later, he was to be one of the key spokesmen for the Catholic hierarchy in the battle for the reform of primary education in the 1820s, leading to the Education Act (1831) that established non-denominational schools.[93] John MacHale, though fully educated in Ireland, was an accomplished linguist and translator.[94] Bartholomew Woodlock (1819–1902), Bishop of Ardagh and Clonmacnoise, had trained at Rome's Pontifical seminary. He co-founded All Hallows College and succeeded Newman as rector of the Catholic University. Woodlock was fluent in Italian, Latin and French.[95]

This handful of examples is indicative of a continuous linguistic dimension in the lives of some influential Irish Catholic clergymen. It should be stressed, at this point, that this is by no means to imply that *only* such Roman Catholic clergymen were multilingual. That would be an absurd proposition for a period when, in the upper echelons of the clergy of all denominations, there was an abundance of foreign-language ability to be found. Indeed – even if their understanding and performance of the spoken word could leave much to be desired –, *all* properly educated Englishmen (and by extension Irishmen)[96] of the nineteenth century were assumed, in addition to their grounding in the classics, to have at least a reading knowledge of a couple of living European languages. It was part of the everyday texture of life to be able, like that quintessential late-Victorian fictional character, Sherlock Holmes, to segue with ease between quoting chunks of Goethe (*auf Deutsch*) and the latest findings in forensic science to issue from Paris (*en français*). Conan Doyle supplies no English translation, the assumption being either that his readers understand the quotations too, or at least expect their sleuth to know his French and German as well as his Latin. This Holmesian syndrome, however aspirational, is presented as the norm throughout educated sections of European society, well into the twentieth century.[97] Our argument here is focused on evidence of language proficiency within Ireland's particular demographic and political structure. Within that frame, being a member of the Roman Catholic clergy entailed a particular linguistic dynamic and texture. If you conduct your daily business in a second or third language, it relativises your first language. Not only did Irish priests and prelates celebrate Mass every day in Latin; many of them also had personal or professional links with their peers outside the English-speaking world.

2.2 Cardinal Paul Cullen, archbishop of Dublin Photograph, by unknown 19th-century Irish photographer. (*No known copyright restrictions.*)

One singular case deserves special mention. The most politically influential of Irish nineteenth-century prelates was Paul Cullen (1803–78), Archbishop of Armagh then Dublin, and Ireland's first cardinal. An ultramontane[98] in his views of papal power, Cullen was an active player in promoting the establishment of the Catholic University and, after his return to Ireland from Rome in 1850 (as we have seen) took the initiative of inviting Newman to be its first rector.[99] He had lived and worked in Rome for 30 years, where he enjoyed an outstanding reputation as one of the ablest scholars of his generation. Having studied at the College of Propaganda Fide, he became its professor of Greek and oriental languages, and continued to work in Rome as rector of the Irish College from 1832. He was fluent in Latin and Italian, and competent in French as well as Hebrew and Greek. At the Propaganda Fide he was 'given charge of the Propaganda's polyglot press, which produced a number of scholarly texts during his tenure'.[100]

As Anne O'Connor has shown, Cullen as archbishop and cardinal deployed his linguistic and translation skills most effectively in advancing political agendas within Ireland as well as exerting influence on English-speaking Catholic countries well beyond Europe. He had an unusually direct line to the Vatican. In his extensive correspondence with Rome, his written Italian was of near-native standard, exemplary in vocabulary, syntax and grammar, while his spoken Italian was also of a high standard.[101] Cullen could have corresponded in Latin with the Vatican, as was customary, but by the middle of the nineteenth century, O'Connor argues, Latin was less useful than Italian for securing immediate access to the corridors of papal power.[102] Significantly, he even resorted to Italian in his correspondence with fellow Irishmen in Rome. Cullen's Italian letters to Tobias Kirby, his successor as rector at the Irish College, for instance, indicate that he clearly intended his message to be circulated, promptly and verbatim, in the right quarters, ensuring speed of communication and eliminating the potential for points being lost in translation.[103]

In discussing Cullen's education as an adolescent at Carlow College (1817–20), Colin Barr quotes from an 1822 source, which allows a glimpse of the kind of language exposure already available at the pre-Victorian seminary. The writer, J. B. Taylor, was a contemporary of Cullen's who had just been appointed to a professorship at the college. He outlines his duties as follows:[104]

> I hear a class of prosody & Italian grammar in the morning, Livy & Juvenal [...] from 10 to 11[,] Greek grammar from 12 to 1[,] Homer from 1 to 2, Cicero & Horace alternately from 2 to 3 – I have six classes of Latin, 4 of Greek, 3 of French, 1 of Italian [...]

Barr points out that the kind of academic education provided by Carlow College was comparable to the standard preparation of students for matriculation at Oxford.[105] However, Cullen's particular case suggests that to be sent on to Rome may have proved to be an altogether different cultural and linguistic experience from being sent to Oxford. The Irishman's experience in the capital of the Papal States, teaching Greek and oriental languages to students from diverse backgrounds, using Italian extensively in his daily life and publishing in various languages, brought an extra dimension to Cullen's exposure to language diversity that was even broader than the Oxford formation, from which, however linguistically rich, a future prelate of the Anglican persuasion might have benefitted.

Where did all of this leave clerical competence in the Irish vernacular? Addressing one of the dilemmas confronting historians of the Irish language, Ciarán Mac Murchaidh couched the problem in the following terms:[106]

> Specifically, the linguistic problem posed [by] a church whose *lingua franca* was Latin and whose officers – priests and bishops – were trained in an environment in which the vernacular – French, Italian, Spanish, Portuguese – was of little use in Ireland, deserve[s] elucidation.

Given the continental education of Ireland's Roman Catholic clergy during the *ancien régime*, and the vestiges of that experience felt up to mid-Victorian times, it is undoubtedly the case that the Irish language must have been the loser in the equation. For much of the early nineteenth century, influential foreign-educated Catholic clerics were, with one or two exceptions, more engaged with continental European languages than with the Irish vernacular.[107] While this did little for the health of the Irish language, it had a profound influence on the acceptance and spread of the study of European languages in Ireland.

TRANSLATION: CHURCH TRIUMPHANT, NATION RESURGENT

Further evidence of the prevailing backdrop of modern foreign languages in Victorian Ireland is found in the sphere of translation, which opened up new currents of transnational exchange with Europe. Anne O'Connor has explored this phenomenon.[108] Two of the translation strands she traces, devotional literature and cultural nationalism, are relevant to our context.

Licensed, after centuries of prohibition, by the twin boons of emancipation (1829) and – 40 years later – disestablishment (1869),[109] the Irish Catholic Church set about displaying its de facto ascendancy over its flock by embarking on a vast church-building programme.[110] This mammoth undertaking echoed a similar renewal of the Church of Ireland's architectural infrastructure that had spanned the closing decades of the Georgian period.[111] The Catholic Church's building boom entailed the importation from Catholic Europe of all the ready-manufactured requirements of worship, including church furnishings, statues, rosaries and printed icons. Some church organs, too, were ordered from Europe, like the one in St Andrews Church, Westland Row, Dublin, which was opened in 1871, with 600 pipes made by the distinguished French organ builder Cavaillé-Coll. There being no Irish church musicians trained in the Catholic liturgy, organists were sought in Belgium and Germany: thus, Aloys Fleischmann 'and his father-in-law, Hans Conrad Swertz, were among the fifty continental organists brought to Ireland by the Catholic bishops from 1860 to 1960'.[112]

A spiritual renewal ran in tandem with these developments: concern for the edification of an increasingly literate faithful led to the importation of streams of pious and devotional texts, to be translated into English from Italian and French, and marketed cheaply by James Duffy (1808/09–71), an influential Dublin printer who enjoyed Church patronage.[113] 'Duffy provided Catholic nationalism with a valuable, cheap and reliable channel for their cause.'[114] These translations, often proselytising in intent and moralising in tone, helped to maintain strong links with certain narrow strands of Counter-Reformation Catholicism.[115] Prominent among the texts were, for example, the works of St Alphonsus Liguori, founder of the Redemptorist Order. O'Connor concludes that the so-called 'devotional revolution' in the nineteenth-century Irish Catholic Church contributed to the Europeanisation of Irish Catholicism.[116] The translation activity also contributed to the Church's anglicisation, since (as Niall Ó Ciosáin observes) 'it produced next to no devotional publishing in Irish, even though Irish-speaking Catholics were numbered in the hundreds of thousands.'[117] Only a handful of devotional texts were translated into Irish by Archbishop John MacHale.[118]

The other radical movement shaping the nineteenth century was of course cultural nationalism, a political force rooted in the philology of the German Romantics, who considered language to be an essential element of cultural identity. The Young Irelander Thomas Davis, in particular, was influenced by Herder and Fichte,[119] and called for modern languages to be given priority over Greek and Latin.[120] Here again, translation played a role in reinforcing Ireland's romantic nationalist sentiment, thereby once again helping the spread of English.[121] From its inception, to boost its Mazzinian construct of unified self-government, the weekly newspaper *The Nation* carried patriotic foreign songs and poems translated into English from French, German and Italian, as well as original verse by Irish writers.[122] This was part of a deliberate policy to align itself with the wave of nationalism running through Europe, from Bohemia to the Balkans, Hungary, Poland, Prussia and the Italian peninsula. In the second issue of the newspaper, John Blake Dillon regretted that contemporary continental literature did not reach Irish shores:[123]

> The literature of the continent has been hitherto a sealed book to the Irish public. [...] Some of the greatest works that have ever seen the light have, within the last few years, been published in Germany and France; and we are utterly ignorant, not only of their contents but of their very names. There are many reasons why we should regret this ignorance of foreign literature. It may be stated as a general truth, that the more intimately acquainted the people of any country are with the sentiments, the actions, and the condition of their neighbours – the more aspiring, the more liberal and the more intolerant of oppression, that people will be.

In an argument relying on rhetoric rather than logic, he singles out French literature as most conducive to the Irish disposition:[124]

> Were we asked which of the European nations it is whose literature is best adapted to the character of the Irish people, we would, without hesitation, point to France. Were we asked which of the nations of Europe possesses a literature most repugnant to that character, we would, with as little hesitation, answer England. It is an indisputable fact, that there are no two nations whose people have more points of resemblance, more passions and prejudice in common, than France and Ireland; and none whose people differ so widely in character and sentiment as England and Ireland. [...] The passages we have selected will serve as an example of that remarkable correspondence between French and Irish sentiment, upon which we have been insisting. Where could we find expressed with more eloquence and truth the two leading passions of the Irish heart – patriotism and piety?

As Anne O'Connor points out, *The Nation*'s editors selected and appropriated foreign literary works, deliberately framing them to suit Young Ireland's ideological agenda. Thus, Petrarch the love-poet was of less interest for their purpose than Petrarch the patriot.[125] The German Romantic poets they translated were those, like Uhland or Rückert, who sang of the wars of liberation against Napoleonic dominance.[126] The paper carried critical pieces about the aggressions of imperial England while extolling the actions and pronouncements of patriots elsewhere and emphasising Ireland's historical ties with foreign places.

What rings loud through the pages of early issues of *The Nation* is its editors' inflated sense of the importance of their own aspirations, and of the inevitability that Ireland's destiny would come to pass. 'Ireland will soon be a nation'; 'The olive growth of nationality is overspreading the provinces, and taking permanent root in the heart of the land.'[127] There is the assumption that, beyond Britain, the rest of the world was watching events in Ireland, as it had, allegedly, during the successful struggle for Catholic Emancipation:[128]

> The world attended us with its thoughts and prayers. The graceful genius of Italy and the profound intellect of Germany paused to wish us well. The fiery heart of France tolerated our unarmed effort, and proffered its aid.

There is certainty that sympathy for Ireland's plight will be forthcoming, and that international friends will be waiting in the wings, on cue to enter the stage and help Ireland confront her ancient foe:[129]

> Let America be told the whole truth of our position, and she will do her best. We can promise for some of the ablest and greatest in France. The French People long to serve us.

Reciprocally, the paper mapped the plight of Ireland's downtrodden people onto that of other nations who aspired to self-determination:[130]

> No! we are not English, thank God, any more than the Italians are Austrians.

> Ireland has been called the Italy of the West, her land so fair, her soul so fiery, her glories so remote, her sorrow so deep, and her slavery so enduring. [...] Our cause is the same as that of Italy – we are provinces resolved to be nations.

There is a generous Mazzinian sweep to these internationalist-nationalist predictions and comparisons. That Mazzini himself was unsympathetic to Ireland's claim to separate nationhood was of no importance.[131] He believed in the destinies of peoples and was happy to re-draw maps; that was enough. Cultural mediation is highly selective; the tropes of nationalism are largely interchangeable, and there are kernels of truth in all mythmaking.

The Nation enjoyed immediate, phenomenal success from its first issue of 15 October 1842 and its high-flown rhetoric and resounding verse went a long way to popularise and articulate the self-image and distinct sense of history of an increasingly literate constituency of Irish readers.[132] The writings of Thomas Davis sowed the seeds of cultural nationalism that was set to flourish over the coming decades. Despite Davis's youth – he died of scarlet fever at the age of 30, in 1845 – his legacy had an incalculable influence on the forging of Irish identity that was to follow. In a public lecture in 1966 to mark the unveiling in Dublin of Edward Delaney's statue of Davis, the historian T. W. Moody observed that a central plank in Davis's construct of Irish nationhood derived from European liberal Romantic nationalism.[133] As well as linking Irish identity to the languages and cultures of Europe, Davis also had the vision to grasp the key importance of the Irish language in the edifice that he and other Young Irelanders were building, even though they did not use that vernacular themselves. In this respect, Davis was a harbinger of the Gaelic League, whose members were to address the issue of the Irish language 50 years later,[134] and who also, as we shall see in Chapter Five, were to align their endeavours, in several respects, with continental Europe. If their language revival flowered as a late Victorian shrub, its roots had been dug deep into the Young Ireland subsoil.

Through translation, the Young Irelanders of the 1840s and 1850s were consciously participating in a European transnational movement of linguistic and cultural mediation that (predictably) peaked in 1848, the year of revolutions.[135] In the cultural export direction, Thomas Moore, in his *Irish Melodies*, had created a hybrid blueprint for Irish nationalists' self-image, by grafting his Anglo-Irish lyrics onto traditional airs. Through translations into half a dozen languages, the bard's *Melodies* brought their quintessential Irish sense of loss and longing to the drawing-rooms of Europe, from Paris to Warsaw.[136] Rendered in Italian by the poet Andrea Maffei, the *Melodies* flowed into the mythical construction of Italian identity, at least within some Italian cultural circles, during the Risorgimento.[137]

In publishing translations of patriotic verse from Europe alongside home-grown ballads in English, the Young Irelanders were in fact adapting and continuing some established tropes from Gaelic Jacobite tradition[138] that prophesied the rout of the occupiers from the land. Irish poetry and folk ballads had conjured up millenarian visions of fleets of continental armies, sailing to reinforce Ireland's struggle against her oppressor.[139] An acquaintance with the literatures of England's enemies could be a form of symbolic resistance to Englishness. This engendered a patriotic rationale for modern-language study – as opposed to any utilitarian value – that was later epitomised by a nationalist commentator in D. P. Moran's *The Leader*, writing in 1908:[140]

> In no country – and it is surprising how seldom men realise it – is the knowledge of modern languages of less *practical* value than in Ireland. [...] To free ourselves from the intellectual control of England is the main purpose with which the study of modern languages can be recommended.

Perhaps not unrelated to reasons like these, attitudes to studying European languages were more constantly positive in Ireland than in England, where the whims of political change could affect the scale and pedagogy of modern-language learning, deciding which languages came in and out of fashion.[141] Monarchs could set trends: the first known manual of Portuguese as a foreign language was printed in London in 1662, on the occasion of the marriage of Charles II to Catherine of Bragança.[142] German became fashionable among affluent English families after Queen Victoria's marriage to Albert of Saxe-Coburg and Gotha in 1840; many parents followed the monarch's example when she hired a German governess for her children.[143] Wars, too, affected language study, both positively and negatively. In 1920, Queen's University Belfast got a lectureship in Spanish instead of Russian, because of the Russian Revolution.[144] One of the many overall effects of the Great War was to promote an increase in university applicants for modern languages.[145] In Britain, the war gave a fillip to interest in learning Spanish, occasionally at the expense of German. On account of anti-German feeling, academics of German or Austrian origin employed in British universities suffered various forms of exclusion such as detention, dismissal or ostracism.[146]

In contrast, the study of modern European languages in Ireland remained relatively unaffected by such political developments. Two striking exceptions were the result of official actions by the Crown rather than swings in fashion on the ground. Max Freund, Belfast's Professor of Modern Languages, was dismissed as a hostile alien in 1914, as were other academics of German provenance working in Britain, while Galway's Professor Valentine Steinberger was a victim of Ireland's domestic insurgence. Rounded up as a suspect sympathiser with the rebels four days after the Easter Rising in April 1916, shipped to Queenstown [Cobh] and detained in Wandsworth Prison, Steinberger died of pneumonia within six months of his release. The Professor had been a pacifist and his elder son was serving in the Royal Navy.[147]

★ ★ ★

The Cambridge historian J. H. Plumb once sweepingly characterised as 'complacent arrogance' a chauvinistic and insular retrenchment from Europe that, in his view, seeped into English culture during the nineteenth century. By the close of the Georgian period, just before Victoria's reign, the successful imperial project gave the English a new self-confidence, whereby[148]

> the maintenance of English ways, the insistence on the superiority of English ideas, led to a withdrawal from European culture as a whole and England in the nineteenth century developed its art and its literature almost uninfluenced by foreign example.

Following the defeat of Napoleon that seemed to stave off, for the time being, dangerous revolutionary ideas emanating from their nearest continental neighbour, this Anglocentrism on the part of the English is understandable. The French Revolution and its turbulent aftermath had given rise to a climate of genuine fear that had led, for the sake of securing Ireland, to the establishment of the Maynooth seminary, the Act of Union and the installation of Martello towers along the east coast. Residual distrust of foreigners remained, foreigners with whom it was in the State's interest to have little to do. In George Eliot's fictional world of *Middlemarch*, the hero Will Ladislaw, as the new editor of the Tipton *Pioneer*, is regarded with deep suspicion because of his Polish forebears.[149]

Matthew Potter asserts that a belief in British superiority grew particularly marked among the Protestant Anglo-Irish during the nineteenth century.[150] By implication, if he is correct, the cultural assumptions of the Irish Catholic community might be thought to have derived from rather different perspectives. Yet the picture can be ambiguous, as for example in the complexity of Irish Catholic responses to the mid-century struggles in the Italian peninsula. While Irish readers of *The Nation* may have been initially swayed by Young Ireland's sympathies for Italian unification, many – perhaps more – of them supported the pro-papal agitation when the papacy was in peril and enlisted in the Irish Papal Brigade that flocked to defend the temporal power of the Pontiff. Conservative Irish Catholics viewed contemporary events in Italy through a confessional lens and, in this instance, their religious allegiance trumped their nationalist fellow feeling.[151]

The 'usual suspects' of Irish historiography, Catholicism and nationalism, are broad and multifaceted realities that subdivide into many strands, without necessarily overlapping in harmony. Together, however, both 'patriotism and piety' (to pick up Blake Dillon's phrase)[152] offered alternative worlds beyond England, and suggested that the cultural centre for many Irish Catholics was based not in Westminster but in the Vatican, not on the Thames but on the banks of the Seine. For an increasing number, that centre lay across the Atlantic.

Of course, plenty of Church of Ireland clergymen also had links with European countries, and some were multilingual. I am concentrating here on the Catholic clergy because allegiance to Rome has been such a defining feature of Irish Christianity since the Reformation, and because Catholicism had such political power in the education culture of the period. The alternative perspectives on Catholic Europe that fed into influential strands of Irish culture inevitably had a bearing on what was taught and studied in schools and universities.

Language, creed and identity had fundamental parts to play in the story of how the academic study of modern languages bedded down early in Victorian Ireland. All three served to differentiate and distinguish between people with different allegiances: Irishness and Britishness, Catholicism and Protestantism. Given the broad cultural and linguistic undercurrents that we have discussed in this chapter – the early-modern foreign-language higher-education experience of Irish people, and the centuries-old linguistic and ideological engagement with Catholic Europe that continued in other forms during the nineteenth century – it would have been surprising had Newman's Catholic University omitted modern European languages from among its foundational disciplines.

In sum, it was not the fact, but rather the timing, of the mid-century arrival of European language study in Ireland's fledgling university sector that seems striking. More by accident than design, the shift from ancient to modern languages appears to have followed a more orderly path within England's universities, which consolidated their modern-language programmes a few decades later than Ireland's, when it was clear there were enough students equipped to take the courses they devised.

But what about the availability of suitably equipped students in Ireland? Our next chapter will explore the extent of language learning at pre-university level in the Irish nineteenth century. It paints a complicated, patchy and uneven picture, shining a light on disparate phenomena peculiar to Irish society which, in the aggregate, prove to be a little more substantial than one might expect. The various historical and linguistic circumstances we have outlined in these opening chapters did not inevitably lead on their own to a pre-eminent position for advanced modern-language study in Ireland. As we shall see, Victorian Ireland possessed an existing educational infrastructure that in practical, logistic ways played an essential part in enabling modern languages, including Irish, to attain the dominant position that they would later hold.

2.3. John Henry Newman, 1844
Chalk drawing by George Richmond, 1844.
© *National Portrait Gallery, London.*

PART TWO: LAYING THE FOUNDATIONS

Varieties and Milestones of Language Education

'I have read more than you would fancy, Mr Lockwood. You could not open a book in this library that I have not looked into, and got something out of also: unless it be that range of Greek and Latin, and that of French; and those I know one from another: it is as much as you can expect of a poor man's daughter.' [Emily Brontë, 1847][1]

'I've been to a day-school too,' said Alice; 'you needn't be so proud as all that.'
'With extras?' asked the Mock Turtle a little anxiously.
'Yes,' said Alice, 'we learned French and music.'
'And washing?' said the Mock Turtle.
'Certainly not!' said Alice indignantly.
'Ah! Then yours wasn't a really good school,' said the Mock Turtle in a tone of great relief. 'Now at ours they had at the end of the bill, "French, music and washing – extra."' [Lewis Carroll, 1865][2]

Les pères de la Congrégation [...] mettront en œuvre le même système d'éducation que dans leurs collèges de France. On apprendra aux étudiants à écrire et à parler le français avec aisance et correctement, mais la culture anglaise aura toujours la première place.
[S. P. Farragher & C. de Mare, 2019][3]

The language of the school was French for a long time and traces of this remained [...] But later the nuns had moved with the times, teaching the courses required for the examining body known as the Royal University and proudly displaying on the long corridors photographs of their graduates, in flowing skirts and pompadour hairstyles, each firmly labelled with her name and the letters B.A. [Eilís Dillon, 1982][4]

Language education and school have been virtually synonymous since schooling began, especially in the elementary stages. Literacy – the rudimentary ability to read and write – is attained by mastering the written code of one's mother tongue. At a more rarefied level, grammar schools and Latin schools were established all over Europe, to teach those of tender years the grammatical structures of Latin, the essential language of the learned. This chapter will outline the varieties of language learning, ancient and modern, in the evolving context of Victorian Ireland and consider some similarities and contrasts with the situation in England. On both sides of the Irish Sea, language provision reflects sharp societal divisions along the fault lines of religion, power, class and gender. We shall see how these compartmentalised networks could sometimes be turned to good advantage.

DIVERSE MODELS OF SCHOOLING

There were several ways of educating the young in nineteenth-century Ireland, whether in domestic or formal school settings. For most of the century, school attendance was neither possible nor compulsory. Wealthy households hired French or German governesses and tutors. Two examples: in December 1863, Johannes Brahms's jilted fiancée, Agathe von Siebold from Göttingen, travelled to work for the Protestant family of the High Sheriff of County Sligo, the Dukes, at Newpark House near Ballymote. She stayed for a year and a half, teaching German, piano, art and Italian to the 19-year-old twin daughters of the household.[5] Twenty-five years later, a Mademoiselle Ditter from Alsace was the first educator of the Plunkett family; this governess taught the children some French poems and songs despite her 'strong hatred of the French'; their mother 'liked only French to be spoken at the dinner table'.[6] One of the children in that Dublin Catholic household was the poet revolutionary Joseph Plunkett, whose idiosyncratic education ran the full gamut thereafter (partly for health reasons), taking in the Catholic University School in Leeson St, Dublin; a Marist boarding school in the Parisian suburb of Passy; erratic attendance at Belvedere College in Dublin; boarding at St George's College, Weybridge in Surrey; evening tutoring from a schoolteacher in Kilternan; and boarding with the Jesuits at Stonyhurst in Lancashire.[7]

3.1 Ballinaboy School (1850s) (*Courtesy of the National Library of Ireland.*)

Some rural families relied on regular visits from itinerant schoolmasters, the private 'hedge-school' teachers who had provided elementary education to the Catholic community during penal times, when it was decreed that no 'person of the popish religion shall publicly teach school, or shall instruct youth in learning in any private house.'[8] In the early nineteenth century, these pay schools were attended by the majority of the school-going population. Their settings could be very rudimentary, and their masters varied considerably in attainment and skills.[9] Greatly revered all over rural Ireland, these popish schoolmasters were eventually supplanted by the State-financed national school teachers set up in 1831, but some were employed by the new regime while others 'lingered on in dwindling numbers until the passing of the Intermediate Act of 1878.'[10] Employing such a master was the solution adopted by the Ó Máille (O'Malley) family dwelling in Connemara's Maam Valley in the barony of An Ros, before the local national school was opened in 1884. The family farmed sheep on some 10,000 acres of mountainy land leased from Lord Leitrim. Just as their father, with two neighbours, had hired a 'hedge'-schoolmaster to teach *them*, three of the Ó Máille brothers engaged a master to teach *their* sons and daughters, collectively.[11] The master, Peaitsín Pheige Ó Máille, who was a native Irish speaker with a knowledge of English, Greek and Latin, lodged by weekly rotation in the brothers' homes in Kilmilkin and Mounterown [*Muintir Eoin*], and taught the cousins as a group, in a barn. Pooled together in this manner, they formed an ample class.[12] A variation on the tutor/governess model, this system of elementary education proved effective for social advancement: among the cousins were a number of future teachers, medical specialists and professors. One of the latter, Tomás Ó Máille, was to be the first professor of Modern Irish Language and Literature at University College Galway.[13]

Other university linguists schooled partly or entirely at home included Ireland's first President, Douglas Hyde, who had been appointed to the first chair of modern Irish at UCD. The son of a clergyman, Hyde learned Irish as a boy by listening to it spoken in the locality in Frenchpark, County Roscommon. Another clergyman's son, the Trinity classicist, Fellow and eventually Provost John Pentland Mahaffy, learned the classics from his father and picked up French and German as a child, having lived in Switzerland and Germany from birth till the age of nine.[14] Hyde and Mahaffy are characters whom we shall have occasion to mention again.

As elsewhere in nineteenth-century Europe, the variety of formal school types available in Ireland was considerable, ranging from privately run small academies[15] to those endowed by the Established Church, and to the new schools set up by Catholics following the Relief Acts from 1782 onwards, which lifted the education restrictions on their religion.[16] Dublin had 15 Catholic charity schools by 1797. New Catholic teaching orders, such as the Presentation sisters' schools founded by Nano Nagle in Cork in the mid-1770s,[17] or the Christian Brothers, whose first school opened in Waterford in 1802, continued to expand their reach, so that by 1825 'the nuns had forty-six schools in the towns and the brothers had twenty-four'.[18] The first diocesan secondary school was St Kieran's College, Kilkenny (1782).

Foreign nationals working in private academies or as individual tutors offered continental language teaching in various settings. A Cork merchant or

3.2 Nano Nagle with Pupils, 1809
Charles Turner engraving, 1809. (© *The Trustees of the British Museum.*)

49

PORTARLINGTON
EDUCATIONAL INSTITUTION.

Principal—Mr. THOMAS ARTHUR, A.B., Native of England, and formerly second Master of the Royal Grammar School of Reading.

EXCLUSIVELY FOR THE SONS OF GENTLEMEN.—NO DAY PUPILS RECEIVED.

IN addition to the soundest instruction in Classics and Science, which is attested by the distinguished career of former Pupils in the University of Dublin, the greatest proficiency can be attained in the Modern Languages, and those accomplishments so essential to the Gentleman. The closing of the English Institutions on the Continent, has induced the Principal to attach to his Institution a Resident Professor of Modern Languages, a native of Germany, Graduate of the University of Paris, and lately Professor in the Royal College of Orleans. Parents will find that this Institution offers to Pupils all the advantages of the best English and Continental Schools, upon very moderate terms, whilst the treatment and domestic arrangements are upon a very superior scale.

The House which is spacious, and which contains large well ventilated rooms, is situated at the entrance of the town, and stands in a pleasure ground of 22 acres in extent.

The following Professors from Dublin visit the Establishment weekly—

PAINTING AND DRAWING.—H. Newton, Esq., Vice-President of the Society of Irish Artists.

DANCING.—Mr. Williams.

FENCING AND DRILLING.—Serjeant Major Goodwin.

THOMAS ARTHUR, Principal.

3.3 Ad for Portarlington Educational Institution, 1848
The Westmeath Independent, 16 September 1848, p. 1 (Courtesy *www. irishnewspaperarchives.com*).

bishop wishing to brush up his rusty French could do worse than attend individual French classes on the South Mall with Claude Marcel, the city's honorary 'French Chancellor' and later Consul from 1816 to 1863. While in Cork he published more than one substantial book on language education, including the two-volume *Language as a Means of Mental Culture and International Communication, or Manual of the Teacher and Learner of Languages* (1853), showing an extraordinary breadth of scholarship and depth of reflection. Marcel has been described as a neglected applied linguist.[19] Modern languages were also on offer in the boarding schools of Portarlington. Some Protestant ascendancy families sent their sons to these schools. Even though they had lost much of their direct connection with France, a network of schoolmasters in the old Huguenot settlement claimed an ability to initiate these boys into the French tongue 'with the strictest grammatical propriety', taking care that they 'not only write, but speak it correctly, and in its pure idiom.'[20] Descendants of Huguenot families were loyal supporters of the Crown. In these schools the sons of landed gentry learned their exclusive role 'as serving the greater British empire, not so much Ireland'.[21] The prominent unionist, Edward Carson, attended Portarlington School and was in touch for the rest of his life with its headmaster, a staunch loyalist.[22]

A small minority of wealthy Catholic families followed the ancestral tradition of sending their male offspring to complete their schooling in France, Spain or the Low Countries.[23] The seventeen-year-old Daniel O'Connell and his brother Maurice had their schooling interrupted in late 1792 while boarding at the English College in Douai, in Flanders. They fled in January 1793 on the day the French King was guillotined.[24] Following the Revolution and the lifting of penal restrictions, many Catholic foundations transferred to English locations. In the second half of the nineteenth century, Irish elite families did likewise, sending their sons to England rather than the Continent, to attend prestigious Catholic boarding schools such as those run by the Benedictines at Ampleforth and Downside or the Jesuits at Stonyhurst. Ciaran O'Neill has pointed out that, as these three schools had originally been founded in the sixteenth and seventeenth centuries to educate English

Catholics on the continent, 'in many ways the nineteenth-century schooling of wealthy Irish Catholics at English Catholic schools is simply a continuation of this Continental recusant period'.[25] In these schools, which were European and transnational in origin, the curriculum was heavily weighted towards the classics and also included French.

The daughters of the same Catholic gentry were frequently sent to be 'finished' in high-status convent establishments in Belgium, France and Germany, run by Sacred Heart or Ursuline nuns, or to be educated by the Irish Benedictines at Ypres, who had been involved in schooling young women since the late seventeenth century.[26] Wealthy Irish Catholics also patronised convent schools in England where, as in other countries, there was a growth in the numbers of foundations, especially after 1830.[27] Significant proportions of Irish-born nuns were members of religious communities in England and in Europe. These schools gave both the religious congregations and their young charges a transnational experience that included modern languages. 'French education was considered especially attractive for girls, the language and the style adding apparently unquantifiable lustre to the young Irish maidens exposed to it.'[28]

By the close of the century, 'the tradition of Continental education for boys faded just as it became even more fashionable for girls.'[29] The option of an elite school abroad was even more common among affluent Protestant families, partly for cultural reasons or out of family tradition, and partly because of the scant number of Protestant secondary schools available in Ireland.[30] 'Throughout the nineteenth century up to three times as many Protestants as Catholics pursued an elite education outside Ireland.'[31]

For Catholics who could afford them, boys' Catholic boarding schools were established in Ireland in the early decades of the century, by the Jesuits at Clongowes Wood, County Kildare (1814) and at Tullabeg, County Offaly (1818) and the Vincentians at Castleknock, County Dublin (1835); these were followed – a generation later – by the Holy Ghost Fathers [today known as The Spiritans] at Blackrock, County Dublin (1860). The Jesuits offered what Ciaran O'Neill calls a 'proto-public school' experience in Ireland for the sons of the Catholic middle class. Mimicking many of the features of an English public school, these elite schools, he argues, accommodated the social aspirations of the boys' parents, whose sons were henceforth free to participate fully in civic society, in industry or business, liberal professions or the imperial civil service.[32] As for the Holy Ghost Fathers, we shall return to their establishment at Blackrock College later in this chapter.

LANGUAGE IN POST-PRIMARY SCHOOLS: FRENCH CONNECTIONS

The rather eclectic range of school type did not yield uniformly positive academic results. Statements made by teaching staff to the Queen's Colleges Commission of 1857–8 frequently decried the inadequate pre-university schooling of their students.[33] Two modern-languages professors – Augustus Bensbach in Galway and Matthias Frings in Belfast – concurred that students were ill-equipped for university courses in French and German. Professor Bensbach declared that his students had no preparation in German and very little in French when they arrived in Galway; Frings asserted that his students entered Belfast unprepared for university study, and that 'very few of them ever saw a French word in their lives'. He made a plea for a basic matriculation examination in one of the languages.[34] By 1858, almost a decade after their foundation, the state of the Queen's Colleges themselves was parlous, not just in languages. They suffered from low student numbers for a variety of reasons – an onerous attendance requirement, a low-status degree, and the competitive advantage enjoyed by Trinity College Dublin, which recruited all the ordinands for the Church of Ireland and counted on links with endowed schools. However, where modern languages were concerned, Trinity's student intake was equally unpromising: 'few of the candidates for university entrance had even a smattering of French.'[35] Things were no better at the CUI, where the general academic standard of incoming students was viewed by Newman and his colleagues as low.[36] Indeed, contemporary accounts, generally, 'paint a rather dismal picture of the quality of the education provided.'[37]

The need for some standardisation at post-primary level was partly addressed by the landmark Intermediate Education (Ireland) Act of 1878, which set up an examination board on the model of the Cambridge and Oxford local annual examinations. The Act enhanced the status of modern languages by including them as examination subjects, and this had a positive effect on the numbers studying both French and German in schools. It was especially beneficial for extending the reach of German.[38] The Act enabled the State to combine a laissez-faire approach to denominational school management and administration with indirect funding of the schools that produced the top examinees. The latter were awarded scholarships and prizes, while their schools reaped financial rewards.[39] The system incentivised competition between schools, as fee income was based on examination results: the more top-performing candidates a school produced, the greater the income. Results were published in national newspapers. In the free-market system operating in the Irish post-primary education landscape, this was not insignificant in changing language study behaviour.[40]

The new legislation had a bearing on another enduring change over the course of the nineteenth century: the education of women, increasing numbers of whom, by the turn of the century, could credibly aspire to seek gainful employment, and even, in a few cases, a university education, thanks to the inclusive policy of the RUI where the admission of female students was concerned.[41] Over the course of the century, Roman Catholic schools for girls mushroomed around Ireland. Many of them were established by nuns, whose numbers and activities were expanding dramatically in other countries of Europe during the same decades.[42] Deirdre Raftery captures the explosive scale of the change: 'While there were only 12 convents and four orders of female religious in Ireland in 1800, by 1900 there were 368 convents and 35 different orders.'[43]

Of particular interest to our theme is the remarkable number of French religious congregations who set up convent boarding schools in Ireland, particularly in the period 1840–80. As Anne V. O'Connor points out:[44]

> It was during Paul Cullen's period of office as archbishop of Dublin (1852–78) that the majority of French teaching orders of women were introduced into Ireland. These orders were: the Sacred Heart (1842), the Faithful Companions of Jesus (1844), St Louis (1859), St Joseph of Cluny (1860), and the Marists (1873). They joined two other European teaching orders already at work in Ireland: the Dominicans (1644) and the Loreto order (1822), a branch of the Institute of the Blessed Virgin Mary. By the end of the century, sixty-two convent boarding schools had been established in Ireland. Out of the total only six were run by Irish religious orders (four Brigidine schools at Tullow, Mountrath, Abbeyleix, Goresbridge, one Mercy convent in Ennis, and one Holy Faith boarding school in Glasnevin, Dublin). This meant in effect that girls' secondary education in Ireland was dominated by religious orders whose

educational views and traditions originated outside Ireland.

Ciaran O'Neill dates the arrival in Ireland of the European model of convent school education to the earliest Ursuline schools, set up in Cork (1771), Thurles (1787), Waterford (1816) and Sligo (1826).[45] French convent boarding schools were influenced by French customs, and to varying degrees the teaching sisters maintained close ties with their mother houses in France. As Deirdre Raftery asserts, 'many Irish women who joined orders of French foundation had their Irish identity diluted by their adoption of French language and culture. They spoke, read and wrote French; they often spent time in France for their novitiate year or for final profession.'[46] Schools advertised the use of French both inside and outside the classroom, and made much of the presence of native speakers of the foreign language taught, allowing pupils 'to speak it fluently and with the purest accent'.[47] An emphasis on perfecting the spoken language is particularly foregrounded, with reports in the national press of girls using French, German, Italian or Spanish in verse recitation or arithmetic exercises.[48] At St Louis convent boarding school in Monaghan in the 1860s, French was reported to be the medium of instruction in senior classes.[49] Annual recitations and plays were performed in French at the convent boarding school run by the Dominicans in Cabra (Dublin).[50] These French communities were, in effect, continuing the tradition of French teaching –

3.4 Two school ads (Pas-de-Calais and Laurel Hill, Limerick, 1845)
Sainte-Marie, Aire, Pas-de-Calais and Convent of the Faithful Companions of Jesus, Boarding School, Laurel Hill, Limerick. *Freeman's Journal*, 28 June 1845, p. 1 (*Courtesy www. irishnewspaperarchives.com*).

while expanding its reach – that had been offered in eighteenth-century academies run by French nationals, clerical and lay.[51]

The school for the daughters of upwardly mobile Catholics, established at Loreto Abbey, Rathfarnham by Mother Teresa Ball in 1822, also prioritised modern languages. Ball went to some trouble to bring to Loreto Abbey continental novices with linguistic skills: in 1851, for example, she asked the community in Munich to send a German novice with 'a good knowledge of her native language, and the capacity to express herself in French or Italian or even in Spanish'. Deirdre Raftery records that 'French language and literature were central to the curriculum, and Ball sent nuns to France to improve their spoken French.

She was especially complimentary of pupils who spoke the language fluently and well'.[52] Speaking foreign languages, like playing the pianoforte or singing, was a social accomplishment for females.[53]

One beneficiary of this education model was the gifted language student Mary Maguire, who was later to marry the author Padraic Colum. At the turn of the twentieth century, she was a boarder at St Louis Monaghan, where she learned French, German, Italian and Latin. A sense of how the French ethos permeated a school in late Victorian Ireland can be gleaned from her account of the experience, published in her autobiography, *Life and the Dream*:[54]

> Class hours and study hours were long, and though we studied books and subjects assembled for us by an educational body called the Intermediate Education Board of Ireland, which at the start must have emanated from the head of some English bureaucrat, the whole way in which this school was conducted and the way we were taught was Continental. [...] In fact my school was French in tradition, having been founded by a French religious order for the education of girls, and we had all sorts of French customs, since the school was not long enough in existence to have become completely Hibernicized. On feast days and birthdays we would kiss each other three times, once on each cheek and once on the lips, as is done in France; we had a French motto for our school and a French coat of arms on our exercise books.

3.5 Ad for Convent of St Louis Boarding School, Monaghan, 1866

Dundalk Democrat, 7 July 1866, p. 5 (*Courtesy www. irishnewspaperarchives.com*).

Mary Colum [*née* Maguire] recalls how every day of this Catholic European education was regimented, and every segment of the clockface was to be spent in a precisely designated way:[55]

> at ten minutes to three I had to study French irregular verbs every day until I knew them and could repeat all the moods and participles without a mistake, and at half past one I had to practice embroidery stitches on a piece of cotton until I could do them well enough to embroider the blue velvet smoking cap which was given me as 'work' to do.

Her love of Latin and her long and laborious apprenticeship to modern languages, combined with her facility for learning them, remained with her in later life, although she criticised the excessively literary emphasis of the teaching, at the expense of the everyday spoken tongue.[56]

St Louis Monaghan was one of the more successful of the new girls' schools at adapting to the new horizons established by the 1878 Act, and at achieving excellent results in national examinations. The Act, which awarded more credit for certain subjects than for others, incentivised academically minded girls' schools to add Latin and Mathematics to their subject range. Before the crucial 1878 landmark, indeed, most girls' schools had offered some modern languages, but girls learning Latin at school had been rare and girls studying Greek practically non-existent.[57] The Intermediate examination's marking system also incentivised wider modern-language ranges. By the last two decades of the century, as we have seen in the case of Mary Colum, St Louis Monaghan was offering not only Latin and French, but German and Italian as well.

Meanwhile, when the establishment (1879) of the Royal University meant that women would henceforth be eligible to be examined for, and awarded, university degrees, some religious orders set up single-sex women's colleges to prepare girls for RUI examinations. At first frowned upon by members of the Catholic hierarchy, this initiative was soon actively promoted, especially by the Archbishop of Dublin, William Walsh. Principally motivated by the fear that Catholic girls might attend a Protestant college like Alexandra[58] instead, the bishops were also beginning to appreciate that teaching nuns ought to hold a university degree. The new women's colleges – run in Dublin by the Dominicans and the Loreto order, and in Cork by the Ursulines – were a winning formula: they prepared able and motivated candidates for both Intermediate and RUI examinations and were to become central to the successful career outcomes of many of the early RUI women students.[59] Enabled to participate in the same examinations as their male peers, from within a space made uniquely for them, females began to be seen as serious contenders for scholarships and even university employment in a way that would have been unheard of only a few decades earlier. While women students in Trinity College Dublin had to wait until 1904 for the same opportunities, RUI's first women graduates of 1884 got a head start that was to prove uniquely valuable for some of them. Oxbridge's women's colleges were even slower to be integrated into the universities' degree structures: Oxford and Cambridge women undergraduates had to wait till 1920 (Oxford) and 1948 (Cambridge) for the chance of an equivalent educational opportunity.[60]

In passing, it is interesting to contrast the success of Catholic convent schools run by teaching sisters who adapted to conditions on the ground, with the fortunes of a small private boarding school, founded, owned and managed by an aristocratic French woman, Héloïse de Mailly, the widow of an Irish clergyman. Her French School, set up in 1864 in Bray, County Wicklow, remained unintegrated with local Irish conditions. As in other French-established schools, French was the language in current daily use in the school.[61] It prepared Protestant young women for Cambridge examinations instead of local Irish ones and, even after independence, taught neither the Irish language nor Irish history. Many of its twentieth-century alumnae went on to study in Trinity College Dublin.[62] The school closed for financial reasons in 1966, when the Irish scheme for free post-primary education was first announced.[63]

THE FRENCH COLLEGE AND UNIVERSITY COLLEGE, BLACKROCK

Modern-language provision also proliferated in boys' second-level schools during the Victorian period.[64] Even before 1837, indeed, it was not unheard of. French was among the broad range of subjects advertised at St Kieran's College, Kilkenny, in its first prospectus. The founding priests announced the opening of an Academy in January

1783 'where Youth will be taught English Grammar, Writing, Arithmetic, French, Latin, Greek, Geography, Mathematics, ancient and modern History, in short every Branch of useful and polite Literature on the most improved Plan'.[65] A glance at seven prospectuses advertising subject provision in schools around the country by the late 1860s – in Dublin and counties Waterford, Cork, Kildare, Offaly and Wexford – shows French available in all of the seven, Italian in six, German in five. Whereas in all of the seven, Latin, Greek and French are core language disciplines, some schools charged extra fees for the other languages.[66] Clongowes Wood offered French, German and Italian, at no extra cost, as did the Protestant St Columba's College, which opened in Stackallan in 1843.[67] In 1855 Foxcroft School, Portarlington, sought a French and German teacher, and was offering both, with Italian, by the 1860s.[68] German and Italian were optional at Portora Royal School, Enniskillen, where Oscar Wilde studied French as a boarder in the 1860s.[69]

By the 1860s, then, foreign languages were extensively present in the Irish intermediate school sector, and were offered by schools catering for the sons and daughters of elite and middle class professionals, urban merchants and established tenant farmers. The curricular pattern in these schools was 'firmly fixed within the humanist grammar-school tradition. Language and literary studies predominated with the classics and English getting pride of place though many pupils got some acquaintance with French.'[70] One school, in particular, is worth singling out: the French College for boys in Blackrock, County Dublin, which offers another instance of a French religious order aligning itself with Ireland's evolving education structures.

The French College, antecedent of today's Blackrock College, was opened in 1860 by a Holy Ghost father, or Spiritan, from northern France, *le père* Jules Leman (1826–80). Having come to Ireland in the previous year with a view to opening a seminary to train missionaries for anglophone Africa, Fr Leman was soon persuaded that post-famine Ireland needed, above all, a secondary school for the sons of the increasingly numerous Catholic middle class. In its early years, the College was staffed entirely – with one exception – by French priests, the last of whom only retired in 1896. Initially, classes were taught through French, French textbooks were imported, and the school followed the French model. French was the language in daily use outside the classroom. When the boys ventured beyond the school grounds,

3.6 French College prospectus, 1860
Blackrock College Archives. (*Courtesy of Blackrock College, Co Dublin.*)

their military style uniforms, modelled on those worn in Second Empire *lycées*, complete with kepis on their heads, earned them a local nickname: 'the Boney boys'.[71] Some cultural adjustment between staff and students was called for in the beginning. One of the French priests found the Irish youths lacked sophistication but were full of righteousness, and was disconcerted by 'leur manque d'ordre, leur tendance à la négligence et un certain laisser-aller' [their disorderly, sloppy ways and devil-may-care attitude]. Another wrote home to say that his English fluency had not improved, because boys had to speak French during recreation.[72]

3.7 French College, Blackrock, 1866: 'Boney Boys'
Pupils in French uniforms 'for public promenades', modelled on French imperial army. Blackrock College Archives. (*Courtesy of Blackrock College, Co Dublin.*)

To judge by the rapid rise in its enrolments and expansion of its buildings and grounds, the new school seems to have responded to an aspiration within its middle-class clientèle. 1860 proved to be a very propitious moment for a French boarding school to open in Dublin. The following press cutting from the *Catholic News*, 1861, is indicative of the targeted niche:[73]

> The establishment of the French College has conferred a boon on many which cannot fail to be appreciated. Heretofore, parents desirous of giving their children a French education, should send them to France for that purpose [...] and to study some time in a French seminary [diocesan college] was deemed indispensable to a good education. Not every person, however, could afford to send his child abroad. But the establishment of the French College offers all the advantages of such an education, without the expense and inconvenience attending a foreign residence.

High standards of attainment were promoted from the outset, with incentives such as weekly 'notes' or assessments and annual prize days. A bi-monthly *Literary Journal* encouraged compositions in verse or prose, written in Latin, Greek or French. Some of these juvenilia were grammatically impeccable.[74]

A flavour of the standard in French expected at Blackrock can be gauged from the astonishingly ambitious course in the language offered by the school. The French Course laid out in the College Calendar for the year 1870–1, for instance, indicates a highly systematic and precisely targeted approach, covering eight years of instruction, and aiming to achieve something not far from the kind of fluency and exactitude in the written language that a pupil in a school in France would be pleased to attain.[75] Starting, in French fashion, with eighth and seventh class, the first two years learning French were spent learning grammar, recitation and reading; these gave way (in sixth and fifth class) to more of the same, with the addition of translation into English. Translation tasks grew gradually more challenging in the senior years, ending up in the final year with translating modern English authors into French. For grammar, a manual called the *French College Grammar* – presumably devised for the school's own Irish learners – was used in the first two years, whereas from sixth class *Otto's French Grammar* was prescribed.[76] Composition from memory (introduced in sixth class) gave way to composing original narratives and letters in third class, moving on to descriptions and more demanding letter-writing tasks in second class, and finally original writing, in prose and verse, in the last year. French history, from the earliest times to the modern day, was included in the syllabus from third class; the history of French literature and the intricacies of French versification were tackled in the two final years. The only year where grammar does not appear as an item in the programme is the final year: instead of grammar, that was the stage when the boys were introduced to literary style. Nor were the sounds and rhythms of the spoken language neglected: every year contained exercises in 'recitation' or 'conversation'.[77] The former probably consisted in rote learning of literary extracts, with the purpose of memorising structures, while the latter presumably involved learning dialogues packed with colloquial phrases.

Like the St Louis sisters, the French Holy Ghost fathers quickly adapted the French College to local conditions, and to changes in Ireland's education system. The College's links with the Catholic University date from as early as 1862. From the moment he assumed the CUI rectorship from April 1861, Newman's successor, Monsignor Bartholomew Woodlock, was intent on expanding the disastrously low student numbers at the ailing institution. With this in mind, links with feeder schools and affiliated schools were established, with varying results.[78] Woodlock had befriended *le père* Leman on his arrival in Ireland,[79] and persuaded the French priest to enter his high-achieving boys for the university's matriculation examinations. Clerical networking led to successful outcomes. Given their thorough grounding in French and other subjects, 'by the early seventies most of the prizes awarded by the Catholic University went to students from the French College.'[80] Over the first decade of the new Intermediate examinations, too, Blackrock boys were consistently top performers.[81]

Taking advantage of the new examination-based recruitment process for the civil service, the French College set up its own Civil Service Department in 1875; this was to run successfully for 35 years. It prepared senior students to sit competitive examinations leading to professional training in the civil service and army, and also in law and medicine. Additional resources were recruited. The 1875 College Calendar Staff List[82] names 13 teachers of modern languages (eleven for French and German; two for Italian and Spanish).

This is impressive, relative to staffing for other subjects on offer: there are ten teachers listed for English and Mathematics, nine for Greek and Latin, three each for Physical Sciences and Music, and two for Drawing. One of the names on the French and German list is 'Revd G. Polin, BA', an individual to whom we shall be returning in Chapter 6.

The 1881 College Prospectus extols the merits of its Civil Service Department as a haven of study, where parents can rest assured that their sons will be cocooned from the dangers of the big city, have their progress and conduct closely monitored and their moral and religious needs taken care of. It highlights another attraction: 'Modern Languages, so much valued at Competitive Examinations, are acquired in the College with much facility, as several of the Professors are natives of France and Germany.'[83]

By 1881, the status of modern languages was further strengthened by the newly established Royal University's matriculation requirement. Candidates had to pass the examination in Latin or Greek *plus* another classical *or modern* language. In practice, for the majority of schools this translated into a requirement for Latin plus a modern language.

At the same moment, also in 1880–1, Blackrock's association with the Royal University was consolidated by the launch of University College Blackrock. This was one of a number of constituent university colleges where students could prepare and present for RUI examinations prior to final degree level. An early prospectus for the new college announces:[84]

> This College has been opened for the benefit of Catholic Students wishing to prepare for the Degrees and Honors [*sic*] of the Royal University, in the Faculties of Arts, Law, and Engineering. It is situated in grounds adjoining the French College and is under the immediate direction of the Revd J. E. Reffé, who is assisted by a large staff of distinguished Professors.

Housed and instructed in Williamstown Castle,[85] University College Blackrock's students continued to score highly in the RUI examinations, consistently outstripping candidates based in the University's own city premises at St Stephen's Green.[86]

RECOGNITION, REGULATIONS AND REPERCUSSIONS

The Blackrock example bears a little more scrutiny, as a reflection of the conditions of the time. We have seen in this chapter how the nineteenth century saw continental influences – especially French – permeate the ethos of various school settings in Ireland, so that the conscious or unconscious association between education and foreign-language learning continued to be taken for granted in those schools and, by extension, percolated into their pupils' family and social circles, reinforcing that particular strand of Irish cultural identity. This trend was helped significantly by three separate developments in education policy and regulations.

Two of these regulatory milestones were significant, particularly for women's language study. In the first place, the 1878 Intermediate Education Act 'exercised a very great influence on the character of secondary education, with a strong grammar school tradition in the studies pursued'.[87] As we have noted, the 1878 Intermediate examination led to an expanded range of languages taught in schools and helped to broaden educational opportunities for female students. Boys' schools, where there was readier access to priests who could teach Latin and Greek, continued to offer the classical languages (worth more marks in the examination) while religious communities running girls' schools could draw on French, German and Italian speakers from among their own congregations to teach those tongues. It is important to remind ourselves that the feature of Victorian language learning we have been highlighting applied to a mere handful of convent schools, within which a few isolated Irish women attained a high degree of proficiency in modern languages, thanks to the religious sisters who had taught them. Without the language provisions in the Intermediate Act, the phenomenon we are talking about might have remained a quaint, passing feature of the education of a small minority of Irish Victorians, and the mainstream study of modern languages, especially French, would not necessarily have followed.

An equally significant change in the regulatory environment came with the University Education (Ireland) Act of 1879 that set up the Royal University of Ireland, with its new matriculation requirements. This shaped language learning in two important ways. After 1880, the option to take a modern language in lieu of one of the classical languages was of immediate and lasting importance, allowing certain girls' schools to capitalise on their existing modern language diversity. Even more significantly, from the outset the RUI recognised women as candidates for the award of a degree. As we shall see in a later chapter, many of the RUI's women students graduated in modern languages, and a cluster of the most able were to become the earliest women professors of modern languages.

Official recognition of middle- and upper-class women's education did not come out of the blue. As education historians have recently chronicled, it was in very large measure thanks to the tireless and coordinated public advocacy by pioneering Protestant women that the right of young women to an intellectual education was finally taken on board by the 1879 Act. Three of these lobbyists should be mentioned: the Presbyterians Margaret Byers (1832–1912) who set up the Ladies' Collegiate School in Belfast (1859, known as Victoria College after 1887) and Isabella Tod (1836–96), prominent member of the Belfast Ladies' Institute, as well as the Quaker Anne Jellicoe (1823–80), who established Alexandra College in 1866.[88] The RUI Act clearly signalled that the doorway into higher education had to include the study of modern languages and of Latin.

Even before these late-Victorian developments, however, modern languages had come to prominence in Ireland during the 1850s, largely because of the gradual recognition they were receiving in England. Following the Northcote-Trevelyan Report of 1854, the civil service appointment process, henceforth to be conducted through public competition (as opposed to patronage or purchase), included French, German and Italian as suitable languages for candidates seeking entry via open public examinations to the Indian Civil Service and to the Royal Military Academy in Woolwich; in 1858, French and German were also included in the first Cambridge Syndicate examinations and their Oxford equivalent set up in 1857.[89]

It is difficult to overestimate the impetus to the study of modern languages that these changes in policy and regulations brought about in Ireland. The Civil Service recognition of French and German in 1855 promoted developments at university level, as university professors were invited to take part in preparing candidates for the new competitive examinations. At Trinity College Dublin, it was the catalyst for a spate of structural reforms, in several disciplines.[90] Where modern languages are concerned, it led to the establishment, a decade later, of Trinity's separate chair of German. According to M.

M. Raraty's account of the College's German Chair,[91] the task of singlehandedly taking charge of two languages (French and German), together with the extra responsibility of organising and teaching public competition classes for the Indian Civil Service, and for admission to the Royal Artillery and Engineers and Royal Military Academy at Woolwich, simply became too onerous for one person. This motivated the Board's decision to divide what had been a two-language post into two separate chairs, one for German and the other for Romance Languages (French, Italian and Spanish), following Professor Abeltshauser's death in 1866. His successor, Albert Maximilian Selss (from Berlin), was to continue Abeltshauser's work by putting German Studies at Trinity on a credible academic footing.[92] While Trinity's language classes for military cadetship candidates only ran for five years, from 1855 to 1860, those for its Indian Civil Service candidates lasted (in modified form) until 1939.[93]

The Catholic University's calendars began to include the regulations for the Open Competition for the Indian Civil Service, and those for admitting Gentlemen Cadets to the Woolwich RMA. Its 1867–8 Calendar, for example, lists the subjects examined at Woolwich: Mathematics, English, History, Geography, Classics (Latin and Greek), French, German, Hindustani, Experimental Sciences, Natural Sciences and Drawing. Specific weightings were assigned to each subject: Mathematics got 3,500 marks, English 1,000, while each of the five other languages (two classical, three modern) was worth 1,500.[94] These tacit valuations of the study of foreign languages were important for their status. Ambitious middle-class families saw avenues to secure employment opening up for their sons. RUI Presidents' Reports highlight successes among its graduates in obtaining Civil Service appointments.[95] The numbers of these Irish graduates were low overall, and fell after 1880, but that mattered less than the cultural and educational significance of signalling the potential usefulness of studying modern languages at university.[96] The popular perception of the Indian Civil Service examination as the end point of modern language study persisted. This is implied in an affectionate reminiscence printed in QCG's *College Annual* (1913), where an imaginary graduate returns to his alma mater and guides his fresher companion around various classrooms:[97]

> We then left the hall of the Muses, and crossing the Quadrangle diagonally, passed through a lofty portal till we reached a doorway on which 'Modern Languages' was inscribed in large black capitals. [...] 'There,' said I, 'you shall spend many pleasant years ere you enter for your Indian Civil Examination.'

It is in the same regulatory context that we should set the Civil Service Department that, as outlined above, opened in Blackrock College.[98] The French priests took a strategic approach to the London Civil Service examinations. In 1874, wishing to test their belief that Irish candidates, though reasonably successful, were failing to reach their true potential, the school's President, Fr Jules Leman, and Dean of Studies, Fr Édouard Reffé, entered one of their brightest scholastics, the nineteen-year-old Hugh O'Toole from County Laois, in a competitive entrance examination for a coveted civil service position. After taking the examination in London, O'Toole was ranked 22 out of 280 candidates, many of them from leading public schools in England. The following year, having been individually coached, he was sent to London again to sit for a senior financial post, and won first place out of a field of 300. Declining the offer of a lucrative civil service position in London, he returned to his clerical studies in Dublin. Although this anecdote is not directly related to foreign-language study – Fr O'Toole later graduated in Science – it illustrates again the French priests' ability to avail of all developmental opportunities that came their way. O'Toole's spectacular examination success in London helped to launch Blackrock's new Civil Service College on a high note. As Fr Hugh O'Toole CSSp, he was to serve as Director of University College Blackrock for over three decades.[99]

It is true, as has often been acknowledged,[100] that the excessively examination-focussed regime heralded by the new environment brought disadvantages in its wake, dampening the natural curiosity of young learners and devaluing the sense that knowledge is to be explored for its own sake. We have been considering only the general benefits of regulatory frameworks in the way they affected the expansion of modern-language provision in Irish secondary schools. A concomitant effect was to embed modern language study in the cultural assumptions of Ireland's upwardly aspiring middle class. In addition, once male and female candidates competed in the same public arena, the new culture helped to explode the myth that females lacked the physical and intellectual calibre to endure the stress of sitting examinations.

MODERN LANGUAGES VERSUS CLASSICS IN IRISH AND ENGLISH SCHOOLS

To what extent did the Irish second-level position align with what prevailed in English elite schools in the same period? For most of the Victorian era, in both countries, schooling was predominantly under clerical control and lay schools were by and large confessional. This is axiomatic for Ireland but also for England, *mutatis mutandis*: in 1872, 'seventy of seventy-two headmasters of England's leading boys' schools were clergymen.'[101] Headmasters in both countries tended to be culturally divided by their different brands of Christianity, heightened by the denominational and political issues of the age. In language provision, too, it turns out that there were broad similarities but also some key disparities between the two islands.

In so far as it is possible to generalise about the English context, given the variables of its decentralised character, some figures seem to indicate that the study of the classics was more deeply entrenched, and its prestige more weighty, in England's all-boys' public schools than in Ireland's elite schools. Take the numbers teaching classics versus those teaching modern languages: 'In 1864, the nine big Public Schools (i.e. privately funded, fee-paying schools) in England had between them 18 teachers of modern foreign languages, compared to 48 for Latin and Greek.'[102] Around the same time, 'Eton was reported to have 31 masters, of whom 26 taught classics, 6 mathematics, 1 history, and none modern languages or science.'[103] If these figures are correct, the subject provision at Eton contrasts sharply with the menu offered in the first prospectus, dated 1860, of the prestigious French College, or (to give it its full title) the *Collège Français de l'Immaculé Cœur de Marie*, Blackrock, County Dublin, where the course of instruction[104]

> embraces the Latin, Greek, Hebrew, English, French, German, Italian and Spanish languages; History and Geography, ancient and modern; Mathematics, Physical and Natural Sciences, Music, Drawing, and the various other branches of a liberal Education.

Such a broad curriculum, it is claimed, 'affords all the advantages of a Continental combined with a sound English education.'[105] In addition, the French priests envisaged a preparatory class for boys who needed to make up for any shortfall in their English and Arithmetic, as well as a special class for practical commercial skills. Fifteen years later, as already noted, with eleven teachers for French and German plus two for Italian and Spanish, as opposed to nine for Greek and Latin, modern languages formed, proportionally, the largest group of teachers on Blackrock's staff.

In the absence of a wider sample, we cannot draw general conclusions, from two schools, about the staffing of classics versus modern languages in elite boys' schools between Ireland and England. Eton may be an outlier. So was Blackrock's French College in many respects. Other schools' staffing figures, in both countries, may yield similar or different results. The report of the Clarendon Commission on public school education (1864) shows considerable variation in practice among public schools themselves. Rugby was offering French and German under Thomas Arnold in the 1830s, as were other public schools such as Shrewsbury and Harrow. Some of the newer public schools, like Cheltenham, had a Modern Department, intended for boys preparing to sit Civil Service examinations; this offered a broad curriculum of subjects that included modern languages while excluding Greek.[106] In Ireland, William Delany SJ, the dynamic rector of Tullabeg who later became President of UCD in its RUI incarnation, was sympathetic to foreign languages, having spent some of his formative years in France and Rome, and this may have created stronger incentives for languages in the university's 'feeder schools' and environs.[107] However, taking the Blackrock figures in isolation, it does seem that modern languages were its strong suit at this period. Perhaps the English public-school model (as cultivated by the Jesuits at Tullabeg and Clongowes) was coloured, at Blackrock, by the significant continental presence on its staff, where eight out of the thirteen modern-language teachers had French, German or Italian surnames: Botrel, Chollet, Polin, Julien, Reffé; Goetner, Haas; Morosini.[108]

In English schools more generally in the early 1800s, French, sometimes with German, was gradually being introduced as an extra subject. A number of schools responded to calls for a broader and more utilitarian curriculum, such as those made by the education reformer and MP (for Waterford) Thomas Wyse, who sympathised with the middle class, 'fed with the dry husks of ancient learning when they should be taking sound and substantial food from the great treasury of modern discovery' and criticised 'the usual stunted course of most of our Grammar Schools' as boiling down to 'a little Latin learnt in a very imperfect manner, with some scraps of Greek to boot'.[109] However, rebalancing the academic curriculum was not always straightforward. In some English schools, objections to modern studies had been raised on the grounds that the school's original charter had not included them. Where the founding mission of the school was the teaching of Latin grammar, no modern languages were to be countenanced.[110] Few if any Irish schools laboured under such constraints. Nor did socially ambitious middle-class families in Ireland demand that their sons' education be dominated by classics. Unlike in England, where a consistently strong parental demand for the high-status model offered by public schools weakened any demand for curricular reform. Indeed, there was every incentive to maintain and even expand an over-specialised classical regime: the vast majority of Oxbridge entrance scholarships were in ancient languages. For all of these reasons, 'classics persisted in the late Victorian public school because of expanding market demand for the social status it continued to symbolize.'[111]

Continuities in classical education were less secure in France's highly centralised education system, where the study of Latin and Greek in schools had been briefly disrupted during the revolutionary period. Already during the ancien régime, some educationalists had begun to question the curricular hegemony of the classics in junior post-primary *collèges*. The Oratorian order of secular priests, more gallican than the Jesuits, were in the vanguard of reformers in the eighteenth century who sought to balance Latin by prioritising more use of French in their classrooms. Not all educationalists agreed with these ideas, and Latin remained essential in the curriculum. However, the so-called *querelle des collèges* – an education debate between ancients and moderns (a familiar theme in French literary history) – may help to explain how the canonisation of works by certain authors of French literature happened during the mid-eighteenth century, and how the French came to treat their vernacular literature as a serious component of tertiary education some decades before the equivalent happened on the other side of the Channel. '*Littérature*', revered by French officialdom, became intrinsic to the sense of French identity constructed by the post-revolutionary nation.[112]

Classical language study also played an important educational role in Victorian Ireland. However it was not the exclusive domain of elite schools. Schools of all kinds taught ancient languages – classical schools, diocesan schools, grammar schools, parochial schools, schools run by religious orders – endowed and private, of all denominations.[113] Ulster's five Royal Free Schools, founded in 1608 by a charter of King James I to educate the sons of plantation settlers,[114] offered a heavy dose of Latin and also some Greek for sacred scripture.[115] It was not unusual for Maynooth seminarians, in the early decades, to have been introduced to Latin while at classical schools run by protestants or dissenters. William Crolly, for instance, future archbishop of Armagh and founder (1833) of St Malachy's College Belfast, had attended a classical school run by a Unitarian minister, in his hometown of Downpatrick.[116] Scientist and priest Nicholas Joseph Callan DD (1799–1864), Maynooth's Professor of Natural Philosophy, was first educated at the Dundalk Classical and Mercantile Academy established by the presbyterian Revd William Neilson, where Latin was the spoken language of the school.[117]

Classical languages persisted with most force in England's elite schools, in some instances well into the twentieth century. In 1965, Flann Campbell reports, Eton had 37 masters teaching classics, 19 science, 13 mathematics, and 19 teaching other languages including English.[118] In Victorian times, such a weighting in favour of the ancient was often accompanied by a disparagement of the modern. Although Thomas Arnold introduced French and German to Rugby (where he was headmaster from 1828 to 1841), he did not believe that the boys would ever learn to speak or pronounce French properly, so it would suffice to teach it grammatically, like a dead language. The inference that a modern language *might as well* be an ancient language could seemingly lend it some prestige. In his evidence to the Clarendon Commission, the Revd H. M. Butler, Harrow's headmaster from 1859 to 1885 (and later Master of Trinity College Cambridge), had deep misgivings about the risk of modern languages 'seriously or dangerously infringing upon the time [usually 12 hours a week] given to what is our main study, *i.e.*, classics'; in his view, to give French or German more hours for training in spoken fluency would 'damage the intellectual tone of the place'.[119] In the 1850s, when asked his opinion on the matter, Eton's headmaster, the Revd C. O. Goodford, expressed the relative educational value of classics to mathematics to modern languages as a ratio of 15:3:1.[120] In short, 'the sole aim of public schools was to discipline and strengthen the mind by teaching subjects which required continuous mental exertion, such as Latin and Greek.'[121]

Although purporting to set up a level playing field in establishing a marking scheme for the Indian Civil Service examinations 'in such a manner that no part of the kingdom, and no class of schools, shall exclusively furnish servants to the East India Company', the authors of the Macaulay Report (1854) betray a similar mindset. Despite asserting that 'in the north of this island the art of metrical composition in the ancient languages is very little cultivated', they still feel obliged to allot twice the number of marks to Greek and Latin over other foreign languages.[122] A decade later, although it recommended more balance between the provision of ancient and modern languages in public schools, the members of the 1864 Clarendon Commission, appointed mainly by old Etonians, themselves classically educated,[123] concluded their report with a glowing endorsement of the uniquely English model of education.

The classics also died hard in Ireland's elite schools for boys, as they did in other European countries. As Flann Campbell observed in 1968, Greek and Latin persisted as a marker of (mostly male) social advantage and privilege. Ireland's 1965 landmark policy document, *Investment in Education*, noted that more boys had sat a recent final school examination in ancient Greek than in German, Italian and Spanish combined.[124] A colourful corroboration of the status of the classics in Irish education, well into the twentieth century, is given by Trinity College's emeritus Regius Professor of Greek, John Dillon:[125]

> [...] a more mainstream European classical education dominated the Protestant schools of the country – as it continued to do down to at least the 1950's, in Protestant and Catholic schools alike. The general feeling then, as I recall it, was that one would continue to do Classics, predominantly or even exclusively, unless and until one was proved hopelessly incompetent, at which stage one would be 'demoted' into Modern Languages, History and English, or, ultimately, Geography and Religious Instruction. Only if one showed an early aptitude for mathematics or science (which I did not) might one break out of this hierarchical structure of subjects.

As we shall discuss later in this book, the NUI's matriculation requirement for Latin or Greek was only dropped, for Arts and Law, in 1974, having been gradually eroded since 1971.[126] A comparable situation in English university requirements[127] allows us to set the late 1960s as the watershed when the hierarchical rivalry between classics and modern languages ended, the sway of the former yielding place to the latter. We shall come back to this watershed in our final chapter.

However, university entry requirements notwithstanding, to return to the 1850s, a headmaster at that period in Ireland would be unlikely to concur with the Revd Goodford's 15:3:1 estimate of educational value. An imbalance of such magnitude would be inconceivable in Ireland, and not only because of the continental influences we have been outlining. In late Victorian and Edwardian England, the classics – in particular, Latin and Roman history – had, if anything, increased in political and philosophical prestige among educators to meet the demands of empire. As Christopher Stray argues, 'the classical strand in what was largely an Oxford-based imperial mission was a powerful one'.[128] Noting how the Latin language was perceived as useful for training the empire's colonial administrators, Flann Campbell charts how a veritable legion of manly Roman virtues – hard work, self-control, discipline, duty, honour, disregard for the body or the emotions, order, loyalty, sacrifice for the public good – became valued models in the training of its functionaries, statesmen and military generals. For a time, he argues, the imperial project prized austere Roman stoicism over effeminate Hellenic hedonism.[129] *Dulce et decorum est pro patria mori.*

Ireland's Catholic headmasters had Latin coordinates, too, but with local bearings. Their world reached out, not to antiquity in the service of colonial rule, but rather, in part, to a latter-day ecclesiastical empire. More significantly, the Irish had for centuries domesticated their study of classical Latin, which still had a lingering, living presence in parts of rural Ireland. This lent another, specifically Irish, dimension to the classics which English people found disconcerting, or even inappropriate. The Home Secretary, Robert Peel, in a House of Commons debate in 1826, complained about the unsuitability of classical learning for the lower orders, and the incongruity of a situation where 'the young peasants of Kerry [...] run about in their rags, with a Cicero or a Virgil under their arms'.[130] In 1868, a parish priest in the same county was applauded by his flock for declaring: 'I make no apology for quoting Latin, for Latin is almost our mother-tongue.'[131]

As we saw in an earlier chapter, Irish men of letters exiled in seventeenth-century Europe, following the disruption of the old order brought about by war and dispossession, had picked up the pieces of a shattered heritage, in order to preserve it in writing and assert its intrinsic value and antiquity. Ireland, in their imagined narratives, was as venerable as ancient Greece and its language as old as the Bible. Irish historians had established a clear continuum running from the ancient world right down to the present. To quote Laurie O'Higgins:[132]

> the Irish language and people were implicated in an international past. Their story belonged with that of ancient Israel, the Scythians, the Greeks and Romans. It was part of a venerable and capacious human story.

This was one reason, O'Higgins argues, for the persistence of classical learning in Ireland's hedge schools. Latin, Greek and Irish were woven together as a sustaining strand of Ireland's cultural identity, that reached further back in time and well beyond the geographical limits of the British Empire.

As Dowling, McManus and O'Higgins amply demonstrate, the teaching of Latin, in particular, permeated the curriculum in Ireland's 'hedge'-schools. Without over romanticising this unique feature of Ireland's underground education history, hedge-schoolmasters, and the learned class they represented, were custodians of an archaic form of cultural transmission, and many of them played a role in antiquarian textual preservation.[133] Although technically 'unlicensed' until 1829, hedge schools vastly outnumbered other forms of elementary schooling when the national schools were introduced in 1831, and a significant number of them ensured continuity with the old order as they became absorbed by the new system.[134]

'Hedge'-schools catered for boys – and even some girls – of all religious denominations, ages and economic means. While the teaching quality presumably covered a broad spectrum, at their best these schools coloured local communities with what W. B. Stanford called 'Ireland's rural Latinity' and 'rustic classicism'.[135] A standard trope in eighteenth-century travellers' accounts of visits to remote parts of Munster, especially County Kerry, is the unexpected presence of Latin or Greek among the poorer inhabitants. One school at Faha in County Kerry, was renowned for its classical training.[136] To cite, from 1797, the testimony of the artist George Holmes:[137]

> Amongst the uncultivated part of the Country, many may be met with who are all good Latin scholars, yet do not speak a word of English. Greek is also taught in the mountainous parts by some itinerant teachers.

Robert Bell, in 1804, had the same impression of 'the sons of some of the most indigent and obscure peasants in Ireland [who had] become acquainted with the best Greek and Roman authors; [and] had the taste to discriminate the beauties contained in them'. The same young lads, he observed, 'frequently conversed with each other in the Latin language; which (by the bye) they spoke much more correctly than English.'[138] The standard of Latin and Greek that could be attained in classical hedge schools – as those with a reputation for teaching classics were called – was capable of preparing abler students for further study, in Ireland or abroad.[139] 'Edmund Burke claimed to have learned more Latin and Greek from an obscure schoolmaster on the banks of the Nore, than he afterwards acquired at the more celebrated places of education, including the university itself.'[140] Reporting on Catholic peasants in the 'wildest districts' of County Derry, the Revd Alexander Ross claimed that 'it is not unusual to meet with good classical scholars; and there are several young mountaineers of the writer's acquaintance, whose knowledge and taste in the Latin poets, might put to the blush many who have all the advantages of established schools and regular instruction.'[141] As each schoolmaster's reputation depended on his erudition, the atmosphere in many cases displayed a rich and sophisticated level of language diversity and esteem for learning. Culturally and socially, both schoolmaster and student teacher (or 'poor scholar') occupied a central place in the community, and were accommodated in cabins and temporary shelters in townlands across rural Ireland.[142]

The subtly contrasting nuances in cultural awareness of the classics between England and Ireland are depicted near the start of Thomas Flanagan's 1979 novel *The Year of the French*. Reflecting on the fictional confrontation between Owen MacCarthy, poet and hedge-schoolmaster, and the Church of Ireland rector at Killala, the Revd Arthur Vincent Broome, John Dillon comments:[143]

> There is a great gulf of mutual incomprehension between them, which the English language, of which MacCarthy has a fair command though a low opinion, does little to bridge. The subject on which they can find most common ground, though even then a ground riven with ambiguities, is their knowledge of the Roman poets. [...] MacCarthy studied Vergil with his master, crouched under a hedge, out of a battered old text carried round the roads in a damp and evil-smelling satchel; while the young Broome, doubtless with equal discomfort, sat in a chilly classroom in one of the great public schools or universities, with stern Protestant forebears looking down on him. But they both read the same stuff.

Consequently, the Irish schoolboys' appreciation of Virgil was primal and emotional rather than critical and philological. Dillon quotes William Carleton's autobiography where he describes himself on the verge of tears when he first read the death of Dido scene in *Aeneid* IV. He had absorbed the classical texts for the stories they contained, not for their grammatical difficulties. For 'schoolboys brought up in the British tradition', Dillon argues, Dido's passion was inevitably toned down 'beneath interesting uses of the Dative and irregularities in the employment of the Subjunctive'.[144]

John Dillon's image of the weather-beaten satchel and the chilly classroom strikingly captures the contrasting sources and processes of traditional classical education in the two islands. Grammar schools had been founded to teach the rules of Latin grammar; however, another pervasive taproot for the transmission of classical languages in Ireland was the 'hedge'-school. On the one hand, a stable model of education grounded in an unbroken tradition for centuries, aligned with the political and legal order; on the other, a precarious and makeshift model, born of rupture, defying the laws of a hostile power. In the one, the imaginative impulse took second place to formal grammatical analysis, while the other may have allowed greater communicative rein to the raw impact of the poetic text.[145]

In addition to Latin and Greek, and occasionally Hebrew, it was not unknown for some 'hedge'-schools to include a modern language – most frequently, French – in their curriculum.[146] There were masters who, having studied in mainland Europe, had abandoned their clerical training and returned to teach rather than preach. For some learners, the language training received in school could lead to higher education, at home or abroad. However, for many others, it had no such utilitarian motivation, and merely generated a residual acquaintance with foreign languages and literatures. This kind of gratuitous language study, a feature of Ireland's education system, is arguably one with increasing relevance for anglophones in the twenty-first century.

The distinctively Irish 'Arcadian love of the classics' was on the wane during the second half of the nineteenth century, partly, in Stanford's view, 'under the influence of the new non-classical national schools'.[147] The phasing out of the 'hedge'-schools, in his view, brought a decline in native classical awareness. Where the balance between classical versus modern languages is concerned, however, there was less entrenched resistance to European languages in Ireland's Victorian secondary schools than in England's. Modern foreign languages as well as classics were given space to thrive.[148]

There was also some balance between ancient and modern at university level. Newman, who hired staff to teach French, German and Italian, tutored CU students in Latin composition, but found many gaps in their knowledge of the ancient world.[149] He recognised that he was a long way from Oxford. Dublin's older university, Trinity College, more invested in classics than the newer establishments, was slower to change. In 1839, speaking at a meeting of Dublin University's College Historical Society,[150] the young Thomas Davis urged his fellow Trinity students to devote their energies to acquiring modern languages. He first warned them that the days of their monopoly of privilege would soon be numbered, given the impending arrival of other universities in the land.[151] Davis decried Trinity's neglect of modern languages, including English and Irish literature. He incited students to rebel against the imbalance with classics, and opined on how the freshman student should spend his time:[152]

Classics! Good sooth, he had better read with the hedge-school boys the History of the Rogues, Tories and Rapparees, or Moll Flanders, than study Homer and Horace in Trinity College. I therefore protest, and ask you to struggle against the cultivation of Greek, or Latin, or Hebrew, while French and German are excluded;[153] and still more strongly should we oppose the cultivation of any, or all of these, to the neglect of English and, I should add, Irish literature.[154]

We might expect such a clarion call from the future editor of *The Nation*, whose name was shortly to become synonymous with Young Ireland. Davis made his plea for modern languages the year Trinity's Classics Professor, J. P. Mahaffy, was born. Yet even Mahaffy, later bellwether don of the College's antiquated establishment who was to have strong misgivings about modern languages constituting suitable university degrees, appreciated the value of knowing German for scientific enquiry, and was very proud of his own mastery of French and German which he had had the good fortune to pick up effortlessly in early childhood abroad, and displayed with panache at international gatherings of scholars.[155]

In fact, as McDowell and Webb argue in their history of the College, Trinity's nineteenth-century undergraduate course managed to stay relatively well balanced, avoiding the over specialisation found in Britain's older liberal universities, where classics was the hallmark of Oxford, pure mathematics was associated with Cambridge and philosophy with Scotland. Dublin University's fellows, too, due to the College's particular examination requirements, displayed a healthy mix of disciplines.[156] A solid foundation in the classics mattered most for undergraduates who hoped to take the university's Scholarship examination in their Senior Freshman year. In that test, the only discipline examined, up to 1856, was classics. Attaining a high standard in Latin and Greek, oral and written, also motivated those who planned to seek Fellowship. Until 1853, Trinity's Fellowships, when vacant, were awarded by examinations conducted *viva voce* in Latin, over four days in front of the Provost, the seven most senior Fellows and the Archbishop of Dublin.[157] As in Oxbridge, classics were of material significance for an Anglican career: understanding the Word of God (*i.e.*, Greek and Latin) was the job of a clergyman. Performance could lead to preferment and – with some luck – the perquisites of clerical office.[158]

MATRICULATION, GENDER, CLASS AND LANGUAGE STUDY

As the syllabi of Irish public examinations and university matriculation requirements together began to shape the provision and take-up of different school subjects, class and religious divides came into play. So did the gender distribution of particular languages. The increased number of girls' convent schools offering modern languages after 1878–9, and the broader range of languages offered, was due in large part to the 'payment-by-results' ethos promoted by the Intermediate examination.

Traditionally, for English girls, the inhibiting 'balance' between classics and modern languages hardly applied, since they were not expected to learn Latin or Greek. This allowed girls to be offered a broader curriculum than boys. In the girls' schools visited by the Taunton Commission (1864–8), only 21 per cent of the girls were studying Latin while almost all studied French and – strikingly – 72 per cent did one of the natural sciences.[159] Girls were therefore more likely than their brothers to study both French and German in schools that offered both. As a German scholar concludes from a sample of English schools in 1891:[160]

> Proportionally [...] French and German were more widely available in girls' schools than in boys' schools – indeed, a higher proportion of the girls' schools (47%) offered German than the proportion of boys' schools offering French (43%). Already in 1868, more girls took German at Senior level than did boys (38 girls, 25 boys), even though there were far more male candidates overall (160 girls, 218 boys).

A broadly similar pattern applied in Ireland, where, conventionally, 'the education offered to middle class girls in schools and by governesses alike, reflected society's expectations as to their future. It consisted of English, history, geography, arithmetic, French (sometimes Italian and German), music, religious instruction and needlework.'[161] When, after 1880, at least one classical language qualification became a *sine qua non* for admission to most of the faculties in the RUI, girls' post-primary schools gradually began to introduce Latin as well. This did not meet with universal approval. In 1883, for instance, the Catholic bishop of Meath expressed the view that exact sciences and 'the Pagan literature of Greece and Rome' were not suitable objects of study for young ladies.[162] For girls, German was often substituted for Greek, and Latin was a novelty. In the absence of expertise on their own staff, some schools, like St Louis Monaghan, enlisted local priests to teach Latin to their more academically ambitious charges.[163]

In this respect, it is interesting to compare the situation in progressive 'modern' schools for middle-class girls in England, like York's Mount School or Bedford's Seminary for Young Ladies, and (later) Cheltenham Ladies' College or North London Collegiate. In the 1860s these offered excellent teaching and an impressively broad curriculum, including science and mathematics, but did not necessarily direct their academically able pupils towards classical languages. A case in point is Cheltenham Ladies' College (opened in 1854), run by Dorothea Beale (herself a gifted mathematician), where one star-ranking pupil in 1871 was awarded first-class marks in eleven subjects, but excluding Latin.[164] Alexandra in Dublin, Belfast Collegiate, or St Louis Monaghan would hardly have made such a key omission. The deficiency struck the Taunton commissioners who recommended that girls' grammar schools take on the study of Latin on top of sciences and modern languages. Ambitious female students complied, and concentrated more and more on classics, bringing a loss to science culture, overall, in girls' education and wiping out feminist reformers' hopes that a new education model could be constructed in which the broad coverage in girls' schools would be taken into consideration for Oxbridge entry. In her history of women's interest in science, *The Scientific Lady*, Patricia Phillips suggests that the perceived superiority of a narrow classical education, synonymous with male excellence, came to matter even more acutely after 1900. During the suffrage struggle, the cream of well-educated women needed to show they were culturally and academically equal to their Eton-educated brothers. The strongly rooted prestige of the classics triumphed, once again.[165]

Statistics show a steady increase in the provision of classical languages to girls in Ireland. The 1881 Irish Census recorded the study of Latin – and Mathematics – by women students as having more than doubled, and those taking Greek more than trebled, over a decade, from a very low base.[166] The numbers of girls taking Latin for the Intermediate examination in 1899 amounted to 2,042,[167] while numbers of female candidates taking

Greek to the end of their schooldays remained minuscule: 'in 1918, one girl and 219 boys passed Greek in the senior grade.'[168]

Apart from university entrance, denominational rivalry was sometimes a powerful motivation for Ireland's Catholic girls' schools to provide Latin: the ambition not to be outdone by progressive new Protestant girls' schools such as Victoria College in Belfast (formerly the Ladies' Collegiate School) or Alexandra College in Dublin. Alexandra had a strong academic ethos from the outset in 1866. Its curriculum included mathematics and science as well as Latin, French, German, Italian, Greek and Hebrew, and it had an institutional connection with Trinity College Dublin, some of whose teaching staff taught there in the later Victorian decades.[169] It was a matter of pride for convent schools to encourage their pupils to achieve better results than Alexandra, who were habitually successful in the Intermediate Certificate.

3.8 Sacred Heart Convent, Leeson Street, garden with cow, 1886–7 Photograph. (*Courtesy of Provincial Archives, Irish/Scottish Province, Society of the Sacred Heart.*)

Within modern languages, French was consistently the most studied in both England and Ireland. In England, the *Educational Annual* of 1891 reported that out of 794 secondary schools of various types, 345 taught French and 217 taught German, with Spanish and Italian following very far behind (6 schools offered Spanish and 4 Italian).[170] Modern-language uptake between French and German appeared even more lopsided in Ireland: in 1905, for instance, out of 9,677 candidates sitting post-primary state examinations, 9,156 took French as opposed to 1,101 taking German.[171] This tallies with the UCD constituent college of the RUI, where pass level French formed the largest language group by far, with other European languages in far less demand.[172]

In reply, then, to the question posed at the end of our previous chapter, we can confirm that, by the end of the nineteenth century, elite secondary schools in Ireland were equipping some students, male and female, with enough knowledge of modern languages for university matriculation. It is of course important to remember that, in those decades, university study was accessible to an extremely small minority of the population at large, male and female. 'In 1871 the census showed that about 22,000 pupils were attending "superior" schools, that is schools which taught a foreign language. By 1911 this had increased to 40,840, but this figure only amounted to 6 per cent of the school-going population';[173] as late as 1930, 93 per cent of Irish people had attended school at elementary level only.[174] If girls tended to study modern languages more than boys, and to study modern languages rather than classics, this only applied to middle-class girls of sufficient means.

Of course, Victorian education was segregated on class lines by design. Britain's new elementary schools, which began to introduce mass literacy in the late 1830s, were intended for the proletarian classes.[175] This was standard received opinion, taken to be in the nature of things. Robert Lowe, MP, a minister who served under Gladstone, in an address delivered at Edinburgh in 1867, while calling for a more practical public-school curriculum that would go beyond the exclusively classical, concluded by rationalising the status quo in the matter of class division:[176]

> The lower classes ought to be educated to discharge the duties cast upon them. They should also be educated that they may appreciate and defer to a higher cultivation when they meet it; and the higher class ought to be educated in a very different manner, in order that they may exhibit to the lower classes that higher education to which, if it were shown to them, they would bow down and defer.

Class determinants were also evident in Ireland's Victorian education landscape. 'Inequality', according to J. P. Mahaffy, 'is and must be the first condition of every society.'[177] Cardinal Paul Cullen, in his 1868 submission to the Powis Commission, expressed the opinion that 'too high an education will make the poor often times discontented and will unsuit them for following the plough or for using the spade or for hammering iron or building walls'.[178]

Ideology and practicality have an admirable tendency to coincide. Sunday schooling, devised by eighteenth-century philanthropists for a rudimentary religious and secular education to be imparted to child labourers in northern England's industrialised cities, necessarily restricted the curriculum to reading, writing and arithmetic. These children worked six long days a week. In Ireland, too, a reduced educational diet for the children of manual labourers was also integral to the culture. Modern languages, increasingly available in some convent school settings, were absent from the menu of the separate Sunday schools for 'servant and labouring classes' run by convent national schools. A Commissioners' Report (1864) on the Convent of Mercy, Ardee, for example, relates:[179]

> There is a separate school for the daughters of shopkeepers, farmers, etc., having an average of about 50. These pupils are taught French and music (vocal and instrumental), in addition to the usual English course; and on every Sunday the nuns open school for two hours, the first hour and a half being devoted to secular, and the remainder to religious instruction. The attendance, so far as I could learn, varies from 60 to 100, and is composed of servants, girls employed daily in the fields, etc. The secular instruction is confined to reading, writing, and a little arithmetic.

In Dundalk, the same congregation ran, on a voluntary basis, a separate Sunday school, where – in addition to moral and religious instruction – the children were taught practical skills such as 'reading, writing, the making up of shop bills, and letter writing, the last principally for those who may, perchance, have an opportunity of emigrating'.[180] This was only marginally broader than the curriculum taught, a century before, in Dublin's first free school for poor girls, set up by Teresa Mulally, with the support of James Philip Mulcaile SJ, in the 1760s: religious instruction, literacy and needlework.[181]

The sphere of convent schooling was itself socially stratified. As Ciaran O'Neill has illustrated, this education brand was much sought after – in Ireland, England and Europe – among the elites of late nineteenth-century society, and some religious congregations were regarded as catering for a more exclusive clientèle than others. These nuns were seen to provide the best way of equipping one's daughters advantageously when facing the marriage market, with their emphasis on accomplishments like music and modern languages, deportment, refined manners and social graces, mingled with the cultivation of 'female' traits such as modesty and self-control.[182] More utilitarian views of the purpose of educating girls were also voiced. The notion of bringing up middle-class girls for a career was contested, and rarely transcended the belief that matrimony and homemaking were the natural destiny for daughters. What was the point, these arguments ran, of teaching a girl how to speak French or play sonatas, if she has not been taught thrift and good housekeeping? Strong opinions on the futility of a convent school education for the practicalities of the real world are aired by the former Irish Party MP Frank Hugh O'Donnell, in his invective against the influence of the Church in Irish education. Here is a sample from his pages:[183]

> Goody-goodyness, and superficiality, and helplessness, trumpery accomplishments, and total unfitness for home and wifehood, these appear to be the darling objects of the saintly and incompetent sisterhoods; who, having forsworn the knowledge and use of the world, devote themselves, for a modest remuneration, to the misinformation and depreparation of the future wives and mothers of the country.

He quotes approvingly from a critique of convent schools published in the *New Ireland Review* in December 1901, which asserts that convent-trained girls are[184]

> reared too softly and foolishly for the life before them [...]. I have heard of convent girls of seventeen and eighteen taking situations in Dublin, and being found incapable of washing a pocket-handkerchief, or of dusting a room without supervision. One, when asked for a corkscrew, brought a dish-cover; she was not acquainted with the names of the commonest appliances to be found in a private house. [...] I have spoken of the probabilities of poor girls marrying poor men, and having to live in a humble cottage, to economise, and learn to spend money to advantage. Of what use to them is a knowledge of fancy-work, of the violin, of the history of England, unless this is accompanied, as it should be, by more solid accompaniments? I despise none of these things in their place, but it should be possible to combine with them the knowledge of how to cook a dinner, avoid disease, and keep children clean, instead of sending them to school in filth and tatters. It may sound prosaic, but I think that if Irish cookery were better, Irish husbands would be more sober.

Perennial determinants of biology, society and ideology gave women students more than one difficulty to contend with. However, beneath the stereotypes there was variety on the ground, and many Irish convent schools did offer a solid academic foundation for further study. It was also an education brand with global reach, up to the twentieth century. The Mercy and Presentation orders set up schools in America, Australia and New Zealand (all anglophone countries). The feminist academic Germaine Greer once described herself as a

Presentation creature and expressed gratitude for her Irish convent education in Australia, where the nuns encouraged her to sit for a scholarship to secondary school.[185] For all its class and gender biases, the expansion of Irish female access to further education is an undeniable feature of the late-Victorian and Edwardian years. Even if it offered relatively narrow career opportunities, at least the door had been opened. The development was rapid. By 1911, an estimated five-fold increase in the educational participation of middle-class Irish women has been noted; even more significantly, 'Ireland was second only to Finland in the percentage of women at university.'[186]

WOMEN OUTSIDE THE WALLS: ERASMUS-CUM-TEFL *ANTE DIEM*

Social background remains a determinant of academic foreign-language study in Ireland as in other Anglophone countries. Mastering another language is still largely an extra accomplishment for the comfortable or privileged, and for those who can afford to engage with the challenge, but it is rarely an intrinsic requirement for employment, due to the global status of English today. In non-Anglophone countries the reverse applies.

The gender bias associated with modern-language learning was also evident when modern languages and women arrived together in the groves of academe. The two newcomers sat side by side. When Irish women first breached the academic citadels, modern languages were a popular degree option for them. The earliest women graduates, who took degrees from the RUI in the 1880s and 1890s, distinguished themselves by earning scholarships and prizes in modern literatures and languages.[187] Two decades later, after their admission to degree status, some of Trinity College Dublin's earliest women students won gold medals in Modern Languages and History. Indeed, the admission of women in 1904 swelled Trinity's numbers in French and German so much that tutors and colleagues from other disciplines had to stand in on a temporary basis. Coinciding with the Board's decision to allow French and German to replace Freshman Greek at pass level, the sudden staff shortage was not helped by the death and retirement of the two incumbents soon afterwards, Professors Selss (German) and Atkinson (Romance languages).[188] Women students contributed to the growth of the College's modern-language departments.[189]

Margaret Ó hÓgartaigh has argued that, while the changes in regulation helped to open up career possibilities for women, the tendency for them to concentrate their studies on modern languages led in some ways to a narrowing of career choice. While a minority of women graduates pursued careers traditionally seen as male only, in practice a choice between two careers faced the vast majority of RUI and NUI women graduates in the watershed period of 1878–1930: teaching and nursing. Since few of them, overall, had studied a classical language at school, many women took a degree in Commerce, 'a favourite choice of students entering without Latin'.[190] Some of these graduates then obtained an education diploma and ended up in the teaching profession by a different route from Arts.[191]

The nexus between education, modern languages and women is illustrated by a custom dating from the 1890s and 1900s, namely, periods of study in Europe undertaken by some young Irish women students. The custom is also a by-product of the gender bias that we have been discussing, as the admission of women to university was neither smooth nor evenly paced. Strictly speaking, this phenomenon sits astride the boundary between post-elementary and third-level education, but such boundaries were more fluid in those days. It was still possible, well into the twentieth century – especially in girls' schools – to remain in primary school until the age of 16, and to prepare public examinations or seek a place on a teacher training course from there.[192]

Taking its cue from the University of London, which admitted women to degrees in 1878, the Royal University of Ireland from its foundation in 1879 – as we have seen – deemed women eligible for degrees, within certain limitations.[193] A quarter of a century later, Trinity College Dublin opened its doors to women undergraduates in Arts and Medicine from 1904 (with restrictions on full participation in College life) and deemed them eligible to take degrees.[194] It is hard nowadays to grasp just how revolutionary a step this was. The very notion of 'ladies' attending the same lectures as young men posed a conundrum beyond the ken of early Victorians. A letter of Newman's (1855) expressed in stark terms his misgivings about admitting both sexes into hearing public lectures held at the newly opened CU. Their presence at Professor Denis McCarthy's poetry lecture, for example, would entirely alter the tone and purpose of the occasion:[195]

> Certainly, if ladies attend the Poetry Lecture, it ceases to be an academical meeting. [...] I do not object to ladies being admitted to Mr McCarthy's lectures, but if so, it is quite impossible that I can send young men with pencil and paper to take down notes.

The admission of women to degree eligibility was increasingly happening in Britain during these later decades of the century, so that by 1895 all but two British universities had capitulated. Oxford and Cambridge were notoriously tardy. The University of Oxford, despite its all-women's colleges at Lady Margaret Hall, established in 1878, and at Somerville, founded the following year, only admitted women candidates for degrees in 1920. Cambridge women students had to wait for degrees until 1948, despite the university having established women's colleges even earlier than Oxford, at Girton (1869) and Newnham (1871). Meanwhile, Oxbridge women attended Lectures for Ladies and sat University degree examinations but were ineligible, on grounds of sex, for the award of a degree.[196]

3.9 Ad for Alberta School, Antrim Road, Belfast, 1888
Northern Whig, 24 October 1888. Post-elementary girls' school run from their home by Louie and Eva Wood, RUI (Belfast) women graduates.

In the midst of developments elsewhere – with the former Queen's Colleges all allowing 'mixed education' from the 1880s (Belfast in 1882, Cork in 1885 and Galway in 1888), and women allowed to attend lectures alongside men in Dublin's Medical School in Cecelia Street, and then with Trinity College's capitulation in 1904 – it became a matter of mounting resentment to women arts students of Dublin's Jesuit-run RUI College in Stephen's Green that they alone were denied access to the same recognition. Whereas, with the exception of medicine and surgery, attendance at lectures was not mandatory at this period, and although the separate women's colleges, run by the Dominicans and Loreto orders, had facilities for them to attend separate lectures when not allowed to attend college on-site, Dublin's RUI women students sought permission to attend in person the same Fellows' lectures as male students, if they wished to do so. Classes, after all, were taught by the same Fellows who would be setting and assessing the examinations that applied to all students. This set women students at a disadvantage. To prepare for the RUI examinations, they had to rely on independent study, extra private tuition or tuition provided by the women's colleges, and (for a few years in the 1900s) by the handful of Junior Fellows who kindly volunteered to give separate 'public lectures' for women students.

Studying at the denominational single-sex colleges – Alexandra College, the Dominicans' St Mary's, Loreto College in Dublin, Victoria College in Belfast or St Angela's in Cork – was in practice the experience of the vast majority of the RUI's women students in the 1890s.[197] Even in the colleges where women were technically permitted to sit in the same lecture rooms as men, entering the hallowed ground of university terrain was not made easy for them. In Cork, 'they often met opposition, resentment and ridicule.'[198] One can appreciate why few of the Royal University's women students enrolled in the three university colleges in the early decades, preferring to pursue their studies in the sheltered spaces made for them. In Trinity College, where they were eligible to take degrees from 1904, special regulations ensured that women would cause the least possible amount of disruption to the traditionally male preserve that was college life. Women undergraduates were socially distanced from their male counterparts. For example, they could not enter the Common Room or the Dining Hall and had to leave the campus by 6pm. Such restrictions, which were not relaxed fully until the 1960s, did not exactly make them feel fully assimilated.[199]

3.10 French College, Blackrock: Castle students, 1892
Students attending University College Blackrock, a constituent college of the RUI. Blackrock College Archives. (*Courtesy of Blackrock College, Co Dublin.*)

The political climate during the 1900s was propitious for bringing women students' grievances to light, as the vexed Irish university question – which had bedevilled successive Westminster administrations for decades – was in the air again, with two commissions of enquiry – the Robertson (1901–03) and the Fry (1906–07) – held in quick succession. A considerable amount of energy was spent, by various representative groups, on lobbying in these forums to alter the unsatisfactory state of affairs. The issue was eventually resolved by the 1908 Universities Act. In 1909, the National University of Ireland admitted men and women on an equal footing to all its colleges.[200]

The unequal treatment of women following admission to the university, which was felt most acutely at UCD, had one consequence that highlights the nexus between women, modern languages and educational attainment. For a small number of middle-class women students of modern languages, protracted continental sojourns were one highly effective response to being barred from attending lectures along with their male peers. Echoing the journeys of Catholic men who, in penal times, had travelled abroad to study for the priesthood or complete clerical training, picking up foreign-language skills into the bargain, a small band of women students now experienced foreign displacement of a different kind. This travel was motivated primarily by a desire to perfect and improve their mastery of foreign languages. The European sojourns of these young women of the late Victorian and early Edwardian period certainly broadened their horizons and the language exposure they gained was extremely enriching. In a couple of cases, the experience led to enhanced career opportunities.

Without unduly labouring the comparison between two historical phenomena of vastly different duration and scale, one might be tempted to hear a faint echo of history repeating itself, at least to the extent that both groups – clerical students in penal times and a tiny group of late Victorian women – experienced discrimination and a denial of full integration at home. However, in the women's case the exclusion proved, in some cases, a kind of liberation. This is adumbrated in 1954 by Professor Mary Macken, reminiscing with fondness on her youth in the RUI, and with gratitude for the role of the Loreto and Ursuline nuns in shaping her own education:[201]

> Sister Eucharia encouraged me already in 1896 to go abroad for language study. She was, like so many of the Women Teaching Orders who have contacts everywhere with the Continent, an expert in finding suitable centres in Germany, France or Italy for students otherwise hard put to it to 'arrive'. I remember with delight my first Paris stay at *L'École Normale*, 39 Rue Jacob, where I lived *en pension* with an interesting group of women brought together in that year, as if specially for my benefit, from various states of Europe and America [...]. The owners of the École were compulsorily laicised nuns; they wore ordinary dress and went about their business on Left or Right Bank of the Seine like any other Frenchwomen. [...] It was a great adventure; one of our compensations for the 'inadequacy' of the early 'Colleges'. The following year it was to be Berlin through the Cork Ursulines and Mary Ryan. Those experiences of mine were not isolated; later Modern Languages 'College' women in the truncated Royal system had continental periods for which they are to this day grateful to the Religious who 'managed' it for them. A Modern Languages B.A. opened up to us then a new world of life and culture.

For some women these periods of study on the continent fundamentally shaped their future lives. Of all the university disciplines, modern European language study was ideally suited to extended periods of living on the continent (not unlike the Erasmus exchange experience today, when it works well). The Mary Ryan evoked by Macken was to hold the chair of Romance Languages in Cork from 1910 to 1938, a promotion that earned her the distinction of becoming the first woman in Ireland to hold a university chair in any subject.[202] Born in Cork in 1873, she was educated by the Ursulines in St Angela's, Patrick's Hill, before matriculating in the RUI in 1891. Part of her time as an undergraduate (1892–3) was spent studying in an Ursuline School in Berlin, followed by a Dominican school in Neuilly-sur-Seine, west of Paris.[203] Mary Macken herself became UCD's first professor of German. While these women linguists did not complete their academic careers in the Victorian era, they had been shaped by their late Victorian upbringing and the regulatory environment in which women sought to achieve equal status.

The same nexus of gender, modern languages and educational opportunity is also found, played in a minor and modulated key, in the case of the Ryans of Wexford (unrelated to Cork's Mary Ryan). The Ryan family of twelve children from a mixed tillage farm of 150 acres at Tomcoole, in Taghmon, outside Wexford town, illustrates how one late Victorian family availed of new educational possibilities through a combination of ambition, ability and circumstance.[204] Six of the eight Ryan daughters attended university. The eldest of the family, Johanna (1877–1942), who matriculated in 1896 and graduated in Arts in 1900, was a member of the Loreto order. She paid close attention to the academic progress of her younger siblings. As Sister Stanislaus, she was reputedly an excellent teacher of mathematics and Latin and made sure that they all reached an acceptable standard in that language, so essential for further study in most disciplines. For her sisters' modern language fluency, she used her connections with Catholic Europe. When the second eldest, Mary Kate, and later some of her younger sisters, Min, Agnes and Chris, showed an interest in studying modern languages, Johanna (known to her family as 'Stan') was instrumental in finding placements in continental convent schools, where they spent extended periods, teaching or speaking English in lieu of board and lodging. The pattern of these expeditions varied: two of them travelled as undergraduates; one went abroad for a year before her matriculation; another sister, Nell, never went to university. Nell, however, had two separate European experiences. Having studied in a convent school in Germany in 1900, she entered the Loreto novitiate in Rathfarnham in 1905 but left the following year, setting out once more to spend 1906–07 as a governess in Spain.

Family letters home have survived. Written from various continental towns in Europe during the 1900s, they give a flavour of the mindset, attitudes and expectations of these late Victorian and early Edwardian rural Irish women. We get a glimpse into how they spent their days in dreary convent boarding schools in Belgium, Germany or France, or (in Nell's case) as governess to a wealthy Spanish family.[205] They confide freely to each other about people of other nationalities whom they meet or with whom they share accommodation; about their homesickness; about the books they are reading; about the blouses they plan to make or the hats they are hoping to purchase. Amidst the gossip and minutiae of their daily lives, the sisters keep reminding each other that the purpose of their time abroad was foreign-language improvement, with a view to educational or career advancement: 'never lose sight of learning French and studying for your future' (Kit, UK, to Min, France, 4 October 1907). Target-language expressions pepper their correspondence, indicating a close engagement with their surroundings: 'I must also give an *Abschiedskaffee* [farewell coffee gathering] on Sunday' (Min, Germany, to Nell, Spain,

19 September 1907); '*enfin, le jeu ne vaut pas la chandelle*' [the game's not worth a candle] (Kit, France, to Min, France, 25 December 1907); 'I shall be quite free – but all alone! *Qu'est-ce que ça me fait?*' [What do I care?] (Kit, France, to Min, France, 27 December 1907); 'Don't repeat my *méchancetés* [catty remarks] or quotations from this letter' (Kit, UK, to Min, Ireland, 25 September 1908). They mention foreign-language reading: 'Next week, when I am finished reading the German book I have now, I shall read a French one. I am going to translate an English book here into German in class with one of my teachers' (Agnes, Germany, to Min, Germany, 4 June 1907); 'I am reading *Iphigenie* now in my class and am studying Goethe. Sr Ludovica is teaching me and she takes a terrible interest in me; so she explains everything grand.' (Agnes, Germany, to Min, Germany, 10 September 1907); 'I can read French and Spanish now [...] Min, if you have got Heine's *Lieder*, my little book, you might send it to me some time. I should like it.' (Nell, Spain, to Min, Ireland, 20 January 1908). Homesickness and financial hardships are brushed aside: 'I don't care what I have to suffer if I can do only what I came abroad for: to learn French and German' (Agnes, Belgium, to Min, Germany, 16 April 1907).[206]

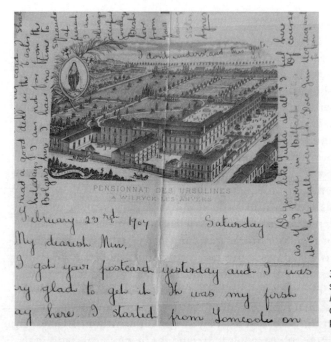

3.11 Letter from Agnes Ryan (Ursuline boarding school, Antwerp), 1907
Agnes (Ursulines, Antwerp) to her sister Min (Loreto college, Fulda), 23 February 1907 (Min Mulcahy papers: NLI Ms 49,528/9/2).

How did language study shape these women's lives? Where did these *séjours linguistiques* take them in future life? Of the six matriculating sisters, five took degrees in modern languages and four of these took a teacher training qualification,[207] a rare commodity at the time. Johanna, as Sister Stanislaus, taught at Loreto College, St Stephen's Green. Mary Kate was the first woman employed to lecture in French at UCD, and she continued to use French throughout her career. Min, Agnes and Chris taught languages, at second and third level. Agnes also did a master's in Irish. Although the teaching careers of the three younger sisters ended upon marriage and motherhood, the time spent in a foreign-language environment was not lost on them and influenced how they brought up their own children.[208]

Of the two unmarried daughters who did not go to university, one (Liz) stayed home all her life, to look after the dairy and run the farmhouse. The other, Nell, despite having spent more time abroad than her sisters, was a committed republican and, like others of her generation, saw Ireland as part of Europe. Yet she would have had little use for German or Spanish in her later life as a political activist and county councillor in Wexford.[209] Nell's case exemplifies one of the arguments of the present book. Ireland's links with continental Europe, and Irish people's historical engagement with foreign-language study, were not always utilitarian. The experience of living in foreign places, immersed in foreign languages and cultures, was educational in itself and of cultural value precisely because it could also be disinterested.

The eighth and youngest Ryan sister, Phyllis (1895–1983), graduated with a BSc in 1916, an MSc in 1917, and then qualified in public analysis in London before setting up her own laboratory in Dawson Street, Dublin. She did not travel abroad to perfect her languages. Yet, although a scientist, she presented three modern languages for her NUI matriculation.

★ ★ ★

What have we learned from this panorama of language study undertaken by the young in Victorian Ireland? The overall trends are broadly comparable with Victorian England where class and gender, and the shift from classical to modern languages, are concerned. However, although the development took the same direction, there are key differences of emphasis and pace. In 'mainland' Britain, modern languages were established at second level before they became normal and widespread in tertiary education curricula. Arguably, Ireland got the order wrong. Before 1878, when the state of Ireland's pre-university level was 'haphazard and underfinanced',[210] it was difficult for Ireland's new university sector to rely on sufficient numbers of students adequately prepared in French or German by schools, even though the Queen's Colleges insisted on a compulsory year of modern-language study as part of the degree programme. Only when modern-language studies were buttressed by other forms of regulatory measures did a more satisfactory situation begin to emerge. The regulations incentivised language study in schools, introducing diversity in the spread of languages offered, although French remained, and still remains, the dominant foreign language in Irish schools.

We have also noted how the gradual replacement of the classics by modern languages, which was the prevailing narrative in both islands, played out differently in Ireland. In England resistance to change was more robust, while in Ireland the hierarchical status of the classics vis-à-vis modern foreign languages had less traction. In some of Ireland's 'hedge'-schools, the traditional assimilation of the classics had been quite distinct. Fitting neither a 'monastic' nor a 'marketplace' label for language learning, and linking the study of Latin and Greek with Ireland's ancient vernacular culture, their unique settings were a far cry from the established schools of late medieval England, which had been set up to teach the grammar of Latin and later Greek, and (as the 1918 Leathes Report noted) 'retained their original purpose unaltered'.[211] In venerable English educational establishments, the weight of tradition was sustained by the numbers of entrance scholarships and distinctions going to Classical Studies in Oxbridge, which in turn channelled abler schoolboys into ancient rather than modern languages.[212] Those who had been schooled in the classics were a class apart, men of influence who knew their ancient Greek or Latin prosody. In High Victorian England, such was the prestige of a classical training that 'a false quantity was still a mark of ill-breeding, and apt quotations from Horace and Virgil were still welcomed in the House of Commons.'[213] Breaking this cultural cycle took time.

In Ireland, ecclesiastical Latin was manifestly present in the Roman liturgy. And Irish links with Catholic Europe were turbocharged by the prevalence of French teaching orders that set up in Ireland in the nineteenth century. Their particular brand of school ensured continuities with continental educational experiences of earlier times. French teaching orders had set up schools in England, too, after the French Revolution, but the proportional scale of the phenomenon was not commensurate between the two countries and had less social impact.

If modern European languages had a head-start (as we have seen) within universities in Victorian Ireland by comparison with the rest of the United Kingdom, European language teaching also had a head-start in relation to Ireland's own vernacular, the study of which spread even later in Irish schools. The presence of this other language obviously constitutes another major distinction to be drawn between England and Ireland. The Irish-language question was increasingly foregrounded by the end of the nineteenth century.

The eight matriculation certificates of the Wexford Ryan family confirm the general trends in late Victorian language study that we have been discussing.[214] These certificates, which span the period 1896 to 1912, tell their own story. Up to 1908, six of the family matriculated at the RUI; the two youngest, Jim and Phyllis, matriculated at the newly constituted NUI. All but one of the eight took Latin. In addition to Latin, one of the sons (Jack) sat Greek instead of a modern language. For their modern language, five of the daughters (Johanna, Mary Kate, Min, Chris, Phyllis) presented French and two (Agnes, Phyllis) presented German as well. The NUI certificates indicate something new: for his matriculation in 1911, Jim, the younger of the two brothers, presented Irish with Latin. The youngest family member, Phyllis, did not need Latin to matriculate in science, and one of her three modern languages in 1912 was Irish.[215]

How did Irish come to be treated as a modern language for university matriculation purposes? That question, and its contentious and transformative context, will be addressed in the following two chapters.

CHAPTER 4

Ancient Celtic: Respectable Roots

As the Irish language is considered the best preserved dialect of the ancient Celtic, a knowledge of it is highly important to the philological scholar and the antiquarian. [...] A knowledge of the Modern Irish is, also, indispensable in travelling through many parts of Ireland where this language is still spoken. The Irish class was established with a view to both these objects. [William Neilson, *c*.1818][1]

It is not a fact that the Irish is a barbarous tongue: it has been, it is true, for a long time the vernacular idiom of a very uncivilized people; but it is an original language, the purest dialect of the Celtic. [Henry Joseph Monck Mason, 1846][2]

And, as I have spoken of the Sanscrit, I beg to recommend the student of the Celtic languages to make himself acquainted, if possible, with that parent tongue. [John O'Beirne Crowe, 1854][3]

It is worth noting that the professional scribe still exists in Ireland, and writes a hand undistinguishable from that of his predecessors many centuries ago. [The Revd R. K. Abbott, 1892][4]

Over the next two chapters, our focus will shift from the study of continental languages to the island's own language. The parallel history of continental and insular language learning in the period exposes characteristic Victorian squabbles, each of them illustrating the contested ascendancy of the modern language over the prestige of older forms. The insular variation on the ancients-versus-moderns theme will be played out right up to the twentieth century. It also demonstrates how the study of Irish served to reinforce existing linguistic ties with Europe while at the same time it opened up new ties, in addition to those we have noted in relation to continental language learning. Irish scholars and teachers, often innovative in their theories and methods, were highly instrumental in shaping the language study agenda of the post-independent Irish State. How that agenda fared in the fledgling independent state will be discussed in our final chapter, which will also speculate on how the repossession of Irish as a European language may conceivably turn out to be an asset in the post-Brexit era, helping to contribute to the pluralism that now animates Irish culture.

Irish in Victorian Universities: A Catalogue of Challenges

If, in the mid-nineteenth century, Irish universities were ready to offer living European languages a curriculum niche alongside Latin and Greek, the story was more complicated for Ireland's own living vernacular. The forces – linguistic and historical, confessional and political – allowing the recognition of modern languages at universities, and their expansion at pre-university level, were re-configured and brought to bear on modern Irish, at the end of the century, suddenly and decisively transforming the fate of the language. In the course of six decades – between the 1840s and the 1890s – the rationale behind the university teaching of Irish was to change dramatically. Proselytising and antiquarian motives were supplanted by the urge to transmit the everyday language of the people as a vital matter of national identity, at all levels of Ireland's education system.

At Trinity College Dublin, since the seventeenth century, occasional efforts had been made to employ an Irish teacher to train clergymen for the conversion of Irish speakers to the reformed church. Irish translations of the Bible and Book of Common Prayer had already been printed.[5] Two centuries later, in 1840, a chair of Irish was set up within the School of Divinity, funded by evangelicals who had grasped the need for an Irish-speaking clergy. Irish only became a Trinity degree component in 1908, and the Irish chair was not separated from Divinity until 1919.[6]

Maynooth's Irish course was likewise pastoral in aim, from a Roman Catholic perspective. Paul O'Brien, appointed in 1802 as the first professor of Irish, taught the language to future priests destined for Irish-speaking parishes. Classes consisted of grammar and translation of biblical passages.[7] This teaching was regarded as ancillary to the core mission of the College, which increasingly conducted its business in two languages, English and Latin.[8] From 1828 to 1876, Irish lessons at Maynooth were given by a very reluctant professor, James Tully, who would have preferred to be engaged in parish work.[9] Although classes were compulsory for seminarians from Irish-speaking dioceses – amounting on average to about one half of the student body – attendance was reportedly poor. 'The professor was uninspiring and the language regarded as doomed.'[10]

Each of the three non-denominational Queen's Colleges which were opened in 1849 had its chair of Celtic Languages and Literature, held by John O'Donovan in Belfast, Owen Connellan in Cork, and Cornelius Mahony in Galway. In the latter two colleges, the use of the philological term 'Celtic' may be misleading. In his account of how the subject fared at Queen's College Galway, Breandán Ó Madagáin reads the term 'Celtic languages' as 'a deliberate euphemism for Irish, a word politically incorrect and unacceptable to the government',[11] and demonstrates convincingly from archival evidence that Cornelius Mahony at Galway was hired to teach Irish, rather than give a general course on Celtic languages. The course consisted specifically in Irish language (grammar and composition) and literature (from the seventeenth to the nineteenth centuries).[12] Cork's first Irish programme, too, devised by Owen Connellan, appears to have covered grammar and colloquial conversation together with literary texts going back to the twelfth century.[13] As well as Celtic languages and their history, he claimed to teach the 'Irish language as now extant, its Grammar, Vocabulary, and Dialects. In this part of the course, the Student will be taught to speak and write the language grammatically.'[14] His examinations tested an ability to discourse on grammatical structures and to translate into and out of Irish.[15]

In all three Queen's Colleges, Celtic courses were blighted by extremely low student numbers, frequently with zero students enrolling, rising to totals like one or two and, on occasion, a couple more.[16] These numbers should be viewed in the context of overall student enrolment: in Galway's early decades, for instance, this 'remained well below one hundred, and would have been lower still but for the presence of a regular supply of northern Presbyterians'.[17] The unsustainable numbers taking Irish were compounded by its marginal academic status and lack of material incentives. To dispel any ambiguity, the General Regulations in Cork include the words 'Special Course Not Required for a Degree' before the course description for 'Celtic Languages'.[18] This contrasted with the requirement to take a modern language. In 1859–60, Cork reported a similar amount of lectures allotted to French (152) and Celtic (149), but a yawning gap in the number of students who took each of the two languages (56 to 8).[19] Not being a degree component, Irish had no scholarships or prizes attaching to it;[20] nor was it recognised as a subject in schools – even in Irish-speaking regions – until 1878, when 'Celtic' was included as an optional language for the Intermediate examination. The credits allotted by that examination indicate its peripheral importance vis-à-vis other languages: Celtic was allowed 600 marks, as against 700 for French and German, and 1,200 for Greek and Latin.[21]

It may be noted, in passing, that experience in English universities shows how optional status can affect the esteem in which a language is held. At King's College London, although modern languages were on the curriculum, they were neither compulsory nor assessed, and student numbers remained consistently low. When the first professor of Spanish at UCL, Antonio Alcalá Galiano, resigned in 1830, the chair was not filled again until 1956.[22] Similarly, Oxford's first Taylorian modern-language classes were optional, or added on as extras for postgraduates.[23] This marginal regime for modern languages in London and Oxford is comparable to the treatment of Celtic in Ireland's Queen's Colleges but contrasts with the relative enjoyment of a core requirement by modern languages in the same Irish colleges. An element of compulsion drives student uptake.

Demoralised, Galway's Cornelius Mahony resigned his chair in 1854 to join the Schools Inspectorate. Cork's Professor of 'Celtic', Owen Connellan, in his submission to the 1857–8 Queen's Colleges Commission, gave a gloomy prognosis for modern Irish:

> I dare say that in consequences of railways and the National Schools, the numbers who speak it will be reduced very much. Perhaps in half a century the reduction will be very great, but still there are parts of Ireland, particularly along the coasts and in the mountains, where it may continue […] for another hundred years.[24]

How accurate is this assessment of the mid-century health of Ireland's vernacular? Whether or not the coming of railway travel altered the balance of linguistic power on the island, it certainly promoted more contacts between languages, as it did in other jurisdictions. However, contacts between English and Irish were there anyway, and were on the increase. As far as national schools are concerned, Professor Connellan was, broadly speaking, correct. The anglicising influence of national schools is a constant factor in subsequent discussions about Ireland's nineteenth-century language shift. Although there were variations in pace according to region, religious denomination and social class, free elementary schooling (since 1831) certainly helped to accelerate the systematic spread of literacy in English into areas that it had not previously reached.[25] By 1849, national schools were catering for almost half a million children.[26] However, the spread of literacy in English was already in train before 1831, especially in towns, and in regions like East Ulster, which in the 1841 Census recorded the highest literacy levels in the country. Presbyterianism, a religion that inherently values education, had driven the establishment of Sunday schools in Ireland since the late 1700s.[27] For well over a century, too, hedge-schoolmasters all over the land had taught children how to read in English, by means of cheaply available chapbooks reprinted from English first editions, availing of a loophole in the 1709 Copyright Act that had omitted to mention Ireland.[28] As Antonia McManus argues, the informal, haphazard hedge-school settings of the eighteenth and nineteenth centuries exposed the young to an eclectic range of English language register, genre and text, of a kind never to be repeated in the formalised State-regulated system that came in their wake.[29]

More pertinent to the university study of Irish is literacy in the vernacular itself. The 1861 Census shows lowest rates of literacy occurring among monoglot Irish speakers.[30] In most cases, there were significant levels of contact between the two languages. Monolingual Irish speakers, for economic reasons, often had a good functional understanding of English, as Mary Daly has shown in the case of migrant labourers from County Donegal who spent several months per annum working in anglophone environments.[31] Effective political action was conducted in English. Although a fluent Irish speaker since early childhood, Daniel O'Connell addressed rallies in the language of power and of parliament.[32] It was not uncommon to find native speakers of Irish whose ability to read and write was limited to English. As some of the Irish texts that made it into print were published in phonetic spelling based on English, it can be assumed that Irish speakers who attained literacy in Irish probably did so by first learning to read and write in English.[33] Thus, while a number of Irish speakers were literate in both languages, everyday Irish culture remained, by and large, oral.

Student enrolment in Irish in the Queen's Colleges was understandably low compared with enrolment in other modern languages since the latter were core components in degree programmes. The relatively low university status of Irish was matched by an absence of socio-economic incentives for studying it, especially in the 1850s, when the trauma of the Great Famine was still very raw. Compounded by death, eviction and emigration, this catastrophe had deeply disrupted the fabric of rural life for those who remained. In the deserted homesteads and depopulated townlands, the Great Hunger put paid to much of the traditional neighbourly gatherings for singing and storytelling in the evening.[34] As Willie Nolan observes, John O'Donovan, 'who from his labours with the Ordnance Survey knew the country better than any living man, was struck by the silence which pervaded Ireland.' In April 1848, O'Donovan advised an expatriate friend not to come back to his native country:[35]

> Do not think of coming here to view our wretched cabins, and our ghastly visages, and famine-stricken bodies. You will see nothing to cheer or please you; not a song is heard from the ploughman or a whistle from the ass driver; but solemn and awful stillness reigns which seems to forebode some dreadful reaction and frightful commotion.

In the immediate aftermath of such desolation, neither Irish speakers nor anglophones viewed the advanced study of Irish as a door to social advancement or employment, let alone a passport for successful emigration; English was the more useful language, if only for reading and responding to letters from emigrant relatives in North America.

In any case, Irish universities at this period were chiefly catering for an anglicised middle class, some of whom also spoke Irish. Since the vast majority of literate Irish speakers were also literate in English, there was all the more need, objectively speaking, for a viable print culture in Irish if there was to be any hope of sustaining the university study of the vernacular. Library resources in that language were lacking. Indeed, perhaps the most intractable impediment to student enrolment in Celtic in this period was the fact that Irish had not been touched to any significant degree by the culture of the printed word. Other languages, since the seventeenth century, had increasingly circulated through print, particularly in Reformation Europe where the study of the Bible in the vernacular was paramount. The Gutenberg revolution did not take root in the Irish language on any meaningful scale. As a recent authority puts it, 'English did not introduce writing to Ireland, but it did introduce an omnipresent writing and print culture which was absent from traditional Gaelic society.'[36]

Irish literature, with its rich store of early manuscripts that vastly outstripped other European languages both in age and in quantity, continued to be produced according to traditional custom, in manuscript form, and copied by a learned class of scribes and poets dependent on patronage. These literati were the descendants of the influential bardic poets of an earlier era who had been retained by chieftain-patrons.[37] After the collapse of that old order at the end of the seventeenth century, they continued to be retained, successively, by different patrons whenever there was a need for transcription or translation. Their presence

'ensured [...] that the medieval form of production and dissemination of texts continued at least to the end of the nineteenth century in Ireland, by which time most other European cultures had long since adopted the printing press to the exclusion of the scribal mode of transmission.'[38]

Leading nomadic lives, they moved from big house to big house or town to town, wherever work came their way. Some tutored young families to complement their precarious livelihood. Sometimes they left manuscripts behind them in the farmhouses where they had been lodging; these contained stories and poems to be read aloud to neighbours who gathered during long winter evenings. 'Books were still luxury items for most people.'[39]

The learned descendants of the bardic schools, then, did not remain in the countryside. The Ó Neachtains, at the centre of a scholarly Gaelic milieu in early eighteenth-century Dublin, portrayed by Liam Mac Mathúna's *The Ó Neachtain Window on Gaelic Dublin, 1700–1750*, had already moved from Roscommon *c*.1670, and mixed with poets and scholars from all four provinces.[40] Patronage had begun to attract them towards the city, where there was a growing demand for manuscript transcription and translation, coming from new patrons among Protestant intellectuals and learned societies, such as the Royal Irish Academy, founded in 1785. Intellectual curiosity about Ireland's heritage gave the native language a respectable status in these circles, for the first time.[41] These new patrons were increasingly taking an antiquarian interest in Ireland's Gaelic past but lacked the linguistic skill to penetrate that past.[42] The poet-scribes were happy to oblige.

Gaelic scholars of the late eighteenth and early nineteenth centuries were competent bilinguals, negotiating their way with ease between English and Irish. Some of them composed macaronic poetry in the two tongues, some composed verse in English as well as Irish.[43] At times they acted as mediators in the community, reading news aloud in public spaces. Economically marginalised, but proud of the archaic cultural heritage of which their way of life was the living embodiment, they were also highly literate. They mingled with Establishment figures with whom they shared interests.[44] Some were avid book collectors and owned extensive personal libraries;[45] many knew other languages as well as Irish and English.[46] They also engaged with print culture: a few of them had launched publication ventures, some of which however ran aground for financial reasons.[47]

From the perspective of the history of the Irish language, there is a sense of a lost opportunity when one speculates on how the labours of these learned scribe-translators of the late eighteenth century could have been harnessed, in the fullness of time, to develop the means to produce printed works in Irish. As things turned out, the potentially transformative cultural collaboration between anglophone antiquarians and Gaelic scholars was set back by the French-aided United Irishmen's uprising (1798) and the Robert Emmet rebellion (1803). The 'green shoots of revivalism manifest in the 1790s', as James Kelly puts it, became associated, in more conservative circles, with political disorder, causing political conservatives to be[48]

> so alarmed by revolutionary agitation in the 1790s and disturbed by the equation of radicalism and hibernicization that their reflective inclination to identify the Irish language with sedition was affirmed in the reactionary environment of the early nineteenth century.

For much of the Victorian period, then, new monolingual reading matter in Irish tended to be handwritten by professional scribes.[49] There was consequently an enormous disparity between the paltry amount of printed Irish books, as against the huge amount available in print in English,[50] especially in new prose fiction. Bilingual authors with ambitions to reach a wider audience naturally aimed for the London market, where there was a demand among the literary reading public for fictional narratives. William Carleton (d.1869) is a case in point. Although one of 14 children brought up through Irish in rural Ireland, and the son of a traditional story-teller and a traditional singer, Carleton chose to write in English. Novels, to quote Vivian Mercier, 'simply did not exist in the Irish language until the twentieth century.'[51] Publications in Irish were weighted towards non-fiction – works of reference such as dictionaries and grammars, religious texts like catechisms and sermons, and poems and ballads. Narratives in Irish persisted via traditional oral storytelling.

The economy of patronage on which this archaic culture depended was plainly ill-suited to the culture of a nineteenth-century university, where assessment by individual written examination was increasingly supplanting older methods of examining that derived from late medieval and renaissance group disputation.[52] This mismatch was compounded by a general disparagement, in language teaching, of the oral language. All language education, from primary to tertiary level, was geared towards cultivating literacy and the written word. At secondary and tertiary level, modern-language teaching had been modelled on the way

Latin and Greek had been imparted for centuries, relying on the tried-and-tested tools of grammar, translation and the use of written texts to illustrate the civilisation expressed in the language. Readily available printed textbooks were an essential ingredient. Owen Connellan's Celtic Studies syllabus is forced to include a caveat: 'The Lectures will be illustrated by reference to Irish MSS, and such publications on Irish Historical and General Literature as are at present accessible.'[53] Before the technology to record speech, universities were not places where a language rich in oral culture could be viewed with much credibility as a self-standing discipline of study.

Could a successful print culture in the Irish language have been introduced in the nineteenth century? There were many practical hurdles to be overcome, not least of which was the typographical one.[54] Printing presses with an Irish fount were mainly located in London or continental Europe; there was no consensus on the variety of Irish to choose for print.[55] Had there been the will, and the financial backing, these difficulties might have been resolved. However, in reality, by the nineteenth century it was already too late: as Louis Cullen points out, printing, to be viable, requires an urban culture, and urban Ireland was by then the most anglicised part of the country.[56] The manuscripts of the old sagas, heroic cycles and related texts were being transcribed and, by and large, edited with critical apparatus in English translation. Therefore, printing in Irish necessarily remained very small-scale.

This lengthy excursus into the state of the Irish language, and of vernacular literacy, helps to explain why so few university students registered to study Irish. It also contextualises why the Queen's Colleges Commission's Report of 1858 recommended that the three chairs of Celtic languages and literature be discontinued when vacancies should next arise. At Belfast, Cork and Galway, they were duly let go. By 1863, all had become dormant, and were to remain so for a number of decades.[57]

It is, however, worth pointing out that even if Irish had been thriving as a functioning vernacular – taught in schools, widely used in administration and commerce, and supported by a print culture and growing literacy[58] – there is still no guarantee that, in the middle of the nineteenth century, university chairs in Irish would have been established. Chairs in other vernacular languages were rare at this period. While French literature was studied at the Sorbonne from the 1820s,[59] English as a university discipline in England was barely in its infancy, taught first at King's College London in the 1840s[60] before gradually finding acceptance in other institutions from the 1860s onwards, thanks to the writings of Matthew Arnold who, as professor of poetry at Oxford from 1857, expounded the political and social importance of literary criticism. Thus, for example, chairs in English literature were established in Glasgow in 1862; in Trinity College Dublin in 1867; in Cambridge in 1911.

When chairs of English literature began to appear in anglophone universities, they tended to include English history; texts were read as illuminating the period in which they were written. Universities that embraced other Celtic vernaculars followed a similar pattern. They were part of philology, history of language, and treated as local or regional cultural phenomena. In France, Breton was beginning to be given teaching space from the 1880s at the University of Rennes, where a chair of Celtic studies was set up in 1903. A Department of Welsh and Celtic Studies was founded at Aberystwyth in 1875; Jesus College Oxford set up a professorship of Celtic in 1876; Edinburgh's chair dates from 1882. Glasgow, where Celtic had been present since the early 1900s (thanks to a bequest), established its chair in

1956.[61] Philology also propelled Aberdeen's Celtic Studies Department, founded in 1916, although its chair dates from 1992.[62]

Rather than considering why Celtic failed to attract students in the Queen's Colleges at Belfast, Cork and Galway, then, the real question to be asked is why the chairs of Celtic were set up there at all, at such an early date. Various reasons may have dictated the decision to include Celtic when the Colleges were founded in 1845: all three universities were located in, or close to, Irish-speaking regions; and the collegiate department at Belfast's Royal Academical Institution had offered Irish from its foundation, although it was mainly taught to students for the Presbyterian ministry.[63] There may also have been political reasons: might it have been a move to mollify some elements of the Roman Catholic hierarchy opposed to the Queen's colleges? Cornelius Buttimer speculates on this possibility.[64] Alternatively, Breandán Ó Madagáin may well be correct in ascribing the decision to the preferences of, and pressures exerted by, certain influential individuals – including, notably, Queen's College Galway's first President, Fr James Kirwan, and also Thomas Larcom, who was Ireland's under-secretary in 1854 when the decision was taken to replace Cornelius Mahony following his resignation, rather than allowing his chair to lapse.[65] These influential individuals shared an interest in common: Celtic antiquities. Their focus was on the remote past of Ireland's language, not its present state. Which brings us to discuss the other face of 'Celtic', so crucial for understanding Irish-language study in the nineteenth century: Celtic philology.

CELTIC PHILOLOGY

The meagre amount of modern Irish in print, the stasis with regard to teaching it and the lack of students registering to study it, were counterbalanced by the abundance of manuscripts in Old and Middle Irish, and the degree of interest they aroused. They were transcribed, edited and translated throughout the nineteenth century, with a view to publication for a largely anglophone (and specialist continental) readership.[66] Antiquarianism continued to flourish after 1800; like-minded amateurs and professionals formed associations to share their common interest, including the Gaelic Society of Ireland (1806) and the Iberno-Celtic Society (1818). The Irish Archaeological Society (1840) merged with the Celtic Society (1845) in 1853 to form the Irish Archaeological and Celtic Society; the Royal Society of Antiquaries of Ireland was founded in 1849; and the literary Ossianic Society was founded in 1853.[67] Government funds supported the RIA in its publications of historical manuscripts, helping to build an invaluable research repository of printed early Irish texts.[68]

In tandem with antiquarian curiosity into the content of Old Irish texts, the language's formal features were also becoming an object of enquiry, thanks to developments in linguistic scholarship being made from the late eighteenth century onwards in European universities, especially in Germany. The new science of language, as early comparative linguistics was called, chimed with the Romantics' search for origins and a growing sense of the relations between Indo-European languages and their putative common ancestor.[69] The close observation of relationships between the words and structures of different languages allowed scholars to establish linguistic families and genealogies, applying to human languages methods analogous to those that were beginning to be used for classifying biological species.[70]

In the case of Celtic languages, scholars had not reached a consensus as to their origins until the decisive publication, in Leipzig, of the two-volume *Grammatica Celtica* (1853), by the Bavarian historian and linguist Johann Kaspar Zeuss (1806–56).[71] Written in Latin, this was the fruit of years of painstaking research carried out in the libraries of Europe that held manuscripts from early medieval Irish monastic foundations such as Würzburg in Bavaria, St Gallen in Switzerland, or Bobbio in Italy. Zeuss scrutinised and transcribed all the Old Irish glosses and commentaries that the expatriate monks had written in the margins of Latin manuscripts. Apart from their precious testimony of the sophisticated level of multilingualism on the part of the monks who generated them, these documents constituted the oldest known corpus of evidence of archaic forms of Irish. Using rigorously scientific methods, Zeuss was able to construct from this material a grammar of Old Irish and to establish incontrovertibly that it was an Indo-European language. An early (posthumous) review of Zeuss's ground-breaking achievement was published by Professor John O'Donovan of Queen's College Belfast:[72]

> In transcribing [scriptural and classical texts], the monks, for the assistance of their own memories, and for the benefit of younger scholars, used to write in the margin the literal Irish translation of every difficult word and phrase. These are the famous glosses of St. Gall and of Milan. Zeuss saw their value, and spared no labour nor expense in copying them out with his own hand. Possessing them, he soon learned more of the really oldest forms and grammar of the Irish language than any man had known before him. There are archaisms preserved in those glosses which were never found in the manuscripts preserved in Great Britain or in Ireland [...]
>
> Ireland has not, as yet, produced any great comparative philologist, and we cannot expect, for some time at least, to see the thread taken up by any competent hand where Zeuss has dropped it: so far, he has distanced all. [...] We must recognise in the *Grammatica Celtica* purely a triumph of comparative philology.

In short, this was a significant milestone in the development of Celtic philology.[73] Thanks to Zeuss, Irish was adjudged the oldest written Celtic tongue of all. The language could finally claim a gold-standard pedigree, and a literature more ancient than England's.

4.1 O'Donovan and O'Curry
John O'Donovan (Professor of Celtic languages and literature, QCB, *d.*1861) and Eugene O'Curry (Professor of Irish History and Archaeology, CUI, *d.*1862). Commemorative Irish postage stamp, issued 1962. (© *An Post. Courtesy of the An Post Museum and Archive.*)

In devising the departmental structure of the Catholic University in 1854, John Henry Newman saw fit to include Celtic studies in its remit. While he envisaged the role of his university as a world 'centre of the Catholicism of the English tongue',[74] he also knew that it should contain an Irish dimension. He recognised the importance of 'Celtic', as part of Ireland's venerable past, within an Archaeology department that would concern itself with 'the language and remains of ancient Ireland'.[75] His appointment of Eugene O'Curry, as Professor of Irish History and Archaeology, was an indication that the rector understood the need to preserve and curate, through transcription, commentary and translation, one of the world's oldest Indo-European tongues. Newman appreciated the printing problem and immediately set about procuring for O'Curry the means of printing with an Irish fount.[76] The preservation of ancient texts, seen in antiquarian and philological terms, was the priority.

When Newman appointed him to the Catholic University chair, Professor O'Curry (1794–1862)[77] was in his 50s, with a lifetime of being steeped in Old Irish texts behind him. Without much formal education, this County Clare man had learned to read and write Irish from his father, a farmer who was also a scholar and collector of manuscripts, and who consorted with other Gaelic scribes and scholars. After various forms of employment – as hedge-school teacher, labourer, scribe – O'Curry had joined one of the Ordnance Survey's topographical and archaeological teams in the 1830s, along with John O'Donovan and George Petrie. O'Curry's job in this mapping of ancient Ireland was to comb early sources, and transcribe 'passages containing place-name lore, history and legend from manuscripts in the Dublin libraries'.[78] After this, in the 1840s, he had been chief cataloguer of Old Irish manuscripts in the RIA, and he worked on some Irish manuscripts in the British Museum.

O'Curry's *Lectures on the Manuscript Materials of Ancient Irish History* (1861) included his university lectures delivered in 1855–6, which had been attended by Newman himself. His three-volume *On the Manners and Customs of the Ancient Irish* was published posthumously in 1873. The second work was reviewed by the founder of the *Revue Celtique*; Henri Gaidoz acknowledges that O'Curry had spent a lifetime reading, collating, copying and translating Old Irish texts, with which nobody could claim to be more familiar than he was, but objects that his approach as a historian lacked the critical faculty required of a scholar:[79]

> Malheureusement il lui manquait [...] surtout le don de la critique. Pour lui, tout ce qu'il trouvait dans ses chers manuscrits irlandais était arrivé; et l'on sait si le fabuleux manque dans les annales de l'ancienne Irlande, ces annales qui racontent l'histoire de l'Irlande dès avant le déluge! Il y a longtemps qu'en France on a cessé de croire à l'existence de Francus, fils d'Hector, dont parlent nos vieilles chroniques. On n'en est pas encore là en Irlande avec les traditions nationales.

> [Unfortunately he lacked [...] above all the critical faculty. For him, everything he found in his precious Irish manuscripts had really happened; and it is well known how much the annals of ancient Ireland are steeped in lore and legend, those annals that tell the history of Ireland from before the Flood! In France we have long since given up believing in the existence of Hector's son, Francus, whom our ancient chronicles talk about. In Ireland, they have not yet reached that stage with their national traditions.]

Unscholarly and unenlightened though it may have appeared to a trained philological French mind, O'Curry's work was all the more influential in Ireland, not only on his students and readers, but also on the creative writers of the next generation, and the perceptions of Irishness conveyed in their dramas and fictions.[80]

Given the international developments in Celtic scholarship, university professors of Irish tended, essentially, to be comparative philologists. Like O'Curry, the first Celticists appointed to the Queen's Colleges were scribes and specialists long apprenticed to the ancient language. And like him, they were mostly men of an earlier era, appointed to university posts as they neared the end of their lives. John O'Donovan (1806–61) is more remembered as a leading editor and translator of Old Irish topographical, historical and legal records, than as professor of Irish at Belfast, where he had no undergraduate students.[81] Similarly, Owen Connellan (1800–69) – our gloomy prognostician of the death of the Irish language – had worked as a scribe for the RIA before his appointment to the Cork chair. The youngest in the group, John O'Beirne Crowe (1824–74), who succeeded Cornelius Mahony to the Galway post in 1854, held it for eight years. A native Irish speaker from County Mayo, he had enrolled in Queen's College Belfast in order to study Sanskrit with Professor O'Donovan, and his research lay firmly in Early Irish textual scholarship. After their chairs were discontinued in 1862, both Connellan and O'Beirne Crowe returned to archival research in Dublin.[82] O'Curry, too, seems to have had few, if any, students at the Catholic University after 1856.[83] When he died in 1862, no replacement was made for over a decade. In spite of this disastrous first showing of the university study of Irish, its eccentric crew of scholars helped to sow the seeds of the Irish cultural revival.[84]

While the study of Early Irish language and society lent academic prestige and historical lustre to the discipline of Celtic Studies, it left little room for studying the language spoken by the dwindling population for whom it was in current use. John O'Donovan saw his role in the Belfast chair as less to teach Irish than to foster an interest in Ireland's past:[85]

> I do not expect to do much in the way of teaching Irish but if I could establish a taste for Historical and antiquarian investigation it would give me much satisfaction. [...] The taste for Irish language and literature will become less and less every year, and therefore I think it of more consequence to work steadily and assiduously to preserve in an intelligible form what historical materials we have than anything that could be done in the way of teaching the language, which will become obsolete in about fifty years.

The challenge of reconciling ancient and modern – the high status of the scholarly antiquarian/philological approach to Old Irish on the one hand, with the low status of studying and transmitting the contemporary living *caint na ndaoine* [the language of the people] on the other – is, as we shall be noting, a challenge also found in relation to the university teaching of other modern languages. It was recognised and graphically articulated by John O'Beirne Crowe in 1854, the year the CU opened. As a postgraduate student in Belfast, O'Beirne Crowe wrote a pamphlet, 'The Catholic University and the Irish Language', in which he berated Newman's University for its neglect of the Irish language. In his view, both approaches to teaching Irish – targeting its development over time as well as its contemporary structures – should be adopted:[86]

> It will not be sufficient that a course of lectures be given annually in the history of Irish literature: the language itself, as it was spoken and written in the days of Columba and Adamnan, and in each succeeding age down to the present, must be taught to the Irish student. For the proper discharge of this office the professor must not be merely a person

who can transcribe old manuscripts and give something like the general sense in a worthless translation, not unfrequently as far from the original as one pole from the other: he must be a scholar, an accomplished adept in antient and modern languages.

The language professor, as a philologist, must have mastery of the entire language, in its ancient and contemporary forms. Comparative philology is essential, but neglecting the contemporary colloquial is not an option either. O'Beirne Crowe even goes further, proposing that all CU students who are natives of Ireland be required to take two undergraduate sessions in 'Hiberno-Celtic',[87] and indeed sees the new college as a way of reviving and extending Irish: 'An opportunity has now arisen not only to prevent the extinction, but to secure the extension of the Irish language.'[88] This role for the university, expressed some 50 years before the Gaelic League's campaign for essential Irish in the new NUI, anticipates the de-anglicising project of Douglas Hyde.

In a rhetorical opening salvo to his argument, the author imagines European Celtic scholars aghast at Ireland's neglect of the descendant of early Irish:[89]

> From the hills of Switzerland and from the plains of Germany dire reproaches shall be flung across the Irish Channel [...]. Pictet of Geneva will exclaim: 'I have proved the affinity of the Celtic languages with the Sanscrit: I have shown that in comparative philology they are indispensable: I have illustrated their importance in the investigation of man's social and political condition previous to the birth of history: and yet these people assign the Celtic no place in the curriculum of their new University!' And Zeuss of Leipzig, in a sober but angry German tone, will say: 'I have spent years upon the investigation of the Celtic languages, and my labours are scarcely heard of in Ireland. I have elucidated the nature of the bond which unites the several dialects, and exhibited their relation, as a whole, to other kindred tongues: and yet the Irish – the purest branch of the Indo-European linguistic tree – receives no countenance in their lately-established Institute! Verily this is a degenerate people – how differently we act in Germany!'

In this melodramatic vision, he is incidentally reminding us of the renewed educational links with Europe that the new developments in Old Irish scholarship were forging. Ireland's Celtic philologists knew that scholars beyond Ireland's shores were interested in what they were doing, and they were increasingly to look to academic journals in languages other than English to place their work and keep abreast of international expertise – journals such as the *Revue Celtique* (established by Gaidoz in Paris in 1870) or the *Zeitschrift für Celtische Philologie* (founded by Kuno Meyer and Ludwig Stern in 1897). This had more than one consequence. It gave a scholarly rationale for studying modern European languages that was specific to Irish researchers, and at the same time opened a new chapter in the history of educational connections between Ireland and continental Europe. Perhaps we should call it, instead, a resuscitation of ancient ghosts, because it was essentially a re-establishing of very old links. After all, it was thanks to the early medieval Irish monks at continental monasteries who had left marginal glosses on their manuscripts, that the mysteries of the ancient Celtic tongue could be more fully elucidated by the latter-day philologists of modern Europe.

RATIONALES FOR THE STUDY OF IRISH: SECTARIAN CONTESTS

In the second half of the nineteenth century, the study of Old Irish found its niche. Even though the university chairs of Celtic remained vacant from the early 1860s, scholarship in Old Irish continued outside the university sphere. A case in point is the astonishing scholarly career of the Victorian polymath Whitley Stokes (1830–1909). This Dubliner worked for the imperial service for two decades as a lawyer in India, where he codified much of Anglo-Indian law; he was also an Indo-European linguistic scholar and a renowned Celticist. By any standards, his publication record was prodigious, running to 'some thirty monographs and more than three hundred scholarly articles'.[90]

While Old Irish enjoyed elevated status, finding a credible rationale for the study of contemporary Irish was a challenge of an entirely different order. In the 1860s, the prestige deficit between learning modern Irish and learning Old Irish could not have been wider. Intermittently outlawed, and long denigrated by the colonisers and now – in the nineteenth century – even by its own speakers, modern Irish enjoyed neither stability (being rich in dialect variation) nor a print culture anywhere near the scale of English, and was fast becoming, by the period in question, a genuinely endangered language. Officially absent from the national school curriculum, the language was taught in a handful of post-elementary schools. There was no strong demand from the public at large that matters should be otherwise, and much evidence to the contrary. Some parents spoke to each other in the native vernacular but to their offspring in English.[91] An 1857 report commented on the islanders of Donegal who inferred, from strangers visiting their shores,

> that prosperity has its peculiar tongue as well as its fine coat [...] and whilst they may love the cadences, and mellowness, and homeliness of the language which their fathers gave them, [...] they long for the acquisition of the 'new tongue', with all its prizes and social privileges. The keystone of fortune is the power of speaking English.[92]

Such evidence of language shift did nothing to help the vernacular's prospects for survival. In the education sphere, the study of Irish contrasts sharply with the study of other modern languages, when we reflect that the mid-1850s – as discussed in our previous chapter – were precisely the years when modern languages were poised to make rapid inroads, at least in elite secondary schools, and would soon be well on the way to becoming established as essential components of the curriculum. There were plenty of reasons, as we have seen, why their provision grew in this period, and plenty of motivating factors for studying them.

Rationales for learning Irish were thinner on the ground. The study of Irish was driven, for most of the century, by two main motivators, one confessional and the other antiquarian. Confessional motivation dictated the provision of Irish at Trinity College and Maynooth. In the latter, the only third-level institution in the country where modern Irish study was compulsory for the future priests of Irish-speaking parishes, the lessons were in the hands of an uninspiring professor who would have preferred to be at parish work.[93] In Ó Cuív's view, 'there seems to be no evidence that the Irish hierarchy ever planned collectively to ensure that the clergy would be competent in both Irish and English.'[94] The efforts of the Established Church to evangelise through Irish were mostly in vain and did not improve the health of the language either.

The native language, for centuries a dispensable pawn in a perennial political and sectarian contest, frequently turned out to be the loser in the country's fractious history. While in other countries, institutional churches had helped to drive print literacy in the majority vernacular, Ireland's anomalous circumstances led to a perverse deviation from this trend whenever an initiative was taken to print confessional material in Irish. The first book ever to be set and printed in Ireland was printed in English, the minority vernacular: the Book of Common Prayer (1551); and the first book to be printed in the majority vernacular (in 1571) was a Reformation catechism, expounding the beliefs of the minority religion.[95] In the history of other Celtic vernaculars, print literacy for religious texts preceded secular, or general, print literacy. In Scotland and Wales, for example, vernacular Scriptures were widely circulated at the Reformation, and Welsh literacy flourished following the evangelical revival of the eighteenth century. Catholic Brittany's thriving nineteenth-century print industry, sustained by a reading public, could be traced to Jesuit missionaries two centuries before who had disseminated popular reading matter printed in Breton.[96] There had been no analogous initiatives taken for Irish. Nor was there an equivalent to the Douai (English Vernacular) Catholic Bible in Irish. The first full Roman Catholic Irish translation of the Bible, *An Bíobla Naofa*, was only brought out in 1981.[97]

In the evangelical climate of Irish Protestantism of the early nineteenth century, there had been a renewed zeal to spread the word of God to Gaelic Ireland by using the vernacular. Circumstances seemed propitious to some evangelisers, not least because of the weak political state of the Roman Catholic Church in the years following the French invasion of the Papal States and deportation of the pope to Paris.[98] However, initiatives to print Protestant religious texts in Irish had always exposed the irreconcilable contradiction, on the part of Ireland's rulers, between the desire to anglicise the 'meere Irish', on the one hand, and the attempt to evangelise them in their own tongue, on the other. Anglicisation and evangelisation could not be carried out simultaneously. Since you can only convert a people to the truth in their native language, you cannot expect them to follow the truth if you also outlaw that language, as one of the Protestant proselytisers pointed out. Henry Joseph Monck Mason, librarian at King's Inns, was a co-founder (in 1818) of The Irish Society for Promoting the Education of the Native Irish through the Medium of Their Own Language, the sole purpose of which was 'to convert the popish natives of Ireland to the Reformed Church, by means of their own language'.[99] In the preamble to his account of the Society's proselytising activities, he is at pains to explain the inherent absurdity of the stance that had been taken at Trinity College in previous centuries:[100]

> Thus when Ussher, in the convocation of 1634, seconded the proposal of Bishop Bedell, to make use of the Irish tongue, as a medium for the spreading of a knowledge of the reformed doctrines among the natives of Ireland, the arguments of his principal opponent – a celebrated person also, Bishop Bramhall – were 'reasons drawn from an act of Parliament, passed in this kingdom in the reign of Henry VIII for obliging the natives to learn the English tongue.' [...] It was for a long time the misfortune of Ireland, to lie barren under the whitening blast of this misrule; [...]. When the admirable Bedell commenced his work of converting the Irish according to the only proper method, and began to be successful, he was plainly told, that he was acting contrary to the interests of the English in Ireland, 'by his endeavouring to make the conquered and enslaved Irish capable of preferment in Church and State, which was the portion of the conquerors.'

When the Irish Society's work of conversion got underway in rural Ireland in the 1820s, several suggestions were made that it should print works in Irish other than the Bible and the Book of Common Prayer. Monck Mason explained that to print other material would be contrary to the Society's *raison d'être* and might run the risk of stimulating the 'Romanist' enemy into printing its own 'poisonous tracts' for the converted (and now literate) peasantry, thereby undoing the Society's good work.[101] The Irish Society need not have worried: the rival 'Romanist' establishment did not respond by printing refutations in Irish to counter the teachings of the so-called *Bioblóirí*. Instead, many priests reacted at parish level by denouncing from the pulpit the (mostly Catholic) schoolmasters who had been hired by the Irish Society, and even excommunicated some parents who had sent their children to the Scriptural classes. The perverse effect of this extreme overreaction to the Irish Society's project was to strike terror into the hearts and minds of their flock. For many years, to read the Bible in Irish, and indeed to read *anything* in Irish (in case it might contain some words of Scripture), was perceived by some Catholics to be tantamount to placing their soul in mortal peril.[102] It was safer to stick to English. As ever, the victim, by default, was the Irish language.

Antiquarian Rationales: Some Pre-Famine Irish Grammars

Yet weaponising the language was not inevitable. Since the eighteenth century there had been post-Enlightenment stirrings of local initiatives taken by voluntary groups of individuals – amateur antiquarians, teachers, bards and scribes, clerics of all creeds – who shared a common purpose: to preserve what remained of a vanishing culture by collecting early Irish manuscripts. Study of the living language was part of this revivalist project, seen in the plethora of Gaelic-oriented societies that had sprung up in the pre-Famine period. Irish grammars were commissioned and produced, to rescue the language and its antiquities from oblivion. Some of these individuals were especially active in the north-east of the country.[103] The Ulster Gaelic Society was founded in 1830 by a Presbyterian industrialist, Robert MacAdam (1808–95), partly in order to disseminate the living language. MacAdam published an Irish dictionary, with the help of a native speaker.[104]

4.2 William Neilson
Miniature cameo portrait. From *Belfast Literary Society 1801–1901* [Centenary Volume] (Belfast, The Linen Hall Press, 1902), p. 53.

An example of an early nineteenth-century professor of Irish is found in another Presbyterian, the Revd William Neilson (1774–1821) from Rademon, County Down. Of Scots planter stock, and the son of a minister-cum-schoolmaster who preached in Irish, Neilson attended the University of Glasgow.[105] As a Presbyterian minister in Dundalk from 1797, he (like his father) preached in the vernacular to his Irish-speaking congregation and set up the interdenominational Dundalk Classical and Mercantile Academy, which offered Hebrew, French and Irish as supplementary to Latin, the language spoken in the school. A founding member of the Gaelic Society (1806), Neilson was author of several books elucidating the grammar of English and ancient Greek; he also published an abbreviated English-Irish dictionary, as well as *An Introduction to the Irish Language* (Dublin, 1808) and a primer for beginners, *Céad Leabhar na Gaoidheilge* (1810). At the age of 31 he was chosen as Moderator of the General Synod of Ulster and was elected to the RIA in 1808. Ten years later, Neilson moved to work in Belfast, as professor of Hebrew, Latin, Greek, Irish and Oriental Languages at the Collegiate Department of the Belfast Academical Institution, where he taught Irish classes thrice weekly until his death in 1821. He learned on his deathbed of his appointment to the chair of Greek at Glasgow, his alma mater.[106]

In the context of Irish-language study, Neilson is a noteworthy figure. His *Introduction to the Irish Language* is of interest both for its form[107] and its content. The content is pedagogically innovative for its time. This practical Irish-language manual was intended for learners whom Neilson imagined to be simply interested in communicating with their fellow humans on their travels. He complements his lessons on grammar and structure with sample conversations in the target language that illustrate a range of everyday situations, such as buying and selling, encounters between travellers and innkeepers, and the like. Many of the dialogues, to quote Aidan Doyle:[108]

> are typical of what we still find in phrasebooks for travellers to foreign countries. On the whole, comparing them to what we know of twentieth-century dialects from the same region, they have an air of authenticity.

A perusal of Neilson's work bears out this opinion, revealing an experienced and skilled language teacher. Comparable with standard European language textbooks before and since, his book starts with the alphabet and sound system before taking his reader through parts of speech and the complexities of the verb system, and on to the rules of syntax. He balances his description of grammatical rules with a constant supply of sample vocabulary, inviting the learner to engage actively with model utterances taken from daily life in order to build further phrases, expanding their vocabulary and mastery of structures as they go along. In comparison, the lists of phrases in another grammar, published in the same year by another language revivalist, William Haliday, *Uraicecht na Gaedhilge: A Grammar of the Gaelic Language* (1808), are less well integrated with the grammatical structures, and fall particularly flat when considered alongside the second section of Neilson's work, which he calls 'Familiar Phrases, and Dialogues'.[109]

Neilson's Part II, printed in English and Irish on facing pages, introduces exchanges based on everyday situations – buying eggs or cloth; visiting a tailor, a dairy, a doctor; travelling; the state of the weather; and so on. The section ends with what Neilson terms an 'original and genuine conversation' that 'furnishes a variety of idiomatical terms and phrases'.[110] The manufacture of 'genuine' dialogues to illustrate the use of the target language in different settings is a standard ploy in early modern European language teaching. All but one of the dialogues are invented by Neilson. Designed to convey to the visitor some notion of the attitudes, beliefs and customs of the people in the locality visited, the alleged authenticity of Neilson's scenarios is cleverly contrived. Thus, a local inhabitant who accompanies the traveller to a forge, so that the traveller can have his lame horse shod, shortens the road by recounting the fortunes of the blacksmith's family and how they had survived the Cromwellian period.[111] Another dialogue, entitled 'The

Country Inn',[112] imagines a scenario where two Ulstermen travelling in the west of Ireland fall into conversation with their innkeeper. After a brief, politely neutral exchange on the unsettled political climate, their host asks the Ulstermen:[113]

> Feadam fòs beit tract air seanacais na tìre, gan diombail. An bfuil mòran do lorg na sean foirgnead, no oibreaca cian arsaiġ eile, le faiceal in bur dtirse?

> We may speak also of the antiquities of the country, without offence. Are there many remains of old buildings, or other ancient works, to be seen in your country?

In response, the two travellers manage, quite plausibly, to mention castles, churches, round towers, 'raths' [ring-forts], caves, engraved stones, standing stones, 'carns' [wayside cairns],[114] 'cromleacs' [megalithic stone circles] and stone-covered beehive chambers. The discussion then turns to whether or not it is prudent to cut down a solitary thorn tree, for fear of drawing the wrath of the little people and goes on to spin a convoluted yarn about a nursing mother, taken by the fairies, who returns to visit on Hallowe'en.[115]

Each part of the book is followed by learned Endnotes that compare points with other languages and lend objectivity to the material. In Note 18 to Section II, for example, we read Neilson's opinion on the folk tale about the fairies, a view that tempers his wish for rural enlightenment with a respect for folklore and a sense of perspective about its provenance:[116]

> This story affords a specimen of the popular superstitions of Ireland. Such fictions prevail, more or less, in all countries, according to the degree of information which the common people possess. And it is much to be regretted that they should be very prevalent in the country parts of Ireland, owing, in a great measure, to the want of more valuable knowledge. There is reason to hope, however, that the decay of such superstitions is not far distant, and that the diffusion of learning will remove every vestige of them. In the meantime, these playful inventions of fancy will serve to amuse the reader; nor will they appear more extravagant than the poetic fictions of ancient times.

In sum, Neilson's grammar gives a sense of discovering a living culture that is distant from the learner's own, as well as offering some useful vocabulary to help the traveller get by. This practical grammar, with its dialogues between travellers and locals foregrounding the everyday spoken word, can be set in the wider context of conversation manuals used in early modern Europe for language learning.[117] It treats the Irish vernacular like a foreign tongue, unfettered by any baggage from its vexed political history.[118]

According to Aidan Doyle, 'William Neilson [...] took a more modern approach to language-learning than his contemporaries.'[119] Certainly, a glance at other pre-Famine Irish grammars makes his stand out. Maynooth's first professor of Irish, Paul O'Brien, wrote *A Practical Grammar of the Irish Language* (1809), that confines itself to stating rules with a few illustrative quotations and extracts from literary texts.[120] Over three decades later, Cork's Professor Owen Connellan produced *A Practical Grammar of the Irish Language* in 1844. After a hundred or so pages of clear grammatical explanation, likewise illustrated by brief manuscript quotations, he appends four pages of Irish text with alternating English translation, of 'Extracts from the Annals of the Four Masters', chronicling the treachery, plunder and slaughter perpetrated by Ireland's invaders.[121] John O'Donovan's

A Grammar of the Irish Language (1845) also gives priority to earlier forms of the language, its history and prosody. His 400-page account of the grammatical rules (illustrated by brief quotations from old texts rather than living everyday situations), is supplemented by a further 20 pages of longer extracts from Irish manuscripts dating from the seventh to the seventeenth century, given in Irish and in translation, and drawn from a variety of sources – hagiographical, devotional, legal, medical and historical.

All of these other grammars, unlike Neilson for his dialogues in Part II, choose a Gaelic fount for the parts written in Irish.[122] The assumption behind them is that the decoding of Old Irish manuscripts was the learner's principal rationale for wanting to learn Irish in the first place. Owen Connellan, in his Preface, says as much:[123]

> I have given many words and phrases collected from ancient Irish MSS, in order to assist the learner in reading the nearly obsolete language in which they are written. While I was myself engaged in studying the ancient manuscripts, I found these phrases and idioms one of the greatest difficulties to be overcome, and the examples now given will supply a key to the elucidation of many passages otherwise perhaps impossible to understand.

John O'Donovan's grammar had been commissioned by the Board of St Columba's College in Stackallan, County Meath, an elite school founded in 1843 to provide a classical education for future clergymen of the established Church of Ireland.[124] Celtic was studied by senior students at the college. A further constituency of learners, external to Ireland, was also targeted. When Professor O'Donovan was awarded the Royal Irish Academy's Cunningham Medal shortly after his grammar appeared, the RIA President's citation mentions that the professor's grammar was meeting 'a want long felt by the philologers of Europe'.[125] This (small) market was composed of Celtic scholars in other countries who sought a knowledge of the structures of modern Irish in order to penetrate the mysteries of Old Irish.

This sample perusal of Irish grammars from before the Great Famine (1845–52) provides a glimpse of how the study of Irish was perceived, and what its study was intended to achieve, in the nineteenth century before the arrival of the Gaelic League. The question *Why study Irish?* appears mainly to have been motivated by preservation and antiquarianism. This instrumentalist rationale saw the acquisition of the living tongue as a means of capturing a rapidly vanishing Gaelic culture. It was essential to train the future scribes and custodians of that cultural repository in order to maintain, for new generations, vital links with the lore, annals and records of the past.

Another motivation, connected with the present, is expressed by Owen Connellan at the end of *his Grammar*'s preface. He hopes that his work may 'establish a medium of communication between the higher and lower orders of society in Ireland'.[126] Neilson's Preface[127] is at once more explicit and pragmatic with the same communication agenda:

> But it is, particularly, from the *absolute necessity* [his italics] of understanding this language, in order to converse with the natives of a great part of Ireland, that the study of it is indispensible [sic]. If Irish be no longer the language of the court, or the senate, yet the pulpit and the bar require the use of it; and he that would communicate moral instruction, or investigate the claims of justice, must be versed in the native tongue, if he expects to be generally understood, or to succeed in his researches. In travelling, and the common occurrences of agriculture and rural traffic, a knowledge of Irish is also absolutely necessary.

To learn Irish in order to communicate with the significant number of people who speak the language is, for Neilson in 1808, a rational proposition: 'while the Irish exists, and *must* exist for many years to come, it is surely reasonable and desirable, that every person should be able to hold converse with his countrymen.'[128]

Neilson's work exemplifies yet another reason for studying Irish: leisured travel.[129] In the days of the grand tour, a useful Italian phrase for a traveller in Italy was *Dov'è il gatto?* [*Where's the cat?*]. The most influential overnight gentleman at an inn would be given the room with the cat, so that no mice would disturb his slumbers.[130] The traveller in Ireland, William Neilson's grammar suggests, would be advised to learn how to ask for the whereabouts of the local forge to shoe his horse: '*Ca mbian Brian gaḃa na ċoṁnaig? [Where does Bryan the blacksmith live?*].'[131] In the Irish context, Neilson's work showed, almost a century before the Gaelic League, that it was possible to imagine learning Irish simply in order to converse with first-language Irish speakers. He hopes that his grammar will address a deficiency in other grammars, intending it to be 'a grammar, by which the learner might be taught to *compose*, as well as to *analyse*'.[132] Like all experienced linguists, Neilson knew that effective grammars generate active learning and production of the spoken language rather than mere comprehension of its dead written forms.

The history of the Irish language is never neutral and often full of surprises. In the light of subsequent history, right up to our own times,[133] it may appear odd that Belfast, of all places, should have hosted the first academic to teach Irish – albeit briefly – in something resembling a non-partisan way, relatively unencumbered by the weight of the language's divisive history. The fact is however less surprising when we consider that William Neilson sprang from the same climate of tolerant and enlightened Presbyterianism that had fuelled Ulster's United Irishmen. He was sympathetic towards Catholic emancipation, president of the Belfast Literary Society for 1819–20, and a prominent member of the Belfast Society for Promoting Knowledge, the group that founded the city's Linen Hall Library.[134] His acquaintances included the constitutionalist reformer William Drennan, one of the founders of the Belfast Academical Institution, where Neilson headed classics in the Collegiate Department and taught Irish and classical languages at the end of his life. Drennan was greatly inspired by the enlightened Antrim schoolmaster David Manson (1716–92), who put into practice, in his Belfast Grammar 'play' school, his innovative principles concerning the need for young children to be amused, and not punished, when learning English.[135] The Belfast Academical Institution, when it opened in 1814, was multidenominational, and unique as a third-level establishment in not requiring its staff or students to declare their religious persuasion. Although in practice the vast majority of its intake were future Presbyterian ministers, it was imbued, in its early years at least, with the liberal and independent spirit of the United Irishmen.[136] The inclusion of Irish in its curriculum is also understandable, given the centrality of the Word of God in Presbyterianism and the fact that from 1833, the General Synod of Ulster made a knowledge of Irish compulsory for clerical students.[137]

* * *

As we have seen, Neilson's approach to language study was exceptional in its day, and the status of Irish, as a language fit to learn, remained anomalous. Since it was a native vernacular, there was no obvious call to study it in a period when English itself was not generally deemed to be an autonomous university discipline for anglophones. At the same time, Irish was, *de facto*, a quasi-foreign language to most of the country's university-going population. Neither a 'modern language' like French or German, in the sense of being spoken by foreigners, nor a classical one like Latin or Greek – despite its ancient Celtic pedigree – it fell between several stools at once, compounding the other daunting challenges besetting it.

The living vernacular therefore lacked a rationale for being given prominence in the academic curriculum. Indeed, as the struggles of the Gaelic League were to prove, it needed such a rationale to be invented before it could be regarded as worthy of study. Such extrinsic requirements are often important factors in language learning. People are generally incentivised to learn another language because they need to learn it, having an end use in mind, or because they are required to learn it by the regulatory environment in which the learning is undertaken.

During most of the Victorian era, both inside and outside the academy, the historicising, philological approach to Irish took precedence, propelled by scholarly curiosity and the need to collect and understand ancient manuscripts before it was too late. To study living languages the better to appreciate earlier or dead language forms was a standard approach to most modern language teaching and learning for much of the nineteenth century.[138] Just as an ability to read and understand German scholarship was perceived as helpful for a better understanding of Latin or Greek literature, Early Irish texts could be better grasped by learning the structures of modern Irish, even if that enterprise was not always seen as possessing great value in and of itself.

In Ireland, the antiquarian drive was also bound up with national identity. All the Irish grammarians we have briefly scrutinised use hyperbole when extolling the age and unique qualities of the ancient language, in the same manner as Owen Connellan, who trusts that his grammar will help people learn 'one of the most ancient, as well as one of the most beautiful and expressive languages of Europe'.[139] This patriotic impetus for the study of Irish, quite separate from its value as an aid to the comprehension of ancient texts, was to come to the fore in the last quarter of the nineteenth century, when it was applied, finally, to the living vernacular.

In the next chapter, our narrative moves into the late Victorian decades and their immediate aftermath, a period that magnified the patriotic rationale for learning the vernacular and was most markedly to shape the language-learning agenda in Ireland over the following century. As always in cultural history, there are continuities amid dramatic ruptures. Seven decades after Neilson's *Introduction to the Irish Language* (1808) was first published, the young Douglas Hyde (1860–1949) learned Irish in County Roscommon by listening and conversing with his Irish-speaking neighbours while teaching himself the written language by using Neilson.[140] The same Douglas Hyde would go on to found the Gaelic League and to be UCD's first professor of Modern Irish. His erudition in Irish, and his activism in promoting its use, contributed to his patriotic credentials to be appointed the first President of Ireland in 1938.

CHAPTER 5

The Modern Irish Battleground

It may cause a moment's distress to one's imagination when one hears that the last Cornish peasant who spoke the old tongue of Cornwall is dead; but, no doubt, Cornwall is the better for adopting English, for becoming more thoroughly one with the rest of the country. [Matthew Arnold, 1867][1]

In order to de-Anglicise ourselves we must at once arrest the decay of the language. [Douglas Hyde, 1892][2]

Irish [...] – not only useless, but a mischievous obstacle to civilisation. [J. P. Mahaffy, 1896][3]

The principles and methods on which Latin and Greek are taught are, in many points, exactly opposed to the methods on which more enlightened teachers are beginning to teach modern languages [...] and the laborious treadmill of Grammar, Dictionary and Exercise-book, which has nearly stifled the dead tongues, has been too much applied to the living. [L. M. Moriarty, 1899][4]

In 1899, [...] disillusionment was still far in the future. On the contrary, the air seemed full of promise, new horizons were opening out in all directions – there appeared to be no limit to what talent and good-will might not achieve. [F. S. L. Lyons, 1964][5]

The oft-recounted tale of how the Gaelic League swept the country at the turn of the twentieth century bears retelling at this juncture, as it is symptomatic of the centrality of language for influential Irish Victorians and their sense of cultural identity. Arguably, the revival of modern Irish would never have occurred without the philological emphasis of the time. It is also germane to one of the main arcs of this narrative, namely the dynamic in language teaching, between conveying spoken and written forms of the language to be taught. Finally, the endeavours of the League will become increasingly relevant after the establishment of independence in 1922.

THE GAELIC LEAGUE AND IDENTITY POLITICS

By the early 1870s, Ireland's political climate had changed sufficiently to generate a new air of confidence and optimism. There was a sense that the country 'might have a future as well as a past'[6]: the Church of Ireland had been disestablished; the Home Rule (or Irish) Party had been founded at Westminster; there was talk of tenants' rights and plans were afoot finally to legislate for land redistribution. Poor harvests in the late 1870s helped to fan the flames of simmering agrarian agitation, seen in the foundation of the Irish National Land League in 1879 and leading to Gladstone's momentous Land Law Act (1881), which was to prove radical in its consequences. Further land acts were to follow right into the early 1920s, transforming the structures of land ownership and ultimately bringing about the repossession of the land by a broad spectrum of its inhabitants.[7]

In tandem with land repossession, these decades also saw concerted efforts to repossess the language. In 1876, yet another cultural society was set up, the Society for the Preservation of the Irish Language [SPIL]. Aiming to preserve and cultivate the living vernacular, especially in those parts of the country where it was still spoken, this broad-based group of advocates included the well-connected: prelates, members of parliament and other dignitaries. It secured some minor concessions in furthering the official recognition of Irish in the educational sphere. At primary level, the Society was instrumental in having Irish introduced as an optional extra subject (taught outside school hours) on the national school curriculum from 1878.[8] However, the option was taken up by minimal numbers of pupils and schools.[9] The concession applied only to Irish-speaking areas, for fifth- and sixth-class children, and schools charged a fee. There was a dearth of inspectors with knowledge of the language, of capable Irish teachers, and of suitable textbooks. The SPIL's primer, *An Chéad Leabhar Gaedhilge* [*First Irish Book*] (1878), was geared towards second-language learners. It was to take two more decades for Irish officially to enter the curriculum in teacher-training colleges, when Eoin MacNeill was appointed supplemental Professor of Irish at St Patrick's College, Drumcondra in 1900.[10]

Also from 1878, at post-primary level, it was at the SPIL's instigation that Celtic was included among the languages examinable in the Intermediate Certificate. Thanks to lobbying from the SPIL, at third level too, Irish (or Celtic, as it was officially labelled) was recognised among the range of modern languages that could be taken, instead of Latin or Greek, in the RUI's matriculation requirement from 1881.

However, while concessions for opening the door to Irish in schools from 1878 mark an important milestone in the history of Irish-language study, their effect was slow, and more symbolic than real. Before 1878, one would be hard put to find an intermediate school advertising Irish on its curriculum. One exception (in this as in other respects) was the elite Church of Ireland boarding school, St Columba's College, which included Irish from its inception in 1843. Founded, as mentioned in Chapter Four, to educate Irish clergymen's sons who might read divinity at Dublin University, there was a proselytising agenda behind the inclusion of Irish in its broad curriculum.[11] Otherwise, Irish was taught in a handful of schools west of the Shannon.[12] After 1878, a trickle of post-primary schools gradually introduced the option of Celtic: the Christian Brothers were quick to introduce the subject, as were the St Louis nuns in Monaghan. At the French College, boys were sitting Intermediate Certificate 'Celtic' by 1885. One of their best candidates, incidentally, was from Alsace.[13] Éamon de Valera studied at the French College from 1898 and enrolled at University College Blackrock in 1900. Revivalism made steady inroads in Blackrock: a motion that Irish should be compulsory in schools and colleges was enthusiastically carried at a turn-of-the-century meeting of the school's debating society.[14] Overall, however, an imbalance with numbers taking other modern languages remained, particularly in girls' schools: in the 1899 Intermediate Certificate examination, for example, 43 girls passed Irish while 457 passed in German and 184 passed in Italian. The relative dearth of girls' schools taking Irish is striking.[15] It confirms a contrast drawn by Tony Fahey between the Christian Brothers and the convent schools: '[The nuns'] concern for the Gaelic past or the Irish language was slow to develop and their cultural leanings, where they had any distinctiveness, tended more towards a provincial fondness for French literary polish.'[16]

Challenges confronting Irish learners were magnified at post-primary level, where the late nineteenth-century curriculum used the study of historical forms of the literary language as a pedagogical model. As Aidan Doyle comments:[17]

> More than in the case of the national schools, the teaching of Irish at secondary level was modelled directly on the teaching of Greek and Latin. The exam in Irish for the Intermediate Certificate tested pupils' knowledge of Early Modern Irish, a version of the language which had not been spoken for nearly 300 years.

This recalls most of the pre-Famine Irish grammars we discussed in Chapter Four, as it reflects the academic approach to teaching modern languages generally found throughout Europe in the nineteenth century. Such pedagogic practices were shortly to be challenged by language-teaching reformers.[18]

The piecemeal educational concessions won by the SPIL were complemented by other cultural developments, such as the founding of *Irisleabhar na Gaedhilge* [*The Gaelic Journal*] in 1882, the first periodical to publish some current affairs in Irish. In Aidan Doyle's estimation, this bilingual monthly 'was by no means a newspaper as we would understand that term, but it did rescue the language from the druidic mists in which it had been shrouded before this.'[19] Occasionally carrying pieces in other languages (Scottish Gaelic, Welsh, French), it included a regular feature called 'Simple Lessons in Irish', written by Maynooth's Professor of Irish, Eugene O'Growney, and targeting anglophone middle-class readers curious about learning the living language. This development was a stepping stone towards the endeavours of the Gaelic League, set up in 1893.

The man most associated with the Gaelic League was its first president, Douglas Hyde. At face value, the third son of a clergyman in Co. Roscommon was a most unlikely candidate to be the chief instigator of an organisation that was to transform the fortunes of the Irish language at the turn of the twentieth century. A Trinity College Dublin graduate in modern literature (1884), Hyde was a very distinguished student. Studying remotely for most of his first two years, he sat term examinations in the college. He came first place in Irish at his entrance examination in June 1880, a subject he took as an elective and in which he won annual prizes. He achieved first class honours standard in German and French and was a first-rank prizeman in Italian.[20] On top of his stellar performance in languages, he was also an outstanding law student when he transferred to Law, being awarded 'the L.L.B. in December 1887, and in April, 1888, the L.L.D. with first class honours – no mean achievement!' The compliment is Mary Robinson's, a reliable source.[21]

Without formal schooling, Hyde had learned spoken Irish from consorting with his neighbours as an adolescent in Co. Roscommon and was deeply affected by the death of the local gamekeeper, the mentor to whom he was most indebted in this regard. He learned to read and write the language with the help of William Neilson's grammar (1808), as already mentioned in Chapter Four.[22] Interested in recording for posterity the folk tales which he had heard in the west, his earliest publications were in that area. As his writings indicate, Hyde developed strong convictions about the need to revive the native language, which he saw as the expression of Irish people's culture and identity. His inaugural address as incoming president to the National Literary Society in November 1892, 'The necessity for de-anglicising Ireland', is a call to arms based on these convictions. He rails against the 'complete Anglicisation, which [...] is, and has been, making silent inroads upon us for nearly a century'[23] and which can only be stalled by restoring the Irish language to its rightful place, 'on a par with – or even above – Greek, Latin, and modern languages, in all examinations held under the Irish Government', should Home Rule be passed. In which case, in Irish-speaking baronies 'where the children speak Irish, Irish shall be taught,' and 'Irish-speaking schoolmasters, petty session clerks, and even magistrates be appointed in Irish-speaking districts.'[24] He calls for an unashamedly chauvinistic promotion of all that is quintessentially Gaelic and Irish, in order to escape the trap of aping English ways while simultaneously resenting them.

Many who heard this idealistic manifesto were perplexed or unimpressed, but a small number of like-minded individuals, including Eoin MacNeill, took it to heart and founded the Gaelic League in the following year. Hyde was elected president of the organisation. They agreed it was essential that their fellow citizens should talk Irish as much as possible. The task of persuading the same citizens – many of whom neither spoke Irish nor wished to do so – was another matter.[25] Yet, within one decade, the tide began to turn.

How did the Gaelic League produce such an extraordinary sea-change in grassroots attitudes towards the Irish language? Brian Ó Cuív observes that the organisation was set up at a timely moment, immediately after the fall and death (1891) of the legendary uncrowned king of Ireland and leader of the Irish Parliamentary Party, Charles Stewart Parnell: 'In the nation-wide despondency following the political débâcle, the language movement offered an outlet for the energies of those with nationalist inclinations.'[26] It certainly provided a focus for cultural nationalists and tapped into latent patriotic pride in the Irish vernacular. As a non-political and broad-church organisation, it united all creeds and walks of life and rapidly established a network of branches throughout every county in Ireland, and even ventured abroad.[27] Branches organised local events and cultural activities like day excursions, céilithe [Irish dances with traditional music], fleadhanna [traditional festivals], they ran regular feiseanna [cultural gatherings with competitions], lectures and competitions. They encouraged the collection and recording of folklore from

5.1 Douglas Hyde in his prime
Irish postage stamp, issued in 1943, the fiftieth anniversary of the Gaelic League's foundation. (© An Post. Courtesy of the An Post Museum and Archive.)

older inhabitants in Irish-speaking parishes.[28] Their annual all-Ireland festivals were a true novelty for the inhabitants of the west of Ireland where, in those days, 'cultural events only took place in large urban centres. It was totally unheard of to bring them out to the countryside, particularly the west of the country, which was underdeveloped in terms of its infrastructure'.[29] In its grassroots structure, the League consciously borrowed the successful model set up by the Gaelic Athletic Association (founded in 1884) for promoting traditional Irish games.[30]

The League's publication division brought out pamphlets, education materials and collections of folklore and in 1899, its weekly newspaper, *An Claidheamh Soluis*, was set up, with Patrick Pearse as its editor from 1903. This publication carried content in Irish and English, targeting a mainly anglophone and urban readership. It printed the words of Irish poems and songs and presented sample bilingual conversations (in two columns) for learners. In its English columns it reported on membership, activities and plans from different branches, and its editorials and letters to the editor consistently advanced the cause of spreading the spoken vernacular, 'the chief rampart of our nationality'.[31] Other organs of the press increasingly included material in Irish, often from a resolutely Irish-Ireland standpoint, during the same period.[32]

In the sphere of education policy, the Gaelic League viewed the concessions won by the SPIL as inadequate. At elementary level, it secured further progress: the passing of legislation in 1900 to make it possible to teach Irish in all national schools, and not just in Irish-speaking areas; and in 1904, a bilingual programme allowing for the teaching of specific subjects through the medium of the vernacular in those areas. Although many Commissioners of National Education were hostile to the introduction of curricular Irish, or at best dubious about its practicability, the League was able to make more headway with Dr W. J. M. Starkie, the Resident Commissioner from 1899. He sympathised in spirit with the proposals and was open to adopting many of the specific changes in teaching methods advanced by League members during the 1900s.[33]

The place of Irish in secondary schools, however, became the subject of a heated public controversy during the Vice-Regal Inquiry into Intermediate Education, held in the early spring of 1899. The Inquiry offered an opportunity for the League to stake a claim for more recognition to be accorded to Irish, which was then still valued at 600 marks, as against 700 for French and German and 1200 for Greek, Latin and English.[34] A group of Trinity dons, however, were of the view that Irish deserved no place at all in the system and ought to be removed from the list of school subjects altogether. A head-on collision was inevitable. Hyde mounted a vigorous defence of the Gaelic League's position, having been goaded into making the case by the particularly cavalier and disparaging remarks on the language and its literature made by the imperious John Pentland Mahaffy, a classicist and ancient historian, and by Trinity College's Professor of Sanskrit and Comparative Philology, Robert Atkinson. Mahaffy, who knew no Irish, expressed his blissfully ignorant opinion that Irish was of no educational value in schools; at best, he conceded, it was interesting for philology, and could be 'sometimes useful to a man fishing for salmon or shooting grouse in the West.'[35] These views had form. A few years before the 1899 enquiry, Mahaffy had opposed the League's plans for the revival of Irish in local administration:[36]

It is only recently that I was sent a pronouncement regarding the Irish (Celtic) language, signed, I grieve to say, by a Protestant bishop and canon, among other names which represent either hostility to England or mere gratuitous folly, recommending that an agitation should be commenced to prevent the appointment of any officials in the south and west who could not speak Irish, and suggesting other means of galvanising into life a most difficult and useless tongue – not only useless, but a mischievous obstacle to civilisation.

Such pronouncements reflected mainstream Victorian English prejudices about the standing of all non-English vernaculars within the United Kingdom. Thomas Arnold's son, the celebrated poet and educationalist Matthew Arnold, who supported the establishment of the Chair of Celtic at Oxford, had other views on the spoken vernaculars.[37] To put Mahaffy in context, it is worth quoting Arnold in some detail:

The fusion of all the inhabitants of these islands into one homogeneous, English-speaking whole, the breaking down of barriers between us, the swallowing up of separate provincial nationalities, is a consummation to which the natural course of things irresistibly tends; it is a necessity of what is called modern civilisation, and modern civilisation is a real, legitimate force; the change must come, and its accomplishment is a mere affair of time. The sooner the Welsh language disappears as an instrument of the practical, political, social life of Wales, the better; the better for England, the better for Wales itself. Traders and tourists do excellent service by pushing the English wedge further and further into the heart of the principality; Ministers of Education, by hammering it harder and harder into the elementary schools. Nor, perhaps, can one have much sympathy with the literary cultivation of Welsh as an instrument of living literature; and in this respect Eisteddfods encourage, I think, a fantastic and mischief-working delusion.

Mahaffy's submission to the Inquiry was supported by Atkinson, who did not know modern Irish either but had produced scholarly editions of early medieval Irish texts. Atkinson argued that modern Irish was an unsettled *patois* rather than a standard language, and merited study for philological purposes only. He dismissed Irish folklore as 'abominable' and deemed early Irish texts to be degrading or silly, of no serious literary value, even offensive to public decency. He would not allow his own daughter to read the *Tóruigheacht Dhiarmada agus Ghráinne* [*The Pursuit of Diarmuid and Gráinne*], the text on the Intermediate Certificate syllabus.[38]

Needless to say, for more reasons than one, these prejudices were a red rag to the Gaelic League bull. Hyde's cogent and extensive apologia for Irish, delivered to the Commission at an oral hearing, was followed by a document marshalling the written support of leading linguistic scholars, from the continent as well as England.[39] Each expressed his incredulity and outrage at the Trinity professors' proposed abolition of Irish as a school subject. This chorus of foreign testimonies helped to demolish the opposition.

The upshot of the controversy was a colossal propaganda victory for the League, particularly as it was fought in full public view, carried in the national press for a number of weeks and drawing other commentators into the fray, mainly on the side of the League. This very public clash did no favours to the old guard at Trinity College, a university where Irish had, after all, been continually taught in the School of Divinity since 1840. However, its teaching had been too narrowly confined to readings from sacred scripture, and Irish attracted few clerical students when monoglot Irish speakers were dwindling in number. All of its Irish professors had been Church of Ireland clergymen and native Irish speakers;

some of them had pretensions to scholarship and even enthusiasm for Irish culture.[40] The attack on the language by Mahaffy and Atkinson served only to compound negative perceptions of Trinity in nationalist circles.[41] While the main bugbear about Catholics studying there, in conservative Catholic opinion, had been 'mixed education' – that is, the integrated education of students from different religious denominations – Trinity was now perceived as 'anti-national' to boot.

Hyde's defence also served to transform the non-sectarian, apolitical Gaelic League into a force for cultural nationalism. Indeed, it was shortly to go further, and align itself with the political struggle for independence, in spite of its founder's principles.[42] It soon became plain that 'after 1899, Irish was no longer just one more school subject; it had acquired a political dimension.'[43] The League's next victory, of enduring influence in the education sphere, was success in its 1908–9 campaign to have Irish made an essential requirement for matriculation in the new National University of Ireland. This radical proposal, spearheaded by Douglas Hyde and Eoin MacNeill and actively supported by Pearse, gave rise to a broad spectrum of opinions among revivalists, not all of whom were totally convinced of its wisdom. Notwithstanding staunch opposition from within the Gaelic League's own ranks – including senior clerics who feared that its adoption could deter potential clerical students, or drive lay Catholic students unqualified in Irish to study in Trinity College – the proposal attracted overwhelming grass-roots support, particularly among the young.[44] 'Large meetings were held throughout the country including one of more than 10,000 supporters in Tuam, County Galway. [...] The campaign culminated in a demonstration by more than 100,000 people in Dublin in September 1909'.[45] The proposal was carried by the newly constituted NUI Senate by 21 votes to 12, to be put into effect from 1913.

As the measure's more ardent campaigners were well aware, the university requirement was crucial for recognition of the language, and for making schools finally take its teaching seriously.[46] Once Irish became mandatory for matriculation in the NUI colleges, there was an immediate knock-on effect on the entire education system. It would now be imperative for post-primary schools to offer Irish if they wished to cater for pupils with professional aspirations. Recognition also led to appointments and expansion at university level: all the colleges of the new NUI appointed chairs of Irish, and its largest constituent member, UCD, broadened Celtic Studies to include four chairs, held by four distinguished scholars.[47] This sudden efflorescence marked a dramatic reversal of the sad collapse of Irish studies in 1862, when the Queen's Colleges suspended their chairs of Celtic.[48] Even Trinity College began to consider Irish as a language for study in its own right. Having established in 1908 that it could be taken as a degree subject,[49] the Board 'rescued' the chair of Irish 'from its clerical doldrums and established it in 1919 as a literary Professorship with a better salary'.[50]

The Gaelic League's successful promotion of the study of Irish, not only at school and university level, but also by running adult evening classes in Irish for its members and establishing Irish teacher training colleges around the country, was meteoric in pace and effect.[51] Cultural nationalist sentiment, impelled by an urgent need to de-anglicise Irish identity, rose to full tide – not to say fever pitch – at the turn of the century. The number of candidates taking Irish in the Intermediate exam, trebling between 1899 and 1902, continued to grow steadily.[52] The study of Irish was enthusiastically embraced, and love of the language, as well as commitment to its renewed vitality, became key markers of what Roy Foster calls the 'robust Anglophobia' of that revolutionary generation of Irish men and women born in the 1870s and 1880s, delineated in his book, *Vivid Faces*.

THE GAELIC LEAGUE AND OTHER MODERN LANGUAGES

All of the League's cultural activities, set up through its extensive network of local branches throughout the country, concerned Irish language and culture.[53] Its elevation of the Gaeltacht – where 'native' speakers of the language could still be found – as an idealised version of the original land of the Gael, unsullied by the mark of the Saxon invader, helped to promote the kind of tourism represented by an emblematic scene in Joyce's short story 'The Dead'.[54] When the annual gathering at his aunts' house takes to the dance floor, the protagonist Gabriel Conroy – an effete cosmopolitan professor of modern languages at the RUI, who wears galoshes in the snow, like they do 'on the Continent' – is chided by his friend and dance partner, Molly Ivors, to whom he reveals his summer travel plans:[55]

> 'O, Mr Conroy, will you come for an excursion to the Aran Isles this summer? We're going to stay there a whole month. It will be splendid out in the Atlantic. You ought to come. Mr Clancy is coming, and Mr Kilkelly and Kathleen Kearney. It would be splendid for Gretta too if she'd come. She's from Connacht, isn't she?'
> 'Her people are,' said Gabriel shortly.
> 'But you will come, won't you?', said Miss Ivors, laying her warm hand eagerly on his arm.
> 'The fact is,' said Gabriel, 'I have just arranged to go —'
> 'Go where?', asked Miss Ivors.
> 'Well, you know, every year I go for a cycling tour with some fellows and so —'
> 'But where?', asked Miss Ivors.
> 'Well, we usually go to France or Belgium or perhaps Germany,' said Gabriel awkwardly.
> 'And why do you go to France and Belgium,' said Miss Ivors, 'instead of visiting your own land?'
> 'Well,' said Gabriel, 'it's partly to keep in touch with the languages and partly for a change.'
> 'And haven't you your own language to keep in touch with – Irish?', asked Miss Ivors.
> 'Well,' said Gabriel, 'if it comes to that, you know, Irish is not my language.'
> Their neighbours had turned to listen to the cross-examination. Gabriel glanced right and left nervously and tried to keep his good humour under the ordeal, which was making a blush invade his forehead.
> 'And haven't you your own land to visit,' continued Miss Ivors, 'that you know nothing of, your own people, and your own country?'
> 'O, to tell you the truth,' retorted Gabriel suddenly, 'I'm sick of my own country, sick of it!'

However, Gabriel's discomfiture derives more from having been labelled a 'West Briton' by the same friend, who has discovered that he writes a weekly literary column in *The Daily Express*.[56] Molly Ivors' kind of Irish patriotism, indeed, tended more often to be exclusively Anglophobic than directed against countries of the European continent. The anxiety over Irish-speaking regions becoming contaminated by English-speaking visitors was so pervasive that other modern languages could even be invoked as a protective measure. The essential point was to avoid using English:[57]

> Persons, with a limited knowledge of Irish, visiting Irish-speaking districts would do well to be careful that in Gaelicising themselves they do not Anglicise the people of the place. I have known visitors to such places who, with the best of intentions in the world, have taught more

English than they have learned Irish. For goodness sake, if they cannot speak Irish let them remain silent or speak French, German, or anything but not make *Béarlóirí* [English speakers] of the Gaels.

It was no coincidence that Joyce set Miss Ivors' Gaeltacht region in the Aran islands on the outer edge of Galway Bay. Considered a paragon of ethnolinguistic purity, cut off from modernity and unsullied by Saxon oppression, these three islands had drawn the attention of antiquarians, archaeologists and ethnographers, botanists and natural history specialists, not to mention artists, writers and language scholars, since the mid-nineteenth century. The visitors had lived among the islanders and published accounts of their findings, describing harsh conditions of island life where human survival was dictated by rhythms unchanged since time immemorial. One such visitor was an RUI undergraduate, Agnes O'Farrelly, who spent summers on Inis Meáin. She was later to be UCD's first woman Professor of Irish.[58]

How did the renewed zeal for learning Irish square with the study of other living languages? In the main, the study of other languages seems to have been taken for granted, not posing any challenge to the teaching or learning of Irish. Many Irish figures from the period appreciated and valued other languages and literatures and maintained an open attitude to studying them. We have pointed out the broad-based language studies of Douglas Hyde. Patrick Pearse took Irish, English and French for his degree and had experience of teaching Irish in various settings: Alexandra College, Westland Row for the Christian Brothers, UCD and Gaelic League colleges.[59] In the view of Séamas Ó Buachalla, Pearse's 'committed nationalism would seem to have been complemented by an enlightened internationalism which advocated for other cultures the acceptability and respect which he demanded for that of his own country.'[60]

Pearse's writings as editor of *An Claidheamh Soluis* (1903–9) reveal a young man keenly interested in current education issues, particularly the highly charged ones surrounding language education. He was truly horrified by the travesty of genuine teaching and learning that he had witnessed in some national schools in Iar-Chonnacht, where the teacher knew no Irish and the children no English.[61] Bilingualism became a special focus for him. In the pages of *An Claidheamh Soluis*, between August 1905 and March 1907, he provided weekly bulletins reporting in detail on the new discoveries concerning best practice in bilingual education that he had witnessed in the classrooms of Belgium during the month of July 1905. Through the good offices of the Belgian ministry, he had paid visits to some 30 educational establishments, from primary to university level,[62] and came back convinced of parallels between Belgium and Ireland where language history was concerned.

Language learning was a constant in Joseph Plunkett's short life too. A recent biography shows him as intent on learning his country's native language as he was in writing or reading French or picking up Italian and Arabic when on a three-month stay in Algiers, for health reasons, in the winter of 1911.[63] He learned Irish at St Enda's, then in Achill, and in summer 1910 at an Irish College in West Donegal, where his creativity was not dampened:[64]

'Coláiste Uladh'

Cloghaneely Irish College
Has a wealth of wit and knowledge,
Not to speak of health and beauty,
Grace and graciousness go leor,
But among its charms entrancing,
Men and maidens, songs and dancing
There is nothing so delightful
As yourself mo mhíle stór.
[...] When the moon is shining palely
On the evening of a céilidhe
And the purple stars are peeping
Through the open College door
There is music on the night
Of the dance and voices laughing
But 'tis laden with the music
Of your voice mo mhíle stór.

Plunkett's first tutor in Irish was another signatory of the proclamation of Easter 1916, the UCD English lecturer Thomas MacDonagh. MacDonagh had taught French and Latin, as well as English, before taking to the fervent pursuit of Irish study through the Gaelic League and becoming the first teacher of language and literature at St Enda's school (1908–10) in its original location in Ranelagh. Along with Edward Martyn, Plunkett and MacDonagh were involved in founding and running the Irish Theatre in Hardwicke Street, Dublin. In addition to producing original plays in Irish or English, one of the goals of that short-lived venture (1914–20) was to stage plays translated from continental languages.[65]

The women of the same revolutionary generation also embraced Irish language and culture with youthful enthusiasm. Antrim-born Máirín McGavock (1894–1972), an executive member of Cumann na mBan who sided against the Anglo-Irish Treaty, was a fluent Irish speaker who held a UCD BA in modern languages (1915) and an MA in German (1916).[66] Agnes Ryan did an MA in Irish and was involved in setting up a branch of Cumann na mBan in Belfast when teaching there. While involved in studying or teaching French or German, the other Ryan sisters frequently allude, in their gossipy letters of the 1900s, to events involving Irish. In their lively accounts of a busy social swirl, they mention League meetings at the London Irish Club, organising flowers from Wexford to decorate a *céilí* hall in Dublin, attending a *fleadh ceoil*, *feis*, or Irish debate, or taking Irish summer courses in Tourmakeady.

Within the women's colleges, debates, lectures, dramatic productions and concerts with an Irish interest blended with other activities to form a mixed cultural and intellectual diet, set up deliberately as extracurricular programmes for the benefit of the student residents. A flavour of the multilingual scope of meetings organised by the 'Literary Academy' at St Mary's Dominican College in Dublin, for example, is given by Margaret Mac Curtain:[67]

In its early days one of the chief functions of the Literary Academy was to sponsor a series of lectures for the public in English and French. These were well attended and of a sufficiently high standard to qualify for the claim of being a course of extra-mural studies. Thus for the Michaelmas term 1893 Mlle. Decoudun gave a magnificent set of lectures of the following themes: Bossuet; La Fontaine; Mme. de Maintenon et Mme. de Sévigné; Boileau; Chateaubriand; and Corneille. [...]

In addition to this emphasis on French literature and culture, the island's own vernacular heritage was given space:

> Irish nationalism, too, found a voice in the Literary Academy and the choice spirits of a new age participated in debates that were becoming bi-lingual. Thus in 1900 Agnes O'Farrelly read a hard-hitting paper, *The Reign of Humbug*, later published as a pamphlet by the Gaelic League, in which she underlined the dangers of 'cosmopolitanism'. In less than two years, the Gaelic revival was in full spate, and Máire Ní Chinnéide, Studentship holder, read a paper in Irish called 'An Craobh Rua'. The chairman was Professor Douglas Hyde and among the speakers to the paper was a man called Pearse. On 4 April, 1906, the first 'Irish' night was held. Josephine O'Sullivan was the auditor and spoke on the 'Schools of Ancient Ireland'. A significant feature of the social gathering was the number of St. Mary's students who answered to it, speaking in Irish, only less fluent, as the *Freeman* puts it graciously, than the Rev. Chairman, Fr. P. S. Dineen, M.A. Finally in December, 1908 a branch of the Gaelic League was founded in St. Mary's. Known to many as Cumann Fódla, it ran classes for beginners and advanced students of Irish at No. 21 Eccles St.

Agnes O'Farrelly, evoked here, had just graduated with an MA in Irish from the RUI, the first woman to do so. She had studied Irish in the Eccles Street women's college with Eoin MacNeill, and persuaded students from other women's colleges to join his classes. A highly influential Gaelic League propagandist, she was later to succeed Douglas Hyde to the chair of Irish in UCD.[68]

Even within the confines of Trinity Hall, the residence for Dublin University's women students that opened in 1908, a touch of revivalism was in the air. Its first Warden, Elizabeth Margaret (Margery) Cunningham from Donegal, had studied modern and medieval languages at Girton in Cambridge and taken a Dublin University degree *ad eundem gradum* in 1906, along with other so-called 'steamboat ladies'.[69] While not going so far as to provide regular lessons in Irish, she was a cultural nationalist and occasionally invited the likes of Æ (George Russell) and Yeats to dine and meet the student residents.[70]

All in all, at the turn of the twentieth century, there is a pervasive sense that the Irish vernacular, so long neglected and undervalued, deserved to be fostered, not exclusively, but to be allowed to find its place among the languages of the world. The study of Irish and the study of European languages were mutually reinforcing. With hopes of Home Rule on the way, members of the Gaelic League were determined not to be 'provincial', an epithet Mahaffy had used when scoffing at their efforts to revive Irish. For Hyde, *au contraire*, the real provincialism was to lose the language completely: it was essential to de-anglicise, at all educational levels, precisely to avoid lapsing into a provincial imitation of England.[71] As he asks rhetorically, in the *Munster News* of 7 July 1909: 'is Ireland going to be Ireland or is it going to be Irelandshire [...], a poor little miserable imitation third-rate English county?'[72]

As a young Gaelic Leaguer, Seán T. O'Kelly was smitten with the Irish language and equally intent on spreading its use on the international stage. In October 1908, representing Dublin Corporation in Rome for Pope Pius X's sacerdotal jubilee, he delivered his address

5.2 John Pentland Mahaffy, classicist, ancient historian, Provost, TCD 1914–1919

Portrait photograph. (Keogh Photographic Collection, 1910–1919. *Courtesy of the National Library of Ireland.*)

in Irish. It was translated into Latin and the Pope thanked him in the diplomatic language, French.[73]

Fin-de-siècle Ireland was a moment of intense cultural possibility, when all strands of society joined forces across 'the traditional barriers of religion and politics' to work towards defining a renewed sense of Irishness.[74] As Liam Mac Mathúna has argued, this collaboration, which bound, in a common purpose, language activists and literary revivalists, owes much to Douglas Hyde's enduring friendship with W. B. Yeats and Lady Augusta Gregory, as well as his links with the broader Irish diaspora in America. For fin-de-siècle revivalists, the Irish vernacular was inseparable from the wider world; consequently, the Gaelic League was broad and outward 'in its heyday and at its highpoint, when the world was a seamless cultural garment, resplendent with a distinctive Irish hue'.[75]

The Gaelic League and the Language Classroom

The Gaelic League did not limit itself to promoting patriotic endeavours expressed through cultural manifestations. Dances, debates and festivals were essential but ultimately ancillary to its core mission, which was the preservation and revival of the language. In turning its energies to language education, the League proved systematic in its organisation and innovative in its teaching methods.

When a bilingual approach for Irish-speaking districts was introduced as an option for national schools in 1904, many primary teachers did not feel equipped to teach through the medium of Irish. In addition, the possibility that the League's proposal for 'essential' Irish in the NUI matriculation might be carried opened vistas of a shortfall in the supply of Irish teachers confident to take on the subject at post-primary level. Planning for ways of meeting the demand for teachers was imperative, both in the school system and in the League's voluntary evening courses in Irish language and culture run for adults.

Sudden policy changes had brought analogous supply issues in other countries. In Germany, for example, when the unified Reich introduced state secondary education for girls in 1872, the study of two foreign languages (i.e., English and French) was made mandatory for *höhere Mädchenschulen* [upper secondary girls' schools]. This led to a shortage of teachers, who had been exclusively male in both girls' and boys' State-run schools. Many German schools called on the services of English or French female native speakers to meet the gap.[76] Such recourse to offshore help was obviously not available for the Irish language, so teachers had to be recruited and trained on the island. First-language

Irish-speaking teachers were especially valued, becoming a precious resource deployed as efficiently as possible and making bilocation a job requirement for the individuals involved. An advertisement for Irish teachers in *An Claidheamh Soluis* specified a required job skill: 'Beidh sé riachtanach dóibh rothaíocht a dhéanamh. [It will be necessary for them to be able to ride a bicycle.]' 'Evidently,' comments Aidan Doyle, 'in 1907 the ability to cycle was the equivalent of a driver's licence nowadays'.[77]

The League's *múinteoirí taistil* [travelling teachers], moving around the countryside on their bicycles, became a familiar phenomenon. These young peddlers of 'a dying language for little or no pay'[78] were motivated by as much zeal as their adult evening students. As depicted by Alice Milligan, their sense of idealism made the weather easier to contend with:[79]

> A man goes by on a wheel with the rain on his face,
> Against the way of the wind, and he not caring;
> Goes on through the winter night towards a lonesome, distant place
> For his heart is hot with the glow of the ancient hero-daring.
>
> He slows on the slant of the hill and must walk the higher road,
> For he knows of an eager crowd that waits in a lighted hall [...]

Where schools were concerned, the Gaelic League knew that the teaching of Irish had to start, first and foremost, with the youngest learners. To a significant degree, it was soon able to claim credit in this regard as attested by the steadily increasing number of primary schools coming on board and of teachers undergoing training during the first two decades of the twentieth century.[80] In the absence of prompt cooperation from the training colleges, the League took teacher training into its own hands. Teachers who were not native speakers, but showed a willingness to learn, were offered intensive training in Irish as well as in methods of teaching it. Once the financial costs were borne by the Commissioners, teachers were able to avail of grant-aided, two-month summer courses run at designated Irish colleges; interested adults who were not professional teachers could also attend. By 1910, the League had opened seven summer training colleges, the earliest of which was Coláiste na Mumhan [Munster College], in Béal Átha'n Ghaorthaidh [Ballingeary] in Co. Cork.[81] Rising numbers of learners testify to the Gaelic League's achievements, on the basis of modest resources. Support for the language in the national schools 'continued to grow so that by 1919–20 it was being taught as an extra subject in 1,525 schools and the bilingual programme was being operated in 232 schools.'[82]

Along with its energetic and thorough organisation another noteworthy feature of the Gaelic League was its innovatory approach to language-teaching methods. It gave primacy to the spoken word, advocating minimal use of the mother tongue (English) in the language classroom and restricting the role of formal grammar and translation. Today we would not expect primary school children, embarking on learning a language, to be given much written language or grammatical rules to process, but at the turn of the last century this was not the case. Some of the literary texts on the 1902 primary school course in Irish would nowadays be reserved for Honours Leaving Certificate or first-year Arts university students.[83] In 1901 the League organised a conference in London for its members to agree on best practice in the teaching of Irish. They decided to target the spoken language above all and much was made of the new science of phonetics. In the packed timetable at their Donegal teacher-training summer course, the first hour of every morning was devoted to phonetics, and for two hours every afternoon, students performed sample classes using the *modh díreach* [direct method] in front of teachers and fellow students.[84] The Australian-born son of Irish emigrants, Rev. Richard O'Daly, D. D. (1865–1930), who was appointed phonetics professor at Ballingeary, had learned Irish as a beginner from classes given by the London branch of the Gaelic League. Having studied in Rome, O'Daly had a keen interest in learning languages – of which he spoke several – and was conversant with the latest ideas about teaching the spoken word, including experimental phonetics laboratories in Europe and America.[85]

In their ambitious espousal of the *modh díreach* [direct method], the Gaelic League organisers were in tune with developments in applied linguistics elsewhere. A new generation of reform-minded modern language teachers was becoming increasingly disenchanted by traditional teaching methods, especially in German education circles, where in most boys' secondary schools English and French were still taught by adopting the methods used for teaching Latin. The beginnings of the German *Neusprachliche Reformbewegung* [Modern Language Reform Movement] date from the last two decades of the nineteenth century, with the publication of Wilhelm Viëtor's landmark pamphlet 'Sprachunterricht muss umkehren!' [Language teaching must change direction!] in 1882. The first issue of the language-teaching journal he founded six years later, *Phonetische Studien* (1888) – renamed in 1894 *Die neueren Sprachen* – listed over 50 collaborators.[86] This young generation of modern language teachers began emphasising an oral/aural approach, with a minimal use of translation into the source language and a maximum use of the target language as a medium of instruction in the classroom, at least in the initial stages of second-language learning. The emphasis on spoken skills was not new: traditional grammar teaching had involved a good deal of rote-learning of phrases, catechism-like, on the *repetitio mater studiorum* principle. What was innovative was to shun the use of the mother tongue in the classroom. Whereas traditional language teaching relied on presenting the materials bilingually, with a liberal use of the mother tongue to explain the vocabulary and grammar of the new language, the reformers frowned upon any bilingual presentation. One of their core tenets was to transmit as far as possible the direct experience of the living culture of the target language's speakers, using the medium of the target language itself. They also jettisoned the practice of using translation exercises as the means of reinforcing grammatical structures.[87]

A sense of the novelty of the changes in methodology can be gauged from considering how languages were still being taught in more traditional settings. Reporting on language teaching at Harrow public school in 1899, L. M. Moriarty warns that the slavish adoption of the classical model is pernicious, and even perverse, for modern languages. He deplores the approach of a typical modern language teacher in the school, who, Moriarty tells us,[88]

> however well he may know the language, does not teach it sufficiently as a *living* tongue. He teaches it much as he teaches Latin – plenty of grammar, plenty of exercises in intricate syntactical rules, copious dictation of elaborate notes over the construe lesson, though the original text is never even read aloud, text books continued, it may be, from term to term like *Virgil* or *Cicero* – but little, if any *dictée*, reading aloud, or repetition, no adequate handling of the tongue as an instrument of *speech*.

Language-teaching reform was in the air in several countries, as scholars and teachers joined in the general turn towards the spoken word. This search for a different approach was partly driven by wider access to education which called into question traditional methods used in teaching the classics. In girls' schools, which had not traditionally taught Latin, teachers were in any case more ready to tackle the spoken language in modern language teaching.[89] In Rhode Island the Berlitz Method can be traced to 1878; in France, the gifted linguist Paul Passy (1859–1940) co-founded the International Phonetic Association, while François Gouin (1831–96) developed what he called the *méthode des séries* or *méthode naturelle* [Series Method, or Natural Method]. Gouin's method derived from the author's personal experience, having observed how his small nephew learned to speak his mother tongue, French, while he himself struggled to learn enough German to follow Philosophy lectures in Berlin. The Series Method also insisted on teaching through the target language. Gouin was less renowned in his native France than in England, where his work was translated at an early stage.[90] The Association Phonétique des Professeurs de Langues Vivantes (later to become the International Phonetic Association), founded in Paris in 1889, 'boasted 743 members by 1896', representing over 20 nationalities.[91]

The new approaches were making inroads in Britain's language-teaching culture and leading to a shortage of fully qualified teachers.[92] The London-born German Walter Rippmann [later Ripman], teacher of French and German, was an early exponent, and disseminated the reforming principles in his textbooks for language teachers. A graduate of Cambridge, where he worked before moving to the University of London, he edited the MLTA's journal, *Modern Language Quarterly* (later *Modern Language Teaching*) from 1897 to 1911. In 1897, Rippmann attended the first European modern languages holiday course at Marburg, after which he became a pioneer in teaching English as a foreign language, running an annual holiday course in direct method practices for foreign teachers of English at the University of London.[93]

The Gaelic League's change in emphasis in second-language pedagogy was, then, by no means a separate indigenous development. The new trends soon filtered through to Ireland's language activists, as they strove to spread the use of Irish, and at the same time minimise the use of English, through every level of Irish society. The Gouin method was taken up by the Gaelic League's small but committed Lee branch in Cork in the late 1890s; by 1901, its London branch was already trying out the Berlitz method of total immersion.[94] Like the members of the Gaelic League, most of the new language reformers in other countries were young and enthusiastic. The debates in their journals betoken the same kind of optimistic passion for the common goal and commitment to reform in modern language teaching. As one commentator observes: 'The 1880s were heady times; and the air of excitement, infecting those within and beyond academia, the sense that language learning is important, is one of enduring value.'[95]

The same transnational idealism informed Patrick Pearse's ideas about language education and, indeed, about education in general.[96] As his articles (1905–7) in *An Claidheamh Soluis* [*ACS*] about Welsh and Belgian bilingualism illustrate, language questions were a constant preoccupation for him, always with the backdrop of Ireland and its Gaeltacht in mind.[97] He was deeply impressed by Belgium's official policies on language pedagogy, which he saw as enlightened and child/learner-centred, favouring the direct method in the early years (*ACS*, 18 and 25 November 1905; *ACS*, 2 December

1905), and by the class teaching he had observed in schools where the policies were put into practice. He was inspired by seeing how language teaching, using the direct method from infant kindergarten level up, was (in his rose-tinted view) helping to overcome the country's linguistic divisions (*ACS*, 23 December 1905). What fired his imagination was the principle that the very first steps in an infant classroom should be taken in the children's vernacular. He witnessed, for example, Flemish-speaking children in a Froebel school in Antwerp physically involved in acting out the everyday situation of preparing a breakfast table, complete with props, verbal exchange and repetition. This particular lesson was performed in the children's mother tongue but would, at a later stage in their schooling, be given to the same children to perform in French. Never slow to compare, the Irish observer invites the reader, 'Imagine the revolution were lessons like this *in Irish only* the order of Infants classes in *Iar-Chonnachta* and the *Déise*.'[98] Bilingual education begins later in the child's schooling. When he visited an *école communale* [municipal school] in the Brussels suburb of Etterbeek with a small Walloon majority, the week's theme for 30 boys (aged 6) in first class involved 'The Wind'. Pearse observed a lesson on windmills taught entirely through French, followed by a totally different aspect of the topic taught through Flemish. The alternating languages, used successively, covered wind from perspectives in art, geography, mathematics, drawing and singing (*ACS*, 3 February 1906).[99]

By far the most detailed accounts in these bulletins concern the language classes Pearse observed, where he reports at length on how teachers, especially in Molenbeek St Jean in Brussels, applied direct method practices for teaching French, Flemish and German using the Series Method, with the help of *images animées* (versatile cardboard figures, teaching aids manufactured in Brussels) and covering model lessons on how to teach verbs, prepositions, adjectives and so on.[100] Some lessons are printed verbatim from Pearse's notes or memory, presumably to suggest that Irish primary teachers could adapt the same ideas for their own classrooms.[101]

Standing down as editor of *An Claidheamh Soluis*, Pearse was soon to apply the same methods in his experimental school at St Enda's [*Scoil Éanna*], which opened in 1908 in Dublin's Ranelagh, and two years later moved to the more outlying area of Rathfarnham. All subjects taught at St Enda's, apart from modern languages, were taught according to the bilingual principles he had seen applied in Belgium: 'the rule is, whether the subject be Christian Doctrine or Algebra, Nature-Study or Latin, to teach the lesson first in Irish and then repeat it in English, or vice-versa. In such subjects as Dancing and Physical Drill English can practically be dispensed with.'[102] Through his educational contacts in Belgium, Pearse was able to organise school exchanges.[103] Irish, the school's main language, was introduced right from day one, but 'in homeopathic doses, and so pleasantly presented as to appear always as a pastime to be enjoyed and never as a task to be learned.'[104] The school's 1909 prospectus describes how the main language of the school is taught:[105]

> In the general curriculum the first place is accorded to the Irish language, which is taught as a spoken and literary tongue to every pupil. The teaching is by attractive modern methods. Object Lessons, Action Games, Pictures, Working Models, 'Images Animées', the Magic Lantern, and other devices of up-to-date Continental teachers being freely adopted. Irish is established as the official language of the School, and is, as far as possible, the ordinary medium of communication between teachers and pupils.

The prospectus goes on to explain how English and continental languages, modern and ancient, fit in to the school's bilingual scheme:

> All Modern Language teaching is on the Direct Method. To boys who are Irish-speaking to start with, English is taught on the Direct Method; and to boys who are English-speaking to start with, Irish is taught on the Direct Method. Foreign languages other than English (French, German, Italian, and Spanish) are taught on the same attractive lines. Under this system it is hoped that every pupil who passes through St. Enda's will, at the end of his course, have obtained a good oral and literary knowledge of at least three modern languages. Latin is taught to all boys in the upper forms, and Greek and Old Irish to such as exhibit an aptitude for classical studies.

When St Enda's moved to Rathfarnham in 1911 and the vacant boys' school premises in Ranelagh was used to open a girls' school, Scoil Íde, the teaching approaches adopted in the boys' school were mirrored. The profile of the girls' school's first manager is unusual but strangely pertinent to our story.[106] Daughter of Young Irelander and editor of *The Nation* Charles Gavan Duffy by his third marriage, Louise Gavan Duffy (1884–1969) was born and brought up in Nice. Aged 18, she visited Ireland for the first time to attend her father's funeral (February 1903) in Glasnevin. Curiosity about her Gaelic roots had haunted her as a teenager – ever since she found an Irish grammar among her father's books and heard that it was a language unknown to him that had been spoken by his mother. Impelled by a consuming interest, she joined the Gaelic League to learn Irish, a language in which she quickly excelled and included in her degree from UCD in 1911. She was to become a noted educationalist, co-founding Scoil Bhríde, an Irish-speaking girls' school in the capital[107] and lecturing on language pedagogy in UCD's Education Department. She held a Cambridge teaching diploma (1913) and her master's thesis (1916) was on French women's education in the early nineteenth century.

Her profile is of interest to this chronicle on a number of counts, not just because of her sex (a later chapter will discuss other professional women linguists of the same period). She also exemplifies another aspect of European–Irish ties in the sphere of language study, that of the Irish diaspora returning to connect with their heritage. Finally, as the daughter of an early Victorian cultural nationalist, Louise Gavan Duffy exemplifies part of the long-drawn-out cultural shift charted in this book. The combined lifespans of father (*b.*1815) and daughter (*d.*1969) well exceed the long nineteenth century of Irish people's engagement in language learning. Bookended politically by Napoleon's defeat at Waterloo and the Hague Summit's commitment to an enlarged European Community, it is a period marked by profound changes at every level of language study.

★ ★ ★

Over the last three chapters we have considered how firstly modern continental languages, and then modern Irish, came to earn a central role in the Irish education system. In Ireland, as elsewhere, the classics set the pedagogic agenda: the way Latin and Greek had been taught, since formal schools began, generally became the model for teaching modern languages in schools. The time-honoured formula involved a curriculum devoted to the study of grammar and the exercise of prose translation, with exposure to extracts from samples of canonical written texts that illustrated the language's culture. Emphasis was placed on the written word.

The trajectory taken by the study of Irish both echoed and departed from this model. As we have discussed, the Victorian period marked two contradictory tendencies with regard to the Irish vernacular: on the one hand, the accelerated ebbing of the living language – even to the threat of extinction – which was undervalued by society and neglected by schools, and on the other hand, an increased prestige attaching to the study of its illustrious ancient ancestor. The golden age of Celtic philology allowed, to an important extent, some continuity with the old bardic schools of scribes and literati, who had sustained the traditional transmission of the language and who adjusted to the new structures of higher learning brought by Irish universities in the mid-century. Even if university students of Celtic were scarce for a few decades, Old Irish was now valued outside the groves of academe, and well beyond Ireland's shores. The emerging discipline established, scientifically, that there was something genuinely separate and unique about Irish heritage that distinguished it from other nations. This was to have lasting effects on cultural nationalism. Thanks to the textual work of the scholars and scribes who edited and translated the ancient sagas, folktales and saints' lives, the cultural world embodied by those texts was filtered through to the anglophone literary and cultural nation-builders of later generations. Then, in the closing years of Queen Victoria's reign, a group of ardent revivalists orchestrated a different approach to the teaching of the modern Irish vernacular that won widespread popular support and succeeded in radically altering the fate of the language.

The pace of cultural change can be glacially slow until sudden historical events, or policy decisions taken by governments or institutions, give the impetus to behavioural changes that redraw the landscape, generating, in their turn, new expectations and assumptions. In the history of how language study became embedded in the formalised architecture of Ireland's education system, certain dates emerge as crucial watersheds. As we have seen, the key gear shift moments for Victorian Ireland's engagement with modern languages include the 1846 Queen's Colleges Board decision to foreground modern language study, the 1855 reform for Civil Service recruitment, the 1878 Intermediate Certificate Act, and the 1880 RUI matriculation requirement. Where Irish is concerned, the milestones of 1878, which gave some recognition to Celtic at both primary and intermediate levels, and of 1880, which saw Celtic included in the RUI matriculation, had little impact on the actual take-up of Irish study in schools. For Irish in schools, the more important dates were the founding of the Gaelic League in 1893, leading both to radical changes in the national school curriculum and teacher training, and to the decision that Irish would be required for the NUI's matriculation examination from 1913. These were the catalysts for enormous cultural change that was to be further reinforced by the coming of political independence. Irish people continue to live with the consequences of these key language policy directions, mostly set in Victorian Ireland.

These developments inevitably give rise to questions. How did the zeal for Irish songs and stories, folklore and folkdances, play out in Irish-language teaching after 1922? How influential in the long run was the modern language reforming approach to teaching Irish? Was the novelty of an approach based on the spoken language sustained? To what extent did it generate similar approaches to the teaching and learning of continental languages? And how did the study of European languages fare alongside the study of Irish?

Before returning to these questions in our final chapter, in order to understand more clearly how things turned out after independence we must first look at the influential individuals who taught modern languages at university level. In Part Three, we shall first profile Victorian Ireland's modern language professors, where they came from and how they approached their work; this will be followed by a chapter appraising two prominent sets of home-grown pioneers at university level from the late Victorian and Edwardian decades: the professors of modern Irish and the first women language professors, and how they exemplify a changing cultural landscape in the years leading to political independence.

5.3 Douglas Hyde, Professor of Modern Irish, UCD, & first President of Ireland
Irish postage stamp, issued in 2010, to commemorate the 150th anniversary of Hyde's birth. (© *An Post. Courtesy of the An Post Museum and Archive.*)

PART THREE: WITHIN THE GROVES OF ACADEME

Profiles and Patterns: Modern Language Professors

Is that the way in which our Irish University is to be Professored? [Edmund Hayes Q. C., 1856][1]

Skill in Greek and Latin versification has indeed no direct tendency to form a judge, a financier, or a diplomatist. But the youth who does best what all the ablest and most ambitious youths about him are trying to do well will generally prove a superior man. [Macaulay Report, 1854][2]

The Science of Language is a science of very modern date. We cannot trace its lineage much beyond the beginning of our century, and it is scarcely received as yet on a footing of equality by the elder branches of learning. Its very name is still unsettled [...]. We hear it spoken of as Comparative Philology, Scientific Etymology, Phonology, and Glossology. In France it has received the convenient, but somewhat barbarous, name of Linguistique. [Max Müller, 1861][3]

Who taught modern languages in Ireland's Victorian universities?[4] Where did the professors come from? How were they selected? What motivated them? What research did they publish? What tactics did they deploy to teach living foreign languages to anglophone or hibernophone students? What kinds of curriculum did they expect their students to follow? Why were some of them controversial figures?

This chapter will consider the earliest professors of modern languages, all of them male and most of them foreign, before moving on, in the following chapter, to discuss the newcomers in the early 1900s: professors of modern Irish, together with Ireland's first women professors, a large number of whom happened to be modern language graduates.

We could open our discussion with Trinity College Dublin, distinguished home (since 1776) of the world's first modern language chairs.[5] However, rather than proceeding chronologically across the Irish universities, rehearsing scholarship already available on individual language departments and professors, our entry point into a broader discussion will be the first appointments at the Catholic University, the least endowed and most anomalous of the four Victorian college foundations. Starting with UCD's Victorian antecedent has some merit. From its rather incidental beginnings as the CUI, the St Stephen's Green college in the capital was to grow into the country's largest university and become an influential driver of the educational and political changes which it is our purpose to describe. Profiling (for the first time) its earliest modern language professors yields useful comparators with appointments made in other colleges, including Trinity, and helps to frame the changes in language learning, over time, that we are charting.[6]

As we shall see, the first four professors employed to teach French and German at the Catholic University – and later at the Jesuit-run University College within the RUI – were atypical in more than one respect. These individuals' biographical traces are unevenly distributed and turn up in unexpected sources. As pioneers in the field, the earliest of them followed paths that nowadays might be viewed as eccentric or haphazard. We shall take them chronologically, before discussing how their profiles compare with those of third-level modern language professors appointed elsewhere in Ireland during Queen Victoria's reign.

EARLY APPOINTMENTS AT THE CUI (UCD)

Peter le Page Renouf

Newman's pick for French Literature, Peter le Page Renouf (1822–97), has been studied, and amply documented, by Kevin Cathcart.[7] Renouf is not however remembered for his work in modern languages. His real interest was ancient history; he became a distinguished scholar in oriental languages, ending his career as Keeper of Egyptian and Assyrian Antiquities at the British Museum. He was knighted in 1896.

The confusion surrounding Renouf's initial CU appointment reflects the chaotic way in which the university was established, and the strange position in which John Henry Newman found himself, dependent as rector on the goodwill of the Irish church hierarchy. The labyrinthine political machinations of Archbishop Cullen's handling of dissent among his fellow bishops led to mysterious delays and uncertainties. In spring 1854, Renouf's correspondence speaks of an offer of a 'lectureship' from Newman, but he is unclear about what the job entailed, and when it was likely to begin. Would it involve history, or literature, or philosophy? Eventually, the appointment was to a lectureship in French literature.[8]

The rector was (justifiably) satisfied with the young man's qualifications as well as his religious affiliations.[9] Extremely versatile, and with broad intellectual interests, Renouf was a bilingual from Guernsey whom Newman had known as a Theology student in Oxford and was (like Newman) an Anglican convert to Roman Catholicism. After stepping down from Oxford following his conversion, he studied oriental languages and church history in Birmingham. When he agreed to take up Newman's offer of a lectureship in French Literature, Renouf was in France. He had been living for several years in

6.1 Peter le Page Renouf, CUI Lecturer in French, CUI. (Meretseger Books. *No known copyright restrictions.*)

an aristocratic household in Besançon, as tutor to the son of the Comte de Vaulchier. This young man, the *vicomte* Louis de Vaulchier, accompanied Renouf to Dublin in autumn 1854 where he was one of the 17 students (including Daniel O'Connell's grandson) to enrol in the CUI in its first year. Both Renouf and his pupil lodged in the university residence known as St Mary's, number 6 Harcourt Street, along with Newman himself and some other students and staff members.[10] Occasional glimpses of life there suggest decorous conviviality: 'After *Pranzo*, the *giovanotti* retired to their drawing-room and I, Newman, and Renouf sat and cosed over some port wine and biscuits for an hour.'[11]

After his marriage (1857) to Ludovica Brentano, niece of the German poet Clemens Brentano, Renouf moved to live in Tivoli Terrace, Kingstown. At work he was increasingly demoralised by low student numbers and an inadequate salary, besides which, his German wife found it difficult to settle in Dublin. She reports to her mother-in-law in 1861: 'It is indeed too bad that Ireland with all its other faults is almost quite at the world's end'.[12] Financial pressures on the young household prompted Renouf to offer to share (with J. B. Robertson, Professor of modern history and geography) the vacant chair of English on the departure of Thomas Arnold in 1862.

Renouf seems to have lectured in French and German for only the first of the nine years he spent in Dublin. By 1855–6[13] he had taken up the chair of ancient history and geography, a post he held until he left Ireland to work in the schools inspectorate in England, in the spring of 1864. He received warm tributes from colleagues on his departure. The man from Guernsey had participated fully in College life from the start, assiduously attending Faculty meetings. Shortly after arriving, he gave an inaugural lecture on 'The Literary History of France', as one of seven public lectures given by staff members. His was fourth in the series; his colleague Augusto Cesare Marani (Italian and Spanish) gave the sixth, on 'The Origin and Rise of the Italian Language and Literature'.[14]

The paucity of students in the CU allowed Renouf time to pursue research interests that were to shape his subsequent career as an Egyptologist at the British Museum. Within a few years, he was teaching himself how to decipher hieroglyphs, and published a paper on the subject in the *Atlantis*, the CU's research journal which he helped to edit.[15] While still in Dublin, he had given an early indication of this final stage in his career: a meeting of the CU's Literary and Historical Debating Society, in February 1857, heard his address on 'The Formation of Alphabets as Illustrated by Egyptian Hieroglyphs.'[16]

This first profile shows how eclectic the academic community could be in a new Victorian university seeking to establish itself in the midst of a myriad of impediments and shortcomings. As we shall see, Renouf's was by no means the only seemingly random academic appointment in mid-nineteenth-century Ireland. In 1854, few, if anyone, had a formal 'qualification' (in the modern sense) to teach modern literature at university level.[17]

L'abbé Félix Schürr

Renouf was replaced by Félix Schürr (1827–1900),[18] about whom we can piece together the briefest of sketches from disparate fragmentary sources. This secular priest from Dambach in Alsace, son of a prosperous winegrower, was born in 1827 and ordained in Paris before leaving Europe as a missionary to work among West Indian slaves. Obliged to return to Paris on contracting yellow fever, he met Archbishop Paul Cullen, who offered him the position of Professor of French and German at All Hallows, Drumcondra, Dublin. As mentioned in Chapter Two above,[19] 'M. F. Abbé Schürr' appears on their staff list for 1853–5. His address is given as 3 St George's Place, North Circular Road, Dublin. He then moved to the CU, having been introduced to Newman by the All Hallows' president, Dr Moriarty.[20] He is listed under French and German on Catholic University staff lists from 1855 to 1870.[21] Given the low student numbers, he had some time for pastoral work in Drumcondra, in addition to his teaching duties.[22]

6.2 Abbé Félix Schürr, CUI Lecturer in French and German, CUI. Press photograph (*The Catholic Press*, Sydney, NSW, Sat. 2 July 1900, p. 11).

The Rev. Schürr also had a connection with Blackrock College. He had studied for a time near Amiens with the congregation of Holy Ghost fathers founded by Fr Francis Libermann, also from Alsace, a Jewish convert to Catholicism. Blackrock's founder, Jules Leman, had studied there at the same period. Schürr proved a valuable 'interpreter and guide' to local customs for the French priests when they first arrived in Ireland.[23]

After 17 years in Dublin, Fr Schürr returned to missionary work, this time as a pioneering priest in the Richmond Valley in New South Wales – at the request of Cork-born Timothy O'Mahony, Bishop of Armidale (a new diocese).[24] He spent the remaining 30 years of his life there and was fondly remembered: 'he always carried a small organ, bringing entertainment and spiritual sustenance through music and song to isolated timber camps and farmers.'[25] His obituarist describes him as, by all accounts, a well-esteemed and kindly pastor, generous and energetic, attracting friends of all creeds. A death notice in the Sydney *Freeman's Journal* (July 1900) describes Fr Schürr as a musical man, and also points out his gift for oral communication in different languages: 'it mattered not whether you spoke English, French, German, or Italian to Father Schürr – they were all one to him. He could read and speak Irish.'[26] This last remark may well be broadly trustworthy, if only because Archbishop Cullen, who hired the French priest, would have recognised a linguist when he met one.[27]

L'abbé Georges Polin

Fr Schürr's successor, l'abbé Georges Polin (d.1889), was another native of Alsace, where French and German have been weaponised by successive regimes since the seventeenth century. During the Franco-German war of 1870–1, a number of French secular priests fled to Ireland and were given refuge in the French College in Blackrock. Fr Polin was one of them. He had been tutoring the sons of the Comte de Leusse, in their château at Reichshoffen in the Bas-Rhin (Lower Rhine) region. The count's older son, Guy, accompanied his clerical tutor to Ireland and enrolled as a pupil in the Blackrock school on 1 September 1872.[28]

Blackrock's refugee priests taught European languages. As we saw in Chapter Three, the College had the capacity to absorb more staff in the early 1870s, when it was expanding its remit to include senior students preparing Civil Service and University examinations.

'L'abbé G. Polin B.A.' appears on its Staff List (Modern Languages) for 1873–5.[29] From 1873, he was also teaching in St Stephen's Green[30] on a temporary basis, having been introduced to the Catholic University's Rector, Monsignor Bartholomew Woodlock. He was appointed to a permanent post in French and German in 1875 and was retained by the Jesuits after the Royal University was set up.[31]

L'abbé Polin held a primary degree and was apparently a gifted linguist with extensive literary interests.[32] Prior to leaving Alsace, he had attended monthly meetings of the *Société littéraire de Strasbourg*, a learnèd society of clerics and lay professionals, Catholic and Protestant. They met to discuss literary works, ancient and modern, but preferably concentrating their deliberations 'sur la littérature française et sur la littérature allemande, ainsi que sur leur corrélation mutuelle' [on French literature and German literature, as well as on their reciprocal connexions]. He had also been teaching in a *petit séminaire* [junior seminary], or Catholic secondary school for boys in Strasbourg.[33]

Polin's profile proved a promising match for his university post. He was made a Royal University of Ireland examiner in 1882 and elected to a fellowship in modern languages in 1884.[34] The fellowship also entailed a chair.[35] During the pioneering years of the campaign for the endowment and equal treatment of women's colleges, l'abbé Polin was among the small group of RUI professors to volunteer to lecture to women students.[36] He was a colleague of Gerard Manley Hopkins, Professor of Classics, during the last years of the poet's life. Both professors died in the summer of 1889.

Édouard Cadic

The profile of UCD's last (and longest-lasting) Victorian Professor of French, the Breton Édouard Cadic (1858–1914),[37] suggests a less eccentric appointment, perhaps because (unlike his predecessors) he was appointed by open competition through Dublin Castle. Born in Guidel, in the Morbihan region of Brittany, he was a miller's son, educated at the Breton *petit séminaire* of Sainte-Anne-d'Auray. This Catholic diocesan school, founded in 1815, harboured a distrust of State exams and only started to prepare students for the national *baccalauréat* in 1872.[38] After that date, its academic standard greatly improved.[39] Which was in time for Cadic, then aged 14. He went on to study literature in Paris and Germany. His doctorate was obtained from Paris.

What first brought him to Ireland is unclear, but he seems to have been working already in Dublin by the age of 20. In October 1877 he is named as an assistant master in French Language and Literature in an ad for a Catholic High School in Kingstown; we find him offering private French classes in Sandymount early in 1879: 'Monsieur Cadic's French Evening Classes for Gentlemen Resume on the 3rd January, at his residence, 133 Tritonville Road, Sandymount. Beginners are taught separately.'[40] Two years later he appears on the staff of the University and Civil Service Institute in Harcourt Street.[41] According to himself, he taught French language and literature in several other educational settings, presumably on an hourly basis, in these early years.[42] This teaching experience introduced the Frenchman to different constituencies of language-learners in an exceptionally varied range of Irish educational settings, from a Protestant school in Kingstown to the Queen's Institute for training impoverished gentlewomen, from Alexandra College to the Roman Catholic Teacher Training College at Drumcondra which had just been opened by the Vincentians in 1875.[43] Hired by the RUI as an examiner in French in 1892, he was appointed fellow and Professor of French and Romanic Philology at University College two years later,[44] and continued to work in UCD after it became a constituent college of the NUI.[45] His career attracted several distinctions: the French Government made him a *chevalier dans l'ordre des Palmes académiques*, an *officier de l'instruction publique* in 1894, and *chevalier de la Légion d'Honneur* in 1900, while the Senate of the RUI awarded him an honorary D.Lit. in 1902.

In University College, Cadic was an enthusiastic and popular professor, who enjoyed teaching abler students and was known for his love of literature.[46] Among the students who passed through his classrooms were George Clancy, Seumas O'Kelly and James Joyce. Richard Ellmann's biography of Joyce records a couple of anecdotes about the young writer as a UCD student (1898–1902) indulging in tomfoolery and pranks to alarm his kindly French professor. Cadic recognised Joyce's genius for verbal invention.[47] Both French professor and student appear in a group photograph taken *c.*1901. Professor Cadic looks saturnine, with an earnest face and a large black moustache.[48]

6.3 Édouard Cadic, RUI Dublin, in Iveagh Gardens. (Seated, second row, third from left.) 1902 Professor of French. In a group photographed after the UCD BA graduation (1902). (Reproduced from the original negative in UCD Special Collections by kind permission of Professor Helen Solterer.)

Sources reveal a man who threw himself into extramural engagements and activities with generosity. As founder and president of the French and German Reading Society and the Modern Languages Society, Cadic entertained groups of students and others who came to read plays in French or German in his own home. A diary entry of Joseph Plunkett's for January 1911 records participation at one of these sessions: 'Fri. 20th. Cough. Franco-German rehearsal in evening at Cadic's. [...] Read at rehearsal. Cadic pleased.'[49] Professor Cadic also chaired student debates[50] and was one of the staff members who gave external lectures on French literary topics for the general public.[51] Indeed, his name crops up again and again in press accounts that summarise the content of his lectures, on French literary or historical figures, delivered in English or in French, to a wide variety of audiences and settings, including University College, the Catholic Commercial Club in Upper O'Connell Street, the Modern Languages Society in Queen's University Belfast, the Theatre of the

Royal Dublin Society in Leinster House, the United Arts Club in Lincoln Place.[52] In today's academic parlance, this extramural engagement with the public would be regarded as excellent cultural 'outreach' and 'impact'.

It is possible that his public persona may also have been favourably regarded in France. Having been decorated for his services to the highly centralised 'instruction publique' [public education] of his home country by spreading its literary culture abroad, Cadic seems to have understood that his work as Professor of French in a foreign university included a role of cultural ambassador. When accepting his *Légion d'Honneur* in 1900, he ends his career summary on an unambiguously patriotic note, describing himself as 'toujours désireux de propager l'amour de son pays et de venir en aide dans l'humble mesure de ses forces à ses compatriotes malheureux' [never failing to spread the love of his country and, in his own small way, to come to the aid of his unhappy compatriots].[53] French cultural diplomacy was very vibrant from the 1870s onwards, with bodies like the Alliance Française being founded in 1883 and the *Bureau des écoles et des œuvres françaises à l'étranger* established in 1910. In the imperial climate of the turn of the twentieth century, Cadic's self-appraisal for the *Légion d'Honneur* adds a further dimension to the role of a French professor abroad.[54]

While he lectured on mainstream French history and literature, Édouard Cadic never lost touch with his native Brittany, and helped to fund some charities in his birthplace, Guidel. His friends included the Breton poet and folklore scholar Anatole Le Braz (1859–1926), who worked at the University of Rennes, and the teacher and novelist Charles Le Goffic (1863–1926).

Coming from the region of France with a Celtic language, the Breton expatriate seems to have felt affinities with Edwardian Ireland. Besides Joyce, another of his former students was Patrick Pearse.[55] Cadic wrote a character reference for Pearse in 1905, and he is listed as one of the invited external contributors to the 1910–11 series of weekly lectures given on half-holidays to pupils of Pearse's bilingual school at St Enda's.[56] As a Breton who kept in touch with Breton writers and scholars, Cadic doubtless understood, and even sympathised with, the motivations of the Gaelic League as well as the ideological debates over compulsory Irish for the NUI matriculation. He joined the League's Executive Committee in 1898[57] and attended (and chaired) meetings of the Irish Committee of the Pan-Celtic Congress at the Royal Irish Academy at the turn of the century.[58]

The French professor was well-liked and respected in Dublin, where he organised a relief collection for victims of the great Seine floods that hit Paris in early 1910.[59] What emerges is a most obliging foreign professor with a presence and visibility in the cultural life of the Edwardian city, reliable enough to be asked to chair meetings and to turn up and lecture on the French literary tradition. At the same time Cadic was well attuned to the hibernophilia of the period. Although it is not certain that he studied Irish himself, it must have been psychologically affirming, for Gaelic League members, to find in their midst a continental language professor whom they regarded as the very model of a cultured French gentleman who acknowledged the importance of *celtitude* [the state of being Celtic]. Such endorsements of the goals of the Irish Revival, from foreign cultural gatekeepers, had considerable weight.

Following a short illness at the close of 1913, the Breton professor died on 9 January the following year. After requiem mass in a packed University Church he was buried before a

6.4 Tombstone of Édouard Cadic (*d.*1914) Glasnevin Cemetery, Dublin. Episcopal chair, designed by William A. Scott, erected 1917. Photographed by Léan Ní Chuilleanáin (2024).

6.4a Tombstone medallion of Édouard Cadic Glasnevin Cemetery, Dublin. Photographed by Léan Ní Chuilleanáin (2024).

large crowd in Glasnevin cemetery, where he lies under an imposing limestone memorial, shaped like an episcopal chair and ornamented with a blend of Celtic and French renaissance motifs.[60] The monument was the work of William Alphonsus Scott, who had also designed the Hiberno-Romanesque memorial tombstone of Eugene O'Growney in Maynooth cemetery.[61] At the monument's unveiling on 1 November 1917, Peter Byrne, C.M., LL.D. praised the deceased in words that paraphrase the epitaph inscribed in Celticised art nouveau script on the stone: 'Édouard Cadic will always live in our memory, and will hold after death, as during life, the first place in our esteem and affection.'[62]

WHAT PATTERNS EMERGE FROM THESE AND OTHER SUCH PROFILES?

In this brief case study of UCD's first four modern language professors, we have seen a shift from Renouf, an Egyptologist rather than a French scholar, to the more 'professional' Cadic, a man trained to the task in Paris, decorated for his services to the French education system, recognised by officialdom consciously engaged in spreading French culture abroad, and much esteemed by those who knew and befriended him in Dublin. This shift reflects the changing cultural context from the 1850s to the turn of the twentieth century.

At the same time, taken as a group, UCD's early appointments in French and German share some commonalities. They were Roman Catholic men, and – leaving Renouf aside – all teachers rather than scholars. There were parallels between the education experience of Irish and French Catholics at this period, which may have helped both Georges Polin and Édouard Cadic feel on familiar ground when working in the CU/UCD. Ireland's denominational private school system must have felt familiar to the Frenchmen, each of whom had experience of a *petit séminaire* – the former as a teacher and the latter as a pupil. While French Catholic diocesan seminaries – *grands séminaires* – were restored in 1801 to allow training for ordination, the *petits séminaires* (like Irish junior seminaries) were boys' boarding schools that admitted pupils not intending to lead a clerical life. Significant for social mobility in rural areas, these Catholic institutions offered a classical education, as well as a Catholic ethos and a strict disciplinary code. Ireland's diocesan schools were culturally similar, even well into the twentieth century.

How representative were these profiles, compared with linguists in other Victorian universities in Ireland?[63] What was the professional context in which they worked? We shall note further echoes – and also contrasts – as we consider profiles of their peers in other institutions, approaching these thematically rather than individually.

Language professors at Irish universities: foreigners, refugees, academics, amateurs

All of the Catholic University's early appointments in modern languages were foreign nationals. This was in line with the rest of Ireland's Victorian modern linguists, both in Dublin University and the Queen's University. They had all come from mainland Europe, until 1869, when Trinity College Dublin appointed one of its own graduates, Anglo-Irishman Robert Atkinson, to romance languages; ten years later, in 1879, Cork filled its modern languages chair with an Irishman and Cork graduate, Owen O'Ryan.

There is a discernible pattern in terms of the linguistic zones from which these Europeans hailed, perhaps due to the manner in which their recruitment was carried out. The CU's narrow head-hunting approach, whereby its first linguists were mostly pursued through personal clerical contacts,[64] contrasts significantly with the public recruitment process followed by the Queen's University when it was set up. The Queen's Colleges process attracted a very wide field of able candidates. These were invited to apply to the Lord Lieutenant by a certain date, submitting testimonials. Applications were received from various parts of Europe, including an abundance of modern linguists with extensive teaching experience, who were interested in working for the Crown in the new universities in Belfast, Cork or Galway.[65]

The upshot was that the CU's Victorian appointments came from peripheral, partly French-speaking regions – the Channel Islands, Alsace and (later, when UCD was part of the RUI) Brittany – while the Queen's Colleges' foreign-born linguists, with one exception, all came from Germanic backgrounds. Cork's first modern language professor, Louis-Raymond de Véricour (Professor, 1849–79), was the only Frenchman appointed out of a total of 60 chairs (in all disciplines) across the three Queen's Colleges in 1849.[66] He was a Swiss-born French Protestant, and his Huguenot identity contrasted with the Roman Catholicism of the Catholic University's appointments. Belfast's Mathias Joseph Frings (Professor, 1849 to 1862), Johann Wilhelm Frädersdorff (Professor, 1862 to 1865) and Albert Ludwig Meissner (Professor, 1865 to 1902), came respectively from Berlin, Hamburg and Jüterbog in Prussia. Galway's first three modern linguists, as their names suggest, were also Germanophone: August(us) Bensbach (Professor, 1849–68), Charles (Karl) Geisler (Professor, 1868–86) and Valentine Steinberger (Professor, 1886–1916, also Librarian from 1902). Bensbach, from Mannheim,[67] was a graduate of Heidelberg, Geisler was from Prussia and Steinberger, who 'had studied in Munich, Rome, Naples, and Paris', was a native of Bavaria.[68] Albert Maximilian Selss, Trinity College's Professor of German from 1866 to 1907, was from the Rhineland.

Foreign nationals could be relied on to know their own language – or languages. Both French priests, Félix Schürr and Georges Polin, were from Alsace, the region where the two 'main' modern languages, French and German, coexisted. This bilingualism had obvious advantages for an Irish university, and the CU was not alone in availing of it. Ignatius Georg Abeltshauser, who was Professor of French and German in Trinity from 1842 to 1866, was also Alsatian.[69] Trinity College's first Professor of French and German was bilingual too: Antoine D'Esca, probably descended from a Huguenot family, had lived as an exile in Berlin.[70]

Not all Victorian professors of modern languages came with a linguistic background. Augustus Bensbach had qualified as a medical doctor in Heidelberg before taking up the first modern language chair in Galway. Before modern language degrees became common, the qualifications to teach them were more fluid than nowadays. In this unregulated labour market, the same could apply to employment in older university disciplines. On his appointment in 1849, Cork's brilliant first professor of mathematics, George Boole, had never studied at a university.[71] When J. P. Mahaffy went up to Trinity in 1855, he was quite unimpressed by its Classicists, one of whom was an economist, and another a mathematician.[72]

However, the majority of Ireland's nineteenth-century modern language professors were native speakers with a teaching background. This was the profile of the CU's Renouf, Schürr, Polin and Cadic, all of whom came with teaching experience, whether in domestic, school or college settings, in France or in Ireland. Prior to taking up their posts, Queen's College Belfast's modern linguists, too, all had a significant range of teaching experience as well as relevant qualifications: Mathias Frings had been a secondary teacher of French in Berlin and then a private instructor of French and German in Dublin for nearly a decade;[73] Johann Wilhelm Frädersdorff had taught German and Dutch for 15 years at the Taylorian Institution in Oxford;[74] Albert Meissner had been a schoolmaster and had then taught classics and modern languages at the Bristol Baptist Academy for 12 years.[75] Cork's Louis-Raymond de Véricour had taught at the *Athénée Royal* in Paris, a prestigious secondary school, and had been principal of the Educational Institution, Twickenham,[76] while Galway's Charles (Karl) Geisler had worked as a language teacher in St Petersburg.[77] His successor Valentine Steinberger came to Galway with even wider experience, having taught in various settings in Ireland since 1879: St Malachy's College, Belfast, Bangor Endowed School and the Belfast Royal Academy, where he had been headmaster of the modern languages department from 1880 to 1886.[78] Trinity's Ignatius Georg Abeltshauser had taught French and German privately in Dublin for over a decade before taking up his chair.[79]

What motivated these foreign gentlemen to remain in the remotest part of north-west Europe, and in several cases to take out British nationality?[80] Apart from economic security,[81] there may have been personal motives. Belfast's Frings married a clergyman's daughter from Croom, Co. Limerick;[82] Galway's Steinberger had married a Coleraine woman in 1880;[83] Trinity's A. M. Selss married a Dubliner.[84] Others – like Georges Polin – had come to Ireland seeking political or religious asylum and, like many refugees before and since, turned to language teaching to earn a living. Indeed, the phenomenon of migrants and refugees teaching their mother tongue when exiled abroad was a common pattern throughout Europe and the new world.[85] Antonio Alcalá Galiano, a political refugee from Spain with no teaching background, was appointed to the first chair of Spanish at University College London in 1828.[86] Likewise, the Rev. Lorenzo Lucena, Taylorian teacher of Spanish at Oxford from 1858, was a convert to the Protestant faith fleeing the Inquisition.[87]

Trinity's Professor of Italian and Spanish from 1824 to 1849, Evasio Antioco Radice, was a political exile from northern Italy. Escaping a death sentence following the Piedmontese Rising in 1821, he had come to work in Dublin after first spending some time in Spain and then in England, with other Italian political exiles. He had contacts with Giuseppe Mazzini, champion of Italian unification and founder of Young Italy. Neither a linguist nor a scholar, he had acquired teaching experience in a military academy for a short period, while serving as a captain in the Sardinian army.[88] The call of Italian politics was too strong, and in January 1849 he resigned from his

6.5 Evasio Radice, Italian and Spanish, TCD Portrait, *c.*1840, by unknown artist. (*Reasonable efforts to contact the Radice family have been made.*)

Dublin post to return to a parliamentary career in Turin, dying of cholera in 1855. While in Trinity, he was an energetic lecturer and seems to have devoted himself to his work with excessive zeal:[89]

> We learn from the Board minutes and the University calendars of the time that he volunteered to deliver lectures in Spanish and Italian literature without fee, that he established the practice that professors of modern languages should be in their chambers three days every week in order to receive pupils; that one day a week he delivered 'a prelection of the literature of some of the southern nations of Europe', that he taught not just Italian and Spanish but also invaded the territory of his colleague, Charles Williomier, professor of French and German, without any recorded objection on the latter's part.

Radice's profile illustrates how individuals without formal qualifications can be highly effective teachers. Ann Frost observes that in Hispanic studies, most nineteenth-century university teachers in British universities were non-specialists, ranging[90]

> through an unorthodox but colourful mix: from native speakers, many of them refugees, who were simply making a living by promoting their native tongue, through Italians, whose language, as a university discipline, was often taught in tandem with Spanish, and sometimes even ranked more highly, to a mixture of poets, writers and intellectuals.

Many apparently unqualified individuals made excellent Spanish teachers, displaying enormous enthusiasm for their subject. The syndrome was confined neither to continental migrants, nor to the Victorian age. Frost cites the case of J. B. Trend. Appointed in 1933 to be the first incumbent of the chair of Spanish at Cambridge, Professor Trend[91] had no official qualifications in Spanish. His degree was in Natural Sciences, but his overwhelming knowledge of, and passion for Spain and things Spanish outweighed all other considerations. He would prove to be a major player in the promotion of Hispanism.

She also cites Irish examples from the twentieth century. W. C. Cooke, appointed to UCC in 1916, was 'a practising solicitor, who had no formal qualifications in Spanish' but had South American contacts; Trinity's eccentric Walter Starkie, appointed to the college's first chair of Spanish in 1926, was 'a popular travel writer, translator and consummate violinist' with a degree in Classics and a passion for Spain.[92] However, as we shall now discover, such flexible criteria for appointments were not without their risks and pitfalls.

A foreign gentleman is unseated: Angeli v. Galbraith (1856)

One of the hardy perennials in learning living languages is the debate about whether to be taught by a native speaker of the target language or to employ a teacher from the learners' language and culture. This long-running debate has come particularly into focus since the late nineteenth century, when qualified graduates began to emerge in countries where the foreign language is studied.[93] There are merits on both sides of the argument. While native speakers have superior command of their mother-tongue and its pronunciation, they sometimes have too shaky a grasp of the learners' own idiom, and of the particular difficulties their language poses for foreign learners, to be effective university teachers. This problem can be especially apparent in the assessment of advanced translation work, where it is important for a professor to be well acquainted with the learner's language.

In 1856, a notorious libel action was heard in the Irish courts, that highlighted precisely the difficulty of assessing the competency and qualifications of foreign-language professors.[94] The case had been simmering for over five years. At stake was the fitness for university teaching of a Trinity College professor, Basilio Angeli, from Lucca in Tuscany. He had been appointed in late 1849 to succeed Evasio Radice when Radice resigned the chair of Italian and Spanish to return to political work in Italy. The new professor had been teaching Spanish and Italian on a commercial basis in Dublin since 1834, when he was 30 years old. However, another Italian, Augusto Cesare Marani, who had stood in for Radice during the latter's absences (on health or political grounds) during the 1840s, confidently expected to succeed him to the vacant post. Marani was unsuccessful in his application and, subsequently, also failed to win his appeal against the College's decision. He argued, on a number of grounds, that Angeli was unfit for the position. Two years later, further allegations of Angeli's incompetence were brought to the attention of the College Board. Three distinguished Junior Fellows – Joseph Allen Galbraith, John Kells Ingram and Samuel Haughton – took Marani's side, possibly convinced of its validity from what they saw of their new colleague, Angeli, in action. Their allegations of falsehoods in the Italian's original application were heard in November 1855,[95] leading to the Board's unanimous resolve that Angeli was 'incompetent to discharge the duties of the Professorship of Italian and Spanish'.[96] He was removed from office; Marani deputised and was eventually appointed professor in 1862.[97]

After his dismissal, Angeli sued for libel and slander against Galbraith. He lost the suit, despite being represented by the distinguished barrister and politician Isaac Butt. McDowell and Webb relate:[98]

> The case was heard in July 1856 at Athy, and for five days a jury of stolid Kildare citizens had to listen to imported Italian witnesses swearing alternately that certain phrases were gross errors or legitimate Tuscan pleonasms. Not surprisingly the jury was unable to agree, and the case had to be re-tried in Dublin in November. After interminable bickering between counsel as to the admissibility of certain evidence the jury indicated that they thought that the plaintiff had made no case that required answer, and judgment was entered for Galbraith.

The deciding document against Angeli was his translation, from English into Italian, of Sir Robert Kane's inaugural address as founding President of Queen's College Cork on 7 November 1849. Sir Robert had commissioned a translation for the purpose of sending it to the Holy See, vainly hoping 'that his sentiments might soften Roman intransigence'[99] against the Queen's colleges. The pivotal testimony was the damning opinion of the translation's quality given in court by Antonio Panizzi, then head of the British Museum and former Professor of Italian and Spanish at the University of London.

Leaving aside the inappropriateness of asking an Irish jury in an open court to assess the quality of a written Italian document, there do seem to have been serious problems with the plaintiff's translation from English, and with his basic language sense.[100] Other factors, brought to light in an unseemly way, included the deficiency of Angeli's command of Spanish, not helped by his refusal to sit an examination in the language set by the College Board. Of more gravity than his language competency, the curriculum vitae that he had submitted with his application for the chair was found to have been misleading, not to say untruthful, in a number of respects. Angeli was found not to have been awarded degrees he implied he had obtained, but to have attended the University of Pisa as a medical student without sitting any examination. It was also revealed that, before taking up the chair, he had worked as an assistant to a *figurista* in the stucco trade, by selling figures made of plaster in the north of England.

The libel case illuminates aspects of university language study in Ireland, 20 years into Victoria's reign, particularly within Dublin University. It yields a sounding of how academics in Ireland's oldest university were coping with the profound changes that were in train, within and outside its walls. Galbraith's defence counsel, Edmund Hayes Q. C., pointed out that modern language professorships were not a sinecure, now that Dublin University had to contend with other universities, and with competitive examinations then barely a year old – examinations in which the three Junior Fellows taking issue with Angeli had a stake:[101]

> thanks be to God, an avenue has been opened up for Irish industry and talent, from which, until lately, we have been entirely excluded. The Competitive Examinations have offered a noble field and incentive to our Irish youth, and, accordingly, no time was lost by my client and his friends, Messrs. Haughton and Ingram, in putting themselves at the head of the movement in the College. They infused new blood into the University, and while Mr. Galbraith and Mr. Haughton are presiding over the Woolwich class, and Mr. Stack and Mr. Jellet and Dr. Ingram over the Indian, the public records of the day testify to the success that has attended their zeal, for we now find gentlemen from Trinity College competing, and successfully competing, with men from the other Universities.

> 9, TRINITY COLLEGE, *August* 23, 1849
>
> MY DEAR SIGNOR ANGELI,—I feel in justice bound to give you the testimonial for which you asked me as to my knowledge of you and your acquirements
>
> I can safely say, that of all the Italians who have taught their own language in Dublin, during the many years which I have lived here, none, as far as my experience goes, has possessed so complete a knowledge of it, or of their literature, that, besides, you possess much general information, and are able to express yourself correctly in the English language.
>
> I have heard many of your pupils express themselves highly pleased with your method, and have myself examined some of them who presented themselves as candidates for prizes, in which they were successful
>
> Moreover, what I consider of great importance, your conduct has been always that of a perfect gentleman, as far as my own observation went, nor did I ever hear anything of you but what was praiseworthy
>
> I remain yours sincerely,
> I. G. ABELTSHAUSER
>
> LR. GLOUCESTER-ST , *September* 12, 1849
>
> MY DEAR SIGNOR ANGELI,—I can have no objection to state, at your request, that I have known you for many years and that I have reason to believe that your literary attainments are of a very high and distinguished kind, and that you possess, in an eminent degree, the faculty of imparting the Italian and Spanish languages to your pupils
>
> I have always considered you a man of respectability as well as ability your command of temper, your gentlemanly manner, combined with your high acquirements in the above-named languages, are such, that I entertain a perfect confidence you will be found, in every respect, adequate to the discharge of your duties, and I sincerely wish you success
>
> Yours truly,
> M J FRINGS,
> *Professor, Queen's College, Belfast*

6.6 Testimonials of Basilio Angeli, Italian and Spanish, TCD (1857) From W. R. Furlong, *Action for Libel: Report of the case of Angeli v. Galbraith* (Dublin, M. H. Gill, 1857), Appendix, p. 500.

The defence also specified the relevance of Italian in the Indian Civil Service examinations. Doing well in the Italian examination could add extra marks to the performance of the best linguists: 'With regard to the Indian class, in order that competitors may distinguish themselves, it is necessary that they should undergo a very searching examination in Italian. Italian is part of their course [...]'.[102]

It was no accident that Hayes alluded to the new Indian Civil Service Examinations: Galbraith, along with other Junior Fellows, were in the vanguard of a new breed of Trinity Fellows, who saw more sharply than their elders, perhaps, the need for their alma mater to move with the times.[103] Still seeing themselves as representing 'our chief University of Ireland', these younger Fellows' awareness of the new rival establishments in Stephen's Green (Dublin), Belfast, Cork and Galway motivated a sense of competition.

In the altered environment, the calibre of modern language professors was of utmost importance. Only a couple of years previously, in 1853 the Dublin University Commission had recommended that 'the study of one Modern Language, at least, should be made compulsory on all candidates for the degree of Bachelor of Arts.'[104] Trinity's Board had ignored this recommendation,[105] but Galbraith and his like had a sense that university teaching of modern languages required more sophistication and depth than language teaching at school level. Witnesses had revealed that the plaintiff, in his classes, was out of his depth when asked 'about the construction of sentences or the difference between languages.' The defence counsel construed that he had a 'knowledge of the language that may do for young ladies' but not for teaching university gentlemen:[106]

> Signor Angeli was not competent to teach Spanish and Italian literature in the way it ought to be taught, not to girls, not to boys, but to men who had learned philosophy, who had studied in the University, men who were competent to discuss the language as philosophers; and a Professor who could not teach it in that way was not worthy of his place as a Professor.

Corinna Salvadori, who alludes to the episode in her account of the fortunes and misfortunes of Italian at Trinity, sees Professor Angeli as perhaps 'more sinned against than sinning'.[107] It is true that he had testimonials from eminent individuals, including the lord lieutenant's private secretary (James Corry Connellan), the president of Queen's College Galway (Rev. Edward Berwick), and two modern linguists (Belfast's Professor Frings and Trinity's

Professor Abeltshauser); and he was able to offer convincing explanations for some, at least, of the alleged 'errors' in his translation of Sir Robert Kane's address.[108] Reading through the minutiae of the legal transcript is like watching a closely contested tennis match, where the evenness of the shots in the endless rallies means the game can go to either player. The triumph of Galbraith, who was hailed by a phalanx of over 500 students and scholars as striking a blow for the protection of the 'fair name' of their University, was by no means a foregone conclusion. Basilio Angeli was unlucky: he had come to work in Trinity College in the pivotal year of 1849. The 1850s brought rapid and far-reaching changes in Ireland's university sector, and the pressures and anxieties arising from those changes were felt most keenly in Dublin's oldest established university. The timing of Angeli's appointment, as much as his deficient academic training, was what led to his dismissal. Conceivably, had he held the chair at an earlier moment, his performance in Spanish and the deficiencies in his teaching style might have been tolerated, and his possibly mendacious curriculum vitae would not have been subjected to such an intense second scrutiny.

Finally, the case shows up the difficulties in appointing a foreign-language professor in an age when, particularly for a new area of study like modern languages, international equivalences between qualifications were unheard of.[109] How could best practice for recruiting modern language professors be determined when the practice itself was barely in its infancy?[110] One of the consequences of the Angeli case, from Trinity's point of view, was to make the College's Board 'feel little enthusiasm for the teaching of modern languages'.[111] The Board was also wary of a change in its function in this regard: from 1862 the appointment of modern language teachers was to pass from the jurisdiction of the Crown to the direct responsibility of the Provost and Senior Fellows of the College.[112]

There was a later, more bitter dispute over academic qualifications, pitting one Queen's College modern language professor against another. After Charles Geisler, who held the Galway chair from 1868 to 1886, was awarded an RUI Fellowship in May 1884, he disappeared and remained absent from his post until his death in Halle in May 1886. This abrupt ending of his career may have occurred because his credentials had been challenged by his Belfast counterpart, the litigious Albert Meissner, a disappointed candidate who believed himself to be better qualified for the vacant Fellowship. Meissner's lobbying even led to the gadfly Tim Healy M.P. challenging the authenticity of Geisler's Göttingen PhD in the House of Commons in August 1884. In November, the Queen's University defended its decision, but Geisler did not return, and his teaching was done by substitutes.[113]

It would be misleading to infer from the foregoing that Victorian linguists tended to be troublesome squabblers. In the main, relations were cordial and collaboration was close between language professors in the different colleges – which was just as well, given the heavy examining load they had to bear and share. Within the four colleges of the RUI, degree examinations were set and assessed in common, and taken in Dublin Castle. By dint of regular meetings and sessions of external examining between institutions, by and large the men got to know and trust each other, and no doubt to pool their wisdom.

Religious allegiances: the vilification of de Véricour

While the religious adherence of a foreign-language professor had little direct academic relevance, it could have cultural or political import in the nineteenth century. In the world of Trinity College, Basilio Angeli was a foreign gentleman in more ways than one: he was an Italian Catholic. Some of the cross-examining during the court case that spelled out the details of his early education in Bagni di Lucca, first with his uncle, a 'Roman Catholic clergyman', and then in a *seminario*, distances him culturally from the Rev. Joseph A. Galbraith, MA, his adversary. By contrast, Evasio Radice, his predecessor, was culturally and politically a different kind of Italian.[114] While in England, Radice and other Italian political refugees had been befriended by dissenting English Protestants who were sympathetic to the emerging Italian nation and anti-papal by definition. He had met his future wife in Norwich in Unitarian circles. One imagines the Radice couple fitting in more easily than Angeli to the social milieu of Dublin University.

True to its royal founder's intentions, that university was of course confessional to its core. The obligation that Trinity's Fellows take holy orders in the Church of Ireland (with few exceptions permitted) was abolished only in 1873, following disestablishment.[115] Trinity's second Professor of French and German, Rev. Francis Bessonnet, had been a minister of the French (Huguenot) church in Dublin.[116] I. G. Abeltshauser, its Professor of French and German from 1842 to 1866, also combined the work of a clergyman with academic life. Ordained in the Church of Ireland shortly after appointment to the chair, he was prebendary of St Audoen's, and in 1859 took up a living at Derralossary in Co. Wicklow. He edited *The Irish Church Journal* for a while.[117] John Pentland Mahaffy, too, was a clergyman, and the son and grandson of clergymen to boot.[118]

Meanwhile, in St Stephen's Green, as we have noted, all four nineteenth-century professors of French and German were Roman Catholics. Two of them were men of the cloth. As for the CU's first Professor of Italian and Spanish, Newman had submitted Marani's name for approval by the archbishops, reassuring them of the Italian's 'high testimonials from persons in Dublin in whose families he had taught,' and Newman had 'heard what is to his credit of his religious profession.'[119] The norm for universities at this period was to be organised on religious lines, and clear confessional loyalties were especially axiomatic for a university whose very existence derived from, and indeed helped to foster, the ethos that took 'mixed' education to mean mixed (and thereby diluted) religious allegiance.[120] Like King's College London, founded in reaction to University College London, the 'godless' College in Gower Street, Dublin's Catholic University was opened to counter the establishment of Ireland's multidenominational Queen's Colleges. The Anglican founders of King's College sought to institute a university that would be utilitarian like their sister college, but strictly denominational at the same time. Its Principal had to be a clergyman, and its teaching staff members of the Church of England.[121]

It is no surprise, then, to find a religious divide between the four Catholic modern linguists holding the chair during the nineteenth-century incarnation of UCD and (with the exception of the disgraced Angeli and his successor, Marani) their non-Catholic counterparts in Trinity College. Of more interest, perhaps, is the fact that their confessional allegiance also set UCD's modern language professors apart from most of their peers in the three new provincial universities during the same period. Although there was no religious test for employment at the secular Queen's Colleges, it is the case that Protestants greatly outnumbered Catholics among the first cohort of recruits.[122] Of the eight foreign modern linguists hired by the Victorian Queen's and later Royal University Colleges, only one was Roman Catholic: Valentine Steinberger in Galway. Charles Geisler, his predecessor, was

Anglican. Galway's first appointment, Bensbach, was the son of a rabbi. Born August Isaac, he was known as Augustus.[123] Certain details about Belfast's first three professors also point to non-Catholic origins: Frings married a clergyman's daughter; Frädersdorff was baptised a Lutheran; and the fact that Meissner had worked as a teacher in Bristol Baptist College suggests a dissenting persuasion.[124] As we have mentioned, Cork's de Véricour was a Huguenot. He was succeeded by two local Irish Catholics, O'Ryan and Butler.

6.7 Augustus Bensbach, QCG
Professor of Modern Languages, Queen's College Galway. Photograph, University Archives, University of Galway. (*Reproduced courtesy of University of Galway.*)

6.8 Tombstone of Augustus Bensbach, QCG (*d.*1868)
Jewish Cemetery, Mannheim. Photographed 1986. © *Zentralarchiv zur Erforschung der Geschichte der Juden in Deutschland in Heidelberg.* (*Courtesy of Mannheims Archiv, Haus der Stadtgeschichte und Erinnerung, Mannheim.*) Inscription reads: 'Hier ruht in Gott Dr Augustus Bensbach, Professor am Queen's College in Galway; geb. 25 Februar 1815 in Mannheim gest. 24 Juli 1868 in Düsseldorf. Friede seiner Asche [Here rests in God Dr Augustus Bensbach, Professor at Queen's College Galway. Born in Mannheim 25 February 1815, died in Düsseldorf 24 July 1868. Peace unto his ashes.]'

In the main, the Queen's Colleges foreign professors participated conscientiously in university life and contributed to the cultural and civic development of the local settings where they worked. As well as mixing with parishioners at Sunday worship, this may have helped some of them settle and feel assimilated. There cannot have been a large community of Jewish expatriates in post-Famine Galway, yet Augustus Bensbach became Vice-President of the Royal Galway Institution.[125] His family background may have helped him to fit into his work in Galway. As the son of a rabbi, he was familiar with a life devoted to studying and interpreting texts for didactic purposes. The youngest of six, Augustus may have found a role model among his siblings. Both sons were adventurous. The eldest sibling, Hayum/Heinrich, had also studied medicine and served as an army doctor in the East Indies.[126] Travelling to the western edge of the British Isles might not have seemed so strange.[127]

In practice, in the sphere of language teaching, the religious criterion per se had less effect than in some other disciplines.[128] Indeed, right from the start, King's College London waived its insistence that language teaching staff be members of the Church of England, since language teachers so often tended to be foreigners.[129] As for the CU/UCD, it should be said in passing that the fact that two of its four Victorian appointments to modern languages were priests probably reflects the hand of archbishop Paul Cullen more than a wish on the part of the CU's rector for a clerically controlled institution. Newman aimed to achieve a balance of lay and clerical appointments on his staff.[130]

Religion could be used as a political weapon, however, in the smouldering sectarian climate of mid-nineteenth-century Ireland. The Queen's Colleges' enemies among the Roman Catholic hierarchy were quick to exploit a minor incident, involving a new modern language professor, as ammunition in their campaign against the new colleges. Just after his appointment to the Cork chair, Louis-Raymond de Véricour published in 1850 a substantial history of Christian civilisation,[131] designed as a textbook. He gave his address as Queen's College Cork on the title page. The book's views on papal power exposed the Munster college to vituperation from the Irish bishops, compounding their sectarian hostility to the Queen's colleges. Their manoeuvres, spearheaded by the Archbishop of Armagh, Paul Cullen, led to the volume being placed on the Vatican's Index of Prohibited Books. Outrageously, they branded Cork's modern language professor as an 'infidel'.[132]

That the Catholic episcopate's overreaction was quite uncalled-for is evident from a mere glance at the book in question. Chronicling the history of the Christian era as central to the moral progress of humanity, it reads like the views of a typical nineteenth-century western historian who believed in a linear and positivist science of history.[133] A few years earlier, in a theoretical work on the *Principles of History*, the author was propagating earnestly Christian views: 'The true idea of Progress is the offspring of Christianity', proclaiming that 'the day will come when there will be but one flock.'[134] Far from being 'dangerous and scandalous', as de Véricour's accusers falsely claimed, the tone of the *Historical Analysis of Christian Civilisation* is respectful with regard to Rome, even if it criticises the extent of the papacy's temporal power. As Kathleen O'Flaherty, Professor of French at Cork a century later, asked: 'It is quite obviously written by a Protestant – but, after all, could one expect him to write like a Catholic?'[135] The author's Preface (dated May 1850) shows an awareness that his approach, with its 'respect for the convictions of all the members of the great human family, may probably expose the Author to many aspersions'.[136] He can hardly have imagined that the publication would risk the loss of a professorship that he had held for hardly a year. Timing was partly the problem: the episode, in itself a storm in a teacup, coincided perfectly with the Roman Catholic Synod of Thurles (August 1850). The French professor fell prey to the machinations of Paul Cullen. The prelate seized on de Véricour as a prime exhibit in his vehement denunciation of 'the system of mixed, or rather irreligious, education introduced in the Queen's Colleges', that helped him canvass support for the Catholic University during the Synod. Cullen's paranoid letters to Rome made de Véricour out to be a dangerous 'open disbeliever' who was intent on corrupting the souls of Cork's Catholic youth.[137]

The manufactured 'scandal' erupted during the same summer of 1850, when de Véricour himself was working in Switzerland, in the library at St Gallen. At a College Council meeting in early August, he was suspended in absentia, with no opportunity to defend himself. Even before he heard about it, the matter was ventilated in correspondence with local newspapers. There were supporters and detractors, with students, both Catholic and Protestant, firmly backing the French professor.[138] Hearing the news in late August, he wrote in his own defence to the editor of the *Cork Examiner*, profusely apologising for his 'pure inadvertence' in giving his College address and stating that his book was not intended, nor ever could be, read as an official college publication since his functions were 'exclusively confined to the modern languages'. He trusts that impartial readers of the work will find evidence of his respect for the Church of Rome.[139] At a September meeting of the Cork College Council, where the Frenchman was able to appear in person, he readily agreed to the Council's request that he remove his workplace address from subsequent editions.[140] Whereupon the matter was resolved as far as the university was concerned. It remained for a Decree placing the book on the Index, engineered by the College's ecclesiastical enemies, to be issued from Rome, in December.[141]

Did the affair motivate de Véricour's unsuccessful bid, in 1862, to move to Queen's College Belfast, where he might have felt more at home as a dissenting Protestant?[142] In the end he served in Cork for three decades. The episode was long remembered by opponents of the Queen's Colleges as a warning against control of appointments by the Chief Secretary.[143] Unconvinced, in 1873, by Dublin Castle assurances that more Catholic academics would be appointed, Paul Cullen believed that the London administration would continue to choose French and German professors who were not reliable on political or religious grounds.[144] After de Véricour's death in 1879, his successor, as will be seen, was a (perfectly worthy) home-grown RUI graduate, Owen O'Ryan.

Research, philology, empire

Compared to de Véricour's, the research output of UCD's earliest modern linguists was low – if not completely absent – with the obvious exception of Peter le Page Renouf, whose capacious publications concerned the ancient world.[145] Although, for Newman, research ranked second to teaching in a professor's list of duties, this did not prevent staff members in other CU arts departments from publishing their work.[146] Indeed, the University provided *The Atlantis*, a periodical for staff members to record their reflections and findings. Its purpose was announced in these terms:[147]

> A periodical, the chief object of which is to serve as a repository of the literary and scientific labours of the members of a University, must necessarily embrace every subject taught within that University – poetry, philosophy, history, philology, archaeology, fine arts, law, political economy, mathematics, and the sciences of experiment and observation.

Modern linguists in other Irish universities engaged in research, with varying degrees of perseverance. When appointed in 1849, all three of the Queen's Colleges modern languages professors had publications to their name,[148] ranging from the slightest to the weightiest of tomes. While Galway's Augustus Bensbach had written a very short sketch of German literature[149] and Mathias Frings in Belfast had published a French grammar for the use of German learners, Louis-Raymond de Véricour came to Cork with a broad and somewhat eclectic publication portfolio under his belt, including *Milton et la poésie épique* (1838), and an extensive survey of *Modern French Literature* (1848). Both of these volumes were over 400 pages in length.[150] The tone and scope of *Modern French Literature*, designed to bring the English-speaking world up to date with writers and politics in post-revolutionary

France, greatly impressed American literati, including the poet and Professor of French, Spanish and Belles-Lettres at Harvard, Henry F. Longfellow.[151] De Véricour continued to produce books on cultural and political history, historiography, literary history and biography, throughout his career.[152] Ten years after coming to Cork, he brought out a substantial 400-page volume on *The Life and Times of Dante*. His work reveals a scholar who is epic in scope and methodical in ordering his ideas, in the mode of nineteenth-century French academic writing. The majority of his books were published in London, in English, in which he expressed himself with ease.[153] There is a consistent breadth and depth to his erudition, which makes him stand out in the Irish context of the time. In terms of broad academic credentials, his research profile puts many of his modern language peers in the shade, and not just his compatriot contemporaries in Stephen's Green. It is worth recalling that Louis-Raymond de Véricour was appointed to Cork in the same year that Basilio Angeli took up his post in Trinity.

Indeed, Cork's broad-minded, virtually bilingual and immensely cultured French historian was in quite a different league from Angeli, Trinity's dismissed Tuscan stuccodore. A popular and well-travelled man of the world, member of a number of learnèd societies in European capitals, de Véricour exuded social graces and elegance, moving with ease in local ascendancy circles. His friend George Boole reported that he was 'an unbounded favourite in Cork especially with the ladies whom he has won over by his lectures, his graceful manner and fine person'.[154] The university appreciated him too. When he died in January 1879 following a short illness, his funeral started in the College, with his coffin 'borne to the hearse in the quadrangle by former students', followed by a procession of 'all the professors, about 100 students, and a large number of the inhabitants of both city and county.'[155] He rests under a memorial stone in the city's St Finbarr's cemetery.

6.9 Tombstone of Raymond de Véricour, QCC (*d.*1879) St Finbarr's Cemetery, Cork. Memorial stone placed over his grave by the President and Professors of Queen's College Cork, and others, 1883. Photographed by Phyllis Gaffney (2024).

Finally, it should be noted that de Véricour was more than just an urbane and enlightened French intellectual, at ease within the predominantly Protestant milieu of Queen's College Cork and its local gentry. There was a scientific dimension to his interests, and life experience, that must have made him look like a surprisingly good fit for a position in the practical university that the Queen's Colleges Board was attempting to set up in the 1840s. In the 1830s, he had spent two years at Hofwyl, near Bern, at the working model farm set up by the Swiss agronomist and educationalist Philipp Emmanuel von Fellenberg. De Véricour's account of what he learned there, *Des Instituts Agricoles et Scientifiques d'Hofwyl*, was published in Paris in 1837.[156] The French professor was a close friend of the mathematics Professor George Boole, whom he had first met in Lincoln, Boole's home town. When both were appointed to chairs in the new Cork College in 1849, they shared lodgings in the city.[157] Both served on the Library Committee, comprising a team of four men who met very regularly to discuss cataloguing and keep track of volumes that went missing when borrowed by colleagues.[158] Both men believed in the diffusion of scientific knowledge to further the progress of humankind.[159]

In comparison with de Véricour's, the research scope of other Queen's Colleges modern language appointments was less concerned with cultural masterworks, focussing instead on language and literary history. Within these fields, however, considerable work was done. All of the Victorians appointed to the Belfast college published language textbooks or literary history. Frings published French and German school-books; Frädersdorff prepared grammars of German, Danish and Norwegian; Meissner produced a German reader, a German grammar, and practical textbooks on French philology, German conversation and English-French prose translation.[160] Galway's Valentine Steinberger published annotated editions of French texts.[161]

With the arrival of Albert Maximilian Selss to take up Trinity's new chair of German in 1866, 'the stage was set for the full development of all aspects of German studies' and Dublin University's reputation as a centre of German studies was secure.[162] As well as practical language exercises and textbooks, he published histories of the German language and German literature, and an edition of Goethe's poetry.[163] The output of Robert Atkinson, Selss's colleague in Trinity, was prolific. Simultaneously holder of two chairs – Romance Languages from 1869 and Sanskrit and Comparative Philology from 1871 – Atkinson was legendary for the range of languages in which he acquired an expertise. A tireless scholar, he edited and published texts in Old and Middle Irish, Anglo-Norman, Coptic, and Old Russian, as well as having some knowledge of Chinese, Arabic, Hindustani, Tibetan, Tamil and Telegu.[164] Trinity's Professor of Old Irish David Greene reported that 'Atkinson was not only a bookman: he spoke French like a native, his Chinese pronunciation was impeccable, he could argue with cab-drivers in St Petersburg'.[165] Such polyglot professors seem a far cry from the narrowing specialisms of today.

In this passion for acquiring and comparing languages, Atkinson typifies a certain breed of nineteenth-century linguistic scholar. This was the age of comparative and historical linguistics, when scholars in the new language sciences were going back to ancient origins and establishing systematic genealogical connections between different species of human tongues.[166] This inevitably gave a panoramic scope to language study. Trinity's first Professor of Italian and Spanish, the Portuguese émigré Antonio Vieyra, wrote on the philological affinities between Arabic, Latin, Persian and Romance languages and also published his philological notes on the *Koran*.[167] The Oxford philologist Max Müller saw 'the long history of the speech of India' as the key to language science, declaring in one of his 1862 introductory lectures that 'it has been truly said that Sanskrit is to the science of language what mathematics are to astronomy.'[168] It was an interest in Sanskrit that led Atkinson to Celtic Studies. Galway's second modern languages professor, Charles Geisler, pursued the study of Celtic philology and Sanskrit for similar reasons. As for Renouf, the CU's first modern linguist, his knowledge of Egyptology may seem to be a far cry from French verbs, but in the wider scheme of things the decoding of hieroglyphs is part of the same intellectual curiosity, compulsive discovery and systematic ordering of knowledge that had driven the French philological prodigy Jean-François Champollion (1790–1832) to decode the Rosetta Stone.[169]

6.10 Charles Geisler, QCG and RUI Galway Professor of Modern Languages, Queen's College and RUI Galway. Photograph, University Archives, University of Galway. (*Reproduced courtesy of University of Galway.*)

In her account of modern language study in Galway, Rosaleen O'Neill mentions Professor Geisler's interest in Sanskrit and Celtic philology.[170] The promoters of Irish culture were sometimes pleased to welcome foreign-language scholars into their ranks, as we saw in the case of Édouard Cadic, but the German linguist may have come to regret this research enthusiasm. In 1882, he was invited to join the Council of the recently founded Gaelic Union,[171] and in 1884 he published a translation from a Middle Irish version of a story from the Alexander legend.[172] This short bilingual text led to a peculiarly vitriolic notice in the *Freeman's Journal*, followed by an equally vituperative riposte after Geisler's brief reply.[173] The anonymous reviewer finds the work rife with errors and careless in its transcription, and pours scorn on Geisler's attempt 'to pass as an Irish-Scholar'. The main thrust of the piece, however, is a venomous *ad hominem* assault on Geisler's reputation, claiming that the only motivation for the modern language professor's admiration for Irish was in order to qualify himself for 'the distinction and emoluments of a Celtic fellowship' in the RUI.[174] Significantly, the fellowship (in modern languages) that Geisler was awarded was announced within weeks, at the end of May.[175] Geisler may have been an amateur in the field of Celtic philology, but the contemptuous tone adopted by his adversary suggests an alarming degree of spite. Who was this anonymous reviewer, who seems familiar with the history and grammar of the Irish language? Geisler's competence in a language that he was not employed to teach but merely interested in researching was shredded in public. To have his reputation impugned, and a few weeks later his qualifications in modern languages queried in the House of Commons, must have made 1884 an *annus horribilis* for the unfortunate German professor, and could indeed have been sufficiently dismaying to motivate his apparently unexplained departure from Galway despite being awarded a fellowship. Whether or not facts can dispel speculation on his reasons for leaving, the salient point of the episode, for our purpose, is to reveal the close engagement with Celtic Studies of a philologically minded professor of French and German from the northern shores of the German empire, who happened to fetch up on Ireland's western seaboard.

Philology was fashionable in the period partly for political reasons. Edward Said sees the new language science as the prevailing European mindset among scholars and historians of the age, embodying 'a peculiar condition of being modern and European, since neither of those two categories has true meaning without being related to an earlier alien culture and time.'[176] The comparatist study of relations between Indo-European languages and their classification into genealogical groups coincided with the age when European powers were bedding down their colonies in other regions of the world: the new trend in language scholarship was intrinsically Eurocentric.[177] Western scholars of language had varying perspectives on the Orient. For the English and Germans, India was 'the *fons et origo* of everything; and then there were the French who had decided after Napoleon and Champollion that everything originated in Egypt and the new Orient.'[178] The eighteenth century had seen the start of a rich vein of scholarly enquiry between individual British imperial administrators and the languages of the Indian subcontinent, the prototype being Sir William Jones (1746–94), father of comparative linguistics. Orientalist and judge of the Supreme Court in Calcutta, Jones founded the Asiatic Society of Bengal in Calcutta (now Kolkata), and reputedly learned up to 28 different languages.[179] In his famous third anniversary discourse delivered to the Society in 1786, Jones established 'beyond doubt the historical kinship of Sanskrit, the classical language of India, with Latin, Greek and the Germanic languages'.[180] Indo-European linguistic scholarship was soon to be a hallmark of German universities, with the first chair of Sanskrit established at Bonn in 1819.[181]

There is no doubt that empire promoted both language contacts and scholarly interest in language learning. This is illustrated by the case of Thomas Prendergast (1807–86). After a career of three decades as a civil servant for the East India Company, he took to producing innovative and bestselling language manuals during his retirement in Cheltenham, despite falling prey to blindness. India's multilingual environment had increased his own linguistic awareness and multicultural sensitivity, and stimulated his interest in taking a fresh approach to the teaching of French, German, Spanish, Hebrew and Latin.[182] He was instrumental in founding a school to teach English to Indian boys.[183] The role of the imperial service in promoting language diversity can also be seen in the motivation behind the Boden Professorship of Sanskrit at Oxford, which was set up in 1832. The first incumbent of the chair, Horace Wilson, had worked for the East India Company, as had the chair's endowing founder, Lieutenant Colonel Joseph Boden. Boden was anxious to facilitate 'the conversion of the natives of India in the Christian Religion, by disseminating a knowledge of the Sacred Scriptures among them, more effectually than by all other means whatever'.[184]

The imperial project valued multilingual formation among its administrators. We have seen how, in Ireland, the study of continental languages got a significant boost from the mid–1850s, with their inclusion in the Indian Civil Service examinations.[185] This led to structural changes in Trinity. The other universities advertised how their courses prepared potential candidates for these open public competitions, reinforcing the message that modern languages were essential to a modern university's palette of career options.[186] Public examinations tested translation skills in both directions along with awareness of literary history, for each modern language. As recommended by the Macaulay Report of 1854 on the Indian Civil Service:[187]

> Several passages in every one of those languages should be set, to be turned into English; passages taken from English writers should be set, to be turned into French, Italian, and German; and papers of questions should be framed which would enable a candidate to show his knowledge of the civil and literary history of France, Italy, and Germany.

University examinations in many respects complied. In its lecture timetabling discussions, the CU's Faculty of Philosophy and Letters showed its awareness of the new context of language study, bearing in mind Woolwich and Civil Service examinations as well as medical science and civil engineering.[188] In 1859, the Faculty agreed to a motion, proposed by the Italian Professor Marani,[189] that premiums should be instituted in order to encourage the study of Modern Languages, admitted to be so important a branch of University education, they being taken up as subjects at the East India, Woolwich, and Sandhurst Competitive Examinations.

This phenomenon may have been a factor explaining an increase in student enrolment for modern languages. In Belfast, for instance, student numbers in the 1860s were more than double those in the 1850s.[190]

At the same moment, Trinity College Dublin founded chairs in Sanskrit and Arabic. In their history of Trinity, McDowell and Webb emphasise how these 1850s developments aligned the College with the imperial administration in London. Among the marble busts on pedestals in the College Library's Long Room gallery, there was one[191]

> of a youngish man of rather prim aspect, in neat mid-Victorian dress, and bearing on its base the rather startling inscription 'Siegfried'. It is not, however, to be regarded as an eccentric aberration of Wagnerian culture, but as a by-product of Macaulay's reforms of the Indian administration.

Trinity's first appointment in Sanskrit, Rudolf Thomas Siegfried, was a young philologist from Dessau near Leipzig. Sadly, he died suddenly in 1863, aged 32. He was replaced by another German philologist, Carl Friedrich Lottner. The post in Arabic, first briefly held by William Wright, was taken over in 1861 by Mir Alaud Ali, who was to hold the chair for almost 40 years. He was a good linguist and soon added Hindustani and Persian to the title of his chair. 'He had no pretensions to original scholarship but gave efficiently the type of teaching that was needed by the Indian Civil Service candidates.'[192]

It should be remembered that Celtic philology, too, was greatly stimulated by the interest in Sanskrit shown by the Crown's colonial representatives, some of whom – like Whitley Stokes – were Irish.[193] Rudolf Siegfried, a close friend of Stokes, had first come to Dublin to look at Celtic manuscripts.[194] His brief time in Dublin was enormously influential for the academic development of Celtic philology in Ireland. Siegfried acted as a crucial human link between continental comparative philologists and Celticists in Ireland. To quote Pól Ó Dochartaigh:[195]

> Understanding Siegfried's influence on and interaction with Irish antiquarians and Celticists during the few years that he was in Ireland is central to understanding how the academic discipline of Celtic philology emerged in Ireland as a branch of the mainland European, and largely German, discipline of comparative philology.

In short, it is no exaggeration to claim that to teach or study a language in the Victorian era was to enter an emerging field, informed by historical and comparative linguistics, which in turn were by-products of the European imperialist drive.

Taken to extremes, the historical–philological approach to language teaching could emphasise comparative linguistic genealogy so much that it could marginalise the living language being studied. When a future Professor of German, Walter Horace Bruford, went up to Cambridge to read German in 1912, he was surprised to find that, at that period,[196]

> Germanists studied Old Irish and Old Icelandic, Gothic, Old High German, Old Saxon and Middle High German, Old Norse and Sanskrit. Even as late as 1925 the only concession to

post-sixteenth-century German literature was *Faust*. It was, as Bruford put it in his diplomatic way in his 1965 Presidential Address to the Modern Humanities Research Association, language and literature 'of a severely philological nature'.

Course content, approaches to teaching and assessment

So far, we have considered divergences – of provenance, religion and research output – among Victorian modern language appointments in Irish universities, as well as the research interests of those who published. What approaches did these linguists take to teaching and assessing their disciplines? How did they organise their courses? While there were some variations, depending on the preferences of individual professors and as fashions changed over time, we also find convergent perennial patterns in the pedagogic culture of the period.

One major common ground is the philological / literary-historical way in which they framed their disciplines. While not going to such lengths as Edwardian Cambridge to establish the pedigrees of French or German, Ireland's modern languages professors also set great store by the historical development of the language being taught, and the earliest forms of its literary texts. In Trinity College Dublin, philology and history of the language were an enduring presence for German. The German examination papers set by Trinity's Professor of French and German in the 1840s and 1850s, Ignatius Abeltshauser, indicate this bias right from his first year in office, as M. M. Raraty notes:[197]

> From the very first paper that Abeltshauser set [...] it is apparent that the tradition of emphasis on philology, on the history and morphology of the German language, and the particular reference to the mediaeval period in literature, which has persisted in German studies in the College even to [the nineteen-sixties], has its roots in the pattern that he set in his first year of university teaching.

Abeltshauser's successor for romance languages, Robert Atkinson, was likewise primarily a comparative philologist.

Professor Abeltshauser was external examiner in French, German and Italian for the Queen's Colleges in the early 1850s, and his approach to teaching was quite in line with theirs. As the Queen's University Vice-Chancellor reported in 1852, honours students were examined[198]

> in the History, Philology, and Grammar of the following modern Foreign Languages, viz: – The French or German. The Candidate will be examined in French and German, or in French, German, and Italian, if he think proper. The Candidate will be required also to translate from the English into the Language or Languages selected by him for examination.

Meissner exemplified the tradition in Belfast. His reports to the President show an emphasis on grammar, canonical authors, and literary history. In line with his research, he lectured on Old German and Old French, especially Anglo-Norman texts, and was primarily a comparative philologist.[199] In Cork, de Véricour gave general lectures on literature and its history, complemented by prescribed texts,[200] and his successors framed their teaching in the same manner. Galway's BA students were all taught the histories of French and German language and literature.[201]

In the Catholic University, modern language syllabi and examinations also covered broad historical surveys. To judge by the university's *Calendar* for 1863, for example, book lists, both general and specific for each language (including English), consisted entirely of histories of the language and literature in question, often written in the target language.[202] A general regulation on the University's organisation of disciplines decrees that modern languages will be arranged 'on the same principles, and in the same manner as for the Greek and Latin languages'; the same *Calendar*'s entry for 'Modern Languages and Modern History' follows 'Ancient Languages and Ancient History'.[203]

Throughout the period, then, modern language assessment was modelled on traditional assessment of Latin, entailing mandatory questions on grammar and translation into the target language. A ruling (1892) of the Royal University is unambiguous in this regard:[204]

> Where Latin or a Modern Language forms part of an Examination, no Candidate shall be adjudged to have passed in that language who does not exhibit a competent knowledge of Grammar and of translation from English into the language. The same rule will apply to Greek, Hebrew, Arabic, and Sanskrit; but translation into those languages will not be required, unless where it is expressly prescribed in the Calendar as forming part of the course for such Examination.

BA assessment 'consisted of translations from and into the target language, with more difficult passages and some grammatical, philological, and literary questions for honours candidates.'[205] In both French and German, the questions tended to elicit factual knowledge, reflecting received ideas that the examiner (like Dickens's Thomas Gradgrind) has in mind – e.g. (for German), 'What are the principal dialects into which the ancient language of the Germans was divided?', 'With which dialect has the Anglo-Saxon most affinity?', 'Upon what dramatic model did Schiller form his style?';[206] or (for French), 'Which are the earliest lasting monuments of the history of French literature?', 'What are considered to be Racine's best plays? Class them according to eminence', 'When did La Fontaine live, and what is the character of his writings?'.[207] Passages or sentences for translation, in both directions and of varying complexity, were intended to illustrate candidates' mastery of 'grammar-rules and idioms'. Candidates were invited to display their grasp of grammatical structures by tackling such questions as 'State the general rule for the use of the tenses of the subjunctive', or 'How are the pronouns *whoever, whosoever, whatever*, translated?'[208]

In the early decades, anthologies of extracts from canonical literary works were often used, to evoke comments on idiomatic peculiarities or lexicographical niceties. Literary texts – largely by canonical authors from the seventeenth and eighteenth centuries – were read less for their intrinsic aesthetic value than for their perceived historical importance, and their use for illustrating 'striking etymologies', 'phonetical changes', 'historic variations of meaning',[209] and acquiring skills in reading or writing the foreign language. The four pillars of literary history, philology, grammar and translation had a very long shelf-life, as Mary Colum testifies, remembering her time at the Stephen's Green college in the 1900s:[210]

> our secondary education had brought us to the nineteenth century in the languages we studied, but now we started at the beginnings of languages and literatures and went step by step through their development down the centuries. We were dosed with linguistics and early texts [...] Then we learned vast quantities of literary history, ancient and modern, the modern

in the languages in which they were written. Some of our teachers, in fact, thought the history of literature more important than the literature itself.

Uninspired by the menu of long-dead authors from foreign lands, not to mention the grammars of Anglo-Saxon, middle high German and medieval French, Colum found a welcome distraction in Edwardian Dublin's theatrical shows and meetings where she could hear living Irish writers read and discuss their work.[211]

Victorian language professors sometimes included contemporary texts in their booklists. Alongside works by dead classical authors, Charles Geisler in Galway prescribed contemporary French comedies for the purpose of teaching idiomatic translation and analysis: *Le Verre d'Eau*, one of over 400 plays written by the highly popular Eugène Scribe and *L'Honneur et l'Argent*, a comedy in verse by François Ponsard. For testing his senior scholarship candidates, Geisler used dramatic dialogue of a very different kind, asking them to transpose a passage of Racinian verse into French prose.[212]

The choice of texts was not exclusively confined to works of literature. For students of German, Augustus Bensbach in Galway prescribed Goethe's *Iphigenie auf Tauris* along with Justus Liebig's (1844) *Chemische Briefe* [Letters on Chemistry].[213] While the Goethe play is standard fare,[214] the work of Liebig, founder of organic chemistry, was a good choice of a non-literary text for medical students, showing an approach similar to what today is called LSP [Language for Special Purposes]. In his 1859–60 syllabus for Cork, de Véricour included Bossuet's *Oraisons funèbres* along with extracts from Étienne Pariset, *Éloges des membres de l'Académie de Médicine*. Bossuet's funeral panegyrics are a model of French classical oratory, but the orations pronounced in eloquent prose by the secretary of the Académie Royale de Médicine at the gravesides of the great men of medical science of nineteenth-century France are a more surprising choice. Perhaps their content was intended to inspire Cork's medical students to advance further frontiers of research.[215]

Both de Véricour and Bensbach prescribed Mignet's (1824) *Histoire de la Révolution Française* [History of the French Revolution].[216] This liberal appraisal of the French revolution, from a French perspective, was in line with the belief that the study of a people's language encompassed the study of their history, reflecting some essential character or identity of their nation. In the middle of the nineteenth century, what date could be more defining for France than 1789?

The examples of prescribed texts just mentioned would have been excessively challenging for the first modern language cohorts in the Queen's colleges. In the early years, student standards were so low that Belfast's Professor Frings resorted to remedial private instruction.[217] Yet there is a sense of gradual improvement over the decades. In 1851, Dr Bensbach reports on the progress of Galway students who had 'nearly without exception, commenced the study of French or German' with him.[218] Almost 30 years later, his successor Geisler records 'the pleasing fact that the majority of first year's Students already knew a good deal of French or German when they entered' the college.[219] By the later Victorian decades, it was possible for abler graduates from all the universities to compete successfully in civil service examinations and find white-collar employment.[220] All of the Queen's Colleges professors were well equipped to offer a broad teaching range, from elementary French and German to comparative philology and medieval texts. Some, like Geisler and Steinberger in Galway, Meissner in Belfast or O'Ryan in Cork, also taught Italian.

What about European languages other than French and German? Italian and Spanish were not taught or assessed in a different manner from French and German. Augusto Cesare Marani was Trinity's last Foundation Chair of Italian before Robert Atkinson's appointment in 1869 to the new chair of romance languages, which combined French, Italian and Spanish. Marani was appointed professor in 1862. Corinna Salvadori concludes that sample examination papers set by the professor conformed to the standard Victorian model of assessment, which sought to appraise candidates' mastery of factual details rather than their ability to reflect critically on what they had absorbed. 'He served the College conscientiously if unremarkably, teaching and examining the limited number of students who presented themselves for Italian and Spanish'.[221] Later Italian papers from the Royal University suggest a broader scope. Thus, BA students in 1888 are invited to write an essay in Italian (on either '*Roma*' or '*Il Teatro Italiano*'), to translate passages, and to answer questions on the history of the language. These elicit a certain display of limited knowledge such as, 'How was Italian affected by the language of the northern invaders?', 'Show how the necessity for a new form of the future tense arose', 'Mention the principal differences between Latin and Italian as to the personal inflections of verbs, with such explanations as you may think fit.'[222]

While in Trinity both Italian and Spanish receded to 'an extra-curricular limbo' during the final decades of the nineteenth century,[223] this was less the case in other universities. Of the two, however, Spanish fared consistently less well than Italian. Even though it was on the CU menu from the beginning, student numbers were low to non-existent. In the RUI colleges, it appears to have been offered if there happened to be students seeking to study it. 'In 1884, the university calendars record that Spanish was being taught and examined, but give no name(s), so possibly just by someone who was paid by the hour.'[224] The exceptionally low take-up for the language is illustrated by a recurrent footnote in the CU and RUI annual Calendars' general regulations, to the effect that candidates intending to present in Spanish should declare their intention to the University at least three months before the date of the Examination, stating whether at Pass or Honours level. In 1892, for example, the same rule applied to candidates intending to take examinations in Spanish, Celtic, Sanskrit, Hebrew or Arabic.[225] Throughout the period, there were consistently far more students studying French than German or Italian.[226]

Why did Spanish attract lower numbers than Italian? Several factors may have contributed, at least in part. Since the days of the grand tour, Italian had got its foot in the door earlier. The Italian language 'in early Victorian times had rivalled and sometimes even displaced French as an elegant accomplishment for well-educated people of either sex.'[227] The view expressed by Renouf that a knowledge of Latin and Italian allowed access to a reading knowledge of Spanish, may have been widespread.[228] Even had Spanish been included along with the three other continental languages as a subject for the Indian Civil Service examinations, it would probably not have been able to rival the position of Italian. The dearth of feeder schools would have been an impediment. In Roman Catholic schools, there was a plentiful supply of clerics able to teach the language of Rome, ensuring that Italian, rather than Spanish, was the option for schools intent on expanding their language range. In universities, prestigious annual student prizes may have favoured some pairs of languages over others. Thus, for example, Rosaleen O'Neill observes that RUI Galway's generous Browne scholarship, awarded to linguists for proficiency in both French and German, may have disincentivised strong candidates from studying other languages.[229] For reasons such as these, the study of Spanish had less visibility in Victorian Ireland than the relative importance it enjoys in the country today.[230]

Teaching and assessing the spoken language

Given their emphasis on literary history, history of the language, knowledge of grammatical rules and ability to write and translate accurately into and out of the foreign language, did Victorian professors also manage to teach and assess their students' practical ability to speak it? In Britain, indications that serious attention was paid to the spoken language can be negative. Robert Lowe, for example, recalled in 1867:[231]

> I have been with a party of half-a-dozen first-class Oxford gentlemen on the Continent, and not one spoke a word of French or German; and if the waiter had not been better educated than we, and known some other language than his own, we might all have starved.

There is evidence that matters may have been different in Irish universities. In language classes, foreign sounds were uttered and heard, and corrected if a teacher saw fit. To quote Trinity's Professor Abeltshauser, in 1856: 'Pronunciation is a matter of great importance, in my opinion, and, therefore, I take the utmost pains to correct everything that is amiss.'[232] Belfast's Professor Frings, in his statement to the Queen's Colleges Commissioners (1858), shows striking sensitivity to this process, which he describes as physiologically arduous for students, who have to train the ear and the tongue in order to pronounce 'words they have

6.11 Valentine Steinberger, RUI Galway Professor of Modern Languages, RUI Galway. Photograph, University Archives, University of Galway. (*Reproduced courtesy of University of Galway.*)

never heard in their lives, and for which they have to be re-modelled in their whole being, as it were, and to get almost different tongues'.[233]

Individual professors occasionally used the target language when teaching honours or scholarship classes. Thus, in QCC, Owen O'Ryan taught Philology through the medium of French;[234] Meissner in Belfast stressed in a textbook (1888) the need to study oral communication, and reported his own practice with his third-year students in French and German: 'The questions and answers are given and returned in French and German respectively. In the second term of the Third Session the Professor delivers Lectures in French and German on those periods of Literature with which the Students have already become somewhat familiarized by their previous studies.'[235] Steinberger in Galway always lectured final-year students through the medium of the language being studied, and believed that a modern language had to be treated as a living language. In his view, literature

151

and history should be the diet of postgraduates, and undergraduates should concentrate on perfecting their ability to communicate in the target language.[236]

By the closing years of the nineteenth century, the ideas of the language reform movement were percolating through to Europe's most westerly island. In this endeavour, Galway was a genuine trailblazer. The belief that colloquial proficiency was attainable for abler students took a scientific turn with Valentine Steinberger. He was proud to have introduced, at the turn of the century, the very first experimental phonetics laboratory to Ireland. This contained a kymograph, an apparatus recently developed in France for teaching pronunciation.[237] Whence this stress on the oral language in Galway? Was it because of the realisation that Galwegians, dwelling on the outer reaches of Europe, had little opportunity to travel or to meet speakers and practise the foreign language in their daily lives?[238] It may be relevant that Steinberger had taught French and German for a number of years in Co. Down, and that his wife was from Coleraine. A former student testifies that the Bavarian professor was conscious of the challenges posed for Ulster speakers by certain foreign sounds.[239]

Apart from communicating with students in the foreign language and correcting their pronunciation, what about the assessment of their oral language skills? How and whether this took place can be difficult to gauge. To take for example Professor Meissner's description of his pedagogic practice:[240]

> The work of the classes, especially during the first two years, is carried on to a great extent by means of *viva voce* questions and answers. Frequent oral examinations are held, and at each meeting of the classes a passage is translated from English into French or German.

What does Meissner mean by 'oral examinations' in this 1867 classroom context? The term may be misleading. Is he referring to regular classroom *assessment* or merely the exchange of words in the foreign language that generally occurs when teaching it? The ambiguity is compounded by the fact that oral examining was by no means confined to language study. In early Victorian times, the assessment of *all* subjects relied on the spoken word. Universities had for centuries tested students *viva voce* and the move towards written examinations was a recent phenomenon. Printed examination papers were so recent, indeed, that the Queen's University Vice-Chancellor's report for 1851–2 actually announces that 'the examination for Honors [*sic*] will be by printed papers.'[241] A detailed oral question and answer (catechetical) examination was the standard mode of conducting all assessment in Trinity College Dublin *c.*1830. For Trinity's quarterly examinations undergraduate classes were divided into groups of 30 or 40 candidates and assigned two examiners, 'one for Classics and one for Science. Both questions and answers were almost entirely *viva voce*...'.[242] The move to written examinations had occurred in Cambridge and Oxford a little earlier; in Dublin University, although some elements of examinations were written, many vestiges of pre-Victorian examining practices survived for decades into the Victorian age.[243]

However, oral examining in modern languages, as generally understood today – i.e., to assess candidates' ability to understand and communicate coherently and intelligibly in the target language – may not correspond, in all respects and cases, to what happened in Ireland's Victorian universities. Meissner's phrase 'oral examinations' could mean the spoken questions and answers that are run of the mill in any language class rather than a formal oral examination as we understand the phrase today.

In Queen's College Galway, an assessment practice used by Augustus Bensbach in the 1850s and 1860s involved a conversation in the target tongue. Galway's candidates for college prizes had to sit for 'a "catechetical examination" on Corneille, conducted in French, or for "conversation in German"'.[244] Rosaleen O'Neill comments on the novelty of this form of assessment:

> This recognition of the importance of the spoken language [...] is perhaps the most interesting feature of the early syllabus, at a time when modern languages as part of university courses were taught, if at all, as 'dead languages' in Dublin and in Britain (Cambridge, for example, did not introduce 'optional conversation' until 1909).

Acknowledging the importance of the spoken language was indeed innovative, at a time when most universities in Britain treated modern languages as dead tongues. The test of a 'conversation' in German certainly sounds like an attempt to treat the language as a living means of communication. However, it is far more likely that the French 'catechetical examination' on Corneille was designed to elicit something other than proficiency in communication – in effect, a variation on the *viva voce*, the manner in which students had been taught and assessed for centuries, testing (in this instance) the candidate's knowledge of Corneille rather than his spoken proficiency in French – i.e., the substance rather than the form of what the candidate uttered.[245]

In the 1830s Evasio Radice lectured on Italian and Spanish literature and was the first to introduce examinations in modern languages in Trinity, testing his students via translation into the target language and conversation.[246] Here again, we cannot tell for certain whether, in the conversation, he was interrogating them to elicit their (factual) knowledge of literature and history, or to assess their oral fluency in the foreign language, or indeed both. Trinity's classics students were examined in 1834 by 'a *viva voce* on the set books'. This involved a performance, with students reading a Latin or Greek text aloud and translating it orally, interrupted by examiners with questions on the choice of words or phrases, on different textual interpretations or on 'philological niceties, historical and other allusions.'[247] The fact that Galway's Professor Bensbach reserved a catechetical oral examination for his best students in French foreshadows a later RUI regulation for borderline Honours candidates in First Year examinations, whereby the ablest candidates in *all* subjects – not just languages – were required to attend an oral examination a fortnight after their written test, if their performance in the written test merited further probing of their knowledge, as a means of deciding how to rank the top-performing candidates.[248] RUI philosophy Fellows resorted to an examining practice for Degree candidates that combined the written and the oral, doubtless reflecting earlier assessment modes: 'One of the examiners read aloud the candidate's answer, and all then discussed it and fixed their award. It took some time perhaps but must have been very effective.'[249]

Oral examining is both time-consuming and labour-intensive, especially when large numbers are involved. In schools, too, when there were moves towards promoting spoken proficiency in modern language teaching, resource constraints were explicitly noted by the 1918 Leathes report. It recommended that oral assessment be 'introduced, where possible'.[250]

In Ireland's universities, while language teaching generally tended to value an ability to write the foreign language accurately over an ability to speak it fluently, there is evidence, within the RUI, especially after 1900, of a growing appreciation of the need for students to achieve spoken proficiency. Mary Colum's memoir distinguishes between her language learning as a boarder in Monaghan in the 1890s and her days at Dublin's RUI. In school, she says, 'not much attention was given to the conversational side of languages, and it was only in my university days that I got to the point of speaking French and German with fair fluency.'[251]

While the RUI's modern language teaching gradually recognised the importance of spoken proficiency,[252] determining whether or how it was tested is however not clear. Oral tests for all modern language students may have been introduced by the NUI after 1908, but the records do not yield sufficient evidence on how such tests were conducted to allow a sense of the examining criteria or tasks involved.[253]

Language study for non-language degrees

It is worth, finally, reminding ourselves of the expectations of general foreign-language competence in Victorian higher education. When perusing lists of prescribed books for subjects outside the domain of modern languages, one is struck by the language diversity in the titles listed. Students would have had difficulties in keeping up with the reading matter by relying on a monoglot approach to study. In the CU *Calendar* for 1863, for example, those enrolled in Political Economy were recommended nine books, only one of which was in English. Its author is John Stuart Mill; of the remainder, seven titles are in French and one is in German.[254] Out of eight text-books listed under Moral Philosophy, one is in Latin, one in French, one in German, two are in English and three in Italian.[255] Many of the textbooks recommended for mathematics and physical sciences are French publications. Queen's College Cork's illustrious appointment in mathematics, George Boole, had taught himself French, German and Italian, in order to keep 'closely in touch with scientific developments on the Continent'.[256] His mathematical thinking was deeply influenced by French mathematicians whose works he had devoured as a youth.[257] In today's globalised world, the need for a reading knowledge of a foreign language in order to access scientific literature is generally funnelled towards English.

This phenomenon helps to explain the Queen's Colleges' insistence on medical and science students studying French or German for a year, and also why they saw fit to appoint a medical doctor as Galway's first Professor of modern languages. We have seen how Professor Bensbach set, as a text book for his medical students taking German, Liebig's *Chemische Briefe*. In their MD language examinations, medical students were given separate tasks, involving the translation of medical texts and questions on medical terminology in the target language, in addition to grammar and literature questions.[258]

The usefulness of knowing French or German, particularly for medical sciences, continued to grow.[259] Professor William Doolin's 1954 reminiscence of the early decades of the CU's Medical School points out that anglophone practitioners in the 1860s were intellectually behind their continental colleagues in some ground-breaking advances in nineteenth-century clinical medicine, the hubs then being Paris for the new discipline of physiology, or Berlin and Vienna for pathology.[260] A knowledge of foreign languages enabled a few Irish medical students to avail of these advances. Thus, Denis J. Coffey, future Professor of physiology (from 1883) and first President of UCD (until 1940), won a studentship in biology to pursue his postgraduate studies in Madrid, Louvain, Munich and Leipzig.[261] Edmond J. McWeeney, future Professor of Pathology and Bacteriology (from 1891), was a highly competent language student, having been to secondary school in St Omer. After taking two concurrent degrees in Arts and Medicine, he was awarded two Studentships – in modern languages and pathology. He used the medical studentship to work for a year with the Czech-born anatomist-pathologist Rokitanski in Vienna, followed by a year 'with Koch, then supreme in bacteriology, at Berlin'.[262] These postgraduate studies led to the UCD Chair of Pathology and Bacteriology, 'the first chair in these young sciences to be established in any University in Britain or Ireland'.[263] This brilliant young medical appointment, MA, MD, was well able, when asked, to assist in examining students in French and German.[264]

★ ★ ★

In the foregoing pages we have assembled disparate data to consider the biographical experience and academic endeavours of a wide cast of professors, mostly of foreign nationality, who were employed to teach modern languages in Irish universities from the 1840s to the 1900s. Relying on their own training in classical languages, these men tended by and large to follow traditional language pedagogy in their approach to teaching, which prioritised accuracy in the written language. Yet, as we have seen, there were by the later decades of the century some emerging trends towards including an element of oral language assessment.

We have discussed traditional approaches to teaching and assessment because not all readers will have studied modern languages at third level, and because – for many of those who have – an exclusive focus on the written language is alien from the way language learning is tackled today. Moreover, as will be outlined in our final chapter, Victorian approaches persisted in Ireland for many years after the Victorian regime was over. In fact, Ireland's history of language learning is particularly revealing of the perennial tension (in pedagogic practice) between pen and tongue. The arrival on the scene of modern-Irish study brought new expectations and experiences of other ways of teaching and learning modern languages, especially with regard to the balance of oral and written language forms. In the extra-mural settings organised by the Gaelic League, the native vernacular was approached through the practical use of the spoken language, and the study of its folk tradition, songs and dances. As we shall see, this pedagogic vision was not shared by all of the vernacular's gatekeepers.

Our next chapter will turn to consider two groups of newcomers to the academic staff of late Victorian and Edwardian universities. Local linguists were appointed, both in continental languages and in Irish, and a number of chairs in modern languages were awarded to women graduates from the RUI.

CHAPTER 7

Home-Grown Language Professors

Let us be as Irish as we can, but let us be European, too. [The Leader, 1908][1]

In the Kulturkampf *of early twentieth-century Ireland, the decision of the Senate of the NUI on [obligatory Irish for matriculation] was probably the only occasion in recent Irish history on which the force of a significant volume of public opinion ensured that language trumped religion as the key marker of Irish cultural identity within the nationalist community in Ireland. [Gearóid Ó Tuathaigh, 2008]*[2]

University Reform was then in the air; [...] the old R.U.I. order was passing. There was little to be said for it in the new age which it had helped to create; such are the ironies of history. [Mary Macken, 1954][3]

In university language department staff lists, foreign names become less dominant from the 1880s. The shift towards local appointments is also found in Britain, but the Irish case differs in two respects. The late Victorian and Edwardian decades introduced two local groups to the staffing of Irish universities: professors of modern Irish and women professors of modern languages. How these changes came about, and in which universities, is worth exploring. The present chapter will consider profiles of these home-grown academics, and the extent to which their Victorian philological studies influenced their work. Showing how change is driven by individuals as well as by institutions, it will argue that developments in modern language staffing both reflected and shaped the Irish university landscape, culturally and politically, during the transition from 'Royal' to 'National' in the years before independence (1922).

Irish-born modern linguists

At Cork, two local men were to lead modern languages through the RUI years up to the founding of the NUI. Owen O'Ryan, QCC's professor of modern languages from 1879, was succeeded by William F. T. Butler in 1895. O'Ryan (1834–95), from Tipperary, was a versatile Cork graduate. Interestingly, his broad balance of expertise in French, German and Italian was mostly attained through life experiences. After distinguishing himself in both classical and modern languages for his 1858 degree, he travelled to Germany, where he studied German at the university of Bonn and also lived in Munich; in 1860 he crossed the Alps to work in Turin for a few years, at the new Italian Ministry for Foreign

Affairs (Italy having recently been united) while also giving private language lessons. He spent the winter of 1865–6 in Florence as a translator, journalist and private language teacher. O'Ryan's final move was northwards, to Paris in 1866, where he worked as a tutor and attended lectures at the Sorbonne and Collège de France, obtaining a diploma in the teaching of English and German.[4] In short, he seems to have been as nomadic and multilingual a European as the mobile Irish churchmen of earlier centuries.

The Cork graduate's own account of these peripatetic graduate years is found in a handwritten application he submitted to Queen's College Galway in September 1868 for the vacant chair of modern languages following the death of Bensbach.[5] The application was warmly supported by Professor de Véricour, who had encouraged his former student to apply. He testifies that O'Ryan[6]

> has acquired a very remarkable knowledge of the languages of Germany and Italy. As to French, it is as familiar to him as his native language; he has been residing in Paris, these last three years, devoted to literary pursuits, and I have had frequent intercourse with him. I believe it would be very difficult to find a candidate for the Galway professorship as qualified as he is for the post.

De Véricour was particularly impressed by O'Ryan's equal mastery of 'the three modern languages taught in the university, aloof from national prejudices, holding the three languages in an equal balance'.[7] The application, however, failed: the post went to Charles Geisler, and O'Ryan had to wait another 11 years for a professorship.

Unsuccessful in his bid for the Galway chair, O'Ryan remained in Paris and embarked on the study of French law but was interrupted by the Franco-Prussian War in 1870, during which time he moved to live in Tours. To quote from his death announcement:[8]

> He returned again to Paris after the campaign, to engage with his usual energy in the twin employment of teaching and study, with which he was still occupied, when, in 1879, he was appointed from among 40 competitors to succeed his old teacher and life-long friend, De Vericour, as Professor of Modern Languages in Queen's College Cork.

Professor O'Ryan was made an examiner and fellow of the RUI and served as College Librarian from 1888.[9] The breadth of his interests, and his keen translation skills, can be gauged from a substantial paper on the Italian poet Leopardi read to the Cork Literary and Scientific Society in 1882.[10] His tenure was cut short by his early death, aged 61.

O'Ryan's broad range of interests was not unique. Several professors combined their language work with other pursuits – legal, religious and administrative. Clongowes-educated William Francis Butler (1869–1930), O'Ryan's successor to the Cork chair in 1895, was a RUI (Dublin) graduate, with an MA and travelling studentship in modern languages (1894). Best known as an historian of Irish land tenure,[11] he also served for four years (1906–10) as registrar for the Cork College. Roman Catholics and nationalists had lobbied QCC in 1875 and 1889, for more home-grown RUI graduates to be employed there. With Butler's appointment, they cannot have had any 'cause to complain'.[12] Fr John F. Hogan, Maynooth's professor of modern languages from 1886, taught French and Italian and (like de Véricour) wrote a serious and well-balanced study of Dante.[13] Other listed local staff members have left fewer traces.[14]

Perhaps the most remarkable local linguist at the RUI during these years was the polyglot professor John James O'Carroll SJ who became something of a legend in academic circles. He appears in University College Calendars of the early 1880s, when the Jesuits took over the College's management. In 1882–3, the Jesuit college in Temple Street became an RUI affiliated college and Fr O'Carroll was an examiner in modern languages. He was at the same time a member of the Irish language, history, and archaeology department.[15] He came to the university with extensive teaching experience at Clongowes Wood, Limerick and Milltown Park in Dublin. He appears to have been an extraordinarily gifted philologist, having mastered over fourteen different languages and dialects, acquired a reading knowledge of eight others and a conversational knowledge of yet another eight. When applying for a professorship in modern languages, he claimed a mastery of French, German, Italian and Spanish, as well as Latin and Greek; in addition, he stated that he had a good knowledge of Portuguese, Dutch, Swedish, Danish and Romanian, along with Icelandic, Anglo-Saxon and Magyar, as well as Polish, Bohemian and Russian, and various Slavonic dialects. He also professed an interest in old forms of the main European languages and their medieval literatures, in addition to being fluent in Gaelic.[16] The application was supported by a string of stellar testimonials from native speaker peers in German, French, Italian and Spanish. All of the distinguished referees – including Professor Max Müller from Oxford – praise the priest's fluency, grammatical accuracy and near-native pronunciation.[17] A lively communicator, Fr O'Carroll worked tirelessly, until his untimely death in March 1889 at the age of 52. A warm appreciation in *The Freeman's Journal*, 6 March 1889, gives an idea of how he kept up his multilingual proficiency:

> He was an indefatigable student, seeking every facility to extend the range of his knowledge. The ships which brought foreigners from distant lands to Dublin sometimes supplied him with teachers; it was not unusual for him to pay a foreign sailor to [...] talk to him the language of Sweden or of Iceland.

Allowing for some possible exaggeration, O'Carroll's profile exemplifies a number of strands we have been noting in Irish linguists of the past. Like other clerics before him (and like his lay counterpart Owen O'Ryan), Fr O'Carroll had used his study time on the continent with considerable profit. Having entered the French Province of the order in Amiens in 1853, he studied theology over the following twenty years at no fewer than seven different Jesuit centres in five European countries: France (Amiens, Laval, Montauban), Austria (Feldkirch), Italy (Rome), the Netherlands (Maastricht) and Poland (Stara Wieś). In each country, he worked at perfecting his knowledge of the local language and was absorbed by language study all his life.

In tune with his time, O'Carroll was also alive to the spirit of the Gaelic Revival. As a middle-class Dubliner, he had taught himself Irish and was a member of the Gaelic Union's Council, serving on a committee of its journal, *Irisleabhar na Gaedhilge* [The Gaelic Journal], to which he regularly contributed. He was an early convert to modern Irish, a language in which he gained enough proficiency to teach and publish research papers. A former student recalled that this linguistic prodigy was not only 'in constant correspondence with the great German philologists who were studying Celtic', but in addition had[18] formed a class in Irish in the College. I was in it. With a foretaste of sentiment, which was in after years to become widespread, Father O'Carroll decided that in learning Irish we should completely abandon the speech of the Sasanach, and the classes were, therefore, conducted in French. I think we should probably have acquired a more firm grip on Irish, and perhaps by this time have earned the *Fáinne*, if our French had been more sure of itself.

IRISH PROFESSORS IN THE GAELIC REVIVAL

We have already discussed, in Chapter Four, the first Victorian cohort of Irish professors at the early Queen's Colleges and the Catholic University, philologists and Old Irish specialists in the main, who attracted few or no students and whose posts had remained vacant since 1862.[19] Our focus here will be on the last quarter of the nineteenth and early years of the twentieth century, when a new wave of professors were appointed to posts in Irish within a very different cultural climate.

As we have seen, the late-Victorian crescendo of cultural nationalism fostered a new confidence among Irish-language enthusiasts. This helped to drive the agenda of the SPIL [Society for the Preservation of the Irish Language], founded in 1876, and its successor, the GL [Gaelic League]. Increased hopes for a future where the Irish people would gain complete sovereignty helped to build support, among the population at large, for the Cinderella of modern languages. In the universities, since the suppression of the original Celtic chairs in the Queen's colleges, and the death of the CU's Eugene O'Curry (1862), Irish, or 'Celtic', had remained without official degree status.[20] At first, the marginal position of the native vernacular at tertiary level impeded any meaningful progress in pursuing the revivalists' aims. In these circumstances, the pursuit of an element of compulsory study of the language is understandable. The uncompromising tactics used to achieve the aims of the new movement were those of a generation simultaneously scarred by raw memories of Famine evictions and emboldened by the successes of the Land League campaign.[21] Language repossession had to follow land repossession.

An increasingly robust strain of Irish-American identity politics was simultaneously burgeoning offshore. Among the post-Famine Irish emigrants in the USA there was a small group of Irish-language literati who continued to copy Irish manuscripts in American libraries, and participated in Hibernophile societies and cultural activities, including giving Irish lessons.[22] This new diaspora, sharply aware of its identity, was to be an important force for spurring on the fight for language recognition on the home front.[23] Things had certainly changed since the immediate post-Famine years.

These transformative cultural trends inevitably filtered through to universities, where a series of appointments to posts in Irish were made during the last three decades of Victoria's reign and into the 1900s. The new generation of Irish professors formed a cast of singular individuals, all Irish-born, from different backgrounds and provinces.[24] Most of them were active members of the Gaelic League or its antecedent, the Society for the Preservation of the Irish Language, albeit some were more active than others in these cultural nationalist organisations. United in the belief that the Irish language had to be revived, they differed on the means to be adopted for achieving that goal. Their public debates frequently divided them along the familiar fault-line between ancient and modern, as some of them preferred a classical and philological approach to the study of Irish while others preferred to put their energies and faith into transmitting the contemporary living vernacular.

We have noted the difficulties, in the early years of the Queen's Colleges, in attracting students of Celtic. In the late Victorian period, a contrary phenomenon emerged: students began to demonstrate a keen interest in the Irish language. Among the expanding range of student societies in Queen's College Belfast, in January 1906 a Gaelic Society [*Cumann Gaedhealach an Choláiste*] was launched under the patronage of the college's president, Rev. Thomas Hamilton. Interest was generated by the Belfast branch of the Gaelic League, founded in 1895. The Gaelic Society had 'the avowed object of re-establishing Irish as the language of Ireland'.[25] It ran Irish classes, competed in *Feiseanna*, organised public meetings, put on dramas and lobbied for the restoration of the Queen's Belfast Celtic chair.[26] Most of its members who took Irish classes were Protestants.[27] In 1907, Trinity College Dublin students founded their own *Cumann Gaelach*.[28]

More significantly, grass-roots enthusiasm for Irish affected university staffing, sometimes happening with surprising speed. Back in January 1874, students at the Catholic University had lobbied for lectures on Irish language and literature. A letter signed by 16 students, politely requesting that lectures in Irish language and literature be set up at an early date, ended with the sentence: 'We hope before the Term is much older to have the opportunity of testifying our zeal.'[29] A temporary lectureship in Irish became a professorship the following October. It was held by Brian O'Looney, a founding member of the SPIL.[30] When the Stephen's Green college came under the auspices of the RUI, Edmund Hogan SJ (1831–1917) was professor of Irish language and history from 1884 to 1909. From Cobh in Co. Cork, Hogan had studied for the priesthood in Belgium and France for 11 years before returning to teach French and German in various Jesuit colleges. As professor he published a number of works of historical and linguistic interest, notably on Irish placenames, and was to be an important mentor in Old Irish for Eoin MacNeill.[31]

While the stirrings of revivalist sentiment among the student body directly led to the re-establishment of Irish on the curriculum in the Stephen's Green college, the zeal of students in QCC was weaker. A notable exception was Osborn Bergin (1873–1950), a young Cork graduate in Classics, who was teaching Classics at Cork Grammar School when he joined Cork's Lee Branch of the Gaelic League. He studied the language so successfully that he was appointed in 1897 to a lectureship in Celtic at his alma mater. The Cork college, first of the old Queen's Colleges to resume the teaching of Celtic studies, had been lobbied to set up the post by the Gaelic League. However, the lectureship, funded by student fees, was unprofitable due to low undergraduate take-up.[32] Bergin's reaction was adventurous. In 1904 he left his native Cork on a travelling studentship to study Old Irish in Berlin. Having taken his doctorate in Freiburg, he was later to hold the Chair of Old and Middle Irish at UCD for 31 years, and was a renowned Celtic scholar.[33]

The greening of the clergy: the turbulence of Father O'Hickey

One of the more dramatic changes wrought by the new cultural climate of the Gaelic revival generation happened in the national Catholic seminary, St Patrick's College Maynooth. Two clerical linguists from the end of the Victorian era left their mark there in noteworthy ways. In a cruelly foreshortened life, Maynooth's professor of modern Irish,

Fr Eugene O'Growney (1863–99), became a founding member and leading light of the Gaelic League.[34] Having started to study the language in earnest in his teens, he was active in promoting it among his fellow clerical students after entering the seminary in 1882, and later published translations into Irish, modern editions of Old Irish texts, and the bestselling *Simple Lessons in Irish*.

In the 1880s the fortunes of Irish were at a low ebb in Maynooth with language classes precariously staffed by annual postgraduate appointments. In 1887 the Scholastic Council even considered doing away with mandatory classes for clerical beginners.[35] This situation was reversed when O'Growney was appointed to the chair in 1891. He ran elementary classes for all students at junior level, increased the class offerings overall and delivered annual lectures on Irish literature and antiquities. After poor health led to his retirement from teaching in 1896 and an early death from tuberculosis,[36] his enthusiasm lived on, as did that of his successor, Michael O'Hickey. By now Maynooth's students were demanding that Irish be used more throughout the college on a daily basis.[37] A successful student society, *Cuallacht Chuilm Cille* [the League of St Columba or Columban League], was set up in 1898 to promote Irish history, language and culture. Patrick Corish, historian of Maynooth, comments:[38]

> Within a few years there was an impressive string of publications, primarily the work of the students themselves, beginning with *Irishleabhar Muighe Nuadhat* [...]. Publication, however, was never seen as the primary aim. Rather, it was proficiency in the language, and this was seen not as an end in itself but as the key to the Irish Catholic religious experience.

The fusion of patriotism and piety created an atmosphere of fervent nationalism in the rank and file of the college community. Maynooth was going decidedly green. All the more understandable, then, that the dismissal of Michael O'Hickey from the chair of Irish in June 1909 should have led to a furore of protest from the student body.[39] O'Hickey had strenuously objected when there were moves in 1904 to dilute the compulsory status of elementary Irish classes in the national seminary. Shortly afterwards, he participated prominently on behalf of the Gaelic League in its 1908–09 campaign to make Irish an essential component for matriculating in the new NUI. In a series of letters to campaign meetings and to the press, O'Hickey excoriated senior clerical members of the University Senate, whom he believed to be opposed to the introduction of 'essential' Irish, using offensive, intemperate language. Unleashing a torrent of ultra-nationalist rhetoric, he accused them of siding with West Britons, the enemies of Ireland, denounced them as traitors to the noble cause of Irish freedom, and called for a black-list to be made of the 'recreant Nationalist Senators'.[40] A clash with his Maynooth superiors was inevitable: once their omnipotence had been challenged the substance of his argument was irrelevant. When asked by the college's Visitors to resign from his teaching position, he refused. Unwisely, he brought his grievance to Rome in April 1910, seeking leave from a Vatican tribunal to appeal in the civil courts against unjust dismissal. His hopes for a fair hearing proved (predictably) naïve. A characteristic five-year stay in the eternal city left the case unresolved, entangled in cumbersome legal procedure. Evidence had to be printed in Latin; to prepare their pleas, advocates worked through Italian. O'Hickey returned to Ireland in the summer of 1916, to a country utterly changed from the one he had left; he died that same winter. Ironically, the Gaelic League's measure had been carried by the NUI Senate in June 1910, 'just after O'Hickey had left for Rome'.[41]

The O'Hickey case shows how the Irish language could ignite extraordinary depths of feeling in the strident politics of the 1900s, and how some professors could be too passionately wed to their subject for their own good. Michael O'Hickey was smitten by an idealised version of an Irish-speaking Ireland. Seán O'Casey admired him as a man of courage and integrity, but by the professor's own admission he was 'strongly, fiercely, savagely'[42] vehement about this one issue, which blinded him to the possibility of reasonable reflection. There were, after all, at least two sides to the question of whether to make Irish a requirement for matriculation in the NUI, and the Gaelic League was itself deeply divided on the matter. From the Maynooth College's point of view, the case for O'Hickey's removal from office was an open and shut one. Intemperate language, intransigence and insubordination were all the more unacceptable in

7.1 Michael O'Hickey, Maynooth Professor of Irish, Maynooth. (*No known copyright restrictions.*)

a college professor who was supposed to be a role model for young seminarians. In his superiors' view, Fr O'Hickey had compromised his position beyond repair.

The professor had his finger on the pulse of nationalist Ireland, however, and the populist view was that he was a martyr to his principles, deprived of his post on account of his patriotic zeal on behalf of his country's native language. In the pages of ACS during the summer of 1909, Patrick Pearse denounced the episcopal Trustees of Maynooth in rhetoric as overblown as O'Hickey's own, and reduced the campaign for essential Irish to a simplistic two-sided issue, Irish-Ireland versus the enemy.[43] A *cause célèbre* both in and of its time, the O'Hickey case illuminates once again how much the Gaelic League campaign divided the younger generation from its elders. In the main, bishops and older clergy opposed the scheme to make Irish essential for matriculation, while younger priests, and the Christian Brothers teaching order, were in favour of the enhanced status of Irish.[44] This reflected a generational divide found amongst the laity at large. O'Hickey attracted widespread student support, and the more prominent among his followers were refused ordination.[45]

The tone of O'Hickey's pronouncements on the language issue shifted the terms of the debate from the merits of studying Irish to a matter of simple patriotism.[46] His dismissal, however, coincided with wider language pressures at Maynooth during the 1900s, a period when the college was facing new resource and timetabling problems. Having obtained university-level recognition on two fronts – the Pontifical charter to confer ecclesiastical degrees in theology from Rome in 1896 had been shortly followed, for arts and science degrees, by Royal University and then National University affiliation – Maynooth College found it difficult to accommodate the new challenges.[47] Conflicting pressures on an already over-demanding curriculum of study were felt acutely in the area of languages, particularly with regard to the level of attainment that students were supposed to reach. Concerns were expressed, both in the Kildare college and in Rome, about the insufficient time devoted to studying the classics and the inadequacy of students' standard of oral Latin for examinations.[48] While Rome insisted that Irish clerical students should pay more attention to Latin (for philosophy and theology) and Greek (for scripture), the Royal University required that written examinations be conducted through English instead of Latin. Among the languages, Irish was now in a doubly weak position: being as yet a non-degree subject, and there being too little time to prepare students for university examinations in Irish, it continued to be relegated to second position by the College authorities.[49] Given this state of affairs, the Gaelic League's proposal to make Irish an essential component for matriculation met with little support from those who steered Maynooth's core curriculum.

These differences of perspective did not stop the wave of Hibernophilia from taking hold of Roman Catholic clergy. During the same late Victorian years, a number of Irish-language revivalists emerged among other men of the cloth. Motivated by the same kind of patriotism, this generation of linguistic clerics included pillars of the Gaelic Revival like Peter O'Leary, Patrick Dineen and Michael Sheehan. All three were influential, in different ways, on the direction taken by Irish study in the post-Victorian years. Inspired by the Gaelic League's calls for new writing in contemporary Irish, Peter O'Leary (1839–1920), better known as An tAthair Peadar Ó Laoghaire, devoted his later years to producing 'a prolific stream of publications from his parochial house in the north Cork countryside'[50] and was to be an exemplary Irish prose stylist for twentieth-century learners. The eccentric Jesuit from Kerry, Patrick Dineen (1860–1934), parted company with the Society of Jesus in 1900 in order to devote his time to writing in Irish, editing Irish texts and preparing the Irish–English dictionary (1904) which still bears his name. He was also an active member of the Gaelic League, and polemical columnist in *The Leader* for over two decades.[51] Thirdly, archbishop Michael Sheehan (1870–1945), who had been a brilliant language student and classicist, went on to pursue postgraduate study in Oxford, Greifswald, Rome and Bonn. Influenced by the Celtic scholar Heinrich Zimmer in Greifswald (1897), he became absorbed by the study of Irish, and in 1906 (co-)founded Ring College, an Irish-language immersion boarding school in Co. Waterford, which continues to host generations of anglophone adolescents who take a year of their schooling entirely through Irish.[52] Last but by no means least among the clerical sons of the revival, mention should be made of the protean scholar, Monsignor Paddy Browne [Pádraig de Brún] (1889–1960). This prodigiously gifted mathematician, who was also a poet, classicist and outstanding linguist, spent his summers in Dunquin in the heart of the Kerry Gaeltacht, translating into Irish the classics of European tradition: Homer, Sophocles, Dante, Racine.[53]

Polemical pioneers: nativists and progressivists[54]

We continue to stray into the post-Victorian years, on the grounds that the essence of a period cannot be fully grasped without sketching what came after it, and arguably because of it. In the transformed Irish-language landscape, while all revivalists were on a mission to save the native vernacular, they were not of one mind on what form of Irish was being revived as the national language. Fundamental questions were raised during this vibrant period of acute linguistic self-awareness. Which of the various dialects of Irish, if any, should take precedence as the standard model for teaching and writing? Which type-font should be used – Roman or Gaelic – in the growing number of publications in Irish? And if there should ever be a consensus reached on simplifying the language's spelling, how would the simplification proceed? In the absence of a centralised public authority to determine policy, these kinds of questions engendered a rich, robust and at times strident public debate during the 1890s and 1900s.[55] Academic contributors to these debates had strong and divergent views on the stakes and variables of Irish study. Several of the questions continued to be contentious after independence, and indeed – some would say – have yet to be resolved.[56]

While the Gaelic League, through the direct method, was expanding the teaching of contemporary spoken Irish in centres throughout the island, there was at the same time a recognition, among revivalists, of the need to transmit older forms of the language, if Irish was to gain credibility in the groves of academe. The School of Irish Learning was set up in Dublin in 1903 by Kuno Meyer (Liverpool professor of German and Celtic scholar), John Strachan (professor of Greek and Celticist at Manchester) and others, to underpin the revival with a scholarly basis, in order to have it taken seriously in Ireland and elsewhere, and to train future Celtic scholars. In July 1903, some 40 students, male and female, gathered for two hours per day, over four weeks, to listen to John Strachan on Old Irish grammar; in September the same year Henry Sweet (Oxford Reader in phonetics) taught the phonetics of modern Irish and Kuno Meyer taught palaeography.[57] In addition to running summer courses in phonetics, philology, palaeography, and Old Irish, taught by visiting scholars from abroad, the School founded the journal *Ériu* which is still in the vanguard of Celtic studies, and awarded travelling studentships to young scholars. Student fees were complemented by voluntary donations and subscriptions from benefactors. The School was incorporated into the Royal Irish Academy in 1925.

This trailblazing initiative served the academy and the revival project very well. It provided a forum for scholars, helping to disseminate research and establish Dublin as a centre for Celtic studies. Through its funding of postgraduate studies it allowed the training of candidates for chairs in the new National University. This was the route taken by UCD's Osborn Bergin and UCG's Tomás Ó Máille, who were both appointed on foot of their doctoral studies abroad, funded by travelling studentships from the School of Irish Learning. The School also, incidentally, helped to maintain direct international links in the field of Celtic studies. More than any other area of scholarship, Celtic studies continued to draw Irish researchers abroad, and keep them in touch with citizens from other countries, especially Germany. German Celticists like Kuno Meyer, Ernst Windisch, or Heinrich Zimmer, were essential interlocutors in the interpretation of Ireland's linguistic past.[58] Irish-German contacts among Celtic scholars were to continue well into the twentieth century.[59]

Celtic scholarship had long been accepted as central to the university's brief, but the fledgling NUI's professors of Irish were not necessarily at one on the university's role in teaching the contemporary Irish language. In making his case for Irish as a prerequisite for NUI matriculation, Eoin MacNeill, UCD's new professor of Early Irish History, drew an important distinction: 'Mere instruction in the Irish language is not university work, it is work for primary and secondary schools.'[60] Universities were for teaching and studying 'old and middle Irish, the philology of the Celtic languages, the literature of modern Irish, and the history and archaeology of Ireland'.[61] This sounds like a familiar view of the role of a university Irish (or Celtic) department, prioritising revival as preservation and transmission of knowledge about the (past) culture of an ancient tongue over revival as extending the presence of the vernacular living language for practical communication in the public sphere.[62]

The lofty academic approach was taken to extremes by the Rev. Professor Richard Henebry (1863–1916), appointed to the first NUI professorship of Irish at UCC in 1909.[63] For Henebry, native speaker from Waterford and linguistic purist, new writing in Irish must contain 'no foreign admixture. English idiom, mannerisms, style, system of thought, must be rigidly eschewed.'[64] The overriding concern should be to conserve the Irish language, to preserve its 'purity and grace' against the 'strange, ungentle touch of the modern renovator'.[65] In a series of caustic critiques of the quality of Irish published by his fellow Gaelic Leaguers, during the winter of 1908–9,[66] Henebry spared no scorn for what he called 'revival Irish', the kind of Irish writing being produced by those – Pearse among them – who had learned Irish as a second language. Even the League's teaching booklets for children are targets: on the League's *An Chéad Leabhar, an chéad chuid* (1908), he recommends: 'If children are to be brought into contact with the living speech in order to learn Irish, they must be carefully kept away from this book.'[67]

Eccentric to the core,[68] Henebry was convinced of the need to retrieve a purer state of the written language than the non-native speaker's variety he disdained. Blithely optimistic about human behaviour, he saw no reason why native Irish speakers could not be weaned off their colloquial (and in his view impoverished) modern idiom, and trained to speak with the fluent classical lucidity and enriched vocabulary of the early modern Seathrún Céitinn [Geoffrey Keating], who had died in 1644:[69]

> Our native Irish speakers, of whatever province soever, can easily by training correct their vernacular to the normal of the last classic writers, subsidizing insensibly by the way much of the splendid spirit of recent philological study, whereby voice would be given once more to a stored-up wealth of words that had long lain silent. The head-waters are abundant to overflowing; we have but to make a staunch in the broken conduit, and the flow will go on copious and sparkling like long ago.

This nativist bias towards returning to ancestral Irish is reflected in the syllabus that Henebry implemented when appointed professor at Cork, as Cornelius Buttimer describes:[70]

> Thus scholars even in First Year Pass were obliged to learn the rudiments of Irish grammar from John Strachan's *Old Irish Paradigms* (Dublin, 1907), a standard handbook of Old Irish (600–900 AD) 'simplified for pupils of modern Irish' in the case of the noun, and from *Sgéalaigheacht Chéitinn* (Dublin, 1909), a primer of seventeenth-century Irish, in the case of the verb. Very few revival works were permitted in the pass courses for all three years; only texts reflecting traditional life-styles such as An tAthair Peadar's *Séadna* were countenanced. The honours courses were of an even more antique flavour. In Second Year, students' practice at writing Irish was to be confined to compositions in the Early Modern Irish idiom (1200–1600 AD), while in Third Year this requirement had reached the earlier, Middle Irish (900–1200) stage. The Third Year syllabus placed a heavy emphasis on Old Irish hagiography and metrics, as well as 'the main principles of Indo-Keltic Philology and of comparative Keltic grammar'.

While such a syllabus sounds, to us, doomed to failure, it may have seemed otherwise in the context of how Victorians had approached language study. All language learning involved the past. Part of the standard pedagogy of the classics in English public schools consisted in producing original lines of verse, in correctly scanned metrical Latin or Greek, as a regular task imposed on young learners.[71] The exercise of writing sentences or passages in an ancient form of a target language encouraged learners to grasp foreign structures and vocabulary.[72] Henebry was Victorian, and Victorian practices of language study permeated his Irish classroom.

That said, Henebry's egregious neglect of contemporary spoken Irish clashed with the practice of his Gaelic League contemporaries,[73] who – as we discussed in Chapter 5 – were determined to bring the contemporary language (caint na ndaoine) into the classroom by prioritising oral expression. Henebry's programme of study could not have been further from the reforming ideals of a Pearse or a Hyde. Nor was the cultivation of seventeenth-century Irish as the only model for new writing seriously entertained by other Celtic scholars. When the kite of opting for Keating's Irish was flown again in 1923, in an essay in Studies by a German Jesuit who had learned Irish, it met little support from local academic respondents.[74]

In the event, Professor Henebry's 'preference for imparting an archaized form of the language was abandoned'[75] by his successor, Tadhg Ó Donnchadha ('Torna'). In any case, even during Henebry's professorship, UCC students were offered alternative forms of Irish to learn and they voted with their feet. They were more attracted to classes in Modern Irish given by a colleague.[76] The pragmatic, progressivist approach won the day. If the language had any hope of surviving, it had to reflect contemporary native usage and could not remain frozen in a supposed golden age of three centuries before.[77]

Yet there were gaps to be filled. Those who argued for the living language to be taught and studied at university were well aware of the need for new writing to emerge in the same contemporary vernacular. 'We have abandoned the archaic style, but a modern Irish prose has not yet been licked into shape.'[78] Further divisions arose on the question of how to model a new literary language on an established tradition that was predominantly oral. If new writing was to spring from the spoken language of the people living in the Gaeltacht, how faithful should writers remain to that source, in terms of themes, style, genre? A central part of the Gaelic League project concerned the collecting and recording, all around the country, of folklore in Irish as told by seanchaithe [storytellers].[79] Some argued that this growing repository of seanscéalta [traditional stories] should be the model for new narrative writing in Irish. The advantages included tapping into a rich store of vocabulary and idiom, as well as salvaging Irish folk wisdom and proverbs from oblivion. Ideally it would also ensure the survival of a 'purer' style and transmit native lore and culture to future generations. On the other hand, purists were unhappy with the quality of some of the recordings, or when English terms were substituted for native utterances. There were inevitable transcription errors that, added to multiple dialect differences, were confusing for learners of the language.[80] More pertinently, commentators and writers in the progressivist camp – Pearse, Pádraic Ó Conaire and others – felt that literary Irish prose needed to move beyond modelling itself on traditional genres and themes if it was to cater for a twentieth-century urban readership. Such writers, in Philip O'Leary's words, 'questioned how a vitally contemporary prose relevant to the concerns of a modern European society could evolve from the folk tales of a rural peasantry.'[81]

There was some sense on both sides. It was important to preserve native tradition as well as go beyond it. The Gaelic Revival project was to build a national language, with all its parts. People needed to master everyday usage, but for the language to be sustained, as a written language, it needed to be enriched and stretched to encompass as many possibilities of expression as possible. In a university teaching context, combining the teaching of Classical with contemporary Irish offered the best route to the future.

7.2 Tomás Ó Máille, UCG
Professor of Irish and Celtic Philology, University College Galway. Photograph, University Archives, University of Galway. (*Reproduced courtesy of University of Galway.*)

To meet this double requirement, two language chairs were set up in UCD when the NUI was established, filled by Hyde in modern Irish and Bergin in early Irish, while at UCC, old Irish was increasingly seen as part of the BA in Celtic Studies and the MA.[82] The 1909 appointments in Galway and Belfast were both born in Connemara, though from different cultural and social backgrounds: Tomás Ó Máille (1880–1938) and Frederick William O'Connell (1876–1929). Ó Máille joined the staff of UCG as professor of Modern Irish Language and Literature. His chair was expanded in the following year to incorporate Celtic philology.[83] This 29-year-old, who remained in the post until his death in 1938, was well qualified to take on both briefs. The youngest of nine surviving children from a family of native speakers in the Maam valley, Co. Galway, mentioned in an earlier chapter,[84] he had been an active member of the Gaelic League, collecting the words of songs from around Corr na Móna, which were later published. Matriculating in 1902, he was an early student at the School of Irish Learning before graduating from the RUI in 1905. On the award of a travelling studentship from the School in 1906, his postgraduate studies to train with eminent Celtic scholars, Rudolf Thurneysen in Freiburg and Heinrich Zimmer in Berlin, allowed him also to include Manchester and Liverpool. His Freiburg doctorate was awarded in 1909.[85]

Ó Máille's was a timely appointment for the Galway college.[86] His application for the chair suggests a teaching approach that would combine Celtic philology with modern literature and language, in the hope that he would 'develop the natural advantages for Modern Irish of the situation of the University College in an Irish-speaking district so as to make it a great centre of Irish learning and Celtic Studies.'[87] While he mostly lectured on philological matters, his publications ranged over Old and Middle, Classical and Contemporary Irish, and were to span philological studies of Old Irish texts as well as linguistic features specific to the Irish used in Connacht. He made valuable recordings of the Irish still spoken in the 1900s and 1920s in the Connacht *Breac-Ghaeltacht* ['speckled' Irish-speaking regions] – i.e., parts of Sligo, Leitrim and East Connacht; and developed a Linguaphone course in modern Irish.[88]

167

Queen's College Belfast sundered its link with the other RUI colleges when the National University of Ireland (NUI) was established (1908). The now independent Queen's University Belfast created a lectureship in Celtic rather than a chair of Irish.[89] QUB's first lecturer in Celtic languages was a Church of Ireland clergyman, Rev. Frederick William O'Connell [Feardorcha Ó Conaill], born in Connemara a few miles from where Tomás Ó Máille grew up. Son of the rector of Omey and Clifden, he was a prodigiously gifted language student at Trinity – winning prizes in Hebrew, German, Irish and classics – and took a literature degree followed by a divinity degree. Appointed in 1909, he resigned his Belfast post in 1925 when his wife died of tuberculosis. Shortly afterwards he moved to Dublin and worked in broadcasting for Dublin's newly established radio station, 2RN, set up in 1926. He was appointed Assistant Director of Broadcasting in 1927. There, 'among his other duties, and because of his linguistic skills, he had charge of correspondence with foreign radio stations.'[90] Sometimes, greetings were broadcast to other linguistic communities. The *Irish Times* of 25 February 1928 reports:[91]

> greetings and messages have been broadcast from 2RN in French, German, Italian, Spanish, Polish, Danish, Norwegian, Esperanto, Hindustani, Arabic and Persian. The polyglot broadcaster is the Assistant Director of 2RN, Dr F. W. O'Connell, who sometimes hides his identity under the literary *nom de guerre* of Conall Cearnach.

When the Irish Free State was doing its best to remain in contact with the wider world, who better than this learned polyglot to send its greetings – in eleven languages, excluding English – at the New Year and other occasions? The former lecturer also sent greetings in Welsh and other Celtic languages and, for his home listeners, broadcast talks in or on the Irish language,[92] 'with the same wide range and playfulness that characterised his essays. He spoke on such subjects as grammar, the tradition of the Wren Boys, and Connaughtmen'.[93]

O'Connell's writings, as unexpected as his career profile, betray a breadth of interests and language expertise. The low uptake of Celtic at QUB may have helped his eclectic range of publications to flourish.[94] As well as producing a grammar of Old Irish, he translated, into and out of Irish, prayers and liturgical texts. He rendered Merriman's *Cúirt a' Mhean oíche* [*The Midnight Court*] (1909) into English and collaborated with his classicist colleague at QUB, professor Robert Mitchell Henry, on translating a seventeenth-century version of a Spanish astronomer, *An Irish Corpus Astronomiae, being Manus O'Donnell's seventeenth century version of the Lunario of Geronymo Cortès* (1915).[95] He translated Stevenson's *Dr Jekyll and Mr Hyde* (1929), and edited Peadar Ó Laoghaire's Irish translation of *Don Quixote* [*Don Cíochóte*] (1921). A humorous, eccentric essayist on all manner of topics, he even tried his hand at fiction, with a collection of magic realist gothic tales (1924), *The Fatal Move and other stories*. His essays reveal a broad-minded cultural nationalist and language revivalist, who situated Ireland's language and history in a very long timespan. O'Connell's arguments for the uniquely practical value of learning Irish are grounded in his own late Victorian philological training: for him, Irish is 'an aid to the study of philology, [...] a preparation for the study of Classics,' and 'a phonetic guide to the acquisition of other languages'.[96]

He could also poke gentle fun at the absurdities of his fellow countrymen. As, for example, in an essay entitled 'Patriotism and Language':[97]

to say that we [Irish Protestants] should have nothing to do with the Irish language because it is spoken principally by Catholics and Nationalists is as sensible as though I refused to go on a tramcar and took 'Shank's mare' because the majority of tram conductors were Orangemen. If it is a question of religion, let them be consistent, let them eschew Latin, for it is the language of 'Popery'.

When in 1929 a road accident cut short his life, he was still in mid-career and would doubtless have continued to record new achievements.

O'Connell's status as a Victorian-born Irish scholar who morphed into a radio broadcaster nudges him over the threshold into the twentieth century, the period discussed in our final chapter. His profile matches one exemplified by other Victorian men of the cloth whose passion for languages, and their interconnections, seems to know no bounds. His radio greetings to the nations of the world in their own languages encapsulate, too, the fiercely independent spirit of the young Free State, wishing to distance itself from England by de-anglicising at every possible opportunity. Within Ireland, O'Connell also

7.3 Frederick William O'Connell, QUB Lecturer, Celtic Languages and Literature, Queen's University Belfast. (*No known copyright restrictions.*)

spans important cultural divides, as a Church of Ireland clergyman whose second wife was Roman Catholic, and as a Connemara-born Irishman who lectured in Irish in Belfast, a city that, before he resigned, had already become capital of the new jurisdiction of Northern Ireland.

During the same pre-independence years, the study of Irish in Trinity was beset by different issues. While NUI professors were absorbed in debating parameters for the language, now that every matriculating student had studied it to a certain level of proficiency, the status of Trinity's Divinity School, where Irish was housed, had been undergoing something of a crisis following Fawcett's Act of 1873.[98] In contrast to the NUI's soaring numbers of students taking Irish, the TCD Divinity School's intake fell after 1900.[99] The College's Celtic Studies Moderatorship, set up in 1907, never drew large numbers of students.[100]

These differences in culture and ethos correlated with an increasing political polarisation between Trinity and the NUI. There is some evidence that, as far back as 1896, Trinity's appointment of (the relatively undistinguished) Protestant clergyman James E. Murphy from the Beara peninsula rather than Douglas Hyde (its brilliant alumnus), had been partly due to fears about Hyde's nationalism.[101] When Irish was decoupled from Divinity in 1919, Murphy's successor, Thomas F. O'Rahilly, put the discipline on a modern footing in Trinity.[102] However, the benign transition in the sphere of Irish was not mirrored by a smooth transition in the political arena. TCD's staff experienced the violent upheavals of the 1914–23 decade in a way that was different from colleagues in other colleges, with their campus depopulated by the engagement of staff and students in combat or other service during World War I, followed by the dawning of a new establishment in Ireland entailing a period of adjustment for ex-Unionists to a changed constitutional order.

PIONEERING WOMEN PROFESSORS OF MODERN LANGUAGES

A pattern requiring explanation

For obvious reasons – not least the shortage of female graduates – none of the Victorian modern languages appointments were women, but in the new century a pioneering cohort of young women scholars was soon recruited to certain academic areas. The NUI (founded in 1908) appointed women professors in arts disciplines: Mary Hayden was UCD's professor of modern Irish history from 1911; Mary Josephine Donovan, also a historian, became UCG's first woman professor in 1914.[103] Modern languages employed the greatest number of women, and the majority of these women linguists were home-grown RUI graduates. Women's university studies were finally bearing fruit, at least in Dublin, Cork and Galway.

Our exploration of this phenomenon will, of necessity, be fragmentary and eclectic. When surveyed as a group, however, interesting facts, patterns and questions emerge despite the gaps in our knowledge. What caused their proliferation in some universities rather than others? How were they treated and judged by their contemporaries? Did they have alternative career opportunities? (What careers had their brothers chosen?) How did they engage with the culture of their time? A variety of possible factors – personal, institutional, logistical, cultural or political – will be canvassed in seeking answers to those questions. The discussion may throw a sidelight on the place of languages, and universities, in the complex culture of post-Victorian Ireland.

Much had changed since Newman's day. He would have been surprised to learn that, within a decade of Queen Victoria's death, young women would not only be lecturing in German, Italian, Spanish, French and Irish in the RUI's Dublin college, but two of them would already be full professors.[104] When the NUI was set up, UCD's new chairs were awarded in German to Mary Macken, and in Italian and Spanish to Maria Degani. Other 1909 appointments were made in French and Irish. These included Mary Kate Ryan, assistant lecturer in French, who (as we have seen) served as acting professor of French when Édouard Cadic fell ill in autumn 1913 and, after his death in January 1914, for the entire duration of the Great War. Agnes O'Farrelly, the new lecturer in modern Irish appointed to assist Douglas Hyde, had to wait until 1932 to be promoted to a chair of modern Irish poetry, which she filled until her retirement in 1947.[105] Women also headed modern languages in Cork and Galway. Cork graduate Mary Ryan (no relation to Mary Kate), who held the first chair of Romance Languages (later redefined as French) in her alma mater from 1910 to 1938, was the first woman to be made professor in any Irish university.[106] In 1910, Waltraut ['Wally'] Swertz was appointed in German[107] and replaced, after her untimely death, by Bridget Lyndsay (*née* Danaher) who ran the department until the arrival in 1920 of Mary Boyle (*née* Curran), who then became professor of German, aged 25, in 1922.[108] In Galway, women were also appointed to the newly defined chair of German: Emily Anderson in 1917, succeeded in 1921 by Margaret Shea (*née* Cooke).

This cluster of women in exalted positions is remarkable, given their previous precarity, and all the more striking when one considers the low ratio of female graduates in the 1890s.[109] The gender change in modern language staffs at Dublin, Cork and Galway shows a sharp cultural shift, largely due to the extension of women's opportunities wrought by Victorian policies such as the Intermediate Education (Ireland) Act in 1878 and the RUI's founding charter in 1879. Arnold Toynbee astutely remarked that significant Education Acts take 20 years for their consequences to be realised.[110]

7.4 The 'Nine Graces': first women graduates, RUI, 1884
Photograph from Anne V. O'Connor and Susan M. Parkes, *Gladly Learn and Gladly Teach: Alexandra College and School 1866–1966* (Dublin, Blackwater Press, 1984), p. 43. (*Courtesy of Alexandra College, Dublin.*)

In contrast, in Trinity College Dublin and Queen's, Belfast, no women were appointed during this period to permanent posts in modern languages. The first female assistant lecturer at Queen's was Elsie McCallum, who had read modern and medieval languages in Cambridge and received a Trinity degree as a 'steamboat lady'. She was employed as an assistant lecturer in modern languages in 1905, renewed annually for five years. Later, she moved into second-level teaching.[111] During the Great War, Queen's hired women to stand in for absent male professors.[112] This work experience did not lead to permanent careers. TCD's first female appointment was the historian Constantia Maxwell, appointed lecturer in 1909 and professor 20 years later. Twenty-five years after that, Belfast got its first woman professor, in Ancient History.[113]

Why was the trend so strong in the NUI colleges – UCC, UCD and UCG? A first answer might be the 'supply chain': Joachim Fischer observes that women outnumbered male candidates for modern language jobs. The gap in German was particularly wide, possibly due to the preponderance of females who had taken German at school — sometimes exceeding a ratio of four to one. For the 1914 Cork chair, only two of the seven candidates were male; one withdrew and one was deemed ineligible.[114] A second factor could be put down to luck: in the early years of the NUI there happened to be a cohort of clever Irish women interested in a language-teaching career. But that was not entirely a matter of chance: these young candidates had presumably chosen language study because it was an area in which girls could undeniably excel, and interesting jobs might be found, whereas some other equally interesting professions were still closed to females: becoming an engineer, an ambassador, or a bishop. And once appointed, the NUI's youthful language professors lasted far into the twentieth century.

7.5 Early woman graduate, RUI Cork, *c.*1890
Photograph, unknown subject. (*Courtesy of University College Cork, Special Collections and Archives.*)

More broadly, the wave of women language academics in the NUI colleges may be a symptom of one of this book's leitmotivs: the strong connections, in Victorian Ireland, between continental language study and Catholic Europe. While in pre-Victorian times, those connections had permeated male clerical experience, the links became feminised in the late nineteenth century. All but one of the women language professors were successful RUI graduates, where women had been appointed as Junior Fellows and Examiners as early as 1893.[115] Some had gained valuable experience lecturing in the women's colleges. The majority were Roman Catholics, who had mostly been convent-educated. Some of them – like Mary Ryan, Mary Macken and Mary Kate Ryan, as we noted in Chapter Three – availed of opportunities, organised by religious orders, to study in educational establishments on the European continent.[116] Rather than studying on the periphery of Europe, a continental placement offered a sensible alternative to RUI female undergraduates who were admitted, but not fully integrated, into the RUI, particularly in its Dublin college. The experience undoubtedly deepened their acquaintance with living foreign languages and cultures, enhancing their employability at a time of university expansion. And this brings us to a fourth factor advantaging women, which might be called 'logistical'. Simply put, the available steps towards an eventual professorship were admirably suited to good female candidates. Under the RUI system there were religious-run colleges offering structured preparatory courses for the university examinations; there were opportunities to study abroad while also gaining teaching experience; there were possibilities of contact with like-minded Europeans within relatively secure and affordable settings. Thus prepared and experienced, a candidate could credibly claim to be ready for work. For some, the award of a travelling studentship enhanced that credibility.

Male language students tended not to follow the same path. Other attractive career openings were available to gifted male language graduates, who would therefore have been less inclined to seek a position teaching English, to perfect their mastery of the spoken foreign language in a continental male boarding school, even if there had been schools wishing to hire such native-speaking English teachers. We have seen how one of the features that emerged with broadening access to post-primary education in Europe was the tendency for more modern languages to be taught in girls' schools than in boys'. Women teachers were therefore in more demand. The phenomenon of women professors, which highlights the Victorian association of modern language learning with girls and women, may thus be seen as a self-fulfilling prophecy or virtuous circle that yielded results in the Edwardian era.

The home-grown appointees to NUI chairs had prepared themselves as thoroughly as possible, under the prevailing conditions. Cork's Mary Ryan, before securing a German lectureship in 1909 and moving to the chair of romance languages in 1910, had graduated with a BA in modern languages (1895) and MA (1896), taught in continental schools, examined as a junior fellow for the RUI and the Intermediate Board, and lectured in two women's colleges.[117] Her younger colleague Mary Boyle had been confined by the war, so her German studies had taken place entirely in Cork, starting with scholarships to the Presentation school where she remembered benefiting from the teaching of one outstanding nun. Following graduation at UCC, she won a travelling studentship in 1918 and undertook postgraduate studies in Zürich. Professor Boyle held the Cork chair for 45 years until 1967.[118] In Galway, Emily Anderson had also studied abroad, but – being Presbyterian – not in convents. Graduating in Galway in 1911 with distinctions in English, French, German and Latin, she did further study in Berlin and Marburg and taught French in a boarding-school in Barbados, before returning in 1917 to take up the new German professorship. Anderson's abiding love of German culture derived from childhood governesses and adolescent sojourns with German families.[119] Her exceptional abilities, as we shall see, were soon transferred to an entirely different arena. Her successor, from Sligo, Margaret Shea [née Cooke] (d.1981) was also a Galway graduate. Following a first-class degree she studied for her MA at Newnham College, Cambridge (a women's college), under the supervision of Professor Karl Breul, the champion of Germanic studies and international understanding who was also the NUI external examiner at the time. Shea's tenure in the Galway chair lasted from 1921 to 1965.[120]

Mary Macken (née Bowler), UCD's foundation professor of German, was a Loreto College alumna. Having studied in Paris and Berlin even before graduating with her BA (1898) and MA (1900), she later used her travelling studentship to study in Cambridge, also with Karl Breul. She was an RUI junior fellow in History from 1905, before becoming the first NUI lecturer in German in 1909, and professor from 1911.[121] UCD's one foreign female appointment hailed from Habsburg-ruled Trieste. Maria Degani applied for the new university's lectureship in German but was appointed instead to a post in Italian and Spanish (1909), which turned into a professorship in 1912, covering both languages.[122] (As will by now have become clear, mastery of several languages was not unusual among academics of that period.) Degani had studied in Padua, Munich and Cambridge, and obtained a teaching diploma and a Gilchrist Travelling Scholarship before working as Inspector for Secondary Schools in England.[123]

Also in UCD, Cavan-born Agnes O'Farrelly, appointed to a modern Irish lectureship in 1909 and (much later) to the chair when Douglas Hyde vacated it in 1932, had studied Irish at the Dominican-run St Mary's University College. The first woman to take an MA in Celtic Studies (1900), she had spent a term at the Collège de France under a renowned Celticist,[124] and lectured in Irish in the Alexandra and Loreto women's colleges. When Mary Kate Ryan – from the large Wexford family we met in Chapter Three – was appointed assistant lecturer in French at UCD in 1909, she had a first-class honours BA (RUI) and a teaching diploma from Hughes Hall, Cambridge University's oldest graduate college (then a teacher-training college),[125] as well as several years' secondary-school teaching in England and Scotland.

Teaching, research and scholarship of women academics

How to evaluate the teaching of colleagues 100 years ago? Modern modes of rating one's professor are mercifully absent, but one finds occasional words of praise from peers, and signs of care for students. Introducing Mary Macken for an honorary doctorate, J. J. Hogan claims that 'her interpretations of Goethe will not be forgotten by any of her pupils.' Professor Macken, in turn, remembers Mary Kate Ryan as a woman of outstanding ability: 'There never was any doubt of her intellectual powers or of her fine teaching quality.' This latter judgment carries some weight, as Macken was a lively, communicative writer and a grateful admirer of inspiring educators such as the Loreto nun, Sister Eucharia, who had guided her own progress in Dublin and Cambridge.[126] Even a hostile comment can testify to conscientious and exacting teaching practices, in the case of Cork's Professor Ryan, to judge by an offensively gendered description penned by one of her more famous undergraduates, the writer Sean O'Faolain. The author in middle age recalled Ryan in an oft-quoted letter to Professor Aloys Fleischmann:[127]

> Mary Ryan – a monster as a professor: a sweet old lady no doubt. Do you know what she used to do? – She used to TEACH us. Sacred Heart – teaching in a University!!!! You know – grammar and syntax and this and that and . . . Oh! And Ah! And groans. And everybody said she was marvellous: because she *did* teach the little ducks, spoonfed them, breastfed them, pre-digested their pap for them.

Her teaching must have worked reasonably well, as she had a 'formidable reputation for sending her postgraduates on to the Sorbonne'.[128] A College obituary described her as 'an exceptionally gifted and inspiring teacher'[129] who energetically and enthusiastically set up the UCC French Society against all the odds and was consistently encouraging and helpful to her students.[130]

Care for the progress made by students is an important aspect of a teaching career. As she prepared to give up her chair of German for a secret posting 'in the Foreign Office', Emily Anderson wrote confidentially to the UCG registrar:[131]

> I am extremely sorry to resign my work in Galway and I do regret leaving my students, some of whom I took a special interest in. I sincerely hope that they will prove to be as thorough as they were promising to become last session.

Mary Kate Ryan saw close contact with students as part of her job description and, fortified by her studies in the Cambridge Training College (subsequently renamed Hughes Hall), she was as much an educationalist as a French specialist. Her expertise in phonetics and language-teaching methodologies led to a supplementary role in UCD as a lecturer on methods for teaching modern languages, including Irish.[132] She writes to her sister Min that some of her new duties included teaching methods for Irish (11 October 1912):[133]

> I have to take a particular interest in the women students, help them about their lessons, notes, etc. – 'Women students, practical side' (there is a minimum of that side here) – and added to that, to give one lecture a week to men and women on Methods of Teaching Modern Languages, French, German and even Irish – [intelligently dealt with]; that (the Irish) is a great feather in my cap, with the C.T.C. Training – during the Hilary Term only. I shall certainly like it.

As regards research and scholarship, it is known that many academics in the early twentieth century published rather little in book form or in scholarly journals, but often contributed to debates in their areas of expertise and based their lectures on serious independent study. Of the cohort that we are considering, the most monumental scholar was Emily Anderson, whose multi-volume works on Mozart and Beethoven were published long after she had moved away from university life. Two other prolific researchers were Mary M. Macken and Mary Ryan, some of whose scholarly output, including erudite reviews, appeared in the pages of *Studies*, the Irish Jesuit journal read mostly by Catholic intellectuals. Although light on footnotes, their contributions were substantial. The Irish lecturer appointed in UCD, Agnes O'Farrelly, writing in English and in Irish, published novels and poetry, an edition of the poems of Seán Ó Neachtain and a bilingual memorial volume in honour of Eoghan O'Growney, who had 'turned from the dry bones of philology to the flesh and blood of the living vernacular'.[134] She also published *Smuainte ar Árainn*, her turn-of-the-century travel diary, jotted down as an undergraduate student on Inis Meáin. In Mary Kate Ryan's case, there was talk of doing an MA with Professor Cadic, but the plan never materialised as he grew ill. A few months after his death in January 1914, the outbreak of war impeded the task of finding a replacement professor and Mary Kate remained at the helm for the duration of hostilities.[135] For an assistant hired on the basis of annual renewal to be suddenly cast in the role of 'Temporary Professor of French', with all the new responsibilities that entailed, was quite a change in her status, and her letters reflect how busy she became.[136] Research and scholarly publications were out of the question.

Naturally, these women's interests reflected their upbringing and education. Mary Ryan was a serious scholar with deep religious convictions. Her writings on authors such as René Bazin and Paul Claudel suggest that what John A. Murphy calls the 'Catholicising of college' was well underway in UCC by the 1920s and 1930s.[137] As well as *Studies*, she wrote for less sophisticated Catholic outlets such as *The Irish Rosary* magazine and the Catholic Truth Society. Her book on Claudel, published in her retirement, offers a detailed analysis of the writer-diplomat's poetry and verse plays. Ryan's command of different languages enabled her to review recent books published in Europe; and her opinions reached a relatively broad constituency of readers.[138] She was decorated as a *chevalier* of the *Légion d'Honneur* by the French Government. From her family circumstances, this recognition might not have appeared out of the ordinary: Mary Ryan was the eldest of four high-achieving siblings. One brother, Sir Thomas, was a Director General in the Indian Civil Service; another, Sir Andrew, K.B.E., C.M.G., was a British diplomat in the Levant; the youngest, Patrick Finbar, O.P., became Archbishop of Port of Spain in Trinidad.[139] None of these professions was open to her, as a female, but within her own sphere, and in her own way, she had done very well.

7.6 Mary Ryan, UCC: first woman professor in Ireland Appointed to the Chair of Romance Languages, University College Cork, 1910. (*Courtesy of University College Cork, Special Collections and Archives.*)

7.7 Mary Macken, UCD
Appointed to the Chair of German, University College Dublin, 1911. At the presentation of her portrait, painted by Margaret Clarke (née Crilly). (Irish Virtual Research Library and Archive. University College Dublin Archives Dept. Tierney/MacNeill Photographs Collection. Press photograph (*Independent Newspapers*). (*Reproduced courtesy of UCD Archives.*)

In his citation for Mary Macken's DLitt, awarded on her retirement from UCD in 1950, Professor J. J. Hogan pointed out the breadth of her teaching coverage, ranging over the whole field of German language and literature from the most archaic texts to the newest experiments, and mastering the difficulties of the 'great newcomers'. Macken's research, he said, tended to focus on 'the Catholic currents in German literature, and all the points where it has touched Irish literature or history'.[140] She was broader than that: her contributions to *Studies* also dealt with social questions, with music (Beethoven, Schubert, Wagner), with politics (the Austrian *Anschluss*, the tension between Nazi and Christian values).[141] Eda Sagarra notes Macken's love of Austria and its culture, and points out her role in drawing the attention of Irish Germanists to Austrian literature.[142] She was involved with the University College Catholic Committee for German and Austrian refugees; and was active, not as a Germanist but as an Irish public intellectual, in women's rights campaigns and public debates such as the 1937 Constitution.[143]

Macken's reminiscences, in her essay for the volume marking Newman's centenary, offer vivid sketches of teachers and colleagues, but remain quite reticent about herself. Some aspects of her personality do emerge quite strongly: her convinced feminism (she believed that women should have equal status with men in their working lives), her international view of Catholicism, her sharp but kindly observation of colleagues. Explicit self-revelation was not the style of the time. Personal and emotional lives tended to remain a closed book, although the modern reader may still enjoy occasional flashes of eccentricity in biographies of post-Victorian women academics. Constantia Maxwell and her sister Euphan kept pet vultures in Dublin Zoo.[144]

Four individual profiles

Some of the women surveyed bear further scrutiny. Whether because of their intrinsic qualities or their response to external circumstances, certain individuals – in German, Italian and Spanish, French, and Irish – mirror their changing times, including the growth of nationalism and the disruptive effects of the Great War.

Emily Anderson (German): cryptology and musicology

If German can claim to be the most 'feminised' of the modern languages during the first decades of the NUI (given the long careers of Professors Macken in Dublin, Boyle in Cork and Shea in Galway), it also framed the shortest professorial career of all. The extraordinary double life of Emily Anderson (1891–1962) has been documented in a recent biography by Jackie Uí Chionna.[145] Galway's first professor of German grew up on the Galway campus as the daughter of the college president, physics Professor Alexander Anderson. On being appointed professor of German in 2017, she immediately reoriented the (more practical) curriculum put in place under Steinberger, expanding the list of prescribed literary texts, and including 'a theoretical knowledge of phonetics as applied to German', with closer study of Middle and Old High German.[146] These curriculum revisions suggest ambitious academic standards, yet within months she was being recruited by British military intelligence and by 1920, after several absences from Galway, she had formally resigned her chair. 'The reasons for her resignation are unknown', wrote Rosaleen O'Neill in her account of modern languages in the Galway College – but the truth of Anderson's sudden career change to codebreaking (with musicology on the side) has now been revealed by Uí Chionna.

Once she had moved to the Foreign Office, working covertly in military intelligence in London, and later in Bletchley Park and Cairo, Anderson's innate qualities as a linguist were given full rein. She was soon recognised as a superb cryptanalyst, with a knack for deciphering the most recalcitrant of enemy messages, whether in coded German, Italian, even Hungarian, through a mixture of painstaking background work, rigorous testing and brilliant conjecture. In her leisure time, she applied her linguistic knowledge to translating important works of European culture, firstly (from Italian) Benedetto Croce's *Goethe* (1923) and later two collections that ensured her a lasting place in the history of music. She is remembered today as the authoritative translator and editor (in three volumes) of *The Letters of Mozart and His Family* (1938), and three volumes of Beethoven's letters (1961). While her cryptanalysis for the war effort earned her an OBE, her edited translations were awarded the German Order of Merit by the Federal Republic of Germany.[147]

Mozart and Beethoven had notoriously illegible handwriting. As Jackie Uí Chionna's biography argues, this was where Anderson's codebreaking skills merged providentially with her expertise in languages and music. Deciphering the composers' eccentric spelling and modes of writing – a US reviewer referred to Mozart's habit of writing 'in reverse and upside down' and the musical annotations of the later Beethoven were described as 'utterly unintelligible, even to another musician' – was an advanced form of cryptology.[148] This labour of love occupied Anderson's spare time for over three decades, and stands as a remarkable feat of unrelenting scholarly organisation.[149] Both publications involved not merely transcribing, deciphering, translating and annotating thousands of autograph letters, organising them in their chronological sequence, but also locating, assembling and authenticating them by means of contacts and correspondence with archivists, librarians, musicologists and publishers all over the world, through stamped addressed envelopes and post-war foreign visits.[150]

Musicologists worldwide greeted both publications with awe and unbounded admiration. Anderson's accomplishments as a translator were marvelled at, from her

177

attention to register – 'Miss Anderson has not shrunk from turning into plain English all the smutty passages in the letters from Mozart to his cousin' – to her meticulous care for annotating the biographical details: 'Rarely can a more detailed, honest and thorough job have been done for the correspondence of any genius.'[151]

Had she studied at an English university, Emily Anderson's individual qualities would doubtless have led to the same career. Her colleagues in the intelligence service included several women language graduates who, like her, had answered the call of duty. The fact that she was born of Irish parents, and brought up in Galway, was incidental to the life she was to lead. It was her particular kind of upbringing, in an academic household where learning how to communicate in a modern foreign language, at a young age, was highly valued, combined with the painstaking and time-consuming 'monastic' approach to learning how to write and translate the language as accurately as possible, learning all about its culture and history along the way, that allowed her latent genius to be deployed to best advantage. She was a perfect fit for the two related pursuits of her life, her day-job of deciphering patterns in coded messages from enemy command, and her hobby of hunting down the right meaning of composers' scribbled messages. In this regard Emily Anderson was an exemplary product of the language-heavy and philology-rich Victorian education model

7.8 Professor Emily Anderson as a campus child, with her mother, sister and governess, c.1901
Standing, held in her mother's right arm, in front of Swiss governess. On steps of the family home – the President's Residence in the Quadrangle of RUI Galway. Appointed to the Chair of German, University College, Galway, 1917. Photograph, University Archives, University of Galway. (*Reproduced courtesy of University of Galway.*)

offered to women of means. In the context of this particular book, her productive genius echoes the passion for decoding Egyptian hieroglyphs illustrated by Peter Lepage Renouf, Newman's first appointment in modern languages to the CUI. Cryptology, graphology and palaeography are not unrelated activities, grounded in philology.[152]

Maria Degani (Italian and Spanish): the importance of being Irish

If Professor Anderson's educational background embodies one particular strand of the age in which she lived, fostering her innate abilities in a particularly positive way, our next case faced an outburst of hostility from external sources. These reveal a facet of Irish popular and political culture of the immediate post-Victorian years.

Professor Maria Degani, alone among the women language professors to have come from outside Ireland, suggests a strange reversal of when the same field had been populated entirely by male foreign nationals. Curiously, it was not her sex, but rather Degani's foreign nationality, that drew populist objections. The crowning insult appears to have been that, although born in Austria-Hungary, Maria Degani had become a naturalised British subject in 1905, and was socially connected with the British administration in Dublin.[153] The *Anglo-Celt*'s correspondent saw her appointment as 'Dublin Castle's pitchforking of foreigners into positions which Irish people were qualified to fill'.[154]

Unfounded rumours ran amok in the press during the summer of 1911, following Degani's successful application, apparently deriving from the vindictive statements of an unsuccessful candidate. They were aired by Shane Leslie in a rabble-rousing denunciation addressed to a Gaelic League meeting in Clones.[155] The new professor's academic qualifications were questioned, as were her teaching competence and the way she had been nominated to posts in two languages that had been advertised separately. Her appointment, Leslie claimed, had been due to her social connections 'with the Viceregal Lodge and other giddy heights;'[156] he had seen written evidence to prove that she could neither 'write, read nor speak, nor translate Spanish with reasonable facility or accuracy' and, 'although she was able to mutter a few words and lisp a few exercises, the students under her could teach her better than she could teach them.'[157] He further alleged that the lectureship in the two languages had been turned into a professorship merely in order to remunerate Degani more handsomely. These allegations were raised during parliamentary questions in the House of Commons, where the Chief Secretary for Ireland defended the decision made by the Dublin Commissioners who had made the appointment.[158] In his response, the Chief Secretary quashed the rumour about the chair of Italian and Spanish being created to reward Degani financially: he asserted that the professorship had been created purely for bureaucratic reasons to comply with the NUI's charter, and that Degani had accepted the new title of Professor while agreeing that her salary would remain the same as it had been while she was called a lecturer.[159]

This was not Shane Leslie's finest hour. When the de-anglicising project was at fever pitch, it is evident that some members of the Gaelic League had no objections to Italian and Spanish being taught, provided they were taught by a local Irish candidate, and not by a British subject who was too close to the Castle for comfort. The so-called 'Degani scandal' – a minor variation, played for a few brief bars, on the Angeli case of half a century before, with overtones of the Maynooth dismissal of O'Hickey – illustrates the democratic workings of the new NUI's style of governance.[160] Dangerously revealing excesses to which the culture of the revival period could go, it is ominously redolent of the kind of extreme nationalist tendencies of decades to come, in the independent Irish State.

Maria Degani taught Italian and Spanish at UCD, singlehanded, until 1938.[161] Respected by her peers, she was a member of the Modern Languages Association. At a summer school hosted by Girton College Cambridge in 1919, she gave a course in Linguistics and a 'brilliant exposition' of the problem of the Adriatic, a contemporary political issue related to the post-war peace settlement understandably close to a woman from Trieste.[162]

Mary Kate Ryan (French) and Agnes O'Farrelly (Modern Irish): activism

Mary Kate Ryan's personal circumstances, as a member of a group of republican siblings, exemplify the changing Ireland in another way. Although she had played no active part in the Easter Rising, she was imprisoned in Mountjoy Gaol for a few weeks in 1916. Mary Macken, looking back, refers to her colleague's experience being held prisoner by the British army as an 'added strain' to her work overload as temporary professor of French.[163]

7.9 Mary Kate Ryan, UCD 1902
Lecturer (and Temporary Professor 1914–18),
French, University College Dublin. Graduation
photograph, 1902. Private collection.

The prisoner herself wrote that students 'sent a great letter of sympathy with grapes and oranges', and she reacted to rumours of deportation to an Oxford prison by writing, 'Oxford would suit me *nearly* as well as Dublin for examining papers.'[164]

Her marriage to prominent republican Seán T. O'Kelly in 1918 cemented her growing nationalism and involvement in the independence movement. As Mrs O'Kelly her name was often gaelicised to Cáit Bean Uí Cheallaigh. When O'Kelly worked in Paris with the Irish provisional government's delegation that vainly tried to persuade the Versailles conference to concede the reality of the Irish State as a *fait accompli*, Mary Kate visited him in Paris as often as possible, finding ways to help the delegation's work by organising dinners in the Grand Hôtel and using her French with persons of influence in order to spread Dublin's message. She found this lifestyle more exciting than marking examinations at home.[165]

The Ryan family was deeply divided over the Anglo-Irish Treaty (1921). Mary Kate opposed the Treaty, and during the ensuing Civil War (1922–3), her husband and close relatives, as well as friends and colleagues, served lengthy prison sentences. Her sister Nell and her brother Jim, imprisoned by a Free State cabinet whose minster for defence was their brother-in-law Richard Mulcahy, went on hunger strike. For Mary Kate, as for members of other divided families all over Ireland, these events brought emotional pressures that took their toll.

Mary Kate Ryan's profile illustrates the extent to which University College Dublin, of all the NUI colleges, was a hotbed of political activists, during those troubled and transformative years. UCD's female appointment in Irish, Agnes O'Farrelly [Úna Ní Fhaircheallaigh], who voted for the 1921 Treaty, embodies their generation just as strongly. A paragon among UCD's women academic activists, she was energetic, intramurally and extramurally, in promoting Irish revivalism and advocating equity for women.[166]

O'Farrelly (1874–1951) was a true child of the 1890s Revival, whose utopian ideals she had assimilated at an impressionable age. She subscribed as an adolescent to the *Weekly Freeman*'s supplement for the young, the 'Irish Fireside Club'. As Ríona Nic Congáil has argued, this journalistic forum was a potent

7.10 Agnes O'Farrelly [Úna Ní Fhaircheallaigh], UCD 1904 Lecturer then Professor of Modern Irish, University College Dublin. Photograph from Agnes O'Farrelly [Úna Ní Fhaircheallaigh], *Leabhar an Athar Eoghan: The O'Growney Memorial Volume* (1904).

force for transmitting the beliefs and values of fin-de-siècle cultural nationalism to the next generation. Presided over by 'Uncle Remus' [*aka* Rose Kavanagh and later Hester Sigerson], the supplement inculcated in its juvenile readers, along with more predictable values – such as an interest in nature, the need for kindness, the joy of discovery through reading books, – a pride in all things Irish and a love of the Irish vernacular.[167] It was a natural progression for O'Farrelly to join the Gaelic League as a young adult. She was to be one of the most influential members of its Executive Committee in the 1900s, especially regarding education policy. At her alma mater, St Mary's women's college, she frequently read papers at student societies and wrote plays in Irish for them to perform.[168] While still a student herself, she spent her summers (1898–1902) on Inis Meáin, the remotest of the Aran Islands, perfecting her spoken Irish and deepening her acquaintance with traditional island life and customs there. In 1899, she set up a women's branch of the Gaelic League on the island that used the schoolhouse on Sundays to teach the women the rudiments of Irish reading and writing. The sessions were so successful that she could claim in 1901 to have seen illiteracy grow rare among women on the island.[169] The phenomenon impressed J. M. Synge:[170]

> [...] every Sunday afternoon three little girls walk through the village ringing a shrill hand-bell, as a signal that the women's meeting is to be held [...].

> Soon afterwards bands of girls – of all ages from five to twenty-five – begin to troop down to the schoolhouse in their reddest Sunday petticoats. It is remarkable that these young women are willing to spend their one afternoon of freedom in laborious studies of orthography for no reason but a vague reverence for the Gaelic. It is true that they owe this reverence, or most of it, to the influence of some recent visitors, yet the fact that they feel such an influence so keenly is itself of interest.

O'Farrelly continued to champion extramural Irish language education as first principal at Cloghaneely Irish College in Co. Donegal (1906) and by chairing the Federation of Irish Language Summer Schools. In later life she spent long periods in the Donegal Gaeltacht, where in the 1930s she helped to promote traditional crafts and cottage industries with a view to combatting the poverty she saw around her.

Her labours in furthering women's rights were equally broad and public-spirited. As one of the founders of the Irish Association of Women Graduates and Candidate Graduates [IAWGCG] (1902), she gave evidence before the Robertson (1902) and Fry (1906) Commissions, arguing for a full co-educational model to apply in the new university (as opposed to a model incorporating an affiliation of the existing single-sex women's colleges).[171] The IAWGCG was ultimately vindicated by the Irish Universities Act (1908). These debates over the place of women in the new university marked a new phase in the feminist agenda of the period, assembling a group of 'exceptional women [...], all Royal University graduates with personal experience of discrimination in the university and teaching fields',[172] who had gained confidence and found a voice to represent themselves. When the NUI was set up, 'gallant comrades in arms' Agnes O'Farrelly and her friend, historian Mary Hayden, were appointed to UCD's first governing body, alongside 28 men.[173] She was not afraid to defend her colleagues' rights.[174] Popular with staff and students alike, she was a founder member and subsequent president of UCD's Camogie Club [the variant of hurling played by women]. She retired in 1947 aged 73.

Other women language graduates

Some women language graduates of the RUI pursued successful careers outside the Irish education sector. Professor Steinberger's habit of encouraging his Galway students to do postgraduate studies is noted by Rosaleen O'Neill. Once the college allowed all students access to internal scholarships and prizes, in the late 1890s, many of the prizewinners were women, and 'as growing numbers of women students successfully took up modern languages, their male counterparts began to direct their energies elsewhere'. QCG's first 'lady scholar' in modern languages was Margaret Aimers, 'who later taught in Odessa'.[175] Steinberger's own daughter, Cécile, wrote a PhD thesis at the university of Paris, published in 1908. Another Galway prizewinner, Janet Hunter Perry, who had majored in French and German for her RUI degree in 1906, was later to be 'possibly the first woman Hispanist to be given an academic post in a British university'.[176] She taught in secondary schools in London and Cornwall before enrolling to do an MA in Spanish at King's College London, where she lectured until her retirement in 1944.[177] She edited and translated a number of texts. An obituary praises 'the very substantial contribution which she made to the growth of Spanish academic studies in London' and reveals that she had studied Arabic and was also proficient in Galician.[178]

A Dublin RUI woman graduate whose career was indirectly shaped by her language and literary studies was Mary Colum (née Maguire) (1887–1957). We have had occasion to quote from her reminiscences, as her early years followed so vividly the path trodden by other women of her generation – educated in St Louis convent boarding school in Monaghan, followed by a modern language degree in Dublin. She then taught for Pearse in Scoil Íde. As a student Colum spent some months in a German convent school, where they took the teaching of music more seriously than at home.[179] She was not destined to have a career in modern languages, but lived with her husband Padraic Colum, a prominent Irish writer, in New York, where she worked as a literary editor and critic, and occasional university lecturer. She more than once expressed her appreciation of the (excessively literary) education provided by the Edwardian Dublin college of the RUI.[180] Mary Colum's abiding love of languages – especially her grounding in Latin – and lifelong habit of moving between several of them at once, had been engendered by her academic and literary education in the European classics, and undoubtedly helped to inform her literary sensibility as a prominent cultural commentator, within certain literary circles of inter-war New York.[181]

These women could work across languages; the barrier between Germanic and Romance tongues did not exist for them. Some women language graduates had distinguished careers outside teaching. Looking back from 1954, Mary Macken recalled an early NUI student, Áine (Neans / Nancy) Wyse Power who, after a primary degree in modern languages, did an MA in Celtic Studies and was awarded a travelling studentship. Despite interruptions caused by the War, she completed her PhD in 1920 in Bonn; in the following year she was sent by the provisional Dáil to set up a diplomatic and trade legation in Berlin, where her skills in networking and her German language proficiency stood her in good stead. She published the *Irish Bulletin* in translation for the German press twice a week, advancing Irish nationalist propaganda. She was pro-Treaty and later became one of the first women principal officers in the Irish Civil Service.[182]

Celtic Studies, which provided outlets for philological work, brought together two Victorian trends – the Irish cultural revival and the feminising of modern language study. Women Celtic scholars came from different social backgrounds. Looking back on her RUI days, Mary Macken recalled Maud Joynt (1868–1940) as a lecturer in German in the old women's colleges. She contrasted Joynt's teaching style with that of a male colleague:[183]

> French was taught by Richard C. Greer, a remarkable grinder who died young. For German Sister Eucharia had secured Maud Joynt, M.A., of Alexandra; she was a distinguished linguist. Unlike R.C. Greer who never spoke French, she invariably used the language of her subject; her German was excellent. In later years the R.I.A. was to know her as worker on the Irish Dictionary, for she had become a Gaelic enthusiast. Relaxing occasionally, she translated poems from both languages.

Joynt, a polyglot in the late Victorian mould, had graduated from the RUI in English, French and German (BA 1889, MA 1890) and taught languages at Methody, Belfast, before pursuing further studies in 1894, in three European cities – Paris, Florence and Heidelberg. On her return, she lectured in the Dublin women's colleges, and was an active campaigner for women's rights to educational opportunities. Maud Joynt's interest in the Irish revival movement dates back to her attending the School of Irish Learning summer schools in 1906 and 1907, followed by a course in Celtic Studies in Liverpool with Kuno Meyer. This led to her appointment to the staff of the RIA in January 1909, as assistant editor of the *Dictionary of Old Irish*. She published several translations and textual editions of early Irish texts and was a much-esteemed colleague at the Academy.[184] Another assistant editor on the Academy's *Dictionary* project was Eleanor Knott, a noted Celtic scholar who moved from lexicographical scholarship to an academic post. She left the RIA in 1928 to take up a lectureship in Irish in Trinity, where she held a special chair of early Irish from 1939 until her retirement in 1955.[185]

Celtic Studies also attracted foreign women, like the German–Polish Celtic folklore scholar, Käte Müller-Lisowski, who spent the 1900s as a student in Jena, Berlin, the Sorbonne, Oxford and London. Beatrix Färber gives an idea of what she studied:[186]

> In Berlin she studies Old Irish with Kuno Meyer; and Swedish, Gothic, Old Icelandic, Danish Ballads, Metrics, and Old German Religion with Andreas Heusler. As a diversion she also studies Mongolian. In Oxford she studies Modern Irish with Sir John Rhys, also 17th Century English. At University College London she studies Old Irish with Robin Flower who had been appointed Honorary Lecturer in Celtic there while working on Irish MSS catalogues in the British Museum.

She lectured in Berlin (1914–20) and did a PhD in Vienna in 1923. Her *Irische Volksmärchen*, a translation from Hyde, ran to over 14 editions. Partly through her contacts with Hyde and other Celtic scholars, Ireland was the site of refuge for herself and her family when fleeing Nazi Germany in 1937.[187]

As Aoibheann Nic Dhonnchadha has shown, Winifred Wulff (1895–1946), a Scottish-born German, also became involved in Celtic Studies. She had been brought up bilingually and educated at a school where French was the main language. Falling victim to multiple sclerosis as a young woman, she had to abandon the study of medicine in London. Moving, for personal reasons, to live with friends in Ireland, she learned Irish, and took a BA (1921) and further degrees in Celtic Studies in UCD (PhD 1931). Wulff later specialised in editing medieval Irish medical texts. In addition to English, German, French and Irish, she was also reputedly competent in Russian, Norwegian, Spanish, Portuguese and Italian.[188]

Women's place: the grammar of cultural change

What does this brief line-up of women language scholars of the 1900s – continental and Celtic – indicate? Once again, it should be reiterated that very small numbers of women achieved positions of academic influence or research scholarship in either modern languages or Irish studies.[189] The fact that there were any women at all nominated to senior appointments is nevertheless symptomatic of the time, when possibilities for third-level or research employment had emerged for them, thanks to late-Victorian policies. Those possibilities were soon to fade. A couple of decades into independent Ireland, as Donal McCartney has noted, the 'promise of the early years' for the general position of women academics began to ebb. The deterioration in status of academic women reflected women's diminishing economic and personal status in Ireland during the 1930s, 1940s and 1950s. The ban on married women's employment in white-collar public service work may have limited female students' options. Initially adopted by governments as a measure to combat unemployment, restrictions like the 'marriage bar' lasted longer in Ireland than elsewhere.[190] McCartney observes that, whereas numbers of women taking primary degrees continued to rise in the early decades of independence, this did not translate into a commensurable increase in the numbers embarking on postgraduate study.[191]

One strand of the debates simmering in the 1900s about how to resolve the Irish university question concerned the role of the denominational women's colleges in whatever settlement would emerge. Lobbyists split into two camps: those who argued for complete equality within a co-educational university, and those who believed that women students would be better served by continuing to attend single-sex women's colleges that would be properly endowed and recognised as affiliates by the new institution, not unlike women's colleges at Oxbridge.[192] The former camp prevailed, for a number of valid reasons. However, this may not have been without downsides. McCartney speculates that, given 'the non-recognition by the NUI of the existing women's colleges, their total disappearance from the scene may well have affected the presence of women in academic life.'[193] This is a view endorsed by the historian of those colleges, Judith Harford, who concludes:[194]

> The opportunities for leadership and advancement enjoyed by women in the single-sex women's colleges were not forthcoming under the new regime, and women students and academics had to fight for meaningful inclusion under the co-educational model.

The visibility of senior role models for women students in everyday university life gradually diminished after the women's colleges turned to ancillary roles – running student hostels, teacher training colleges, or secondary schools. For modern language students, in particular, the single-sex colleges for women students run by religious orders – a distinctive feature of Ireland's late Victorian denominational divide and of the RUI period – had offered valuable opportunities for periods of study in educational centres on the continent.[195]

Women may have won their battle for a co-education model, and within the NUI women academics participated in college life on an equal footing with their male colleagues, serving on committees, and even the governing body, and playing other administrative roles.[196] They were not, however, paid equally for this equal work. A gender pay gap was taken for granted for many decades to come.

In 1911, in Earlsfort Terrace's new National University, women were still perceived as a novelty in the public eye, and as creatures for whom social accomplishments still mattered. This can be inferred from the following press account of an 'At Home' afternoon tea for women students, hosted in the rooms of the Dean of Residence by UCD's women academics in December 1911:[197]

> Mrs Macken, Miss Hayden, and Miss O'Farrelly received the guests, while Miss Degani and Miss Ryan occupied themselves in initiating a concert programme. Some excellent instrumental music was contributed by the Misses McCarthy, Brazil, Collins, and O'Carroll. The Misses Clancy, Hogan, Roddy, and Mullett added much to the enjoyment of the afternoon by their splendid rendering in Irish and English of some of our best known songs. Miss Cunniffe gave a pianoforte solo and Misses Rea and Miss Brady some selections on the violin and piano. Mrs Rooney sang by request 'The Snowy Breasted Pearl.' Miss Kavanagh interested the audience by a witty German monologue, and Caitlín ni Conchubhar delighted everybody present by some excellent specimens of Irish dancing.

The piece is penned by 'Our Lady Correspondent.' It is difficult to imagine the same level (or style) of press coverage for gatherings of male students to read French and German plays hosted by their (male) professors, such as the one Joseph Plunkett attended in Professor Cadic's house in January of the same year.[198] Cultural history is a slow bake.

POLITICAL ALLEGIANCES IN A CHANGING UNIVERSITY LANDSCAPE

It remains curious that, unlike the NUI's readiness to hire women on a permanent basis in its first decade, no female modern linguist obtained a permanent senior appointment in Dublin University (Trinity) or Queen's University Belfast. At the moment when Ireland's tripartite university structure emerged in 1909, consisting of DU, the NUI and QUB, a chasm was clearly discernible between staffing at Trinity and Belfast, on the one hand, and in the NUI colleges on the other. Our account of the new professors of Irish and the women language professors has so far revealed one side of that chasm. While the fledgling NUI was anxious to set up an institution within an Irish frame of reference, the other two universities continued to see their role in a different cultural context.[199] If the recruitment ethos in Belfast and Trinity was more conservative, was this because these universities instinctively aligned themselves to a British academic model where it was still a rarity to find any women academics in senior posts?[200] When one speculates in this way, there is an obvious danger of imputing bias on the basis of a tiny sample. The opposite danger, of course, is the denial of bias when the sample strongly suggests its presence. Any presumed favouritism towards women in most Southern Irish universities was in any case a fleeting phenomenon.

The staffing of modern languages in 1900s Belfast and Trinity, with one exception, mirrored the cultural and political divide. Mainly British and Protestant males, the linguists employed in these two universities were neither Irish nationalists, nor continental, nor Catholic, and show a tight network of mobility between the two colleges. The single exception was Saxony-born Max Freund, who had studied in Leipzig and Paris, and taught for a year in Liverpool, before his appointment to Queen's College Belfast at the age of 24. He served as Professor of modern languages from 1903 to 1909 and – from 1909, when QUB split modern languages into two chairs – as Professor of German and Teutonic Philology. While at home in summer 1914 he was dismissed from Queen's as a hostile alien; he then served his Kaiser on the eastern front, where he was wounded, almost fatally.[201]

7.11 Max Freund, QUB, 1979 (aged 100)
Professor of French and German, RUI Belfast, and (from 1908) Professor of German, Queen's University Belfast. *(Courtesy of Woodson Research Center, Fondren Library, Rice University, Houston Texas, where Freund was Professor of German 1925–47.)*

Freund's successors were from the largely unionist milieu then dominant at Trinity. The dismissed German professor was replaced by a local Belfast man, Robert Alan Williams, who had worked in Trinity in Anglo-Saxon and German since the death of Selss in 1907.[202] After Williams retired in 1932, his successor, Gilbert Waterhouse, also moved north from Trinity. Waterhouse, as Trinity's professor of German from 1915, distinguished himself in April 1916 as a Lieutenant in Trinity College's Officer Training Corps, sniping at rebels from the roof of the College.[203] A year later, he took a public stand on the need to study German as part of the war effort. He knew the country well, having studied in Berlin and lectured in English for three years at Leipzig. In May 1917, he delivered a public lecture in Trinity, later published, entitled 'The War and the study of German', arguing that the one purpose of undertaking German studies was to defeat the 'desperate and dastardly enemy':[204]

7.12 Gilbert Waterhouse, TCD and QUB
Professor of German, Trinity College Dublin, and (from 1933) Queen's University Belfast. Photographic print, *c.*1920. *(Courtesy of Patricia Dunlop, granddaughter of Waterhouse.)*

Germany can be beaten as decisively in the lecture room as in the workshop, the counting house, or on the field of battle. [...] If we refuse to study German literature, we cannot understand the German in his many moods, and if we are unwilling to understand him, we are depriving ourselves of the power to beat him in whatever walk of life he cares to challenge us.

Knowing the language of one's enemy is a long-established rationale for studying a foreign language; putting the case in such a combative tone, in mid-1917, shows Waterhouse's political views to be unambiguously pro-British.[205]

QUB's French appointment in 1909 was an equally loyal subject of the Crown. Belfast's first professor of romance philology, Douglas Lloyd Savory from Palgrave in Suffolk, was 'perhaps the most active of the university unionists'.[206] He was part of the QUB's delegation to London, in 1912–13, to discuss the future governance of the university in the event of Home Rule.[207] Savory had studied at Oxford, Paris, Bern and Lausanne, and worked at Goldsmith's College in London and the University of Marburg before taking up his Queen's post. His publications included a co-translation of Paul Passy's work on the sounds of French, suggesting an interest in how to include phonetics in his teaching.[208] When elected to represent QUB as a unionist MP in 1940, he resigned the chair of French,[209] which was to remain vacant for the duration of the war. Savory put his language skills to use in the war effort: during the 1914–18 war he worked in naval cryptanalysis for the Royal Navy and acted as interpreter between de Gaulle and Churchill during the war of 1939–45. His DIB biographer, Ian Montgomery, depicts him thus:[210]

> Often described as a Pickwickian figure, Savory was a well-known house of commons 'character' and his frequent interventions on Irish affairs were treated with tolerant amusement by most of his fellow MPs. His pomposity and verbosity attracted the attention of the satirist 'Myles na Gopaleen' [...]. Many northern nationalists found his strident unionism less amusing and he was frequently portrayed as a sectarian extremist.

In Trinity College Dublin, the chair of Romance languages had been filled by Thomas Brown Rudmose-Brown, after a brief hiatus following Robert Atkinson's retirement and death (1908).[211] Rudmose-Brown felt allegiance to no State, perhaps least of all to post-independence Ireland. He was later – much to the concern of colleagues anxious that Trinity maintain a low profile by avoiding public debate on matters political or religious – loudly vocal in his attacks on the clericalised Irish Free State.[212]

An appendix to the 1918 Leathes Committee's Report on Modern Languages illustrates dramatically the political divide within the Irish universities during the Edwardian years. A letter from 31 professors and readers of modern languages – all of them males – is appended to the report.[213] These 'gentlemen obedient servants' decry the dearth of chairs of modern languages and call for improvements in staffing as well as a range of reforms in curriculum and conditions. Four of the signatories are attached to Irish universities: the professors of French and German at Trinity, Rudmose-Brown and Waterhouse, and at Belfast, Savory and Williams. The conspicuous absence of names attached to the National University of Ireland is perhaps explained when one reflects that, when the evidence for the Report was being assembled between August 1916 and April 1918, the modern language professors and acting professor in UCC and UCD were all females (and therefore overlookable), while UCG's one male modern language professor, Liam Ó Briain, was either a guest of his majesty or on active service in the War of Independence.[214]

The line-up of university professors of modern languages, on the eve of independence, indeed reveals wide political and cultural differences that were to endure for well into the twentieth century. To cite the example of French: in 1920, each of the four male professors of French was to hold the chair for three decades or more; each was influential in distinct ways. While the staunch unionism of Douglas Lloyd Savory was in tune with the majority culture in Queen's University Belfast where he held the chair (1909–40), the other three men – Thomas Brown Rudmose-Brown (Trinity, 1909–42), Liam Ó Briain (Galway,

1917–59), and Roger Chauviré (UCD, 1918–48) – indicate how these language chairs, too, were emblematic of contrasting strands in Ireland's cultural and political history.

Trinity's Rudmose-Brown (1878–1942) was an independent-minded freethinker who despised all political-isms. Of Scots-Danish parentage, he was educated at Aberdeen and Grenoble; in his research he concentrated on French and Provençal literature, specialising in contemporary living writers, with whom he was in personal contact. This was very daring for a professor of French in 1909, when the standard approach to teaching literature was still 'historical, not to say archeological'.[215] In this, he contrasts strikingly with the philological interests of his Victorian predecessor, Robert Atkinson. As a critic he valued the transcendent and gratuitous beauty of individual poetic expression that is totally devoid of didactic or political message.[216] Rudmose-Brown was a formative influence on the young Samuel Beckett and described his brilliant student in 1929 as 'un de mes élèves les plus intelligents, grand ennemi de l'impérialisme, du patriotisme, de toutes les Eglises' [one of my most brilliant students, sworn enemy of imperialism, patriotism and all religious creeds].[217] It takes one to know one.

If the Trinity appointment in French disapproved of the Ireland where he worked, Galway's professor of romance languages, Liam Ó Briain (1888–1974), was perfectly aligned with the cultural climate of the new State. A freedom-fighting Dubliner and zealous revivalist, he was a brilliant linguist who took an MA in French (1910) before studying Old Irish on a travelling studentship in Berlin, Bonn, Freiburg and Paris. He left an imprint on the cultural life of Galway by co-founding, with Micheál Mac Liammóir and Hilton Edwards in 1928, *Taibhdhearc na Gaillimhe*, the city's Irish-language theatre. He energetically took part in staging many of his own Irish translations of plays from French, Spanish and English, which were performed there over the years, illustrating in a very real way his passionate belief in the value of European languages for the cultural enrichment of the Irish language.[218] This larger-than-life character was awarded an honorary doctorate by the NUI in 1974. Micheál Mac Liammóir delivered an oration at his graveside. Seán Mac Réamoinn remembered his former professor vividly, with genuine gratitude:[219]

> to his students he was a godsend. I was one of them during the doldrum years of the second World War, and, at a time when the doors and windows were bolted, he was a one-man Open University. And he was magnificent proof that a love of tradition could live with an openness to new and radical ideas, that an Irishman could be a European, that a Jackeen could be a Gael.

Franco-Irish cultural mediation in the opposite direction is encapsulated by the work of Professor Roger Chauviré (1880–1957), who arrived in Dublin from Anjou in January 1919 to take up the UCD chair of French, vacant since the death of Cadic and provisionally held by Mary Kate Ryan during the Great War. An outsider who had never set foot in Ireland and who was not confident in his command of English when he arrived, Chauviré became quite fascinated by the country, its history and its culture. For this veteran of the trenches who had written his doctoral thesis for the Sorbonne on the French political philosopher Jean Bodin, the prospect of observing part of the British empire turning into not one but two separate polities, before his eyes, must have been an enthralling one. He made the country his home and stayed in UCD until the end of his career. Most of his publications were inspired by Ireland, including works of history, travel books, translations

7.13 Roger Chauviré, UCD
Professor of French, University College Dublin, 1918–48. Pen and ink drawing by Seán Keating. (*Courtesy of Seán Keating Estate.*)

from Old Irish, essays on contemporary politics and short stories set in Irish history, as well as two novels based on recent Irish history, the first set in 1916 and the second in the aftermath of the War of Independence.[220] Professor Chauviré was a gifted communicator. At least three former students – authors Kate O'Brien, Mary Lavin and Máire Mhac an tSaoi – later recorded their admiration for his teaching.[221] He made close friends among several colleagues within and outside UCD and was firmly convinced of the ancient pedigree of Ireland's unique cultural heritage.[222] Irish academics in the early post-independence years were understandably preoccupied with their own land as they fashioned its future. Chauviré helped to convey that Irish self-positioning to a French reading public. Like Édouard Cadic, the previous French citizen to hold the UCD chair, Chauviré saw his role as that of a cultural ambassador, or *agent de propagande française* [French propagandist]; but unlike Cadic, he published copiously. In reality he was a cultural ambassador in two directions, conveying Ireland and Irish history to a French reading public while at the same time spreading an appreciation of French literature and history to Irish students.

★ ★ ★

The group biographies of language academics sketched in the foregoing two chapters suggest some general conclusions about the evolving context of language study during the Victorian period and the two decades leading to independence and partition.

Professors of modern languages – foreign nationals for most of the nineteenth century – had no need to debate what their subjects were. French or German or Italian had relative stability of grammar, lexis and structure, born of centuries of print culture and standardised spelling, illustrated in a range of canonical works of literature and upheld by institutions like France's Académie Française or Italy's Accademia della Crusca, ensuring prestige and respectability in court, literary and intellectual circles. Dialectal forms were widely disregarded. When professors of modern Irish were appointed, after the NUI vote in favour of 'essential Irish' was carried in 1909, they were keenly aware of the relatively low prestige of vernacular Irish. Hence the debates among professors and scholars about which form of Irish to teach, or what model of literary language to propose to Irish writers of the future.

Political engagement is another distinction that divides the two groups of professors. Victorian Ireland's foreign nationals did not, on the whole, trespass on local sensibilities. If they did, it was inadvertently, like the unfortunate Louis-Raymond de Véricour and Charles Geisler. Professors of modern Irish, on the other hand, were politicised by definition. On a mission to save a linguistic and cultural patrimony from extinction, they approached their task with patriotic zeal. Some became politicised even further and engaged in separatist nationalism; in addition, some female colleagues pursued equal opportunities for women.

The group of women academics, taken together, offer striking illustrations of Ireland's rapidly changing social and political landscape, where they formed a broad church within a Roman Catholic matrix. The family background of Cork's Professor Mary Ryan (*b.*1873), which included the colonial administrative careers of two brothers (in the Levant and India) and the episcopal career of the third in the British West Indies, smacks of an earlier Victorian generation than that of an Agnes O'Farrelly (*b.*1874) or a Mary Kate Ryan (*b.*1878). Rather than propping up earth-spanning empires, some of Mary Kate's family spent their energies helping to shape their own new independent Ireland.

Political reverberations were hard to avoid in the Edwardian years. One consequence of the shift, in modern language appointments, towards hiring local Irish-born scholars, male and female, was to point up the chasm between the ethos of DU and QUB on one side and the NUI on the other. This cultural separateness was probably inevitable. The 1908 Irish Universities Act, copper-fastening three State-funded universities in Ireland, effectively recognised three culturally distinct traditions – DU (Trinity), modelled on Oxbridge, continuing to represent the old Anglican ascendancy; QUB, a civic model, non-denominational in theory, but in reality associated with unionism and Presbyterianism; and the federal NUI, also non-denominational on paper, but unmistakably and boldly Catholic and nationalist in practice.[223] Consequently, 'relations between the three universities were to remain for many years neither friendly nor hostile, but virtually non-existent'.[224]

The cultural legacy of Victorian Ireland continued to shape the language education of Irish people in practical ways. For most of the twentieth century, a relatively heavy loading of language study remained essential requirements for matriculation in the NUI colleges in Cork, Dublin, Galway and Maynooth. Our concluding chapter will look at how that Victorian legacy has played out since independence. It will speculate on rationales for foreign-language learning in today's globalised world, as well as the challenges that beset anglophones who pursue that goal at a moment of history when English pervades the planet as never before. The discussion may at times seem to wander far from Victorian Ireland, but we may also recognise some familiar perspectives on perennial issues – the place of humanities in a modernising education system, the contrast between pure and applied study, the impact of foreign hegemonies on local identities, the role of institutions in sustaining elites, the impacts of regulatory frameworks, the dynamics of culture and policy – which had also confronted Ireland's Victorian forebears.

PART FOUR: BEYOND THE VICTORIANS

CHAPTER 8

Shifting Language Perspectives

The life of a language depends on its being spoken as a mother-tongue by a community of speakers. If it is written as well, so much the better, but if it is written and spoken only by learners, then ultimately it will become a dead language. [Aidan Doyle, 2015][1]

A Uachtaráin, agus a chairde... [Her Majesty Queen Elizabeth II, 2011][2]

I still wrestle with the idea of anglophones learning foreign languages. Here the utilitarian argument is weakest of all. [Simon Kuper, 2021][3]

Hiberno-English: a resistant way of speaking the English language, a language we never asked for. [Blindboy Boatclub, 2020][4]

Even cultural history may still have many futures. [J. J. Lee, 1989][5]

This concluding chapter will consider how language learning has fared in Ireland since independence and partition. Did continental language study compete with the study of Irish? How did language teaching differ between the two jurisdictions, North and South? What are the prospects and the issues at stake for Irish people who study languages today, in a time of global anglicisation?

In 1920, Trinity's professor of German, Gilbert Waterhouse, hailed the 1918 Leathes Committee's Report on Modern Languages as a 'Magna Carta' for modern languages but noted 'the unaccountable omission of Ireland' from its terms of reference – an omission which he then proceeds to justify:[6]

> The teaching of modern languages in Ireland has no feature sufficiently remarkable to warrant separate treatment. The difficulties and conditions are the same and the measures and remedies suggested by the Report are just as applicable to Ireland as to any other part of the United Kingdom.

Waterhouse was only partly right. While the challenges in mastering foreign languages were indeed similar for English speakers on both sides of the Irish Sea, there were also, as we have seen, significant variations in the language learning cultures of the two islands. These were to increase after Irish independence in 1922.

Enormous cultural changes have affected Ireland in recent decades, including the influence of new media, membership of the European bloc, huge population growth, substantial inward migration, growing prosperity, the arrival of digital technology, the effects of sectarian warfare, the flowering of new language communities due to multinational immigration. Rather than attempting to account for all these developments, we propose to focus on three significant shifts affecting language study over the past 100 years. One was specifically Irish, the other two were international. In the first place, there was the southern Irish regime's focus on consolidating the language revival policies of the Gaelic League. A second shift, impossible to predict in 1921, was the abandonment, within a few decades, of the centuries-old symbiotic relationship between the study of classical languages and university education. Thirdly, and perhaps most significantly, there has been the spread of English on an unprecedented global scale. This triple re-alignment – involving Irish, Latin and English – definitively distances Irish people today from the language culture of their Victorian forebears and has altered the dynamics of language learning on the island, not just at university level. While the impact of these shifts, which are of vastly different dimensions, has varied widely over the course of the century, any speculation on future prospects and needs for language learning has to be framed within this transformed context.

All of these ruptures in the Victorian status quo have taken place against a backdrop of broader changes in linguistic thought. Advances in applied linguistics since the second world war have swung the pendulum diametrically away from the Victorian paradigm.[7] The move towards more pragmatic communicative targets is just one illustration of radically altered teaching and assessment practices that have become the norm.

It was in the 1970s that changing international views of language education began to be felt most decisively in Ireland. Our assessment of the Victorian language legacy will therefore start with the first five decades of independence, up to that tipping point. Across the two half-centuries of independence, we shall chart shifting regulatory pressures, institutional and governmental, affecting Irish and European languages, and see how language study worked under, or against, new regulations. Inevitably, the focus will fall on the southern State, crossing the border briefly to consider divergences in language learning between Northern Ireland and the south. The second part of the chapter also considers the impact of further significant changes since the 1970s: dropping mandatory classics, joining the European bloc, and ever-increasing anglicisation.

REGULATORY FRAMEWORKS (1922–1970s)

Institutional regulation: NUI matriculation language requirements

The ways in which universities organise the transmission of knowledge and culture have a material effect on modern western societies, not least because third-level entry requirements influence the pre-tertiary school curriculum. Thus, Victorian and Edwardian universities set the linguistic agenda for post-independence Ireland. Although university attendance was enjoyed by a very small elite at that period, and indeed for many decades thereafter, the power of that elite was in inverse proportion to its size.[8] It shaped and formed the assumptions and expectations of future generations at a key moment in Ireland's cultural history.

After 1922, Irish was given pride of place as the country's first official language. Yet Irish and modern continental languages were granted a central position in the new regime's education system, partly because the NUI continued to apply its broad matriculation requirements for language competence. University entrants still had to demonstrate a satisfactory standard, not only in Latin or Greek, but also in at least one modern language and in Irish. Although these entry requirements have been gradually eroded, and although their overall impact has been attenuated by the arrival or expansion of new third-level institutions with less stringent language prerequisites, the broad language requirement was applied throughout most of the past century, and still pertains, in part, in some highly sought degree programmes in the four colleges of the NUI.[9] This was particularly significant when the alma mater of the vast bulk of Irish graduates was an NUI college.[10] It was, then, an important policy cornerstone that dictated the language take-up of Irish citizens for a large part of the twentieth century.

Despite some tensions, the National University of Ireland has, in the main, been a source of continuity and stability in language provision.[11] During the first five decades since independence, its Senate left the language regulations untouched. Perhaps this was partly due to what Ronan Fanning dubbed 'the grotesquely long tenure'[12] of Éamon de Valera as NUI Chancellor; he served from 1921 (just before independence) to 1975 (two years after Ireland had joined the EEC). The longest-serving chancellor of a conservative institution, he was also the chancellor who most embodied stagnation.[13]

A strong association between the NUI and the Irish language stems from its origins as a solution to the Irish university conundrum that had bedevilled British administrations for decades. In 1908, the 'Royal' University of 1880 gave way to a 'National' University at a moment when the Gaelic League was at the height of its hold on Irish national sentiment. Indicatively, when de Valera succeeded the first Chancellor, Archbishop William Walsh, he was welcomed at his inauguration in two languages. Linda O'Shea Farren relates:[14]

> De Valera was formally received as Chancellor of the NUI on Saturday, 19 November 1921 in an elaborate ceremony, at which two addresses of welcome from Convocation were presented to the Chancellor – one in Irish read by Michael Hayes and one in Latin read by Michael Tierney. Indeed, it was commented upon in the media that, with the exception of the brief speech of Dr Denis Coffey, then President of University College Dublin, no word of English was spoken during the ceremonial proceedings.

Besides keeping faith with Irish, the NUI has at the same time done much to promote the study of continental languages.[15] Rather than being locked in a zero-sum competition, the two aspirations, for Irish and for European languages, were reciprocally sustaining, making it difficult to diminish the status of one without damaging the other. This echoes the mindset of early revivalists who paid commensurate esteem to Irish and foreign languages. As Eoin MacNeill argued in 1909, the continent of Europe had for centuries been the multilingual site where the Irish language had developed. During penal times it had been 'written, read, spoken and sung among the exiled Irish nobility at the court of St Germain', and cultivated in the Irish colleges; he also opined that the study of modern Irish had a positive effect on the study of other languages.[16] The revivalists knew that Irish Studies needed to maintain connections with German and French Celtic scholarship. Indeed, some of them saw continental languages and cultures as vital to the general national project of de-Anglicisation. Liam Ó Briain, Galway's professor of romance languages who (as we have seen) translated European plays for staging in the Irish-language theatre, is a case in point. The translations were to serve the revival of the vernacular.[17] Ó Briain had studied Old Irish on the continent during his studentship. The politician and academic Michael Hayes, who succeeded Agnes O'Farrelly as UCD's professor of Irish, had earned a first-class MA in French (1920).[18] Such intersecting cultural positions may help to explain how the broad language matriculation requirement, for both Irish and a modern language as well as a classical language, in addition to English, was to remain intact for so long.

Irish revival: rise, fall, survival

In the wider public arena, the focus on the native language reigned supreme. The fostering of Irish, designated first official language in the 1937 Constitution, was a core education policy of the independent State, and even predated the State's own foundation.[19] The first Dáil (1919) appointed a minister for Irish before a minister for Education.[20] It also employed an official Irish translator.[21] Compensating for past neglect, successive governments poured energy and resources into the teaching and use of the language and can, on the whole, claim credit for having staved off its total extinction. The 1922 education programme aimed at 'the strengthening of the national fibre by giving the language, history, music, and tradition of Ireland their natural place in the life of Irish schools.'[22] The language became a compulsory subject in all national schools, and (by 1934) an obligatory requirement for obtaining a school Leaving Certificate (established in 1925) or civil service employment.[23] Initiatives in the 1920s, in line with Gaelic League ideals and gaining broad popular support, included incentivising Irish as a medium of instruction in schools, primary and secondary, and reforming teacher-training programmes to ensure Irish language competence of national school teachers. Infant classes in national schools were to be conducted entirely through Irish. Despite practical problems and resistance from the national teachers' union (INTO), there is evidence that these policies were generally bearing some fruit by the 1940s.[24]

Aspirations for a distinctly Irish Ireland, and for an Irish-speaking bilingual nation, involved cultivating a self-image whereby the definition of 'Irish/ness' was the antithesis of 'English/ness'. De-anglicising measures adopted in the early decades of independence – with varying degrees of success – included the establishment of *An Gúm* (1935), the State's Irish-language publication company; the attempt in the *Caighdeán Oifigiúil* (1948, revised ten years later) to standardise regional varieties of Irish and simplify its grammar and spelling; and the classification of Irish legal terminology in *Téarmaí Dlí* (1957). Irish placenames and signposts were restored (or issued for the first time) to towns and townlands, counties, cities and streets throughout the land. Translations were to serve all age groups: the classics of children's literature from the nations of the world were published in Irish, as were school textbooks and classics of world literature for adults.[25] Indeed, the emphasis placed by the cultural gatekeepers on subsidising translation rather than original writing meant that 'many of the most talented Irish-language writers of the time earned their living from the surreal task of producing Irish-language versions of Shakespeare, Dickens', and other works readily available in the original.[26]

All in all, the achievements of the Irish revival were remarkable, given the considerable challenges of the cultural change that had been set in motion. It has to be admitted, however, that the shift towards Irish as the dominant language in the national schools was by no means an unalloyed success. In the first years of the transition, many primary teachers continued to feel inadequately prepared for the momentous change in their working lives. Some suffered painfully, some left the profession. Looking back, seven decades later, on his initiation to a boys' school in the early 1920s, UCD's Professor of Latin, John O'Meara, sympathised with the plight of his teacher in Eyrecourt, Co. Galway:[27]

> The Master, in fact, was a very pleasant man in the normal way. He worked under almost impossible conditions. His modest apprentice-training had not prepared him to teach the Irish language. Yet certain educational pundits had assured the new Irish Government after 1922 that the desired revival of Irish could be achieved in some five years or so. Crash courses in the language were held for primary school teachers during the summer months. Our Master, being no longer young, made slow progress with these; he evidently did not have his heart in the venture. His attempts, therefore, to teach what became a central subject were pathetic, which much reduced his self-esteem before the knowing 'scholars'.

We must feel some sympathy for teachers, obliged in mid- or late-career to become learners and proponents of an unfamiliar language in which they had little competence – a language de facto foreign but *de iure* their first national language. For many whose mother-tongue was English, the Irish language was a *straniera in patria* [stranger in her own land] – as Tullio de Mauro, Italy's language historian, tagged the literary language of Tuscany that the Italian State imposed in schools all over Italy as the unifying national tongue after 1859. It took decades to establish the Tuscan language over other dialects, and for illiteracy levels to fall below 50 per cent.[28] Yet Italian was linguistically much closer to its regional dialects than Irish was to English. One might also mention that the diffusion throughout France, during the nineteenth century, of French as a school subject was no straightforward matter either. And this in a country also enjoying an already well-established literary language, fostered and promoted since the sixteenth and seventeenth centuries by royal decrees and the centres of power and influence. French remained a minority language for the first three decades of the nineteenth century, reserved as the everyday language of a culturally powerful literate minority. The French landmass was speckled with *patois* and fewer than 50 per cent of the population could read and write the *langue nationale* (as French had been designated from the Revolution onwards).[29] In Ireland, demographically much smaller than Italy or France, the complexity of reviving a language with a variety of competing forms was extremely daunting, and lively debates were to continue throughout the early years of independence concerning the best way to establish an agreed written model. Aidan Doyle observes that literacy in Irish 'remained the preserve of language-learners for the most part.'[30] With subsidies driving authors' creative energies to write with only schools and learners in mind, the concentration on the education sphere did little to foster independent writing in Irish of books that readers might enjoy reading.[31]

Peaking in the mid-1940s, the revival strategy was to enter a pattern of slow decline.[32] Many possible factors can help to explain how this happened. Initially, the novel pedagogic approach to language study contributed to the Gaelic League's phenomenal success with the public. Irish classes in the 1900s offered a style of language learning that most of the first generation of learners had never experienced before, foregrounding songs and stories, pronunciation exercises and spoken fluency, while in other modern language classrooms the diet had generally consisted in rules of grammar, morphology and prosody as well as the decoding of venerable texts. For a couple of decades, modern Irish became an adventurous, exciting subject to study.[33] And also to teach: Agnes O'Farrelly reported on classes in Cloghaneely Irish College, where 'all the old ideas about language teaching had to be scrapped. We set out, very inexperienced, but full of faith and enthusiasm, and we kept trying new ideas.'[34]

Many marriages were hatched at Gaelic League Irish classes, a fact that may have given the language a special kind of nostalgia in the hearts and minds of that cohort of the population. Their descendants, in the grip of de Valera's economic policies, can hardly have shared the same pitch of excitement. A generation or two later, when learning the language had morphed from a way of resisting the old British oppressor into the prosaic business of nation-building, or when – to quote Declan Kiberd – 'a Gaelic movement conceived with the greatest idealism had declined into a cynical state agency',[35] how could the enthusiasm of the initial revival years be sustained?

Weary disenchantment is discernible, for example, in a wartime contribution to *The Bell* from an anonymous national teacher with 16 years' work experience behind him. As he confides to the reader: 'I do an average day's work, but lacking fanaticism it is unequal to the overwhelming task of reviving a language which is *in extremis*.'[36] He has grave doubts about the practical use of Irish in the world beyond the school, a world where his pupils are besieged by English:[37]

> I contemplate that I am educating youngsters the majority of whom will clean out from cows, brush streets, ornament street corners, bring bags from Railway Stations, all of which tasks are performed in the *lingua franca* of manual labour.

An imagined encounter with a past pupil brings out the chasm between teacher and taught:[38]

> perhaps on my way home from school I meet a bright scholar of former years perched on the chariot of a milk-float, a boy who was one of my most fluent Gaelic speakers. I speak to him in Irish. He looks at me with that truculent faintly-entertained superciliousness of first puberty as if I had addressed him in Syro-Chaldaic or fifteenth-century Armenian! [...] He drives off with a grimace at a street audience as if to say: 'This simpleton is actually at that stage all these years!'

Although policy programmes prioritised spoken competence in Irish, striking the balance between oral and written language in the classroom was genuinely difficult,[39] all the more so as teachers whose first language was Irish were growing thinner on the ground. The direct method requires an ability to speak the target language to a high level of fluency and comprehensibility. As Aidan Doyle points out, it was easier to learn codified written forms than to acquire an ability to converse in Irish with its several regional varieties of pronunciation.[40] In practice, using the direct method can be extremely taxing for individual teachers, requiring considerable performance and communication skills.

Spoken language can be difficult to assess objectively, without external verification.[41] The challenge of finding enough examiners, not to mention establishing clear and fair criteria with standardised norms for conducting oral examinations, doubtless proved daunting for the limited resources available. The first Leaving Certificate oral examination in Irish was only introduced in 1960. Quite apart from financial and logistical pressures, once examinations in Irish came to represent an important threshold in the lives of young Irish citizens – with serious consequences for their future lives and careers should they fail – teaching and assessing the language were perhaps inevitably to lapse into safer, more reliable methods that lent themselves more readily to scrutiny. Kiberd again synthesises what happened:[42]

> Whereas Hyde had excited the youth of his generation with a challenge to repossess their heritage, to the young people of a later era the language appeared not so much a gift as a threat. Irish was studied in the most emasculated manner imaginable, as a heartbreaking discipline of grammar and syntax rather than as a living language. Worse still, this hyper-academic method of study detached Irish from its natural milieu, from the native music and dances which could have proved so valuable in exciting the interest of young people.

In the view of some commentators, the most egregious failing of early policymakers was to neglect traditional 'Irish Speakers' (for whom Irish was a mother tongue or first language). These felt increasingly marginalised.[43] The goal of preserving the Gaeltacht as a pre-modern and primordial space, minimally uncontaminated by modernity, meant that insufficient official attention was paid to the material livelihood of its inhabitants. Limited tourism based on language could not redress economic hardship. A testimony to the Gaeltacht Commission of 1925–6 strikingly links the futility of using Irish with a familiar tale of emigration:[44]

> 'Meirice Mecca na Gaeltachta. Níl sa bhaile ach an dealús agus an t-ocras. [...] Ní haon mhaith dóibh a gcuid Gaolainne. Thar lear atá an uaisleacht agus an saibhreas – thall atá an t-ór le bailiú ar na sráideanna.' [America is the Mecca of the Gaeltacht. There is only misery and hunger at home. [...] Irish is no good to them. Nobility and wealth is abroad – there is gold to be gathered on the streets over there.]

Even within the education sphere, the State tended to neglect the small minority of its citizens who were first speakers of the native vernacular. Irish-language teaching was aimed at the majority, who were learning Irish as a second language. University curricula in Irish remained largely 'characterised by an emphasis on linguistics and literary history, their reading lists dominated by scholarly editions of earlier work [...] or by more modern works written for learners, not for people with a serious, not to say professional, interest in contemporary literature'.[45]

In the long run, then, the language's preferential status in education may have been counter-productive, fuelling resentment among those who were elevated as its exemplary speakers as well as the scores of school-leavers whose future depended on learning enough Irish to pass an examination. The compulsory Irish measure had its share of critics, well before those of the more organised Language Freedom Movement of the 1960s. An editorial in *The Bell* in February 1943 declares that 'We have choked the Irish cat with Gaelic butter' and fears that 'the so-called revivalists – vivisectionists would be more like it – have done irreparable harm to the Language.'[46] Some four decades later, Declan Kiberd deemed compulsory Irish to have been disastrous and self-defeating, causing the language to become 'fatally identified in the popular mind with trouble at school, irregular verbs and tight-faced schoolteachers.'[47]

The language's absence of uniformity did not help. The lack of a standard spelling was inimical to teachers and learners alike, as Myles Dillon opined in 1929:[48]

> Anyone who has taught Irish is aware of the need for agreement on the question of spelling. At present no law runs, and every writer feels free to introduce reforms. Obviously the teacher's work is more difficult as a result. [...] But even worse is the effect on the learner. As no rules of spelling are absolute, he abandons himself to anarchy, and Irish may become a training in carelessness.

Uniformity was hard to establish. When attempts to standardise regional variations in orthography were made by the eventual publication of the *Caighdeán Oifigiúil* [Official Standard] (1947; revised in 1958, and again in 2017), they came too late and were generally ignored.[49] The Official Standard pleased nobody and has continued to attract criticisms. Mícheál Ó Siadhail characterised it as deeply flawed, amounting to a 'ragbag of half-systematic and half-random choice'; in Alan Bliss's opinion, it was a source of 'great harm to the cause of the Irish language' with invidious results for native speakers and learners alike.[50] The absence of agreed rules for dialect and orthography has impeded the grammatically-minded learner, and foreigners accustomed to a stable language system in print form. Dialectal differences continue to confuse learners, as they did Gustav Lehmacher, the German Jesuit who had made an attempt to learn Irish in 1923:[51]

> The foreigner who wishes to learn Irish, at any rate in the early stages of his study, has no interest whatsoever in dialects. What he wants is to learn *the* Irish language, not this or that particular dialect of the same.

For some or all of the above reasons, the Irish revival did not materialise as revivalists had hoped. However, why or how it did not go according to plan is ultimately less significant than the fact that the revival was attempted at all. The Irish State, quasi-paranoid lest it should lapse into a monoglot anglophone country, has constantly reminded its citizens of their Irish-speaking hinterland or Gaelic alter ego. Despite its glaring faults, what was achieved by this strategy was by no means insignificant.[52] The project came at the moment in history when it had a chance of some success; and it would have been hardly conceivable had its movers and shakers not themselves been steeped in the philological scholarship and language study of the Victorian period chronicled in this book or had Ireland's education culture not been open to the idea of language learning.

It is also the case that, no matter what measures were adopted to protect it, Irish – like most languages – was ill-equipped to withstand the unrelenting pressure from the rise of global English. All the more so as, during precisely the same interwar period, on both sides of the Atlantic, a vast amount of energies and resources were being systematically mobilised to promote the English language as a universal form of global communication.[53] In 1923, the very moment when the new Irish State was starting to implement its Irish-language policy, the pioneering Institute for Research in English Teaching [IRET] was founded in Tokyo by the linguist and phonetician Harold Palmer (1877–1949). This body, as the world's first institution of its kind, launched its *Bulletin* in the same year. It marks a significant step in the trend towards a more scientific period of research into language teaching.[54] Considering the influence that applied linguistics was later to have on language education, not just in English, the Tokyo Institute was a harbinger of things to come.[55]

Modern languages since independence

With most official attention focussed on reviving Irish, other modern languages received less formal scrutiny in independent Ireland. Britain's pioneering Leathes Committee had looked into the state of modern language teaching and made recommendations for improvement in 1918; the first Irish Government strategy for foreign languages in education, 'Languages Connect', was published a century later, in 2017.[56]

We have seen the importance of the NUI language requirement, but how the twin modern language teaching goals – prioritising Irish while retaining European languages – were accommodated in practice by schools in the fledgling State is less easy to pinpoint with precision. There was some local variation. Initially, Protestant schools were less enthusiastic about the new status of Irish lest it interfere with the teaching of existing languages like Latin and French.[57] Subject provision changed dramatically, especially in schools for boys. Irish had already replaced German by the early 1900s in the Christian Brothers' school in Richmond Street, Dublin. Liam Ó Briain remembers: 'That very year in which I joined the Preparatory Grade class, German was swept away completely at one fell stroke and Irish took its place.'[58] Inevitably, the privileged status of Irish brought a decline in the uptake of modern languages in general, and not just German. Maynooth's modern European languages suffered a severe drop in student numbers in the mid-1920s, where the polyglot Jean-Louis Rigal, appointed to succeed Professor John F. Hogan in 1914, was competent to teach three languages but had no students of German or Italian and only a handful in French. And this in a college where, 20 years previously, 'every student entering Maynooth had a good knowledge of French' and many had a working knowledge of the other two. Celtic Studies in Maynooth, on the other hand, found itself short-staffed due to a surge in student enrolments.[59] Clerical students knew which way the wind was blowing.

Yet, anecdotal evidence suggests that insular and continental language learning could co-exist fruitfully, with little friction. The sense of Irishness as a portal to both modern European languages and the classics remained very real in some milieux, as for example in Máire Cruise O'Brien's idyllic account of her 'golden childhood', spent between the Kerry Gaeltacht and student stage performances in Loreto Hall (Dublin) where she played parts from Aeschylus or Racine in her uncle's Gaelic translations – the same uncle Paddy (Browne) who spoke only Irish in the household and taught her Latin at the age of six and Greek at the age of ten. Studying classics at St Flannan's diocesan school in Ennis in the 1940s, Anne Enright's father translated from Greek into Irish.[60] Even in the 1990s, my own children were translating Virgil into Irish at a Dublin *Gaelscoil*, thanks to an inspirational Latin teacher. Irish-medium *Gaelscoileanna* appear to foster a relative ease in acquiring foreign-language skills.[61]

A detailed account of how school teaching and assessment of modern languages evolved from 1925 to the 1970s is beyond the scope of this book, but a passing glance at Leaving Certificate or matriculation examination papers from that time reveals the extent to which teaching remained for the most part wedded to nineteenth-century approaches. John Coolahan's assertion that the Irish secondary school system remained strongly anchored in traditional humanities pedagogy and a curriculum derived from the grammar school model, undoubtedly applies to the modern language sphere.[62] Thus, French and German papers involved translation into and out of the target language, as well as questions on prescribed poems, plays and prose. This gave an academic and literary slant to foreign-language study, requiring (in theory) a high standard of literacy, and some proficiency in reading and writing. Not that this standard was always met with ease. Mechanical workarounds could also be found. In a plea for better French teaching in secondary schools, UCC's Professor Kathleen O'Flaherty painted a dismal picture:[63]

> Answers to possible examination questions are dictated to a class in bad French and then learnt by heart. [...]. The same cause explains the amazingly weird and wonderful sounds which, to the average First Year students, symbolize the French tongue. Of course, no native speaker can understand; but then, our secondary school children do not have oral examinations, so why bother? [...] Truly, we are a gullible people: parents and children still imagine that French is taught in our schools.

In theory, O'Flaherty asserts, a graduate could be put in front of a French class with a degree in subjects other than French. Unlike Britain, there was no requirement for language teachers to have spent time in France or Germany or Italy or Spain. She continues:[64]

> In the Six Counties, where the Government can hardly be accused of fostering Irish, a man must reside for a certain period in the Gaedhealtacht before being allowed to teach this subject. We are not so particular, either for our national language or for any other.

Most of all, she blames the 'powers-that-be' – presumably, the State's Department of Education – for indifference to standards and willingness to be 'perfectly content with "French as she is spoke"' on the emerald isle.[65]

The French themselves were unhappy about how their language was being neglected. Alfred Blanche, the French Consul in Dublin, corresponded with the Quai d'Orsay in 1921–2, expressing concerns that the new status of Irish could pose a risk to the privileged position that had been enjoyed by French in Irish schools. He saw the teaching of French as excessively traditional, lacking modern methods and native speakers, and considered it to be in danger of being relegated to 'une langue moderne quelconque qu'on étudie si le temps le permet' [a random modern language to be taken up if time allows], due to curriculum pressure from other languages such as Irish, Latin, Greek and English. The study of French, he claimed, was in a period of steep decline, particularly in boys' schools. He suggested three measures which the ministry might consider introducing (teacher exchanges, scholarships for in-service summer courses, annual phonetics courses for teachers) to counter Ireland's absorption in 'le tourbillon de l'américanisme' [the whirlwind of Americanism].[66]

At that time and for many years to follow, there were no oral examinations. The Irish language requirement for all permanent teachers, regardless of what they taught, would naturally have impeded the permanent employment in schools of target-language teachers from abroad. The dearth of teachers with mother-tongue French mostly affected oral expression in terms of accent. Some Irish school-leavers might have an excellent grounding in French grammar but their spoken French was that of their local teacher.

In German, too, the written language continued to be prioritised over the spoken. Joachim Fischer speculates that the excessively literary German school curricula could have been due to the employment of non-Germanophone professors of German in Irish universities, and that this may have led to the downgrading, in schools, of practical spoken language skills.[67] Foreigners were certainly growing less visible in schools: as French religious sisters died they were replaced by local non-native speakers; the last of the French Spiritans had retired in 1896,[68] shortly before the French College changed its name to Blackrock College. While oral examinations in Irish were introduced in 1960,[69] oral examinations in other modern languages were piloted in the period 1982 to 1986.

Some ground-breaking changes began to appear in the mid-1960s. These were in large measure due to the advocacy of the Irish-language activist Colmán Ó hUallacháin, a Franciscan philosopher who had studied applied linguistics in Washington DC.[70] On his return, he directed *An Teanglann*, a State-funded Language Centre in Gormanston College, Co. Meath. In this dedicated space, Ireland's first language laboratory, language teachers and researchers could become familiar with new aural methodologies and how to use them in the classroom. Grants for language laboratories in schools were made available during the late 1960s and early 1970s. Out of these mid-1960s initiatives, new post-primary audio-visual courses for French, German and Spanish were developed.[71] Once again, as with the Gaelic League at the turn of the century, Irish was ahead of modern languages where methods of teaching the spoken language were concerned.

In Britain's schools, the oral component also began to be taken seriously during the 1960s.[72] Advocates for reform in the 1880s and 1890s had been hampered by the low status of spoken foreign languages and the scant training in spoken language skills for teachers themselves. In a climate of deeply entrenched traditional methods and aims of language pedagogy that included the regular use of English in the classroom and in translation exercises, non-target-language speakers were regarded as preferable to native target-language speakers.[73] Just as the 1918 Leathes Committee had reported, teaching methods may have evolved a little, but 'the examinations in modern languages are modelled too closely on Classical tradition.'[74] The guiding rationale for studying a foreign language remained access to the language's literary culture. Even if speaking French was unattainable, one could at least appreciate the verse dramas of Racine.

In influential British universities, traditional Victorian pedagogy continued to hold sway. At Oxbridge, the Leathes Report commented, 'the place assigned to philology and medieval language was too prominent.'[75] John le Carré's perfect spy, Magnus Pym, as a student reading German literature in a fictional interwar Oxford, is not entirely atypical; his avatars could readily be identified up to the 1960s:[76]

> He threw himself afresh upon the German muse and scarcely faltered when he discovered that at Oxford she was about five hundred years older than she had been in Bern, and that anything written within living memory was unsound. But he quickly overcame his disappointment. This is quality, he reasoned. This is academia. In no time he was immersing himself in the garbled texts of mediaeval minstrels with the same energy that, in an earlier life, he had bestowed on Thomas Mann. By the end of his first term he was an enthusiastic student of Middle and Old High German. By the end of his second he could recite the *Hildebrandslied* and intone Bishop

Ulfila's Gothic translation of the Bible in his college bar to the delight of his modest court. By the middle of his third he was romping in the Parnassian fields of comparative and putative philology, where youthful creativity has ever had its fling.

In Ireland too, university curricula for modern languages remained, by and large, minimally innovative. While individual professors may have nibbled at the edges of the prevailing literary canon by prescribing contemporary authors, the standard model involved close textual analysis of canonical works from the middle ages to the late nineteenth century, translation both into and out of the target language, and some time devoted to language history. The spoken language, though present in the curriculum, was given proportionately less time. Some professors taught through the medium of the foreign language, some institutions deployed target-language tutors for weekly conversation classes, and oral examinations were undervalued in assessment processes.[77]

Overall, the rhythms and style of education experienced by many independent citizens had the sort of timelessness evoked by Seamus Heaney, who recalled his time as a boarder at St Columb's Diocesan College in Derry, with its 'humanist emphasis on languages' as basically the experience of European Christian civilisation from AD 400 to AD 1940 or 50.[78]

There was a kind of stasis about this educational world, frozen in time and insulated from the outside world in a way that mirrored the isolationism of Ireland after independence, a period when intellectual exchange with other cultures receded. Psychologically, linguistically and economically cut off from the world, Ireland was socially resistant to change. It was, in Eda Sagarra's words, 'in almost every respect a static, hierarchical and paternalist society, one in which the accident of your birth would generally determine your whole life'.[79] The naïve ideology of de Valera's Ireland is recalled by John O'Meara in a hard-hitting description of a well-known Christian Brothers pamphlet from his youth, *Éire, Sean is Nua* [Ireland, Old and New]:[80]

> Ireland of the future, according to this crude and simple document, was to have all its problems solved: full employment on land and sea, and in factories; the best food products in the world; self-sufficiency; love of Jesus and Mary; no emigration except of missionary priests, nuns and brothers; the Irish language heard everywhere; admiring tourists; and the reunion of the country. Things looked simple to de Valera and the Brothers; but resumed colossal emigration to England in the fifties began the rude awakening from an understandable but dangerous dream.

It was high time to wake up from the dream, 'to shut the door on the past and to move forward', as Ken Whitaker and Seán Lemass clearly understood by the end of the 1950s.[81] Politically and economically, Ireland began to open up to the modern world in the 1960s. Emigration started to fall; negotiations on joining the Common Market were initiated. Educationally, efforts to improve school participation rates began to target the socially disadvantaged. Notable among the achievements of these years were the landmark statistical survey of infrastructure and trends for forecasting education requirements, published as *Investment in Education* (1965)[82] and the introduction of free post-primary education in 1967. New schooling models at post-primary level emerged, in the form of comprehensive and community schools. Later, the establishment of institutes of technology and national institutes of higher education was to expand the range of tertiary educational opportunities. The fruits of these initiatives began to be harvested from the 1970s on.

NORTH AND SOUTH: DIVERGENT POLICIES, DIVERGENT CULTURES

From the beginning of the island's partition into two jurisdictions, different perspectives on language learning emerged. These were most saliently reflected in the status of Irish on each side of the border but other features, such as the assessment of spoken languages, were also strikingly different in Northern Ireland.

Irish language study in Northern Ireland

Unsurprisingly, the independent State's Irish revival measures were not welcomed by the unionist jurisdiction of Northern Ireland. In 1928, the Cosgrave government responded cautiously to the activist policy recommendations of the *Coimisiún na Gaeltachta* [Gaeltacht Commission], partly due to the Taoiseach's worries about their effects on possible reunification.[83] This caution gave all the more impetus to the zealous revivalism of the succeeding Fianna Fáil administration (1932–48). As John Bowman has argued, de Valera's prioritising of language revival over unity was ultimately partitionist.[84] Politically, the goals of gaelicisation and unification were at odds: the more politicised the Irish language south of the border became, the wider the wedge driven along the border. In the North, language activists were regarded with deep suspicion by the Unionist majority, summarised by the slogan 'Scratch a Gaelic Leaguer and you'll find a Fenian'.[85]

Yet that simplistic slogan is not the whole story. Long before partition, as Roger Blaney has illustrated, Presbyterians and other dissenters had cultivated a strong tradition of interest in, and knowledge of, the island's vernacular heritage. Protestants were represented in significant numbers among early Gaelic League branches that opened in Belfast in the 1890s: one of the League's first northern branches was on the city's Shankill Road.[86] Even after the League adopted its separatist political stance in 1915, 'respect for cultural nationality continued to be a significant, if immeasurable, ingredient of Irish Presbyterianism.'[87] Personal reminiscences of elderly Northerners from both sides of the region's political and cultural divide, who grew up during the decade before partition, bear testimony to a complementary and overlapping heritage.[88]

That said, the cause of Irish did not have many powerful champions in the industrial city of Belfast. The independent QUB established in 1909 was, to quote Gearóid Ó Tuathaigh, 'an early acknowledgement of the confessional and cultural distinctiveness and demands of Ulster unionism which would soon take constitutional form in the partition of 1921.'[89] Yet QUB included a post in Irish, the first since the death of John O'Donovan in December 1861. The post was partly set up in response to lobbying by five Roman Catholic members of the Senate. Although a professorship was requested, it was created as a lectureship in Celtic languages and literature, and first filled by a Church of Ireland clergyman, Rev. F. W. O'Connell (already profiled in Chapter Seven). The relegation to lectureship status was probably more significant than the reversion to the older nomenclature, 'Celtic'.[90] In 1911–12, when the Gaelic League offered Queen's an annual grant towards transforming its Irish post into a chair, the university turned down the offer on financial grounds. Moody and Beckett comment: 'The plea of financial difficulties was not unfounded; but it is likely that a similar offer on behalf of some other subject would have been more sympathetically considered.'[91]

One cannot pigeonhole every individual according to their religion. Ernest Blythe, the Irish politician, Minister for Finance, promoter of An Gúm and later director of Dublin's Abbey theatre, was a separatist Ulster Protestant whose passion for the Irish-language revival drew him south of the border. His Presbyterian maternal relatives had been Gaelic speakers.[92] QUB's professor of classics Robert Mitchell Henry, central in designing the independence of Belfast's new university in 1908, was a home ruler. Of dissenter background, he sympathised with the Gaelic League and was one of the lobbyists for restoring the teaching of Irish in the Belfast College.[93]

Despite such nuanced perspectives on the language, predictable confessional and political divides are seen in the distribution of Irish-language study in schools in Northern Ireland since 1921. A growth in Irish-language use in the north-east of the island, probably due to the endeavours of the Gaelic League, was stunted during the early decades of partition.[94] The region's last native Irish speakers died in Co. Tyrone in 1970, and in Co. Antrim in 1983.[95] In inverse proportion to Dublin's obsession with Irish revival, the Stormont administration's indifference to the language is seen in the dearth of official data: no question regarding the Irish language was asked in the Northern Ireland census until the 1991 census.[96]

In 1972, Tomás Ó Fiaich reported that Irish had been 'tolerated rather than encouraged by the State. It is taught in about 150 primary schools, roughly one in nine of the total number [...],' while 'at post-primary level it is available in most Catholic schools and in only a couple of others.'[97] Thus, while boarders at Derry's Catholic diocesan college of St Columb's learned Irish in school, as did students attending St Dominic's High School for Girls run by the Dominicans in Belfast (where Irish was taught to a very high standard), and went to practise speaking it in the Gaeltacht,[98] Enniskillen's Church of Ireland Portora boys did not. James Sharkey evoked the way in which Irish was kept alive at St Columb's, giving pupils a familiarity with both traditions in the divided region:[99]

> We certainly, in our history studies, had a sense of Britain's contribution to the world. Of course, we were skeptical about it. But, importantly, we also had a substantial engagement with the Gaelic tradition. This was something quite unusual, and in the unionist tradition they wouldn't have had this engagement. We had it from a historical perspective (that is, the long view of Irish history) and also in terms of the resurgence of Irish literature, sometimes called 'the Hidden Ireland' of Munster or, more recently, 'the Hidden Ulster', the poets of the eighteenth century. St Columb's was one of the most important defenders of the northern tradition in Irish, in the language, in its validity, in its dialects.

Since the early 1970s, Irish-language regulatory frameworks in Northern Ireland have shifted in other directions, as have the demands of activists. With the emergence of a new, more confident generation of Northern Catholics – what Heaney called the '11-plus generation of Catholic scholarship boys',[100] civil rights discourse began to include language rights. *Bunscoil Phobal Feirste*, Northern Ireland's first Irish-medium primary school, was opened in West Belfast in 1971, with nine pupils. By 2010 its pupils reached almost 300. The phenomenon of early language immersion schools for Irish has continued throughout the region, with over 80 schools both urban and rural, mostly pre-school and primary, by 2004.[101] To some effect: among the features of his native Belfast, post-Troubles, Gerald Dawe singled out the presence of the Irish language: 'Far from being an underground and repressed language in twentieth-century Belfast, spoken Irish is now a dynamic and empowering mark of cultural identity for nationalists.'[102]

Irish – unlike Welsh in Wales – remains outside the core curriculum in Northern Ireland's schools, with optional status as a modern language among other European languages. In line with trends in England, modern language study enjoyed a rise in the 1990s, before falling out of favour in the new millennium, due to changes in language education policy.[103] Irish 'became the second most popular language for the GCSE (intermediate) examination in Northern Ireland, after French, from 1988 to 2002,'[104] but falling numbers taking languages since the 2003 peak affect Irish as much as other languages. Nonetheless, despite drops in take-up, attitudinal surveys reveal strong support for keeping Irish alive in Northern Ireland and there is broad agreement that the language is one part, although not a necessary part, of being Irish.[105] Even among some unionists.[106]

Political developments have brought more secure funding to the region. The 1998 Belfast Agreement gave legal recognition to Irish as it did to Ulster Scots; it also led to the cross-border initiative to promote minority languages, An Foras Teanga. Its Irish arm, Foras na Gaeilge, was established the following year.[107] Several reports and statistical surveys on the study and use of the Irish language in Northern Ireland have been conducted, many of them funded by European agencies, such as the regional dossier prepared by Mercator. St Mary's University College Belfast offers a B.Ed. Honours (Bilingual) degree for Irish-medium teachers.[108] West Belfast's pirate radio station, Raidió Fáilte (1985), now enjoys an Ofcom licence; its elegant modern building houses a bilingual café and a cultural centre which has been called 'the best community radio facility in all of Ireland'.[109]

These policy initiatives, underscored and supported by Europe and symptomatic of the peace process of recent decades, in themselves demonstrate that the language continues for the most part to be the preserve of a minority, embroiled in deeply divergent political divisions. Sadly, the distortions of cultural nationalism and identity politics have not yet run their course, with the Language Act continuing to be used for political ends since the enactment of the Good Friday agreement. The more feverish the local sectarian temperature, the more irrational seem attempts made to stop relations becoming normalised: Irish-medium schools that are confessionally desegregated can meet with deep-set resistance of a kind all too familiar in Northern Ireland.[110] While Irish in the Republic has recently begun to embrace new speakers from well beyond the island's shores, north of the border the language has increasingly been identified with one side of a narrow and local culture war. Efforts to reclaim the region's venerable Irish patrimony, on a neutral ground, have been stymied. However, even in the absence of a functioning regional executive, the Identity and Language (Northern Ireland) Act was voted into law by the UK parliament in December 2022.

Yet even in Northern Ireland, linguistic polarisation does not always have to map onto political polarisation. In 1992, William Smith opened his lecture at a symposium in Belfast on 'The Irish Language and the Unionist Tradition' with an anecdote recalling his first venture into Irish language study as a loyalist prisoner in Long Kesh during the early 1970s. During exercise in the prison yard, he was intrigued by the sounds of republican prisoners in another compound talking to each other in Irish. When he persuaded one of them to teach him the language, they could be seen seated on either side of two fences and a roadway; after a couple of months the prison authorities facilitated the cross-community lessons by allowing Smith to move beyond his yard and sit on the roadway with just one fence between republican teacher and loyalist student.[111] When an Irish teacher was engaged to teach Irish in both compounds, the republicans refused the teacher on the grounds that he had the wrong Irish, which they called 'Fianna Fáil Gaelic' – probably because it was not Donegal Irish, the variety familiar to them. Smith ends his reminiscence on a wise note:[112]

> When I think back to those days in the prison camp, with the gun towers, the guard dogs, and the rows of razor wire which housed thousands of prisoners of opposing factions, I think of the tolerance that existed, and that two insignificant prisoners sat on each side of the fence talking Irish, and sometimes wondering what all this was about.

Modern languages in Northern Ireland: a brief comment

As regards practical arrangements for language learning in schools, important divergences emerged between the two jurisdictions immediately after partition. From the 1920s on, the Northern Ireland curriculum required oral assessment for modern language students.[113] Significantly, this rule included Irish. Assessing the spoken component at language examinations shows a serious effort to engage with the strong recommendations of the Leathes Report. A residency requirement for language teachers was also in force, meaning in practice that aspiring teachers had to spend 'at least three months in the country where the language was spoken, or in the case of Irish, in a district where Irish was the ordinary everyday language of the people.'[114] Such regulatory rigour contrasted with the Republic, where a graduate in any subject was deemed qualified to teach all Leaving Certificate subjects, and language teachers faced no residency requirement. The July 1939 Feis gathering at Ballycastle, Co. Antrim, was told that Irish was not given separate treatment as the 'national' language of the region, but 'the Belfast authorities were in some respects more thorough in regard to Irish than were the Dublin authorities.'[115] The northern regime's Gaeltacht residency requirement was later praised by those lobbying for the introduction of a similar scheme for Irish teachers in the South.[116]

Written assessment for modern languages in each jurisdiction still conformed to the Victorian literary model,[117] but a significant divergence in the overall assessment of school leavers lay in the narrow subject range (normally as few as three subjects) taken by A-level candidates as against the broader curriculum promoted by the Leaving Certificate south of the border. This relative specialisation may have affected language provision and raised expectations of higher standards among the public in Northern Ireland. The A-level regime sat well with the 1918 Leathes Commission's belief that learning one modern language well was better than doing two or three badly.[118]

We may, finally, note the drastic cull of languages offered at northern universities. In the 1990s, QUB began to cut its range of language departments – Arabic (Semitic Studies), Russian (Slavonic Studies), Italian, and finally German – while in 2015–19 'a similar fate befell all first-degree courses in modern languages at Ulster University, leaving just Irish and Linguistics as areas of postgraduate research.'[119] Such closures may signal a more 'corporate' view of higher education than in the south, or merely the continuing alignment of Northern Ireland's tertiary education sector with the rest of the UK, where language departments, already undermined by the downgrading of foreign languages in British schools, have also been shrunk or jettisoned by many universities.

SHIFTING CONTEXTS OF LANGUAGE LEARNING SINCE THE 1970s

The old certainties that sustained Victorian approaches to language education were losing their grip from the 1970s. This did not happen just in Ireland but was correlated with several trends both global and local.

In the first place, Ireland's change of language-learning culture has to be understood within the wider context of twentieth-century linguistic thought, shaped by Saussure, Jakobson, Sapir, Bloomfield, Chomsky and others. One broad outcome has been the rise of descriptive or synchronic (as opposed to historical and diachronic) linguistics.[120] In the narrower sphere of foreign-language learning, a new consensus on goals and methods has emerged since the second world war. The pendulum has swung away from prioritising grammatical rules towards a functional or communicative style of teaching, informed by evidence-based research into how humans acquire foreign languages. Advances in applied linguistics, and the scientific description of language-learning processes, have led to a concern with teaching communicative and creative competence along with the four skills of listening, speaking, reading and writing the language being studied, rather than just teaching grammatical accuracy and vocabulary in isolation.

With the attention of applied linguistics research focussed on the process rather than the results of second language learning, the student's utterances in the target language have moved centre stage. As part of the learner's individual 'interlanguage', these imperfect utterances are regarded as an important step in the process of learning any language. Even if they deviate from a native speaker's way of communicating the same message, the learner's attempts may succeed in communicating something, however ungrammatically. From the learner's point of view, there is less concern with 'right' and 'wrong' formulations; the essential thing is to communicate.[121]

The tendency towards prioritising communicative skills while tolerating 'errors', reducing the time spent on formal grammar teaching, and avoiding translation, shifts language teaching in schools far away from Victorian approaches to the same task. Yet, as McLelland points out, late twentieth-century pedagogic orthodoxy is 'anything but new'.[122] The new trend should be viewed not so much as a radical change but rather as a pendulum swing, back to pre-Victorian times, when language teaching had not yet become dominated by the methods for teaching the classics.[123]

Shifting regulations, shifting sociolinguistics: the Irish language

International trends in language pedagogy made their presence felt during a time of important reversals in some of the local regulatory frameworks that had shaped Irish language classrooms since the establishment of the State.

Five decades into independence, fissures in governmental language policy were showing. The 1965 'White Paper on the Restoration of the Irish Language' showed that official State aspirations had by then changed, towards bilingualism rather than restoration.[124] Partly in response to civil society advocates who campaigned for a different weighting of language study, the 'requirement to pass Irish in order to be awarded the Leaving Certificate and the Irish Language entrance examination for the civil service' was abolished in 1973–4.[125] State-funded schools however are still obliged to teach Irish and the language remains as a matriculation requirement, with exemptions of different sorts, in four of Ireland's universities.[126]

This radical reversal of a Leaving Certificate regulation that dated back to 1934 has been welcomed by many. In recent decades, a more relaxed approach to the study of Irish in schools has allowed more positive perceptions to grow among a 'new generation, which is learning Irish for pleasure rather than bonus examination points'.[127] In primary classrooms, for example, Irish literacy has been reformed by new teaching methods.[128] Enriching possibilities have emerged for framing the language as part of Ireland's heritage and connecting it with other forms of cultural expression such as traditional music or sport. Non-governmental advocacy groups like *Gael Linn* have been fundamental in harnessing contemporary culture to promote a sense of Gaelic modernity, more aligned with the future than the past; and attitudinal surveys since the mid-1970s have shown consistently that two-thirds of Irish people approve of the Irish language as a cultural marker worth maintaining and transmitting in schools, while deprecating the older requirement for school leavers to pass Irish in order to pass the Leaving Certificate.[129]

The picture is not all positive, however. Some language advocates are dismayed by the removal of Irish from its core position in the final school examination. They view this volte-face as a form of betrayal, exposing the 'paralysis of political will allied to bureaucratic obstruction' among those charged with formulating the State's language policy.[130] In 1981, Séamas Ó Buachalla concluded his account of 150 years of Irish-language educational policy on a pessimistic note. He saw the revival as deficient in 'a continuity of measures and a coherent resource availability independent of party interest and ministerial whim' and blamed the 'weakness of our political will' combined with 'an inadequate understanding of the complexity of the task'.[131] Advocates continue to worry about the long-term future of the language and are alarmed by ever-declining competence (as measured by traditional expectations).

Meanwhile, the language itself, like all living languages, is evolving rapidly, amid unprecedented sociolinguistic changes. Its 'language community' now consists almost entirely of new speakers. A plurality of *Gaeltachtaí* [pockets of Irish-speaking areas], far more diverse than the officially designated regions of the past, points to a redefinition of the Gaeltacht concept.[132] The fixed mapping of Gaeltacht areas where 'native' speakers dwell, first undertaken in the mid-1920s, is therefore problematic. Indeed, by the lights of today's linguistics, the very concept of 'native' speakers smacks of 'the remnants of Romanticism linking language, nation and territory'.[133] Language use is more fluid than what can be contained within geographical boundaries, and the outmoded ethnolinguistic cartography of the past cannot indicate the interconnectedness and variety of today's Irish speakers, who cover a multitude of levels of competence and may be found living anywhere and everywhere, in Ireland and overseas.[134]

Since the late 1960s, in particular, there has been an increase in urban users of Irish, with the enormous popularity and spread of *Gaelscoileanna* [Irish-medium schools, both primary and secondary] in places outside traditional Gaeltacht or Irish-speaking regions. Some of these new Irish speakers have been the driving force behind the vibrant recent phenomenon of Irish-language community radio, born of minority-language rights activism. Originating in Gaeltacht communities disillusioned over the State's neglect of the language, the activism first took the form of cooperative initiatives and grass-roots pirate radio stations. The staff of the newest urban radio stations, many of them past pupils of *Gaelscoileanna* and not 'native-speaking' by definition – expose the need for alternatives to traditional categories like 'native' speakers. They also challenge older models of Irish-language broadcasting led by identity politics. The alternative music and content that these volunteers broadcast motivates them more than the colloquial Irish medium they speak on air.[135] We have come a long way – or perhaps a short way – from the launch of 2RN in 1926, when Hyde 'stressed the importance of an Irish radio station for bolstering national identity.'[136] Replacing ethnolinguistic models of 'native speaker', these urban mediascapes are accelerating the process of evolution that all vernaculars undergo, for good or ill, whenever usage spreads.

Following decades of emigration – amounting at times to depopulation – Ireland's novel experience of immigration (since the 1990s) has further widened the cohorts of people who study the Irish language. Some visitors from other countries and continents learn to speak Irish fluently.[137] New Irish residents and citizens can come to the language without historical baggage and be unafraid to speak it. This phenomenon again points to a need to revise the categories and policy goals of the past, given that some 17 per cent of Irish citizens today have been born outside the State.[138] 'Irish speakers' no longer necessarily identify as 'Irish'. 'If Ireland is to become a multicultural society, then the Irish language can no longer function as a badge of identity for just one section of the community, those who claim descent from putative Gaelic ancestors.'[139] We may be moving beyond the binary Romantic equation of language with nation. How would an Edwardian professor of Irish react to the news that the person currently charged with promoting and maintaining the Irish language in a Kerry Gaeltacht is a Russian from Moscow?[140] Or if he heard a Chinese student being interviewed by an Irish fellow student, in Irish, on the UCD Gaeltacht website?[141] Or read about a Ukrainian refugee who moved to Ireland with her family in spring 2022, having learned Irish in Belfast?[142] Such is the globalised world in which languages – not just English – can be acquired and sustained today.

Arguably, as more immigrants study the language, Irish people become aware of it in different ways from the past, viewing it as an enrichment or an emblem of diversity rather than the failed imposition of a compulsory monoglot culture. In theory, too, the study of Irish should promote an appreciation of issues confronting minoritised-language study in other countries. Because of their own language history and their study of Irish, Irish people have more respect for languages other than English and (perhaps) an instinctive sense of how languages can come under threat, in unexpected ways and in relatively short periods of time.

On balance, then, considerable goodwill continues to be expressed about the Irish language since the 1960s. Opportunities for learning and speaking it abound, at least at a colloquial level, in a variety of unregulated and unprecedented settings. Today's Irish speakers form a collective *breac-ghaeltacht*, to recoin an old term in a more appropriate way, as John Walsh argues.[143] Overall, while Irish language advocates and practitioners tend to be filled with dismay – even anger – at the State's reluctance to formulate enlightened language policies to redress a continuing decline in usage and levels of competence, there are nevertheless some tiny green shoots to suggest that all is not yet lost.

Decommissioning the classics, pendulum swings in modern languages

Also in the 1970s, the Republic of Ireland was to witness a second educational tipping point, occurring in the context of broadening participation and curriculum review. This was the abandonment of a classical language requirement for university entry, which had amounted – in the vast majority of Irish secondary schools – to a de facto Latin requirement.[144] Of all the shifting regulatory measures taken since 1970, this was the most radical departure from Victorian Ireland's education landscape.

It should be stressed that the abandonment of the classics requirement was part of a common trend where post-war governments in the west were aspiring towards social inclusion by building societies based on social justice. Classical languages were generally viewed as socially elite and too exclusive during a period of widening access to further education.[145] Oxford and Cambridge removed their Latin entry requirement for non-classics candidates in 1960.[146] Continental western European universities also took decisions that eroded the prestige of classical languages, leading to the final overthrow of the *empire pluriséculaire* [centuries-old hegemony] of Latin.[147]

In Ireland, Trinity revised its requirement for entry to a pass degree in 1953, relieving freshmen 'of the necessity to take Latin unless they so wished' – a change soon followed by the dropping of compulsory Latin from matriculation requirements.[148] In QUB, following previous adjustments to matriculation regulations, 1959 marked the end of a classics requirement for medical students in the Northern Ireland university.[149] During the winter of 1972–3, the NUI's constituent colleges deliberated on which courses and Faculties should continue to require Latin (or Greek) for matriculation. Their varying recommendations to the NUI Senate led to the regulation being gradually phased out.[150] By 1974 the rubric for Arts and Law had been altered to read 'a third language accepted for matriculation'.[151]

This tipping point was also in line with the Catholic church's decision, taken at the Second Vatican Council, to abandon the practice of using Latin for public worship. In a bid to return to the origins of the early church, when mass was celebrated in the local language, and in order to include the faithful in worship, altars were turned around to face the flock. Latin missals were translated into spoken languages.[152] In Ireland, the first vernacular masses were celebrated in March 1965. For Irish Catholicism, this was a seismic moment. People wondered if the Vatican was now conceding ground to Protestantism, and speculated on what might give way next: priestly celibacy or an all-male priesthood? (These expectations were to prove premature.) Where language learning is concerned, it compounded the collapse in student take-up of the classics. As W. B. Stanford reported in 1976: 'In the decade 1964–74 15 schools in the Irish Republic ceased to teach Greek. Only eight remain. Latin, which until recently had strong ecclesiastical support, has maintained itself better, but now shows signs of a similar decline.'[153]

The magnitude of the change can be appreciated when we recall how competence in Latin and Greek had been the *sine qua non* for anybody wishing to study anywhere, at home or abroad, and for learnèd foreign travellers. To remove this pre-eminence was not only to remove what had been the bread and butter of everyday study for well over a millennium; it also disrupted centuries-old cultural continuities. As John O'Meara put it, 'the mind of Europe – and to a considerable extent the world – has been formed by the same Graeco-Roman education experienced by St Augustine of Hippo in the 4th century, Montaigne in the 16th, and Arnold Toynbee in the 20th.'[154] Latin and Greek played such a central part in the schooling of all European writers educated before 1922 that, to quote another Classics professor, John Dillon, 'whatever their attitudes to classical culture, whatever the torments they endured in the process of learning the language, they had to relate to it, if only by opposition.'[155] Consequently, the removal of that classical core obscures full appreciation of how the minds and sensibilities of our forebears were formed.[156] The worst fears of the late Victorian classics brigade, who had stoutly resisted the establishment of university degrees in modern languages, were being realised. The long-term impact of this cultural watershed remains to be fully assessed.[157]

The decommissioning of the classics by the early 1970s was the culmination of two centuries during which classics had been on the wane. In his (1976) book on Ireland's engagement with the classical tradition, Professor Stanford identified Trinity's (1776) modern languages chairs as the starting point of that decline:[158]

> The foundation of two professorships in French with German, and in Italian with Spanish, at Trinity College in 1776 marked the beginning of a new era, though the classicists managed to keep the sphere of influence of these innovations out of the normal courses for undergraduates until over a hundred years later.

Stanford criticised the stultifying manner in which classics had been taught in some nineteenth-century schools.[159] Things did not improve much, if we are to believe John O'Meara's account of the woeful way Latin had been taught in many secondary schools, prompting his own central role in setting up the Classical Teachers Association, which led to a measure of influence on curriculum development. Badly taught Latin was worse than no Latin at all. Above all, by the 1970s, a classical education was perceived as socially divisive: neither Latin nor modern languages were taught in Vocational Schools, effectively ruling out the possibility of anybody schooled there accessing the liberal professions. Both O'Meara (UCD Professor of Latin) and Ó Catháin SJ (UCD Professor of Education,) were opposed to the NUI matriculation requirement of a classical language for all NUI students.[160]

The 1970s mark a related trend: the re-positioning of modern languages in the education sphere. Gradually taking the place of the classics, living languages became the sole foreign-language element to be cultivated in schools. *Les anciens* having been put out to grass, it was now over to *les modernes*. Dismantling centuries of education tradition did not happen overnight: in Ireland's secondary schools, Latin enjoyed a protracted twilight.[161] As long as there were teachers who had an acquaintance with Latin, Victorian language teaching approaches persisted. The literary and grammatical curriculum began to disappear as teachers retired and schools discontinued Latin. The change brought slow, almost imperceptible consequences to the language classroom. After the 1970s, modern language teachers could no longer assume that their abler school leavers could handle complex syntax and obscure literary verb tenses, or even short novellas and poems in a foreign language. In universities, modern language courses began gradually to phase out philology and history of the language.[162]

In English-speaking countries like Ireland, the removal of school Latin has served to distance learners from the structures of other modern foreign languages that bear more evident marks of Latin morphology, conjugations and declensions. Without the convenient comparison with Latin, a more inflected language than English, it can be difficult for teachers to teach, or learners to grasp, the conventions of agreement in gender or number, and the complexities of verb conjugations. Even German, largely Latin-free in its lexis, but heavily inflected in its syntax, becomes slightly less manageable for learners once the complications of Latin grammar have been excised from the core curriculum. Adrift from Latin, for centuries the key to a deeper understanding of language structures, anglophone language-learners find themselves a little further away from mastering other languages in their written form.

Soon, however, these gaps began to matter less, as the pendulum in modern language teaching was swinging towards communicative competence and an emphasis on oral and aural skills. The twentieth century's communications media par excellence – radio, film, television, pop songs – were finally embraced, and drove rapid changes in traditional language pedagogy, all of which tied in with the democratisation of language-teaching provision.[163] As Christopher Brumfit told a Dublin gathering of modern language teachers in 1986, the exposure to foreign languages came to be viewed as a right, rather than a privilege offered to what he called 'a pre-selected elite of quasi-classicists.' He continued:[164]

> No longer could fluent mother-tongue literacy be taken for granted (if it ever really could); [...] it was assumed that straightforward conversation needed to be taught, and the traditional sources of fluency activity in earlier language teaching, reading and composition, were not so readily available for those who were not classified as readers or writers in their mother tongues.

The early 1980s were a turbulent period for modern language teachers in Ireland. Between 1982 and 1986, policy changes initiated by the Department of Education led to new language syllabuses at Leaving Certificate and Intermediate Certificate, introducing listening and speaking tests.[165] The Government was finally addressing what had been obvious to teachers: while the nineteenth century had been devoted to the written word, the twentieth was the century of spoken media.[166] Re-setting the balance between oral and written has completely changed the goals and expectations of language learning. A series of MLTA [Modern Language Teachers Association] Conventions were held during this time of sweeping changes, the Proceedings of which reveal a confusing pace of pressures and challenges. A flavour of the period reads as follows:[167]

> teachers have been called upon to intensify the fight to secure an aural/oral component in Leaving Certificate exams in modern languages; they have continued to be bombarded with propaganda on behalf of (various versions of) the communicative approach to language teaching; there has been no let-up in the stream of new course books and supplementary materials that eager salesmen would like them to buy; and now (rather suddenly, as it seems)

they must live with the reality of oral exams and listening tests and the additional burden that these impose on an already overcrowded school timetable.

On the positive side, teachers have adjusted well, over time, to the new emphasis on oral and aural skills, and the diminished literary and written component has not been as catastrophic as some had feared. At its best, in the hands of a gifted teacher, backed up by attractive materials, printed and aural, and by the sophisticated mixed-media textbooks and websites of today, the communicative approach involves learning to use grammatical structures appropriately and is capable of producing 'a curriculum and a methodology which both enables learners to buy themselves cups of coffee *and* leads them towards reading Racine or Flaubert, Goethe or Fontane'.[168] Third-level language study has also been adapting, in Ireland as elsewhere, to the switch from traditional liberal arts goals to more practical skills. Ireland's expanding university sector – including five technological universities [incorporating former institutes of technology] – has set up new degree courses combining applied languages with vocational disciplines such as law, business, information technology or hospitality and tourism management.

New European alliances

Meanwhile, roughly coinciding with the adieu to Latin and expanding access to education, Ireland's membership of the European Economic Community arrived in 1973. This has brought many benefits – economic, political, and also linguistic. Since joining forces with the nations of Europe in the early 70s, Ireland has been able to forge new kinds of alliances with the continent. Modern languages student enrolment soared. Through the Erasmus student exchange scheme, introduced in 1987 by an Irish EU Commissioner, Peter Sutherland, Irish undergraduates have spent periods of university study abroad and made personal contacts with their continental peers. Graduates have been able to find work, in a range of sectors and services, within other Member States. More recently, citizens from eastern European accession countries have enriched the variety of languages heard in workplaces, streets, shops, buses and trains, all around Ireland. Irish people today experience a daily kaleidoscope of different languages in their midst.[169] The palette of languages recognised for assessment in the Leaving Certificate examination has broadened considerably. A winning combination of EU membership, English language, and a spread of other languages makes Ireland a natural site for EMEA headquarters of multinationals. We noted how new opportunities in the Indian Civil Service incentivised language learning in Victorian times; today, the benefits of foreign languages arrive naturally on our shores, in the form of foreign people.

Within the EU, Ireland wields the world's most useful language not as an owner but as a squatter, and as one language among many, which may enable a more co-operative mindset. Membership of the EU has, perhaps paradoxically, also brought long-term benefits for Irish-language study. As a Member State of a supranational organisation where plurilingualism is enshrined as a foundational principle,[170] Ireland finds its ancestral language placed in a relationship of parity within a multilingual federation of nations. This delivers it from being locked in a binary struggle against the language of the Saxon.[171] Ireland's native vernacular has gained in confidence and optimism, enriched by further translation contacts with a broadening range of languages other than English. An official language of the Communities since 1973,[172] Irish has been a working language of Europe since 2007. Full official status (meaning that EU documents must be available in Irish) in place since 1 January 2022 brings a demand for Irish graduates with translation skills. Here at last is a material incentive for mastering Irish that would have been unthinkable a generation ago.

Multilingualism is a defining feature of the EU. David Best explains that Europeans are doing their level best 'to muddle along by at least trying to speak the same language, that is, all 24 versions of it.'[173] 'Muddling along' is enabled by translation. Umberto Eco's famous dictum – *La lingua dell'Europa è la traduzione* [The language of Europe is translation] – reflects the fact that European citizens have a right to be heard in the European Parliament by deputies who speak their language, and to read European laws drafted in their own language. Since official status came fully into force in January 2022, the need for translators and lawyer-linguists with skills in Irish has grown more acute. All of this suggests that Europe, by a curious loop of history, is where the long-term survival of Irish is, once again, guaranteed. The last Gaeltacht may well flourish, not among the Irish Franciscans in Louvain, but within the language services in Brussels.

On the surface, the study of modern languages in Irish society generally appears to be alive and well. It has never been more accessible or more consensual to the motivated learner. Cultural institutes (of France, Germany, Italy, Spain) offer courses at all levels. A small privileged group of Irish schoolgoers can avail of content-based approaches to language learning by attending the *Lycée français d'Irlande* or its Eurocampus partner, *St Kilian's Deutsche Schule*. Both schools, based in Dublin, promote European citizenship.[174] The Common European Framework of Reference provides a useful tool, for learners and teachers alike, for gauging levels of competence across individuals, sectors and situations. There is a thriving language-learning industry that churns out a wealth of new materials for mastering the spoken and written code of foreign languages, potentially of enormous benefit to learners – from audiovisual and text-based approaches to mobile phone apps and eBooks supplemented by digital listening and speaking units. Irish is available on DuoLingo.[175] Although this is a profitable industry, at least some of these aids are relatively low in cost and can be attempted by individuals on a do-it-yourself basis. This is a blackboard jungle where a Victorian linguist visitor would be totally lost, and from which it would take more than a Virgilian digital native to extricate him.

Since EU enlargement, however, there are some fresh anxieties. The new Member States joining the EU in 2004, 2007 and 2013 doubled the number of official languages; and, particularly with the accession of countries from the former eastern bloc, enlargement has brought a discernible increase in the use of English as a working language within the day-to-day business of the European institutions. During the Brexit debate, a British politician claimed with some justification that 'bad English' is now the official language of the European Union. French-speaking countries have been the most vocal proponents of EU multilingualism, motivated largely by a desire 'to stem the unstoppable rise of English as the institutions' *lingua franca*.'[176] However, there remains the EU's fundamental obligation to communicate with its citizens in their own language. While, for practical purposes, the common language may tend to be English between officials of different nationalities meeting in Brussels, their official communications will always be in the individual idioms of the different Member States. So, multilingualism will persist on some level, 'no matter what the doomsayers may claim'.[177]

Following the European Year of Languages (2001), the EU set as a minimum target for all Europeans the ability to communicate in their mother tongue plus two foreign languages. This target, as Attracta Halpin observes, corresponds in effect to what had been the prevailing matriculation language requirement of the NUI for decades.[178] The Irish government's response was to publish an ambitious strategy for foreign languages in education, 'Languages Connect' (2017), the fruit of three years' research and deliberations among stakeholders.[179] The document insists on the importance and value of learning foreign languages for individuals and society as well as for competitive international trade in a globalised world, and identifies a number of ways to increase both the range of languages offered (from Europe and beyond) and the numbers of students studying them within the current Irish education system.[180] It points out the potential linguistic resource that could be tapped in the future, among the new Irish, who hail from almost 200 countries of the world.[181] The government strategy led to an academic symposium held in UCC, on the theme 'When English is not enough'.[182] The participants welcomed 'Languages Connect' while cogently arguing remedies to address its salient defects. Among the many challenges discussed in the strategy, one observation surfaces repeatedly, in the document itself and in the academic papers responding to it: a recognition that 'the global dominance of English and its status as a *lingua franca* gives rise to the mistaken belief that "English is enough" and can result in complacency or lack of motivation to learn other languages.'[183]

A new scale of anglicisation: English as lingua franca

After the revival of Irish and the disposal of Latin, the arrival of global English is the third major language shift affecting language study in post-Victorian Ireland. The hegemony of English is not something that stealthily crept up since the second world war and the rise of information technologies. As already noted, the interwar period had seen deliberate steps being taken by Britain and America to develop English as a world language that would be instrumental for diplomatic soft power in cultural relations overseas. 'Global English' later came to denote the English language used as a genuinely supranational means of communication, stripped of references to a specific nation or culture.[184] Indeed, the phenomenon had already been delineated in a prescient essay published in 1922 by a linguist whom we have already profiled, the Rev. Frederick William O'Connell ['Conall Cearnach']:[185]

> If the present rate of progress be maintained – and everything points to its acceleration rather than its retardation – English, already the language of the British Isles, North America, Australia, New Zealand, and part of Africa, will in another hundred years be the official language of Mexico, Brazil, and the greater part of Africa; while it will have replaced Hindustani as the inter-tribal speech of all India. English-speaking missionaries will have familiarised all Heathendom with its sound, and it will be taught as an essential subject in the schools of China and Japan, as well as those in Europe. By the year 3000 AD three-eighths of the world's population will be English-speaking monoglots, and the remaining five-eighths bilinguists and polyglots having English as one of their languages. [...] We may assume that about the year 6000 AD the whole earth will be of one speech, and that speech English. [...] The language of the future will be English but it will not be [the] English of Shakespeare or Milton or Ruskin.

Brilliant though he was, O'Connell underestimated the speed and scope of change: the sway of English has expanded unstoppably thanks to the global internet and new economic and geopolitical structures of the late twentieth century. This poses real challenges for anglophones wishing to master another language. One hundred and fifty years ago, as we have seen, there were certain tangible benefits to be gained from learning a foreign language. In our day these are less evident, especially when compared to the position of non-anglophones, for whom competence in English is an essential requirement for work in tourism, transport and many other sectors, including information technology.[186]

International transport developments illustrate the language learning reversal. In the nineteenth century, railways increased connections between different language users, broadening peoples' awareness of the variety of other tongues and occasionally whetting the appetite to study them. However, for sound safety reasons, twentieth-century aviation has funnelled this interest more narrowly: pilots and air traffic controllers need proficiency in English. Aviation English is the de facto language of civil aviation, a crucial skill in instantaneous communication that can be a matter of life and death.

When most of the motivation flow is in the opposite direction, it grows more difficult to persuade anglophone learners to put the effort into studying a foreign language. As members of a multilingual federation engaged in global trading activity, Irish people pursuing the study of another language often find themselves thwarted by linguistically competent foreigners who wish to communicate with them in English. 'Try going to Sweden and speaking bad Swedish. You'll be forced into English in seconds.'[187] For learners, efforts to practise the target language can prove frustrating. Irish citizens have never travelled back and forth as much, and at the same time they have never had less need to learn a foreign language for practical purposes. More often than not, when they travel to European destinations, they are given little opportunity to interact in the language of the foreigner. This feature has grown exponentially in recent decades: Simon Kuper points out that millennials in Europe constitute the 'first global generation in which tens of millions of people from outside the English-speaking world speak perfect English.'[188] Every interlocutor encountered by Irish citizens travelling to major urban or tourist centres – in travel, transport or hospitality – tends to transact the exchange in the new *lingua franca*. 'Amsterdam and Copenhagen are already effectively bilingual. Berlin and Paris aren't far behind.'[189] In the knowledge sector the same applies: Irish students can take a degree in other European cities where teaching is largely or entirely through English. Many masters courses stipulate that the thesis has to be written in English. Today, all specialists, in any discipline, require some acquaintance with English.[190]

A 2006 Eurobarometer study found that the Irish and the British were the Europeans least capable of holding a conversation in a foreign language.[191] Two decades earlier, Joe Lee commented in like manner on Irish people's language skills:[192]

> Knowledge of English has opened some doors for the Irish. It has, ironically, helped close many others. It has made the Irish bad linguists. They have been able to assume, in contrast to small countries who kept their languages, that once they had English as their vernacular, they need learn nothing else.

Even today, Ireland 'still struggles to meet the growing need to communicate with the rest of the world in languages other than English'.[193] It is harder for Irish foreign-language learners to show that they are not 'bad linguists' per se; they can be 'bad linguists' through circumstances beyond their control, deriving from the global reach of the Anglobubble. Yet – as we have seen –, multilingualism, and openness to language diversity, have very deep roots on the island: early Irish scribes and monks had a remarkably stable grasp of their own written language, which allowed them to move comfortably between Latin and Irish, and to dazzle their continental peers with their wit and conversational agility.[194] In later centuries, one of the common tropes of Irish elegies is praise for the richly textured language skills of the defunct.[195] While in the remote past the Irish student had learned Latin as a passport to social advancement, ambitious medical and scientific Irish graduates from late Victorian universities used their reading knowledge of German or French to keep up with their field of research. Nowadays, it is rare to find places abroad where the writ of English does not run. With pervasive English-language media in the ascendant, Irish students are no longer guaranteed total immersion in the foreign language and culture they are studying.

Of course there are also positives. Anglicisation, another linguistic legacy from Victorian Ireland, is in some respects a golden egg. In today's interconnected world, Irish people can tune in directly to the voices of politicians in Washington or Sydney, Edinburgh or London, or access the latest fruits of scientific research anywhere on the planet. Knowledge comes to them already packaged in English. Ireland's tourism sector benefits enormously. The same applies to Irish graduates seeking employment overseas: no longer preaching Catholicism, nowadays they travel the globe with a TEFL qualification. Irish journalists broadcast in English for international channels of Deutsche Welle, Euronews or France 24 as well as the BBC or CNN. In many ways, the English language, once decried as an instrument of oppression, can now be seen as the most valued asset bequeathed to the country by a bountiful next-door neighbour.

Of Ireland's sense of cultural identity separate from Britain, Garret FitzGerald wrote: 'The fact that in some ways it became even more strongly marked when both countries came to use the same language makes the cultural divergence even more striking.'[196] The divergence is linguistically notable: both use English, but the variety used by Irish people deviates in several ways from standard English.[197] As postcolonial readings of Anglo-Irish literature tell us, Ireland's particular language history has left the Irish unable to claim full ownership of either of their two official languages. Having never completely assimilated English, they Hibernicised it instead. The historic language shift over the course of the nineteenth century leaves few Irish people fully at home in their official first language. Most have to learn Irish in school and not the cradle. The long 'transformation of one culture into the idiom of another', to quote Seamus Deane, has meant that 'the foreign thereby would become Hibernicized and the native Anglicized.'[198] The resulting hybridity has enriched the language diversity of the two islands. Irish writers – like Synge, Joyce or Beckett (to name but three dead male ones) – have often been at their most creative when crafting forms of Hiberno-English deviant from British modes of expression.

A hyphenated linguistic identity is the norm for citizens of the Eurozone in countries where bilingualism is more evident than in Ireland. But the ascendancy of English in today's world means that Ireland's case differs fundamentally from that of others. The asymmetry between English and Irish has been magnified exponentially in recent decades. With Ireland's linguistic identity located somewhere between a raucous trumpet and a lilting tin whistle, its citizens have persistent everyday access to one of the planet's most widespread and powerful languages while at the same time remaining partially, and occasionally, still in touch with one of its oldest and most fragile.

★ ★ ★

How durably did Victorian legacies shape Ireland's education scene? Comparisons across time reveal continuities and discontinuities. Victorian colleges have proved resilient, growing and adapting to new conditions. Schools founded by continental religious orders have held their own among other types of school, although boarding schools have shrunk and teaching personnel have changed. Modern languages remain relevant as access to education expands. French still predominates; Spanish is rising. Classics have declined in schools, but university research forges ahead and Classical Civilisation offers innovative degree programmes. University languages extend their coverage (Chinese, Korean, Japanese, Arabic) and their potential pairings (Business, Law, European Studies). Celtic scholarship persists in universities and research institutes, albeit in reduced circumstances. We saw how Victorian government regulations and policy incentivised foreign language study through competitive Civil Service examinations. Similarly, the administration of the independent State fostered Irish language study. Today, language degrees of various kinds can lead to the European (not Indian) Civil Service.

One area of tenacious traditionalism, in Ireland and Britain, concerned the pedagogy and assessment of written language. Some recommendations in the 1918 Leathes Report – introducing oral tests; funding study grants for poorer students; requiring residence abroad before and after graduation; hiring temporary foreign assistants; making phonetics mandatory and philology optional; prescribing more contemporary literature – proved too radical (or costly) for many institutions. Cultural change takes more than worthy parliamentary proddings.

Excessive compulsion created long-term problems for the first official language of the Free State, where education policy was skewed by anxious oversight of modern Irish teaching, combined with a blithe absence of policy on continental languages. These deficiencies were eventually overtaken by other forces: social and political change, advances in technologies and applied linguistics. When (in 1973) compulsory Irish was set adrift from its policy moorings within the Leaving Certificate regulations, the NUI's matriculation policy continued to support Irish by specifying the language as a *sine qua non* for ambitious school leavers planning to proceed to higher education. But even that institutional bulwark was not everlasting. The NUI's central place in educational culture was undermined when the Universities Act of 1997 cut most of its traditional powers, devolving greater autonomy to its constituent colleges, now renamed universities.[199] The old model looked outdated in a globalised era of competing universities, hungry for students, funding and 'ratings'. Like federal universities elsewhere, the NUI plays a reduced role in a changed marketplace.[200]

Cultural practices and government policies sometimes run on divergent tracks, leading to benign coincidences. In the independent State, Irish-language advocates pushed policymakers to adopt strong regulations on teaching and assessing oral Irish, which in turn caused the goals of the Irish revival to be applied in all modern language classrooms. Meanwhile, the educational regime in Northern Ireland, a polity deeply suspicious of Irish revivalism, bolstered the continued position of spoken assessments in all languages, including Irish (when it was taught). Through all the vicissitudes of culture and policy, Irish and continental languages have somehow survived as rivals, but also allies, adapting to a rapidly changing world where the humanities, as ever, are under pressure.

Amid the institutional forces propelling change, the real protagonists of education are of course the students whose lives are changed by what they learn, and in what company. Newman's 'multitude of young men' mixing freely and learning from one another, were eventually joined by their sisters. Photographic evidence from the Victorian period includes intriguing group portraits: the 'Boney Boys' of Blackrock, the professors and classmates of Joyce, the women graduates of the Royal University known as 'The Nine Graces'. A recently discovered image, beautifully composed, of ten young women graduates from Queen's College, Belfast, offers a further testament to what the Victorians achieved in enlarging horizons and opportunities in higher education, all over Ireland.[201]

8.1 Ten Graces of Belfast
First women graduates at RUI, Belfast, c.1884 (*Courtesy of Queen's University Belfast Students' Union.*)

CODA

Language learning teaches us [...] that there is a dazzling inexactness about translation, that we have no monopoly on meaning, that there is a richly endowed world outside ours which has a place for us if only we let it in. [President Mary McAleese, 2001][1]

The decision to learn a foreign language is to me an act of friendship. [...] The decision to teach a foreign language is an act of commitment, generosity, and mediation. It's a promise [...] to guide your pupils toward insights, ideas, and revelations that they would never have arrived at without your dedication, patience, and skill. [John le Carré, 2017][2]

Susan Parkes saluted the achievements of Ireland's higher education in the nineteenth century, which had served to establish the principle of open access and 'to lay the foundation of a university structure that was acceptable to the majority, had a high reputation in the country, and offered the potential for development'.[3] This book has traced another legacy of Ireland's Victorian universities: their ambitious agenda for language study, reflecting historical traditions while simultaneously responding to needs of the time. We have seen the enormous intellectual investment made by Victorian scholars in mastering languages, ancient and modern, from a communicative as well as a philological point of view. These custodians of culture wielded considerable influence, with the result that the study of languages became integral to education structures while access to learning was being broadened, new career openings were appearing, and new political debates were emerging.

A complex set of circumstances helps to account for the growth potential of foreign languages in Victorian Ireland. The country's perennial engagement with Catholic Europe, *inter alia*, fostered an openness to learning other languages and to flows of ideas from beyond the Anglosphere. To illustrate all the factors involved we have ranged eclectically over biographical and institutional history, cultural history, education and translation history to show how the roots of progress, though scattered, were sufficiently tenacious to allow European languages official recognition on all nineteenth-century university curricula in Ireland, sooner than was the case in England and Scotland.

Ireland's mid-century educational establishments embraced modern languages partly for utilitarian reasons. Within a decade, the Indian Civil Service competitions helped foreign language study to become an expected component of a university arts degree alongside classical languages. Within a generation, the Intermediate Education (Ireland) Act and the RUI's admission of women to take degrees added other strong incentives. But while foreign and classical languages were rather easily accommodated, the Irish language claimed its place in university admissions and school curricula in a more fractious fashion.

The study of Irish was all the more entrenched after independence, having been borne on a tide of nationalist sentiment, when there were pressing concerns for the language's very survival.

Victorian Ireland, with its cultural aspirations and fine stable of adventurous scholars, proved to be fertile ground for linguistic science and pedagogy to thrive. Although the subject area was not as staffed and organised as university departments of more recent times, there was room for some big beasts and serious research. Modern languages and (later) Irish became embedded in universities and schools, mutually sustaining each other in the emerging education landscape. Arguably, the late-Victorian roots of the Irish revival might not have flourished as vividly had it not been for the philological training and nationalist sentiment of its champions. From a cultural and political point of view, the revival occurred at just the right time.[4]

The present study has identified some continuities, eccentricities and even scandals that might be thought characteristic of our topic. The linguistic aspect of Irish people's engagement with Europe has persisted from Carolingian monks to Counter-Reformation clerics and poets, and the Erasmus students and TEFL teachers of today. The Victorian era, pivotal for the political and cultural implications of language study, was an age of versatility when polyglots and polymaths were given free rein; it was also a time when language study seems to have been a higher-stakes pursuit than today. In our professorial profiles, we have chronicled three cases of fevered litigation over potential or actual professorial dismissals – de Véricour in Cork, Angeli in Trinity and O'Hickey in Maynooth – each of which reveals how high the stakes could be: in the de Véricour case, the stark sectarianism of education and society in Victorian times; in Professor Angeli's case, the move towards taking modern languages seriously in universities; and, in the O'Hickey case in Maynooth, the passions associated with studying the Irish vernacular in the immediate post-Victorian years.[5] These three cases are, in their own odd way, emblematic of the prominence – or pitfalls – of language study in Ireland over a century ago.

Our Victorian panorama has framed a familiar series of shifts in education patterns: from ancient languages to modern; from social elites to broader access; from male bastions of learning to open institutions that eventually include females; and – in the case of Irish-language study – from exclusion to compulsion. In Ireland as elsewhere, there were shifts among the contextual parameters of language study. Broadly mirroring economic and social, technological and ideological changes, the pendulum swung from pen to tongue, from written text to audio, from monastery to marketplace, from Gradgrind to Google. These new realities coexist with global English, challenging some traditional rationales for language learning.

★ ★ ★

We have seen the connection between Victorian philology and the ethos of empire, with a concomitant rise in cultural nationalisms and their assertion of the importance of national and vernacular languages. It may seem appropriate that the two remaining anglophone nations of the EU, post-Brexit, are countries carrying vestiges of a colonial past. In both Ireland and Malta, English remains an immensely valuable calling-card, while the autochthonous national language has been raised to the status of official EU language:

a double benefit.[6] Maltese (a Semitic language of Arabic origin) is spoken by 371,000 inhabitants and, like Irish, exists in an asymmetric relationship to English.[7]

If English is the *lingua franca*, why continue to study other living languages? Persuasive incentives might include personal connections, curiosity about another culture, intellectual satisfaction, even embarrassment at being monoglot.[8] However, utilitarian rationales for the collective study of foreign languages are harder to pin down. Often, education policies dictate take-up. In England, universities have been shedding their language requirements since the late 1960s;[9] and numbers studying languages at GCSE level have been shrinking since 2004, when the foundation status that made a foreign language compulsory was dropped.[10]

Ireland's self-image includes the notion that we somehow remain open to embracing cultures from other places. It is not clear how far our language teaching establishment can claim credit for this – as against, say, our tradition of emigration or the natural agility of a marginal people – but the language dimension in the education system has at least ensured that Irish identity is not reduced to the monolingual. However, this linguistic openness may not match how others see us. We feel we 'know' other languages, having had some exposure to learning them, but European interlocutors may not always be impressed by Irish people's linguistic fluency, perceiving it instead as the inferior foreign-language competence of a people steeped in an 'Anglo-Saxon' cultural sphere. Such a perception would be heightened as Europeans continue to raise their English-language skills to ever-greater heights, realising that to be heard on the world stage today, the message has to be expressed in perfectly cadenced English. Recent estimates of the global drive to English are striking:[11]

> About 1.5 billion people are learning English, roughly 10 times more than are learning French, Chinese, Spanish, German, Italian and Japanese put together, estimates the German linguist Ulrich Ammon. And the more people who speak English, the more useful English becomes.

History is never entirely predictable, but trends like this indicate that English is guaranteed to retain its EU 'procedural' status despite the UK's recent departure from the bloc.[12] Citizens of Ireland and Malta will continue to be the only two 'native' English-speaking Member States among the 23 other official language communities, but according to one recent estimate, English is now studied by 98 per cent of EU schoolchildren.[13] In the next generation, some continental Europeans will have become so proficient that they will compete directly in the Anglosphere, against native speakers. Some already are.

Meanwhile, the Irish government's 'Languages Connect' strategy identifies the expansion of Ireland's foreign-language capabilities as crucial for global competition:[14]

> English may be a global lingua franca but, in the world of international business, knowledge of English is increasingly taken for granted. It is companies with additional language capabilities and an understanding of local cultures that will enjoy competitive advantage in new but also in existing markets.

Although English appears to suffice for most transactions, it is often vital to know the language (and culture) of one's interlocutor. Important soundings can take place outside the formal meeting – in cafés, corridors, airports, trains. The requisite linguistic and cultural knowledge for such exchanges is not arrived at overnight.

Yet, as we have seen, utilitarian rationales for learning and using languages have never been all-pervasive and can be completely irrelevant when the language in question has a strong emotional or ideological appeal, as when some idealists of the Irish revival wrote in Irish for a tiny readership, renouncing the vast English-language market. Knowledge of Irish had become, and still remains, a particular token of Irish identity;[15] it is also a separate key to the island's heritage, and thus of special interest to historians and other writers. If a distinctive portion of primary documents and records were, because of their language, unavailable to even the best historians, they could only produce a distorted or partial narrative of the past, and one harder to debate and reconsider.

Looking back on 60 years of Ireland's statehood in December 1981, Ken Whitaker, champion of the country's economic recovery, expressed the hope that, on the Irish language front, 'voluntary bilingualism' would prevail by the end of the twentieth century.[16] A wildly optimistic idea, but perhaps some scholars will continue to engage with all periods and forms of the Irish language; much manuscript material remains to be mined, and there are many knowledge gaps to be researched.[17] There is an international dimension to this. One of the most recent Centres for Irish Studies was launched at the Julius-Maximilians-Universität in Würzburg, during the Covid-19 pandemic.[18] Würzburg's patron saint is Kilian, a seventh-century Irish missionary, and the university library holds precious Old Irish glosses from the eighth century, but the new Centre has Irish cultural interests reaching down to the present day. An ancient book, in an ancient vernacular, forges new links.

Within and between countries, within and between languages, translation remains fundamental. For all the importance of oral culture or artificial intelligence, there is still a need for more reflective or 'monastic' approaches to language learning, that spend time, effort and concentration to foster close reading and careful editing of written texts. Accurate knowledge of grammatical structures, an appreciation of semantic nuances, idioms and tones, sensitivity to the creative ambiguities and the long history of languages: these are competences essential to the translator and to the culture. John le Carré remarked that the most conscientious editors of his novels were 'not those for whom English is their first language, but the foreign translators who bring their relentless eye to the tautological phrase or factual inaccuracy.'[19] Complex technical, legal, political, or literary texts still require live human input to transpose them with clarity (and the appropriate emotional tone) from one speaker, one writer, one language to another speaker, writer, language. Learning how to read the zones where languages and cultures intersect with each other most closely, and learning what individual languages can and cannot do, still take time, and deep education.[20]

At the other end of the spectrum, introducing languages in the primary school curriculum can sow the seeds of awareness for adults of the future. Language educators stress the benefits of exposure to other languages and cultures at an early age.[21] Welcoming the diversity of languages in schools is easier today than in a Victorian classroom, given the array of European and world languages represented in Ireland's newest generation.

Concerns are frequently expressed about the rate of language extinction around the globe.[22] Preserving language diversity can be important for actual biodiversity. This point of view has been argued, for instance, from the wealth of ecological knowledge and practical *savoir-faire* to be derived from the abundance of Irish words that relate to local marine fauna and flora, used among traditional fishing communities along the west coast of the island.[23] Geopolitical arguments have also been plausibly made – in relation to Russian hacking of sensitive US political websites, for example – that the use of English itself, so ubiquitous on the worldwide web as to be easily mastered by hostile foreign agents, runs serious risks of breaches of cybersecurity and direct manipulation of gullible people by malicious propaganda from abroad.[24] Lesser-used languages may sometimes escape enemy targeting.[25]

The case of the Strasbourg Oaths, a sort of birth certificate for the French language, may be the ultimate example of foreignness, not sameness, as a guarantee of safety and trust. Linguists have always contributed to international and cross-border understanding. One of the earliest proofs that colloquial languages had grown so distant from Latin, as to be regarded as distinct tongues in themselves, is found in a ninth-century bilingual military pact sworn in Strasbourg, between two grandsons of Charlemagne, that they would help each other reciprocally if attacked by their brother: the *Serments de Strasbourg* [Strasbourg Oaths] of 842 CE. The army of Ludwig I, King of the (Germanic) East Franks, heard Charles the Bald, King of the (Romance-speaking) West Franks, swear the oath of mutual assistance in a proto-Germanic tongue, while Ludwig swore in the Romance tongue so that Charles's men would understand his promise. The Rhine, then as now, marked the linguistic border between Francophones and Germanophones. 'Each army of troops thus heard the leader of their potential enemies addressing them, and not in an incomprehensible foreign tongue but in their own idiom.'[26] In times of international tension it is crucial to understand the language of one's adversary and to leave one's monoglot comfort zone for one crucial moment. A scrupulous attention to accuracy and detail is the mark of a useful linguist. The codebreaking work of Britain's German scholars at Bletchley Park helped in the war effort against the Nazis.[27] From Emily Anderson to Samuel Beckett or Mary Elmes (1908–2002), Irish linguists have translated across cultures in times of need.[28] While Ukrainians communicate on their mobile phones, in perfect English, with anglophone TV and radio journalists, anglophones also need reliable linguists who can interpret what is going on in Russia. Wars tend to be fought, and peace made, with contested assumptions couched in words. Intelligence work involving a precise understanding of the enemy's use of language, in its cultural context, might lead to more effective engagement. Through difference, sameness can perhaps be reached.

The Strasbourg Oaths of 842, at the heart of the historical French/German linguistic divide, represent what the EU means in Europe, a continent that has been both bellicose and polylingual for centuries. You need to understand the language and culture of your enemies, but also those of your friends and partners. Like the Indian Civil Service in Victorian times, the EU continues to require language graduates who are competent in more than one language. If Ireland wishes to be fully European, it needs to galvanise all the resources it can muster to encourage take-up and expansion in the range of LOTES (languages other than English, including Irish) available for study.[29] Incentivising people with aptitudes and interests in pursuing a career using languages – insular, continental, global – will require imagination and sustained commitment.

★ ★ ★

All the various strands touched on in the foregoing pages – the linguistic, confessional, and nationalist seams of Ireland's cultural geology – are symptoms of a long history, of the kind of slow-baked changes that the medieval historian Georges Duby would call a *mouvement de profondeur*. Cultural history deals in long perspectives. The roots of England's Euroscepticism are as firmly embedded in the *longue durée* of England's cultural history as are the roots, in Irish cultural DNA, of Ireland's historical affinities with continental Europe. Roy Hattersley, former British Labour politician, affirmed in an opinion piece in 2017:[30]

> When I was a student, opponents of the nascent common market called the idea of a European alliance 'political Catholicism.' At the time I denied what I thought a libel. Now, still an unreligious European, I am not so sure. Catholicism teaches that there is a world beyond the local parish. Had there been no Reformation, England would have been spared the folly of Brexit.

Ach sin scéal eile [But that is another story].

Notes

PREFACE

1. Arlie Russell Hochschild, *Strangers in Their Own Land: Anger and Mourning on the American Right* (New York, 2016).
2. Occasional references are made to Scotland, distinctive for its early modern educational development with universities dating from the fifteenth century. If Wales seems neglected, that is also for chronological reasons: the federal university of Wales (1893) is a comparatively late foundation.
3. John Gallagher, *Learning Languages in Early Modern England* (Oxford, 2019), p. 2.
4. Conor Cruise O'Brien (ed.), *The Shaping of Modern Ireland* (London, 1960) and Eugenio Biagini & Daniel Mulhall (eds), *The Shaping of Modern Ireland: A Centenary Assessment* (Sallins, 2016).

CHAPTER I: IRISH UNIVERSITIES: WHY ALL THE LANGUAGES?

1. Thomas Arnold, 'Rugby School – use of the Classics' (*Quarterly Journal of Education*, 1834), in *The Miscellaneous Works of Thomas Arnold, D. D. Collected and Republished* (London, 1845), p. 348.
2. Nicola McLelland, 'French and German in British schools (1850–1945)', in *Documents pour L'Histoire du Français Langue Étrangère ou Seconde* 53 (2014), pp 109–24 (online edn, 2017, p. 7).
3. Michael Sanderson (ed.), *The Universities in the Nineteenth Century* (London, 1975).
4. Charles Colbeck, *On the Teaching of Modern Languages in Theory and Practice* (Cambridge, 1887), pp 2–3.
5. In England, Karl Breul, Cambridge's first lecturer (later professor) in German, trained women students who later became language teachers. Breul examined in several universities, including the RUI and NUI. See Roger Paulin, 'Breul, Karl Hermann (1860–1932)', *Oxford Dictionary of National Biography* (published online 27 May 2010, revised 19 May 2011), https://doi.org/10.1093/ref:odnb/61616, 3 August 2023; *Calendars of the Royal University of Ireland*, 1883–1909 (NLI).
6. This contrasted with the beginnings of tighter State involvement at primary level, particularly since 1831, when Chief Secretary Stanley set up the government-financed Irish national schools. These co-existed with private primary schools.
7. In 1860, Queen's College Cork (a university founded in 1849) records twelve students attending who were 'under 16 years of age' and fourteen aged 'from 16 to 17 years of age'. *Report of the President of Queen's College Cork*, 1859–60, p. 3.
8. Tony Fahey, 'State, family and compulsory schooling in Ireland', in *The Economic and Social Review* 23 (1992), pp 369–95 (pp 375–6).
9. In 1911, for example, no more than six per cent of Ireland's school-going population attended schools that taught a foreign language: John Coolahan, *Irish Education: Its History and Structure* (Dublin, 1981), p. 55.
10. President's Reports from the Queens' University of Ireland Colleges (1850s–70s) devote more space to their students' pastoral care and religious observance than to academic matters.
11. 'In the later eighteenth century and the first half of the nineteenth, one-half of Cambridge graduates and two-thirds of those from Oxford went into Holy Orders' (Sanderson, *The Universities in the Nineteenth Century*, p. 2).
12. On various unsuccessful attempts to found universities in Ireland, see Charles H. Murray, 'The founding of a university', in *University Review* 2 (1960), pp 10–22 (pp 10–11). Since the easing of penal restrictions (on religious grounds) in the 1780s, Trinity had begun to admit members of other faiths on certain conditions.
13. For a useful summary of the complicated political stakes in the 1840s leading to Peel's decision, see Gearóid Ó Tuathaigh, 'The establishment of the Queen's Colleges: Ideological and political background', in Tadhg Foley (ed.), *From Queen's College to National University: Essays on the Academic History of QCG/UCG/NUI, Galway* (Dublin, 1999), pp 1–15.

14. On this complicated institutional history, see for example: Anon., 'The results of Newman's campaign in Ireland', in *Studies: An Irish Quarterly Review* 2 (1913), pp 898–905; Colin Barr, 'The failure of Newman's Catholic University of Ireland', in *Archivium Hibernicum* 55 (2001), pp 126–39; Colin Barr, *Paul Cullen, John Henry Newman, and the Catholic University of Ireland, 1845–1865* (South Bend and Leominster, 2003); Donal McCartney, *UCD: A National Idea: The History of University College Dublin* (Dublin, 1999); Donal McCartney, 'Joyce's UCD', in Anne Fogarty and Fran O'Rourke (eds), *Voices on Joyce* (Dublin, 2015), pp 65–75; Fergal McGrath, SJ, *Newman's University: Idea and Reality* (Dublin, 1951); Murray, 'The founding of a university'; J. J. Hogan, 'The Newman heritage: The Catholic University of Ireland, 1854–1883' [Radio broadcast, aired on Raidió Éireann 25 April 1954], in Michael Tierney (ed.), *Struggle with Fortune: A Miscellany for the Centenary of the Catholic University of Ireland, 1854–1954* (Dublin, 1954), pp 213–21. See Coolahan, *Irish Education*, pp 105–28, on Irish university structures in the nineteenth century.

15. In 1846, a Protestant evangelist evoked the College's origin in unambiguous terms: 'This seminary was founded chiefly for the education of a Protestant ministry' (Henry Joseph Monck Mason, *History of the Origin and Progress of the Irish Society, Established for Promoting the Education of the Native Irish, Through the Medium of Their Own Language* (2nd edn, Dublin, 1846), p. 6). Another constituency, specified in the Charter, was young gentlemen who, by travelling into foreign lands for education purposes, risked being 'infected by popery' (James Lydon, 'The silent sister: Trinity College and Catholic Ireland', in C. H. Holland (ed.), *Trinity College Dublin and the Idea of a University* (Dublin, 1991), pp 29–53 (p. 31). Revealingly, in the seventeenth century, Trinity's Professor of Divinity was often referred to as 'Professor of Theological Controversies' (R. B. McDowell and D. A. Webb, *Trinity College Dublin 1592–1952: An Academic History* (Cambridge, 1982), p. 11).

16. Lay students could attend Maynooth from 1800 to 1817 (Patrick J. Corish, *Maynooth College 1795–1995* (Dublin, 1995), pp 41–2, 64). Its pontifical university status dates from 1896. Derry's Magee Presbyterian College of theology was set up in 1865.

17. For an authoritative account of how the Queen's Colleges were founded, see T. W. Moody and J. C. Beckett, *Queen's, Belfast 1845–1949: The History of a University* (2 vols, London, 1959), vol. 1, pp xxxv–lxvii, pp 1–83.

18. Although the episcopate was divided on the issue, their synodal decree was unanimous. William Crolly and Daniel Murray, in favour of working with the new colleges, failed to win support. The Synod of Thurles was the first formal gathering of the Irish episcopacy held since 1642.

19. Barr, *Paul Cullen, John Henry Newman, and the Catholic University of Ireland, 1845–1865*, pp 73–90.

20. Barr, 'The failure of Newman's Catholic University of Ireland'; Barr, *Paul Cullen, John Henry Newman, and the Catholic University of Ireland, 1845–1865*, pp 133–76, 221–3. Right from the 1850s, the prolonged absences from Dublin of both its rector, Newman, in Birmingham and its vice-rector, Patrick Leahy, in Thurles hardly helped the institution to get off the ground (ibid., pp 149–53).

21. The CUI's medical faculty had already been established in 1837 and accredited by the RCSI; it was purchased by Newman in 1854. See Barr, *Paul Cullen, John Henry Newman, and the Catholic University of Ireland, 1845–1865*, p. 157.

22. Barr, 'The failure of Newman's Catholic University of Ireland', p. 136; cf. McCartney, *UCD*, p. 15; Barr, *Paul Cullen, John Henry Newman, and the Catholic University of Ireland, 1845–1865*, pp 131, 221–2. Patrick O'Flynn, *A Question of Identity: The Great Trinity & UCD Merger Plan of the 1960s* (Dublin, 2012), p. 10, Table 1.1, gives comparative figures for students attending the three Queen's Colleges. [His source is Moody and Beckett, *Queen's, Belfast 1845–1949*, vol. 1, p. 149.]

23. McDowell and Webb, *Trinity College Dublin*, pp 253–4.

24. McCartney, 'Joyce's UCD', p. 69.

25. Cited in McCartney, 'Joyce's UCD', p. 65.

26. Cited in ibid., p. 66.

27. On the campus design at Queen's College Cork, for example, see John A. Murphy, *The College: A History of Queen's/University College Cork, 1845–1895* (Cork, 1995), pp 27–33.

28. Murray, 'The founding of a university', p. 14.

29. McDowell and Webb, *Trinity College Dublin*, p. 57. See also Corinna Salvadori, '*Dove 'l sì sona*: two hundred and thirty years of Italian in Trinity College Dublin', in Cormac Ó Cuilleanáin, Corinna Salvadori and John Scattergood (eds), *Italian Culture: Interactions, Transpositions, Translations* (Dublin, 2006), pp 13–28 (pp 13–14); and Francis M. Higman, 'Modern languages in Trinity

College, Dublin 1776–1976', in *Hermathena* 121 (1976), pp 12–17 (p. 14). On traditional rationales, see Nicola McLelland, *Teaching and Learning Foreign Languages: A History of Language Education, Assessment and Policy in Britain* (London and New York, 2017), pp 39–47.

30. Jane Austen, *Pride and Prejudice* [1813], Chapter 8 (New York, 1950), vol. 1, p. 306); *Persuasion* [1817], Chapter 20 (New York, 1950), vol. 2, pp 680–1.

31. Jennifer Flegg, *The French School, Bray, Remembered: A History of The French School, Bray 1864–1966* (Dublin, 2006), p. 192.

32. https://www.st-andrews.ac.uk/modern-languages/about/; https://research-repository.st-andrews.ac.uk/handle/10023/5570, 12 November 2020.

33. Cited in the Leathes Report, 'Modern Studies, being the report of the committee on the position of Modern Languages in the educational system of Great Britain' (London, 1918), pp 87–8.

34. An influential figure in public school history, Thomas Arnold (1795–1842) was the father of Matthew Arnold, poet and cultural critic, and also of the Roman Catholic convert Thomas Arnold, whom Newman appointed to the CU Chair of English in Dublin in 1857.

35. Thomas Arnold, 'Rugby School – use of the Classics', in *Quarterly Journal of Education*, ISSUE (1834), reprinted in *The Miscellaneous Works of Thomas Arnold, D. D. Collected and Republished* (London, 1845), pp 347–61 (accessed via Google Books, 26 April 2021), p. 347. Rugby's emphasis on original composition (writing original essays in Latin) was gradually to wane, in favour of prose composition, or translation into Latin. This was 'an acknowledgement that Latin was no longer a tool for international composition': Anne Leslie Saunders, 'The value of Latin prose composition', in *The Classical Journal* 88 (1993), pp 385–92 (p. 387).

36. Arnold, 'Rugby School – use of the Classics', p. 349.

37. Ibid., p. 351.

38. See Saunders, 'The value of Latin prose composition', on arguments for and against the pedagogical value of translation into Latin.

39. Arnold, 'Rugby School – use of the Classics', p. 348.

40. See below, Chapter Three.

41. Cf. the distinction drawn by Harold Palmer, a pioneer in the teaching of English as a foreign language, between 'conscious' versus 'unconscious', or 'studial' versus 'spontaneous' learning: the intellectual grasp of a foreign language versus its assimilation on a colloquial level (Harold E. Palmer, *The Principles of Language-Study* (London, 1922, revised edn, ed. R. Mackin, London, 1964), pp 1–15, 127–8).

42. This is illustrated by many of the case studies in all three volumes of Nicola McLelland and Richard Smith (eds), *The History of Language Learning and Teaching* (3 vols, Cambridge, 2018).

43. Giuseppe Baretti, *Easy Phraseology for the Use of Young Ladies, Who Intend to Learn the Colloquial Part of the Italian Language* (London, 1775), cited in Vilma De Gasperin, 'Giuseppe Baretti's multifarious approach to learning Italian in eighteenth-century Britain', in McLelland and Smith (eds), *The History of Language Learning and Teaching*, vol. 1, pp 156–72 (p. 167). When teaching Italian to the young members of the Thrale household in London, Baretti favoured the oral approach, using dialogues and role-play (De Gasperin, pp 167–9). He declined an invitation to teach in Trinity College Dublin, on grounds of advanced age (Salvadori, '*Dove 'l sì sona*: two hundred and thirty years of Italian in Trinity College Dublin', p. 14).

44. The bedding down and diffusion of national languages, through mass education, took time, and varied in pace between countries. Factors such as a national postal service and military conscription contributed to the decline of dialect. See for example Peter Rickard, *A History of the French Language* (London, 1974), p. 124; or Anna Laura Lepschy and Giulio Lepschy, *The Italian Language Today* (London, 1977), pp 34–7 (p. 36). On European modernist authors turning to use dialect forms in their work precisely at the historical moment when these forms were ebbing from everyday discourse, see Barry McCrea, *Languages of the Night: Minor Languages and the Literary Imagination in Twentieth-Century Ireland and Europe* (New Haven and London, 2015).

45. See the use of these terms by Sabine Doff, '"Let girls chat about the weather and walks": English language education at girls' secondary schools in nineteenth-century Germany', in McLelland and Smith (eds), *The History of Language Learning and Teaching*, vol. 2, pp 87–97 (pp 88–90).

46. i.e., the grammar of post-medieval 'new Latin', pruned of some of the barbarisms that humanists had found in late medieval Latin.

47. Sonya Kirk, 'Grammar–translation: tradition or innovation?', in McLelland and Smith (eds), *The History of Language Learning and Teaching*, vol. 2, pp 21–33, takes a rigid definition of the 'grammar–translation' approach.

48. Spoken fluency in Latin was no longer required outside the Vatican. Hungary dropped Latin as its language of administration in 1844, when Hungarian was adopted as the national language. The French monarch had decreed in favour of the French vernacular for administrative and legal purposes as early as 1539.

49. On the spread of the written examination as a means of assessment, see Christopher Stray, *Classics Transformed: Schools, Universities, and Society in England, 1830–1960* (Oxford, 1998), pp 49–54. Cambridge and Oxford were both using printed examination papers from 1828, partly because the pressure of undergraduate numbers led to the breakdown of universal oral assessment (Christopher Stray, 'The shift from oral to written examination: Cambridge and Oxford 1700–1900', in *Assessment in Education: Principles, Policy & Practice* 8 (2001), pp 33–50.

50. Michael Pye, *Antwerp: The Glory Years*, p. 79. Cf. John Gallagher, *Learning Languages in Early Modern England* (Oxford, 2019), p. 125.

51. Michèle Cohen, 'From "glittering gibberish" to the "mere jabbering" of a *bonne*: The problem of the "oral" in the learning and teaching of French in eighteenth- and nineteenth-century England', in McLelland and Smith (eds), *The History of Language Learning and Teaching*, vol. 2, pp 1–20; Doff, 'Let girls chat about the weather and walks.'

52. Karl von Reinhardstöttner, *Ueber das Studium der Modernen Sprachen an den Bayerischen Gelehrten-Schulen: Ein Beitrag zu den Ideen über die Reorganisation der Gymnasien* (Landshut, 1868), cited in Doff, 'Let girls chat about the weather and walks', pp 89–90 [my adjustment of her translation].

53. George Eliot, *The Mill on the Floss* [1860], Book 2, Chapter 1 (London, 2010), p. 162.

54. John Dillon, 'The classics in Trinity', in Holland (ed.), *Trinity College Dublin*, pp 239–54 (p. 239). In Rome's Pontifical universities, Latin as the vehicle for teaching, assessment and everyday communication was abandoned only in the late 1960s, after the Second Vatican Council.

55. Stray, *Classics Transformed*, pp 48–9. Cf. the school memories of Queen's College Galway's classicist D'Arcy W. Thompson, as related in T. P. O'Connor, 'D'Arcy W. Thompson: An old schoolmaster and a new system', in *UCG: A College Annual* 1 (1913), pp 9–15 (p. 13): in boarding school from the age of seven, the child had to 'grapple with the difficulties of one unknown tongue through the medium of another tongue, almost equally unknown'.

56. William Riley Parker, 'Where do English departments come from?', in *College English* 28 (1967), pp 339–51 (p. 341).

57. This was partly due to post-Enlightenment interest in comparative linguistics. The anonymous author of 'The organisation of the study of modern languages in the University of Cambridge', in *The Modern Quarterly of Language and Literature* 1:4 (1899), pp 322–6, is at pains (p. 322) to stress the quality and substance of the relatively recent modern languages tripos, where lectures were 'not merely on "French" and "German", but dealt with old and modern French and German texts, philology (history of the language, historical grammar), metre, and literature, and also with subjects belonging to Romance and Germanic philology'.

58. Andrew R. Linn, 'Modern foreign languages get a voice: The role of journals in the reform movement', in McLelland and Smith (eds), *The History of Language Learning and Teaching*, vol. 2, pp 145–60. These specialised journals, some of which are still running, include *Englische Studien* (1877), *Zeitschrift für Romanische Philologie* (1877), *Französische Studien* (1880), *Anglia: Zeitschrift für Englische Philologie* (1881), *Romanische Forschungen* (1883), *Phonetische Studien* (1888, renamed in 1894 *Die Neueren Sprachen: Zeitschrift für den Neusprachlichen Unterricht*). Some of them were associated with the modern language teaching reform movement, on which see below, pp 115–6. The *Modern Language Review* can be traced back to 1897, and *Modern Languages Quarterly* to 1892 (Eda Sagarra, 'The centenary of the Henry Simon Chair of German at the University of Manchester (1996): Commemorative address', in *German Life and Letters* 51 (1998), pp 509–24 (p. 517).

59. Nicola McLelland, 'The history of language learning and teaching in Britain', in *The Language Learning Journal* 46 (2018), pp 6–16 (p. 9). The Modern Language Association (America) was founded in 1883.

60. Thus, the 1830 prospectus for University College School, London, explains that German – introduced after French – is taught so that pupils may avail of 'the valuable assistance afforded by the labours of German philologists towards the right study of Classical Literature'. Cited in Nicola

McLelland, 'French and German in British schools (1850–1945)', in *Documents pour l'Histoire du Français Langue Étrangère ou Seconde* 53 (2014), pp 109–24, http://journals.openedition.org/dhfles/4089, 23 October 2020 (online edn).

61. Ann Frost, 'The emergence and growth of Hispanic Studies in British and Irish universities', AHGBI [Association of Hispanists of Great Britain and Ireland] (2019), online report, p. 4, https://www.hispanists.org.uk/news/ahgbi-publication-the-emergence-and-growth-of-hispanic-studies-in-british-and-irish-universities/, 28 April 2021. Cf. Alan Bacon, 'English literature becomes a university subject: King's College, London as pioneer', in *Victorian Studies* 29 (1986), pp 591–612; and Parker, 'Where do English departments come from?'. The Queen's College Belfast chair of history and English literature, for example, was separated into modern history and English literature only in 1909, at the foundation of Queen's University Belfast (Moody and Beckett, *Queen's, Belfast*, vol. 1, p. 393; vol. 2, pp 592–3).

62. Thomas Hughes, *Tom Brown's School Days* (New York and London, 1857), Chapter 1.

63. McLelland, 'French and German in British schools' [online edn].

64. Colbeck, *On the Teaching of Modern* Languages, p. 4.

65. In 1850, there were four universities in England and four in Scotland: Oxford (eleventh century), Cambridge (thirteenth century), St Andrews (fifteenth century), Glasgow (fifteenth century), Aberdeen (sixteenth century), Edinburgh (sixteenth century), Durham (1832), University of London (1836). https://en.wikipedia.org/wiki/List_of_UK_universities_by_date_of_foundation, 12 November 2020.

66. https://www.kcl.ac.uk/study/undergraduate/courses/history-and-modern-languages-with-a-year-abroad-ba, 12 November 2020. University College London offered modern languages from 1829 (draft publication, by Matilde Gallardo Barbarroja and Nicola McLelland, kindly forwarded to the author by Nicola McLelland, August 2023).

67. https://en.wikipedia.org/wiki/Faculty_of_Medieval_and_Modern_Languages,_University_of_Oxford, 12 November 2020; Frost, 'The emergence and growth of Hispanic Studies in British and Irish universities', p. 8. Oxford's Taylor Institution (the Taylorian) was built in the mid 1840s to provide teaching and library space for the study of European languages. The Chair of Modern European Languages was abolished in 1858, when its second incumbent, Max Müller, became Professor of Comparative Philology instead.

68. Anon., 'The organisation of the study of modern languages in the University of Cambridge'; https://en.wikipedia.org/wiki/List_of_professorships_at_the_University_of_Cambridge, 12 November 2020.

69. https://www.st-andrews.ac.uk/modern-languages/about/ 12 November 2020.

70. http://ourhistory.is.ed.ac.uk/index.php/Faculty_of_Arts 12 November 2020.

71. Durham University Library, Archives and Special Collections subject guide: Modern Languages and Cultures, libguides.durham.ac.uk/mlac/asc, 20 November 2020.

72. Anon., 'The organisation of the study of modern languages in the University of Cambridge', p. 323, n. 2. The University of Glasgow, too, was offering modern languages as part of its curriculum of studies, according to an advertisement in the *Belfast Newsletter* as early as October 1789 (Máire Kennedy, *French Books in Eighteenth-Century Ireland* (Oxford, 2001), p. 33).

73. Frost, 'The emergence and growth of Hispanic Studies in British and Irish universities', p. 4. Cf. Stray, *Classics Transformed*, pp 141–6, on evolving career contexts at Cambridge in the period 1870 to 1920.

74. Stray, *Classics Transformed*, p. 129.

75. 'The University of Cambridge: The age of reforms (1800–82)', in J. P. C. Roach (ed.), *A History of the County of Cambridge and the Isle of Ely: Volume 3, the City and University of Cambridge* (London, 1959), pp 235–65. Oxford's Corpus Professorship of Latin dates from 1854. TCD's chair of Latin dates from 1861. Medical students at Trinity were taught and examined in 'what was intended to be Latin' until well into the nineteenth century (W. B. Stanford, *Ireland and the Classical Tradition* (Dublin, 1976), p. 187). It was perhaps difficult to conceive of a separate chair when Latin was the everyday language of learning and teaching, and when English, too, was only gradually emerging as a university discipline in its own right.

76. McLelland, 'French and German in British schools'.

77. French was the official language of the courts until 1731 (McLelland, *Teaching and Learning Foreign Languages*, p. 37, n. 6).

78. Extermann, Blaise, 'L'allemand scolaire en Suisse romande entre langues nationales, langues internationales et dialectes (XIXe–XXIe siècles)', in McLelland and Smith (eds), *The History of Language Learning and Teaching*, vol. 2, pp 98–112 (p. 102). See also Ritchie Robertson, 'Tides of Germany' [review of Peter Watson, *The German Genius: Europe's Third Renaissance* (New York, 2010)], *Times Literary Supplement* 1 October 2010, pp 7–8 (p. 7): 'When England had only two universities, Germany had about fifty, intended to train clerics and administrators. [. . .] Instead of passively acquiring established knowledge, students were expected to learn how to do original research, helped by the new institution of the research seminar.'

79. George Eliot, *Middlemarch*, Book 2, chapter 21 (Penguin Classics edn, London, 1994), p. 208. Published in 1871–2, the novel is set in 1829–32.

80. J. R. Woodhouse, 'Serena, Arthur (1852/3–1922)', *Oxford Dictionary of National Biography* https://doi.org/10.1093/ref:odnb/52527, 2 February 2021.

81. Luis G. Martínez del Campo, 'A utilitarian subject: The introduction of Spanish language in British schools in the early twentieth century', in McLelland and Smith (eds), *The History of Language Learning and Teaching*, vol. 2, pp 179–95 (p. 180). Cf. McLelland, *Teaching and Learning Foreign Languages*, p. 15. Oxford's King Alfonso XIII Professorship of Spanish was established by a Chilean politician in 1927. Cambridge's Chair of Spanish was set up in 1933 (Frost, 'The emergence and growth of Hispanic Studies in British and Irish universities', pp 23–4).

82. Leathes Report, Appendix IV (2), p. 251.

83. M. M. Raraty, 'The chair of German, Trinity College, Dublin 1775–1866', in *Hermathena* 102 (1966), pp 53–72 (p. 68); Salvadori, '*Dove 'l sì sona*: two hundred and thirty years of Italian in Trinity College Dublin', p. 19.

84. Maria Do Céu Fonseca, 'Londres et les britanniques dans l'ancienne grammaticographie du portugais langue étrangère (XVIIe–XIXe siècles)', in McLelland and Smith (eds), *The History of Language Learning and Teaching*, vol. 1, pp 173–91 (pp 181–4 and p. 190 n. 3); Raraty, 'The chair of German, Trinity College, Dublin 1775–1866' p. 54; Salvadori, '*Dove 'l sì sona*: two hundred and thirty years of Italian in Trinity College Dublin', pp 14–20; Higman, 'Modern languages in Trinity College, Dublin 1776–1976', p. 14; McDowell and Webb, *Trinity College Dublin*, pp 271–2. Vieyra published a Portuguese–English dictionary and grammar, both of which ran to several editions.

85. Máire Kennedy, 'Antoine D'Esca: First professor of French and German at Trinity College Dublin (1775–1784)', *Long Room* 38 (1993), pp 18–19.

86. Murphy, *The College*, p. 18; Rosaleen O'Neill, 'Modern languages', in Tadhg Foley (ed.), *From Queen's College to National University*, pp 360–83 (pp 360–1).

87. Cited in Moody and Beckett, *Queen's, Belfast*, vol. 1, p. 43.

88. Cited in O'Neill, 'Modern languages', p. 360.

89. Moody and Beckett, *Queen's, Belfast*, vol. 1, pp 41–3.

90. Ibid., p. 44.

91. Ibid., p. 43.

92. On the CU's broad and balanced curriculum, see McGrath, *Newman's University*, pp 300–12.

93. Stanford, *Ireland and the Classical Tradition*, pp 61–2.

94. Barr, *Paul Cullen, John Henry Newman, and the Catholic University of Ireland, 1845–1865*, p. 205. On the Thurles subcommittee, pp 58–62.

95. Moody and Beckett, *Queen's, Belfast*, vol. 1, p. 298; O'Neill, 'Modern languages', p. 368.

96. Moody and Beckett, *Queen's, Belfast*, vol. 1, p. 298.

97. Frost, 'The emergence and growth of Hispanic Studies in British and Irish universities', p. 4. Cf. Leathes Report, pp 4–9.

98. https://en.wikipedia.org/wiki/Victoria_University_of_Manchester, 22 November 2020; University of Manchester Department of German Archives, https://archiveshub.jisc.ac.uk/search/archives/7d53bb62-3b7b-3754-9b8f-ff388bd6d7c7, 22 November 2020. See also Su Coates, 'Manchester's German gentlemen: immigrant institutions in a provincial city (1840–1920)', *Manchester Region History Review* 5:2 (1991–2), Manchesterrsquos_german_gentlemen_immigrant_institutions_in_a_provincial_city_1840-1920rdquo.pdf, 22 November 2020. On Manchester University's role as cradle of twentieth-century German scholarship in Britain, see Sagarra, 'The centenary of the Henry Simon Chair of German at the University of Manchester'.

99. Sagarra, 'The centenary of the Henry Simon Chair of German at the University of Manchester' pp 513–14.

100. Gilbert Carr, 'Literary historical trends and the history of the German syllabus at Trinity College, Dublin, 1873–1972', in *Hermathena* 121 (1976), pp 36–53 (pp 39–40).

101. Moody and Beckett, *Queen's, Belfast*, vol. 1, pp lxv–lxvi (p. lxvi). Cf. Frost, 'The emergence and growth of Hispanic Studies in British and Irish universities', p. 5.

102. Kennedy, *French Books in Eighteenth-Century Ireland*, p. 166.

103. As documented in John Stocks Powell, *Schooling in Ireland: A Clustered History 1695–1912* (Tullamore, 2020).

104. Kennedy, *French Books in Eighteenth-Century Ireland*, p. 24. Cf. Thomas J. Morrissey, SJ, *Irish Jesuits in Penal Times 1695–1811: Thomas Betagh and his Companions* (Dublin, 2020), p. 23.

105. Kennedy, *French Books in Eighteenth-Century Ireland*, pp 17–21. In Table 1, 'French schoolbooks printed in Ireland', pp 169–71, Kennedy draws up a list of 67 titles, all published between 1721 and 1810. The vast majority were produced in Dublin, apart from five in Cork and one in Galway. Some titles are reprints. As school textbooks tend to be treated as ephemera and discarded on account of overuse or poor repair, this is a minimum estimate of the total number.

106. Ibid., pp 26–9. Cf. her Table 2, 'Schools and teachers teaching French: a provisional list', pp 172–82. Kennedy estimates over three hundred establishments and teachers (p. 27). Given the limitations of her source materials, this figure is doubtless conservative.

107. Kennedy, *French Books in Eighteenth-Century Ireland*, p. 25.

108. Richard Lovell Edgeworth, *Essays on Professional Education* (London, 1809), p. 123.

109. Ibid., p. 388.

110. Ibid., p. 123. Cf. Kennedy, *French Books in Eighteenth-Century Ireland*, pp 25, 28–9.

CHAPTER 2: LANGUAGE, CREED, IDENTITY

1. Hugh Trevor-Roper, *The Rise of Christian Europe* (London, 1960), p. 84.

2. Brian Friel, *Translations*, Act Two scene One (London, 1981; reprint 2000), p. 50.

3. The last instance of a will in Irish dates from 1675 in the Burren (L. M. Cullen, 'Patrons, teachers and literacy in Irish: 1700–1850', in Mary Daly and David Dickson (eds), *The Origins of Popular Literacy in Ireland: Language Change and Educational Development 1700–1920* (Dublin, 1990), pp 15–44 (p. 30)).

4. Mary Phelan, *Irish Speakers, Interpreters and the Courts, 1754–1921* (Dublin, 2019). The failings of the procedure were graphically illustrated by the judicial murder of Myles Joyce, an innocent monoglot Irish speaker implicated in the Maamtrasna murders in Connemara (1882). See Margaret Kelleher, *The Maamtrasna Murders: Language, Life and Death in Nineteenth-Century Ireland* (Dublin, 2018).

5. Mícheál Mac Craith, 'Dochum glóire Dé agus an mhaitheasa phuiblidhe so / For the glory of God and this public good: The Reformation and the Irish language', *Studies* 106:424 (2017–18), pp 476–83.

6. Kevin Whelan, *Religion, Landscape and Settlement in Ireland: From Patrick to the Present* (Dublin, 2018), pp 44–5.

7. Ibid., p. 84.

8. Ibid., pp 48–79.

9. See Ciarán Mac Murchaidh, 'The Catholic Church, the Irish mission and the Irish language in the eighteenth century', in James Kelly and Ciarán Mac Murchaidh (eds), *Irish and English: Essays on the Irish Linguistic and Cultural Frontier, 1600–1900* (Dublin, 2012), pp 162–88; Liam Mac Mathúna, 'Verisimilitude or subversion? Probing the interaction of English and Irish in selected warrants and macaronic verse in the eighteenth century', in Kelly and Mac Murchaidh (eds), *Irish and English*, pp 116–40; and Niall Ó Ciosáin, 'Pious miscellanies and spiritual songs: Devotional publishing and reading in Irish and Scottish Gaelic, 1760–1900', in Kelly and Mac Murchaidh (eds), *Irish and English*, pp 267–82; Daly and Dickson (eds), *The Origins of Popular Literacy in Ireland*; Patricia O'Connell, *The Irish College at Santiago de Compostela, 1605–1769* (Dublin, 2007), p. 132; Nicholas M. Wolf, 'The Irish-speaking clergy in the nineteenth century: Education, trends, and timing', in *New Hibernia Review/Iris Éireannach Nua* 12 (2008), pp 62–83; Aidan Doyle, *A History of the Irish Language: From the Norman Invasion to Independence* (Oxford, 2015), pp 96–8; Brian Ó Cuív, 'Irish language and literature, 1845–1921', in W. E. Vaughan (ed.), *A New History of Ireland, vol. 6: Ireland under the Union, II (1870–1921)* (Oxford, 1996), pp 385–435, pp 385–91; Garret FitzGerald, *Irish*

Primary Education in the Early Nineteenth Century: An Analysis of the First and Second Reports of the Commissioners of Irish Education Inquiry, 1825–6 (Dublin, 2013). The decline of Irish was marked by significant local variations of pace and degree, on which see Cullen, 'Patrons, teachers and literacy in Irish'; FitzGerald, *Irish Primary Education in the Early Nineteenth Century*; and Mary E. Daly, 'Literacy and language change in the late nineteenth and early twentieth centuries', in Daly and Dickson (eds), *The Origins of Popular Literacy in Ireland*, pp 153–66; but overall, the trend was unidirectional. For cartographic illustrations of this trend, see the language community maps reproduced in Doyle, *A History of the Irish Language*, p. 130 (*c*.1800), p. 131 (*c*.1851) and p. 166 (1891); and in Ó Cuív, 'Irish language and literature, 1845–1921', pp 387–8, for 1851, 1891 and 1911. For an analysis of the long cultural retreat from the Irish language, see Seán de Fréine, *The Great Silence* (Dublin, 1965).

10. Doyle, *A History of the Irish Language*, p. 129; Ó Cuív, 'Irish language and literature, 1845–1921', pp 386–9.

11. Benedict Anderson, *Imagined Communities: Reflections on the Origins and Spread of Nationalism* (London, 1983, revised edn 1991). This theory of the rise of the early modern nation-state posits the emergence of imagined political communities who share standardised vernaculars, thanks to the invention of the printing press, and its exploitation by entrepreneurs in the book trade.

12. As memorably portrayed in Brian Friel's play *Translations* (1980). It should be said that the anglicised names were drawn up by scholars, who paid meticulous attention to etymology, orthography and local traditions.

13. Pierre-Jakez Hélias, *Le Cheval d'orgueil* (Paris, 1975); Jean-Luc Le Cam, 'Le parcours de Pierre-Jakez Hélias vu par l'historien de l'éducation ou la mythologie de l'école républicaine', in *Hélias et Les Siens: Helias Hag e Dud*, Colloque inaugural du Pôle Universitaire Pierre-Jakez Hélias (Sept. 2000), Centre de Recherche Bretonne et Celtique, Quimper, 1 (2001), pp 87–113.

14. Maria Tymoczko, 'Language interface in early Irish culture', in Michael Cronin and Cormac Ó Cuilleanáin (eds), *The Languages of Ireland* (Dublin, 2003), pp 25–43 (pp 30–6).

15. Jean-Michel Picard, 'The Latin language in early medieval Ireland', in Cronin and Ó Cuilleanáin (eds), *The Languages of Ireland*, pp 44–56; Ní Bhrolcháin, Muireann, *An Introduction to Early Irish Literature* (Dublin, 2009), pp 13–19; Tymoczko, 'Language interface in early Irish culture'. On classical learning in pre-Viking Ireland, see W. B. Stanford, *Ireland and the Classical Tradition* (Dublin, 1976), pp 1–18.

16. Keith Busby, *French in Medieval Ireland, Ireland in Medieval French: The Paradox of Two Worlds* (Turnhout, 2017), pp 10–19. The colonists spoke a variety of medieval French, variously labelled.

17. Stanford, *Ireland and the Classical Tradition*, pp 25–6; Seán P. Ó Mathúna, *William Bathe, SJ, 1564–1614: A Pioneer in Linguistics* (Amsterdam/Philadelphia, 1986), pp 33–4; Eric Haywood, *Fabulous Ireland/Ibernia Fabulosa: Imagining Ireland in Renaissance Italy* (Bern, 2014), pp 149, 167 n. 26.

18. Gillian O'Brien, 'The 1825–6 Commissioners of Irish Education reports: Background and context', in FitzGerald, *Irish Primary Education in the Early Nineteenth Century*, pp 42–3 (p. 43); cf. Michael Cronin, *Translating Ireland: Translation, Languages, Cultures* (Cork, 1996), p. 120; Wolf, 'The Irish-speaking clergy in the nineteenth century', p. 79, p 81; Antonia McManus, *The Irish Hedge School and Its Books, 1695–1831* (Dublin, 2002), p. 13 n. 30. See also below, pp 64–8.

19. Frank Hugh O'Donnell, *The Ruin of Education in Ireland and the Irish Fanar* (London, 1902), p. 30.

20. Cited in McManus, *The Irish Hedge School and Its Books, 1695–1831*, p. 127; and in Laurie O'Higgins, *The Irish Classical Self: Poets and Poor Scholars in the Eighteenth and Nineteenth Centuries* (Oxford, 2017), p. 115.

21. Thomas O'Connor, 'Irish Colleges abroad until the French Revolution', *Encyclopedia of Irish History and Culture*, https://www.encyclopedia.com/international/encyclopedias-almanacs-transcripts-and-maps/irish-colleges-abroad-until-french-revolution, 16 November 2020; John J. Silke, 'Irish scholarship and the Renaissance, 1580–1673', in *Studies in the Renaissance* 20 (1973), pp 169–206; John J. Silke, 'The Irish abroad in the age of the Counter-Reformation, 1534–1691', in T. W. Moody, F. X. Martin and F. J. Byrne (eds), *A New History of Ireland, vol. 3: Early Modern Ireland, 1534–1691* (Oxford, 1976), pp 587–633; Benignus Millett, 'Irish literature in Latin, 1550–1700', in Moody, Martin and Byrne (eds), *A New History of Ireland*, vol. 3, pp 561–86; Patricia O'Connell, *The Irish College at Alcalá de Henares, 1649–1785* (Dublin, 1997); Patricia O'Connell, *The Irish College at Lisbon, 1590–1834* (Dublin, 2001); O'Connell, *The Irish College at Santiago de Compostela, 1605–1769*; Kevin

Whelan, 'Paris: Capital of Irish culture', in Pierre Joannon and Kevin Whelan (eds), *Paris: Capital of Irish Culture: France, Ireland and the Republic, 1798–1916* (Dublin, 2017), pp 33–76 (pp 33–7); Liam Chambers, '"Une maison de refuge": The Irish Jesuit college in Poitiers, 1674–1762', in Mary Ann Lyons and Brian MacCuarta, SJ (eds), *The Jesuit Mission in Early Modern Ireland, 1560–1760* (Dublin, 2022), pp 227–50. On Louvain, see Doyle, *A History of the Irish Language*, pp 73–4.

22. Mac Craith, 'Dochum glóire Dé agus an mhaitheasa phuiblidhe so'; Ó Corráin, Ailbhe, 'Slán agaibh a fhir chumtha, a poem by Giolla Brighde Ó hEódhasa', paper read at a Study Day to mark the retirement of Damian McManus, TCD, 21 May 2021 (Zoom transmission).

23. Margaret Mac Curtain, 'O'Daly, Daniel (Dominic; Domingos do Rosario)', DIB.

24. Jason Harris and Keith Sidwell, 'Introduction: Ireland and *Romanitas*', in Jason Harris and Keith Sidwell (eds), *Making Ireland Roman: Irish Neo-Latin Writers and the Republic of Letters* (Cork, 2009), pp 1–13 (p. 5).

25. There was no shortage of examples, from Isidore of Seville to Edmund Spenser. On the range of French perspectives, see Éamon Ó Ciosáin, 'Le merveilleux et l'espace européen: L'Irlande et les Irlandais dans la littérature médiévale française (XIIe–XVe siècles)', in Phyllis Gaffney and Jean-Michel Picard (eds), *The Medieval Imagination: Mirabile Dictu: Essays in honour of Yolande de Pontfarcy Sexton* (Dublin, 2012), pp 158–92; and Busby, *French in Medieval Ireland, Ireland in Medieval French*. For Italian Renaissance attitudes, see Haywood, *Fabulous Ireland / Ibernia Fabulosa*.

26. O'Higgins, *The Irish Classical Self*, pp 15–36. The Irish, they alleged, could trace their ancestry to biblical times; as for their language, it was the fourth ancient language to emerge from the tower of Babel, along with Latin, Greek and Hebrew.

27. White was hailed as a 'polyhistor' by Rader of Munich, and much esteemed by (the protestant) Archbishop Ussher. He claimed that he turned to history and hagiography in order 'to defend the injured reputation of the Old Irish with whom I, and my fathers for four hundred years, have shared a common fatherland' (cited in George A. Little, 'The Jesuit University of Dublin, c.1627', in *Dublin Historical Record* 13 (1952), pp 34–47 (p. 39).

28. For White, see Terry Clavin, 'White, Stephen', DIB. White was sent back to Ireland to teach in the short-lived Jesuit university that ran in Dublin from 1628 to 1629 (Little, 'The Jesuit University of Dublin, c.1627', pp 38–9). For a recent analysis of White's rhetorical skills, see Jason Harris, 'A case study in rhetorical composition: Stephen White's two *Apologiae* for Ireland', in Harris and Sidwell (eds), *Making Ireland Roman*, pp 126–53.

29. On Keating and his influence, see Vincent Morley, 'The popular influence of *Foras feasa ar Éirinn* from the seventeenth to the nineteenth century', in Kelly and MacMurchaidh (eds), *Irish and English*, pp 96–115. Cf. Bernadette Cunningham, 'Seventeenth-century historians of Ireland', in Edel Bhreathnach and Bernadette Cunningham (eds), *Writing Irish History: The Four Masters and their World* (exhibition catalogue, Dublin, 2007), pp 52–9; and Bernadette Cunningham, 'Keating, Geoffrey (Céitinn, Seathrún)', DIB.

30. Bernadette Cunningham, 'Writing the Annals of the Four Masters', in Bhreathnach and Cunningham (eds), *Writing Irish History*, pp 26–33. Ó Cléirigh, who left Ireland for the continent before 1621, was engaged to return in 1626 for the purpose of hagiographical research. He spent eleven years in Ireland transcribing written records of saints' lives. For the context in which he and other scribes worked, see Raymond Gillespie, 'The Ó Cléirigh manuscripts in context', in Bhreathnach and Cunningham (eds), *Writing Irish History*, pp 42–51.

31. Millett, 'Irish literature in Latin, 1550–1700', p. 585. The essays in Harris and Sidwell (eds), *Making Ireland Roman*, abundantly illustrate the point.

32. O'Connell, *The Irish College at Lisbon, 1590–1834*, p. 45; Mac Murchaidh, 'The Catholic Church, the Irish mission and the Irish language in the eighteenth century', pp 163, 168–70; Liam Swords, 'History of the Irish College, Paris, 1578–1800: Calendar of the papers of the Irish College, Paris', in *Archivium Hibernicum* 35 (1980), pp 3–233 (p. 62 par. 241) (Paris, 1 June 1736); see also p. 102 par. 403 (Paris, 9 August 1761): a bursary for two young students, on condition they agree 'to live in the Irish community so as to preserve the Irish language'.

33. Helga Robinson-Hammerstein and Charles Benson, *A Bohemian Refuge: Irish Students in Prague in the Eighteenth Century* (exhibition catalogue, Dublin, 1997), pp 5–6.

34. de Fréine, *The Great Silence*, p. 125; J. G. Simms, 'The Irish on the continent, 1691–1800', in T. W. Moody and W. E. Vaughan (eds), *A New History of Ireland, vol. 4: Eighteenth-Century Ireland, 1691–1800* (Oxford, 1986), pp 629–56 (pp 644–5).

35. Ó Mathúna, *William Bathe, SJ, 1564–1614*, p. 48.

36. O'Connell, *The Irish College at Alcalà de Henares, 1649–1785*, p. 50; O'Connell, *The Irish College at Santiago de Compostela, 1605–1769*, pp 36–7. These disciplines formed the trivium, or three elementary skills of the seven liberal arts.

37. The Douai community (set up in 1568) relocated to Reims for 15 years. Other English and Scots colleges were set up for example in Rome, Paris and Valladolid. Tridentine colleges, called after the Council of Trent (1545–63), were seminaries established by the papacy to tighten the training of Roman Catholic clergy in confronting the reformed churches.

38. Eamon Duffy, *A People's Tragedy: Studies in Reformation* (London, 2020), pp 66–82, p. 81.

39. Ibid., p. 80.

40. Ibid., p. 75.

41. Rulhière, Claude Carloman de, 'Sur les disputes', in *Oeuvres de Rulhière*, vol. 6 (Paris, 1819), pp 332–8 (p. 335). [My translation.]

42. Montesquieu, *Lettres persanes*, ed. Paul Vernière (Paris, 1960), XXXVI, p. 79. [My translation.] He goes on (*loc. cit.*) to explain the provenance of these disputatious seminarians: 'on a vu une nation entière, chassée de son pays, traverser les mers pour s'établir en France, n'emportant avec elle, pour parer aux nécessités de la vie, qu'un redoutable talent pour la dispute' [a whole nation, driven from its own land, has been seen crossing the seas to settle in France, equipped to confront life's daily needs with nothing more than a fearsome propensity to disputatiousness]. [My translation.]

43. MacMurchaidh, 'The Catholic Church, the Irish mission and the Irish language in the eighteenth century', p. 169. Swords, 'History of the Irish College, Paris, 1578–1800', p. 69 par. 262: the younger students 'acquire perfect French but lose their Irish which renders them incapable of serving on the Irish mission. Being obliged to speak Irish is not practicable. They have to beg their daily bread and are completely dependent on the charity of the French'.

44. O'Connell, *The Irish College at Alcalà de Henares, 1649–1785*, pp 107–8; O'Connell, *The Irish College at Santiago de Compostela, 1605–1769*, p. 138.

45. Thomas O'Connor, 'Irish Colleges abroad until the French Revolution'; O'Connell, *The Irish College at Alcalà de Henares, 1649–1785*, pp 92–3; O'Connell, *The Irish College at Santiago de Compostela, 1605–1769*, pp 130–2. 'Old English' in this context denotes the descendants of Ireland's first (medieval) influx of Anglo-Normans, many of whom had assimilated with native Irish families. (On their Catholicism, see Whelan, *Religion, Landscape and Settlement in Ireland*, pp 69–79.)

46. Simms, 'The Irish on the continent, 1691–1800', pp 645–6; Thomas O'Connor, 'Irish Colleges abroad until the French Revolution'; Whelan, 'Paris: Capital of Irish culture', p. 36. Some abandoned their clerical garb for other walks of life: e.g., John William O'Sullivan turned soldier (Simms, 'The Irish on the continent, 1691–1800', pp 635–6); or Nicholas Madgett (*d.*1813), ordained at Toulouse in 1767, later left the priesthood to work as interpreter and translator for the *Directoire*, France's revolutionary government. Cf. C. J. Woods, 'Madgett, Nicholas', DIB.

47. Whelan, *Religion, Landscape and Settlement in Ireland*, p. 39, n. 46; cf. Raymond Murray, 'Plunkett, St Oliver', DIB. John Gleeson, 'Translation in the shifting sands of the French Revolution: Nicholas Madgett (1738–1813) and John Sullivan (1767–1802)' [paper, TCD French Department Research Seminar, 20 February 2024], gives a vivid sense of the precarious lives of such translators who survived political upheavals through their wits and linguistic agility.

48. See https://www.jesuitarchives.ie/o-neachtain-peadar-1709-1756-jesuit-priest, 27 October 2022; Cathal Ó Háinle, 'Ó Neachtain, Tadhg', DIB. Cf. Liam Mac Mathúna, *The Ó Neachtain Window on Gaelic Dublin, 1700–1750*, Cork Studies in Celtic Literatures, vol. 4 (Cork, 2021), pp 25–6.

49. On the Gaelic urban milieu of the Ó Neachtain family, see Mac Mathúna, *The Ó Neachtain Window on Gaelic Dublin, 1700–1750*.

50. Tadhg Ó Neachtain, '"Ochlán Thaidhg Uí Neachtain"/"Tadhg Ó Neachtain's Lament"', in Samuel K. Fisher and Brian Ó Conchubhair (eds), *Bone and Marrow/Cnámh agus Smior: An Anthology of Irish Poetry from Medieval to Modern* (Winston-Salem, NC, 2022), pp 520–31 (pp 522–3). [Bilingual edition; English translation, by Liam Mac Mathúna, reproduced with kind permission of Liam Mac Mathúna and Wake Forest.] One of Peadar's teachers, the Jesuit Maolra Ó Bruin [Fr Milo Byrne], was involved in setting up the Jesuits' classical school in St Mary's Lane Dublin in 1713 (Thomas J. Morrissey, SJ, *Irish Jesuits in Penal Times 1695–1811: Thomas Betagh and his Companions* (Dublin, 2020), p. 18). On the Jesuit curriculum's emphasis on Latin style, as laid out in the *Ratio Studiorum* which was mandatory in Jesuit schools from 1599, see Jason Harris, 'The Latin style of the Irish

Litterae Annuae Societatis Jesu', in Mary Ann Lyons and Brian MacCuarta SJ (eds), *The Jesuit Mission in Early Modern Ireland, 1560–1760* (Dublin, 2022), pp 63–81 (pp 64–7).

51. Tadhg Ó Neachtain, 'Ochlán Thaidhg Uí Neachtain', pp 524–5.

52. For the Restoration period, see Martin Foerster, '"The best teachers in the world": Jesuit schooling in Ireland, 1660–90', in Lyons and MacCuarta (eds), *The Jesuit Mission in Early Modern Ireland, 1560–1760*, pp 208–26. In contrast, priests trained by mendicant friars in unofficial and remote seminaries tended to be less competent in Latin (Whelan, *Religion, Landscape and Settlement in Ireland*, p. 38).

53. Amalio Huarte, 'El. P. Paulo Sherlock: Una autobiografia inédita', in *Archivium Hibernicum* 6 (1917), pp 156–74; O'Connell, *The Irish College at Santiago de Compostela, 1605–1769*, pp 68–72.

54. On Bathe's life and career, see Ó Mathúna, *William Bathe, SJ, 1564–1614*. Grandnephew of Gerald FitzGerald, Earl of Kildare, he was also a noted musical scholar and practitioner, and wrote a manual for the efficient teaching of music and singing.

55. Ó Mathúna, *William Bathe, SJ, 1564–1614*, p. 80. Cf. O'Higgins, *The Irish Classical Self*, p. 40; Silke, 'Irish scholarship and the Renaissance, 1580–1673', pp 203–5. On the use of sentences and dialogues in different languages, juxtaposed in columns, a widespread traditional method for language learning in early modern Europe, see John Gallagher, *Learning Languages in Early Modern England* (Oxford, 2019), pp 55–100; Nicola McLelland, *Teaching and Learning Foreign Languages: A History of Language Education, Assessment and Policy in Britain* (London and New York, 2017, pbk edn, 2018), pp 85–94. For Bathe, it may have been modelled on how his great-grandmother was said to have learned to speak Irish fluently on arriving in Kildare in the early 1500s (Ó Mathúna, *William Bathe, SJ, 1564–1614*, p. 105 n. 13).

56. For an account of the various editions and imitations of the *Ianua*, and an appraisal of its influence on the history of language teaching, see Ó Mathúna, *William Bathe, SJ, 1564–1614*, pp 77–110. Comenius, the great Bohemian educator, acknowledged Bathe in his own *Ianua*. Although Bathe's work has been overshadowed by later (improved) versions, Ó Mathúna (p. 78) sees the Irishman's 1611 Preface as 'an important milestone in the history of language teaching and vocabulary analysis. His ideas on frequency and about the categorisation and limitation of lexis, several hundred years before the advent of electronic recording and computing facilities, were very advanced indeed.'

57. Vincent Morley, 'Ó Coileáin, Seán "Máistir" (O'Collins, John)', DIB. For other instances of the connection between study abroad and classical 'hedge'-school masters, see O'Higgins, *The Irish Classical Self*, p. 111 n. 40, p. 113.

58. O'Higgins, *The Irish Classical Self*, pp 81–2.

59. Mary Ann Lyons and Brian MacCuarta, SJ, 'Introduction', in Lyons and MacCuarta (eds), *The Jesuit Mission in Early Modern Ireland, 1560–1760*, pp 15–28. Cf. Bernadette Cunningham, 'Popular preaching and the Jesuit mission in seventeenth-century Ireland', in the same volume, pp 82–100. On Dublin's short-lived Jesuit university, set up in the late 1620s, see Little, 'The Jesuit University of Dublin, c.1627'.

60. Morrissey, *Irish Jesuits in Penal Times 1695–1811*. To secure the Crown's power in Ireland, a series of restrictive measures (or 'penal laws') against the lives and liberties of Roman Catholics were passed during the seventeenth and early eighteenth centuries. The degree of severity with which these laws were locally enforced varied considerably.

61. Morrissey, *Irish Jesuits in Penal Times 1695–1811*, passim. The suppression of the Jesuits in Catholic Europe (with some exceptions) lasted from 1761 to 1814. On the effects of the Jesuits' expulsion in France (1761–64), where one third of post-primary schools known as *collèges* were run by them, see Gemma Tidman, *The Emergence of Literature in Eighteenth-Century France: The Battle of the Schoolbooks* (Liverpool, 2023).

62. O'Higgins, *The Irish Classical Self*, p. 44 n. 36, citing R. C. Cole, 'Private libraries in eighteenth-century Ireland', in *Library Quarterly* 44 (1974), pp 231–47. For confiscated books see O'Higgins, *The Irish Classical Self*, p. 38.

63. Nor was the Irish Catholic diaspora composed solely of scholars. Large contingents of Irish émigrés went abroad to enlist in the armies of Europe or to pursue successful careers in trade or liberal professions. For an overview, see Simms, 'The Irish on the continent, 1691–1800'; for the Italian peninsula, see Patricia A. O'Sullivan, 'The "Wild Geese": Irish soldiers in Italy, 1702–1733', in the Italian Cultural Institute's *Italian Presence in Ireland* (Dublin, 1964), pp 79–114; for Bohemia, see Robinson-Hammerstein and Benson, *A Bohemian Refuge*; or for influential Irish émigrés at Habsburg courts, see Declan Downey, 'Wild Geese and the double-headed eagle: Irish integration in Austria

c.1630–c.1918', in Paul Leifer and Eda Sagarra (eds), *Austro-Irish Links Through the Centuries* (Vienna, 2002), pp 41–57.

64. His application for the chair was first turned down for language reasons: he would have to improve his Czech or German (Robinson-Hammerstein and Benson, *A Bohemian Refuge*, pp 30–2).

65. Máire Kennedy, *French Books in Eighteenth-Century Ireland* (Oxford, 2001), pp 49–65 passim, especially pp 57–8.

66. His predecessor, James Caulfeild, first earl of Charlemont (1728–99), had also spent nine formative years in Europe and the eastern Mediterranean, on the grand tour. Five of them were lived in Italy, a country the peer claimed to have 'loved as a mistress' (Maurice James Craig, *The Volunteer Earl: Being the Life and Times of James Caulfeild, First Earl of Charlemont* (London, 1948), p. 216). He spoke fluent Italian and wrote a three-volume history of Italian poetry.

67. Kennedy, *French Books in Eighteenth-Century Ireland*, p. 54. She adds that Kirwan 'conformed to the established church to inherit the family estates' after the death of his elder brother. One of his biographers claimed Kirwan was familiar with ten languages: English, Latin, Greek, Hebrew, French, German, Italian, Spanish, Irish and Swedish.

68. Ibid., p. 59. On Irish accents and foreign tongues, Betsy Sheridan, younger sister of the playwright Richard Brinsley Sheridan, described her Irish doctor in Bath speaking French in public 'to hide his Brogue' (ibid.). On Roche, see also Patrick Long, 'Roche, James', DIB.

69. Thomas O'Connor, 'Irish Colleges abroad until the French Revolution' (concluding sentence).

70. Kevin Collins, *Catholic Churchmen and the Celtic Revival in Ireland, 1848–1916* (Dublin, 2002), p. 84; Colin Barr, 'MacHale, John', DIB; Wolf, 'The Irish-speaking clergy in the nineteenth century', p. 64; Fergal McGrath, SJ, *Newman's University: Idea and Reality* (Dublin, 1951), p. 92.

71. https://en.wikipedia.org/wiki/St._Patrick%27s,_Carlow_College, 19 November 2020; Jim Moriarty, 'Carlow College adapts to changing times', *Irish Times*, 4 August 2003.

72. Patrick J. Corish, *Maynooth College 1795–1995* (Dublin, 1995), pp 60, 77. Cf. Michael Turner, 'The French connection with Maynooth College, 1795–1855', in *Studies: An Irish Quarterly Review* 70 (1981), pp 77–87; https://avergeen9.wixsite.com/maynoothcemetery/lists-c1pd6, 4 November 2020.

73. Corish, *Maynooth College 1795–1995*, p. 60.

74. Ibid. Cf. Turner, 'The French connection with Maynooth College, 1795–1855'. The textbooks of Delahogue and Anglade were still in use many years after the decease of their authors. Much of the content was outmoded by the mid-nineteenth century, reflecting the theology of the pre-revolutionary French church, and helped to earn Maynooth the labels of Gallicanism in politics and Jansenism in theology.

75. https://www.maynoothuniversity.ie/french, 4 November 2020.

76. https://en.wikipedia.org/wiki/Matthew_Kelly_(historian), 24 November 2020. 'Belles-lettres' in early modern university curricula meant instruction in oratory and rhetoric, for training in oral communication and written composition.

77. In the early days, French was taught for two hours per week, before breakfast on Tuesdays and at 1.00pm on Saturdays, while English was given four evening sessions per week (Corish, *Maynooth College 1795–1995*, pp 74–5).

78. *Battersby's Catholic Directory, Almanac and Registry of the Whole Catholic World* (Dublin, 1860), pp 272–3.

79. Matthew 28: 19–20.

80. Corish, *Maynooth College 1795–1995*, pp 95–6. For a history of All Hallows, see Kevin Condon, *The Missionary College of All Hallows 1842–1891* (Dublin, 1986).

81. https://allhallows.ie/missionary-college/publications/, 23 November 2020.

82. *Second Annual Report of the Missionary College of All Hallows, Drumcondra, Dublin (1849)* (Dublin, 1850), p. 8.

83. *Ninth Report of All Hallows College, Drumcondra, Dublin (1858)* (Dublin, 1858), p. 64.

84. *First Annual Report of the Missionary College of All Hallows, Drumcondra, Dublin (1848)* (Dublin, 1849), p. 38.

85. *Seventh Report of All Hallows College, Drumcondra, Dublin (1853)* (Dublin, 1855), pp 72–3.

86. Father Stanislas OSFC, 'An Irish Capuchin pioneer', in *The Capuchin Annual* (1930), pp 71–84.

87. Ibid., p. 75.

88. Condon, *The Missionary College of All Hallows 1842–1891*, p. 112, on Vincennes Indiana; pp 118–19, on Sioux City Iowa; and on the substantial numbers of All Hallows priests in the dioceses of California, p. 86, 116, 242, n. 26.

89. Italian was taught by one of its co-founders, Bartholomew Woodlock, who was also professor of dogmatic theology: Colin Barr, *Paul Cullen, John Henry Newman, and the Catholic University of Ireland, 1845–1865* (South Bend, 2003), p. 184.

90. Including Irish. Seán de Fréine (*The Great Silence*, p. 127) cites continuous requests (from 1784 to the early twentieth century) for Gaelic-speaking pastors, to work with Irish emigrants in places as scattered as Australia, the West Indies, Canada, Newfoundland, Maine and Philadelphia.

91. *Seventh Report of All Hallows College*, p. 92. The 'Propaganda College' is the headquarters of the Vatican's *Sacra Congregatio de Propaganda Fide*, set up in 1622 and tasked with coordinating the spread of the Roman Catholic Faith to all the peoples of the world.

92. Anne O'Connor, *Translation and Language in Nineteenth-Century Ireland: A European Perspective* (London, 2017), 30–1; Patrick Geoghegan, 'Lanigan, John', DIB.

93. https://en.wikipedia.org/wiki/James_Warren_Doyle, 19 November 2020; McManus, *The Irish Hedge School and Its Books, 1695–1831*, passim; and Thomas McGrath, 'Doyle, James ("JKL")', DIB.

94. O'Connor, *Translation and Language in Nineteenth-Century Ireland*, p. 77; Cronin, *Translating Ireland*, pp 114–15; Barr, 'MacHale, John'.

95. Liam Rigney, 'Woodlock, Bartholomew', DIB.

96. On Daniel O'Connell's language education, see Grace Neville, '"I got second in Latin, Greek, and English, and eleventh in French": Attitudes to language(s) in the correspondence of Daniel O'Connell (1775–1847)', in Wesley Hutchinson and Clíona Ní Ríordáin (eds), *Language Issues: Ireland, France, Spain* (Brussels, 2010), pp 77–90.

97. Bernd Marizzi, 'An overview of the history of German language learning and teaching in the Iberian peninsula, with a particular focus on textbooks for German as a language for special purposes (LSP) in Spain', in Nicola McLelland and Richard Smith (eds), *The History of Language Learning and Teaching* (3 vols, Cambridge, 2018), vol. 2, pp 113–26 (p. 117), quotes the twentieth-century Spanish chemist Enrique Moles: 'Un científico que, además del suyo, no conoce como mínimo dos idiomas, es un analfabeto [A scientist who, apart from his own language, does not know at least two languages, is illiterate].' A similar view is taken by some scholarly journals today.

98. That is to say he sided with those Catholics who believed in absolute papal authority in matters of dogma. In French church history, there was a long-running tension between 'ultramontanes' and 'Gallicans', the two camps differing on the respective powers they ascribed to the papacy ('beyond the mountains', i.e. the Alps) and to the local French ('Gallican', of Gaul) episcopate.

99. On Cullen's uneasy relations with Newman, see Barr, *Paul Cullen, John Henry Newman, and the Catholic University of Ireland, 1845–1865*.

100. Ibid., p. 74. On Cullen's intellectual abilities, see ibid., pp 74–6, and passim.

101. He was able to converse with the French Prince Imperial, Napoleon III's son and heir, whom he showed around Maynooth's grounds in July 1857. The prince's Italian was better than his French. (Corish, *Maynooth College 1795–1995*, p. 171.)

102. Anne O'Connor, 'Translating the Vatican: Paul Cullen, power and language in nineteenth-century Ireland', in *Irish Studies Review* 22:4 (2014), pp 450–65. On Cullen's hyper-conservatism and ultramontane politics, and his enormous influence on mid-Victorian Irish Catholicism, see Colin Barr, 'Paul Cullen, Italy and the Irish Catholic imagination, 1826–70', in Colin Barr, Michele Finelli and Anne O'Connor (eds), *Nation/Nazione: Irish Nationalism and the Italian Risorgimento* (Dublin, 2014), pp 133–56.

103. Barr, *Paul Cullen, John Henry Newman, and the Catholic University of Ireland, 1845–1865*, p. 114. Cf. *The Italian Correspondence of Cardinal Paul Cullen*, translated and edited by Anne O'Connor (forthcoming, Irish Manuscripts Commission). After the Synod of Thurles, Cullen's letters show his desire to control recalcitrant bishops: 'The bishop of Galway is old and very confused. He was never fit to act as a bishop'; the bishop of Cork 'believes he is something, but in reality however, he is nothing' (to Tobias Kirby, 21 October 1851); 'the bishop of Killaloe [...] has become dropsical'; 'the bishop of Dromore is totally deaf and is no longer fit to govern his diocese' (to Giacomo Filippo Fransoni, 8 October 1850). [These letters were kindly sent to the author by Anne O'Connor.]

104. Letter from J. B. Taylor to Cullen, 1822, cited in Barr, *Paul Cullen, John Henry Newman, and the Catholic University of Ireland, 1845–1865*, pp 74–5.

105. Barr, *Paul Cullen, John Henry Newman, and the Catholic University of Ireland, 1845–1865*, p. 75.

106. Mac Murchaidh, 'The Catholic Church, the Irish mission and the Irish language in the eighteenth century', p. 163. [My amendments to printed text.]

107. The most notable exception being John MacHale, on whom see Collins, *Catholic Churchmen and the Celtic Revival in Ireland, 1848–1916*, pp 80–95. This balance would be redressed, later in the century, as more of the clergy came to appreciate and study Irish. See below, pp 160–3.

108. O'Connor, *Translation and Language in Nineteenth-Century Ireland*.

109. The landmark Catholic Emancipation (Ireland) Act (1829), associated with Daniel O'Connell, allowed Roman Catholics to become MPs and hold public office for the first time. An equally significant milestone was the Irish Church Act (1869), which ended the privileged status of the (Protestant) Church of Ireland. Both acts in effect conceded the demographic imbalance of the two religious communities in Ireland.

110. 'In the hundred years after Emancipation, twenty-four cathedrals or pro-cathedrals and over 3,000 substantial churches were erected' (Willie Nolan, 'Land reform in post-Famine Ireland', in John Crowley, William J. Smyth and Mike Murphy (eds), *Atlas of the Great Irish Famine, 1845–52* (Cork, 2012), pp 570–9 (p. 579).

111. 'Publication of early 19th-century architectural albums online', Church of Ireland Historical Society website, http://churchofirelandhist.org/the-weekend-read-publication-of-early-19th-century-architectural-albums-online/, 10 September 2023.

112. Ruth Fleischmann, 'Aloys Fleischmann: Bavarian musician and civilian prisoner of war, 1916–1919', in Tom French (ed.), *Oldcastle Camp 1914–1918: An Illustrated History* (Navan, 2018), p. 126. Swertz had arrived in Cork in 1879; Fleischmann moved there to replace him, with his wife, Tilly Swertz, in 1906. Her sister, Waltraut ['Wally'], was briefly to hold the chair of German in UCC. See below, p. 170. Cf. Mary Regina Deacy, 'Continental organists and Catholic church music in Ireland, 1860–1960' (M.Litt. dissertation, NUIM, 2005).

113. Brian Maye, 'Fit to print – Brian Maye on pioneering publisher James Duffy' [An Irishman's Diary], *The Irish Times*, 21 June 2021; Cf. C. J. Woods, 'Duffy, James', DIB; O'Connor, *Translation and Language in Nineteenth-Century Ireland*, pp 48–69; Tony Farmar, *The History of Irish Book Publishing* (Stroud, 2018), pp 39–40.

114. Farmar, *The History of Irish Book Publishing*, p. 40.

115. O'Connor, *Translation and Language in Nineteenth-Century Ireland*, pp 39–110. As Duffy was the official publisher for the Dublin archdiocese, the texts translated tended to reflect Archbishop Cullen's ultramontane tendencies. Anne O'Connor, 'The languages of transnationalism: Translation, training, and transfer', in *Éire–Ireland* 51 (2016), pp 14–33 (p. 28), makes the point that, in general, what got translated from French did not include contemporary novels, for example, which were considered too risqué for their Irish readership, by translators and publishers alike.

116. O'Connor, *Translation and Language in Nineteenth-Century Ireland*, p. 224. This is conceivably one of the roots of Irish Catholic devotion to modern continental saints, such as Thérèse de Lisieux (1873–97), the Curé d'Ars (1786–1859) or Margaret Mary [Marguerite Marie] Alacoque (1647–90).

117. Ó Ciosáin, 'Pious miscellanies and spiritual songs', p. 282.

118. O'Connor, *Translation and Language in Nineteenth-Century Ireland*, p. 77; Cronin, *Translating Ireland*, pp 114–15.

119. Joachim Fischer, 'The eagle that never landed: Uses and abuses of the German language in Ireland', in Cronin and Ó Cuilleanáin (eds), *The Languages of Ireland*, pp 93–111; p. 95.

120. O'Connor, *Translation and Language in Nineteenth-Century Ireland*, p. 25; Thomas Davis, 'The young Irishman of the middle classes' (1848), in Seamus Deane (ed), *The Field Day Anthology of Irish Writing* (3 vols, Derry, 1991), vol. 1, pp 1,269–86 (pp 1,272–3); and see below, pp 68–9.

121. Cronin, *Translating Ireland*, pp 116–17.

122. O'Connor, *Translation and Language in Nineteenth-Century Ireland*, pp 145–68. She estimates (O'Connor, 'The languages of transnationalism', p. 21) that 'in the 1840s 36 percent of these translations were from German; 31 percent from French; 18 percent from Irish; 9 percent from Italian; 2 percent from Latin, and 4 percent from other languages'.

123. John Blake Dillon, 'Continental literature', *The Nation*, 22 Oct. 1842.

124. Ibid.

125. O'Connor, *Translation and Language in Nineteenth-Century Ireland*, pp 155–63.

126. Fischer, 'The eagle that never landed', p. 94.

127. 'Our nationality', *The Nation*, 29 April 1843.

128. 'The history of the agitation', *The Nation*, 28 December 1844.

129. 'Something is coming', *The Nation*, 29 April 1843.

130. Thomas Davis, 'Ireland and Italy', *The Nation*, 25 February 1843.

131. Denis Mack Smith, *Mazzini* (New Haven, 1994), pp 156–7; E. J. Hobsbawm, *Nations and Nationalism Since 1780: Programme, Myth, Reality* (Cambridge, 1990), p. 31; cf. R. Dudley Edwards (ed.), *Ireland and the Italian Risorgimento: Three Lectures by Kevin B. Nowlan, R. Dudley Edwards, T. Desmond Williams* (Dublin, c.1958).

132. T. W. Moody, 'Thomas Davis and the Irish nation', in *Hermathena* 103 (1966), pp 5–31 (pp 19–21).

133. Ibid., p. 19.

134. On Davis as a forerunner of the Gaelic League, see ibid., p. 23. Cf. Ó Cuív, 'Irish language and literature, 1845–1921', pp 398–9 and passim.

135. O'Connor, 'The languages of transnationalism', pp 17–21; O'Connor, *Translation and Language in Nineteenth-Century Ireland*, pp 145–68.

136. Harry White, 'The sovereign ghosts of Thomas Moore', in Martin Fanning and Raymond Gillespie (eds), *Print Culture and Intellectual Life in Ireland, 1660–1941* (Dublin, 2006), pp 164–85; Fintan O'Toole, 'Fashioning the airs that we breathe', *Irish Times*, 24 December 2005. Archbishop MacHale's Irish translations of Moore (1842), in their turn, re-fashioned the *Melodies* for the consumption of the Irish-speaking community.

137. Emanuela Minuto, 'The reception of Thomas Moore in Italy in the nineteenth century', in Barr, Finelli and O'Connor (eds), *Nation/Nazione*, pp 193–205.

138. Exemplified by Charles Gavan Duffy's 'The Irish Rapparees: A Peasant Ballad' (1850), which opens with: 'Righ Shemus he has gone to France and left his crown behind: – / Ill-luck be theirs, both day and night, put runnin' in his mind!' See Martin MacDermott (ed.), *The New Spirit of the Nation* (London, 1894), pp 176–9 (p. 176).

139. On classical tropes found in Irish political vision poems or *aislingí*, see O'Higgins, *The Irish Classical Self*, pp 71–5; on Irish Jacobite poems, see Doyle, *A History of the Irish Language*, pp 83–5, p. 109; and on the persistence in local folk memory of the French invasion at Killala, see Guy Beiner, 'Mapping the "Year of the French": The vernacular landscape of folk memory', in Edric Caldicott and Anne Fuchs (eds), *Cultural Memory: Essays on European Literature and History* (Oxford, 2003), pp 191–208. Cf. *An Duanaire 1600–1900: Poems of the Dispossessed, Dánta Gaeilge curtha i láthair ag* Seán Ó Tuama with verse translations by Thomas Kinsella (Mountrath, 1981), pp 148–55: poems 49 and 50 by Aogán Ó Rathaille; and pp 186–91: poem 59 by Eoghan Rua Ó Súilleabháin. In this last poem, the arrival of the Stuart saviour 'le *fleet* d'fhearaibh Laoisigh 's an Spáinnigh' [with a fleet of Louis' men, and the Spaniard's] will herald the new age. On the wider political and historical implications of these vision poems, see Mícheál Mac Craith, review of Breandán Ó Buachalla, *Aisling Ghéar Na Stiobhartaigh agus an tAos Léinn 1603–1788, Eighteenth-Century Ireland/Iris an Dá Chultúr* 13 (1998), pp 166–71.

140. Quoted in Joachim Fischer, *Das Deutschlandbild der Iren, 1890–1939: Geschichte – Form – Funktion* (Heidelberg, 2000), p. 467. ('Chanel', in D. P. Moran's *The Leader*, 17 October 1908, p. 206.)

141. Michèle Cohen, 'From "glittering gibberish" to the "mere jabbering" of a *bonne*: The problem of the "oral" in the learning and teaching of French in eighteenth- and nineteenth-century England', in McLelland and Smith (eds), *The History of Language Learning and Teaching*, vol. 2, pp 1–20; Luis G. Martínez del Campo, 'A utilitarian subject: The introduction of Spanish language in British schools in the early twentieth century', in McLelland and Smith (eds), 3 vols (Cambridge, 2018), *The History of Language Learning and Teaching*, vol. 2, pp 179–95; Nicola McLelland, 'The history of language learning and teaching in Britain', in *The Language Learning Journal* 46 (2018), pp 6–16; Ann Frost, 'The emergence and growth of Hispanic Studies in British and Irish universities', online report, AHGBI [Association of Hispanists of Great Britain and Ireland], 2019.

142. Maria Do Céu Fonseca, 'Londres et les britanniques dans l'ancienne grammaticographie du portugais langue étrangère (XVIIe–XIXe siècles)', in McLelland and Smith (eds), *The History of Language Learning and Teaching*, vol. 1, pp 173–91.

143. Nicola McLelland, 'French and German in British schools (1840–1945)', in *Documents pour L'Histoire du Français Langue Étrangère ou Seconde* 53 (2014), pp 109–24, http://journals.openedition.org/dhfles/4089, 23 October 2020.

144. Frost, 'The emergence and growth of Hispanic Studies in British and Irish universities', p. 29.

145. Ibid., p. 22. Cf. Eda Sagarra, 'The centenary of the Henry Simon Chair of German at the University of Manchester (1996): Commemorative address', in *German Life and Letters* 51 (1998), pp 509–24, pp 516–17. In 1918, the report of the Leathes Parliamentary Committee on the position of modern languages recommended (pp 217–19) the expansion of modern language departments, as well as better conditions for staff.

146. Christopher T. Husbands, 'German-/Austrian-origin professors of German in British universities during the First World War: The lessons of four case studies', in *LSE Research Online* (2013), pp 1–61, http://eprints.lse.ac.uk/49797, 28 November 2020; Frost, 'The emergence and growth of Hispanic Studies in British and Irish universities', p. 20; Sagarra, 'The centenary of the Henry Simon Chair of German at the University of Manchester (1996), pp 514–16.

147. Rosaleen O'Neill, 'Modern Languages', in Tadhg Foley (ed.), *From Queen's College to National University: Essays on the Academic History of QCG/UCG/NUI, Galway* (Dublin, 1999), pp 360–83, pp 373–4; Stephanie Klapp, 'Death by wrongful humiliation – the story of Valentine Steinberger', *Galway Advertiser*, 4 February 2021. Cf. below, Ch. 6, passim (Steinberger) and Ch. 7, p. 186 (Freund). For a fellow captive's warm tribute to the kindly and stoical professor, and his ordeal as a captive of the Crown, see 'The late Professor Steinberger', in *UCG: A College Annual*, 1916–17, pp 44–5. In December 1916, the NUI Senate complemented its vote of condolence for the loss of the German professor by setting up a chair of German henceforth distinct from its chair of Romance Philology. There was anti-German sentiment in Cork and Galway during the First World War, but it was mitigated by nationalist sentiment after 1916 (John A. Murphy, *The College: A History of Queen's/University College Cork, 1845–1895* (Cork, 1995), pp 198–201; O'Neill, 'Modern languages', pp 373–4). Fischer, *Das Deutschlandbild der Iren, 1890–1939*, points out that Irish attitudes to Germany and German culture remained generally on an even keel up to 1939.

148. J. H. Plumb, *The First Four Georges* (London, 1956), pp 34–5.

149. George Eliot, *Middlemarch*, Book 2, Chapter 37 (Penguin Classics edn, London, 1994), pp 357–9.

150. Matthew Potter, 'William Monsell: A Roman Catholic Francophile Anglo-Irishman', in Leon Litvack and Colin Graham (eds), *Ireland and Europe in the Nineteenth Century* (Dublin, 2006), pp 77–88, p. 82. Potter's essay illustrates how the Anglo-Irish Unionist MP William Monsell did not conform to type. This convert to Roman Catholicism was a friend of both Newman and Gladstone, and his second wife was a French noblewoman. He had close contacts with the upper echelons of French liberal Catholicism, and felt at home in Paris and Rome as much as London.

151. See Ciarán O'Carroll, 'The Irish papal brigade: Origins, objectives and fortunes', in Barr, Finelli and O'Connor (eds), *Nation/Nazione*, pp 73–95; Jennifer O'Brien, 'Irish public opinion and the Risorgimento, 1859–60', in ibid., pp 110–30; Barr, 'Paul Cullen, Italy and the Irish Catholic imagination, 1826–70', in ibid., pp 133–56; and Andrew Shields, '"That noble struggle": Irish conservative attitudes towards the Risorgimento, c.1848–70', in ibid., pp 157–75.

152. Blake Dillon, 'Continental literature'.

CHAPTER 3: VARIETIES AND MILESTONES OF LANGUAGE EDUCATION

1. Emily Brontë, *Wuthering Heights* (1847), Chapter 7.

2. Lewis Carroll, *Alice's Adventures in Wonderland* (1865), Chapter 9.

3. 'The fathers of the Congregation will set up the same education system as in their colleges in France. Students will learn to write and speak French fluently and correctly, but English culture will always have priority.' [My translation.] Seán P. Farragher and C. de Mare, 'Le Père Jules Leman et la fondation du collège de Blackrock', in *Mémoire Spiritaine*, 5:5 (2019), pp 37–62.

4. Eilís Dillon, *Inside Ireland* (London, 1982), p. 146.

5. I am indebted to Gerry Murphy, composer and musicologist, for these details.

6. Honor O Brolchain, *Joseph Plunkett* (Dublin, 2012), p. 25.

7. Ibid., passim.

8. 'An act to prevent the further growth of popery' (8 Anne c 3), 1709, cited in Antonia McManus, *The Irish Hedge School and Its Books, 1695–1831* (Dublin, 2002), p. 16. Cf. Áine Hyland and Kenneth Milne (eds), *Irish Educational Documents* (vol. 1, Dublin, 1987), pp 45–9 (p. 49).

9. Whether or not hedge schools had generally been located outside, on the sunny side of a roadside hedge, this was not the case by the 1800s. Kevin Whelan, 'Between: The politics of culture in Friel's *Translations*', in *Field Day Review* 6 (2010), pp 7–27 (p. 14), cites the *OED* for one derivation of the use of 'hedge' as a pejorative prefix, to mean 'untrained', 'informal'.

10. McManus, *The Irish Hedge School and Its Books, 1695–1831*, p. 242. On the absorption of some hedge schoolmasters after 1831, see Mary Daly, 'The development of the National School system, 1831–40', in Art Cosgrove and Donal McCartney (eds), *Studies in Irish History Presented to R. Dudley Edwards* (Dublin, 1979), pp 150–63.

11. Breandán Ó Madagáin, 'Irish: A difficult birth', in Tadhg Foley (ed.), *From Queen's College to National University: Essays on the Academic History of QCG/UCG/NUI, Galway* (Dublin, 1999), pp 344–59 (pp 355–7). This cooperative system of households hiring a master to teach the families together is attested in other parts of Ireland: see L. M. Cullen, 'Patrons, teachers and literacy in Irish: 1700–1850', in Mary Daly and David Dickson (eds), *The Origins of Popular Literacy in Ireland: Language Change and Educational Development 1700–1920* (Dublin, 1990), pp 15–44 (p. 18).

12. One of the younger children was my maternal grandfather, Michael George O'Malley, M.Ch., FRCS, the sixth son and second youngest of 14 siblings. Another family numbered 13 children. Michael O'Malley's reminiscences, written in the late 1950s, recall stories about the colourful schoolmaster who had taught his older siblings (Sheila Mulloy, 'Memories of a Connemara man', in *Journal of the Clifden & Connemara Heritage Group* 2 (1995), pp 33–46 (pp 37–8).

13. See also below, p. 167. Like his cousin Michael, Tomás Ó Máille was born late enough to attend the new school in the valley. His schoolteacher was one of his older sisters, who had been educated by the private schoolmaster (Ruairí Ó hUiginn, 'Tomás Ó Máille', in Ruairí Ó hUiginn (ed.), *Léachtaí Cholm Cille* 27 (Maynooth, 1997), pp 83–122 (pp 83–5).

14. W. B. Stanford and R. B. McDowell, *Mahaffy: A Biography of an Anglo-Irishman* (London, 1971), pp 6–14, 16–17.

15. Dublin, for example, had an estimated 50 or more small private ladies' seminaries by 1860. See Scoilnet teaching resources on the Intermediate Education Act (1878), available at http://womeninhistory.scoilnet.ie/content/unit4/exhibpast.html, 7 March 2023.

16. John Coolahan, *Irish Education: Its History and Structure* (Dublin, 1981), pp 56–61.

17. T. J. Walsh, *Nano Nagle and the Presentation Sisters* (Monasterevin, 1959, reprinted 1980). In the 1760s, Nagle had risked falling foul of the law by opening several schools for the children of Cork's poor, and had persuaded the Ursulines to set up a school for girls in Cork in 1771. See Jessie Castle and Gillian O'Brien, '"I am building a house": Nano Nagle's Georgian convents', in *Irish Architectural and Decorative Studies* 19 (2016), pp 54–75 (pp 58–61, 66). On Nagle's advisory role for Teresa Mulally in Dublin, see Thomas Morrissey, *Irish Jesuits in Penal Times 1695–1811: Thomas Betagh and his Companions* (Dublin, 2020), p. 55.

18. McManus, *The Irish Hedge School and Its Books, 1695–1831*, p. 30.

19. Claude Marcel (1793–1876) was married to a Cork Catholic. See J. C., 'Notes and queries: Two Franco-Cork professors', in *Journal of the Cork Historical and Archaeological Society* 15 (1909), pp 99–100 (p. 100). Cf. Nicola McLelland, 'The history of language learning and teaching in Britain', in *The Language Learning Journal* 46 (2018), pp 6–16 (p. 11), and Richard Smith, 'Claude Marcel (1793–1876): A neglected applied linguist?', in *Language and History* 52 (2009), pp 171–81. Marcel's 1853 work on language education can be accessed via Google Books.

20. Advertisement, *Dublin Evening Post*, 14 February 1784, p. 1. Reproduced in John Stocks Powell, *Schooling in Ireland: A Clustered History 1695–1912* (Tullamore, 2020), p. 129.

21. Stocks Powell, *Schooling in Ireland*, p. 114.

22. John Stocks Powell, *Carson's School, Portarlington: Edward Carson and his Headmaster, Francis Hewson Wall* (York, 2018).

23. Ciaran O'Neill, *Catholics of Consequence: Transnational Education, Social Mobility, and the Irish Catholic Elite 1850–1900* (Oxford, 2014), pp 161–203; cf. Máire Kennedy, *French Books in Eighteenth-Century Ireland* (Oxford, 2001), pp 31–2.

24. Fr Nicholas Schofield, 'The last days of the English College in Douai', https://rcdow.org.uk/news/the-last-days-of-the-english-college-in-douai-/, 9 May 2021. O'Connell witnessed some frightening mob behaviour during the Terror, one of the standard reasons cited to explain his preference for non-violent constitutional politics.

25. O'Neill, *Catholics of Consequence*, p. 73.

26. The Counter-Reformation English Benedictine convent at Ypres passed to Irish nuns in 1682. The community, known locally as *De Iersche Damen* or *les Dames d'Ypres*, ran a successful boarding-school for affluent English and Irish Catholic girls until the nuns took refuge in Ireland at the outbreak of war in 1914. Shortly thereafter they set up a school at Kylemore Abbey, County Galway. See Deirdre Raftery and Catherine Kilbride, *The Benedictine Nuns and Kylemore Abbey: A History* (Newbridge, 2020).

27. O'Neill, *Catholics of Consequence*, p. 171: 'There were just 24 convents in England and Wales in 1810, but anything up to 596 convents by 1900.' For figures for Ireland, see below, Ch. 3, notes 42 and 44.

28. O'Neill, *Catholics of Consequence*, p. 188. It should be said, however, that at Ypres the Irish Benedictines taught through English (Raftery and Kilbride, *The Benedictine Nuns and Kylemore Abbey*, p. 22).

29. O'Neill, *Catholics of Consequence*, p. 203.

30. One Protestant boys' school in Ireland, St Columba's College, was undoubtedly an elite establishment (ibid., p. 10); so was Portora Royal School in Enniskillen. As for girls, Margaret Byers, the progressive founder of Victoria College Belfast (formerly Ladies' Collegiate), felt that Protestant girls had lost out educationally, there being few schools available to them compared to the range of convent schools open to Catholic girls (Margaret Ó hÓgartaigh, 'A quiet revolution: Women and second-level education in Ireland, 1878–1930', in *New Hibernia Review/Iris Éireannach Nua* 13 (2009), pp 36–51, p. 42). This was despite the Protestant middle class outnumbering their Catholic counterparts.

31. O'Neill, *Catholics of Consequence*, p. 10.

32. Ciaran O'Neill, 'Jesuit education and the Irish Catholic elite', in *Espacio, Tiempo y Educación* 6 (2019), pp 99–120.

33. Liam O'Malley, 'Law', in Foley (ed.), *From Queen's College to National University*, pp 16–124, p. 82; Rosaleen O'Neill, 'Modern languages', in Foley (ed.), *From Queen's College to National University*, pp 360–83, pp 363–4; Stanford and McDowell, *Mahaffy*, pp 16–17.

34. *Report of the Queen's Colleges Commission*, 1858, pp 22–3; cf. Frank Hugh O'Donnell, *Mixed Education in Ireland: The Confessions of a Queen's Collegian* (2 vols, London, 1870), vol. 1, *The Faculty of Arts*, pp 147–9. Cork's professor Raymond de Véricour was more sanguine about most of his students' level of French by 1858, although he found the first-year university programme had too many subjects. (*Report of the Queen's Colleges Commission*, p. 195.)

35. Stanford and McDowell, *Mahaffy*, p. 16.

36. Colin Barr, *Paul Cullen, John Henry Newman, and the Catholic University of Ireland, 1845–1865* (South Bend and Leominster, 2003) pp 218–19.

37. Coolahan, *Irish Education*, p. 61.

38. Joachim Fischer, 'The eagle that never landed: Uses and abuses of the German language in Ireland', in Michael Cronin and Cormac Ó Cuilleanáin (eds), *The Languages of Ireland* (Dublin, 2003), pp 93–111 (p. 97).

39. Hyland and Milne (eds), *Irish Educational Documents*, vol. 1, Introduction, pp 18–19.

40. O'Neill, *Catholics of Consequence*, p. 15, explains how the system satisfied key education stakeholders, cementing denominational divisions while entailing 'no standardization, no inspectorate and no direct state involvement'. On the genesis of the 'payment-by-results' scheme that shaped Ireland's Intermediate Certificate Act, and the different influence of both Blackrock College's Holy Ghost Fathers and Tullabeg's Jesuits in its conception, see O'Neill, *Catholics of Consequence*, pp 59–60. Seán Farragher narrates the Blackrock perspective, in Seán P. Farragher, CSSp, and Annraoi Wyer, *Blackrock College 1860–1995* (Dublin, 1995), pp 52–4; and in Seán P. Farragher, CSSp, *The French College Blackrock 1860–1896* (Dublin, 2011), pp 173–5, 190–2 and 213–33.

41. This important phenomenon has been well documented: see for example, Mary Cullen (ed.), *Girls Don't Do Honours: Irish Women in Education in the 19th and 20th Centuries* (Dublin, 1987); Deirdre Raftery, 'The higher education of women in Ireland, *c.*1860–1904', in Susan M. Parkes (ed.), *A Danger to the Men? A History of Women in Trinity College Dublin 1904–2004* (Dublin, 2004), pp 5–18; Judith Harford, *The Opening of University Education to Women in Ireland* (Dublin, 2008); Ó hÓgartaigh, 'A quiet revolution'; Claire Rush, 'Women who made a difference: The Belfast Ladies' Institute, 1867–1897', in Judith Harford and Claire Rush (eds), *Have Women Made a Difference? Women in Irish Universities, 1850–2010* (Bern, 2010), pp 29–53; Deirdre Raftery, 'The "mission" of

nuns in female education in Ireland, *c.*1850–1950', in *Paedagogica Historica* 48 (2012), pp 299–313 (https://doi.org/10.108000309230.2011.568624).

42. In Ireland, there were 120 nuns in 1801, 1,500 by 1851, rising to *c.*8,000 by 1901 (Tony Fahey, 'Nuns in the Catholic Church in Ireland in the nineteenth century', in Cullen (ed.), *Girls Don't Do Honours*, pp 7–30 (p. 7)).

43. Raftery, 'The "mission" of nuns in female education in Ireland, *c.*1850–1950', online open access, n.p.

44. Anne V. O'Connor, 'The revolution in girls' secondary education in Ireland, 1860–1910', in Cullen (ed.), *Girls Don't Do Honours*, pp 31–54 (p. 37). Traditional French convent schooling was Archbishop Cullen's preferred model for the education of girls: it was necessarily different from boys' education, and offered an 'attractive alternative to the growing power of the state and of anglicisation' (ibid., p. 42). The spread of this model was made possible by the growing population in Ireland during the nineteenth century, coinciding with an unprecedented increase in numbers of women entering religious life in Catholic Europe. On the latter phenomenon, comparing Ireland, France, Prussia and the Netherlands, see Fahey, 'Nuns in the Catholic Church in Ireland in the nineteenth century', pp 7–10.

45. O'Neill, *Catholics of Consequence*, p. 169. Originally an Italian order, the Ursulines arrived in Cork from Paris, in response to an invitation by Nano Nagle. Cf. Walsh, *Nano Nagle and the Presentation Sisters*, pp 55–93; and Gerardine Meaney, Mary O'Dowd and Bernadette Whelan, *Reading the Irish Woman: Studies in Cultural Encounter and Exchange, 1714–1960* (Liverpool, 2013), pp 61–4.

46. Deirdre Raftery, '"*Je suis d'aucune Nation*": The recruitment and identity of Irish women religious in the international mission field, *c.*1840–1940', in *Paedagogica Historica* 4 (2013), pp 513–30 (pp 513–14), DOI: 10.1080/00309230.2013.800123.

47. Advertisement for the Sacred Heart of Mary Convent, Lisburn, County Antrim (1875), quoted in O'Connor, 'The revolution in girls' secondary education in Ireland', p. 38.

48. Anne O'Connor, 'The languages of transnationalism: Translation, training, and transfer', in *Éire–Ireland* 51 (2016), pp 14–33 (pp 24–5).

49. O'Connor, 'The revolution in girls' secondary education in Ireland', pp 38–9.

50. Ibid., p. 39.

51. Kennedy's provisional list of schools and teachers is peppered with French names (Kennedy, *French Books in Eighteenth-Century Ireland*, pp 172–82). One such academy was a boarding school for 'young ladies' run by Mrs Molyneux. A small advertisement claims: 'As she particularly professes the French language, it shall be that of her House', and her care for the morals, manners and improvement of her charges will be complemented by lessons in French, English, History, Geography, *Use of the Globes* and 'all sorts of useful and ornamental Work'. (*Dublin Evening Post*, 8 June 1809. Reproduced in Stocks Powell, *Schooling in Ireland*, p. 201.)

52. Deirdre Raftery, *Teresa Ball and Loreto Education: Convents and the Colonial World, 1794–1875* (Dublin, 2022), p. 129. A knowledge of modern languages was intrinsic to the ethos of the IBVM (Loreto order) from its foundation: see Harford, *The Opening of University Education to Women in Ireland*, p. 110.

53. Foreign languages enhanced a young woman's marriage prospects and were also an insurance, offering the possibility of a position as governess in the event of misfortune. See Mary Hatfield, *Growing Up in Nineteenth-Century Ireland: A Cultural History of Middle-Class Childhood and Gender* (Oxford, 2019), pp 126–7. On the gendering of 'polite' discourse, see Michèle Cohen, *Fashioning Masculinity: National Identity and Language in the Eighteenth Century* (Abingdon, 1996).

54. Mary Colum, *Life and the Dream* (New York, 1947, 1958; revised edn, Dublin, 1966), p. 22.

55. Ibid., p. 16.

56. Ibid., pp 22–3.

57. Anne O'Connor, *Translation and Language in Nineteenth-Century Ireland: A European Perspective* (London, 2017), pp 26–9.

58. Alexandra College (from 1866) provided Protestant girls with an exceptionally academic education.

59. Harford, *The Opening of University Education to Women in Ireland*, pp 99–128; Judith Harford, 'Women and the Irish University Question', in Harford and Rush (eds), *Have Women Made a Difference?*, pp 7–28; Margaret Mac Curtain [Sister Benevenuta], 'St Mary's University College', in *University Review* 3 (1964), pp 33–47. Cf. below, pp 74–7; 170–2; 184–5.

60. Lucinda Thomson, 'The campaign for admission, 1870–1904', in Parkes (ed.), *A Danger to the Men?*, pp 19–54 (p. 53). Cf. 'The rising tide: Women at Cambridge', https://www.cam.ac.uk/stories/the-rising-tide; and 'A short history of women's education at the University of Oxford', https://www.history.ox.ac.uk/article/a-short-history-of-womens-education-at-the-university-of-oxford, both accessed 15 April 2023.

61. Cf. Madame Terson's Huguenot Academy at Clontarf, immortalised in the memoirs of Lady Morgan [aka Sydney Owenson], who boarded there for three years in the 1790s. See Meaney, O'Dowd and Whelan, *Reading the Irish Woman*, pp 59–60. The school had originally been set up in Portarlington.

62. Two of Trinity's earliest cohort of women graduates had attended the French School in Bray (Susan M. Parkes, 'The first decade, 1904–14: A quiet revolution', in Parkes (ed.), *A Danger to the Men?*, pp 55–86 (p. 61). The link was to continue for many decades.

63. Jennifer Flegg, *The French School, Bray, Remembered: A History of The French School, Bray 1864–1966* (Dublin, 2006).

64. Anne O'Connor, *Translation and Language in Nineteenth-Century Ireland*, pp 28–9.

65. Cited in Hyland and Milne (eds), *Irish Educational Documents*, vol. 1, pp 194–5.

66. UCD James Joyce Library, Special Collections, Catholic University of Ireland *Calendar*, 1867–8, unpaginated appendix. The prospectuses are from the following schools: CUS Leeson St, Dublin; CU High School, Waterford; St Colman's, Fermoy; Clongowes Wood, County Kildare; St Stanislaus, Tullamore; St Francis Xavier, 6 Gt Denmark St, Dublin; St Aidan's, Enniscorthy. Cf. UCD James Joyce Library, Special Collections, Catholic University of Ireland *Calendar*, 1863, p. 60, on St Flannan's CU High School, Ennis: 'French is part of the ordinary business of the School. German, Italian, Drawing, Music, etc are extra charges.' Cf. Anne O'Connor, 'The languages of transnationalism', pp 23–4, which mentions modern languages being advertised, during the 1840s, as curricular subjects for boys' schools in Ennis, Lismore, Portarlington and Gt Brunswick St, Dublin.

67. Clare Sargent, 'Singleton, Sewell and the ideal of a school: St Columba's College, Stackallan and St Peter's College, Radley', https://victorianweb.org/history/education/radley/ideals.html, 31 March 2021. St Columba's later moved to Rathfarnham, Co. Dublin.

68. Stocks Powell, *Schooling in Ireland*, p. 165.

69. Davis Coakley, *Oscar Wilde: The Importance of Being Irish* (Dublin, 1994), pp 77, 83. Wilde, who read Classics at Trinity, wrote *Salomé* (1891) in French.

70. Coolahan, *Irish Education*, p. 53.

71. S. Farragher, CSSp, and C. de Mare, 'Le Père Jules Leman et la fondation du collège de Blackrock, en Irlande' in *Mémoire Spiritaine* 5 (2019), pp 37–62 (p. 50). De Mare back-translates *boney boys* as 'les petits bonapartes' [little Bonapartes]. *Boney* was a popular British nickname for Napoleon Bonaparte.

72. Ibid., pp 47–8.

73. Reproduced in Farragher and Wyer, *Blackrock College 1860–1995*, p. 13.

74. Samples of literary juvenilia are reproduced in ibid., p. 29.

75. Teaching at junior level was done by French clerical students spending a year in Ireland; after 1879, with the new public examinations, the French system of studies became harder to sustain (Farragher, *The French College Blackrock 1860–1896*, p. 299).

76. Emil Otto (1813–78), theologian and philologist at the University of Heidelberg, was a prolific author of grammars and language-teaching textbooks in German and French. His *French Conversation Grammar* (c.1864), continued to be revised and in print well into the twentieth century. See Nicola McLelland, *German Through English Eyes: A History of Language Teaching and Learning in Britain, 1500–2000* (Wiesbaden, 2015), pp 91–4; and *Teaching and Learning Foreign Languages: A History of Language Education, Assessment and Policy in Britain* (London and New York, 2017; pbk edn, 2018), pp 101–3. On the publisher's role in this success, see Rolf Kemmler and María José Corvo Sánchez, 'The importance of the "method Gaspey-Otto-Sauer" amongst the earliest Portuguese textbooks of the German language', in *Language & History* 63 (2020), pp 120–38.

77. *Calendar of the French College, Scholastic Year 1870–71*, pp 85–96 (Blackrock College Archives, Blackrock College, County Dublin).

78. Barr, *Paul Cullen, John Henry Newman, and the Catholic University of Ireland, 1845–1865*, pp 186–92. There were 37 CU-affiliated schools by 1874 (Coolahan, *Irish Education*, p. 61).

79. Coincidentally, they had been fellow-students of canon law while in Rome in 1856–7 (Farragher and de Mare, 'Le Père Jules Leman et la fondation du collège de Blackrock, en Irlande', pp 44–5). This specific example of Catholic clerical networking led to further cooperation.

80. Farragher and Wyer, *Blackrock College 1860–1995*, p. 53.

81. Ibid., p. 54.

82. Reproduced in ibid., p. 50.

83. Reproduced in ibid., p. 51.

84. Reproduced in ibid., p. 70.

85. The Castle and its grounds, on property adjoining the school's land, had been procured by the Spiritans in 1875 (ibid., pp 42–5).

86. Fergal McGrath, SJ, *Newman's University: Idea and Reality* (Dublin, 1951), p. 60; Donal McCartney, *UCD: A National Idea: The History of University College Dublin* (Dublin, 1999), p. 18; Farragher and Wyer, *Blackrock College 1860–1995*, pp 53–4, 69.

87. Hyland and Milne (eds), *Irish Educational Documents*, vol. 1, p. 19.

88. Harford, *The Opening of University Education to Women in Ireland*, pp 10–46; Rush, 'Women who made a difference'.

89. J. G. Dewey, 'The education of a ruling caste: The Indian Civil Service in the era of competitive examination', in *English Historical Review* 88 (1973), pp 262–85; McLelland, 'The history of language learning and teaching in Britain', p. 9; cf. *The Macaulay Report on the Indian Civil Service* (1854), in *The Fulton Report* (1968), Appendix B (pp 119–28), p. 122, https://www.civilservant.org.uk/library/1854-Macaulay_Report.pdf, 4 September 2023. Two 1854 reports on reforming the civil service – in the UK (Northcote-Trevelyan) and in India (Macaulay) were printed as appendices to the 1968 Fulton Report.

90. *The Book of Trinity College Dublin, 1591–1891: Tercentenary Celebration presented by the Provost and Senior Fellows of Trinity College, Dublin, July 1892* (Dublin, 1892), pp 122–3.

91. M. M. Raraty, 'The chair of German, Trinity College, Dublin 1775–1866', in *Hermathena* 102 (1966), pp 53–72 (p. 68).

92. Gilbert Carr, 'Literary historical trends and the history of the German syllabus at Trinity College, Dublin, 1873–1972', in *Hermathena* 121 (1976), pp 36–53; Raraty, 'The chair of German, Trinity College, Dublin'; and Francis M. Higman, 'Modern languages in Trinity College, Dublin 1776–1976', in *Hermathena* 121 (1976), pp 12–17.

93. Raraty, 'The chair of German, Trinity College, Dublin', p 72 n. 11.

94. Catholic University of Ireland *Calendar*, 1867–8, p. cliii. Examinations in French, German and Hindustani included a dictation test. There were slight variations in the examination marking scales between Woolwich and the East India Company.

95. See for example *The Report of the President of Queen's College, Galway*, vol. 5, 1888–9, pp 6–7.

96. The Queen's Colleges Commission of 1858 reported on the appointment in 1855 of two Irish students (from Cork and Galway) to Writerships in the East India Company; this was followed by the success of another Cork graduate in 1856 and of three from Belfast in 1857 (Cited in Hyland and Milne (eds), *Irish Educational Documents*, vol. 1, p. 332.) On the Indian Civil Service competition and Oxbridge during the second half of the nineteenth century, see Dewey, 'The education of a ruling caste'; for numbers, see ibid., p. 276, Table 1 ('Universities attended by ICS recruits, 1855–1896').

97. Queen's College Galway, *College Annual*, 1913, 'Arts notes', p. 58.

98. See above, pp 58–9.

99. Farragher and Wyer, *Blackrock College 1860–1995*, pp 49–50.

100. Critics include Patrick Pearse in *The Murder Machine* (1912).

101. Flann Campbell, 'Latin and the elite tradition in education', in *The British Journal of Sociology* 19 (1968), pp 308–25, p. 321 n. 2 (citing G. Baron, *Society, Schools and Progress in England* (Oxford, 1965), p. 5). It was only in the 1890s that the 'embedded tradition that a headmaster must be a classicist and in Anglican orders began to crumble' (Christopher Stray, *Classics Transformed: Schools, Universities, and Society in England, 1830–1960* (Oxford, 1998), p. 189).

102. Nicola McLelland, 'French and German in British schools (1850–1945)', in *Documents pour l'histoire du français langue étrangère ou seconde* 53 (2014), pp 109–24 (online edn, 2017, p. 6, paragraph 16 – citing Karl Peter Ortmanns, *Deutsch in Grossbritannien: Die Entwicklung von Deutsch als Fremdsprache von den Anfängen bis 1985* (Stuttgart, 1993), p. 28).

103. Campbell, 'Latin and the elite tradition', p. 309 (citing Edward C. Mack, *Public Schools and British Opinion since 1860* (New York, 1941), p. 36).

104. Reproduced in Farragher and Wyer, *Blackrock College 1860–1995*, p. 8.

105. Christopher Stray speculates on the persistently narrow focus of British, as opposed to continental, education by observing that Britain's industrial revolution had occurred when scientific knowledge was of a 'relatively low order'. France and Prussia experienced industrialisation a century later when more advanced scientific and technical knowledge made science an essential element of school programmes (Stray, *Classics Transformed*, pp 27–8). Mathematics and science have continued to be undervalued in Britain, according to Simon Kuper, *Chums: How a Tiny Caste of Oxford Tories Took Over the UK* (London, 2022), pp 37–9.

106. Derek Gillard, *Education in England: A History* (City, 1998; online publication, 2018), Chapter 5, http://www.educationengland.org.uk/history, 26 March 2022.

107. He had entered the Jesuit order in Amiens and studied Theology in Rome's Pontifical Gregorian University – https://www.jesuitarchives.ie/delany-william-1835-1924-jesuit-priest, 3 December 2020. In his evidence before the Fry Commission (1906–7), Fr Delany made a special case for modern language study at university. (Mary M. Macken, 'Women in the University and the College: A struggle within a struggle', in Michael Tierney (ed.), *Struggle with Fortune: A Miscellany for the Centenary of the Catholic University of Ireland, 1854–1954* (Dublin, 1954), pp 142–65 (p. 159).)

108. Farragher, *The French College Blackrock 1860–1896*, p. 177, reproduces the staff list for 1875.

109. Gillard, *Education in England*, Chapter 5, passim; he quotes from Thomas Wyse, *Education Reform* (1837).

110. Gillard, *Education in England*, Chapter 5. For the numerous endowed schools in England and Wales that had been teaching literacy in Latin since early modern times, see https://en.wikipedia.org/wiki/List_of_English_and_Welsh_endowed_schools_(19th_century), 3 February 2023.

111. Stray, *Classics Transformed*, p. 183. The best primary source on Victorian public schools is the report of the Clarendon Commission (1864). From this, Stray (pp 185–6) calculates how much classics dominated the average weekly timetable of 20 lessons: eleven were for classics, three for mathematics, two each for modern languages, natural science, and music/drawing. Cf. Patricia Phillips, *The Scientific Lady: A Social History of Woman's Scientific Interests 1520–1918* (London, 1990), pp 238–41.

112. Gemma Tidman, *The Emergence of Literature in Eighteenth-Century France: The Battle of the School Books*, Oxford Studies in the Enlightenment (Liverpool, 2023), relates how the French eighteenth century was when modern notions of *littérature* were forged, and when something called *la littérature française* was taught for the first time (in 1751 at the École Royale Militaire). Cf. Thierry Gouault, 'L'enseignement des langues anciennes au collège de l'Oratoire du Mans au XVIIIe siècle: Une remise en cause du latin et du grec?', in *Annales de Bretagne et des Pays de l'Ouest* 124 (2017), pp 57–73, online edn, 2019, paragraphs 14–22, 36–41, http://journals.openedition.org/abpro/3666, 7 October 2023; Serge Tomamichel, 'Le latin dans l'enseignement secondaire français: Formes et légitimités sociales d'une discipline scolaire entre monopole et déclin (XVIe–XXe siècles)', in *Espacio, Tiempo y Educación* 4:2 (2017), pp 209–26 (pp 217–18), doi:http://dx.doi.org/10.14516/ete.141, 7 October 2023.

113. See the list in Laurie O'Higgins, *The Irish Classical Self: Poets and Poor Scholars in the Eighteenth and Nineteenth Centuries* (Oxford, 2017), Appendix D, pp 232–86. (Her source is the 1834 Returns Connected to the Second Report of the Commissioners of Public Instruction, 1834. The schools are listed by ecclesiastical province and diocese.)

114. During the Ulster Plantation, English and Scottish settlers were granted confiscated land holdings of the region's rebellious Gaelic chieftains; the latter went into exile following the defeat at Kinsale.

115. Royal Schools were established in Armagh, Cavan, Dungannon, Portora and Raphoe. For a description of the classes and timetable at Cavan Royal School in 1788, see Michael Quane, 'Cavan Royal School', in *The Journal of the Royal Society of Antiquaries in Ireland* 100 (1970), pp 39–66 (p. 52).

116. Ambrose Macaulay, 'Crolly, William', DIB.

117. William Reville, 'Callan, Nicholas Joseph', DIB. Cf. Séamas Ó Saothraí, 'William Neilson DD MRIA (1774–1821)', in *Journal of the County Louth Archaeological and Historical Society* 22 (1989), pp 20–8 (p. 24). On Neilson, cf. below, pp 96–101.

118. Campbell, 'Latin and the elite tradition', p. 309.

119. Cited in Michèle Cohen, 'From "glittering gibberish" to the "mere jabbering" of a *bonne*: The problem of the "oral" in the learning and teaching of French in eighteenth- and nineteenth-century

England', in Nicola McLelland and Richard Smith (eds), *The History of Language Learning and Teaching* (3 vols, Cambridge, 2018), vol. 2, pp 1–20 (p. 9).

120. Campbell, 'Latin and the elite tradition', p. 321 n. 7.

121. Cohen, 'The problem of the "oral"', p. 9. Inevitably, some voices ran counter-current, like the highly critical plea to parents to stop sending their children to 'Classical' academies to the neglect of more useful knowledge (Anon., 'On the abuse of the Classics', in *Educational Magazine* 2 (October 1835), pp 270–7), or Robert Lowe's argument in favour of a broader curriculum, *Primary and Classical Education* (Edinburgh, 1867). On mid-Victorian challenges to the exclusively classical education model, see Stray, *Classics Transformed*, pp 83–113.

122. *The Macaulay Report* (1854), p. 123.

123. Stray, *Classics Transformed*, p. 86.

124. Campbell, 'Latin and the elite tradition', p. 319. His source is *Investment in Education* (Dublin, 1965), pp 276–7.

125. John Dillon, 'Some reflections on the Irish Classical tradition', in *The Crane Bag* 3 (2) [*Anglo-Irish Perspectives*], (1979; 1982 reprint), pp 448–52 (pp 449–50).

126. Communication from Dr Attracta Halpin, former Registrar, NUI, 10 February 2021. Cf. below, pp 194–6; 212–3.

127. McLelland, 'French and German in British schools', online edn, p. 18 n. 12.

128. Stray, *Classics Transformed*, p. 54.

129. Campbell, 'Latin and the elite tradition', pp 310–13; on the Classical influences – especially Roman ones – that permeate the work of Rudyard Kipling, see Paul MacKendrick, 'Kipling and the nature of the Classical', in *The Classical Journal* 52 (1956), pp 67–76. Cf. A discussion on Marcus Aurelius, 'In Our Time', BBC Radio 4, 25 February 2021.

130. *Parliamentary Debates*, Hansard, new series, 15, 20 March 1826, 21. Cited in Gillian O'Brien, 'The 1825–6 Commissioners of Irish Education reports: Background and context', in Garret FitzGerald, *Irish Primary Education in the Early Nineteenth Century: An Analysis of the First and Second Reports of the Commissioners of Irish Education Inquiry, 1825–6* (Dublin, 2013), pp 1–43 (p. 43 n. 155); cf. McManus, *The Irish Hedge School and Its Books, 1695–1831*, p. 126. Cf. W. B. Stanford, *Ireland and the Classical Tradition* (Dublin, 1976), p. 25.

131. Michael Cronin, *Translating Ireland: Translation, Languages, Cultures* (Cork, 1996), p. 120, citing Stanford, *Ireland and the Classical Tradition*, p. 27. (Stanford's source is J. A. Gaughan, *Listowel and Its Vicinity* (Cork, 1973).)

132. O'Higgins, *The Irish Classical Self*, p. 29.

133. P. J. Dowling, *The Hedge Schools of Ireland* (London, 1935; revised edn, Cork, 1968), pp 12, 85–6. Not all were itinerant; some taught from their own simple dwellings: see Hyland and Milne (eds), *Irish Educational Documents*, vol. 1, p. 69.

134. Dowling, *The Hedge Schools of Ireland*, p. 33; McManus, *The Irish Hedge School and Its Books, 1695–1831*, p. 21, 57; O'Higgins, *The Irish Classical Self*, p. 151; Appendices C and D, given by O'Higgins, pp 213–86, indicate, among other data, their geographical spread. On the degree of continuity between those hedge schools of the 1820s that had been *de facto* Catholic parochial schools and the new national schools, see Daly, 'The development of the National School system', who finds that 'a majority of schools which had become national schools by 1840 were already in existence prior to 1831.' (p. 156).

135. Stanford, *Ireland and the Classical Tradition*, pp 25–33 (esp. pp 27, 30).

136. McManus, *The Irish Hedge School and Its Books, 1695–1831*, p. 128.

137. George Holmes, *Sketches of Some of the Southern Counties of Ireland* (London, 1801), p. 151, cited in Dowling, *The Hedge Schools of Ireland*, pp 39–40. Cf. O'Higgins, *The Irish Classical Self*, p. 123. For other witnesses, see ibid., pp 38–41 and passim; McManus, *The Irish Hedge School and Its Books, 1695–1831*, pp 125–30; Hyland and Milne (eds), *Irish Educational Documents*, vol. 1, pp 69–73.

138. Robert Bell, *Description of the Condition and Manners as Well as the Moral and Political Character, Education, etc. of the Peasantry of Ireland* (London, 1804), cited in Hyland and Milne (eds), *Irish Educational Documents*, vol. 1, p. 72.

139. Dowling, *The Hedge Schools of Ireland*, p. 25, 33, 42, 55. Robert Bell noted: 'The ultimate object which they had in view was that of being admitted into the Romish Priesthood.' Cited in Hyland and Milne (eds), *Irish Educational Documents*, vol. 1, p. 73. (One may of course wonder if the young lads

were pulling the legs of George Holmes and Robert Bell, and knew more English than they cared to admit.)

140. McManus, *The Irish Hedge School and Its Books, 1695–1831*, p. 129.

141. In a parochial survey, 1814–19. Cited in O'Higgins, *The Irish Classical Self*, p. 134.

142. Dowling, *The Hedge Schools of Ireland*, pp 72–81; O'Higgins, *The Irish Classical Self*, pp 53–98 and passim. Cf. McManus, *The Irish Hedge School and Its Books, 1695–1831*, pp 69–106, on the social context of schools and schoolmasters. On 'poor scholars', see Hyland and Milne (eds), *Irish Educational Documents*, vol. 1, pp 72–3.

143. Dillon, 'Some reflections on the Irish Classical tradition', p. 448.

144. Ibid., p. 449; cf. McManus, *The Irish Hedge School and Its Books, 1695–1831*, p. 130. Cf. Campbell, 'Latin and the elite tradition', p. 316: 'The students of Balliol had a limerick which sums up the problem: "There once were some lectures on Homer – / But I think the name's a misnomer; / Verbs, nouns and articles / Verbs, nouns and particles / But uncommonly little of Homer".'

145. Hedge schoolmasters commonly relied on pupils 'rehearsing', i.e., committing material to memory by oral repetition. See Dowling, *The Hedge Schools of Ireland*, pp 45–54; and McManus, *The Irish Hedge School and Its Books, 1695–1831*, pp 109–10.

146. Cf. O'Higgins, *The Irish Classical Self*, Appendices C and D.

147. Stanford, *Ireland and the Classical Tradition*, p. 30; cf. pp 33–41. He partly links the decline in the quality of Ireland's classical teaching to the waning of the hedge school culture. That loss was classicism's loss.

148. The relative imbalance in the respective weightings accorded to modern languages and the classics in the Irish Intermediate examination was redressed in 1902. (Fischer, 'The eagle that never landed', p. 97.)

149. Stanford, *Ireland and the Classical Tradition*, pp 62–4.

150. Thomas Davis, 'The young Irishman of the middle classes' (1848), in Seamus Deane (ed), *The Field Day Anthology of Irish Writing* (Derry, 1991), vol. 1, pp 1,269–86.

151. Ibid., pp 1,269–70: 'The college in which you and your fathers were *educated*, from whose offices seven-eighths of the Irish people are excluded by religion [...] that institution seems no longer to monopolise the education-funds of Ireland.'

152. Ibid., p. 1,273.

153. Davis's own footnote, inserted at this point, reads: 'There are professors of French, German and Italian, and medals are given once a year to promote such studies; but they form no part of the graduate course, or even the fellowship, and the provisions for teaching them are notorious mockeries.'

154. English and history were badly neglected at Trinity during these decades. See Stanford and McDowell, *Mahaffy*, p. 16; on Irish, see below, pp 83, 107–8, and Ch. 5, n. 40. On Davis and Irish, see Jean-Christophe Penet, 'Thomas Davis, "The Nation" and the Irish language', in *Studies: An Irish Quarterly Review* 96 (2007), pp 433–43.

155. Stanford and McDowell, *Mahaffy*, pp 16–17, 50, and passim. On resistance, within Trinity's establishment, to the encroachment of modern on classical languages, see Carr, 'German syllabus at Trinity College, Dublin', pp 39–40.

156. McDowell and Webb, *Trinity College Dublin*, pp 119–21; 128–9.

157. In addition, up to 1840, Trinity's fellows were required to be celibate; the requirement for them to be ordained in the Established Church (with some dispensations) was repealed in 1873. (McDowell and Webb, *Trinity College Dublin*, pp 97–110.) On Trinity's classical courses in the nineteenth century, see Stanford, *Ireland and the Classical Tradition*, pp 56–9.

158. Stanford and McDowell, *Mahaffy*, pp 25–6; Stray, *Classics Transformed*, pp 60–1.

159. Patricia Phillips, *The Scientific Lady*, p. 242.

160. McLelland, 'French and German in British schools', online edn, 2017, p. 5, paragraph 15. The source for the figures cited is Karl Peter Ortmanns, *Deutsch in Großbritannien*.

161. Eileen Breathnach, 'Women and higher education in Ireland (1879–1914)', in *The Crane Bag* 4 (1) [*Images of the Irish Woman*], (1980; 1982 reprint), pp 560–7 (p. 560).

162. Ó hÓgartaigh, 'A quiet revolution', p. 43.

163. Scoilnet teaching resources on the Intermediate Education Act; Ó hÓgartaigh, 'A quiet revolution', p. 44.

164. Phillips, *The Scientific Lady*, pp 245–8. The eleven subjects examined were: scripture, history, literature, geography, French, German, geology, chemistry, Euclid, arithmetic and algebra.

165. Phillips, *The Scientific Lady*, pp 248–9, 251–5.

166. Ó hÓgartaigh, 'A quiet revolution', p. 36: 'The number of females studying Latin had increased from 292 to 770; in the case of Greek, from 35 to 122; and in mathematics from 510 to 1,082.' Cf. Raftery, 'The higher education of women in Ireland, *c*.1860–1904', pp 12–14.

167. Raftery, 'The higher education of women in Ireland, *c*.1860–1904', p. 13.

168. Ó hÓgartaigh, 'A quiet revolution', p. 49.

169. Ibid., p. 42; McDowell and Webb, *Trinity College Dublin*, p. 344; Harford, *The Opening of University Education to Women in Ireland*, pp 24–35. 'While only 245 Catholic women were receiving instruction in Latin in 1891, this number had increased to 941 by 1901.' For the study of mathematics, the increase over the same decade went from 812 to 2,107 (ibid., p. 118).

170. McLelland, 'French and German in British schools' (online edn, 2017), p. 4, paragraph 12. Her source is again Karl Peter Ortmanns.

171. Joachim Fischer, *Das Deutschlandbild der Iren, 1890–1939: Geschichte – Form – Funktion* (Heidelberg, 2000), p. 631, extrapolated from Table 2.2. The discrepancy is consistent over three decades. The figures show even more starkly the gender breakdown for studying these two modern languages. See Fischer, 'The eagle that never landed', pp 97–8.

172. *A Page of Irish History: Story of University College, Dublin 1883–1909*, compiled by Fathers of the Society of Jesus (Dublin and Cork, 1930), pp 212–13. Higher level class sizes were much smaller in the advanced modern languages degree course, a degree that required three languages.

173. Coolahan, *Irish Education*, p. 55.

174. Ó hÓgartaigh, 'A quiet revolution', p. 41.

175. Paddy Lyons, 'Ireland, Britain, and mass literacy in nineteenth-century Europe', in Leon Litvack and Colin Graham (eds), *Ireland and Europe in the Nineteenth Century* (Dublin, 2006), pp 89–100.

176. Lowe, *Primary and Classical Education*, p. 32.

177. Stanford and McDowell, *Mahaffy*, p. 49.

178. John Logan, 'Sufficient to their needs: Literacy and elementary schooling in the nineteenth century', in Daly and Dickson (eds), *The Origins of Popular Literacy in Ireland*, pp 113–37 (p. 130). Stanford, *Ireland and the Classical Tradition*, p. 28, cites a Church of Ireland rector who berated peasants for sending their sons to learn dead languages: in his view, Latin and Greek were for the well-to-do.

179. Quoted in Scoilnet teaching resources on the Intermediate Education Act.

180. Ibid. Cf. Linde Lunney [as Linda Lunny], 'Knowledge and enlightenment: Attitudes to education in early nineteenth-century East Ulster', in Daly and Dickson (eds), *The Origins of Popular Literacy in Ireland*, pp 97–111 (pp 102ff).

181. Morrissey, *Irish Jesuits in Penal Times 1695–1811*, pp 48–55.

182. O'Neill, *Catholics of Consequence*, pp 161–89; Mary Hatfield, *Growing Up in Nineteenth-Century Ireland*, pp 126–68.

183. Frank Hugh O'Donnell, *The Ruin of Education in Ireland and the Irish Fanar* (London, 1902), p. 152.

184. Cited in ibid., p. 157, quoting from *The New Ireland Review*, December 1901.

185. Quoted in Scoilnet teaching resources on the Intermediate Education Act.

186. Ó hÓgartaigh, 'A quiet revolution', pp 49–50, p. 49.

187. Harford, *The Opening of University Education to Women in Ireland*, pp 117–18. Cf. below, pp 170–85.

188. McDowell and Webb, *Trinity College Dublin*, pp 402–3. Professors Selss and Atkinson died in 1907 and 1908 respectively.

189. Susan M. Parkes, 'A danger to the men? Women in Trinity College Dublin in the first decade, 1904–1914', in Harford and Rush (eds), *Have Women Made a Difference?*, pp 55–75 (p. 63). Cf. McDowell and Webb, *Trinity College Dublin*, p. 349; Carr, 'German syllabus at Trinity College, Dublin', pp 40–1.

190. Macken, 'Women in the University and the College', p. 163. Science did not require Latin either.

191. Ó hÓgartaigh, 'A quiet revolution', pp 37–8.

192. Ibid., pp 40–1.

193. For the background to the RUI decision, see Harford, *The Opening of University Education to Women in Ireland*, pp 74–98; and Harford, 'Women and the Irish University Question'.

194. Parkes, 'The first decade'; Parkes, 'A danger to the men?'; cf. McDowell and Webb, *Trinity College Dublin*, pp 341–53. Since 1868, it had run examinations for women that led to the award of a certificate (Parkes, 'A danger to the men?', p. 56).

195. Extract from letter, Newman to T. Scratton, 17 January 1855. (Cited in McGrath, *Newman's University*, p. 351.)

196. Oxbridge was slow for practical and cultural reasons: difficulties of accommodating women in colleges' cramped living quarters; stout conservative resistance from the old guard; long-established tradition of forming men for Anglican ministry. Today's mixed-sex regime is relatively recent. In the early 1970s, when I started postgraduate studies in Cambridge, only four of its 30 colleges then admitted women. On Cambridge, see 'The rising tide: Women at Cambridge'. The last Oxbridge college to capitulate was Magdalene College, Cambridge, in 1988. A conservative element in its student body wore black armbands to mark the change. (Remark heard at a lecture by Dr Ben Griffin on 'The Rising Tide', Girton College, Cambridge, September 2019.)

197. Harford, 'Women and the Irish University Question', p. 9; and Harford, *The Opening of University Education to Women in Ireland*, p. 80, 92.

198. Virginia Teehan, 'An Irishwoman's Diary', *The Irish Times*, 28 Jun. 2010. Cf. John A. Murphy, *The College: A History of Queen's/University College Cork, 1845–1895* (Cork, 1995), pp 129–30.

199. Parkes, 'The first decade, 1904–14'; Parkes, 'A danger to the men?'. In the main, Trinity's women students and staff complied, and were grateful for the concessions that had been made. On the 1960s position of women in Trinity, see the 2016 documentary 'WiSER – All Changed' produced by Angie Mezzetti for TCD's Centre for Gender Equality and Leadership, https://www.tcd.ie/tcgel/resources/multimedia.php, 20 May 2023.

200. McCartney, *UCD: A National Idea*, pp 72–84; Murphy, *The College*, pp 127–31; Breathnach, 'Women and higher education in Ireland'; Harford, 'Women and the Irish University Question'; and (for the case of Trinity), Raftery, 'The higher education of women in Ireland, *c*.1860–1904'.

201. Macken, 'Women in the University and the College', pp 152–3. Sister Mary Eucharia IBVM was a much-lauded teacher at the Loreto women's college at 53, St Stephen's Green. On Professor Mary Macken, see below, pp 173, 176.

202. Murphy, *The College*, p. 130.

203. On Professor Mary Ryan, see below, Chapter Seven, p. 175 and passim.

204. Family correspondence, curated in the last years of her life by the youngest member, Phyllis Ryan. It contains over 400 items, now in NLI MSS Collection, List 178 (Seán T. Ó Ceallaigh and the Ryans of Tomcoole). The family members were as follows: Johanna [Jo] (1877–1942), Mary Kate [Kit] (1878–1934), Liz (1880–1958), Nell (1881–1959), Martin (1883–1929), Mary Josephine [Min] (1884–1977), Michael (1886–1952), Jack (1887–1960), Agnes (1888–1967), Christina [Chris] (1890–1976), Jim (1892–1970), Phyllis (1895–1983). Chris was my maternal grandmother.

205. The year 1907 was a particular year for family separation: Mary Kate was teaching in Southwark; Nell was a governess in San Sebastián; Min was teaching in Fulda (Germany), and then in Rouen; Agnes was teaching at an Ursuline school in Antwerp before moving to a school in Darmstadt.

206. NLI MSS Collection, List 178: MS 48,444/1/28; MS 48,444/2/27; MS 48,444/2/36; MS 48,444/2/37; MS 48,445/1/8; MS 48,444/1/14; MS 48,444/2/24; MS 48,445/1/2; MS 48,444/1/9.

207. For papers relating to Min Ryan's time as a postgraduate teacher-training student at St Mary's College Paddington, and as a staff member of North London Collegiate School for Girls, see NLI MSS Collection, List 178, 'Papers of Mary Josephine (Min) Ryan, Tomcoole, Wexford, 1901–1917', MSS 49,528/16/1; 49,528/16/2; 49,528/13.

208. On Mary Kate Ryan, see below, pp 173, 174, 175, 179–80; and Phyllis Gaffney, '"Assistant something-or-other in the new university": Life and letters of Mary Kate O'Kelly (1878–1934)', in Harford and Rush (eds), *Have Women Made a Difference?*, pp 105–26. It was expected, as part of the texture of adolescence, for the daughters of the next generation to spend a summer staying with a family in continental Europe.

209. The most radical revolutionary of all the Ryans, Nell spent the most time in gaol. Imprisoned, in Ireland and England, for several months after the 1916 Rising, she was on extended hunger strike during the Civil War in 1923. Her interest in foreign languages helped her pass the time when detained in Aylesbury: in September 1916 she wrote home for her Otto's Grammar and enjoyed studying Russian and Persian. Nell's siblings, and some of her in-laws, were involved in politics on both sides of the Treaty divide. Min, who married Richard Mulcahy, and Agnes, married to Denis McCullough,

were pro-Treaty. Their brother Jim, later a Fianna Fáil minister and parliamentary representative, was anti-Treaty, as were the two sisters who married the prominent republican Seán T. O'Kelly: first Mary Kate and after her early death, Phyllis. (Seán T. O'Kelly was a revolutionary, an ersatz diplomatic statesman, then a mainstream politician, and ultimately succeeded Douglas Hyde as president of Ireland.)

210. Coolahan, *Irish Education*, p. 116.

211. Leathes Report, 'Modern studies, being the report of the committee on the position of Modern Languages in the educational system of Great Britain' (London, 1918), p. 3.

212. Ibid., pp 4–5, 19.

213. Ibid., p. 5. In this context, 'false quantity' means mispronouncing a vowel by ignoring its metrical length, when quoting Latin verse. The use of Latin quotations in the House of Commons had declined by the 1880s, a symptom of widening diversity among elected representatives (Stray, *Classics Transformed*, pp 65–6). Yet Britain's Victorian classicists could still become very exercised by scholarly debates, as for example in the pages of *The Academy*, in the 1870s, about the correct and 'scientific' pronunciation of Latin (ibid., pp 126–31). As a 1923 critic asserted, concerning the excessive philology of old-style dons: 'They are profound in Greek particles or the Latin subjunctive: in politics they are on the level of the daily paper' (ibid., p. 146, citing Gilbert Norwood, 'Is there a case against modern Classical scholarship?', in *London Mercury*, October 1923, pp 612–20.)

214. I am grateful to the Registrar, NUI, for information on seven of these matriculations.

215. Phyllis certainly used Irish in later life, and her school French and German were occasionally useful to her as the second wife of Ireland's second president.

CHAPTER 4: ANCIENT CELTIC: RESPECTABLE ROOTS

1. William Neilson, *An Account of the System of Education in the Belfast Academical Institution* (Belfast, c.1818), p. 3.

2. Henry Joseph Monck Mason, *History of the Origin and Progress of the Irish Society, Established for Promoting the Education of the Native Irish, Through the Medium of Their Own Language* (2nd edn, Dublin, 1846), p. 14.

3. John O'Beirne Crowe, *The Catholic University and the Irish Language* (Dublin, 1865), p. 14.

4. The Revd R. K. Abbott, BD, LittD, 'The Library', in *The Book of Trinity College Dublin 1591–1891: Tercentenary Celebration Presented by the Provost and Senior Fellows of Trinity College, Dublin*, July 1892 (Dublin, 1892), p. 168.

5. R. B. McDowell and D. A. Webb, *Trinity College Dublin 1592–1952: An Academic History* (Cambridge, 1982), pp 9–10, 189. William Daniel, an early Fellow, translated the New Testament (1602) and Book of Common Prayer (1608). Provost Bedell's Old Testament was printed in 1685. Cf. Máirtín Ó Murchú, 'Irish language studies in Trinity College Dublin', in *Hermathena (Quatercentenary Papers)* (1992), pp 43–68 (pp 48–52): During the provostship of Narcissus Marsh (elected Provost 1678), Paul Higgins, a priest who had been educated in Rome but conformed to the Established Church upon returning to Ireland, was engaged to teach Irish-speaking scholars to read and write Irish; he also preached a weekly Irish sermon in College Chapel. Ó Murchú believes that instruction in Irish, intended to educate Irish-speaking ordinands, was more or less continuously present in Trinity in the period c.1678–1730.

6. McDowell and Webb, *Trinity College Dublin*, pp 517 n. 20; 164, 190–01.

7. Patrick J. Corish, *Maynooth College 1795–1995* (Dublin, 1995), p. 53, 75.

8. Corish, *Maynooth College*, pp 74–5; Brian Ó Cuív, 'Irish language and literature, 1845–1921', in W. E. Vaughan (ed.), *A New History of Ireland, VI: Ireland under the Union, II: 1870–1921* (Oxford, 1996), pp 385–435 (p. 392). Corish (*Maynooth College*, p. 116) points to the neglect of practical communication skills in Maynooth's nineteenth-century training: 'If preparation for preaching was defective, training in catechetics did not exist.'

9. Ibid., p. 75, 116, 213.

10. Ibid., p. 116. Cf. Leon Ó Broin, 'The Gaelic League and the Chair of Irish in Maynooth', in *Studies: An Irish Quarterly Review* 52 (1963), pp 348–62 (p. 349).

11. Breandán Ó Madagáin, 'Irish: A difficult birth', in Tadhg Foley (ed.), *From Queen's College to National University: Essays on the Academic History of QCG/UCG/NUI, Galway* (Dublin, 1999),

pp 344–59 (p. 344). T. W. Moody and J. C. Beckett, *Queen's, Belfast 1845–1949: The History of a University* (2 vols, London, 1959), vol. 1, p. 51 n. 4, quote from William Smith O'Brien, in a letter of 1 July 1845: 'Any proposal to establish a professorship of Irish in the new colleges would only be laughed to scorn in the house of Commons.' The term 'Celtic' also masked the fact that Irish was being endowed by government.

12. Ó Madagáin, 'Irish: A difficult birth', pp 349–51. John O'Beirne Crowe, Mahony's successor, included lectures on the history of Celtic languages and literature, but concentrated on teaching Irish, both modern and ancient.

13. Cornelius G. Buttimer, 'Celtic and Irish in College 1849–1944', in *Journal of the Cork Historical and Archaeological Society* 94 (1989), pp 88–112 (p. 90).

14. *Report of the President of Queen's College Cork*, 1859–60, p. 29.

15. See for example ibid., p. 64, Sessional Examinations in Celtic Languages, Junior and Senior Classes.

16. Ó Madagáin, 'Irish: A difficult birth', p. 349, 351, 352; John A. Murphy, *The College: A History of Queen's/University College Cork, 1845–1895* (Cork, 1995), p. 66, 80; C. G. Buttimer, 'Celtic and Irish in College 1849–1944', p. 91; Moody and Beckett, *Queen's, Belfast*, vol. 1, p. 128, 170, and vol. 2, p. 718, Appendix III (B) 'Professorial emoluments'. (Professors' fee income was an indicator of student numbers.) Belfast fared worst of the three, with zero enrolment in Celtic over the period; of the other two, Cork did marginally better than Galway.

17. Gearóid Ó Tuathaigh, 'The establishment of the Queen's Colleges: Ideological and political background', in Foley (ed.), *From Queen's College to National University*, pp 1–15 (p. 14).

18. *Report of the President of Queen's College Cork*, 1859–60, p. 29.

19. Ibid., p. 6.

20. As Owen Connellan observed at the 1858 Commission: *Report of the Queen's Colleges Commission*, 1858, p. 195.

21. P. J. Mathews, 'Hyde's first stand: The Irish language controversy of 1899', in *Éire/Ireland* 35 (2000), pp 173–87 (p. 174).

22. Ann Frost, 'The emergence and growth of Hispanic Studies in British and Irish universities', online report, AHGBI [Association of Hispanists of Great Britain and Ireland], 2019, pp 5–6.

23. Ibid., p. 8.

24. Quoted in Murphy, *The College*, p. 80. As we shall see, Belfast's Professor John O'Donovan, whose interest in Irish appears to have been predominantly antiquarian, saw the modern language as 'obsolete in about fifty years' (cited in Breandán Ó Buachalla, *I mBéal Feirste Cois Cuain* (Dublin, 1968), p. 239).

25. Mary Daly and David Dickson (eds), *The Origins of Popular Literacy in Ireland: Language Change and Educational Development 1700–1920* (Dublin, 1990). For nuances, see in particular Mary E. Daly, 'Literacy and language change in the late nineteenth and early twentieth centuries', pp 153–66; Garret FitzGerald, 'The decline of the Irish language, 1771–1871', pp 59–72; Graeme Kirkham, 'Literacy in North-West Ulster, 1680–1860', pp 73–96.

26. Aidan Doyle, *A History of the Irish Language: From the Norman Invasion to Independence* (Oxford, 2015), p. 118.

27. Linde Lunney [as Linda Lunny], 'Knowledge and enlightenment: Attitudes to education in early nineteenth-century East Ulster', in Daly and Dickson (eds), *Origins of Popular Literacy*, pp 97–111.

28. Antonia McManus, *The Irish Hedge School and Its Books, 1695–1831* (Dublin, 2002), pp 11–14. Cf. Tony Farmar, *The History of Irish Book Publishing* (Stroud, 2018), pp 32–3.

29. McManus, *Irish Hedge School*, passim, and Appendices, pp 245–53. Cf. P. J. Dowling, *The Hedge Schools of Ireland* (London, 1935; revised edn, Cork, 1968), pp 62–71; Gillian O'Brien, 'The 1825–6 Commissioners of Irish Education reports: Background and context', in Garret FitzGerald, *Irish Primary Education in the Early Nineteenth Century: An Analysis of the First and Second Reports of the Commissioners of Irish Education Inquiry, 1825–6* (Dublin, 2013), pp 1–43 (p. 24).

30. Kirkham, 'Literacy in North-West Ulster', p. 84; cf. McManus, *Irish Hedge School*, p. 239: 35 per cent of Catholics could read and write.

31. Daly, 'Literacy and language change'.

32. On O'Connell's pragmatism with regard to the use of Irish, see Doyle, *A History of the Irish Language*, pp 108–13. O'Connell hoped that his daughters would master several foreign languages; he himself handled spoken and written French with ease. See Grace Neville, '"I got second in Latin,

Greek, and English, and eleventh in French": Attitudes to language(s) in the correspondence of Daniel O'Connell (1775–1847)', in Wesley Hutchinson and Clíona Ní Ríordáin (eds), *Language Issues: Ireland, France, Spain* (Brussels, 2010), pp 77–90 (pp 83–6).

33. Niall Ó Ciosáin, 'Printed popular literature in Irish 1750–1850: Presence and absence', in Daly and Dickson (eds), *Origins of Popular Literacy*, pp 45–57 (pp 47–8, 52).

34. John Crowley, William J. Smyth and Mike Murphy (eds), *Atlas of the Great Irish Famine, 1845–52* (Cork, 2012), passim.

35. John O'Donovan, letter to Daniel MacCarthy, 1 April 1848 [NLI, MS 132 (19)]. Cited in Willie Nolan, 'Land reform in post-Famine Ireland', in Crowley, Smyth and Murphy (eds), *Atlas of the Great Irish Famine*, pp 570–9 (p. 570).

36. Doyle, *A History of the Irish Language*, p. 68.

37. They wrote in a high linguistic register, known as Classical Irish, which enjoyed a prestige similar to that of Latin of the first century BCE. (Doyle, *A History of the Irish Language*, pp 25–6). For this paragraph I rely on: L. M. Cullen, 'Patrons, teachers and literacy in Irish: 1700–1850', in Daly and Dickson (eds), *Origins of Popular Literacy*, pp 15–44; Lesa Ní Mhunghaile, 'Bilingualism, print culture in Irish and the public sphere, 1700–c.1830', in James Kelly and Ciarán Mac Murchaidh (eds), *Irish and English: Essays on the Irish Linguistic and Cultural Frontier, 1600–1900* (Dublin, 2012), pp 218–42; Muireann Ní Bhrolcháin, *An Introduction to Early Irish Literature* (Dublin, 2009; reprinted 2011). Some of them chronicled the Famine in Irish, in verse or prose: see the account of first-hand witnesses given in Neil Buttimer, 'The Great Famine in Gaelic manuscripts', in Crowley, Smyth and Murphy (eds), *Atlas of the Great Irish Famine*, pp 460–72.

38. Meidhbhín Ní Úrdail, *The Scribe in Eighteenth- and Nineteenth-Century Ireland: Motivations and Milieu* (Münster, 2000), p. 30; and passim, for an account of the milieu and motivations of the Ó Longáins, a family of professional scribes that ran for four successive generations through the eighteenth and nineteenth centuries. A number of émigré Irish scribes were still active in the United States up to the second decade of the twentieth century (Meidhbhín Ní Úrdail, 'Patrick Ferriter (1856–1924): An Irish scholar at home and abroad', in *American Journal of Irish Studies* 15 (2009), 164–94). Cf. Ó Cuív, 'Irish language and literature, 1845–1921', pp 414–16.

39. Doyle, *A History of the Irish Language*, p. 144. Some of the scribes and poets also ran 'pay' (or hedge-) schools: Dowling, *The Hedge Schools of Ireland*, pp 85–6.

40. Liam Mac Mathúna, *The Ó Neachtain Window on Gaelic Dublin, 1700–1750* (Cork, 2021), pp 27–57 and passim. The Ó Neachtains' literary works reveal a vibrant and sophisticated intellectual community, creatively coping with economic and political adversity. Mac Mathúna concludes (p. 91) that 'in the skilled hands of the Ó Neachtains, the Irish language was a versatile medium, one which was capable of adapting to a wide range of registers in prose and poetry', equally at home 'in its ornate bardic inheritance' as in 'the pithy and functional documenting of current affairs'.

41. In Ireland, antiquarianism dates back to the 1740s (James Kelly, 'Irish Protestants and the Irish language in the eighteenth century', in Kelly and Mac Murchaidh (eds), *Irish and English*, pp 189–217), and curiosity about Ireland's antiquities was further fuelled by the Celtic craze following the publication in 1760 of MacPherson's *Ossian* (Doyle, *A History of the Irish Language*, pp 88–90).

42. Kelly, 'Irish Protestants and the Irish language in the eighteenth century'; Ní Mhunghaile, 'Bilingualism, print culture in Irish and the public sphere'.

43. Liam Mac Mathúna, 'Verisimilitude or subversion? Probing the interaction of English and Irish in selected warrants and macaronic verse in the eighteenth century', in Kelly and Mac Murchaidh (eds), *Irish and English*, pp 116–40; Ní Mhunghaile, 'Bilingualism, print culture in Irish and the public sphere'; Doyle, *A History of the Irish Language*, pp 85–8; Ní Úrdail, *The Scribe in Ireland*.

44. Laurie O'Higgins, *The Irish Classical Self: Poets and Poor Scholars in the Eighteenth and Nineteenth Centuries* (Oxford, 2017), pp 54–5.

45. Ní Mhunghaile, 'Bilingualism, print culture in Irish and the public sphere', pp 232–4.

46. Ibid.; Cullen, 'Patrons, teachers and literacy in Irish'.

47. Ní Mhunghaile, 'Bilingualism, print culture in Irish and the public sphere', pp 234–7.

48. Kelly, 'Irish Protestants and the Irish language in the eighteenth century', p. 216.

49. Ó Ciosáin, 'Printed popular literature in Irish'; Niall Ó Ciosáin, 'Pious miscellanies and spiritual songs: Devotional publishing and reading in Irish and Scottish Gaelic, 1760–1900', in Kelly and Mac Murchaidh (eds), *Irish and English*, pp 267–82; Dáithí Ó hÓgáin, 'Folklore and literature in Ireland: 1700–1850', in Daly and Dickson (eds), *Origins of Popular Literacy*, pp 1–13 (pp 3–5). Poetic

compositions in traditional metre were slow to disappear over the nineteenth century (Ó Cuív, 'Irish language and literature, 1845–1921', p. 424).

50. Declan Kiberd, Editorial, in *The Crane Bag* 5 (2) [*The Irish Language and Culture*], (1981; 1982 reprint), pp 835–7 (p. 835): 'When Douglas Hyde founded the Gaelic League in 1893, he discovered to his horror that there were only six books in Irish print throughout the country.' Irish writing in English could be published in Dublin or in London, making it part of a worldwide market.

51. Vivian Mercier, *Modern Irish Literature: Sources and Founders*, edited and presented by Eilís Dillon (Oxford, 1994), p. 46. Similarly, the minuscule amount of Irish language journalism, in contrast with the Victorian English-language press, is itself an indicator of low monoglot Irish literacy. On journalism in the Irish language, see Regina Uí Chollatáin, 'Newspapers, journals and the Irish revival', in Kevin Rafter (ed.), *Irish Journalism Before Independence: More a Disease Than a Profession* (Manchester, 2011), pp 160–73.

52. Christopher Stray, 'The shift from oral to written examination: Cambridge and Oxford 1700–1900', in *Assessment in Education: Principles, Policy & Practice* 8 (2001), pp 33–50; *The Book of Trinity College Dublin, 1591–1891: Tercentenary Celebration Presented by the Provost and Senior Fellows of Trinity College, Dublin, July 1892* (Dublin, 1892), pp 123–4.

53. *Report of the President of Queen's College Cork*, 1859–60, p. 29.

54. On the complexities of the 'script–print dialectic', see Ní Úrdail, *The Scribe in Ireland*, pp 221–5.

55. Ó Ciosáin, 'Printed popular literature in Irish', pp 48–9.

56. Cullen, 'Patrons, teachers and literacy in Irish', pp 39–40.

57. Ó Madagáin, 'Irish: A difficult birth', p. 353; Murphy, *The College*, p. 150; Moody and Beckett, *Queen's, Belfast*, vol. 1, p. 412.

58. Census data show illiteracy levels in Ireland falling from 53 per cent in 1841 to 14 per cent in 1901 (John Coolahan, *Irish Education: Its History and Structure* (Dublin, 1981), p. 7).

59. 'La Sorbonne au XIXe siècle: Le temps des grands travaux sous la Troisième République', website of the Sorbonne, https://www.sorbonne.fr/la-sorbonne/histoire-de-la-sorbonne/la-sorbonne-au-xixe-siecle-le-temps-des-grands-travaux-sous-la-troisieme-republique/, 11 November 2023.

60. William Riley Parker, 'Where do English departments come from?', in *College English* 28 (1967), pp 339–51 (p. 345); Alan Bacon, 'English literature becomes a university subject: King's College, London as pioneer', in *Victorian Studies* 29 (1986), pp 591–612. Bacon argues that F. D. Maurice, one of the earliest promoters of English literature, who taught it at King's College London from 1840 to 1853, can be seen as a forerunner of Matthew Arnold. He valued vernacular literature as particularly suitable for the middle classes, and for promoting English national consciousness as well as social cohesion.

61. Ó Madagáin, 'Irish: A difficult birth', p. 344. For Glasgow, see 'The Gaelic story at the University of Glasgow', https://sgeulnagaidhlig.ac.uk/20th-c-department-of-celtic/?lang=en#, 5 September 2023.

62. Donald E. Meek, '*Beachdan Ura à Inbhir Nis*/New Opinions from Inverness: Alexander Mac Bain (1855–1907) and the foundation of Celtic Studies in Scotland', in *Proceedings of the Society of Antiquaries in Scotland* 131 (2001), pp 23–39.

63. Moody and Beckett, *Queen's, Belfast*, vol. 1, pp xlv–xlvi.

64. C. G. Buttimer, 'Celtic and Irish in College 1849–1944', p. 89.

65. Ó Madagáin, 'Irish: A difficult birth', pp 345–8.

66. One exception in this regard was the output of John O'Daly (1800–78), who published some traditional verse in Irish with no English translation. Cf. Mercier, *Modern Irish Literature*, pp 26–7; Ó Cuív, 'Irish language and literature, 1845–1921', pp 398–9.

67. Doyle, *A History of the Irish Language*, p. 139; Ní Úrdail, *The Scribe in Ireland*, pp 200–04.

68. Ó Cuív, 'Irish language and literature, 1845–1921', pp 396–7. On the Academy Scribe Seosamh Ó Longáin (*d.*1880), see Ní Úrdail, *The Scribe in Ireland*, pp 119–33.

69. See below, Chapter Six, pp 144–7.

70. An example of a pre-Darwinian may be seen in Jean-Baptiste Lamarck, the French botanist (1744–1829).

71. On Zeuss, see D. Ellis Evans, 'The heroic age of Celtic philology', in *Zeitschrift für Celtische Philologie* 54 (2005), pp 1–30 (pp 6–8); Dáibhí Ó Cróinín, 'Johann Caspar Zeuss (1806–56)', *Irish Times* ('An Irishman's Diary'), 7 August 2006; Charles Dillon, '"Ability and industry scarcely credible": Johann Kaspar Zeuss and *Grammatica Celtica*', blog post, RIA website, 3 April 2017; Ó Cuív, 'Irish language and literature, 1845–1921', pp 397–8.

72. John O'Donovan and Jakob Grimm, 'Zeuss's *Grammatica Celtica*', in *Ulster Journal of Archaeology* 7 (1859), pp 11–32 (p. 14).

73. For an overview of the emerging branch of linguistic study concerned with Celtic languages, see Evans, 'The heroic age of Celtic philology'.

74. Newman's *Memorandum* to synod, 1854, cited in Fergal McGrath, SJ, *Newman's University: Idea and Reality* (Dublin, 1951), p. 298. The CUI was to serve the same purpose for the 'English tongue' as that served for French by the Université Catholique de Louvain. On Paul Cullen's view of Louvain's Catholic University as the template for Ireland to follow, see Colin Barr, *Paul Cullen, John Henry Newman, and the Catholic University of Ireland, 1845–1865* (South Bend and Leominster, 2003), pp 76–8.

75. McGrath, *Newman's University*, p. 305.

76. Ibid., p. 321 n. 1.

77. Diarmuid Ó Catháin, 'O'Curry (Curry, Ó Comhraí), Eugene (Eoghan)', DIB; cf. 'Papers of Eugene O'Curry (1796–1862)', biographical section, https://digital.ucd.ie/view/ivrla:2620 (5 April 2021). See also Bernadette Cunningham, 'A candle for Eugene O'Curry or the cataloguer's revenge', blog post, RIA website, 19 July 2017.

78. Mercier, *Modern Irish Literature*, p. 12. According to one estimate of O'Curry's Ordnance Survey work (1835–42), he consulted about 30,000 pages of manuscript (Ó Catháin, 'O'Curry, Eugene').

79. Henri Gaidoz, review of 'On the manners and customs of the Ancient Irish [Des mœurs et des coutumes des Anciens Irlandais]', in *Revue Celtique* 2 (1873–5), pp 260–4 (p. 261). [My translation.]

80. Vivian Mercier sees O'Curry's 1863 volume 'without exaggeration as the prime source book of the Literary Revival': Mercier, *Modern Irish Literature*, pp 16–19 (p. 16).

81. His chair at Queen's College Belfast is not even mentioned in the NLI blog on him; Mercier (*Modern Irish Literature*, p. 12) describes the post as 'an honorary position'. He did deliver annual public evening lectures in Belfast, free of charge, on the language, laws and customs of the ancient Irish (Moody and Beckett, *Queen's, Belfast*, vol. 1, p. 170).

82. On Connellan: Paul Rouse, 'Connellan, Owen (1800–69)', DIB. For a sense of his scholarship as seen in his correspondence with the antiquarian John Windele, see Denis O'Leary, 'The first professor of Irish in QCC', in *Cork University Review* 8 (1947), pp 37–44. On O'Beirne Crowe: Ó Madagáin, 'Irish: A difficult birth', pp 351–3; Diarmuid Breathnach and Máire Ní Mhurchú, 'Crowe, John O'Beirne (*c*.1824–74)', ainm.ie.

83. Barr, *Cullen, Newman, and the CUI*, p. 209.

84. In some respects Ireland's early Celtic professors echo the achievements, despite adversity, of Alexander Mac Bain, the scholarly Inverness headmaster portrayed by Donald Meek as 'the finest Professor of Celtic that Scotland never had' (Meek, '*Beachdan Ura à Inbhir Nis*', p. 36).

85. RIA ms, cited in Breandán Ó Buachalla, *I mBéal Feirste Cois Cuain*, p. 239.

86. John O'Beirne Crowe, 'The Catholic University and the Irish language' (pamphlet, dated Belfast, 1854; printed in Dublin, 1865), p. 7. He apparently tried to have the pamphlet suppressed shortly after he wrote it, not long after taking his Belfast degree (Breathnach and Ní Mhurchú, 'Crowe, John O'Beirne').

87. Could this element of compulsion be based on his own experience of the Queen's Colleges' modern languages requirement for undergraduates?

88. O'Beirne Crowe, 'The Catholic University and the Irish language', p. 15.

89. Ibid., p. 6.

90. Elizabeth Boyle and Paul Russell (eds), *The Tripartite Life of Whitley Stokes (1830–1909)* (Dublin, 2011), p. 3 n. 10. Cf. the eulogistic obituary of Stokes by Richard Henebry, 'Whitley Stokes', in *The Celtic Review* 6 (1909), pp 65–85.

91. Ó Cuív, 'Irish language and literature, 1845–1921', pp 394–5.

92. P. J. (later Sir Patrick) Keenan, report to the National Education Board, from Donegal, 1857. Cited in Ó Cuív, 'Irish language and literature, 1845–1921', p. 395.

93. James Tully: see above, p. 83.

94. Ó Cuív, 'Irish language and literature, 1845–1921', p. 392. There were of course individual bishops and priests who used and valued Irish.

95. Farmar, *The History of Irish Book Publishing*, p. 29; Doyle, *A History of the Irish Language*, pp 46–7.

96. Niall Ó Ciosáin, 'Printed popular literature in Irish', pp 51–2.

97. Translated from Hebrew, Aramaic and Greek, by Pádraig Ó Fiannachta, published by An Sagart, Maynooth.

98. Jacqueline Hill, 'Whitley Stokes Senior (1763–1845) and his political, religious and cultural milieux', in Boyle and Russell (eds), *Whitley Stokes*, pp 14–28 (pp 16–25). Whitley Stokes senior, Professor of Medicine in Trinity, was the grandfather of the Celtic scholar. He was a member of the Irish Society.

99. Henry Joseph Monck Mason, *History of the Origin and Progress of the Irish Society, Established for Promoting the Education of the Native Irish, Through the Medium of Their Own Language* (2nd edn, Dublin, 1846), p. 8.

100. Ibid., pp 5–6.

101. Ibid., p. 10. He adds, significantly, that, after three or four years in the field the Society noticed that learners who had mastered the art of reading Irish were now keen to learn how to read English as well. The Society printed its Irish works in phonetic English spelling; it made a collection of translated sermons in 1847 (Ó Cuív, 'Irish language and literature, 1845–1921', p. 393).

102. See the evidence cited in Doyle, *A History of the Irish Language*, pp 120–3.

103. For an account of the activities and difficulties of one of these societies, in County Louth in the 1830s, see Seán Duffy, 'Antiquarianism and Gaelic Revival in County Louth in the pre-Famine era', in *Journal of the County Louth Archaeological and Historical Society* 21 (1988), pp 343–68.

104. Doyle, *A History of the Irish Language*, pp 138–40; Roger Blaney, *Presbyterians and the Irish Language* (Belfast, 1996), pp 56–63.

105. For religious reasons it was customary for Irish Presbyterians to go to Scotland rather than Trinity College Dublin for their university education.

106. Ó Saothraí, Séamas, 'William Neilson DD MRIA (1774–1821)', in *Journal of the County Louth Archaeological and Historical Society* 22 (1989), pp 20–8; Ó Buachalla, *I mBéal Feirste Cois Cuain*, pp 59–64; David Murphy, 'Neilson, William (Mac Néill, Uilliam)', DIB; Kate Newmann, 'William Neilson (1774–1821): Teacher and writer', http://www.newulsterbiography.co.uk/index.php/home/viewPerson/1239, 23 March 2021. On the Belfast Academical Institution before the founding of Queen's College Belfast, see Moody and Beckett, *Queen's, Belfast*, vol. 1, pp xliv–liii.

107. For Irish language historians it reveals the variety of Irish then spoken in south-east Ulster. Its modern Irish pages are printed in aspirated roman fount. (Ó Saothraí, 'William Neilson', p. 26); Blaney, *Presbyterians and the Irish Language*, p. 58; Ní Úrdail, *The Scribe in Ireland*, p. 224 n. 117). It uses Gaelic fount for the shorter Part III, 'Extracts from Irish books and manuscripts.'

108. Doyle, *A History of the Irish Language*, pp 154–5.

109. Haliday wrote under the assumed name of Edmond O'Connell.; for biographical information, see https://en.m.wikisource.org/wiki/Dictionary_of_National_Biography,_1885-1900/Haliday,_William, and Eoghan Ó Raghallaigh, 'Haliday, William', DIB', 3 April 2021. Like Neilson, Haliday works from the alphabet and sound system to more complex syntactic structures; brief quotations from ancient texts are used to illustrate the latter, and his lists of common phrases, or 'Dialogues', laid out in two columns of English and Irish (pp 134–54), are perfunctory. The Irish is printed in a Gaelic fount, and the book includes a section on Prosody. See his work on https://digital.nls.uk/108990860.

110. William Neilson, *An Introduction to the Irish Language* (Dublin, 1808), Part II, p. 46.

111. Ibid., pp 46/47–60/61: '*Brian Gaḃa*/Bryan the Blacksmith'.

112. Ibid., pp 60/61–84/85: '*Teaċ oiḋeaċta tuaiḋte*/The Country Inn'.

113. Ibid., pp 64/65. Neilson had lived through the 1798 insurrection in Dundalk, during which he was wrongly arrested after preaching in Irish. He may have been mistakenly linked to Samuel Neilson of the United Irishmen (Ó Saothraí, 'William Neilson', pp 22–3).

114. On Counter-Reformation burial rites and their impact on the Irish landscape, see Kevin Whelan, *Religion, Landscape and Settlement in Ireland: From Patrick to the Present* (Dublin, 2018), pp 82–106 (pp 86–9 for wayside stone cairns).

115. Neilson, *An Introduction*, Part II, pp 68/69–84/85.

116. Ibid., Notes to Part II, p. 88.

117. See John Gallagher, *Learning Languages in Early Modern England* (Oxford, 2019), pp 55–100; cf. Nicola McLelland, *German Through English Eyes: A History of Language Teaching and Learning in Britain, 1500–2000* (Wiesbaden, 2015), pp 24–5; and Nicola McLelland, *Teaching and Learning Foreign Languages: A History of Language Education, Assessment and Policy in Britain* (London and New York, 2017; pbk edn, 2018), p. 49.

118. This was not Neilson's only language-learning book. His 1804 *Greek Exercises in Syntax, Ellipsis, Dialects, Prosody and Metaphrasis* ran to eight editions by 1846. His Irish grammar, published by subscription, and used, presumably, by his pupils in Dundalk and later Belfast, ran to two editions (1808 and 1843). The demand for modern Irish was not as high as for ancient Greek.

119. Doyle, *A History of the Irish Language*, p. 154.

120. Paul O'Brien, *A Practical Grammar of the Irish Language* (Dublin, 1809). This was commissioned by Maynooth as a reference grammar for clerical students.

121. The years covered run from 1171 to 1188 CE (Owen Connellan, *A Practical Grammar of the Irish Language* (Dublin, 1844), pp 125–8). As a translator of the Annals into English, Connellan was very familiar with the subject matter.

122. Neilson's Part III, 'Extracts from Irish books and manuscripts', conforms to expectations; it includes extracts from the Bible and the Deirdre legend in old script. It is much briefer than the other sections, as if the author had run out of steam.

123. Connellan, *A Practical Grammar*, Preface, p. 8.

124. Until 1849 the school was located at Stackallan House, County Meath, before moving to the location it still occupies in the hills of south county Dublin.

125. 'Address of the President, on presenting the gold medals to Sir William R. Hamilton, to the Revd Samuel Haughton, to the Revd Edward Hincks, DD, and John O'Donovan, Esq.', in *Proceedings of the Royal Irish Academy (1836–1869)* 4 (1847–50), pp 193–210 (p. 208).

126. Connellan, *A Practical Grammar*, loc. cit.

127. Neilson, *An Introduction*, p. x.

128. Ibid., pp x–xi.

129. On cultured travel motivating foreign-language learning, see McLelland, *Teaching and Learning Foreign Languages*, pp 49–50.

130. Personal communication from the late Eilís Dillon, referring to the Victorian travels in Italy of her grandfather, the art historian George Noble, Count Plunkett.

131. Neilson, *An Introduction*, pp 46/47.

132. Ibid., p. xi.

133. The Irish Language Act, announced on 18 June 2021, shows how Irish can provoke or reflect political polarisation in Northern Ireland: see, for example, Susan McKay, 'The DUP has a new leader, but language is still Northern Ireland's sticking point', *The Guardian*, 24 June 2021.

134. Ó Saothraí, 'William Neilson', pp 27–8. Ó Buachalla, *I mBéal Feirste Cois Cuain*, amply illustrates how Belfast was a thriving centre for enlightened cultural and language revivalists in the early nineteenth century. Cf. *Belfast Literary Society 1801–1901* [Centenary Volume] (Belfast, 1902).

135. These notions of sparing the rod and encouraging play in elementary schooling foreshadowed some of the educational ideas propounded by reformers like Locke, Rousseau or Lancaster. On Manson, see 'Life of David Manson', in *The Belfast Monthly Magazine* 6 (1811), pp 126–32; Richard Froggatt, 'David Manson (1726–1792): Teacher', NUB, http://www.newulsterbiography.co.uk/index.php/home/viewPerson/1124, 24 March 2022; and Linde Lunney, 'Manson, David', DIB.

136. Moody and Beckett, *Queen's, Belfast*, vol. 1, pp xliv–liii (pp xlvi–xlvii). Cf. Ó Buachalla, *I mBéal Feirste Cois Cuain*, pp 46–8, on the Institution's mission to promote the pursuit of useful knowledge for all, in a spirit of harmony and tolerance. Some of its staff members defended their freedom of thought unwisely when, in 1816 on St Patrick's Day, they raised a glass to France and the Revolution. Their grant was withdrawn for a decade (ibid., p. 64). It became the '*Royal Belfast Academical Institution*' in 1831 and is the ancestor of today's grammar school locally known as 'Inst'.

137. Duffy, 'Antiquarianism and Gaelic Revival', p. 357; Blaney, *Presbyterians and the Irish Language*, p. 76.

138. This is asserted, and illustrated, by many of the contributors to Nicola McLelland and Richard Smith (eds), *The History of Language Learning and Teaching* (3 vols, Cambridge, 2018). See in particular Sabine Doff, '"Let girls chat about the weather and walks": English language education at girls' secondary schools in nineteenth-century Germany', vol. 2, pp 87–97 (p. 91).

139. Connellan, *A Practical Grammar*, Preface [one page long, np].

140. Doyle, *A History of the Irish Language*, p. 171.

CHAPTER 5: THE MODERN IRISH BATTLEGROUND

1. Matthew Arnold, *On the Study of Celtic Literature* (London, 1867), p. 24.

2. Douglas Hyde, 'The necessity for de-Anglicising Ireland', lecture to Irish National Literary Society (Dublin, 1892); extract in Seamus Deane (ed.), *The Field Day Anthology*, vol. 2, pp 527–33 (p. 532).

3. Cited in Stanford and McDowell, *Mahaffy: A Biography of an Anglo-Irishman* (London, 1971), p. 109.

4. L. M. Moriarty, 'Some notes on methods and aims of modern language teaching in public schools', in *The Modern Quarterly of Language and Literature* 1 (1899), pp 326–30.

5. F. S. L. Lyons, 'George Moore and Edward Martyn', in *Hermathena: a Dublin University Review* 98 (1964), pp 9–29.

6. Vivian Mercier, *Modern Irish Literature: Sources and Founders*, edited and presented by Eilís Dillon (Oxford, 1994), p. 26.

7. R. V. Comerford, 'The politics of distress, 1877–82', in W. E. Vaughan (ed.), *A New History of Ireland, VI, Ireland under the Union, II: 1870–1921* (Oxford, 1996), pp 26–52; Willie Nolan, 'Land reform in post-Famine Ireland', in John Crowley, William J. Smyth and Mike Murphy (eds), *Atlas of the Great Irish Famine, 1845–52* (Cork, 2012), pp 570–9. Members of the established church had held 'a virtual monopoly of power and wealth in the island. By 1775 only 5% of the land of Ireland was still retained by the three-quarters of its inhabitants who were Roman Catholics': Garret FitzGerald, *Reflections on the Irish State* (Dublin, 2003), p. 138. Such statistics reveal the magnitude of the land redistribution initiative.

8. It may be pertinent that Scottish Gaelic had just been admitted as a school subject in the Highlands (Adeline Tissier-Moston, 'The campaign for the recognition of the Irish language in National Schools (1878–1904)', in Wesley Hutchinson and Clíona Ní Ríordáin (eds), *Language Issues: Ireland, France, Spain* (Brussels, 2010), pp 91–103 (p. 97 n. 17).

9. Séamas Ó Buachalla, 'Educational policy and the role of the Irish language from 1831 to 1981', in *European Journal of Education* 19 (1984), pp 75–92 (p. 78): From 1878 'to the end of the century the number of schools seldom rose above 1% of the total and the total number of pupils examined never exceeded 2000 out of a total enrolment of 800,000'.

10. Brian Ó Cuív, 'Irish language and literature, 1845–1921', in Vaughan (ed.), *New History of Ireland, VI*, pp 385–435; Aidan Doyle, *A History of the Irish Language: From the Norman Invasion to Independence* (Oxford, 2015), pp 165–7; Ó Buachalla, 'Educational policy', pp 77–9; Nóirín Ní Nuadháin, 'The teaching of Irish 1900–1926: Influences from abroad reflected in proposed methodologies and textbooks', unpublished postgraduate thesis in Applied Linguistics, Trinity College Dublin, 1983–4, p. 52.

11. Clare Sargent, 'The Fellows of St. Columba's College, Stackallan', https://victorianweb.org/history/education/stcolumba/1.html, and 'Singleton, Sewell and the ideal of a school: St Columba's College, Stackallan and St Peter's College, Radley', https://victorianweb.org/history/education/radley/ideals.html, both accessed 31 March 2021; Ciaran O'Neill, *Catholics of Consequence: Transnational Education, Social Mobility, and the Irish Catholic Elite 1850–1900* (Oxford, 2014), pp 10–11.

12. Ó Cuív, 'Irish language and literature', mentions the Catholic diocesan college of St Jarlath in Tuam and a Galway school endowed by James Hardiman (p. 396 n. 3), and refers to Irish being introduced into schools in County Clare in the 1860s, due to the advocacy of William Smith O'Brien (p. 398 n. 2).

13. Eugène Berbach opted to take Celtic instead of mathematics (which he found difficult, being accustomed to decimal measurement). Later, as a priest, he taught Irish in Blackrock. See Seán P. Farragher, CSSp, *The French College Blackrock 1860–1896* (Dublin, 2011), p. 336, p. 366.

14. *Minutes of the French College Debating Society*, 2 November 1902. The first speaker compared the revival of Irish to the recent restoration of the 'language of Bohemia' (Czech). (Blackrock College Archives.) Cf. Farragher, *The French College Blackrock 1860–1896*, pp 524, 538.

15. Tomás Ó Fiaich, 'The great controversy', in Seán Ó Tuama (ed.), *The Gaelic League Idea*, RTÉ Thomas Davis Lectures 1968–9 (Cork, 1972), pp 63–75 (pp 66–7). By 1899, ten boys' schools, all run by the Christian Brothers, 'had a dozen or more pupils presenting Irish at the four State examinations' (ibid., p. 66). Almost all of the passing female candidates in the 1899 Intermediate Examination were attending St Louis Monaghan.

16. Tony Fahey, 'Nuns in the Catholic Church in Ireland in the nineteenth century', in Mary Cullen (ed.), *Girls Don't Do Honours* (Dublin, 1987), pp 7–30 (p. 23).

17. Doyle, *A History of the Irish Language*, p. 168.

18. Nicola McLelland, 'The history of language learning and teaching in Britain', in *The Language Learning Journal* 46 (2018), pp 6–16 (pp 11–12). On the reform movement, see below, pp 115–16.

19. Doyle, *A History of the Irish Language*, p. 169.

20. Mary Robinson, 'Douglas Hyde (1860–1949): The Trinity connection', in *Hermathena (Quatercentenary Papers)* (1992), pp 17–26 (p. 19); cf. Corinna Salvadori, '*Dove 'l sì sona*: two hundred and thirty years of Italian in Trinity College Dublin', in Cormac Ó Cuilleanáin, Corinna Salvadori and John Scattergood (eds), *Italian Culture: Interactions, Transpositions, Translations* (Dublin, 2006), pp 13–28 (p. 20).

21. Robinson, 'Douglas Hyde', p. 19. Mary Robinson, Ireland's first woman president, is also a distinguished lawyer; she served as Reid Professor of Constitutional and Criminal Law at Trinity from 1969 to 1975.

22. See above, p. 101. For an account of Hyde's formative years, see Doyle, *A History of the Irish Language*, pp 170–7.

23. Douglas Hyde, 'The necessity for de-anglicising Ireland', p. 528.

24. Ibid., p. 533.

25. Doyle, *A History of the Irish Language*, p. 178. In 1893, very few younger people in Ireland could speak Irish.

26. Ó Cuív, 'Irish language and literature', p. 403. The revelation of Parnell's affair with Mrs Katharine O'Shea and their subsequent marriage had split his party in two and scandalised Catholic opinion.

27. By 1907, there were 599 branches, of which only 34 were Dublin-based (ibid.). Branches in London and New York ran Irish classes and cultural activities for Irish expatriates. On Hyde's successful lecturing and fundraising tours in the United States (1905–6), see Liam Mac Mathúna, 'Douglas Hyde's intellectual links with John Quinn, Lady Gregory and W.B. Yeats', in Liam Mac Mathúna and Máire Nic an Bhaird (eds), *Douglas Hyde: Irish Ideology and International Impact* (*Éigse: A Journal of Irish Studies*, Occasional Publications 3) (Dublin, 2023), pp 51–78 (pp 73–5).

28. On the success of the League's early Oireachtas folklore competitions see Philip O'Leary, '*Seanchuidhthe, Séadna*, Sheehan, and the "Zeitgeist": Folklore and folklife in Gaelic fiction of the early revival', in *Proceedings of the Harvard Celtic Colloquium* 9 (1989), pp 43–99 (pp 44–5).

29. Doyle, *A History of the Irish Language*, p. 188.

30. Aoife Whelan, '*Irish Independent* coverage of Douglas Hyde's vision for a de-anglicised Ireland', in Mac Mathúna and Nic an Bhaird (eds), *Douglas Hyde*, pp 79–97 (pp 95–6).

31. 'More intrigue', *An Claidheamh Soluis*, 25 January 1902.

32. Whelan, '*Irish Independent* coverage of Douglas Hyde's vision for a de-anglicised Ireland'.

33. Ní Nuadháin, 'The teaching of Irish 1900–1926', pp 11, 64; Ó Buachalla, 'Educational policy', pp 79, 80. It is perhaps relevant that Dr Starkie was a distinguished Greek scholar, who had served for two years as President of University College Galway, as well as holding chairs in English Literature and History, and Moral Science; he was Roman Catholic (Arthur Keaveney, 'Classics in Victorian Galway', in Tadhg Foley (ed.), *From Queen's College to National University* (Dublin, 1999), pp 326–43 (pp 330–1); and Tadhg Foley and Fiona Bateman, 'English, history, and philosophy', in Foley (ed.), *From Queen's College to National University*, pp 384–420 (pp 395–6).) His son Walter was Trinity's professor of Spanish and lecturer in Italian literature, and his daughter Enid, Reader in French Literature at Somerville College, Oxford, was a distinguished biographer of Baudelaire, Rimbaud and Flaubert. Starkie's sympathy for the cultural importance of language study sprang from deep personal conviction and the revivalists' disinterestedness impressed him.

34. P. J. Mathews, 'Hyde's first stand: The Irish language controversy of 1899', in *Éire/Ireland* 35 (2000), pp 173–87 (pp 173–4).

35. W. B. Stanford and R. B. McDowell, *Mahaffy: A Biography of an Anglo-Irishman* (London, 1971), pp 104–5. Cf. David Greene, 'Robert Atkinson and Irish studies', in *Hermathena* 102 (1966), pp 6–15; Mathews, 'Hyde's first stand'; Ó Fiaich, 'The great controversy', pp 66–70.

36. Cited in Stanford and McDowell, *Mahaffy*, p. 109. In a previous essay (1882), Mahaffy had referred to Irish as an 'out-of-the-way and troublesome language' (ibid., p. 105).

37. Matthew Arnold, *On the Study of Celtic Literature* (London, 1867), p. 12, cited in Alan Bliss, 'The standardization of Irish', in *The Crane Bag* 5 (2) [*The Irish Language and Culture*], (1981; 1982 reprint), pp 908–14 (p. 908).

38. Mathews, 'Hyde's first stand', pp 177–8, argues that Atkinson's attack betrays an imperialist prejudice typical of colonial print-capitalist cultures. Aidan Doyle points out that the *Pursuit of Diarmuid and Gráinne* text, then on the syllabus, was unsuitable for use in secondary schools, not because of its depraved morality, but rather because of its fiendish linguistic difficulty (Doyle, *A History of the Irish Language*, p. 183). On Atkinson as an Irish scholar, see Greene, 'Robert Atkinson and Irish studies', and on Mahaffy's trenchant attitudes regarding Irish, see Stanford and McDowell, *Mahaffy*, pp 104–12.

39. The transcript of the Vice-Regal Inquiry was published as 'The Irish language and Irish intermediate education', Gaelic League pamphlets 13, 15 and 16 (Dublin, 1901); pamphlet 16 carried Hyde's written memorandum lodged in response to Atkinson. This document appended verbatim letters from Georges Dottin in Rennes, Ernst Windisch in Leipzig, Holger Pedersen in Copenhagen, Heinrich Zimmer in Greifswald, Christian Stern in Berlin, Alfred Nutt in London, Owen Edwards in Oxford, Kuno Meyer in Liverpool. Hyde's evidence to the Inquiry, 60 pages in all, was by far the longest (Mathews, 'Hyde's first stand', p. 175 n. 7).

40. Máirtín Ó Murchú, 'Irish language studies in Trinity College Dublin', in *Hermathena (Quatercentenary Papers)* (1992), pp 43–68 (pp 61–4), gives a brief account of the five appointments to the Divinity Irish chair and makes a plea for their reappraisal: Thomas de Vere Coneys, from County Mayo (1840); Daniel Foley, from County Kerry (1852); Thaddeus O'Mahony, from County Cork (1861); James (Séamas) Goodman, also a Kerryman (1879); James E. Murphy, from the Beare peninsula in County Cork (1896). Goodman displayed a keen interest in Irish language and music (Ó Cuív, 'Irish language and literature', p. 393).

41. R. B. McDowell and D. A. Webb, *Trinity College Dublin 1592–1952: An Academic History* (Cambridge, 1982), pp 363–5; Stanford and McDowell, *Mahaffy*, pp 104–12. Mathews, 'Hyde's first stand' (p. 186), observes that the controversy also pointed to a generational divide in Trinity, between older dons, entrenched in a colonial mindset, and younger intellectuals with other ideas. The Senior Fellows were an ageing constituency: by 1897, the youngest of them was aged 70 (Stanford and McDowell, *Mahaffy*, p. 194).

42. Hyde eventually resigned his presidency in 1915, when the organisation explicitly aligned itself with the struggle for political independence. See Doyle, *A History of the Irish Language*, pp 205–10; and Earnán de Blaghd, 'Hyde in conflict', in Ó Tuama (ed.), *The Gaelic League Idea*, pp 31–40.

43. Doyle, *A History of the Irish Language*, p. 183.

44. Brendan Walsh, '"Frankly and robustly national": Padraig Pearse, the Gaelic League and the campaign for Irish at the National University', in *Studies* 103 (2014), pp 318–30; R. F. Foster, *Vivid Faces: The Revolutionary Generation in Ireland 1890–1923* (London, 2014), pp 58–9. Cork's student body in the 1900s had more mixed views on the Irish Question. Cornelius G. Buttimer, 'Celtic and Irish in College 1849–1944', in *Journal of the Cork Historical and Archaeological Society* 94 (1989), pp 88–112 (pp 96–7). The Cork College's Academic Council voted against compulsory Irish, favouring instead matriculation with no compulsory subjects (Donal McCartney, 'University College Dublin', in Tom Dunne et al. (eds), *The National University of Ireland Centenary Essays* (Dublin, 2008), pp 87–99 (p. 91)).

45. Walsh, 'Frankly and robustly national', p. 324.

46. Walsh, 'Frankly and robustly national', p. 323.

47. R.A.S. Macalister in Celtic archaeology, Eoin MacNeill in early Irish history, Douglas Hyde in modern Irish and Osborn Bergin in early Irish.

48. See above, pp 83–93.

49. McDowell and Webb, *Trinity College Dublin*, p. 517 n. 20.

50. Ibid., p. 191. Irish was added to Trinity's Modern Languages Moderatorship in 1927 (ibid., p. 448).

51. Walsh, 'Frankly and robustly national', p. 325. Cf. Ó Cuív, 'Irish language and literature', pp 402–12, for an account of the League's achievements; and Ó Tuama (ed.), *The Gaelic League Idea*.

52. Mathews, 'Hyde's first stand', p. 181. Cf. Ó Cuív, 'Irish language and literature', p. 407: 'In 1890 only 18 out of 230 boys who sat for the senior grade examination (that is, 7.8 per cent) took Irish. By 1900 the proportion had risen slightly to 25 out of 309 (8.1 per cent). But in 1910 the situation was

very different for by then the figures were 295 out of 550 (53.6 per cent), and by 1919 805 out of 1,116 (72.1 per cent).'

53. See for example the account in Doyle, *A History of the Irish Language*, pp 187–200.

54. The tourism represented by middle-class Dubliners heading west to practise Irish on the Aran islands echoes the Ulstermen venturing across the Shannon in William Neilson's Irish-language dialogues.

55. James Joyce, *Dubliners* (Harmondsworth, 1914; 1956 reprint), pp 178, 186–7.

56. 'But she had no right to call him a West Briton before people, even in joke.' (Ibid., p. 188.) A *Dublin Daily Express* ran from 1851 to 1921.

57. *An Claidheamh Soluis*, 19 October 1907. Cited in Doyle, *A History of the Irish Language*, p. 200.

58. Ríona Nic Congáil (ed.), Úna Ní Fhaircheallaigh [Agnes O'Farrelly], *Smaointe ar Árainn* [Thoughts on Aran] (Dublin, 2010), pp 74–5, 77. Agnes O'Farrelly first published her diary about life on Inis Meáin in 1902. Some of the most eminent exponents of Ireland's island cultures have been scholars from abroad. Nic Congáil points out (pp 77–83) the two-way influence between islanders and visitors. On O'Farrelly, see below, pp 112, 170, 173, 175, 180–2.

59. Ruth Dudley Edwards, *Patrick Pearse: The Triumph of Failure* (London, 1977; pbk edn 1979), p. 108 and passim. Students he taught at UCD found him awkward and earnest; James Joyce, who was one of them, found him boring and took to learning Norwegian instead (ibid., p. 29).

60. Séamas Ó Buachalla (ed.), *A Significant Irish Educationalist: The Educational Writings of P.H. Pearse* (Cork, 1980), p. xxiv.

61. P. H. Pearse [Pádrac MacPiarais], '"Education" in the West of Ireland', *Guth na Bliadhna* (Edinburgh, 1905), reprinted in Ó Buachalla (ed.), *A Significant Irish Educationalist*, pp 313–16.

62. Ó Buachalla (ed.), *A Significant Irish Educationalist*, p. x.

63. Honor O Brolchain, *Joseph Plunkett* (Dublin, 2012), pp 137–68. He was also involved with the Irish Esperanto Association founded in September 1907 (ibid., pp 64–5).

64. Ibid., pp 80–1, 84–5, and 93–100 (pp 97–8).

65. Lawrence William White, 'MacDonagh, Thomas', DIB. He taught French, Latin and English at Rockwell College, and History, English and French at St Kieran's Kilkenny.

66. Caitriona Beaumont, 'How a photograph uncovered my grandmother's republican activism during the Irish revolution', *The Conversation.com*, 17 October 2022. McGavock was a founding teacher at the Irish-language school, Scoil Bhríde.

67. Margaret Mac Curtain [Sister Benevenuta], 'St Mary's University College', in *University Review* 3 (1964), pp 33–47 (p. 42). The 'Literary Academy' was founded in 1889.

68. Nic Congáil (ed.), *Smaointe ar Árainn*, p. 73. O'Farrelly requested that the teaching of Irish be provided in the college.

69. There was a reciprocal agreement between the three ancient universities of Dublin, Oxford and Cambridge, whereby a person deemed to have met the degree requirements at one university could take out the degree in either of the other two. The fact that Trinity College Dublin admitted women in 1904 brought an influx of Oxbridge women graduates who turned up on the mailboat to collect their parchment at a Commencements ceremony the following day. The scheme proved so popular that Trinity was accused of selling its degrees and the College discontinued it after three years. Appropriately, the moneys were sufficient to be put towards setting up the women's residence at Trinity Hall. (Susan M. Parkes, 'The "steamboat ladies", the First World War and after', in Susan M. Parkes (ed.), *A Danger to the Men? A History of Women in Trinity College Dublin 1904–2004* (Dublin, 2004), pp 87–112.) Cf. McDowell and Webb, *Trinity College Dublin*, pp 351–2.

70. Susan M. Parkes, 'The first decade, 1904–14: A quiet revolution', in Parkes (ed.), *A Danger to the Men?*, pp 55–86 (pp 75–8).

71. Mathews, 'Hyde's first stand', p. 182.

72. Hyde, in *Munster News*, 7 July 1909. Quoted in Andreas Hüther, 'A transnational nation-building process: philologists and universities in nineteenth-century Ireland and Germany', in Leon Litvack and Colin Graham (eds), *Ireland and Europe in the Nineteenth Century* (Dublin, 2006), p. 110.

73. https://www.cso.ie/en/releasesandpublications/ep/p-1916/1916irl/cpr/coir/stk/, 18 August 2023. In the same vein, the business of the Irish Republic's first Dáil assembly in January 1919 was conducted in Irish, with translations provided in English and French.

74. F. S. L. Lyons, 'George Moore and Edward Martyn', in *Hermathena* 98 (1964), pp 9–29 (p. 10).

75. Mac Mathúna, 'Douglas Hyde's intellectual links with John Quinn, Lady Gregory and W.B. Yeats', p. 78.

76. Sabine Doff, '"Let girls chat about the weather and walks": English language education at girls' secondary schools in nineteenth-century Germany', in Nicola McLelland and Richard Smith (eds), *The History of Language Learning and Teaching* (3 vols, Cambridge, 2018), vol. 2, pp 87–97 (pp 93–4).

77. Doyle, *A History of the Irish Language*, p. 186.

78. Ibid., p. 187.

79. Cited in Ní Nuadháin, 'The teaching of Irish 1900–1926', p. 42. She cites a pamphlet by A. Ó Muimhneacháin, *Na Múinteoirí Taistil* (1966).

80. See Séamas Ó Buachalla, 'Educational policy and the role of the Irish language from 1831 to 1981', in *European Journal of Education* 19 (1984), pp 75–92 (p. 84), Table 1; he views the 1904 bilingual programme, and its handling by the Gaelic League, as a 'watershed in the curricular history of the Irish language' (p. 82).

81. Ibid., pp 82–3. In 1910, there were two Gaelic League training colleges in Donegal, one each in Mayo, Cork, Kerry and Antrim; and in Leinster College, Dublin; by 1915, there were 17 such colleges; by 1920, 23 Irish training colleges for teachers had been set up by the League (Walsh, 'Frankly and robustly national', p. 325).

82. Ó Cuív, 'Irish language and literature', p. 407.

83. Ní Nuadháin, 'The teaching of Irish 1900–1926', p. 7. Similarly, the primary-level curriculum for Latin, an extra subject in the upper years, included some Caesar and Virgil, as well as translation into Latin; primary school optional French included grammar, as well as translation in both directions (ibid., p. 16).

84. Ní Nuadháin, 'The teaching of Irish 1900–1926', p. 44. The daily timetable also included listening to a *seanchaí* telling a folktale, lessons on written Irish, *sean-nós* singing, history lectures and debates.

85. Ní Nuadháin, 'The teaching of Irish 1900–1926', pp 46–7. O'Daly was author of a book on Irish phonetics, *How to Speak Irish* (1905), and *Phoneology* (1908).

86. Doff, 'Let girls chat about the weather and walks', pp 90–1; Andrew R. Linn, 'Modern foreign languages get a voice: The role of journals in the reform movement', in McLelland and Smith (eds), *The History of Language Learning and Teaching*, vol. 2, pp 145–60 (p. 153); cf. Nicola McLelland, *German Through English Eyes: A History of Language Teaching and Learning in Britain, 1500–2000* (Wiesbaden, 2015), pp 109–33; Anna Morpurgo Davies, *History of Linguistics, Volume IV, Nineteenth-Century Linguistics* (London, 1998), pp 294–6.

87. McLelland, 'The history of language learning and teaching in Britain', pp 11–14; Nicola McLelland, *Teaching and Learning Foreign Languages: A History of Language Education, Assessment and Policy in Britain* (London and New York, 2017; pbk edn, 2018), pp 105–7. The extent to which the mother tongue was used in classrooms varied considerably in practice.

88. L. M. Moriarty, 'Some notes on methods and aims of modern language teaching in public schools', in *The Modern Quarterly of Language and Literature* 1 (1899), pp 326–30 (p. 328). Two decades later, a similar imitation of classical teaching methods in England was noted by the Leathes Report, 'Modern Studies, Being the Report of the Committee on the Position of Modern Languages in the Educational system of Great Britain' (London, 1918), pp 9–10, 181, and passim.

89. Doff, 'Let girls chat about the weather and walks', pp 92–7.

90. On Maximilian Berlitz, see https://en.wikipedia.org/wiki/Maximilian_Berlitz, 2 August 2023; McLelland, *Teaching and Learning Foreign Languages*, pp 106–7. On Gouin, see https://fr.wikipedia.org/wiki/Fran%C3%A7ois_Gouin, 2 August 2023.

91. Gerhard J. Stieglitz, 'The Berlitz method', in *The Modern Language Journal* 6 (1955), pp 300–10; Linn, 'Modern foreign languages get a voice', p. 157.

92. Leathes Report, pp 10–12.

93. McLelland, *German Through English Eyes*, pp 118–23; Nicola McLelland, 'Ripman [*formerly* Rippmann], Walter (1869–1947)', ONDB; McLelland, 'The history of language learning and teaching in Britain', pp 13–14. Cf. Etain Casey, 'Walter Ripman and the University of London holiday course in English for foreign teachers 1903–1952' (unpublished doctoral thesis, University of Oulu, 2017).

94. Buttimer, 'Celtic and Irish in College 1849–1944', p. 93; Ní Nuadháin, 'The teaching of Irish 1900–1926', pp 54–5.

95. Linn, 'Modern foreign languages get a voice', p. 158.

96. Ó Buachalla (ed.), *A Significant Irish Educationalist*, introductory essay, 'A significant Irish educationalist', pp ix–xxv (p. xxiv). Pearse's interest in Belgium was, it seems, first kindled by a book he had reviewed: T. R. Dawes, *Bilingual Teaching in Belgian Schools*. He had already written about Belgian bilingualism in *ACS* from 23 January 1904 (ibid., pp xi, 31–4).

97. Ibid., p. 258: Belgian independence from the Dutch had occurred, Pearse argued, on account of linguistic oppression. The new kingdom set up in 1830, he writes, 'owed its origin to a language question. The *causa causans* of the Revolution was the attempt of the Dutch Government to outlaw the speech of the Walloon' (*ACS*, 19 August 1905), ibid. For the text of Pearse's published articles on 'Belgium and its Schools', see Ó Buachalla (ed.), *A Significant Irish Educationalist*, pp 254–310.

98. i.e., West Connacht and County Waterford. Pearse, in Ó Buachalla (ed.), *A Significant Irish Educationalist*, p. 279 (*ACS*, 6 January 1906).

99. For other examples of such 'object lessons' in the classroom, see McLelland, *German Through English Eyes*, pp 112–15, 125.

100. Ó Buachalla (ed.), *A Significant Irish Educationalist*, pp 287–308 (*ACS*, 3 March 1906; 29 September 1906; 13 October 1906; 27 October 1906; 17 November 1906; 24 November 1906; 1 December 1906; 5 January 1907; 26 January 1907; 2 February 1907; 16 February 1907; 2 March 1907). On using realia and images in language teaching, see McLelland, *German Through English Eyes*, pp 114–15.

101. Pearse's published observations of language classrooms in 1905 Brussels (*ACS*, 5 August 1905–9 March 1907), can be compared to those of Mary Brebner, who used a Gilchrist travelling scholarship to observe realia being used during foreign-language lessons in 1897 Germany. Mary Brebner's *The Method of Teaching Modern Languages in Germany* (London, 1898), was in its third edition by 1904. In effect, Pearse was advocating the new pedagogy for Irish teachers, just as Brebner had done for foreign-language teachers in England.

102. Pearse, 'By way of comment', June 1909, in Ó Buachalla (ed.), *A Significant Irish Educationalist*, p. 325.

103. Ó Buachalla (ed.), *A Significant Irish Educationalist*, p. xxiv.

104. Pearse, 'By way of comment', p. 325.

105. Ó Buachalla (ed.), *A Significant Irish Educationalist*, p. 318.

106. Mary Kotsonouris, 'Duffy, Louise Gavan', DIB.

107. In Scoil Bhríde she taught French, and even Latin, by the direct method (Ní Nuadháin, 'The teaching of Irish 1900–1926', pp 59–60).

CHAPTER 6: PROFILES AND PATTERNS: MODERN LANGUAGE PROFESSORS

1. Edmund Hayes Q.C., defence counsel, *Galbraith v. Angeli* (1856), Report of the case (Dublin, 1857; reprinted New Haven, CT, 2021), p. 86.

2. Macaulay Report on the Indian Civil Service (1854), included as Appendix B to the Fulton Report (1968), pp 119–28 (p. 123), https://www.civilservant.org.uk/library/1854-Macaulay_Report.pdf, 4 September 2023.

3. Friedrich Max Müller, *Lectures on The Science of Language* (London, 1861), pp 3–4.

4. For reference, see Table 1, Professors of Modern Languages in Ireland's Universities (1776–1921), pp 311–13 below.

5. Historical studies of Trinity's modern language departments include Gilbert Carr, 'Literary historical trends and the history of the German syllabus at Trinity College, Dublin, 1873–1972', in *Hermathena* 121 (1976), pp 36–53; Richard Cox, 'A curious history: two hundred years of modern languages', in C. H. Holland (ed.), *Trinity College Dublin and the Idea of a University* (Dublin, 1991), pp 255–69; Francis M. Higman, 'Modern languages in Trinity College, Dublin 1776–1976', in *Hermathena* 121 (1976), pp 12–17; Máirtín Ó Murchú, 'Irish language studies in Trinity College Dublin', in *Hermathena (Quatercentenary Papers)* (1992), pp 43–68; M. M. Raraty, 'The chair of German, Trinity College, Dublin 1775–1866', in *Hermathena* 102 (1966), pp 53–72; Corinna Salvadori, '*Dove 'l sì sona*: two hundred and thirty years of Italian in Trinity College Dublin', in Cormac Ó Cuilleanáin, Corinna Salvadori and John Scattergood (eds), *Italian Culture: Interactions, Transpositions, Translations* (Dublin, 2006), pp 13–28.

6. A number of studies have been published on modern language departments in the other RUI colleges. For example, see Breandán Ó Madagáin, 'Irish: A difficult birth', in Tadhg Foley (ed.), *From Queen's College to National University: Essays on the Academic History of QCG/UCG/NUI, Galway* (Dublin, 1999), pp 344–59; Rosaleen O'Neill, 'Modern languages', in ibid., pp 360–83. For Cork, see Cornelius G. Buttimer, 'Celtic and Irish in College 1849–1944', in *Journal of the Cork Historical and Archaeological Society* 94 (1989), pp 88–112. Passing references to individual language departments and professors can be found in institutional histories, such as T. W. Moody and J. C. Beckett, *Queen's, Belfast 1845–1949: The History of a University* (2 vols, London, 1959); John A. Murphy, *The College: A History of Queen's/University College Cork, 1845–1895* (Cork, 1995); Patrick J. Corish, *Maynooth College 1795–1995* (Dublin, 1995); R. B. McDowell and D. A. Webb, *Trinity College Dublin 1592–1952: An Academic History* (Cambridge, 1982); and Donal McCartney, *UCD: A National Idea: The History of University College Dublin* (Dublin, 1999).

7. Kevin J. Cathcart (ed.), *The Letters of Peter le Page Renouf by Peter le Page Renouf (1822–97)* (4 vols, Dublin, 2003), vol. 3, *Dublin 1854–1864*, Introduction, pp xi–xxix. Cf. Fergal McGrath, SJ, *Newman's University: Idea and Reality* (Dublin, 1951), passim.

8. Colin Barr, *Paul Cullen, John Henry Newman, and the Catholic University of Ireland, 1845–1865* (South Bend and Leominster, 2003), p. 126. The tone of Newman's letter of 20 February 1854 is intriguing: 'what your work would be and what your remuneration, it is impossible to calculate at first. We are making a great *experiment*' (Cathcart (ed.), *Letters of Renouf*, vol. 3, p. 3). The appointment was for three years at £150.00 per annum. Correspondence between the two men in spring 1854 indicates that Renouf already expressed a keen interest in moving to a post in Christian antiquity, should the French post fail for some reason (ibid., p. xviii).

9. 'Mr. Renouf is a native of Guernsey, and speaks English and French with equal facility. He is a classical scholar, well versed in Theology and History.' (Newman to the archbishops, 3 October 1854, cited in McGrath, *Newman's University*, p. 324.)

10. Incidentally, this was the same building that was to become the headquarters of Sinn Féin in 1910. See Éanna Ó Caollaí, 'Uimhir a 6 Sráid Fhearchair: finné ar stair na hÉireann', *The Irish Times*, 12 April 2021. For the CU's first batch of students, see Donal McCartney, *UCD: A National Idea*, pp 5–8.

11. Letter, John Hungerford Pollen (Professor of Fine Arts), 13 May 1855. Cited in McGrath, *Newman's University*, p. 359. (McGrath gives many such testimonies to daily life in the CU during Newman's time there.)

12. Letter, Ludovica to Mary Renouf, 29 June 1861 (cited in Cathcart (ed.), *Letters of Renouf*, vol. 3, p. xxi.)

13. Ibid., p. 22, n. 2.

14. McGrath, *Newman's University*, p. 345. Cf. Cathcart (ed.), *Letters of Renouf*, vol. 3, p. 5, n. 2. On Marani, see below, pp 134, 138, 150, and Ch. 6, n. 97.

15. Cathcart (ed.), *Letters of Renouf*, vol. 3, pp xx–xxi. This paper was very well received by Egyptologists in England. Renouf's lifetime contribution to Egyptology is evident in the list of his publications (1841 to posthumous); ibid., pp 322–3. Cf. Kevin J. Cathcart, 'Renouf, Peter Le Page', DIB.

16. Cathcart (ed.), *Letters of Renouf*, vol. 3, p. 83, n. 3; James Meenan (ed.), *Centenary History of the Literary and Historical Society of University College Dublin 1855–1955* (Tralee, 1955), p. 6.

17. The PhD (doctorate), nowadays regarded as a standard entry to university academic work, did not come into Irish or British universities until 1920 (http://trinitynews.ie/2010/03/old-trinity-a-90-degree-university/, 3 March 2023).

18. McGrath, *Newman's University*, p. 502; Cathcart (ed.), *Letters of Renouf*, vol. 3, p. 22; S. Farragher, CSSp, and C. de Mare, 'Le Père Jules Leman et la fondation du collège de Blackrock, en Irlande', in *Mémoire Spiritaine* 5:5 (2019), pp 37–62 (p. 45, n. 25); Louise T. Daley, 'Schurr [*sic*], Felix (1827–1900)', in *Australian Dictionary of Biography*, vol. 6 (Melbourne, 1976), p. 197; 'Death of Abbé Schurr, V.G.', *Freeman's Journal* (Sydney, NSW), 21 July 1900, p. 15; *Seventh Report of All Hallows College, Drumcondra* (Dublin, 1855). Schürr's name first appears in the minutes of a CU Faculty meeting held 3 November 1856 (UCD Archives, CU/4, Minutes of the Council of the Faculty of Philosophy and Letters, 26 June 1856–25 January 1878).

19. See above, p. 36. For more on Schürr, see Ch. 6, notes 18, 22, 24, 26, 27, and 130.

20. Seán P. Farragher, CSSp, *The French College Blackrock 1860–1896* (Dublin, 2011), p. 408; Kevin Condon, *The Missionary College of All Hallows 1842–1891* (Dublin, 1986), p. 82.

21. His name appears in the Catholic University of Ireland *Calendar*, 1855–6, printed in early summer 1856 (Cathcart (ed.), *Letters of Renouf*, vol. 3, p. 22, n. 2).

22. Louise Daley, 'Schurr, Felix (1827–1900)', says that Schürr worked in an institution for the blind in Dublin. If so, this was probably St Joseph's Asylum for the Male Blind, founded in Drumcondra by the Carmelites in 1859. There is documentary evidence (1865) of his working as chaplain to Dr Lynch's private lunatic asylum, Hartfield, Drumcondra: see DDA/AB4/b/327/2/IV/25 [Dublin Diocesan archives].

23. Farragher, *French College*, p. 408; Farragher and de Mare, 'Le Père Jules Leman et la fondation du collège de Blackrock, en Irlande,' p. 44.

24. Paul Cullen, who had 'engineered' the appointment of three cousins of O'Mahony, was indirectly involved. See Anthony Fisher, OP, 'A Glorious Future for the Infant Diocese of Armidale: The emerging Church in New England', in *Australasian Catholic Record* 99:1 (2022), pp 86–95, n. 27. Schürr features in other Australian sources, such as https://trove.nla.gov.au/newspaper/article/146500583/17325443 and https://trove.nla.gov.au/newspaper/article/106334704, 18 August 2021. Cf. 'Death of the Venerable Abbe Schurr: The apostle of the North Coast', *The Catholic Press* (Sydney, NSW), 21 July 1900, p. 11.

25. Zoe Satherly, 'History under the hammer', *Daily Telegraph* (Australia), 8 July 2005, https://www.dailytelegraph.com.au/news/nsw/lismore/history-under-the-hammer/news-story/c0a99443fe7b2da8087e6f4c026e9c1a, 18 August 2021.

26. 'Death of Abbé Schürr', *Freeman's Journal*, p. 15. It is entirely possible that the French priest could have picked up some Irish at All Hallows. See Condon, *The Missionary College of All Hallows 1842–1891*, pp 141–7, on deficiencies in the use of English among some students of the College in its early years.

27. His command of written English, on the other hand, was not universally admired: Cf. a letter of Renouf's to John Dalberg Acton, April 1862: 'Neither Marani nor Schürr write English' (cited in Cathcart (ed.), *Letters of Renouf*, vol. 3, p. 124).

28. Farragher, *French College*, p. 177. Guy de Leusse's younger brother, Charles, spent four months in the College in January–April 1884: Blackrock College Archives, *Blackrock College Ledger*, 1867–72.

29. See above, p. 59. Seán P. Farragher, CSSp, and Annraoi Wyer, *Blackrock College 1860–1995* (Dublin, 1995), pp 49–50.

30. A holograph letter from Paul Cullen to Tobias Kirby (Irish College, Rome), 7 December 1873, mentions that 'Abbé Polin is teaching French and German in the Catholic University' (Kirby Collection Catalogue, Pontifical Irish College, Rome, Part 4, 1867–73, p. 1206). Cf. UCD Archives, CU/4, Minutes of the Council of the Faculty of Philosophy and Letters, 1 December 1873.

31. Farragher, *French College*, p. 164; Anon., 'The results of Newman's campaign in Ireland', in *Studies: An Irish Quarterly Review* 2 (1913), pp 898–905 (p. 904); UCD Archives, CU/4, Minutes of the Council of the Faculty of Philosophy and Letters, 26 February 1875, 6 July 1875.

32. On Blackrock College's 1875 staff list, Polin is the only priest, out of 16, with the letters 'B.A.' after his name (list reproduced in Farragher, *French College*, p. 177). Cf. *A Page of Irish History: Story of University College, Dublin 1883–1909*, compiled by Fathers of the Society of Jesus (Dublin and Cork, 1930), p. 98.

33. *Bulletin de la Société littéraire de Strasbourg*, 1862, https://gallica.bnf.fr/ark:/12148/bpt6k5505224v/f6.image.r=Polin%20%20petit%20seminaire?rk=21459;2 (29 November 2020).

34. McCartney, *UCD: A National Idea*, p. 426 (Chapter 3, n. 1).

35. *A Page of Irish History*, p. 74.

36. McCartney, *UCD: A National Idea*, p. 73; *A Page of Irish History*, p. 456.

37. *A Page of Irish History*, pp 212–13; J. Daniel, 'Édouard Cadic ... un "enfant de Locmaria"', *Terre et Mer / An Douar Hag ar Mor: Bulletin Municipal de la ville de Guidel*, Guidel, 61, January 2010, p. 2; National Archives (France), Légion d'honneur_dossier, 19800035/231/30555, 'CADIC Edouard Marie', available on the Léonore database, https://www.leonore.archives-nationales.culture.gouv.fr/ui/notice/62164, 17 January 2023.

38. The post-Restoration French church had an uneasy relationship with the State, and church–state tensions were particularly felt in the field of education, with leading churchmen taking different standpoints on contentious issues like the limits of secularism and state control. (See Jean Leflon, 'Les petits séminaires de France au XIXe siècle', in *Revue d'histoire de l'Église de France* 61 (1975), pp 25–35.)

39. Ibid., p. 32, n. 23.

40. Advertisements, *Freeman's Journal*, 15 October 1877, p. 4; and 3 January 1879, p. 4.

41. Advertisement, *Freeman's Journal*, 9 February 1881. The Institute was a preparatory college for university entrance and civil service examinations, cadetships and legal apprenticeships.

42. See National Archives (France), Légion d'honneur_dossier, 'CADIC Edouard Marie'. The file includes a career summary, dated 30 August 1900, in Cadic's hand, submitted to the Grande Chancellerie of the Légion d'honneur. He lists Corrig School Kingstown, Royal Terrace School, Morehampton School, Rutland School, Alexandra College, the Queen's Institute and St Patrick's Training College Drumcondra.

43. On the Corrig School, see Arnold E. Bousfield, *Corrig School, Kingstown* (Bray, 1958). On the Queen's Institute: see Patricia Phillips, 'The Queen's Institute, Dublin (1861–1881): the first technical college for women in the British Isles', in Norman McMillan (ed.), *Prometheus's Fire: A History of Scientific and Technical Education in Ireland* (Kilkenny, 1995), pp 446–63; and Linde Lunney, 'Corlett, (Ada) Barbara', DIB.

44. Having landed this prize, why he applied (unsuccessfully) for the vacant modern languages chair in Cork the following year is unclear (National Archives, CSORP 1895/3921, application from E. Cadic, 29 February 1895). [An attempt to view this document, listed in the CSORP Catalogue for 1895, proved unsuccessful.]

45. The RUI post entailed examining work for other bodies such as the Intermediate Board, the Civil Service Commissioners and the War Office.

46. *A Page of Irish History*, pp 212–13.

47. Richard Ellmann, *James Joyce* (1st edn, New York, 1959), pp 61–2. On Joyce's Italian lecturer at UCD, see Fran O'Rourke, 'Joyce's early aesthetic', in *Journal of Modern Literature* 34 (2011), pp 97–120 (p. 102). Charles Ghezzi, SJ, was an influential mentor, and their one-to-one philosophical and aesthetic debates revealed the student's excellent command of Italian.

48. Reproduced in McCartney, *UCD: A National Idea*, pp 40–1.

49. Cited in Honor O Brolchain, *Joseph Plunkett* (Dublin, 2012), p. 106. Joseph Plunkett, although not himself a registered student, mixed in student circles. The play in question was Henri Meilhac's *L'été de St Martin* (1896).

50. For example, among the activities mentioned by Mary Kate Ryan in a letter to her sister Min (in London), 27 March 1911: 'I have an exam paper to prepare and Chris has a French debate with Cadic presiding next Friday.' (NLI, Manuscripts Collection, List No. 178 (Seán T. Ó Ceallaigh and the Ryans of Tomcoole), MS 48,445/5/6.)

51. In 1903, Cadic gave a public lecture on Lamartine. See *A Page of Irish History*, pp 231–4 (p. 234).

52. Thus, for example, we find him in March 1901 lecturing at the Catholic Commercial Club in Upper O'Connell Street on 'A Royal Martyr – Louis XVII' (*Irish Daily Independent*, 9 March 1901, p. 2); in March 1905 he gave a public lecture (in French) in University College on Joseph de Maistre (*Irish Independent*, 3 March 1905, p. 6); in December 1908 he addressed the Modern Languages Society in Queen's University Belfast on Madame de Staël (*Belfast Newsletter*, 4 December 1908, p. 6); in February 1909 he lectured (in French) at the Theatre of the Royal Dublin Society, Leinster House, on Sully-Prudhomme (*Evening Herald*, 20 February 1909, p. 3); in December 1909 he addressed the United Arts Club, Lincoln Place, on 'L'aviation littéraire du dix-septième siècle' (*Freeman's Journal*, 3 December 1909, p. 5); in March 1911 he again gave a lecture (in French) to the Royal Dublin Society on Edmond Rostand's play *Chantecler* (*Freeman's Journal*, 2 March 1911, p. 5).

53. National Archives (France), Légion d'honneur dossier, 'CADIC Edouard Marie', career summary (30 August 1900). This self-appraisal is redolent with the language of cultural diplomacy, and with the French sense of victimhood after the defeat of 1870–1. It may be relevant that the award was given to Cadic in Wissembourg [Weissenburg] in Alsace, a town overrun by Prussia in 1870.

54. Cadic's career summary also states that he had occasionally stood in for the French chancellor at the French consulate, a detail that may suggest some official link with Paris.

55. Pearse took his RUI Arts degree (English, Irish, French) in 1901–02, having attended lectures in his final year: see Ruth Dudley Edwards, *Patrick Pearse: The Triumph of Failure* (London, 1977; pb edn 1979), pp 24–5. On Pearse's idealistic approach to bilingual education, see ibid., pp 104–10.

56. *Sgoil Éanna Prospectus, 1910–11* (St Enda's School, Rathfarnham). See Chapter Five above, pp 117–8.

57. 'Central Executive Meeting', *Evening Echo*, 18 October 1898, p. 1. His name appears in the diary of Joseph Plunkett as one of a number of people Plunkett had met at a League Oireachtas meeting on 1 August 1911 (cited in O Brolchain, *Joseph Plunkett*, pp 126–7).

58. 'Pan-Celtic Congress', *Freeman's Journal*, 2 March 1900; 'Celtic Association', *Freeman's Journal*, 15 October 1900 and 12 June 1902.

59. French and Irish citizens contributed to the fund, which amounted to £91, or *c.*£13,700 today: letter from Cadic, *Freeman's Journal*, 5 February 1910, p. 8; 'Succour for Flood Victims', *Irish Independent*, 24 February 1910, p. 8.

60. The monument was financed by Cadic himself, who had set aside funds from his estate, valued at over £8,000. One of his executors was the mathematician Sir Joseph McGrath, first registrar of the NUI. Cadic was unmarried. On O'Growney, see below, pp 160–1.

61. Scott was UCD's professor of architecture. He is best known for the O'Growney memorial and for restoring the Ballylee tower-house (County Galway) for W. B. Yeats. See Jeanne Sheehy, *The Rediscovery of Ireland's Past: The Celtic Revival 1830–1930* (London, 1980), pp 134–42.

62. 'Dublin Tribute to Esteemed French Citizen', *Freeman's Journal*, 2 November 1917, p. 8.

63. For ease of navigation through the various appointments discussed, together with their dates and institutions, see Table 1, 'Professors of Modern Languages in Ireland's Universities (1771–1921)', pp 311–13 below.

64. Thus, Newman knew Renouf; and Schürr, Polin and Cadic were already available in Dublin. The (unsuccessful) Queen's Colleges applications that lie in files in the National Archives show a far wider range of provenance and allegiance.

65. National Archives, CSORP 1849/65 and CSORP 1849/176, contain applications from mostly unsuccessful candidates. These files provide a treasure trove of professors who give an account of themselves in print or in manuscript, briefly or at length, accompanied by all sorts of testimonials.

66. Murphy, *The College*, p. 34, specifies the nationalities of those first appointed to the Queen's College chairs, from a field of over 500 applicants: 'forty-two were Irish, fifteen were English or Scottish, two were German and one was French'.

67. Born in Karlsruhe on 25 February 1815, his family was from Mannheim. (Karlsruhe, Generallandesarchiv 390, Nr. 2859); information kindly supplied by Markus Enzenauer (Mannheim municipal archives).

68. O'Neill, 'Modern languages', p. 369; cf. p. 367 and p. 361. O'Neill claims Steinberger was a native of Alsace, but Bavaria is stated as his region of origin in the 1901 and 1911 census (See Stephanie Klapp, 'Death by wrongful humiliation – the story of Valentine Steinberger', *Galway Advertiser*, 4 February 2021). Cf. 'Roamer: disturbing story from a hundred years ago resonates disquietingly today', *Belfast Newsletter*, 25 August 2016.

69. O'Neill, 'Modern languages', pp 369–74.

70. Máire Kennedy, *French Books in Eighteenth-Century Ireland* (Oxford, 2001), pp 34–5.

71. Des MacHale, *The Life and Work of George Boole: A Prelude to the Digital Age* (Cork, 2014).

72. W. B. Stanford and R. B. McDowell, *Mahaffy: A Biography of an Anglo-Irishman* (London, 1971), pp 18–19.

73. Moody and Beckett, *Queen's, Belfast*, vol. 1, p. 167; vol. 2, p. 610.

74. Ibid., vol. 1, pp 167–8; vol. 2, pp 610–11.

75. Ibid., vol. 1, pp 168–70; vol. 2, p. 611; Meissner's naturalisation papers, June 1860 (National Archives (UK), HO 1/96/3256).

76. For Twickenham, see *Athenaeum*, January 1842, p. 1.

77. O'Neill, 'Modern languages', p. 366. There is some doubt about the university where Geisler had been awarded his doctorate, but he 'would appear to have held both a PhD and a DLitt' (ibid., p. 367.)

78. Ibid., p. 369.

79. Raraty, 'The chair of German, Trinity College, Dublin 1775–1866', p. 62.

80. Those who naturalised include Trinity College's Evasio Radice in 1837 (Enrico Francia, 'Radice, Evasio', *Dizionario Biografico degli Italiani* 86 (2017)) and Albert Maximilian Selss in 1862 (National Archives (UK), HO 1/103/3742); Belfast's Albert Ludwig Meissner in 1860 (National Archives (UK), HO 1/96/3256); and Galway's Valentine Steinberger in 1913 (National Archives (UK), HO 144/1069/190325).

81. Professors could charge fees per student on top of their basic annual salary, which for the Queen's Colleges stood at £200 in 1850. In the RUI, professors were entitled to receive additional income from

fellowships and examinerships. The former were valued at £100 and the latter at £75 or £100 per annum in 1883 (*Belfast Telegraph*, 9 June 1883, p. 3).

82. Moody and Beckett, *Queen's, Belfast*, vol. 2, p. 610.

83. 'Roamer', *Belfast Newsletter*, 27 June 2016; Klapp, 'Death by wrongful humiliation', *Galway Advertiser*, 4 February 2021.

84. Grace Catherina Maffett: https://www.stirnet.com/articles/selectfams/HamiltonMemoirs/CH20.html, 18 August 2021.

85. The nomadic refugee existence, and multiple career changes, of Mozart's famous librettist, Lorenzo da Ponte, led to a post (at the age of 76) as the first professor of Italian at New York's Columbia University in 1825. See Paul Hond, 'How Mozart's librettist became the father of Italian Studies at Columbia: The curious cross-continental tale of Lorenzo da Ponte', in *Columbia Magazine*, winter 2020–1. On precarious expatriates multitasking in early modern England, see John Gallagher, *Learning Languages in Early Modern England* (Oxford, 2019), pp 53–4 and passim.

86. Ann Frost, 'The emergence and growth of Hispanic Studies in British and Irish universities', online report, AHGBI [Association of Hispanists of Great Britain and Ireland], 2019, pp 5–6.

87. Ibid., p. 8.

88. Salvadori, '*Dove 'l sì sona*', pp 15–16; Margaret C. W. Wicks, *The Italian Exiles in London 1816–1848* (Freeport, NY, 1937; reprint, 1968); Francia, 'Radice, Evasio'.

89. Salvadori, '*Dove 'l sì sona*', p. 15. He undertook extra duties in spite of being ill, in the mid-1840s (McDowell and Webb, *Trinity College Dublin*, p. 224).

90. Frost, 'Hispanic Studies in British and Irish universities', p. 42.

91. Ibid., p. 2; cf. ibid., p. 24: 'His travels to Spain brought him into contact with luminaries like Federico García Lorca and Manuel de Falla, and his interest in music took him all over the country, and became one of the constants of his writing.'

92. Ibid., pp 30–1.

93. Nicola McLelland, 'The history of language learning and teaching in Britain', in *The Language Learning Journal* 46 (2018), pp 6–16 (pp 8–9).

94. W. R. Furlong, *Action for Libel: Report of the Case of Angeli v. Galbraith* (Dublin, 1857; Yale Law Library reprint, 2021). Cf. McDowell and Webb, *Trinity College Dublin*, pp 224–5; Salvadori, '*Dove 'l sì sona*', pp 16–18; Murphy, *The College*, p. 41.

95. The Junior Fellows were prompted to act in 1855, when the Board nominated Angeli for an honorary LLD.

96. Cited by Edmund Hayes, Q.C., counsel for Galbraith (Furlong, *Action for Libel*, p. 88).

97. In the meantime, Marani was working for the CU, having been Newman's pick for Italian and Spanish since 1854 (Cathcart (ed.), *Letters of Renouf*, vol. 3, p. 87, n. 6). He was an assiduous attender of Faculty meetings and even stood for election on two occasions, but his name is crossed out at a meeting of 10 July 1862 and disappears from CU lists and calendars thereafter (UCD Archives, CU/4, passim.) Before his appointment to the Trinity chair, it was perfectly feasible for the Italian lecturer to move between the two universities, given low student numbers and the proximity of the two locations.

98. McDowell and Webb, *Trinity College Dublin*, pp 224–5.

99. Murphy, *The College*, p. 41. Kane was himself a Roman Catholic.

100. For example, the best he could come up with to render the ubiquitous term of address 'Ladies and Gentlemen' caused much mirth in court: he translated it as 'Signori d'ambo i sessi' [literally, *Gentlemen of both sexes*] (Furlong, *Action for Libel*, p. 68 and passim). Translation into one's own mother tongue can be a telling test of a non-native's nuanced understanding of the source language.

101. Ibid., p. 87.

102. Ibid.; cf. p. 204.

103. McDowell and Webb, *Trinity College Dublin*, p. 234, describe Galbraith and Haughton as 'two of the more active and outward-looking of the Junior Fellows', who saw the potential of the new competitive climate for providing outlets for graduates.

104. Cited in Áine Hyland and Kenneth Milne (eds), *Irish Educational Documents* (vol. 1, Dublin, 1987), p. 328.

105. McDowell and Webb, *Trinity College Dublin*, p. 215.

106. Furlong, *Action for Libel*, p. 87.

107. Salvadori, '*Dove 'l sì sona*', p. 17.

108. For the testimonials, see Furlong, *Action for Libel*, Appendix H, pp 499–500 (for his testimonials) and Appendix B, pp 486–92 (for Angeli's comments on the prosecution's list of errors).

109. These are notoriously difficult to determine, even in our own times, when the increased complexity and sheer multiplicity of degrees and diplomas can defy institutional and international norms and standards.

110. That said, the calibre of the publicly appointed Queen's Colleges' first modern linguists suggests more rigorous vetting standards of recruitment than elsewhere.

111. McDowell and Webb, *Trinity College Dublin*, p. 225. On the pre-Victorian history of Trinity's modern languages chairs, occupied by five men in 25 years, see Raraty, 'The chair of German, Trinity College, Dublin 1775–1866', pp 53–60.

112. As recommended by the Dublin University Commission report (1853). Cf. McDowell and Webb, *Trinity College Dublin*, pp 213, 224–5. The removal of Angeli had been initially stymied by the role of the Crown in his original appointment (ibid., p. 224). Cf. Raraty, 'The chair of German, Trinity College, Dublin 1775–1866', pp 64–5.

113. O'Neill, 'Modern languages', pp 366–8; cf. University of Galway James Hardiman Library, Bursar's Office (Correspondence), BU Box 8, B/176. On Meissner's 'difficult, touchy, pugnacious' character, see Moody and Beckett, *Queen's, Belfast*, vol. 1, pp 168–70. Geisler's absence from QCG, which remains unexplained, also followed a savagely hostile review of a work he published the same year: on which see below, p. 144.

114. Radice had Waldensian sympathies (Francia, 'Radice, Evasio') and was buried in the English Cemetery in Genoa (Marco Cazzulo, 'Evasio Radice: "Britain, this great country"', https://cazzulo. altervista.org/evasio-radice-britain-this-great-country/, 15 August 2021.) The Waldensians, considered heretical by Catholicism, had centuries-old roots in northern Italy, and had garnered sympathy from English Protestants at least since John Milton (cf. the 1655 sonnet 'On the late massacre in Piedmont', which opens on a prayer: 'Avenge, O Lord, thy slaughtered saints, whose bones / Lie scattered on the Alpine mountains cold').

115. McDowell and Webb, *Trinity College Dublin*, pp 106–7. Cf. Stanford and McDowell, *Mahaffy*, pp 25–6, on the effect of disestablishment on the status of Trinity's clerical fellows.

116. Raraty, 'The chair of German, Trinity College, Dublin 1775–1866', p. 56.

117. Raraty, 'The chair of German, Trinity College, Dublin 1775–1866', pp 62–3. Born in Strasbourg in 1806, Abeltshauser had come to Ireland as the son of the bandmaster of Cork's regiments and had maintained a business as a 'Professor of the French and German Languages' at different Dublin addresses for well over a decade before graduating with a Trinity degree in 1842 (ibid., p. 62). He presumably converted to the Church of Ireland from his original Lutheran or Huguenot persuasion. (McDowell and Webb, *Trinity College Dublin*, p. 271.)

118. Stanford and McDowell, *Mahaffy*, pp. 25–6, 127–43, and passim.

119. McGrath, *Newman's University*, p. 324.

120. James Lydon, 'The silent sister: Trinity College and Catholic Ireland', in Holland (ed), *Trinity College Dublin and the Idea of a University*, pp 29–53 (pp 34–5), points out that, in practice, these religious divisions were less pronounced in the student body, especially in the first half of the nineteenth century. Many eminent Catholics attended Trinity, including John Blake Dillon; and Daniel O'Connell sent his sons there. More surprisingly, Michael Slattery, future president of Maynooth and archbishop of Cashel, was also a Trinity alumnus. Paul Cullen himself had been first educated by the Quakers at Ballitor, near Athy, County Kildare. Attitudes hardened and polarised later in the century.

121. Frost, 'Hispanic Studies in British and Irish universities', p. 6.

122. On the basis of surviving evidence, reasons for the imbalance cannot be determined with certainty (Moody and Beckett, *Queen's, Belfast*, vol. 1, p. 67). For statistics and a full discussion, see Juliana Adelman, 'Communities of science: the Queen's Colleges and scientific culture in provincial Ireland, 1845–1875', unpublished PhD dissertation, NUIG, 2006, pp 99–106.

123. The names 'August Isaac' are carved on his tombstone, in Mannheim's Jewish Cemetery. Unlike many Jewish graves in the city, his tomb escaped desecration in 1938. See https://www.marchivum. de/de/juedischer-friedhof/a2-08-04-bensbach-august-drisaak (accessed 8 March 2023). He died suddenly in Düsseldorf in May 1868, having spent two months staying with his sister and her family in Mannheim. (Information from Mannheim police registers, kindly forwarded to me by Markus Enzenauer.)

124. Moody and Beckett, *Queen's, Belfast*, vol. 2, pp 610–11. For Geisler's religion: *Belfast Telegraph*, 9 June 1883, p. 3.

125. Bensbach, who believed in the usefulness of knowledge, proposed extra-murals for the public and opening the university's library to the citizens of Galway (O'Neill, 'Modern languages', p. 365). He served on the University's Library Committee; as Dean of the Literary Division (Arts Faculty) he was perhaps over-zealous (see Liam O'Malley, 'Law', in Foley (ed.), *From Queen's College to National University*, pp 16–124 (p. 84).

126. The Dutch East Indies were able to attract German medical personnel partly due to changing conditions in the profession at home. See Philipp Teichfischer, 'Transnational entanglements in colonial medicine: German medical practitioners as members of the health service in the Dutch East Indies (1816–1884)', in *Revue d'histoire sociale et culturelle de la médecine, de la santé et du corps*, 10 (2016) [Guerre, maladie, empire], pp 63–78 [https://doi.org/10.4000/hms.1035].

127. Information about Bensbach's family kindly supplied by Markus Enzenauer, who searched the *Familienbögen* [civil family registers] in Mannheim's municipal archives [Marchivum], on my behalf.

128. The scientific disciplines were considered highly exposed to a professor's religious beliefs. See Adelman, 'Communities of science', pp 91–9, for the fraught confessional context of the late 1840s, and pp 99–106 for the initial Queen's Colleges appointments in the sciences, where Roman Catholics were under-represented.

129. Frost, 'Hispanic Studies in British and Irish universities', p. 6.

130. McGrath, *Newman's University*, p. 502. In 1858, the year of Newman's departure, the CU's teaching staff numbered thirty-two, five of whom were priests. Félix Schürr was the odd one out among these five clerics: his subject, modern languages, contrasts with the areas of scripture or theology taught by the other four.

131. Louis-Raymond de Véricour, *Historical Analysis of Christian Civilisation* (London, 1850) [502 pp]. De Véricour was first and foremost a historian. When seeking a Queen's College appointment, in December 1848, he had applied for a post in modern languages or history (Murphy, *The College*, p. 34). The book is dedicated to the influential French historian and politician François Guizot, also of Huguenot stock, whose ideas it espouses. Guizot wrote testimonials for the younger man. Paul Cullen alleged that de Véricour was a 'nephew of Guizot' in a note to archbishop Manning in 1873 (Murphy, *The College*, p. 48), doubtless meaning that de Véricour was a protégé of the politician.

132. Murphy, *The College*, pp 46–8; Adelman, 'Communities of science', p. 102.

133. Kevin Lambert, 'Victorian stained glass as memorial: an image of George Boole', in Minsoo Kang and Amy Woodson-Boulton (eds), *Visions of the Industrial Age, 1830–1914: Modernity and the Anxiety of Representation in Europe* (Burlington, 2008), pp 205–26 (pp 218–20).

134. These ecumenical views were quoted in a review of de Véricour's *Principles of History*, in *The Leeds Times*, 30 August 1845. De Véricour expounds analogous views on the moral and Christian necessity for historical enquiry in 'The study of history', in *Transactions of the Royal Historical Society* 1 (1875), pp 9–37.

135. K. O'Flaherty, 'Random notes on Q.C.C. in the Fifties', in *Cork University Record* 10 (1947), pp 26–8 (pp 27–8).

136. De Véricour, *Historical Analysis of Christian Civilisation*, p. vi.

137. *The Italian Correspondence of Paul Cullen*, translated and edited by Anne O'Connor (forthcoming, Irish Manuscripts Commission): letters from Cullen to Alessandro Barnabò, 16 June 1850 and 9 August 1850. [Eight letters mentioning de Véricour (June 1850–January 1851) were kindly forwarded to me by Anne O'Connor.]

138. See for example *Cork Examiner*, 12 August 1850; *Waterford News and Star*, 23 August 1850.

139. Louis-Raymond de Véricour, 'To the Editor of the Southern Reporter' (28 August 1850), *Cork Examiner*, 6 September 1850. The book's London publisher, John Chapman, endorsed it in the *Cork Examiner*, 9 September 1850, as did an anonymous 'Roman Catholic layman', *Cork Examiner*, 29 November 1850.

140. Murphy, *The College*, p. 47.

141. *Cork Examiner*, 20 January 1851, p. 3. Anne O'Connor (trans. and ed.), *The Italian Correspondence of Paul Cullen* shows Cullen as the instigator of this Decree: see his letters to Alessandro Barnabò (16 June 1850) to Tobias Kirby (21 October 1850), to Bernard Smith (27 October 1850) and to Tobias Kirby (20 January 1851).

142. Two items from de Véricour relating to the Belfast vacancy are listed in the Catalogue for 1862 (CSORP): National Archives, CSORP/1862/11554 and CSORP/1862/11595. Cf. 'Queen's College Belfast', *Cork Examiner*, 18 April 1862, p. 3. The successful candidate for the Belfast chair in 1862 was Johann Wilhelm Frädersdorff.

143. The Chief Secretary was a minister of the Crown and member of Cabinet responsible for British administration in Ireland.

144. Murphy, *The College*, p. 48.

145. For a list of Renouf's scholarly publications, mostly on Egyptology, from 1841 to after his death, see Cathcart (ed.), *Letters of Renouf*, vol. 3, pp 322–3. The apparent absence of research undertaken by Schürr, Polin and Cadic contrasts with the splendid publication record of Roger Chauviré, the next incumbent of the chair of French at UCD (1918–1948), on whom see Phyllis Gaffney, '*Une certaine idée de l'Irlande*, or the professor as propagandist: Roger Chauviré's Irish fictions', in Phyllis Gaffney, Michael Brophy and Mary Gallagher (eds), *Reverberations: Staging Relations in French since 1500. A Festschrift in Honour of C.E.J. Caldicott* (Dublin, 2008), pp 390–403; Phyllis Gaffney, 'Roger Chauviré's perspective on 1916 and its aftermath', in Pierre Joannon and Kevin Whelan (eds), *Paris: Capital of Irish Culture: France, Ireland and the Republic, 1798–1916* (Dublin, 2017), pp 215–26; and below, pp 188–9.

146. McCartney, *UCD: A National Idea*, pp 64, 4–5, 12; Barr, *Cullen, Newman, and the CUI*, p. 209.

147. Catholic University of Ireland *Calendar*, 1863, p. 62.

148. Literary histories and grammars, for the most part: see 'List of professors recently appointed', *Anglo-Celt*, 10 August 1849.

149. Augustus Bensbach, *Kurze Skizze der Deutschen Literatur* (London, 1847).

150. The Milton volume, which published his lectures at the Athénée Royal de Paris, was favourably reviewed in 'De Véricour's lectures on Milton', in *The Monthly Review* 2 (July 1838), pp 342–51. His *Modern French Literature* ran to ten editions in the 1840s. He had also written on model farms in Switzerland and contributed articles on sawflies and wood wasps to a British Museum catalogue. These last may have been translations, from French or German into English: he later translated an Austrian play from German.

151. Louis-Raymond de Véricour, *Modern French Literature* (Boston, 1848), Editor's Preface, p. iv.

152. In the QCC fire of 15 May 1862, he allegedly lost other work in progress: see *Cork Examiner*, 22 May 1862. On the fire, see Murphy, *The College*, pp 82–94.

153. He even lectured for a term in Cork on English language history and structure, replacing a colleague who was 'indisposed' (*Report to the Queen's Colleges Commission*, 1858, p. 195). His near-native command of English doubtless came from his years living in England, including as principal of the Educational Institution, Twickenham. His wife was English. Although one reviewer of his Dante book admired his expertise but not his English style (*North American Review* 87:180 (July 1858), pp 257–8), the American editor of the French literature book, W. Staughton Chase, could find only 'occasional infelicities of expression' in his English (de Véricour, *Modern French Literature*, Editor's Preface, p. v).

154. George Boole, letter to Mary Ann (November 1849), quoted in Des MacHale and Yvonne Cohen, *New Light on George Boole* (Cork, 2018), p. 73. Cf. ibid., pp 113–14, 121.

155. *Belfast Newsletter*, 10 January 1879, p. 8.

156. *Athenaeum*, January 1842, p. 1; cf. Adelman, 'Communities of science', pp xi–xvii, on the importance of agricultural science and education, especially in Cork and Dublin, during the period 1845–75.

157. MacHale, *The Life and Work of George Boole*; MacHale and Cohen, *New Light on George Boole*. Boole expressed his delight at the news of de Véricour's appointment: 'An intimate friend of mine, Mr De Vericour, who is now visiting at Lord Mavern's nearby, is appointed to the chair of modern languages in the same college. This will be very pleasant for me' (Boole to Mary Davis, 13 August 1849, quoted in MacHale and Cohen, *New Light on George Boole*, pp 264–5.)

158. De Véricour was an assiduous attender: see UCC Boole Library Archives, Class no. U.376, Minute Book of the Library Committee, 1850–1885.

159. Boole was involved with Cork's Cuvierian Society, set up in 1835 (Murphy, *The College*, pp 7–9), and promoted the education of the working class; de Véricour spoke to the Cork Literary and Scientific Society, founded in 1820 (MacHale, *The Life and Work of George Boole*, p. 253). On Cork's voluntary societies, see Adelman, 'Communities of science', pp 118–54.

160. Moody and Beckett, *Queen's, Belfast*, vol. 2, pp 610–11. For Meissner, see also Nicola McLelland, *German Through English Eyes: A History of Language Teaching and Learning in Britain, 1500–2000* (Wiesbaden, 2015), pp 101, 110, 362.

161. As College Librarian from 1902, Steinberger also produced, single-handed, a printed catalogue (1913) of the university's entire collection of 'over 30,000 volumes as well as numerous miscellaneous papers and reports' (O'Neill, 'Modern languages', p. 372).

162. Raraty, 'The chair of German, Trinity College, Dublin 1775–1866', p. 68.

163. Joachim Fischer, *Das Deutschlandbild der Iren, 1890–1939: Geschichte – Form – Funktion* (Heidelberg, 2000), pp 479–81, sees Selss as an influential figure for German studies in Irish education at the turn of the twentieth century, as he lectured in Alexandra College, examined for the RUI and was a member of the Board of Intermediate Education. Politically liberal, he was interested in social questions and was not afraid to include contemporary works of literature in his teaching.

164. McDowell and Webb, *Trinity College Dublin*, pp 272, 313–14; Higman, 'Modern languages in Trinity College, Dublin 1776–1976', p. 15.

165. David Greene, 'Robert Atkinson and Irish studies', in *Hermathena* 102 (1966), pp 6–15 (p. 14). Atkinson's aversion to modern Irish, displayed at the Vice-Regal Inquiry of 1899 (see above, p. 106), seems curiously at odds with his passion for languages in general.

166. Benedict Anderson, *Imagined Communities: Reflections on the Origins and Spread of Nationalism* (London, 1983; revised edn, 1991), pp 70–5 and passim; Friedrich Max Müller, *Lectures on the Science of Language* (London, 1861). Cf. R. H. Robins, *A Short History of Linguistics* (London, 1967; fourth edn, 1997), pp 189–221.

167. Raraty, 'The chair of German, Trinity College, Dublin 1775–1866', p. 54; Corinna Salvadori, '*Dove 'l sì sona*', pp 14–15; Higman, 'Modern languages in Trinity College, Dublin 1776–1976', p. 14.

168. Max Müller, *Lectures on the Science of Language*, p. 166.

169. Any ancient artefact with an inscription satisfied the passion for deciphering the secrets of antiquity.

170. O'Neill, 'Modern languages', p. 367. Geisler offered lectures on Sanskrit and Hebrew: see *Report of the President of Queen's College Galway*, 1877–8, p. 22.

171. *Irish Examiner* [Cork Examiner], 20 December 1882. The Gaelic Union, a forerunner of the Gaelic League, was founded in March 1880.

172. Charles Geisler (ed.), *Epistil Imaralait eter Alexandir ocus Dindimus rí na mBragmanda* [Controversy between Alexander the Great and Dandamis, Chief of the Brahmans], *Leabhar Breac*, vol. 1, 211A, Irish Texts from Ancient Manuscripts, First series, part 1 (Dublin, 1884).

173. 'Literature: Irish Texts for [*sic*] Ancient Manuscripts', *Freeman's Journal*, 21 April 1884, p. 6; 'Irish Texts From Ancient Manuscripts', *Freeman's Journal*, 16 May 1884, p. 7. Geisler responded briefly, 24 April 1884, p. 7.

174. The RUI's 26 fellowships, valued at a maximum of £400 per annum, were paid in full to Fellows at the Dublin college. Fellows attached to the other colleges had their salaries increased to that amount. See Patrick Semple, 'The Royal University', in Michael Tierney (ed.), *Struggle with Fortune: A Miscellany for the Centenary of the Catholic University of Ireland, 1854–1954* (Dublin, 1954), pp 51–60 (pp 51–2).

175. 'University Intelligence. Royal University of Ireland. Election of Four New Fellows', *Freeman's Journal*, 30 May 1884, p. 6. There were two modern languages fellowships awarded: to Geisler (QCG) and Polin (UCD).

176. Edward W. Said, *Orientalism: Western Conceptions of the Orient* (Harmondsworth, 1991; 1978 edn), p. 132.

177. With all the racist and colonial implications of empire: classification posited some languages as superior, others as inferior (ibid., passim). Cf. Tore Janson, *Speak: A Short History of Languages* (Oxford, 2002), pp 75–6.

178. Said, *Orientalism*, p. 137 (citing Benjamin Constant); cf. Robins, *A Short History of Linguistics*, p. 169.

179. See https://www.britannica.com/biography/William-Jones-British-orientalist-and-jurist, https://royalasiaticsociety.org/sir-william-jones-1746-1794/, https://www.britannica.com/topic/Indo-European-languages/Establishment-of-the-family#ref603272, all accessed 22 November 2021.

180. Robins, *A Short History of Linguistics*, p. 168.

181. Ibid., pp 169–70.

182. Marjorie Perlman Lorch, 'Investigating the biographical sources of Thomas Prendergast's (1807–1886) innovation in language learning', in Nicola McLelland, and Richard Smith (eds), *The History of Language Learning and Teaching* (3 vols, Cambridge, 2018), vol. 2, pp 127–44. Prendergast based his 'mastery' method on the way children acquire language by oral repetition of segments of speech. In several respects, these ideas prefigure those of the Reform Movement of the 1890s. Cf. Nicola McLelland, *Teaching and Learning Foreign Languages: A History of Language Education, Assessment and Policy in Britain* (London and New York, 2017), pp 104–5.

183. Perlman Lorch, 'Investigating the biographical sources of Thomas Prendergast's (1807–1886) innovation in language learning', pp 136–7.

184. H. M. Chichester, revised by Philip Carter, 'Boden, Joseph', *Oxford Dictionary of National Biography*. The chair's proselytising aim was rescinded by the University in 1882. Learning Sanskrit to convert the Indians, like learning Irish to convert the Irish, was not destined for resounding success.

185. See above, pp 95–6.

186. For example, *Report of the President of Queen's College Cork*, 1859–60, p. 12; *Report of the President of Queen's College Belfast*, 1869–70, p. 12; Catholic University of Ireland *Calendar*, 1867–8, p. cxlviii.

187. Macaulay Report, p. 122.

188. UCD Archives, CU/4, Minutes of the Council of the Faculty of Philosophy and Letters, 4 and 6 November 1856 (pp 11–13).

189. UCD Archives, CU/4, Minutes of the Council of the Faculty of Philosophy and Letters, 19 December 1858 (p. 76). The meeting – an adjourned one – was held on a Sunday 'immediately after Mass'.

190. QCB's enrolment figures of modern language students between 1849 and 1869 yield an average of 39 students per annum in the first decade, as opposed to 109 students per annum in the following decade. (See *Report of the President of Queen's College Belfast*, 1869–70, pp 12–13.)

191. McDowell and Webb, *Trinity College Dublin*, pp 232–4 (p. 232).

192. Ibid., p. 234. For Siegfried, see Pól Ó Dochartaigh, 'A shadowy but important figure', in Elizabeth Boyle and Paul Russell (eds), *The Tripartite Life of Whitley Stokes (1830–1909)* (Dublin, 2011), pp 29–43. J. V. Luce, *Trinity College Dublin: The First 400 Years* [Quatercentenary Series] (Dublin, 1992), p. 104, reports that 180 Trinity graduates were recruited between 1855 and 1912.

193. See above, p. 94.

194. Siegfried had been learning Welsh in Wales.

195. Ó Dochartaigh, 'A shadowy but important figure', p. 42.

196. Eda Sagarra, 'The centenary of the Henry Simon Chair of German at the University of Manchester (1996): Commemorative address', in *German Life and Letters* 51 (1998), pp 509–24 (p. 514). Bruford was the Schröder professor of German at Cambridge in the 1950s.

197. Raraty, 'The chair of German, Trinity College, Dublin 1775–1866', p. 64. He appends (p. 69) a sample paper from 1843, set by Professor Abeltshauser. The questions are mostly rudimentary or quiz-like, encouraging candidates' ability to memorise rather than to reason or evaluate. For comparable bias in UK schools and universities, see McLelland, *German Through English Eyes*, pp 103–8.

198. *Report on the Condition and Progress of the Queen's University in Ireland, for the Year 1851–52*, by the Rt Hon Maziere Brady, Vice-Chancellor of the University (Dublin, 1852), p. 32.

199. Moody and Beckett, *Queen's, Belfast*, vol. 1, p. 168: 'Meissner's ideal was Max Müller'.

200. *Report of her Majesty's Commissioners Appointed to Inquire into the Progress of the Queen's Colleges*, 1858, p. 195.

201. O'Neill, 'Modern languages', pp 363, 366.

202. Catholic University of Ireland *Calendar*, 1863, pp 65–6.

203. Ibid., p. 42.

204. Royal University of Ireland *Calendar*, 1892, p. 30. This ruling is comparable with the assessment tasks set by the earliest public examinations for schools (Higher Level) set by the UCLES (University of Cambridge Local Examinations Syndicate): see McLelland, *Teaching and Learning Foreign Languages*, pp 127–73 (pp 135–40).

205. O'Neill, 'Modern languages', p. 364.

206. *Report of the President of Queen's College Galway*, 1852, p. 40.

207. *Report of the President of Queen's College Cork*, 1859–60, p. 63.

208. *Report of the President of Queen's College Cork*, 1876–7, p. 74.

209. *Report of the President of Queen's College Galway*, 1875–6, Appendix, p. 18.

210. Mary Colum, *Life and the Dream* (New York, 1947, 1958; revised edn, Dublin, 1966), pp 82–3.

211. Mary Colum, *Life and the Dream*, pp 79–80, 82–3.

212. O'Neill, 'Modern languages', p. 366; on the same page, O'Neill cites a former student who had found Geisler to be a humorous and lively teacher. Cf. Geisler's report to the College President, in *Report of the President of Queen's College Galway*, 1875–6, p. 18.

213. O'Neill, 'Modern languages', p. 363. Presumably the non-literary text (of some 200 pages) was read in extracts.

214. I can vouch, from personal experience, that *Iphigenie auf Tauris* was on the Leaving Certificate (Honours) German syllabus in 1968.

215. Etienne Pariset (1770–1847) was a member of the Société de Protection des Animaux. As was de Véricour himself, who read a paper against cruelty to animals, 'The claims of the dumb creation', in Dublin in 1869 (see *The Westminster Review* 36 (July and October 1869), p. 261).

216. Presumably in extracts: Mignet's history ran to two volumes.

217. Moody and Beckett, *Queen's, Belfast*, vol. 1, p. 167.

218. *Report of the President of Queen's College Galway*, 1850–1, p. 58, item 26.

219. *Report of the President of Queen's College Galway*, 1877–8, pp 21–2 (p. 21).

220. O'Neill, 'Modern languages', pp 364–5, on distinguished QCG language graduates who entered the colonial civil service or who pursued careers in journalism or teaching. Geisler offers his lectures on Sanskrit to undergraduates studying Sanskrit and Hindustani, to 'prepare for the competitive Indian Civil Service Examinations' (*Report of the President of Queen's College Galway*, 1877–8, p. 22). Cf. Catriona Mulcahy, Cork's university archivist, on diverse employment opportunities availed of by Cork's Victorian graduates in far-away places: 'This week Queen Elizabeth II will visit the Tyndall National Institute at University College Cork', 'An Irishwoman's Diary', *The Irish Times*, 17 May 2011. See also C. J. Dewey, 'The education of a ruling caste: The Indian Civil Service in the era of competitive examination', in *The English Historical Review* 88 (1973), pp 262–85.

221. Salvadori, *'Dove 'l sì sona'*, p. 18.

222. NUI Archives, NUI, RUI examination papers, 1888, pp 126–7.

223. McDowell and Webb, *Trinity College Dublin*, p. 272.

224. Frost, 'Hispanic Studies in British and Irish universities', p. 10.

225. Royal University of Ireland *Calendar*, 1892, p. 44.

226. Queen's College Cork President's Reports, for example, illustrate the wide disparity between numbers studying French versus German. Thus, in 1859–60 this was 56:0; in 1877–8 it was 86:0; in 1881–2 it was 140:5; in 1882–3 it was 31:3; and in 1885–6 it was 24:4. (*Report of the President of Queen's College Cork*, 1859–60, p. 6; ibid., 1877–8, p. 58; ibid., 1881–2, p. 13; ibid., 1882–3, p. 13; 1885–6, p. 17.)

227. McDowell and Webb, *Trinity College Dublin*, p. 272.

228. Cathcart (ed.), *Letters of Renouf*, vol. 3, pp 83–4, n. 6.

229. O'Neill, 'Modern languages', p. 370.

230. On the case of Spanish in the UK, see McLelland, *Teaching and Learning Foreign Languages*, pp 14–16, 191–3.

231. Robert Lowe, *Primary and Classical Education: An Address Delivered Before the Philosophical Institution of Edinburgh* (Edinburgh, 1897), p. 26.

232. I. G. Abeltshauser, public lecture on modern language study, Trinity College Dublin, 1856, cited in Raraty, 'The chair of German, Trinity College, Dublin 1775–1866', pp 66–7.

233. *Report of her Majesty's Commissioners Appointed to Inquire into the Progress of the Queen's Colleges*, 1858, p. 22.

234. Queen's College Cork *Calendar*, 1881, p. 67.

235. *Report of the President of Queen's College Belfast*, 1867, p. 18. Meissner (*Practical Lessons in German Conversation*, 1888) is quoted in McLelland, *German Through English Eyes*, p. 110. Meissner was a member of the Berlin branch of the Reform Movement (ibid., p. 362).

236. O'Neill, 'Modern languages', pp 371–2.

237. Ibid. The *Report of the President of Queen's College Galway*, 1899–1900, p. 6, mentions the recent purchase of an *'appareil inscripteur* as used by Professor Rousselot of the Collège de France [...] for the experimental study of Phonetics.' On early experimental phonetics in England during the early 1900s, see Michael Ashby, 'Experimental phonetics at University College London before World War I', First International Workshop on the History of Speech Communication Research (HSCR 2015),

Dresden, September 2015, available online at the ISCA Archive (accessed 30 July 2023). Cf. Michael Ashby and Joanna Przedlacka, 'Technology and pronunciation teaching, 1890–1940', in McLelland and Smith (eds), *The History of Language Learning and Teaching* (3 vols, Cambridge, 2018), vol. 2, pp 161–78.

238. O'Neill, 'Modern languages', pp 365–6.

239. Ibid., p. 371, alludes to the memoir of a former student, Micheál Breathnach, who was a fluent Irish speaker. He recalled that Professor Steinberger frequently asked him to utter foreign words, to demonstrate to the class the professor's belief that the Irish language contained all the sounds needed for the correct pronunciation of French.

240. *Report of the President of Queen's College Belfast*, 1867, p. 18.

241. *Report on the Condition and Progress of the Queen's University in Ireland, for the Year 1851–52*, p. 31.

242. McDowell and Webb, *Trinity College Dublin*, pp 122–7 (p. 124). The *viva voce* questions were in some cases printed after the examination had taken place, and the printed examination paper itself was a very recent invention: Cambridge in 1827, Oxford in 1830. Cf. W. B. Stanford, *Ireland and the Classical Tradition* (Dublin, 1976), pp 57–8.

243. For Trinity Fellowships, 'a proposal in 1856 that the classical part of the examination be conducted entirely by written papers was defeated, and a significant part of the examination in all subjects was still conducted *viva voce*' (McDowell and Webb, *Trinity College Dublin*, p. 232). In many countries even today, the written examination is by no means the exclusive mode of assessing school-leavers: e.g., the French *baccalauréat* or the Italian *maturità*. Candidates are examined orally in some subjects and in writing for others, depending on their balance of disciplines presented.

244. O'Neill, 'Modern languages', p. 363. Cf. *Report of the President of Queen's College Galway* (1850–1), p. 65.

245. In 1863, the handful of chosen candidates from Blackrock's French College who underwent an oral examination in public, before a panel of examiners presided over by the CU's rector, may well have been performing a *soutenance*, or *viva voce* display of their knowledge, rather than an oral French examination, held in a more private space, specifically to assess their skill in understanding and performing the spoken foreign language (Farragher and de Mare, 'Le Père Jules Leman et la fondation du collège de Blackrock, en Irlande,' pp 52–3). On traditional language learning that relied on oral memorisation and question-and-answer methods, see McLelland, *German Through English Eyes*, p. 11 and passim; and John Gallagher, *Learning Languages in Early Modern England* (Oxford, 2019), pp 125–6.

246. Salvadori, *'Dove 'l sì sona'*, pp 15–16.

247. See the 1834 College 'grinder' cited in Stanford, *Ireland and the Classical Tradition*, p. 57.

248. See for example Royal University of Ireland *Calendar*, 1892, General Regulations, p. 41. Cf. other RUI calendars from the 1890s. Students of Latin or Greek were penalised for false quantities when reading ancient texts aloud at oral examinations (Royal University of Ireland *Calendar*, 1906, p. 35).

249. Semple, 'The Royal University', p. 53. Eda Sagarra's 1954 UCD degree examinations in history included an assessment on Irish history set for honours history students that ran over three full-day sessions, involving a written essay examination on the first day, followed by students 'critiquing each other's work' on the second day and discussing the exercise on the third. A *viva voce* session rounded this off, in front of the entire History department. See Eda Sagarra, *Living with My Century* (Dublin, 2022), p. 49.

250. Leathes Report, 'Modern Studies, Being the Report of the Committee on the Position of Modern Languages in the Educational system of Great Britain' (London, 1918), p. 195.

251. Mary Colum, *Life and the Dream*, p. 22.

252. O'Neill, 'Modern languages', p. 370.

253. NUI calendars, from 1908–9 onwards, state that there will be a *viva-voce* examination in each language, including Irish. This suggests that all modern language students had to take an oral examination.

254. Catholic University of Ireland *Calendar*, 1863, pp 66–7.

255. Ibid., p. 66.

256. MacHale, *The Life and Work of George Boole*, p. 50.

257. Ibid., p. 103. William Rowan Hamilton, Trinity's Professor of Astronomy and Astronomer Royal of Ireland, was another linguistic prodigy, mastering a dozen languages by the age of 12 (McDowell and Webb, *Trinity College Dublin*, pp 111–12).

258. O'Neill, 'Modern languages', p. 364.

259. Once again, George Eliot strikes the right note in her fictional doctor–scientist hero, Tertius Lydgate, whose new-fangled ideas about treating patients, regarded with hostility by the people of Middlemarch, come from his studies in Edinburgh and Paris (George Eliot, *Middlemarch* (1871)). Lydgate, social *déclassé* and first doctor-hero of English fiction, takes an approach to his profession that is informed by the pioneering work of the late-eighteenth-century French anatomist and physiologist Xavier Bichat. (For the historical and scientific background to the character's genesis, see Patrick J. McCarthy, 'Lydgate, "The new, young surgeon" of *Middlemarch*', *Studies in English Literature, 1500–1900*, 10, No. 4 [Nineteenth Century] (Houston, 1970), pp 805–16.)

260. William Doolin, 'The Catholic University School of Medicine (1855–1909)', in Tierney (ed.), *Struggle with Fortune*, pp 61–81 (pp 67–8).

261. Ibid., p. 76.

262. Ibid.

263. Ibid.

264. The name Edmond J. McWeeney, MD (Pathology) appears in lists of RUI assistant examiners in Modern Languages (Royal University of Ireland, *Calendar*, 1896 and 1897.)

CHAPTER 7: HOME-GROWN LANGUAGE PROFESSORS

1. *The Leader*, 15 August 1908.

2. Gearóid Ó Tuathaigh, 'The position of the Irish language', in Tom Dunne et al. (eds), *The National University of Ireland 1908–2008* (Dublin, 2008), pp 33–43 (pp 40–1).

3. Mary Macken, 'Women in the university and the college: a struggle within a struggle', in Michael Tierney (ed.), *Struggle with Fortune: a Miscellany for the Centenary of the Catholic University of Ireland, 1854–1954* (Dublin, 1954), pp 142–65 (p. 153).

4. 'Death of Professor O'Ryan, FRUI', *Freeman's Journal*, 26 February 1895, p. 5.

5. National Archives, CSORP/1868/12422, Owen O'Ryan to the Under-Secretary, 10 September 1868.

6. National Archives, CSORP/1868/12422, Testimonial from Raymond de Véricour, 8 August 1868.

7. National Archives, CSORP/1868/12422, Raymond de Véricour to Sir Robert Kane, 9 August 1868. Kane also endorsed O'Ryan as 'a person at once perfectly qualified, an Irishman, a Roman Catholic and a member of the Queen's University' (National Archives, CSORP/1868/12422, Kane to Chief Secretary, 11 August 1868).

8. 'Death of Professor O'Ryan, FRUI', *Freeman's Journal*, 26 February 1895, p. 5.

9. John A. Murphy, *The College: A History of Queen's/University College Cork, 1845–1895* (Cork, 1995), p. 369, Appendix A.

10. Owen O'Ryan, 'Giacomo Leopardi', lecture to the Cork Literary and Scientific Society, 16 February 1882 (Dublin, 1883), reprinted in Marco Sonzogni (ed.), *Or Volge l'Anno / At The Year's Turning: an Anthology of Irish Poets responding to Leopardi* (Dublin, 1998), pp 259–86.

11. J. A. Murphy, *The College*, p. 135; Paul Rouse, 'Butler, William Francis Thomas', DIB. His books include *The Lombard Communes: A History of the Republics of North Italy* (1906), *Confiscation in Irish History* (1917), and *Gleanings from Irish History* (1925).

12. J. A. Murphy, *The College*, pp 134–5 (p. 135).

13. Patrick J. Corish, *Maynooth College 1795–1995* (Dublin, 1995), p. 258. This Clare man (1858–1918), later President of Maynooth, had studied in St Sulpice in Paris, and in Freiburg im Breisgau (ibid., pp 302 and 461). On his Dante study (1899), see Cormac Ó Cuilleanáin, 'Dante's adventures in Ireland, 1785–2021', in Massimo Bacigalupo (ed.), *Dante nel mondo* (Genova, 2022), pp 152–80 (p. 160).

14. At St Stephen's Green, one Bryan O'Donnell looked after French between Polin's death in 1889 and Cadic's arrival in 1892 (*A Page of Irish History: Story of University College, Dublin 1883–1909*, compiled by Fathers of the Society of Jesus (Dublin and Cork, 1930), p. 212; Royal University of Ireland *Calendar*, 1891, pp 23–4). Could he be the Bryan O'Donnell, MA, who did an English

adaptation of Frédéric Loliée, *Prince Talleyrand and his Times*, published by John Long in London in 1911 (online advertisement, accessed via Abebooks, 18 August 2021)? We may never know.

15. *A Page of Irish History*, p. 83. His name appears alongside the names of two other Jesuits in Celtic Studies: Denis Murphy, SJ and Edmund Hogan, SJ.

16. Ibid., pp 127–8.

17. Ibid.; 'The late Father O'Carroll S.J.', in *The Irish Monthly* 17 (1889), pp 209–15.

18. 'Recollections of W.H. Brayden', *A Page of Irish History*, pp 123–6 (pp 124–5). Brayden was a future editor of *The Freeman's Journal*.

19. See above, pp 83–93.

20. Ó Madagáin cites the example of problems encountered by individual students wishing to take Irish to degree level, in University College Galway in the 1900s. See Breandán Ó Madagáin, 'Irish: A difficult birth', in Tadhg Foley (ed.), *From Queen's College to National University: Essays on the Academic History of QCG/UCG/NUI, Galway* (Dublin, 1999), pp 344–59 (p. 354).

21. The indelible trauma of the Famine on survivors, and its legacy on the next generation, are forcefully brought out by the opening pages of Kevin Whelan's detailed unpacking of the densely layered reverberations in Joyce's short story 'The Dead' (Kevin Whelan, 'The memories of "The Dead"', in *The Yale Journal of Criticism* 15 (2002), pp 59–97).

22. See the examples discussed by Meidhbhín Ní Úrdail, 'Patrick Ferriter (1856–1924): An Irish scholar at home and abroad', in *American Journal of Irish Studies* 15 (2019), pp 164–94.

23. On revival periodicals among Irish-Americans in the US, see Regina Uí Chollatáin, 'A new Gaelic League idea? The global context', in Liam Mac Mathúna and Máire Nic an Bhaird (eds), *Douglas Hyde: Irish Ideology and International Impact* (Dublin, 2023), pp 15–49.

24. Thus, out of 12 appointments made between 1873 and 1909, six were from Munster, three from Connacht, two from Leinster and one from Ulster. Some were rural, others urban; some were native speakers, others had learned Irish as a second language. Some were Catholics, others not; some were clerics, others lay. See Table 2, Professors of Celtic/Irish in Ireland's Universities (1800–1921), pp 314–5 below. The Table is limited to professors of language or literature. A more inclusive grouping would include people like Eoin MacNeill, professor of early Irish history, whose work advanced research into early and medieval Irish (see Patrick Maume and Thomas Charles-Edwards, 'MacNeill, Eoin (John)', DIB).

25. T. W. Moody and J. C. Beckett, *Queen's, Belfast 1845–1949: The History of a University* (2 vols, London, 1959), vol. 1, pp 370–1. Cf. Roger Blaney, *Presbyterians and the Irish Language* (Belfast, 1996), pp 185–6.

26. *Q.C.B.* 7/4 (22 February 1906); 8/1 (November 1906); 9/4 (February 1908). The substance of these items, from various issues of QCB's student magazine (a rare periodical), were kindly provided to me by Jennifer FitzGerald (pers. comm., 5 February 2022).

27. Blaney, *Presbyterians and the Irish Language*, p. 185. In 1905–6 there were 25 Catholic students at QCB, out of a total student body of 403 (ibid.).

28. Eda Sagarra, 'From the pistol to the petticoat? The changing student body 1592–1992', in C. H. Holland (ed.), *Trinity College Dublin and the Idea of a University* (Dublin, 1991), pp 107–27 (pp 121–2).

29. UCD Archives, CU/4, Minutes of the Council of the Faculty of Philosophy and Letters, 15 February 1874, Students' letter, dated 26 January 1874, inserted in the Faculty Minutes.

30. UCD Archives, CU/4, Minutes of the Council of the Faculty of Philosophy and Letters, 13 October 1874 . It is not clear where the Clareman O'Looney (1828–1901) had studied classical Irish, but he had worked as a copyist and translator. See Lesa Ní Mhunghaile, 'Ó Luanaigh (O'Looney), Brian', DIB.

31. See Eoghan Ó Raghallaigh, 'Hogan, Edmund Ignatius', DIB; and Gerard Murphy, 'Celtic Studies in the university and the college', in Michael Tierney (ed.), *Struggle with Fortune: A Miscellany for the Centenary of the Catholic University of Ireland, 1854–1954* (Dublin, 1954), pp 121–41 (pp 130–1).

32. David Murphy and Linde Lunney, 'Bergin, Osborn Joseph', DIB; Cornelius G. Buttimer, 'Celtic and Irish in College 1849–1944', in *Journal of the Cork Historical and Archaeological Society* 94 (1989), pp 88–112 (pp 93–4); J. A. Murphy, *The College*, p. 150. Cf. Ó Madagáin, 'Irish: A difficult birth', p. 354, n. 42; and Buttimer, p. 95: 'Bergin had only two pupils for the duration of his involvement with the lectureship.'

33. Murphy and Lunney, 'Bergin, Osborn Joseph', DIB. The Cork lectureship was continued by Bergin's successor, Éamonn O'Donoghue, an Irish-speaking League member (Buttimer, 'Celtic and Irish in College 1849–1944', pp 95–6). Bergin was to be the first Director of the School of Celtic Studies at the Dublin Institute for Advanced Studies (1940).

34. See the biographical note by Lesa Ní Mhunghaile, 'O'Growney, Eugene (Eoghan Ó Gramhnaigh)', DIB.

35. Corish, *Maynooth College*, p. 213.

36. His remains, brought back from Los Angeles to Ireland in 1903, were buried in the college cemetery after a large public funeral lasting four days; they were finally laid to rest in a Celtic mausoleum installed in 1905. (Ibid., pp 287–8.) The archaising mausoleum, reputedly modelled on St Kevin's Church in Glendalough, was (like Cadic's monument) designed by William Alphonsus Scott.

37. Thus, for example, students spontaneously began to recite the nightly rosary in Irish and requested that the book read at supper be an Irish text (Ibid., pp 284–5).

38. Ibid., p. 285. The publications, generously funded, included some of the college's manuscripts (ibid., p. 286). Brian Ó Cuív, 'Irish language and literature, 1845–1921', in W. E. Vaughan (ed.), *A New History of Ireland, vol. 6: Ireland under the Union, II (1870–1921)* (Oxford, 1996), pp 385–435 (p. 408, n. 3), describes Michael O'Hickey as 'prime mover' behind the society's establishment.

39. Corish, *Maynooth College*, pp 288–96; Leon Ó Broin, 'The Gaelic League and the Chair of Irish in Maynooth', in *Studies: An Irish Quarterly Review* 52 (1963), pp 348–62; Tomás Ó Fiaich, 'The great controversy', in Seán Ó Tuama (ed.), *The Gaelic League Idea*, RTÉ Thomas Davis Lectures 1968–9 (Cork, 1972), pp 63–75 (pp 70–3); RTÉ Radio One, *Documentary on One*, 8 December 1979: 'Dismissal of Father Michael O'Hickey'; Lucy McDiarmid, *The Irish Art of Controversy* (Dublin, 2005), pp 50–86.

40. McDiarmid, *The Irish Art of Controversy*, pp 60–6 (p. 63).

41. Ibid., p. 232, n. 6.

42. Cited in Corish, *Maynooth College*, p. 289.

43. See for example the ACS extracts reproduced in Séamas Ó Buachalla (ed.), *A Significant Irish Educationalist: The Educational Writings of P.H. Pearse* (Cork, 1980), pp 233–7, 239–42.

44. Aidan Doyle, *A History of the Irish Language: From the Norman Invasion to Independence* (Oxford, 2015), p. 184.

45. Corish, *Maynooth College*, p. 292. The individuals found other routes to ordination following this setback.

46. 'The campaign for the Irish language requirement, in Dr O'Hickey's vision of it, was indistinguishable from the cause of Irish nationalism.' (McDiarmid, *The Irish Art of Controversy*, p. 65.)

47. Corish, *Maynooth College*, pp 240–8; 257–66.

48. While English had begun to take over as a teaching medium, oral examinations continued to be conducted in Latin (Ibid., p. 245). Some of the staff, like the theology professor Walter McDonald, were not convinced that an examination conducted through Latin was the best way of discerning the ablest theologians, as it led students to avoid complicated questions and 'to trot out commonplaces' (Walter McDonald, *Reminiscences of a Maynooth Professor* (Cork, 1967) p. 238; cf. pp 135–6).

49. Corish, *Maynooth College*, pp 289–90. From June 1906, all Maynooth students took the RUI matriculation examination (ibid., p. 261).

50. John A. Murphy, 'Ó Laoghaire, Peadar (An tAthair Peadar; O'Leary, Peter)', DIB. The stream of publications ran to almost 500 items.

51. Eoin Mac Cárthaigh, 'Dineen, Patrick Stephen', DIB.

52. Maurice Cronin, 'Sheehan, Michael', DIB. Ring College is situated in a (partly) Irish-speaking district of County Waterford.

53. See Lawrence William White, 'De Brún, Pádraig (Browne, Paddy)', DIB; and Máire Cruise O'Brien, *The Same Age as the State* (Dublin, 2003). On a travelling studentship, De Brún had studied in Paris for his doctorate (1912) before holding the Maynooth chair of physics and theoretical physics (1914–45). He chaired the council of the Dublin Institute for Advanced Studies (set up by the State in 1940), where he was instrumental in offering asylum to Erwin Schrödinger during the war.

54. These terms, borrowed from Philip O'Leary, *The Prose Literature of the Gaelic Revival, 1881–1921* (Pennsylvania, 1994), do not precisely label individuals. Rather they help to frame different tendencies among revivalists. Cf. Doyle, *A History of the Irish Language*, pp 252–61.

55. Doyle, *A History of the Irish Language*, pp 215–30.

56. See for example Mícheál O'Siadhail, 'Standard Irish orthography: An assessment', in *The Crane Bag* 5:2 (1981; 1982 reprint), pp 903–7; Alan Bliss, 'The Standardization of Irish', in ibid., pp 908–14. There was a bias towards Munster Irish, which, according to Doyle, *A History of the Irish Language*, p. 228, 'was probably due to the strong influence of Peadar Ó Laoghaire and Patrick Dineen, the man whose 1904 dictionary fixed the spelling of Irish; both of them were speakers of Munster dialects. Academics in particular were drawn to the Irish-speaking regions of the south.'

57. For an account of the first summer school, see 'Sgoil Árd-Leighinn na Gaedhilge / School of Irish Learning: Report of First Session, 1903', in *Ériu* 1 (1904), pp 9–12.

58. Andreas Hüther, 'A transnational nation-building process: philologists and universities in nineteenth-century Ireland and Germany', in Leon Litvack and Colin Graham (eds), *Ireland and Europe in the Nineteenth Century* (Dublin, 2006), pp 101–11, highlights the role played by Celtic philologists in Irish nation-building. On Ernst Windisch, see Eleanor Knott, 'Ernst Windisch, 1844–1918', in *Studies* 8 (1919), pp 264–7; on Zimmer (1851–1910), see Aidan Breen, 'Zimmer, Heinrich', DIB; and on Meyer (1858–1919), see idem, 'Meyer, Kuno', DIB. Joachim Fischer, *Das Deutschlandbild der Iren, 1890–1939: Geschichte – Form – Funktion* (Heidelberg, 2000), pp 631–40, Appendix 3 ('Irische Studierende an deutschen Universitäten'), lists 54 Irish students who studied at German universities between the 1880s and 1939. Of this number, the largest cohort – 19 – studied Celtic philology. Cf. ibid., pp 496–504.

59. Some contacts may have prompted the welcome given to individual scholars fleeing persecution: Osborn Bergin knew the prodigious philologist Ernst Lewy, who came to Ireland from Berlin in 1937, and lectured in Sanskrit, Old Slavonic and Finno-Ugric in UCD during the war before being given a chair in the RIA. (See Gisela Holfter, 'Akademiker im irischen Exil: Ernst Lewy (1881–1966)', in *German Life and Letters* 61 (2008), pp 363–87; and 'Lewy, Ernst', DIB.) Another Hitler émigré, the successful lawyer Ernst Scheyer (1890–1958), arrived in Ireland from Silesia in 1939 and eventually found stable employment transmitting his love of German literature to Trinity students in 1947, for the last decade of his life. (See Gisela Holfter, 'Ernst Scheyer', in Holfter (ed.), *German-Speaking Exiles in Ireland 1933–1945* (Leiden, 2006), pp 149–69.)

60. Eoin MacNeill, 'Irish in the National University of Ireland: a plea for Irish education' (Dublin, 1909), p. 46. (UCD James Joyce Library, Special Collections, 34.G.3/12.)

61. Ibid.; for MacNeill and Irish studies, see G. Murphy, 'Celtic Studies in the university and the college', pp 131–7.

62. See John O'Beirne Crowe, 'The Catholic University and the Irish language' (pamphlet, dated Belfast, 1854; printed in Dublin, 1865), discussed above, Chapter Four, pp 92–3; cf. Uí Chollatáin, 'A new Gaelic League idea?', p. 31.

63. Buttimer, 'Celtic and Irish in College 1849–1944', pp 97–100. Henebry had studied at Maynooth and taken a doctorate in Old Irish in Greifswald, under Zimmer, before working as professor of Celtic at the Catholic University in Washington DC He 'was the first native Irish-speaker to receive formal modern linguistic training. He received his doctorate from Greifswald (1898) for a thesis on the dialect of Waterford' (Eoghan Ó Raghallaigh, 'Henebry, Richard (de Hindeberg, Risteard)', DIB).

64. Richard Henebry, 'A plea for prose', in *The Gaelic Journal* 4:41 (June 1892), pp 141–4 (p. 143).

65. Ibid.

66. Henebry's weekly columns on 'Revival Irish', appeared in *The Leader*, November 1908–March 1909.

67. Richard Henebry, 'Revival Irish', *The Leader*, 6 March 1909, pp 58–9 (p. 59).

68. This rings loud from Ó Raghallaigh, 'Henebry, Richard (de Hindeberg, Risteard)', DIB.

69. Henebry, 'A plea for prose', p. 142; cf. Doyle, *A History of the Irish Language*, p. 226. On Keating, see above, Chapter Two, p. 28.

70. Buttimer, 'Celtic and Irish in College 1849–1944', pp 97–8 (p. 98).

71. Christopher Stray, *Classics Transformed: Schools, Universities, and Society in England, 1830–1960* (Oxford, 1998), pp 69–71, on classical verse composition as part of the texture of daily life in a public school. In Thomas Hughes, *Tom Brown's School Days* (New York and London, 1857), 'doing your verses' was a daily chore for the boy protagonists, who invent a variety of shortcuts to ease the pain (see in particular Chapters 3 and 9). The less daunting task of prose composition, in the sense of translation of prose passages from English to the target language, gradually took over during the later nineteenth century.

72. In a similar vein, a manual of Old French grammar, published in the 1970s, includes sentences for translation from English to Old French: see E. Einhorn, *Old French: A Concise Handbook* (Cambridge, 1974).

73. Indeed, he was something of a *bête noire* in Revival circles (Buttimer, 'Celtic and Irish in College 1849–1944', p. 97).

74. Gustav Lehmacher, SJ, 'Some thoughts on an Irish literary language', in *Studies: an Irish Quarterly Review* 12 (1923), pp 26–32. The piece drew reactions (pp 32–44) from a number of respondents, including Thomas O'Rahilly, Osborn Bergin, Tomás Ó Máille and Frederick William O'Connell.

75. Buttimer, 'Celtic and Irish in College 1849–1944', p. 101.

76. The colleague was Éamonn O'Donoghue, brother of Tadhg. Buttimer, 'Celtic and Irish in College 1849–1944', pp 98–9, gives telling statistics on numbers of students taking Early Irish and Modern Irish for the years 1909–15: those opting for the former were steadily outnumbered by the latter, especially after the die had been cast on the question of essential Irish for NUI matriculation. Students opted to learn the Irish that would guarantee them employment after graduation.

77. Hyde, as a collector of modern Irish manuscripts, was aware that the contemporary language, like all languages, was constantly evolving, even in written form: see Richard Sharpe, 'Destruction of Irish manuscripts and the National Board of Education', in *Studia Hibernica* 43 (2017), pp 95–116. On the transformations wrought on the language itself by the very process of reviving it, see Doyle, *A History of the Irish Language*, pp 215–62.

78. Frederick William O'Connell, in his response to Lehmacher, 'Some thoughts on an Irish literary language', *Studies* 12 (1923), pp 36–7 (p. 37).

79. The League published more folklore than educational material. See Philip O'Leary, 'Seanchuidhthe, *Séadna*, Sheehan, and the "Zeitgeist": Folklore and folklife in Gaelic fiction of the early Revival', in *Proceedings of the Harvard Celtic Colloquium* 9 (1989), pp 43–99 (pp 43–8).

80. Ibid.

81. Ibid., p. 51.

82. Buttimer, 'Celtic and Irish in College 1849–1944', p. 101.

83. Ó Madagáin, 'Irish: A difficult birth', p. 355. Galway initially set up two Irish chairs in the new university, but failed to fill the proposed Celtic Philology professorship.

84. See above, Chapter Three, p. 49. Cf. Ruairí Ó hUiginn, 'Tomás Ó Máille', in Ruairí Ó hUiginn (ed.), *Scoláirí Gaeilge: Léachtaí Cholm Cille* 27 (Maynooth, 1997), pp 83–122; Lesa Ní Mhunghaile, 'Ó Máille, Tomás', DIB.

85. Ó Madagáin, 'Irish: A difficult birth', pp 358–9, gives details of his curriculum vitae, gleaned from his application for the NUI chair. His studentship was courtesy of Mrs Alice Stopford Green, who had the vision and generosity to fund it as well as Osborn Bergin's, in the same year. Under Celtic scholars in foreign parts, Ó Máille studied Old Irish, Celtic Philology, Sanskrit, Greek, Breton and Welsh. His MA thesis, 'The language of the Annals of Ulster', was later published as a book.

86. 'With the appointment of Ó Máille, Irish in UCG can be said to have at last been put on a secure footing, in contrast with the difficulties of the previous century.' (Ó Madagáin, 'Irish: A difficult birth', p. 359.)

87. Ó Máille, application, cited in Ó Madagáin, 'Irish: A difficult birth', p. 359.

88. Ó hUiginn, 'Tomás Ó Máille'. He was finicky about his students' spoken Irish. See the anecdote recorded by Jackie Uí Chionna, *An Oral History of University College Galway, 1930–1980: A University in Living Memory* (Dublin, 2019), p. 174: having accidentally knocked a student off a bicycle when at the wheel of his car, Ó Máille corrected the student's Irish usage in the exchange that followed.

89. Moody and Beckett, *Queen's, Belfast*, vol. 1, pp 412–13. Ibid., vol. 2, p. 641, Appendix I (G), shows that no professorial appointment in 'Celtic' was made in Belfast between 1861 and 1945.

90. Lesa Ní Mhunghaile, 'O'Connell, Frederick William', DIB. Cf. Reggie Chamberlain-King, 'F.W. O'Connell: Master of strange tongues', introduction to Conall Cearnach [Frederick William O'Connell], *The Fatal Move* (Dublin, 1924; Swan River Press edn, 2021), pp vii–xxxv; idem, 'Conall Cearnach (1875–1929)', in *The Green Book: Writings on Irish Gothic, Supernatural and Fantastic Literature* 11 (Dublin, 2018), pp 60–4.

91. 'Irish personalities in the public eye', *Irish Times*, 25 February 1928, p. 4.

92. The broadcasting schedule for 11 July 1927, p. 5, for instance, announces for 7.30 to 7.45 'Gaedhilg: Conall Cearnach'. On his Welsh, cf. *Irish Times*, 25 February 1928, p. 4; and 'Dublin literary man killed by bus', *Irish Times*, 26 October 1929, p. 5.

93. Chamberlain-King, 'F.W. O'Connell', p. xxxi.

94. A perusal of the statistics in a sample of QUB *Vice-Chancellors' Reports* for the period 1910–25 suggests that enrolment for Celtic rarely exceeded 20 students. (Information kindly supplied by Jennifer FitzGerald.)

95. Professor Mitchell Henry, brother of the painter Paul Henry, was (along with O'Connell) one of the very few academics at QUB who espoused the nationalist cause. See Edith Hall, 'Sinn Féin and Ulysses: Between Professor Robert Mitchell Henry and James Joyce', in Isabelle Torrance and Donncha O'Rourke (eds), *Classics and Irish Politics, 1916–2016* (Oxford, 2020), pp 193–217.

96. F. W. O'Connell, 'The practical value of Irish', in F. W. O'Connell, *The Writings on the Walls* (Dublin, 1915), pp 80–5 (p. 80). Cf. his 'Irish the master key to linguistics', in ibid., pp 86–96.

97. In O'Connell, *The Writings on the Walls*. Cited in Chamberlain-King, F.W. O'Connell p. xi.

98. On this tangled issue see R. B. McDowell and D. A. Webb, *Trinity College Dublin 1592–1952: An Academic History* (Cambridge, 1982), pp 379–87.

99. Ibid., p. 502, Appendix 2, Fig. 2: 'Number of qualifications awarded annually in Divinity, Medicine and Engineering, plotted as five-year running averages'.

100. Ibid., pp 414–15. It did however produce serious scholarship in Celtic philology.

101. Ibid., p. 550, n. 23. Máirtín Ó Murchú, 'Irish language Studies in Trinity College Dublin', in *Hermathena* (*Quatercentenary Papers*) (1992), pp 43–68 (pp 63–4), is less dismissive about Murphy's scholarship.

102. Ó Murchú, 'Irish language Studies in Trinity College Dublin', pp 64–5.

103. Hayden (BA 1885, MA 1887) was a noted campaigner for equal opportunities for women. On Donovan, see Marie Coleman, 'O'Sullivan, Mary Josephine Donovan', DIB.

104. See Table 3, 'NUI's First Women Professors (Modern Languages, including Irish)', p. 316.

105. Donal McCartney, *UCD: A National Idea: The History of University College Dublin* (Dublin, 1999), pp 83, 100.

106. Macken, 'Women in the university and the college', p. 143, cites earlier cases of women professors in other European countries. In the UK, Edith Morley became professor of English at University College Reading in 1908 (not without opposition), and Caroline Spurgeon was the first woman professor in the University of London. See Renate Haas, 'Caroline F. E. Spurgeon (1869–1942): First woman professor of English in England', in Jane Chance (ed.), *Women Medievalists and the Academy* (Madison, 2005), pp 99–109 (p. 101).

107. Swertz was promoted to a chair the following year. Having spent the summer of 1914 with relatives in Germany, she found it impossible to travel back to Ireland once the war broke out. She died in Germany from tuberculosis in 1915. (Ruth Fleischmann, 'Aloys Fleischmann: Bavarian musician and civilian prisoner of war, 1916–1919', in Tom French (ed.), *Oldcastle Camp 1914–1918: An Illustrated History* (Navan, 2018), pp 125–66 (p. 127).) Swertz had arrived in Cork in 1879; cf. above, Chapter Two, p. 39, n. 112.

108. J. A. Murphy, *The College*, p. 376. Cf. Fischer, *Das Deutschlandbild der Iren, 1890–1939*, pp 485–6.

109. Cf. Judith Harford, *The Opening of University Education to Women in Ireland* (Dublin, 2008), p. 94: 'In the period 1891 to 1900, 417 women students were awarded the degree of BA and twenty-nine women were awarded the degree of MA. A further twenty-five women were awarded the degree of MB, seven the degree of LLB, and six the degree of MD for the same period.' In Galway in 1908, for example, when Emily Anderson completed her first year, there were eleven females out of a total student body of 120. (Jackie Uí Chionna, *Queen of Codes: The Secret Life of Emily Anderson, Britain's Greatest Female Codebreaker* (London, 2023), p. 15.) For Cork, see J. A. Murphy, *The College*, pp 130–1.

110. See Seamus Deane on the impact of the 1947 Education Act on Northern Ireland (Maurice Fitzpatrick (ed.), *The Boys of St Columb's* (Dublin, 2010), pp 89–90).

111. I am grateful to Jennifer FitzGerald for calling Elsie McCallum to my attention (pers. comm., 15 February 2022).

112. Jennifer FitzGerald, '"The Queen's girl": Helen Waddell and women at Queen's University Belfast, 1908–1920', in Judith Harford and Claire Rush (eds), *Have Women Made a Difference? Women in Irish Universities, 1850–2010* (Bern, 2010), pp 77–104 (p. 93). Temporary posts were held by Maude Clarke in history, Rubie Warner in English and Hedwig Moore in French.

113. Professor Kathleen Atkinson. See Martina McKnight and Myrtle Hill, '"Doing academia" in Queen's University Belfast', in Harford and Rush (eds), *Have Women Made a Difference?*, pp 189–217 (p. 190).

114. Fischer, *Das Deutschlandbild der Iren, 1890–1939*, p. 488. For numbers of male versus female students taking German in Irish secondary schools, see ibid., pp 626–9; for numbers of male versus female students taking French and German at Intermediate and Leaving Certificate levels, see ibid., pp 631–2. On German study in UK schools and universities during and after the Great War, see F. E. Sandbach, 'German Studies in the British Isles since 1914', in *Monatshefte für deutsche Sprache und Pädagogik [Jahrbuch 1927]* (Madison, 1926), pp 22–37. For the collapse in numbers of male students taking German during the war, see ibid, pp 27–8. This may already have been a factor in 1914 in Cork.

115. Women's names appear in lists of Junior Fellows and Examiners of RUI *Calendars*.

116. See above, pp 74–80.

117. St Mary's in Dublin and St Angela's in Cork. See Margaret Mac Curtain [Sister Benevenuta], 'St Mary's University College', in *University Review* 3 (1964), pp 33–47 (p. 41); 'Professor Mary Ryan', UCC heritage website, https://www.ucc.ie/en/heritage/history/people/ucc-staff/prof-mary-ryan (accessed 22 August 2023); Timothy O'Connor, 'Remembering one of the trailblazers of our education system', *Irish Examiner*, 7 March 2020; J. A. Murphy, *The College*, pp 130–1, 187. See also *Evening Echo*, 17 June 1961; *Evening Herald*, 17 June 1961; 'Professor Mary Ryan, D.Litt.', in *UCC Record* 37 (Easter 1962), pp 21–5.

118. Conversation, 2 February 2023, with Professor Boyle's daughter, Dr Ita Kirwan (also a German scholar). Cf. *A Century of Scholarship: Travelling Students of the National University of Ireland* (Dublin, 2008), pp 101, 103. Her sharp observations of life in the Swiss city appeared in print. See Mary Curran, 'Impressions of Zürich', in *Studies: An Irish Quarterly Review* 9 (1920), pp 613–19.

119. Rosaleen O'Neill, 'Modern languages', in Tadhg Foley (ed.), *From Queen's College to National University: Essays on the Academic History of QCG/UCG/NUI, Galway* (Dublin, 1999), pp 360–83 (p. 375); Uí Chionna, *Queen of Codes*, pp 11–12, 15–17, 23–6.

120. O'Neill, 'Modern languages', pp 377–9; and 381–2. On Anderson, see below, pp 177–8.

121. Macken, 'Women in the university and the college'; 'Retirement gift to woman professor', *Irish Independent*, 9 March 1951.

122. McCartney, *UCD: A National Idea*, p. 29.

123. *Irish Independent*, 16 April 1910, p. 6; *Freeman's Journal*, 22 August 1911; *Irish Independent*, 27 October 1911, p. 6. She worked in the Inspectorate from 1905 to 1908. On Mary Brebner, also a Gilchrist travelling scholar, see above, Chapter Five, n. 101.

124. Henri D'Arbois de Jubainville.

125. Set up in 1885 to admit women graduates, Hughes Hall was then called the Cambridge Training College for Women Teachers. See Margaret Bottrall, *Hughes Hall 1885–1985* (Cambridge, 1985).

126. J. J. Hogan, 'Mary M. Macken: An appreciation', in *Studies* 39 (1950), pp 315–18 (pp 315–16); Macken, 'Women in the university and the college', pp 160, 150–4. Sister (later Mother) Eucharia (1860–1929), born Elizabeth Ryan, had expertise in classical and modern languages. The Loreto sisters ran a hostel for Roman Catholic student teachers in Cambridge for a few years in the early 1900s. (Deirdre Bryan, 'Ryan, Elizabeth (Mary Eucharia)', DIB.) Mary Kate Ryan, Maria Degani and Agnes O'Farrelly had postgraduate teaching diplomas.

127. O'Faolain to Fleischmann, n.d. but January 1949, cited in J. A. Murphy, *The College*, p. 231. O'Faolain was equally dismissive, on opposite grounds, of UCC's professor of English, W. F. P. Stockley: 'Alas, as a teacher he was a comical figure. [...] His mind was like a lady's sewing basket after a kitten had been through it. His lectures were a host of bright scraps of quotation and casual references all jumbled colourfully together without order, sequence or evident purpose.' (Sean O'Faolain, *Vive Moi! An Autobiography* (London, 1965), pp 131–2.)

128. Margaret Mac Curtain, 'The 1940s: Women academics at University College Cork', in Harford and Rush (eds), *Have Women Made a Difference?*, pp 127–37 (p. 130).

129. 'Professor Mary Ryan, D.Litt.', p. 22.

130. Ibid., p. 23.

131. Letter from Emily Anderson to Fr Hynes, college registrar, 22 July 1918 (cited in Uí Chionna, *Queen of Codes*, p. 46).

132. The Ryan sisters' correspondence frequently allude to the pronunciation of foreign languages; Kit mentions taking a course on French phonetics in London (January 1907), and a *stage* in Paris

(1908). She was certainly aware of the importance of the spoken language and advises her sisters on relevant textbooks.

133. NLI, Manuscripts Collection, List No. 178 (Seán T. Ó Ceallaigh and the Ryans of Tomcoole), MS 48,445/6/10, Mary Kate Ryan to her sister Min, 11 October 1912. By 'C.T.C.' she is referring to the Cambridge Training College for teachers.

134. Agnes O'Farrelly, 'The reign of humbug', Gaelic League pamphlet 10 (Dublin, 1901), p. 10.

135. McCartney, *UCD: A National Idea*, pp 83, 100.

136. Her colleague Agnes O'Farrelly worked on her behalf as a member of the Governing Body to obtain commensurate remuneration for doing the work of two. See Phyllis Gaffney, '"Assistant something-or-other in the new university": life and letters of Mary Kate O'Kelly (1878–1934)', in Harford and Rush (eds), *Have Women Made a Difference?*, pp 105–26 (pp 113–14). The French chair was eventually filled by Roger Chauviré, who arrived in February 1919 and stayed until his retirement in 1948. Mary Kate was promoted to a statutory lectureship in 1925, which brought permanence of employment. She retired for health reasons and died in Germany in 1934.

137. J. A. Murphy, *The College*, p. 233. For a list of her publications, see UCC's heritage website on Mary Ryan.

138. See, for example, her well-written and imaginative appraisal of a Spanish professor of Arabic's book on Muslim sources for Dante's topography of the Otherworld, 'A Dante discovery', in *Studies: An Irish Quarterly Review* 10 (1921), pp 425–36; or her informed review of a new book on Voltaire, 'Alfred Noyes on Voltaire', in *Studies* 26 (1937), pp 281–95.

139. Thomas's sudden death was recorded in *The Brisbane Courier*, 13 March 1934, p. 12 ('Death of India's postal chief'), and appreciations were voiced by members of the Legislative Assembly at New Delhi, Monday 12 March 1934. He was lauded on all sides for his honesty, good humour and fairmindedness and as the type of man 'which enable the British Government to rule in India'. (See *Legislative Assembly Debates, Official Report*, 12 March 1934, vol. 3, no. 1, 'Death of Sir Thomas Ryan', New Delhi, Government of India Press, 1934, pp 2073–6.) Cf. David Morray, 'Ryan, Sir Andrew', DIB; William Murphy, 'Ryan, Finbar', DIB. The second brother, Andrew, a linguist like his sister, served as the last dragoman in Constantinople; see his posthumous memoir, *The Last of the Dragomans* (London, 1951).

140. Hogan, 'Mary M. Macken', pp 315–16; Fischer, *Das Deutschlandbild der Iren, 1890–1939*, p. 488.

141. Hogan, 'Mary M. Macken', p. 318, lists her articles in *Studies*.

142. Eda Sagarra, 'Austrian literature in Ireland', in Paul Leifer and Eda Sagarra (eds), *Austro-Irish Links Through the Centuries* (Favorita Papers, special edn, Vienna, 2002), pp 143–61 (p. 147).

143. Gisela Holfter and Horst Dickel, *An Irish Sanctuary: German-speaking Refugees in Ireland 1933–1945* (Berlin, 2017), p. 310; and Joyce Padbury, *Mary Hayden, Irish Historian and Feminist 1862–1942* (Dublin, 2021), passim.

144. Frances Clarke, 'Maxwell, Constantia (Elizabeth)', DIB.

145. Uí Chionna, *Queen of Codes*. Cf. Roisin Healy, 'The lives of Emily Anderson: Galway professor, music historian, and British intelligence officer', https://mooreinstitute.ie/2017/03/20/lives-emily-anderson-galway-professor-music-historian-british-intelligence-officer/, 25 October 2022.

146. O'Neill, 'Modern languages', p. 375. For BA Honours students she revised his course on the history of German literature.

147. O'Neill, 'Modern languages', p. 376, quotes from a glowing review of the remarkable qualities of Anderson's translation work.

148. Uí Chionna, *Queen of Codes*, pp 126, 241.

149. Ibid., pp 105–29, 235–82.

150. Her Mozart volumes contained over 900 letters; the Beethoven volumes contained over 1,570 letters, 230 of which had never been previously published, and 33 of which 'had previously missing pages restored' (Ibid., pp 350, n. 15, 278).

151. *The Times*, 20 August 1938, cited in ibid., p. 127; and *The Times*, 10 October 1961, cited in ibid., p. 278.

152. Anderson observed, in a 1961 radio interview broadcast after the publication of her Beethoven letters, that to read the composer's handwriting required years of familiarity. On the difficulty of the task, she commented, 'It's rather like dealing with papyri.' (Ibid., pp 285–7 (p. 286).)

153. *Freeman's Journal*, 13 August 1910, p. 9: she had attended a Vice-Regal Lodge reception for Canadian school teachers in August 1910. She was naturalised in 1905.

154. *Anglo-Celt*, 12 August 1911, p. 7.

155. For the transformation of John Randolph Leslie (educated at Eton and Cambridge) into a kilted Catholic Irish Nationalist, see Charles Lysaght's profile, 'Leslie, John Randolph ('Shane')', DIB.

156. *Kilkenny People*, 12 August 1911; cf. *Freeman's Journal*, 22 August 1911.

157. *Kilkenny People*, 12 August 1911, p. 2; cf. *Tipperary Star*, 26 August 1911, p. 8. A moment's reflection points up the absurdity of this contention: a native Italian speaker with language expertise could handle Spanish with little difficulty. The verb 'lisp', associated with childishness, is demeaning and sexist.

158. *Irish Independent*, 21 August 1911, p. 4; *Freeman's Journal*, 22 August 1911; *Irish Independent*, 27 October 1911, p. 6.

159. *Freeman's Journal*, 22 August 1911.

160. The NUI's governing body comprised 10 local authority representatives out of a total of 34, and local government was a source of funding. The assumption that senior appointments could be debated in the public arena, and that applicants had to canvass support from county councillors who sometimes felt entitled to interfere, lasted until the 1960s, when more academic assessment and appointment procedures were brought in. See Patrick O'Flynn, *A Question of Identity: The Great Trinity & UCD Merger Plan of the 1960s* (Dublin, 2012), pp 24–5, 24, n. 7, 53.

161. Ann Frost, 'The emergence and growth of Hispanic Studies in British and Irish universities', online report, AHGBI [Association of Hispanists of Great Britain and Ireland], 2019, p. 30. Her public lectures on Dante and introductory course in Spanish are advertised in the *Irish Independent*, 16 April 1910, p. 6, and 13 October 1910, p. 4. Upon retirement Degani returned to England and died in Cambridge in June 1942. A Girton College scholarship in Italian still bears her name.

162. K. T. Butler, 'The Italian Summer School at Cambridge, July 28–August 16 1919', Modern Languages Association, *Year Book of Modern Languages*, 1920, pp 198–201 (p. 200). For a contemporary view of the problem facing the post-war peace conference – how to balance the claims of a victorious Italy against the aspirations of Southern Slavs wishing to form their own kingdom – see V. R. Savić, 'The problem of the Adriatic', in *The North American Review* 206 (1917), pp 885–93. For Tony Judt, *Postwar: A History of Europe Since 1945* (New York, 2005; Random House Vintage edn, London, 2010), pp 140–2, that particular east-west meeting-point remained a very knotty problem, even after two world wars, and there were genuine fears it might spark a third conflagration.

163. Macken, 'Women in the university and the college', p. 160.

164. NLI, Manuscripts Collection, List No. 178, MS 48,446/2 (Mary Kate [Kit] Ryan, Mountjoy, to her father, 15 May 1916) and MS 48,446/7 (Mary Kate [Kit] Ryan, Mountjoy, to her mother, 24 May 1916). Cf. Phyllis Gaffney, 'Assistant something-or-other', p. 116. Ryan was involved with Cumann na mBan in 1914, but the increased work responsibilities that year meant she had less time to be as politically active as her sisters and brothers.

165. On this period of her life, see Gaffney, 'Assistant something-or-other', pp 116–18; and on her vicarious proto-diplomatic work in Paris on behalf of the Provisional Irish government (1919–January 1922), see Gaffney, '*When we were very young*: University College Dublin's French Department and the fight for Irish freedom', in Éamon Maher and Grace Neville (eds), *France–Ireland: Anatomy of a Relationship. Studies in History, Literature and Politics* (Bern, 2004), pp 203–23 (pp 211–14).

166. Born Farrelly, she gaelicised her surname in her student days and also used the Irish form of her name. For her biography, see Marie Coleman, 'O'Farrelly, Agnes Winifred', DIB; Ríona Nic Congáil, *Úna Ní Fhaircheallaigh agus an Fhís Útóipeach Ghaelach* (Dublin, 2010).

167. Ríona Nic Congáil, 'Fiction, amusement, instruction: The Irish Fireside Club and the educational ideology of the Gaelic League', in *Éire–Ireland* 44 (2009), pp 91–117; Nic Congáil, *Úna Ní Fhaircheallaigh*, pp 44–63. Parallels can surely be drawn between the *Weekly Freeman*'s initiative and the growth in children's literature in the late nineteenth century. In France and Italy, too, literacy had exposed the need for suitable reading material for the young, at a time when the prevailing idiom was nationalist.

168. Harford, *The Opening of University Education to Women in Ireland*, p. 120. Her rant against 'cosmopolitanism', in 'The reign of humbug', a paper read to the college's Literary Academy in December 1900, reveals her uncompromising espousal of a utopian Irish Ireland ideal. (O'Farrelly, 'The reign of humbug'.)

169. Nic Congáil, *Úna Ní Fhaircheallaigh*, pp 80–6.

170. J. M. Synge, *The Aran Islands*, ed. Tim Robinson (London, 1992), p. 68, cited in Úna Ní Fhaircheallaigh [Agnes O'Farrelly], *Smaointe ar Árainn* [Thoughts on Aran], ed. Ríona Nic Congáil (Dublin, 2010), p. 79.

171. Harford, *The Opening of University Education to Women in Ireland*, pp 128–68.

172. Senia Paseta, 'Achieving equality: women and the foundation of the university', in Tom Dunne et al. (eds), *The National University of Ireland 1908–2008: Centenary Essays* (Dublin, 2008), pp 19–32 (pp 26–7). The women she mentions are Mary Hayden, Agnes O'Farrelly and Alice Oldham. The IAWGCG changed its name to the National University of Ireland Graduates' Association in 1914. Cf. Padbury, *Mary Hayden*, pp 116–38.

173. Macken, 'Women in the university and the college', p. 147. Cf. McCartney, *UCD: A National Idea*, p. 79. O'Farrelly's commitment to bettering women's lives never waned. In 1937 she was a prominent opponent of the draft constitution's measures curtailing employment rights for women. One of the founders of the Dublin Soroptimist Club (1938) and its first president, she was later to assume the presidency of the Irish Federation of University Women (1937–9) and of the National University Women Graduates' Association (1943–7).

174. At one meeting of the governing body she allegedly 'sustained a stand-up battle' with UCD's President Coffey on behalf of Mary Kate Ryan, who she claimed had been underpaid by the college while doing Cadic's work as well as her own (NLI, Manuscripts Collection, List No. 178, MS 48,445/1, Mary Kate Ryan to her sister Min, [n.d.] January 1914).

175. O'Neill, 'Modern languages', p. 373.

176. Frost, 'The emergence and growth of Hispanic Studies in British and Irish universities', p. 21. Frost sees Hunter Perry as 'another example [...] of an academic who came to Spanish from another subject'.

177. Her thesis, a critical edition of a renaissance Spanish manuscript at the British Museum, was published by the University of London press in 1927.

178. 'Janet Hunter Perry, 1884–1958', in *Bulletin of Hispanic Studies* 35 (1958), pp 177–8.

179. Mary Colum, *Life and the Dream* (New York, 1947, 1958; revised edn, Dublin, 1966), pp 37–9. Cf. Maureen Murphy, 'Colum, Mary Catherine ('Molly')', DIB. Mary Colum's time in the German school most likely took place after 1905, to judge by her allusion (p. 38) to French nuns there who felt exiled from their homeland. (The French State initiated its secularist regime, introducing the *loi de séparation des Églises et de l'État*, that year.)

180. See for example, her review of Herbert Gorman's *James Joyce* (New York, 1940), in *The Saturday Review*, 16 March 1941, pp 10, 16.

181. Twice recipient of Guggenheim fellowships, she moved to Paris for a time to work on an account of the origins of modernism. On her love of Latin and her flair for translation, see her *Life and the Dream*, pp 22–4.

182. Macken, 'Women in the university and the college', p. 156; Marie Ann O'Brien, 'A century of change: The (in)visibility of women in the Irish Foreign Service, 1919–1929', in *Irish Studies in International Affairs* 30 (2019), pp 73–92 (pp 75–6). Cf. Michael Kennedy, 'Power, Ann ("Nancy") Wyse', DIB.

183. Macken, 'Women in the university and the college', p. 152. Cf. pp 155–6, where she recalls other women from her student days who had been drawn to Irish studies.

184. Íde Ní Thuama, 'Joynt, Maud Anna Evans', DIB; Karen de Lacey, '"A rich and gentle mind" – Maud Joynt and the 1911 Census', blog post (RIA website), https://www.ria.ie/news/library-blog-library/rich-and-gentle-mind-maud-joynt-and-1911-census, 2 September 2023; Fischer, *Das Deutschlandbild der Iren, 1890–1939*, p. 503.

185. Eoghan Ó Raghallaigh, 'Knott, (Philippa Marie) Eleanor (1886–1975)', DIB.

186. Beatrix Färber, 'Life and works of Käte Müller-Lisowski', CELT, Corpus of Electronic Texts (University College Cork). (18 September 2023)

187. See 'The Lisowski story', in Holfter and Dickel, *An Irish Sanctuary*, pp 27–9; and ibid., pp 175, 230–1, 374.

188. Diarmuid Breathnach and Máire Ní Mhurchú, 'Wulff, Winifred Mary Paula (1895–1946)', ainm.ie; Beatrix Färber, 'Life and work of Winifred Wulff', CELT, Corpus of Electronic Texts (University College Cork). (18 September 2023) (Färber relies on three articles by Aoibheann Nic Dhonnchadha.)

189. In the new UCD, for instance, three women were appointed out of a total of 45 professorships, and one of the six statutory lectureships went to a woman. Of the four senior appointments that went to women, three were linguists. (McCartney, *UCD: A National Idea*, p. 83.)

190. The Civil Service Regulation Act, requiring women to resign from established pensionable posts on marriage, was introduced in 1924. For Ireland's primary teachers the marriage bar lasted from 1933 to 1958. The restrictions were not totally removed from Irish law until the 1970s, after EEC membership.

191. McCartney, *UCD: A National Idea*, p. 84. Entrenched positions against women over-qualifying themselves persisted well into the following century, and not only in Ireland. Eda Sagarra, *Living with My Century* (Dublin, 2022), p. 59, recalls hearing a professor in 1950s Vienna telling women doctoral students in his class that they would do better to stay at home and learn how to knit.

192. The different positions were voiced to the Robertson and Fry Commissions. For a clear account of the various stakeholders, see Judith Harford, 'Women and the Irish University Question', in Harford and Rush (eds), *Have Women Made a Difference?*, pp 7–28.

193. McCartney, *UCD: A National Idea*, p. 84. Women who ran important educational institutions were often nuns who did not hold senior academic titles. Subordinate women knew their place.

194. Harford, *The Opening of University Education to Women in Ireland*, p. 173; 'Women and the Irish University Question', p. 24.

195. The original function of the Roman Catholic women's colleges was clouded in ambiguities: they were neither convent secondary schools nor 'approved' student hostels, nor yet establishments on a par with Oxbridge women's colleges. The precise role they had actually played in preparing women students for their RUI degrees was very soon forgotten, once the transition to the NUI had been made.

196. The 1908 Universities Act stipulated women's eligibility for all offices in the NUI. In Trinity, by contrast, women were admitted to fellowships only in 1967. (O'Flynn, *A Question of Identity*, p. 103, n. 11.)

197. *Irish Independent*, 19 December 1911, p. 6. Cf. Harford, *The Opening of University Education to Women in Ireland*, pp 89–91, on similar public interest in the RUI's first women graduates in 1884.

198. Honor O Brolchain, *Joseph Plunkett* (Dublin, 2012), p. 106. Plunkett's diary entry is dated 20 January 1911. Cited above, p. 128.

199. Fischer, *Das Deutschlandbild der Iren, 1890–1939*, p. 490. See McDowell and Webb, *Trinity College Dublin*, pp 423–76, on TCD's finely balanced period of adjustment to the Free State in the decades after 1921. In Belfast, the vast majority of the Queen's University community was anxious to remain as attached as possible to 'mainland' Britain.

200. The difficulties encountered by women in securing permanent academic employment in the UK are illustrated by the case of Helen Waddell, brilliant Belfast graduate and Oxford researcher of the first calibre. She ended up working in publishing, but continued to produce first-class medieval scholarship that has stood the test of time. See FitzGerald, 'The Queen's girl'; and Jennifer FitzGerald, 'Helen Waddell (1889–1965): The scholar-poet', in Chance (ed.), *Women Medievalists and the Academy*, pp 322–38. Many were highly accomplished linguists. Cf. Mary Dockray-Miller, 'Mary Bateson (1865–1906): Scholar and suffragist', in ibid., pp 67–78; and Haas, 'Caroline F. E. Spurgeon (1869–1942)'. Spurgeon did her doctorate on Chaucer through French, at the Sorbonne.

201. Freund's writings during the war were unmistakably anti-English (Fischer, *Das Deutschlandbild der Iren, 1890–1939*, pp 489–90). After the war he lectured in English in Giessen and Marburg, before leaving Europe in 1925 for a post at Rice University, in Houston Texas. He became an American citizen and worked in Texas until retirement in 1947. He died aged 101, in 1980. His papers indicate an interest in the eighteenth century and in translation. When in Belfast he had been interested in revival literature, and he later translated George Moore. For information on Freund, with useful further weblinks, see https://second.wiki/wiki/max_freund and https://scholarship.rice.edu, 27 September 2023. Cf. Moody and Beckett, *Queen's, Belfast*, vol. 2, p. 611; 'Prize will honor late Rice professor emeritus, Freund', https://ricehistorycorner.com/wp-content/uploads/2018/04/max-freund-article-1980126.jpg and https://scholarship.rice.edu/bitstream/handle/1911/34769/37.pdf, 13 February 2022.

202. Moody and Beckett, *Queen's, Belfast*, vol. 2, pp 611, 613. Fischer, *Das Deutschlandbild der Iren, 1890–1939*, pp 481–2, sees Williams as more of an Anglo-Saxonist than a Germanist. (His one publication was on an episode in *Beowulf*, Cambridge, 1924.)

203. Dorothy Dunlop, *1916 and Beyond the Pale* (Croydon, 2016), pp 110–13.

204. Gilbert Waterhouse, 'The War and the study of German', 29 May 1917, pp 21, 24, cited in Fischer, *Das Deutschlandbild der Iren, 1890–1939*, p. 482.

205. In contrast, the proclamation launching the 1916 Rising referred to Britain's enemies as 'gallant allies in Europe'. On Waterhouse, see Fischer, *Das Deutschlandbild der Iren, 1890–1939*, pp 482–3; Sagarra, 'The centenary of the Henry Simon Chair of German at the University of Manchester (1996): Commemorative address', in *German Life and Letters* 51 (1998), pp 509–24 (pp 515–16); and Eda Sagarra, 'Waterhouse, Gilbert', DIB. Waterhouse took part in the Allied Naval Armistice Commission's Inspection of the German Fleet in December 1918 (see his report, in Dunlop, *1916 and Beyond the Pale*, pp 149–62), and served in the Foreign Office's Naval Intelligence Division in 1939 (see https://www. thebritishacademy.ac.uk/publishing/memoirs/humanities-scholars-who-worked-military-intelligence-second-world-war/, 21 September 2023).

206. Moody and Beckett, *Queen's, Belfast*, vol. 1, p. 451.

207. Ibid., vol. 2, p. 612; Fischer, *Das Deutschlandbild der Iren, 1890–1939*, pp 489–90.

208. Moody and Beckett, *Queen's, Belfast*, vol. 2, p. 612.

209. See Ian Montgomery, 'Savory, Sir Douglas Lloyd', DIB. He continued to work in politics until 1955.

210. Ibid. Montgomery also credits Savory for his work on behalf of a number of minority groups in Europe after the second world war, in Poland, South Tyrol, South Slesvig and Heligoland.

211. When Atkinson retired the year before his death in 1908, the gap was filled for a couple of years by Maurice Alfred Gerothwohl (McDowell and Webb, *Trinity College Dublin*, p. 403).

212. Ibid., pp 429–30. See also below, p. 188.

213. Leathes Report, 'Modern Studies, Being the Report of the Committee on the Position of Modern Languages in the Educational System of Great Britain' (London, 1918), Appendix 3, pp 250–8.

214. The Leathes Committee, appointed in August 1916, reported in April 1918. On Liam Ó Briain's political activism, see O'Neill, 'Modern languages', p. 377.

215. Roger Little, 'Beckett's mentor, Rudmose-Brown: Sketch for a portrait', in *Irish University Review* 14 (1984), pp 34–41 (p. 36).

216. T. B. Rudmose-Brown, *French Literary Studies* (Dublin and London, 1917).

217. Little, 'Beckett's mentor, Rudmose-Brown', p. 37; cf. Vivian Mercier, *Beckett / Beckett* (Oxford, 1977; pb edn, 1979), pp 34, 74–5.

218. O'Neill, 'Modern languages', pp 376–81; Paul Rouse, 'Ó Briain, Liam', DIB.

219. Mac Réamoinn, *Irish Times*, 13 August 1974, cited in O'Neill, 'Modern languages', p. 380.

220. On Chauviré, see Phyllis Gaffney, 'When we were very young'; '*Une certaine idée de l'Irlande*, or the professor as propagandist: Roger Chauviré's Irish fictions', in Phyllis Gaffney, Michael Brophy and Mary Gallagher (eds), *Reverberations: Staging Relations in French since 1500. A Festschrift in Honour of C.E.J. Caldicott* (Dublin, 2008), pp 390–403; and 'Roger Chauviré's perspective on 1916 and its aftermath', in Pierre Joannon and Kevin Whelan (eds), *Paris Capital of Irish Culture: France, Ireland and the Republic, 1798–1916* (Dublin, 2017), pp 215–26.

221. See Gaffney, '*Une certaine idée de l'Irlande*, or the professor as propagandist', pp 402–3, n. 17.

222. His friends included the O'Kellys (Seán T. and his two wives), Pádraig de Brún, Michael Hayes, the de Valeras, and many others. His *Contes ossianiques* (Paris, 1949) betray his admiration for the uniquely Irish version of European civilisation.

223. John Coolahan, 'From Royal University to National University, 1879–1908', in Dunne et al. (eds), *The National University of Ireland 1908–2008*, pp 3–18 (p. 18). Cf. Gearóid Ó Tuathaigh, 'The position of the Irish language', in ibid., pp 33–43 (p. 34).

224. McDowell and Webb, *Trinity College Dublin*, p. 379. In the 1950s, Trinity students dubbed UCD 'the hedge school in Earlsfort Terrace' while for UCD students Trinity was 'an extension of the British Empire' (Sagarra, *Living with My Century*, p. 67). In 1960 the President of UCD, Michael Tierney, described the relationship between UCD and TCD as a 'truceless cold war' (O'Flynn, *A Question of Identity*, p. 92). Divisions were exacerbated by the Catholic bishops' ban on Catholics attending Trinity (1875–1970), vigorously enforced by Dublin's Archbishop John Charles McQuaid (ibid., pp 47–9). More official rapprochement between the universities began to form in the early 1970s.

CHAPTER 8: SHIFTING LANGUAGE PERSPECTIVES

1. Aidan Doyle, *A History of the Irish Language: From the Norman Invasion to Independence* (Oxford, 2015), p. 261.

2. [*'President, friends...'*] Queen Elizabeth II, opening her address at State Dinner, Dublin Castle (18 May 2011).

3. Simon Kuper, 'The case for diving into another language', *Financial Times*, 21 April 2021.

4. David Chambers ['Blindboy Boatclub'], foreword to Terence Patrick Dolan (ed.), *A Dictionary of Hiberno-English* (Dublin, 1998; 3rd edn, Dublin, 2020).

5. John Joseph Lee, *Ireland, 1912–1985: Politics and Society* (Cambridge, 1989), p. 674.

6. Gilbert Waterhouse, editorial, in *The Year Book for Modern Languages* (Cambridge, 1920), pp 1–9 (pp 1–2).

7. R. H. Robins, *A Short History of Linguistics* (London, 1967; fourth edn, 1997), pp 222–76; Nicola McLelland, *Teaching and Learning Foreign Languages: A History of Language Education, Assessment and Policy in Britain* (London and New York, 2017), pp 105–23.

8. In 1963, the proportion of school leavers who went on to university after school remained under four per cent of the age cohort: John Coolahan, 'The National University of Ireland and the changing structure of Irish higher education, 1967–2007', in Tom Dunne et al. (eds), *The National University of Ireland 1908–2008: Centenary Essays* (Dublin, 2008), pp 261–79 (p. 261). In Ireland today, '54 per cent of people aged 25–64 have third-level qualifications' (Fintan O'Toole, *Irish Times*, 14 January 2023).

9. The four NUI colleges are Maynooth University, University College Cork, University College Dublin and University of Galway. While NUI STEM candidates no longer require a language other than English and Irish, three languages (English, Irish and another language) still remain essential for Arts & Humanities, Commerce, Law, Medicine. (Attracta Halpin, 'The role of the National University of Ireland in language learning and language research and scholarship', in Patricia Maguire (ed.), *Foreign Language Learning and Ireland's* Languages Connect *Strategy: Reflections following a symposium organised by the National University of Ireland with University College Cork* (Dublin, 2019), pp 4–6 (p. 4).

10. Garret FitzGerald, Foreword, in Dunne et al. (eds), *The National University of Ireland 1908–2008*, pp xiii–xx (p. xviii).

11. Ibid., pp xvi–xviii, mentions three sources of tension over the University's hundred years: Irish as a matriculation requirement, Catholic hierarchy attempts to reduce the institution's non-denominational character, and tensions between the federal centre and its constituent members seeking autonomy.

12. Ronan Fanning, 'T. K. Whitaker, 1976–96', in Dunne et al. (eds.), *The National University of Ireland 1908–2008*, pp 146–62 (p. 149). During his tenure, de Valera's more fleeting incarnations included President of the Dáil, Leader of the Opposition, Taoiseach, President of the League of Nations, and President of Ireland. Fanning, 'De Valera, Éamon ('Dev')', DIB, observes that, when boarding in the French College Blackrock, de Valera had not been inclined towards the rampant hibernophilia among some of his peers, and only set his mind to learning Irish and joining the Gaelic League in 1908. As a relative latecomer to revivalism, he may have had the 'zeal of the convert'.

13. John Walsh, 'Eamon de Valera, 1921–75', in Dunne et al. (eds.), *The National University of Ireland 1908–2008*, pp 135–45. In 1921, de Valera was sole nominee for the Chancellorship (Nóirín Moynihan, 'The archives held in the National University of Ireland', in Dunne et al. (eds.), *The National University of Ireland 1908–2008*, pp 245–56 (p. 255)).

14. Linda O'Shea Farren, 'The role of Convocation', in Dunne et al. (eds.), *The National University of Ireland 1908–2008*, pp 228–45 (p. 235). She also alludes to the revivalist credentials of the longest-serving chair of Convocation (1955–84) and co-founder of Gael Linn, Dónall Ó Móráin.

15. Halpin, 'The role of the National University of Ireland in language learning and language research and scholarship'.

16. Eoin MacNeill, *Irish in the National University of Ireland: A Plea for Irish Education* (Dublin, 1909), pp 26, 38–9.

17. Liam Ó Briain, 'The Irish revival and modern languages', in UCG *Annual* 6 (1928–9), pp 15–18; and Rosaleen O'Neill, 'Modern languages', in Tadhg Foley (ed.), *From Queen's College to National University: Essays on the Academic History of QCG/UCG/NUI Galway* (Dublin, 1999), pp 360–83 (pp 378–9). On Ó Briain, cf. above, p. 188.

18. Diarmaid Ferriter, 'Hayes, Michael', DIB.

19. John Walsh, *One Hundred Years of Irish Language Policy, 1922–2022* (Oxford, 2022), p. 142.

20. Séamus Ó Buachalla, 'Educational policy and the role of the Irish language from 1831 to 1981', in *European Journal of Education* 19 (1984), pp 75–92 (p. 84). The minister, Seán Ó Ceallaigh, was president of the Gaelic League. Ó Buachalla ascribes this gesture less to the centrality of language policy than to the goal of securing ecclesiastical approval for the nascent independent State, since the Roman Catholic hierarchy remained hostile to centralised State control of education.

21. Brian Ó Cuív, 'Irish language and literature, 1845–1921', in W. E. Vaughan (ed.), *A New History of Ireland, VI: Ireland under the Union, II: 1870–1921* (Oxford, 1996), pp 385–435 (p. 413, n. 3).

22. *Notes for Teachers: Irish* (Dublin, n.d., c.1944), p. 55 (kindly shown to the author by Nóirín Ní Nuadháin). These Department of Education notes from the early 1940s, redolent of the ideology of their time, show that careful planning and coherent thinking went into advising primary teachers on working through the medium of Irish in the classroom.

23. Compulsory Irish for school leavers was phased in gradually. See Áine Hyland and Kenneth Milne (eds), *Irish Educational Documents*, vol. 2 (Dublin, 1992), p. 189.

24. Ó Buachalla, 'Educational policy and the role of the Irish language from 1831 to 1981', p. 84, and passim, for an informative and succinct account. Cf. Walsh, *One Hundred Years of Irish Language Policy, 1922–2022*.

25. On translation and the new administration, see Michael Cronin, *Translating Ireland: Translation, Languages, Cultures* (Cork, 1996), pp 153–6. On Irish translations of the classics of children's literature, see Órla Ní Chuilleanáin, *Tíortha na hÓige: Litríocht Ghaeilge na nÓg agus Ceisteanna an Aistriúcháin* (Dublin, 2014), pp 41–108.

26. Barry McCrea, *Languages of the Night: Minor Languages and the Literary Imagination in Twentieth-Century Ireland and Europe* (New Haven and London, 2015), p. 40. The over-emphasis on translation was controversial. For further details and statistics, see Philip O'Leary, *Gaelic Prose in the Irish Free State, 1922–1939* (Dublin, 2004), pp 376–406 (pp 387–9); and *Writing Beyond the Revival: Facing the Future in Gaelic Prose, 1940–1951* (Dublin, 2011), pp 153–218 (pp 174–83).

27. John O'Meara, *The Singing-Masters* (Dublin, 1990), p. 19.

28. Bruno Migliorini and T. Gwynfor Griffith, *The Italian Language* (London, 1966), p. 404; Anna Laura Lepschy and Giulio Lepschy, *The Italian Language Today* (London, 1977), pp 34–7. Cf. McCrea, *Languages of the Night*, pp 48–60. For an anthology of Italian poetry in dialect, see Franco Brevini (ed.), *La Poesia in Dialetto: Storia e testi dalle origini al Novecento* (3 vols, Milan, 1999).

29. Gérard Vigner, 'Depuis quand enseigne-t-on le français en France? Du *sermo vulgaris* à l'enseignement du français langue maternelle', in *Études de linguistique appliquée* 123–4 (2001), pp 425–44 (p. 429). Military service, mandatory for males after 1889, accelerated the spread of French.

30. Doyle, *A History of the Irish Language*, p. 249. Cf. pp 261–2.

31. As argued magisterially in the work of Philip O'Leary (*Gaelic Prose in the Irish Free State* and *Writing Beyond the Revival*).

32. Ó Buachalla, 'Educational policy and the role of the Irish language from 1831 to 1981', pp 87–9.

33. Breandán Ó Madagáin, 'Irish: A difficult birth', in Foley (ed), *From Queen's College to National University*, pp 344–59 (p. 353, n. 41), quotes a student of Irish at QCG/UCG who looks back (in the 1960s) with nostalgia at the 'draíocht a bhain le gluaiseacht na Gaeilge sna laethanta sin' [magic connected with the Irish movement in those days].

34. *Derry Journal*, 16 July 1907, p. 6. Cited (in her biography of Agnes O'Farrelly) by Ríona Nic Congáil, *Úna Ní Fhaircheallaigh agus an Fhís Útóipeach Ghaelach* (Dublin, 2010), p. 210.

35. Declan Kiberd, Editorial, in *The Crane Bag*, 5 (2) [*The Irish Language and Culture*] (1981; 1982 reprint), pp 835–7 (p. 835). *The Crane Bag*, a short-lived Irish Studies journal founded by Mark Hederman and Richard Kearney, ran from 1977 to 1985.

36. A National Teacher, 'Gaelic – with the lid off', in *The Bell* 3 (1941), pp 221–8 (p. 223).

37. Ibid., pp 223–4.

38. Ibid., p. 224.

39. The Gaelic League's draft education programme for a free Ireland (1918) had stressed the need for spoken competence at *all* levels: see Áine Hyland and Kenneth Milne (eds), *Irish Educational Documents*, vol. 1 (Dublin, 1987), pp 189–91; Walsh, *One Hundred Years of Irish Language Policy, 1922–2022*, pp 142–3. However, oral assessment in Irish was not introduced before 1960, while communicative approaches to Irish teaching came on stream after 1989.

40. Doyle, *A History of the Irish Language*, pp 227–30 (p. 229). 'To this day, there is no agreed standard pronunciation of Irish' (p. 230). Cf. ibid., pp 237–8.

41. A subcommittee of modern language teachers in England understood these challenges all too well. See Modern Language Association, *Report on Higher School Certificate Examinations* (London, n.d., c.1926), pp 22–5. (Pamphlet kindly shown to me by Áine Hyland.)

42. Kiberd, Editorial, in *The Crane Bag*, 5 (2), p. 835.

43. Walsh, *One Hundred Years of Irish Language Policy, 1922–2022*, pp 77–139. Cf. Doyle, *A History of the Irish Language*, pp 204–5.

44. Statement to the Gaeltacht Commission from the Christian Brothers (Dublin, 9 June 1925). Cited in Walsh, *One Hundred Years of Irish Language Policy, 1922–2022*, p. 102.

45. O'Leary, *Gaelic Prose in the Irish Free State*, p. 18.

46. The Editor, 'Gaelic – The truth', in *The Bell* 5 (February 1943), pp 336–40 (p. 337).

47. Kiberd, Editorial, in *The Crane Bag*, 5 (2), p. 836.

48. Myles Dillon, 'Irish in the universities', in *Studies: An Irish Quarterly Review* 18 (1929), pp 124–30 (p. 128).

49. See Malachy O'Rourke, 'Writing the wrongs', *Irish Times*, 26 September 1998.

50. Mícheál Ó Siadhail, 'Standard Irish orthography: An assessment', in *The Crane Bag*, 5 (2), p. 904; Alan Bliss, 'The Standardization of Irish', in ibid., pp 908–14 (p. 912).

51. Gustav Lehmacher, SJ, 'Some thoughts on an Irish literary language', in *Studies* (1923), pp 26–32 (p. 26). Cf. Walsh, *One Hundred Years of Irish Language Policy, 1922–2022*, pp 154–5.

52. For a succinct summary of the revival's achievements, see Doyle, *A History of the Irish Language*, pp 237–8. Walsh, *One Hundred Years of Irish Language Policy, 1922–2022*, ends his critique with a balanced judgment: 'neither an unmitigated disaster nor a roaring success' (p. 319), seeing 'grounds for hope and opportunities for growth' (p. 320).

53. For a recent account of the fortunes of English language teaching around the globe during the 1920s and 1930s, see Michael G. Malouf, *Making World English: Literature, Late Empire, and English Language Teaching, 1919–1939* (London, 2022).

54. Nicola McLelland, *Teaching and Learning Foreign Languages*, p. 107. Cf. Malouf, *Making World English*. The Tokyo IRET is now called the IRLT [Institute for Research in Language Teaching].

55. Malouf, *Making World English*, p. 12; McLelland, *Teaching and Learning Foreign Languages*, pp 107, 193–7; Richard Smith, 'Harold E. Palmer, IRLT and "Historical sense" in ELT', in *IRLT Journal* 12 (Journal of the Institute for Research in Language Teaching, Tokyo: special issue to celebrate the Institute's 90th anniversary, 2013), pp 1–8 [pre-publication version].

56. 'Languages Connect: Ireland's Strategy for Foreign Languages in Education 2017–2026' (Dublin, 2017) (www.education.ie). This document was propelled by the EU's target of 'mother tongue plus two', following the European Year of Languages (2001). On the strategy's Irish context, see Jennifer Bruen, 'Languages Connect: What does Ireland's first government strategy for foreign-languages-in-education mean for Irish universities?', in Maguire (ed.), *Foreign Language Learning and Ireland's Languages Connect Strategy*, pp 7–20 (pp 7–8). For background information on Ireland's foreign-language deficit, see Jennifer Bruen, 'Towards a national policy for languages in education: The case of Ireland', in *European Journal of Language Policy* 25 (2013), pp 99–114. For a list of UK policy documents related to language learning that runs to ten pages for the years 2018 to 2013, see McLelland, *Teaching and Learning Foreign Languages*, pp 202–13.

57. Margaret Ó hÓgartaigh, 'A quiet revolution: Women and second-level education in Ireland, 1878–1930', in *New Hibernia Review / Iris Éireannach Nua* 13 (2009), pp 36–51 (p. 46). Máire Cruise O'Brien [née Mhac an tSaoi] reports that French was introduced in Alexandra primary school when she was aged six, four years before Irish (Máire Cruise O'Brien, *The Same Age as the State* (Dublin, 2003), p. 116).

58. Ó Briain, 'The Irish revival and modern languages', p. 15.

59. Patrick J. Corish, *Maynooth College 1795–1995* (Dublin, 1995), p. 321.

60. Cruise O'Brien, *The Same Age as the State*, pp 80–1; Anne Enright, 'Censorship in Ireland', in *London Review of Books* 35:6 (21 March 2013).

61. Éamon Ó Cofaigh, 'Learning French through Irish: the impact of bilingualism on the acquisition of French as a third language (L3)', in Maguire (ed.), *Foreign Language Learning and Ireland's Languages Connect Strategy*, pp 39–46.

62. John Coolahan, *Irish Education: Its History and Structure* (Dublin, 1981), pp 80–104.

63. Kathleen O'Flaherty, 'The teaching of modern languages', in *Cork University Record* 2 (1944), pp 41–3.

64. Ibid., p. 42; cf. Leathes Report, 'Modern Studies, Being the Report of the Committee on the Position of Modern Languages in the Educational system of Great Britain' (London, 1918), pp 74–5, 213. An oral Irish examination was in place in Northern Ireland since the 1920s (Coolahan, *Irish Education*, p. 80).

65. O'Flaherty, 'The teaching of modern languages', p. 43. Since the relatively recent prioritising of oral language competence, modern language teachers today must have spent time in a region where the foreign language is spoken. The minimum duration, however, is a mere four weeks.

66. Alfred Blanche, 'Enseignement du français dans les écoles de l'Irlande', 21 October 1921 (French Diplomatic Archives, Nantes, Œuvres françaises à l'étranger, no. 33, CADN C22/7).

67. Joachim Fischer, *Das Deutschlandbild der Iren, 1890–1939: Geschichte – Form – Funktion* (Heidelberg, 2000), p. 489.

68. Seán P. Farragher, CSSp, and Annraoi Wyer, *Blackrock College 1860–1995* (Dublin, 1995), p. 99.

69. Coolahan, *Irish Education*, p. 81.

70. He was adviser to the Department of Education and instrumental in campaigning for applied linguistic research to be done on the Irish language; he served as first Director of ITÉ [Institiúid Teangeolaíochta Éireann], the Linguistics Institute of Ireland established in 1967. See Lawrence William White, 'Ó hUallacháin, Colmán', DIB; and Walsh, *One Hundred Years of Irish Language Policy, 1922–2022*, pp 163–9.

71. In 1966, the Department of Education's inspectorate carried out Buntús Gaeilge, the first frequency-based linguistic analysis of conversational Irish in Gaeltacht areas. This led to the first audio-visual method applied to Irish – Tomás Ó Domhnalláin's highly influential (and still popular) *Buntús Cainte*, which subsequently led to the development of post-primary courses in modern languages: *Écouter et Parler, Entendir e Hablar, Verstehen und Sprechen*. Ó Domhnalláin was director of ITÉ from 1973 to 1979. (Áine Hyland, '*Buntús Gaeilge* (1966) and its aftermath', unpublished paper, 2022; kindly shown to me by Áine Hyland.)

72. McLelland, *Teaching and Learning Foreign Languages*, pp 148, 153; she dates Britain's first school language laboratory to Salford in 1962; within five years, there were 200 laboratories (p. 110).

73. Ibid., pp 66–9; Michèle Cohen, 'From "glittering gibberish" to the "mere jabbering" of a *bonne*: The problem of the "oral" in the learning and teaching of French in eighteenth- and nineteenth-century England', in Nicola McLelland and Richard Smith (eds), *The History of Language Learning and Teaching* (3 vols, Cambridge, 2018), vol. 2, pp 1–20 (p. 16); Leathes Report, pp 144–8.

74. Leathes Report, p. 127; cf. p. 195. The Modern Language Association Subcommittee's 'Report on Higher School Certificate Examinations' finds examination standards that are well beyond average learner capabilities.

75. Leathes Report, p. 7.

76. John le Carré, *A Perfect Spy* (London, 1986), pp 258–9. Little had changed by the 1950s when, according to Eda Sagarra, tenured staff still didn't 'bother to teach' spoken German (Eda Sagarra, *Living with My Century* (Dublin, 2022), p. 69).

77. This necessarily general overview, of several languages and diverse institutions, is based on impressions and personal experience. Closer scrutiny may lead to more nuance, as indeed do the reminiscences of other practitioners. Trinity's four-year degree, allowing an intercalated year abroad, improved the spoken language skills of students. For German, see the individual testimonies of Germanists assembled in Gisela Holfter (ed.), *Rückblicke und Reflexionen: A History of German Studies in Ireland* (Trier, 2023).

78. Maurice Fitzpatrick, *The Boys of St Columb's* (Dublin, 2010), interview with Seamus Heaney, pp 66, 67. The poet opted for French rather than Greek. Greek was for boys who might have a vocation for the priesthood.

79. Sagarra, *Living with My Century*, p. xi.

80. O'Meara, *The Singing-Masters*, p. 34.

81. T. K. Whitaker, 'Economic development' (Dublin, 1958); extract reprinted as T. K. Whitaker, 'Shut the door on the past', in John Bowman (ed.), *Ireland: The Autobiography. One hundred years of Irish life, told by its people* (Dublin, 2016), pp 237–9 (p. 239). Whitaker considered the Irish language (which he loved and believed in keeping alive) outside the realm of economics. On Ireland's slow and

stumbling embrace of modernity, see Fintan O'Toole, *We Don't Know Ourselves: A Personal History of Ireland since 1958* (London, 2021).

82. Áine Hyland, 'The Investment in Education Report 1965 – recollections and reminiscences', in *Irish Educational Studies*, 33 (2014), pp 123–39.

83. The Gaeltacht Commission was an attempt (1925–6) to map the regions where Irish was still the everyday language of inhabitants. Walsh, *One Hundred Years of Irish Language Policy, 1922–2022*, pp 90–139, takes it as a policy case study. In practice, he points out, approximately 40 per cent of the recommendations were adopted by the Cosgrave government (p. 131).

84. John Bowman, 'De Valera: did he entrench the partition of Ireland?', in Paul Brennan (ed.), *Eamon de Valera* (Paris, 1986), pp 35–54. Cf. Garret FitzGerald, *Reflections on the Irish State* (Dublin, 2003), pp 174–5.

85. Cathal O'Byrne, quoted in Breandán Ó Buachalla, *I mBéal Feirste Cois Cuain* (Dublin, 1968), p. 273.

86. Christopher D. McGimpsey, lecture to seminar on 'The Irish language and the Unionist tradition', Ulster People's College, Belfast, 9 May 1992, in Pilib Mistéil (ed.), *The Irish Language and the Unionist Tradition* (Belfast, 1994), pp 7–16 (pp 10–11).

87. Roger Blaney, *Presbyterians and the Irish Language* (Belfast, 1996), pp 175–215 (p. 183). Cf. Pádraig Ó Snodaigh, 'Hidden Ulster revisited', in *The Crane Bag* 5 (2), pp 876–8.

88. Alison Murphy, *When Dublin Was the Capital: Northern Life Remembered* (Portaferry and Vancouver, 2000).

89. Gearóid Ó Tuathaigh, 'The position of the Irish language', in Dunne et al. (eds.), *The National University of Ireland 1908–2008*, pp 33–43 (p. 34).

90. This is argued in T. W. Moody and J. C. Beckett, *Queen's, Belfast 1845–1949: The History of a University* (2 vols, London, 1959), vol. 1, p. 407.

91. Ibid., vol. 1, p. 413. The chair of Celtic was briefly restored from 1945 to 1947 (ibid., vol. 2, p. 641.) Nowadays Queen's has an Institute for Irish Studies.

92. Patrick Buckley, 'Blythe, Ernest (de Blaghd, Earnán)', DIB; Blaney, *Presbyterians and the Irish Language*, pp 206–8. As Minister for Finance, Blythe made sure that schools teaching through Irish were adequately funded.

93. Linde Lunney, 'Henry, Robert Mitchell', DIB; Blaney, *Presbyterians and the Irish Language*, p. 185. After his retirement he moved to live in Bray, County Wicklow and was attached to TCD. Cf. Edith Hall, 'Sinn Féin and *Ulysses*: Between Professor Robert Mitchell Henry and James Joyce', in Isabelle Torrance and Donncha O'Rourke (eds), *Classics and Irish Politics 1916–2016* (Oxford, 2020), pp 193–217.

94. As revealed by Census data from 1911 compared to 1901. See Diarmait Mac Giolla Chríost, *The Irish Language in Ireland: From Goídel to Globalisation* (Abingdon, 2005), p. 135.

95. Mercator-Education report, *Irish: The Irish language in education in Northern Ireland* (2nd edn) (Leeuwarden, 2004), with financial support from the Fryske Akademy and the European Commission (DGXXII: Education, Training and Youth), p. 2 (accessed online, 7 October 2023); and Glens of Antrim Historical Society, 'Lament for Seamus 'Bhrian' Mac Amhlaigh', 12 February 2006 (https://antrimhistory.net/lament-for-seamus-bhriain-mac-amhlaigh/, 18 October 2023).

96. In 1991, the census asked householders 'whether persons aged 3 years or over could either speak, read or write Irish. It also contained a category for those with no knowledge of Irish'. The question was identical in wording to the question concerning Gaelic in Scotland's census of the same year. (*The Northern Ireland Census 1991 Summary Report* (Belfast, 1992), p. xii (3.35), p. vi (1.15) and p. viii (2.10).)

97. Tomás Ó Fiaich, 'The great controversy', in Seán Ó Tuama, (ed.), *The Gaelic League Idea* (Cork, 1972), pp 63–75 (pp 74–5).

98. Seamus Heaney recalls a stay with fellow-students in the Donegal Gaeltacht in Rosguill, at Easter 1960, in 'The Gaeltacht', a pastiche of an early Dante sonnet, 'Guido, i' vorrei'. He sees his poem as 'the wildtrack of our gabble': Heaney, *Electric Light* (London 2001). For recollections of the teaching of Irish at St Columb's, see Fitzpatrick, *The Boys of St Columb's*, p. 29 (Edward Daly), p. 97 (Eamonn McCann), pp 125–6 (Phil Coulter).

99. Ibid., p. 154.

100. Ibid., p. 57. That is, the first cohort of Roman Catholics who benefited from the 1947 Education Act and availed of free secondary education, having passed the Eleven Plus examination. The

interviewees of Fitzpatrick's book, all educated at St Columb's, were members of that new generation of educated Catholics that was to transform ways of thinking about Northern Ireland.

101. Padraig O Duibhir, 'Gaeilge labhartha na bpáistí i scoileanna lán-Ghaeilge i dTuaisceart na hÉireann: The spoken Irish of pupils in Irish-medium schools in Northern Ireland', in SCoTENS [Standing Conference on Teacher Education, North and South]-funded report (2010).

102. Gerald Dawe, *My Mother-City* (Belfast, 2007), p. 99.

103. See McLelland, *Teaching and Learning Foreign Languages*, p. 181.

104. Walsh, *One Hundred Years of Irish Language Policy, 1922–2022*, p. 152.

105. Mac Giolla Chríost, *The Irish Language in Ireland*, pp 162–71.

106. See, for example, the case of the East Belfast Turas Irish language project's founder, Linda Ervine MBE: 'Linda Ervine on her mission to preserve and advance the Irish language', *Belfast Telegraph*, 1 April 2023.

107. It replaced Bord na Gaeilge (in the south), not uncontroversially: see Walsh, *One Hundred Years of Irish Language Policy, 1922–2022*, pp 238–9.

108. https://www.stmarys-belfast.ac.uk/academic/education/courses/bed/ime_english.asp, 17 October 2023.

109. Walsh, *One Hundred Years of Irish Language Policy, 1922–2022*, pp 291–302 (p. 291).

110. See for example the cases cited in Susan McKay, 'The Irish language can give us all a sense of home – if we save it from sectarianism', *Guardian*, 10 August 2021.

111. William Smith, lecture to seminar on 'The Irish language and the Unionist tradition', in Mistéil (ed.), *The Irish Language and the Unionist Tradition*, pp 17–23 (pp 17–19).

112. Ibid., p. 19.

113. Assessment at Ordinary level included reading a passage aloud, conversing on everyday matters and taking a dictation; the Advanced level sought to test more sophisticated levels of self-expression (Revd T. Foy, 'Oral examination – an absurd situation', *Roscommon Herald*, 12 February 1971). On the history of oral assessment in the UK generally, see McLelland, *Teaching and Learning Foreign Languages*, pp 146–8.

114. Foy, 'Oral examination – an absurd situation'; cf. *Irish Press*, 19 January 1971; *Irish Independent*, 29 January 1971. Northern Ireland's regime for modern language education was often cited by advocates for oral assessment to be introduced south of the border, during the early 1970s.

115. *Irish Independent*, 3 July 1939. The speaker, District Justice Louis J. Walsh, Letterkenny, also noted the large number of Protestant children winning prizes in the Irish language competitions.

116. 'Gael-Linn praise Northern education authorities policy on language', *Strabane Chronicle*, 6 July 1963.

117. See for example, Ministry of Education for Northern Ireland, Secondary School Certificate 1933 and 1935 examinations in French taken at Portora Royal School, Enniskillen in 1933 and 1935 [family papers].

118. Leathes Report, pp 27 (pars 89, 90), 28 (par 93), 31 (par 106), 61 (Conclusion 17). We have noted in earlier chapters how Ireland's broader school curriculum contrasted with a narrower one in UK schools. On debates about how many languages learners should study, see McLelland, *Teaching and Learning Foreign Languages*, pp 182–3.

119. Colin Walker and Tony Williams, 'German at Queen's University Belfast', in Holfter (ed.), *Rückblicke und Reflexionen*, pp 63–74 (p. 74). Cf. Monika Unsworth, 'Epic battle to save classical studies at Queen's', *Irish Times*, 29 August 2002.

120. For further details, see Robins, *A Short History of Linguistics*, pp 222–76.

121. McLelland, *Teaching and Learning Foreign Languages*, pp 116–20.

122. Ibid., p. 119.

123. McLelland concludes that the real contribution of the twentieth century to the history of language teaching is twofold: empirical research has come to drive language policy, and technological innovation has transformed the processes of language learning. Ibid., pp 123–5.

124. Walsh, *One Hundred Years of Irish Language Policy, 1922–2022*, pp 141–94; he describes this change of tack as tantamount to 'a retreat from overt gaelicisation' (p. 194). On official Irish language policy, I have made extensive use of his (mainly critical) history.

125. Ibid., pp 144, 214. The advocates were the LFM [Language Freedom Movement], an organisation founded in the 1960s. Cf. John Horgan, 'Strong language', *Irish Times*, 9 January 2022.

126. Walsh, *One Hundred Years of Irish Language Policy, 1922–2022*, pp 193–4. The four universities are Maynooth (NUIM), Cork (UCC), Dublin (UCD), Galway (UOG). Exemptions include some non-humanities subjects, and individual circumstances that make Irish-language proficiency impracticable.

127. Kiberd, Editorial, in *The Crane Bag*, 5 (2), p. 837. Cf. Bruce Stewart, 'On the necessity of de-Hydifying Irish cultural criticism', in *New Hibernia Review / Iris Éireannach Nua* 4 (2000), pp 23–44 (p. 40). Bonus points, awarded to candidates answering State examination papers through Irish, were designed to encourage Irish-medium teaching of subjects other than Irish and to recognise candidates' additional efforts, possibly compensating for their difficulties in finding the best range of textbooks required.

128. Nóirín Ní Nuadháin, 'Putting a bit of spice into reading of Irish in the primary school', in Tina M. Hickey (ed.), *Literacy and Language Learning: Reading in a First or Second Language* (Dublin, 2006), pp 1–22.

129. See Ó Buachalla, 'Educational policy and the role of the Irish language from 1831 to 1981', p. 88; Kiberd, Editorial, in *The Crane Bag*, 5 (2), p. 836; Michael Cronin, 'The Gaelic hit factory', review of *Scéal Ghael-Linn* by Mairéad Ní Chinnéide (Inverin, 2014), in *The Dublin Review of Books* (November 2014); The 1975 CILAR [Committee on Irish Language Attitudes Research] survey reported 68 per cent of respondents believed that Irish should remain as an obligatory school subject (Walsh, *One Hundred Years of Irish Language Policy, 1922–2022*, p. 186); this is almost identical to the 67 per cent declaring positive attitudes towards the Irish language given in *The Irish Language Survey*, published in 2015 by the ESRI [Economic and Social Research Institute]: see Merike Dermody and Tania Daly, 'Attitudes towards the Irish Language on the Island of Ireland' (Dublin, 2015).

130. Gearóid Ó Tuathaigh, 'The decline of the Irish language,' in J. J. Lee (ed.), *Ireland: 1945–1970* (Dublin, 1979), pp 111–23; extract reprinted in Bowman (ed.), *Ireland: The Autobiography*, pp 312–13 (p. 313).

131. Ó Buachalla, 'Educational policy and the role of the Irish language from 1831 to 1981', p. 90.

132. 'The Irish language – a linguistic crisis?', Oireachtas Library & Research Service Note (September 2016), pp 1–25 (p. 2). For details on recent census estimates of Irish language speakers, see Walsh, *One Hundred Years of Irish Language Policy, 1922–2022*, pp 29–34.

133. Ibid., p. 21.

134. A curious feature of Irish springs from its double status, simultaneously denoting an official national language and an idiom used by a minority of citizens. This sociolinguistic reality is (unintentionally) expressed by official signposting in the Gaeltacht itself where, as Ronan Barré points out, 'des panneaux indiquent généralement l'entrée d'un Gaeltacht mais aucun signe n'indique au voyageur de passage qu'il en est sorti [signposts generally mark the entry to an Irish-speaking area but no signpost tells the passing traveller that he has left it behind]'. (Ronan Barré, 'L'irlandais peut-il seulement être une langue?', in Wesley Hutchinson and Clíona Ní Ríordáin (eds), *Language Issues: Ireland, France, Spain* (Brussels, 2010), pp 141–51 (p. 142).)

135. For an interesting account of broadcasting policy since 1922, including recent case studies of Dublin's Raidió na Life and Belfast's Raidió Fáilte, see Walsh, *One Hundred Years of Irish Language Policy, 1922–2022*, pp 249–304.

136. Ibid., p. 250.

137. Like the interviewees in a TG4 documentary by Hector Ó hEochagáin, 'Éire Nua' (30 September 2021).

138. Walsh, *One Hundred Years of Irish Language Policy, 1922–2022*, p. 318.

139. Doyle, *A History of the Irish Language*, p. 267.

140. In 2019, Viktor Bayda was appointed Oifigeach Pleanála Teanga [language-planning officer] in the Iveragh Gaeltacht in County Kerry. See 'Victor Bayda': https://en.wikipedia.org/wiki/Victor_Bayda (3 October 2023).

141. 'Interview with Junhan Zhang' on ucd.ie/irish/en/global (accessed June 2022).

142. Nadia Dobrianska, 'Níl an fuinneamh agam gach masla a thugtar dúinn mar Úcránaigh a fhreagairt, ach tá ceann amháin nach féidir liom scaoileadh leis [I do not have the energy to respond to every insult given to us as Ukrainians, but there is one that I cannot let pass]', *Tuairisc*, 9 March 2022. She can be heard on Raidió Fáilte giving an interview in Irish: 'An Úcráin – Ag caint le Nadia Dobrianska' (13 May 2022), https://soundcloud.com/raidio-f/an-ucrain-ag-caint-le-nadia-dobrianska-1352022 (accessed 4 September 2022).

143. Walsh, *One Hundred Years of Irish Language Policy, 1922–2022*, pp 44–6, and passim. The term *Breac-Ghaeltacht* ['speckled' Irish-speaking region] – as opposed to *Fíor-Ghaeltacht* ['true' Irish-speaking region] – was first used in the 1920s by the Gaeltacht Commission to designate areas such as County Waterford's Déise, where Irish speakers were scattered among English speakers. In reality, Walsh argues, the term is appropriate for all populations that are culturally and linguistically hybrid, and is highly relevant to describe Irish-language speech communities today. Hugo Hamilton used the word creatively in the title of his fascinating memoir of a German–Irish childhood, *The Speckled People* (London, 2003).

144. J. J. Lee refers to 'compulsory Irish and virtually compulsory Latin' before free post-primary education was introduced in 1967 (Lee, *Ireland, 1912–1985*, p. 131). He links this overemphasis with the neglect of science and modern European languages. Cf. O'Toole, *We Don't Know Ourselves*, pp 121–2.

145. Flann Campbell, 'Latin and the elite tradition in education', in *The British Journal of Sociology* 19 (1968), pp 308–25; Vigner, 'Depuis quand enseigne-t-on le français en France?'; Serge Tomamichel, 'Le latin dans l'enseignement secondaire français: formes et légitimités sociales d'une discipline scolaire entre monopole et déclin (xvie–xxe siècles)', in *Espacio, Tiempo, Educación* 4:2 (2017), pp 209–26 (doi:http://dx.doi.org/10.14516/ete.141).

146. Ancient Greek was required for admission to Oxford up to 1920. In 1960, Cambridge substituted 'one of Greek or Latin' by a requirement for any two languages. By 1967 this was reduced to one language. However, public schools, which insisted on Victorian classical learning, continued to supply 'seedbeds of social exclusion' (Christopher Stray, *Classics Transformed: Schools, Universities, and Society in England, 1830–1960* (Oxford, 1998), p. 12). Cf. Simon Kuper, *Chums: How a Tiny Caste of Oxford Tories Took Over the UK* (London, 2022).

147. Tomamichel, 'Le latin dans l'enseignement secondaire français,' p. 224.

148. John V. Luce, *Trinity College Dublin, the First 400 Years* (Dublin, 1992), p. 156.

149. Moody and Beckett, *Queen's, Belfast*, vol 2, pp 503–4; Minutes of Senate of QUB, 26 May 1959.

150. See NUI Archives, NUI, Dublin, Minutes of NUI Senate, 10 November 1972, item 5; 7 December 1973, item 8.

151. Attracta Halpin, email to the author, 10 February 2021. A 'third' language means after English and Irish.

152. ICEL, The International Commission on English in the Liturgy, was set up in Rome in 1963.

153. W. B. Stanford, *Ireland and the Classical Tradition* (Dublin, 1976), pp 245–6. See, For the downward trend in take-up of Leaving Certificate Latin, Ancient Greek and Classical Studies since the 1980s, see Table 4, 'Numbers of candidates taking classics at Leaving Certificate (1980–2022)', p. 317 below.

154. John O'Meara, 'Augustine versus the love of women', BBC Radio 3, 24 January 1972 (typescript).

155. John Dillon, 'Some reflections on the Irish classical tradition', in *The Crane Bag* 3 (2) [*Anglo-Irish Perspectives*] (1979; 1982 reprint), pp 448–52 (p. 450).

156. One cannot help wondering whether Joyce was aware of the additional linguistic liminality that future readers of his *Ulysses* would experience. The novel, structured on Homer's *Odyssey*, was published just as Ancient Greek was dropped as a matriculation requirement for Oxford, when the tide for classical education was beginning to turn in the British isles.

157. Classics continue to resurface in other guises. Greek and Roman Civilisation has become a discipline in its own right. (A pioneering RUI professor in this regard, UCD's professor of Greek, Henry Browne SJ, founded the college's classical museum and used a kinematograph to convey classical art, artefacts and architecture; he even advocated teaching a non-linguistic course on the classical world: Stanford, *Ireland and the Classical Tradition*, pp 65–6.) Ireland's rich classical tradition continues to manifest itself in translation, with poets and playwrights mining Greek and Roman texts to appropriate them in different ways (see Brian Arkins, 'Irish appropriation of Sophocles' *Antigone* and *Philoctetes*', in Michael Cronin and Cormac Ó Cuilleanáin (eds), *The Languages of Ireland* (Dublin, 2003), pp 167–78). On new chains of continuity in Irish appropriations of classical authors since independence, see Torrance and O'Rourke (eds), *Classics and Irish Politics 1916–2016*.

158. Stanford, *Ireland and the Classical Tradition*, pp 33–4. He refers to the 'hand of doom' (p. 33).

159. Ibid., pp 33–41. Comparable criticism, for English schools, is found in Stray, *Classics Transformed*.

160. John O'Meara, 'Remembering Archbishop McQuaid, U.C.D. and reform of Irish education', in *Studies* 92 (2003), pp 340–8 (pp 344–6).

161. Stray, *Classics Transformed*, p. 293, likewise refers to 'a kind of Indian summer' for classics in England, between 1920 and 1960.

162. With considerable variation, institutional and departmental, depending on local staffing. For example, UCD's French Department in the 1990s had four medievalists, none of whom exclusively confined their work to medieval French. For other universities, where German is concerned, see Holfter (ed.), *Rückblicke und Reflexionen*.

163. See McLelland, *Teaching and Learning Foreign Languages*, pp 180–1.

164. Christopher Brumfit, 'Must language teaching be communicative?', in David Little, Bebhinn O Meadhra and David Singleton (eds), *New Approaches in the Language Classroom: Coping With Change* [Proceedings of the Second National Modern Languages Convention (31 January–1 February 1986)] (Dublin, 1986), pp 11–19 (p. 14).

165. David Little, 'Concluding remarks', in Little, O Meadhra and Singleton (eds), *New Approaches in the Language Classroom*, p. 114. Gemma Hussey, Minister for Education (1982–6), introduced aural and oral examinations.

166. The Language Teachers' Associations, the RIA's National Committee for Modern Language Studies and its National Modern Language Commission had all lobbied in vain, since the early 1970s, for a compulsory oral component in the Leaving Certificate language examinations.

167. David Little and Eugene Davis, 'Facing the challenge of new technologies: interactive video and the AUTOTUTOR project', in Little, O Meadhra and Singleton (eds), *New Approaches in the Language Classroom*, pp 26–33 (p. 26). Cf. Bebhinn Ó Meadhra, Bill Richardson and Cormac Ó Cuilleanáin (eds), *Languages in the 1990s* [Proceedings of the Third National Modern Languages Convention (29–30 January 1989)] (Dublin, 1989).

168. Brumfit, 'Must language teaching be communicative?', p. 15.

169. See Cronin and Ó Cuilleanáin (eds), *The Languages of Ireland*.

170. Domenico Cosmai, *The Language of Europe. Multilingualism and Translation in the EU Institutions: Practice, Problems and Perspectives*, translated and edited by David Albert Best (Brussels, 2007), pp 29–49; for the relevant language policy, Regulation no. 1, 15 April 1958, see ibid., pp 48–9.

171. Cronin, *Translating Ireland*, p. 188, refers to translation from other languages helping 'to deliver Irish from the fatality of one language pair with its troubled contexts'.

172. There are many minority languages in the EU without official language status. One of the arguments for Irish gaining that status was its position as an official language of the State.

173. David Best, Cosmai, *The Language of Europe*, Introduction, pp 17–25 (p. 18).

174. See https://ie.ambafrance.org/Qu-est-ce-que-le-LFI and https://en.wikipedia.org/wiki/St_Kilian%27s_German_School#History, both accessed 7 March 2023.

175. What would have been the result, for the history of Irish usage, had Raidió na Gaeltachta been set up along with 2RN in the 1920s, or TnaG [now TG4] along with RTÉ in the 1960s?

176. Cosmai, *The Language of Europe*, p. 189. In France itself, fears about English encroachment on the French language go back a few decades. For a recent account, see Lara Marlowe, 'Académie Française sounds alarm about the increasing use of English', *Irish Times*, 21 February 2022.

177. Cosmai, *The Language of Europe*, p. 191.

178. The EU's 2001 target of 'mother tongue plus two' is formulated in https://eur-lex.europa.eu/legal-content/EN/TXT/HTML/?uri=LEGISSUM:c11044&from=PT, 24 October 2023. Cf. Halpin, 'The role of the National University of Ireland in language learning and language research and scholarship', p. 4. Cf. Bruen, 'Towards a national policy for languages in education' [online edn], p. 4.

179. 'Languages Connect', cited above at n. 56.

180. 'Languages Connect', Chart 2, p. 27, gives the numbers of candidates who sat foreign-language examinations in the 2016 Leaving Certificate: 25,757 students took French, 7,615 German, 6,579 Spanish, 512 Italian; there were 333 candidates taking Russian, 326 Japanese and 110 Arabic; while 17,947 took no foreign language. For the spread of languages in the 2022 Leaving Certificate, see Table 5, 'Numbers of candidates taking Languages at Leaving Certificate (2022)', p. 318 below.

181. 'Languages Connect', p. 40. Statistics from the 2016 Census indicate the following large groups of foreign nationals: Poles, Lithuanians, Romanians, Latvians, Brazilians, Spaniards and Italians (ibid., p. 14).

182. The symposium's proceedings were published by the NUI: Maguire (ed.), *Foreign Language Learning and Ireland's* Languages Connect *Strategy*.

183. 'Languages Connect', p. 17.

184. For an account of the key players' varying perspectives, including the role of the Carnegie Foundation, see Malouf, *Making World English*. 'World English' took on several meanings, from being understood as a means of best conveying Britishness and British culture overseas to being increasingly accepted as an instrument of communication that is truly 'global', denoting no particular people or culture.

185. 'The language of the future', in *Old Wine and New Wine* (Dublin, 1922), reissued in Conall Cearnach, *The Fatal Move [and other stories]*, ed. Reggie Chamberlain-King (Dublin, 2021), pp 79–83 (pp 80–1). O'Connell may not be quite right in every detail, but he was not the only one to notice. The Leathes parliamentary committee reported in 1918 that, although Britons 'need to know foreign peoples and foreign lands, the very general use of English throughout the world is an actual impediment to them in the acquisition of such knowledge' (Leathes Report, p. 207). For twenty-first-century perspectives, see Tore Janson, *Speak: A Short History of Languages* (Oxford, 2002), pp 232–66; and for the relative current health of the Irish language, see Liam Mac Cóil, 'Irish – one of the languages of the world' ['An Ghaeilge: Ceann de theangacha an domhain', translated by Michael Cronin], in Cronin and Ó Cuilleanáin (eds), *The Languages of Ireland*, pp 127–47 (pp 135–8).

186. Four languages are regarded as 'world' languages today: Arabic, English, Mandarin and Spanish. We are concerned with English for obvious reasons.

187. Simon Kuper, 'Globish just doesn't cut it any more', *Financial Times*, 11 January 2018.

188. Ibid.

189. Ibid.

190. Simon Kuper, 'The best place to build a life in English? The Netherlands', *Financial Times*, 25 April 2019, discusses how the hard-headed trading Dutch are capitalising on their ability to be a post-Brexit European English-language economy of choice for non-Europeans.

191. Leigh Oakes and Martin Howard, 'Foreign language motivation in a globalised world: The case of languages other than English (LOTEs)', in Maguire (ed.), *Foreign Language Learning and Ireland's Languages Connect Strategy*, pp 26–34 (p. 26.)

192. Lee, *Ireland, 1912–1985*, p. 667.

193. Michael Brophy, 'On the opportunities and challenges of implementation: Connecting with *Languages Connect* in higher education', in Maguire (ed.), *Foreign Language Learning and Ireland's Languages Connect Strategy*, pp 21–5 (p. 23).

194. Maria Tymoczko, 'Language interface in early Irish culture', in Cronin and Ó Cuilleanáin (eds), *The Languages of Ireland*, pp 25–43; Jean-Michel Picard, 'The Latin language in early medieval Ireland', in ibid., pp 44–56; and Muireann Ní Bhrolcháin, *An Introduction to Early Irish Literature* (Dublin, 2009; 2011 reprint), pp 14–15.

195. Laurie O'Higgins, *The Irish Classical Self: Poets and Poor Scholars in the Eighteenth and Nineteenth Centuries* (Oxford, 2017), pp 58–68.

196. FitzGerald, *Reflections on the Irish State*, p. 15.

197. On deviations (from standard English) in Hiberno-English, see Terence P. Dolan, 'Translating Irelands: The English language in the Irish context', in Cronin and Ó Cuilleanáin (eds), *The Languages of Ireland*, pp 78–92. Cf. Dolan's *A Dictionary of Hiberno-English: The Irish Use of English* (Dublin, 1998), Introduction to the first edn, pp xx–xxviii; and Blindboy Boatclub, foreword to the third edn (Dublin, 2020).

198. Seamus Deane (ed.), *The Field Day Anthology of Irish Writing* (3 vols, Derry, 1991), vol. 1, p. 1056.

199. The NUI's association with Irish may well remain ingrained on the public mind, however. In 2006, following a row over individual universities' independent entitlement to award honorary degrees, the registrars of the (now more autonomous) universities responded to the NUI Senate's protest by asserting their autonomy and suggesting that the Senate might consider a new role for the NUI as 'an academy and educational trust dedicated to graduate education, research and scholarship in Irish language, literature and culture, with the potential to be a world leader in Irish Studies'. The incident sparking the row was UCD's Ryder Cup honorary degrees ceremony held at the K Club (an elite golf club and resort in County Kildare). See 'The future of the National University of Ireland: the consensus view of the NUI Registrars', p. 2, cited in Tom Dunne, 'Coming to Terms with the 1997 Act: The National University of Ireland Senate, 1997–2007', in Dunne et al. (eds), *NUI Centenary Essays*, pp 280–7 (p. 285).

200. See, in particular, Coolahan, 'The National University of Ireland and the changing structure of Irish higher education, 1967–2007'; and Dunne, 'Coming to terms with the 1997 Act'. Ireland now has 13 universities.

201. This photograph of Belfast's RUI women graduates surfaced in 2019 when discovered by chance in the QUB Student Union building. See Shannon Devlin, 'Queen's First Women', https://www.qub. ac.uk/research-centres/CentreforPublicHistory/Blog/ShannonDevlinBlog/.

CODA

1. President Mary McAleese, address to the RIA Modern Languages Annual Research Symposium, on 'Translations: Paradigms of linguistic and cultural transformation', UU Coleraine (9 November 2001).

2. John le Carré, 'Why we should learn German', *The Guardian*, 2 July 2017.

3. Susan M. Parkes, 'Higher education, 1793–1908', in W. E. Vaughan (ed.), *A New History of Ireland, VI: Ireland under the Union, II: 1870–1921* (Oxford, 1996), pp 539–70 (p. 540).

4. Likewise, Garret FitzGerald argues on economic and political grounds that Irish independence itself was 'secured almost at the latest date at which it could have been usefully achieved'. See FitzGerald, *Reflections on the Irish State* (Dublin, 2003), pp 1–24 (p. 14).

5. The ruckus over the appointment of Professor Degani in UCD (see above, pp 178–9) seems to have involved no greater issues than prejudice and jobbery. The demise of Professor Geisler in QCG (see above, pp 137, 144) remains slightly mysterious, but it is remarkable that his 'case' was ventilated in the House of Commons as though it were a great scandal.

6. Malta's current population is under half a million, while the Republic of Ireland's is just over five million (https://www.worldometers.info/world-population/, 17 August 2023).

7. European Commission data (2012) cited in https://en.wikipedia.org/wiki/Maltese_language#, 17 August 2023.

8. On shame or embarrassment as a motivator, see Leigh Oakes and Martin Howard, 'Foreign language motivation in a globalised world: The case of languages other than English (LOTEs)', in Patricia Maguire (ed.), *Foreign Language Learning and Ireland's Languages Connect Strategy: Reflections following a symposium organised by the National University of Ireland with University College Cork* (Dublin, 2019), pp 26–34.

9. Nicola McLelland, 'French and German in British schools (1850–1945)', in *Documents pour l'histoire du français langue étrangère ou seconde* 53 (2014), pp 109–24, n. 12: 'The requirement for foreign languages was dropped entirely by universities from the late 1960s onwards'.

10. Nicola McLelland, *Teaching and Learning Foreign Languages: A History of Language Education, Assessment and Policy in Britain* (London and New York, 2017; pb edn, 2018), p. 181. Cf. Rebecca Smithers and Ben Whitford, '"Free fall" fears as pupils abandon languages', *The Guardian*, 25 Aug. 2006.

11. Simon Kuper, 'Globish just doesn't cut it any more', *Financial Times*, 11 January 2018.

12. The matter was raised at an Italian seminar in 2016: https://www.terminologia.it/index. php/2016/11/25/translation-is-the-language-of-europe-umberto-eco/?lang=it, 11 February 2023.

13. Simon Kuper, 'The case for diving into another language', *Financial Times*, 21 April 2021.

14. 'Languages Connect: Ireland's Strategy for Foreign Languages in Education 2017–2026' (Dublin, 2017), p. 40.

15. On the Irish language as a marker of cultural identity, see J. J. Lee, *Ireland, 1912–1985: Politics and Society* (Cambridge, 1989), pp 658–74 (p. 662).

16. T. K. Whitaker, 'Sixty years on: Achievement and disappointment', *Irish Times*, 4 December 1981, p. 9.

17. Muireann Ní Bhrolcháin, *An Introduction to Early Irish Literature* (Dublin, 2009; 2011 reprint), pp 151–2.

18. It was launched on 24 April 2021.

19. Le Carré, 'Why we should learn German'.

20. McLelland, *Teaching and Learning Foreign Languages*, pp 199–200, contrasts the uninspiring and limiting goals of language learning laid out by contemporary education policy documents with more

challenging and substantial goals presented to former generations. The pendulum has perhaps swung too far.

21. John Harris and Denise O'Leary, 'A third language at primary level in Ireland: An independent evaluation of the Modern Languages in Primary Schools Initiative', in Marianne Nikolov (ed.), *Early Learning of Modern Foreign Languages: Processes and Outcomes* (Bristol, 2009), pp 1–14.

22. On the world's endangered languages, see Michael Krauss, 'The world's languages in crisis', in *Language* 68 (1992), pp 4–10; and Gary F. Simons and Melvyn Paul Lewis, 'The world's languages in crisis: a 20-year update', in Elena Mihas, Bernard Perley, Gabriel Rei-Doval and Kathleen Wheatley (eds), *Responses to Language Endangerment* [Studies in Language Companion Series 142] (Amsterdam, 2013), pp 3–20. Cf. Kevin Whelan, 'Between: The politics of culture in Friel's *Translations*', *Field Day Review* 6 (2010), pp 7–27 (p. 27).

23. Manchán Magan, 'The hundreds of Irish words for sea and sea life', *Irish Times*, 9 January 2021. Cf. Manchán Magan, *Listen to the Land Speak: A Journey Into the Wisdom of What Lies Beneath Us* (Dublin, 2022).

24. Simon Kuper, 'The problem with English', *Financial Times*, 12 January 2017.

25. For intelligence reasons, Irish army officers on United Nations duty occasionally text each other in Irish and Irish diplomats regularly communicate in Irish to frustrate eavesdroppers.

26. Anthony Harvey, *How Linguistics Can Help the Historian* (Dublin, 2021), p. 29. In traditional philological textbooks, the Strasbourg Oaths are presented as one of the earliest 'monuments' of the French language.

27. Eda Sagarra, 'The centenary of the Henry Simon Chair of German at the University of Manchester (1996): Commemorative address', in *German Life and Letters* 51 (1998), pp 509–24 (p. 522).

28. For Anderson, see Jackie Uí Chionna, *Queen of Codes: The Secret Life of Emily Anderson, Britain's Greatest Female Codebreaker* (London, 2023). Beckett's meticulous language work for the French resistance has been well rehearsed by his biographers: see James Knowlson, *Damned to Fame: the Life of Samuel Beckett* (London, 1996), pp 297–318 (pp 307–11). For Elmes, see Clodagh Finn, *A Time to Risk All* (Dublin, 2017).

29. As set out in the recent government strategy, 'Languages Connect'.

30. Roy Hattersley, 'Had there been no Reformation would England have been spared Brexit?', *Irish Times*, 25 February 2017. It may not be entirely coincidental that Simon Kuper, in a recent study of his fellow students at Oxford, many of whom were to become ardent Brexiters, finds that 'the most Brexity degree among MPs in 2016 was classics: six of the eight classicists in the Commons voted Leave' (Simon Kuper, *Chums: How a Tiny Caste of Oxford Tories Took Over the UK* (London, 2022), p. 40).

Timeline of Events, Institutions, Policies Mentioned in this Book*

(* Key developments for language-learning noted in bold type)

pre-VICTORIAN:

1570s	**First continental Irish Colleges for Roman Catholics (RC) set up, an offshore education model that runs until the French Revolution**
1592	**Trinity College (Dublin University) founded by Queen Elizabeth I [TCD, DU, 'Trinity']**
1607	Flight of the Earls
1608	Royal Free Schools founded in Ulster (for sons of Plantation settlers) by King James I
1609–10	Douai Old Testament
1611	Franciscans' Irish College at Louvain acquires a printing press with Irish characters William Bathe, SJ, *Ianua Linguarum* [Door to Languages]
1620s/30s	*Annála Ríoghachta Éireann* [*Annals of the Four Masters*] is transcribed
*c.*1634	Seathrún Céitinn [Geoffrey Keating] finishes *Foras Feasa ar Éirinn* [Compendium of Knowledge about Ireland]
1690	Battle of the Boyne
1693	John Locke, *Some Thoughts Concerning Education*
1728	Peadar Ó Neachtain sets sail for Santiago
1761–1814	Suppression of the Jesuits in parts of Catholic Europe
1771	Ursulines set up their first school for girls in Ireland (in Cork)
1776	**Trinity's Provost John Hely-Hutchinson founds two modern languages chairs (French with German; Italian with Spanish), first of their kind in the world**
mid–1770s	Presentation Sisters are founded by Nano Nagle
1782	St Kieran's College, Kilkenny, is founded (first RC diocesan secondary school)

1782–93	Removal of penal restrictions on Catholics by a series of Relief Acts
1784	William Jones sets up the Asiatic Society of Bengal
1785	Royal Irish Academy [RIA] is founded
1789	French Revolution
1795	**Royal College of St Patrick, Maynooth, County Kildare, is founded as a Roman Catholic seminary [Maynooth College; later to share its campus with NUI Maynooth]**
1798	United Irishmen's uprising
1801	Act of Union of Great Britain and Ireland
1802	Christian Brothers open their first school for boys in Waterford
1803	Robert Emmet rebellion
1806	Gaelic Society of Ireland is founded
1808	William Neilson, *An Introduction to the Irish Language*
1809	Richard Lovell Edgeworth, *Essays on Professional Education*
1814	Jesuits found Clongowes Wood College, County Kildare (boys' RC boarding school) Belfast Academical Institution opens
1815	Battle of Waterloo: defeat of Napoleon Bonaparte
1818	Jesuits found Tullabeg, County Offaly (boys' RC boarding school) Iberno-Celtic Society is founded Irish Society for Promoting the Education of the Native Irish through the Medium of their Own Language is set up
1819	Chair of Sanskrit is established at the University of Bonn
1822	Loreto Abbey Rathfarnham, County Dublin, is founded (RC girls' boarding school)
1826	University College London is founded
1829	Roman Catholic Relief Act [Catholic Emancipation] King's College London is founded
1829–42	Ordnance Survey of Ireland
1830	Ulster Gaelic Society is founded
1830s	System of national education is set up in Ireland (primary level)
1832	Boden professorship of Sanskrit in Oxford established
1833	St Malachy's College, Belfast, is founded

1835   Vincentians found Castleknock College, County Dublin (RC boys' boarding school)

VICTORIAN:

1842   Missionary College of All Hallows, Drumcondra, Dublin, is founded (RC seminary)

Oct. 1842   First issue of Young Ireland's *The Nation*

1843   St Columba's College, Stackallan, County Meath, is founded (Church of Ireland boys' boarding school, later moved to Rathfarnham, County Dublin)

1845–52   The Great Famine

1845   Robert Peel announces multidenominational Queen's University of Ireland [QUI]

1846   Resolutions of the Irish Queen's Colleges Board include modern language chairs and deem modern languages to be an essential degree component

1849   Queen's Colleges are opened (in Belfast, Cork, Galway) [QCB, QCC, QCG]
                Royal Society of Antiquaries of Ireland founded

1850   Synod of Thurles, first Roman Catholic plenary synod held in Ireland since 1642

1852–79   Paul Cullen becomes archbishop of Dublin

1853   Irish Archaeological and Celtic Society founded
                Ossianic Society founded
                Johann Kaspar Zeuss, *Grammatica Celtica*

1854   Northcote-Trevelyan Report on the Organisation of the Permanent Civil Service

1854–79   Catholic University of Ireland founded (later University College, and University College Dublin) [CU / CUI / UCD; occasionally '[St] Stephen's Green' or 'Earlsfort Terrace']

1854–8   John Henry Newman becomes rector of the CUI

late 1850s   Modern languages become subjects in open public examinations for entry to the Indian Civil Service and the Royal Military Academy at Woolwich and in Oxbridge Syndicate examinations

1857–8   Queen's Colleges Commission of Inquiry

1859   St Louis sisters set up schools in Ireland, including in Monaghan
                Ladies' Collegiate School (from 1887 Victoria College) is set up in Belfast

1860	Holy Ghost Fathers found the French College, Blackrock, County Dublin (RC boys' boarding school)
1861	Bartholomew Woodlock succeeds Newman as CUI rector Eugene O'Curry, *Lectures on the Manuscript Materials of Ancient Irish History*
1863	Queen's Colleges Chairs of Celtic are suspended
1864	French Protestant School for Girls founded in Bray, County Wicklow Clarendon Commission's Report on (fee-paying) boys' public schools in England
1866	Alexandra College (school for girls) is set up in Dublin TCD divides its two-language post (French and German) into two separate chairs: one in German and one in Romance Languages (French, Italian, Spanish)
1868	Taunton Commission's Report on girls' grammar schools in England
1869	Irish Church Act [Disestablishment of the Church of Ireland]
1870	*Revue Celtique* is founded
1873	Eugene O'Curry, *On the Manners and Customs of the Ancient Irish*
1875	Civil Service Department set up at the French College, Blackrock, County Dublin
1876	Society for the Preservation of the Irish Language [SPIL] founded
1878	**Intermediate Education (Ireland) Act** Celtic becomes an optional extra in national schools in Irish-speaking areas, and is included among languages for examination Berlitz (immersive) method for language learning is set up
1879	Irish National Land League is founded St Columb's College, Derry, is founded
1879–80	**University Education (Ireland) Act sets up the Royal University of Ireland [RUI], incorporating the three Queen's Colleges (Belfast, Cork, Galway), the Catholic University (Dublin) and several other constituent colleges; the RUI's matriculation examination requires students to have a satisfactory level of Latin or Greek plus another classical *or* modern language; in addition, it deems women eligible to take degrees**
1880	Gaelic Union is founded University College Blackrock is founded as a constituent college of the RUI
1882	*Irisleabhar na Gaedhilge* [The Gaelic Journal] is founded (bilingual monthly) Wilhelm Viëtor, *Sprachunterricht muss umkehren!* [Language teaching must change direction!]

1883	Alliance Française is founded
1884	**RUI's first cohort of women graduates**
1885–93	**To complement Alexandra College in Dublin and Victoria College in Belfast, RC single-sex colleges are set up to prepare women students for university examinations: in Cork by the Ursulines (St Angela's from 1887) and in Dublin by the Dominicans (Eccles Street from 1885, later in St Mary's University College from 1893) and the Loreto Sisters (Loreto College St Stephen's Green from 1893)**
1891	Death of Charles Stewart Parnell
1892	Modern Languages Teachers' Association is founded (England) Douglas Hyde, 'The necessity for de-Anglicising the Irish nation' (presidential address to the National Literary Society, Dublin)
1893	**Gaelic League [GL] is founded (Dublin)**
1895	Belfast branch of GL is founded
1897	*Zeitschrift für Celtische Philologie* is founded
1899	*An Claidheamh Soluis* is founded (Gaelic League's weekly newspaper) [ACS] Vice-Regal Inquiry into Intermediate Education
1900	Irish is recognised as a subject for all national schools
1901–2	Robertson Commission [Royal Commission on University Education (Ireland)]

post-VICTORIAN:

1902	Irish Association of Women Graduates and Candidate Graduates [IAWGCG] is founded
1903	The School of Irish Learning [*Sgoil Árd-Leighinn na Gaedhilge*] is set up in Dublin
1904	**Trinity College deems women eligible to take degrees** Optional bilingual programme for national schools in Irish-speaking districts
1906	Irish-language school is set up in Ring College [Coláiste na Rinne], County Waterford Queen's College Belfast's student Gaelic Society is founded
1906–7	Fry Commission [Royal Commission on Trinity College and the University of Dublin]
1907	TCD sets up a Celtic Studies Moderatorship TCD's Cumann Gaelach (student Irish Society) is founded
1908	Trinity Hall opens (residence for TCD's women students)

July 1908	**Irish Universities Act establishes the National University of Ireland [NUI], to include University College Cork [UCC], University College Dublin [UCD], University College Galway [UCG] and (later) Maynooth** **Queen's College Belfast becomes Queen's University Belfast [QUB]**
1908–9	GL campaign for 'essential' Irish: that Irish be a required matriculation subject for NUI
1909	Dismissal by Maynooth of its Irish professor, Fr Michael O'Hickey Mary Ryan is first woman to be appointed professor (Romance Languages, UCC)
1910	GL's 'essential' Irish measure is carried by NUI Senate
1913	**'Essential' Irish for NUI matriculation comes into effect: NUI's matriculation requirements stipulate a satisfactory level in a classical language, a modern European language and the Irish language**
1914	Dismissal of Queen's University Belfast's Professor Max Freund as a hostile alien
1916	Easter Rising Arrest of University College Galway's Professor Valentine Steinberger
1916–18	Leathes Report (Parliamentary Committee on the Position of Modern Languages in the Educational System of Great Britain)
Dec. 1918	General election in Ireland brings landslide victory for nationalist Sinn Féin party
1919	Dáil Éireann (provisional unicameral Irish parliament) declares Irish independence at its first meeting (January); a large number of its MPs are in prison, and its proceedings, conducted mainly in Irish, are translated into English and French. TCD's chair of Irish is separated from the School of Divinity
1919–21	Irish War of Independence [Anglo-Irish War]
Nov. 1920	Government of Ireland Act sets up Northern Ireland
May 1921	Partition of the island (two separate jurisdictions)
Dec. 1921	Anglo-Irish Treaty concludes the War of Independence
1921–75	Eamon de Valera serves as Chancellor of the NUI

post-INDEPENDENCE:

6 Dec. 1922	Self-governing independent Irish Free State is set up (under the terms of the 1921 Treaty)

1922–3   Irish Civil War

1923   Institute for Research in English Teaching [IRET] is founded in Tokyo

1925   Leaving Certificate examination is established
School of Irish Learning is incorporated into the RIA

1927   Dr Frederick William O'Connell [Conall Cearnach] is appointed Assistant Director of Broadcasting, Dublin's 2RN

1934   Leaving Certificate 'compulsory Irish' is introduced

1935   An Gúm, the State's Irish-language publication company, is set up

1937   Constitution designates Irish as the State's first official language

1940   DIAS (Dublin Institute for Advanced Studies) set up by the State, includes a School of Celtic Studies

1948   *Caighdeán Oifigiúil* [Official standardised and simplified version of Irish] is published (revised 1957, 2017)

1953   Gael Linn is set up

1957   *Téarmaí Dlí* [classification of Irish-language legal terminology] is published

1960   Leaving Certificate oral examination in Irish is introduced

1963   *Coimisiún um Athbheochan na Gaeilge* [Commission on the Restoration of the Irish Language] [CRIL]

1965   *Investment in Education*
White Paper on the Restoration of the Irish Language

1966   *Buntús Gaeilge* is undertaken by Department of Education inspectorate

1967   Free post-primary education is introduced

1971   *Bunscoil Phobal Feirste*, first Irish-medium primary school in Belfast, is founded

1973   Ireland joins the European Economic Community
Requirement to pass Irish in order to pass the Leaving Certificate is abolished

1981   *An Bíobla Naofa* (first complete Irish translation of the Roman Catholic Bible)

1982–6   Oral and aural components are introduced in modern language examinations

1985   Raidió Fáilte, West Belfast's first Irish-language pirate radio station, is set up

1987   Erasmus [European Community Action Scheme for the Mobility of University Students] is introduced

1991   Northern Ireland Census starts to include a section on the Irish language

1997   Universities Act

1998   Belfast [Good Friday] Agreement gives legal recognition to Irish and to
            Ulster Scots

2001   European Year of Languages
            Council of Europe's Common European Framework of Reference for
            Languages [CEFR]

2017   'Languages Connect: Ireland's Strategy for Foreign Languages in Education
            2017–2026'

2022   Full official status for Irish within the EU
            Identity and Language (Northern Ireland) Act voted into law by UK
            Parliament

Table 1: Professors of Modern Languages in Ireland's Universities (1776–1921)

University	Name	Appointment	From	Creed	Provenance
CUI / UCD	Peter le Page Renouf	French and German	1854	RC	Guernsey
	Augusto Cesare Marani	Italian and Spanish	1854	RC	Italy
	Félix Schürr	French and German	1855	RC	Alsace
	Georges Polin	French and German	1873	RC	Alsace
	Édouard Cadic	French and German	1892	RC	France (Brittany)
	Maria Degani	Italian and Spanish	1909	RC	Trieste
	Mary Macken (*née* Bowler)	German	1909	RC	Ireland (Co. Cork)
	Mary Kate O'Kelly (*née* Ryan)	French *(lecturer)*★	1909	RC	Ireland (Co. Wexford)
	Roger Chauviré	French	1918	RC	France (Touraine)
DU (TCD)	R. Antonio Vieyra Transtagano	Italian with Spanish	1776	Prot	Portugal
	Antoine D'Esca	French with German	1776	Prot	Berlin
	Bessonnet, Hamilton, Kildahl, Martini, Aymot★★	French / German / French with German	1785	Prot	[various]
	Charles Williomier	French with German	1801	Prot ?	France ?
	Evasio Radice	Italian with Spanish	1824	Prot	Italy (Piemonte)
	Ignatius G. Abeltshauser	French with German	1842	Prot	Alsace (Strasbourg)
	Basilio Angeli	Italian with Spanish	1849	RC	Italy (Lucca)
	Augusto Cesare Marani	Italian with Spanish	1862	RC	Italy
	Albert Maximilian Selss	German	1866	Prot	Rhineland

University	Name	Appointment	From	Creed	Provenance
	Robert Atkinson	Romance languages	1869	Prot	England
	Maurice Alfred Gerothwohl	Romance languages	1907	*Jewish?*	British
	Robert Alan Williams	German	1907	Prot	Ireland (Belfast)
	Thomas B. Rudmose-Brown	Romance languages	1909	?	England
	Gilbert Waterhouse	German	1915	Prot	England (Yorkshire)
QUI Belfast	Mathias Joseph Frings	French and German	1849	Prot	Prussia
	Johann Wilhelm Frädersdorff	French and German	1862	Prot	Hamburg
	Albert Ludwig Meissner	French and German	1865	Prot	Prussia
	Maximilian Freund	French and German	1903	Prot	Saxony
	Maximilian Freund	German	1909	Prot	Saxony
	Douglas Lloyd Savory	Romance philology	1909	Prot	England (Suffolk)
	Robert Alan Williams	German	1915	Prot	Ireland (Belfast)
QUI Cork	Louis-Raymond de Véricour	French German Italian	1849	Prot	France (Paris)
	Owen O'Ryan	French and German	1879	RC	Ireland (Tipperary)
	William F. Butler	French and German	1895	RC	Ireland (Co. Down)
	Mary Ryan	Romance languages	1910	RC	Ireland (Cork)
	Waltraut [Wally] Swertz	German	1910	RC	Ireland (Cork)
	Bridget Lyndsay (*née* Danaher)	German	1915	RC	Ireland
	Mary Boyle (*née* Curran)	German	1921	RC	Ireland (Cork)
QUI Galway	Augustus Bensbach	French and German	1849	Jewish	Mannheim
	Charles [Karl] Geisler	French and German	1868	Prot	Prussia
	Valentine Steinberger	French and German	1886	RC	Bavaria
	Richard J. Conroy	Spanish	1916	RC ?	Ireland
	Liam Ó Briain	Romance languages	1917	RC	Ireland (Dublin)

University	Name	Appointment	From	Creed	Provenance
	Emily Anderson	German	1917	Prot	Ireland (Galway)
	Margaret Cooke [Shea]	German	1921	RC	Ireland (Co. Sligo)
Maynooth	Hugh O'Rourke	English and French	1862	RC	Ireland (Co. Galway)
	John F. Hogan	Modern Languages	1886	RC	Ireland (Co. Clare)
	Jean-Louis Rigal	Modern Languages	1914	RC	France (Aveyron)

* Acting Professor of French (1914–18), after the death of Professor Édouard Cadic and during the First World War.

** For Trinity's various 'licensed grinders' in the closing years of the 18th century, see M. M. Raraty, 'The chair of German, Trinity College, Dublin 1775–1866', in *Hermathena*, 102 (1966), pp 53–72.

Table 2: Professors of Celtic / Irish in Ireland's Universities (1800–1921)

University	Name	Appointment	From	Creed	Provenance
CUI / UCD Dublin	Eugene O'Curry	Irish history and archaeology	1854	RC	Co. Clare
	Brian O'Looney	Irish language and literature	1874	RC	Co. Clare
	Edmond Hogan, SJ	Irish language, literature, archaeology	1884	RC	Co. Cork
	John James O'Carroll, SJ	language and literature (*lecturer*)	1880s	RC	Dublin
	Osborn Bergin	Early Irish	1909	Prot	Cork
	Douglas Hyde	Modern Irish	1909	Prot	Co. Roscommon
	Agnes O'Farrelly	Modern Irish	1909	RC	Co. Cavan
DU (TCD) Dublin	Thomas De Vere Coneys	Irish [Divinity chair]	1840	Prot	Co. Mayo
	Daniel Foley	Irish [Divinity chair]	1852	Prot	Co. Kerry
	Thaddeus O'Mahony	Irish [Divinity chair]	1861	Prot	Co. Cork
	James [Séamas] Goodman	Irish [Divinity chair]	1879	Prot	Co. Kerry
	James E. Murphy	Irish [Divinity chair]	1896	Prot	Co. Cork
	Edward John Gwynn	Celtic languages (*lecturer*)	1907	Prot	Co. Donegal
	Thomas F. O'Rahilly	Modern Irish	1919	RC	Co. Kerry
QCB/QUB Belfast	John O'Donovan	Celtic languages and literatures	1849	RC	Co. Kilkenny
	Frederick William O'Connell ['Conall Cearnach']	Celtic languages and literatures (*lecturer*)	1909	Prot	Co. Galway
QCC/UCC Cork	Owen Connellan	Celtic languages and literatures	1849	RC	Co. Sligo
	Osborn Bergin	Celtic	1897	Prot	Cork
	Éamonn O'Donoghue	Irish (*lecturer*)	1904	RC	Co. Cork

University	Name	Appointment	From	Creed	Provenance
	Richard Henebry	Irish	1908	RC	Co. Waterford
	Tadhg O'Donoghue ['Tórna']	Irish	1916	RC	Co. Cork
QCG/UCG Galway	Cornelius Mahony	Celtic languages and literatures	1849	RC	Co. Cork
	John O'Beirne Crowe	Celtic languages and literatures	1854	RC	Co. Mayo
	Tomás Ó Máille	Modern Irish and Celtic philology	1909	RC	Co. Galway
SPCM Maynooth	Paul O'Brien	Irish	1804	RC	Co. Meath
	Martin Loftus	Irish	1820	RC	Connaught
	James Tully	Irish	1828	RC	Co. Galway
	Eoghan O'Growney	Irish	1891	RC	Co. Meath
	Michael O'Hickey	Irish	1896	RC	Co. Waterford

Table 3: NUI's First Women Professors
(Modern Languages, including Irish)

College	Name	Appointment	Chair	Creed	Provenance
UCC	Mary Ryan	1909 Romance languages	1910–38	RC	Ireland (Cork)
	Waltraut [Wally] Swertz	1910 German	1911–15	RC	Ireland (Cork)
	Bridget Lyndsay (*née* Danaher)	1915 German	1915–21	RC	Ireland
	Mary Boyle (*née* Curran)	1920 German	1922–67	RC	Ireland (Cork)
UCD	Mary Macken (*née* Bowler)	1909 German	1911–50	RC	Ireland (Co. Cork)
	Maria Degani	1909 Italian and Spanish	1912–38	RC	Trieste
	Mary Kate O'Kelly (*née* Ryan)	1909 French (*lecturer*)	(1913–18) [*]	RC	Ireland (Co. Wexford)
	Agnes O'Farrelly	1909 Modern Irish (*lecturer*)	1932–47	RC	Ireland (Co. Cavan)
UCG	Emily Anderson	1917 German	1917–1920	Presb	Ireland (Galway)
	Margaret Shea [*née* Cooke]	1921 German	1921–65	RC	Ireland (Co. Sligo)

[*] Acting Professor of French, following the death of Professor Édouard Cadic and during the First World War.

Table 4: Numbers of candidates taking classics at Leaving Certificate (1980–2022)

YEAR	LATIN (toal no. of candidates)	ANCIENT GREEK (total no. of candidates)	CLASSICAL STUDIES (total no. of candidates)
1979–80	23,610	707	---
1987–8	1,314	35	484
1996–7	310	17	1,359
2007–8	122	6	766
2022	80	*fewer than 10*	526

Sources: Department of Education Statistical Reports (Dublin: Stationery Office) and (post-2003) Department of Education, State Examinations Commission, State Examinations Statistics, https://www.examinations.ie/statistics/, 27 November 2023.

Table 5: Numbers of candidates taking languages at Leaving Certificate (2022)

Leaving Cert 2022	Total	Total	overall
SUBJECT	higher	lower	
Ancient Greek	fewer than 10	fewer than 10	fewer than 10
Arabic	172	28	200
Classical Studies	499	27	526
English	43,757	13,484	57,241
French	15,454	5,696	21,150
German	6,275	1,851	8,126
Irish	24,441	23,520	47,961
Italian	461	80	541
Japanese	219	52	271
Latin	80	*fewer than 10*	81–89
Lithuanian	174	12	186
Mandarin Chinese	280	*fewer than 10*	281–289
Polish	789	29	818
Portuguese	131	*fewer than 10*	132–141
Russian	407	12	419
Spanish	7,104	2,436	9,540

Source: Department of Education, State Examinations Commission, State Examinations Statistics, https://www.examinations.ie/statistics/, 27 November 2023.

List of Works Consulted

'Address of the President, on presenting the gold medals to Sir William R. Hamilton, to the Revd Samuel Haughton, to the Revd Edward Hincks, D.D., and John O'Donovan, Esq.' in *Proceedings of the Royal Irish Academy (1836–1869)*, 4 (1847–50), pp 193–210.

Adelman, Juliana, 'Communities of science: The Queen's Colleges and scientific culture in provincial Ireland, 1845–1875', PhD dissertation, NUIG, 2006.

Akenson, D. H., 'Pre-university education, 1870–1921', in Vaughan (ed.), *New History of Ireland, vol. 6*, pp 523–38.

Anderson, Benedict, *Imagined Communities: Reflections on the Origins and Spread of Nationalism* (London: Verso, 1983; revised edn 1991).

An Duanaire 1600–1900: Poems of the Dispossessed, Dánta Gaeilge Curtha i Láthair ag Seán Ó Tuama with Translations into English Verse by Thomas Kinsella (Mountrath: Dolmen Press, 1981).

Anon., 'The organisation of the study of modern languages in the University of Cambridge', in *The Modern Quarterly of Language and Literature*, 1, 1899, pp 322–6.

Anon., 'The results of Newman's campaign in Ireland', in *Studies: An Irish Quarterly Review*, 2, 1913, pp 898–905.

A Page of Irish History: Story of University College, Dublin 1883–1909, compiled by Fathers of the Society of Jesus (Dublin and Cork: Talbot Press, 1930).

Arkins, Brian, 'Irish appropriation of Sophocles' *Antigone* and *Philoctetes*', in Cronin and Ó Cuilleanáin (eds), *The Languages of Ireland*, pp 167–78.

Arnold, Matthew, *On the Study of Celtic Literature* (London: Smith, Elder & Co., 1867).

Arnold, Thomas, 'Rugby School – Use of the Classics', in *Quarterly Journal of Education*, 1834; reprinted in *The Miscellaneous Works of Thomas Arnold, D.D. Collected and Republished* (London: Fellowes, 1845), pp 347–61.

Ashby, M., 'Experimental phonetics at University College London before World War I', First International Workshop on the History of Speech Communication Research, (Dresden, September 2015), ISCA Archive, http://www.isca-speech.org/archive [accessed 30 July 2023].

Ashby, Michael, and Joanna Przedlacka, 'Technology and pronunciation teaching, 1890–1940', in McLelland and Smith (eds), *The History of Language Learning and Teaching*, vol. 2, pp 161–78.

Athenaeum, January 1842.

Austen, Jane, *The Complete Novels of Jane Austen*, 2 vols (New York: Random House, 1950).

Bacigalupo, Massimo (ed.), *Dante nel Mondo* (Genova: Accademia Ligure di Scienze e Lettere, 2022).

Bacon, Alan, 'English literature becomes a university subject: King's College, London as pioneer', in *Victorian Studies*, 29, 1986, pp 591–612.

Baretti, G., *Easy Phraseology for the Use of Young Ladies, Who Intend to Learn the Colloquial Part of the Italian Language* (London: G. Robinson and T. Cadell, 1775).

Barr, Colin, 'MacHale, John', DIB.

Barr, Colin, 'The failure of Newman's Catholic University of Ireland', in *Archivium Hibernicum*, 55, 2001, pp 126–39.

Barr, Colin, *Paul Cullen, John Henry Newman, and the Catholic University of Ireland, 1845–1865* (South Bend: University of Notre Dame Press and Leominster: Gracewing, 2003).

Barr, Colin, Michele Finelli and Anne O'Connor (eds), *Nation / Nazione: Irish Nationalism and the Italian Risorgimento* (Dublin: UCD Press, 2014).

Barr, Colin, 'Paul Cullen, Italy and the Irish Catholic imagination, 1826–70', in Barr, Finelli and O'Connor (eds), *Nation / Nazione*, pp 133–56.

Barré, Ronan, 'L'irlandais peut-il seulement être une langue?', in Hutchinson and Ní Ríordáin (eds), *Language Issues*, pp 141–51.

Battersby's Catholic Directory, Almanac, and Registry of the Whole Catholic World (Dublin: John Mullany, The Catholic Publishing and Bookselling Company, 1860).

Beaumont, Caitriona, 'How a photograph uncovered my grandmother's republican activism during the Irish revolution', The Conversation.com, 17 October 2022.

Beiner, Guy, 'Mapping the "Year of the French": The vernacular landscape of folk memory', in Caldicott and Fuchs (eds), *Cultural Memory*, pp 191–20.

Belfast Literary Society 1801–1901: Historical Sketch with Memoirs of some Distinguished Members [Centenary volume] (Belfast: The Linenhall Press, 1902).

Best, David, 'Introduction to the 1st English edn', in Cosmai, *The Language of Europe*, pp 17–25.

Bhreathnach, Edel, and Bernadette Cunningham (eds), *Writing Irish History: The Four Masters and their World* [exhibition catalogue, TCD Long Room Hub] (Dublin: Wordwell, 2007).

Biagini, Eugenio and Daniel Mulhall, eds, *The Shaping of Modern Ireland: A Centenary Assessment* (Sallins: Irish Academic Press, 2016

Blake Dillon, John, 'Continental literature', *The Nation*, 22 October 1842.

Blaney, Roger, *Presbyterians and the Irish Language* (Belfast: Ulster Historical Foundation, 1996).

Blindboy Boatclub, Foreword to T. P. Dolan, *A Dictionary of Hiberno-English* (3rd edn).

Bliss, Alan, 'The standardization of Irish', in *The Crane Bag*, 5 (2) [*The Irish Language and Culture*] (1981; 1982 reprint), pp 908–14.

Bottrall, Margaret, *Hughes Hall 1885–1985* (Cambridge: Rutherford Publications, 1985).

Bousfield, Arnold E., 'Corrig School, Kingstown' [pamphlet] (Bray: The Dargle Press, 1958).

Bowman, John, 'De Valera: did he entrench the partition of Ireland?', in Brennan (ed.), *Eamon de Valera*, pp 35–54.

Bowman, John (ed.), *Ireland: The Autobiography. One Hundred Years of Irish Life, Told by Its People* (Dublin: Penguin Ireland, 2016).

Boyle, Elizabeth, and Paul Russell (eds), *The Tripartite Life of Whitley Stokes (1830–1909)* (Dublin: Four Courts Press, 2011).

Boyle, Elizabeth, and Paul Russell, 'Introduction', in Boyle and Russell (eds), *Tripartite Life of Whitley Stokes*, pp 1–13.

Brayden, W. H., 'Recollections of W. H. Brayden', in *A Page of Irish History*, pp 123–6.

Breathnach, Diarmuid, and Máire Ní Mhurchú, 'Crowe, John O'Beirne (c.1824–1874)', ainm.ie.

Breathnach, Diarmuid, and Máire Ní Mhurchú, 'Wulff, Winifred Mary Paula (1895–1946)', ainm.ie.

Breathnach, Eileen, 'Women and higher education in Ireland (1879–1914)', in *The Crane Bag*, 4 (1) [*Images of the Irish Woman*] (1980; 1982 reprint), pp 560–7.

Brebner, Mary, *The Method of Teaching Modern Languages in Germany, Being the Report Presented to the Trustees of the Gilchrist Educational Trust on a Visit to Germany in 1897, as Gilchrist Travelling Scholar* (London: C. J. Clay and Sons, 1898).

Breen, Aidan, 'Meyer, Kuno', DIB.

Breen, Aidan, 'Zimmer, Heinrich', DIB.

Brennan, Paul (ed.), *Eamon de Valera* (Paris: Presses Sorbonne Nouvelle, 1986).

Brevini, Franco (ed.), *La Poesia in Dialetto: Storia e Testi Dalle Origini al Novecento*, 3 vols (Milan: Mondadori, 1999).

Brontë, Emily [Ellis Bell], *Wuthering Heights* (1847).

Brophy, Michael, 'On the opportunities and challenges of implementation: connecting with *Languages Connect* in higher education', in Maguire (ed.), *Foreign Language Learning and Ireland's* Languages Connect *Strategy*, pp 21–5.

Bruen, Jennifer, 'Towards a national policy for languages in education: The case of Ireland' [Vers une politique nationale pour les langues dans l'éducation: le cas de l'Irlande], in *European Journal of Language Policy*, 5, 2013, pp 99–114.

Bruen, Jennifer, '*Languages Connect*: What does Ireland's first government strategy for foreign-languages-in-education mean for Irish universities?', in Maguire (ed.), *Foreign Language Learning and Ireland's* Languages Connect *Strategy*, pp 7–20.

Brumfit, Christopher, 'Must language teaching be communicative?', in Little, O Meadhra and Singleton (eds), *New Approaches in the Language Classroom*, pp 11–19.

Bryan, Deirdre, 'Ryan, Elizabeth (Mary Eucharia)', DIB.

Buckley, Patrick, 'Blythe, Ernest (de Blaghd, Earnán)', DIB.

Bulletin de la Société littéraire de Strasbourg, 1862, https://gallica.bnf.fr/ark:/12148/bpt6k5505224v/f6.image.r=Polin%20%20petit%20seminaire?rk=21459;2 [accessed 29 November 2020].

Busby, Keith, *French in Medieval Ireland, Ireland in Medieval French: The Paradox of Two Worlds* (Turnhout: Brepols, 2017).

Buttimer, Cornelius G., 'Celtic and Irish in College 1849–1944', in *Journal of the Cork Historical and Archaeological Society*, 94, 1989, pp 88–112.

Buttimer, Neil, 'The Great Famine in Gaelic manuscripts', in Crowley, Smyth and Murphy (eds), *Atlas of the Great Irish Famine*, pp 460–72.

Caldicott, Edric, and Anne Fuchs (eds), *Cultural Memory: Essays on European Literature and History* (Oxford: Peter Lang, 2003).

Campbell, Flann, 'Latin and the elite tradition in education', in *The British Journal of Sociology*, 19, 1968, pp 308–25.

Carr, Gilbert, 'Literary historical trends and the history of the German syllabus at Trinity College, Dublin, 1873–1972', in *Hermathena*, 121, 1976, pp 36–53.

Carroll, Lewis [Charles L. Dodgson], *Alice's Adventures in Wonderland* (1865).

Casey, Etain, 'Walter Ripman and the University of London holiday course in English for foreign teachers 1903–1952', PhD dissertation, University of Oulu, 2017.

Castle, Jessie, and Gillian O'Brien, '"I am building a house": Nano Nagle's Georgian convents', in *Irish Architectural and Decorative Studies*, 19, 2016, pp 54–75.

Cathcart, Kevin J. (ed.), Peter le Page Renouf, *The Letters of Peter le Page Renouf (1822–97), vol. 3: Dublin 1854–1864* (Dublin: UCD Press, 2003).

Cathcart, Kevin J., 'Renouf, Peter le Page', DIB.

Cazzulo, Marco, 'Evasio Radice: "Britain, this great country"', on the website *Genova, ieri, oggi e domani*, http://cazzulo.altervista.org/evasio-radice-britain-this-great-country/ [accessed 15 August 2021].

Chamberlain-King, Reggie, 'Conall Cearnach (1875–1929)', in *The Green Book: Writings on Irish Gothic, Supernatural and Fantastic Literature* 11, May 2018, pp 60–4.

Chamberlain-King, Reggie, 'F. W. O'Connell: Master of strange tongues', Introduction to O'Connell [Conall Cearnach], *The Fatal Move*, pp vii–xxxv.

Chambers, Liam, '"Une maison de refuge": the Irish Jesuit college in Poitiers, 1674–1762', in Lyons and MacCuarta (eds), *The Jesuit Mission*, pp 227–50.

Chance, Jane (ed.), *Women Medievalists and the Academy* (Madison: University of Wisconsin Press, 2005).

Chauviré, Roger, *Contes Ossianiques* (Paris: Presses Universitaires de France, 1949).

Chichester, H. M., revised by Philip Carter, 'Boden, Joseph', ODNB.

Clarendon Report: *Report of Her Majesty's Commissioners Appointed to Inquire Into the Revenues and Management of Certain Colleges and Schools, and the Studies Pursued and Instruction Given Therein*, vol. 1 (London: HM Stationery Office, 1864).

Clarke, Frances, 'Maxwell, Constantia (Elizabeth)', DIB.

Clavin, Terry, 'White, Stephen', DIB.

Coakley, Davis, *Oscar Wilde: The Importance of Being Irish* (Dublin: Town House, 1994).

Coates, Su, 'Manchester's German gentlemen: Immigrant institutions in a provincial city (1840–1920)', in *Manchester Region History Review*, 5:2, 1991–2, pp 21–30.

Cohen, Michèle, *Fashioning Masculinity: National Identity and Language in the Eighteenth Century* (Abingdon: Routledge, 1996).

Cohen, Michèle, 'From "glittering gibberish" to the "mere jabbering" of a *bonne*: The problem of the "oral" in the learning and teaching of French in eighteenth- and nineteenth-century England', in McLelland and Smith (eds), *The History of Language Learning and Teaching*, vol. 2, pp 1–20.

Colbeck, Charles, *On the Teaching of Modern Languages in Theory and Practice* (Cambridge: Cambridge University Press, 1887).

Coleman, Marie, 'O'Farrelly, Agnes Winifred', DIB.

Coleman, Marie, 'O'Sullivan, Mary Josephine Donovan', DIB.

Collins, Kevin, *Catholic Churchmen and the Celtic Revival in Ireland, 1848–1916* (Dublin: Four Courts Press, 2002).

Colum, Mary, review of *James Joyce* by Herbert Gorman (New York: Farrar & Rinehart, 1940), *Saturday Review*, 16 March 1941, pp 10, 16.

Colum, Mary, *Life and the Dream* (New York, 1947, 1958; revised edn, Dublin: Dolmen, 1966).

Comerford, R. V., 'The politics of distress, 1877–82', in Vaughan (ed.), *New History of Ireland, vol. 6*, pp 26–52.

Condon, Kevin, *The Missionary College of All Hallows 1842–1891* (Dublin: All Hallows College, 1986).

Connellan, Owen, *A Practical Grammar of the Irish Language* (Dublin: B. Geraghty, 1844).

Coolahan, John, *Irish Education: Its History and Structure* (Dublin: Institute of Public Administration, 1981).

Coolahan, John, 'From Royal University to National University, 1879–1908', in Dunne et al. (eds), *The National University of Ireland 1908–2008*, pp 3–18.

Coolahan, John, 'The National University of Ireland and the changing structure of Irish higher education, 1967–2007', in Dunne et al. (eds), *The National University of Ireland 1908–2008*, pp 261–79.

Corish, Patrick J., *Maynooth College 1795–1995* (Dublin: Gill & Macmillan, 1995).

Cosgrove, Art, and Donal McCartney (eds), *Studies in Irish History Presented to R. Dudley Edwards* (Dublin: University College Dublin, 1979).

Cosmai, Domenico, *The Language of Europe. Multilingualism and Translation in the EU Institutions: Practice, Problems and Perspectives*, translated and edited by David Albert Best (Brussels: Éditions de l'Université de Bruxelles, 2007).

Cox, Richard, 'A curious history: two hundred years of modern languages', in Holland (ed.), *Trinity College Dublin*, pp 255–69.

Craig, Maurice James, *The Volunteer Earl: Being the Life and Times of James Caulfeild, First Earl of Charlemont* (London: The Cresset Press, 1948).

Cronin, Maurice, 'Sheehan, Michael', DIB.

Cronin, Michael, *Translating Ireland: Translation, Languages, Cultures* (Cork: Cork University Press, 1996).

Cronin, Michael, 'The Gaelic hit factory', review of *Scéal Ghael-Linn* by Mairéad Ní Chinnéide (Inverin, Cló Iar-Chonnacht, 2014), in *The Dublin Review of Books*, November 2014.

Cronin, Michael, review of *Teasáras Gaeilge–Béarla / Irish–English Thesaurus* by Garry Bannister (Dublin: New Island, 2023), *Irish Times*, 6 May 2023.

Cronin, Michael, and Cormac Ó Cuilleanáin (eds), *The Languages of Ireland* (Dublin: Four Courts Press, 2003).

Crowley, John, William J. Smith, and Mike Murphy (eds), *Atlas of the Great Irish Famine, 1845–52*, (Cork: Cork University Press, 2012).

Cruise O'Brien, Conor (ed.), *The Shaping of Modern Ireland,* (London: Routledge & Kegan Paul, 1960)

Cruise O'Brien, Máire, *The Same Age as the State* (Dublin: The O'Brien Press, 2003).

Cullen, L. M., 'Patrons, teachers and literacy in Irish: 1700–1850', in Daly and Dickson (eds), *Origins of Popular Literacy*, pp 15–44.

Cullen, Mary (ed.), *Girls Don't Do Honours: Irish Women in Education in the 19th and 20th Centuries* (Dublin: Women's Education Bureau, 1987).

Cunningham, Bernadette, 'Keating, Geoffrey (Céitinn, Seathrún)', DIB.

Cunningham, Bernadette, 'Writing the Annals of the Four Masters', in Bhreathnach and Cunningham (eds), *Writing Irish History*, pp 26–33.

Cunningham, Bernadette, 'Seventeenth-century historians of Ireland', in Bhreathnach and Cunningham (eds), *Writing Irish History*, pp 52–9.

Cunningham, Bernadette, 'A candle for Eugene O'Curry or the cataloguer's revenge', blog post, RIA website https://www.ria.ie/news/library-library-blog/candle-eugene-ocurry-or-cataloguers-revenge#, 19 July 2017 [accessed 1 November 2023].

Cunningham, Bernadette, 'Popular preaching and the Jesuit mission in seventeenth-century Ireland', in Lyons and MacCuarta (eds), *The Jesuit Mission*, pp 82–100.

Curran, Mary, 'Impressions of Zürich', in *Studies: An Irish Quarterly Review*, 9, 1920, pp 613–19.

Daley, Louise T., 'Schurr [*sic*], Felix (1827–1900)', ADB.

Daly, Mary, 'The development of the National School system, 1831–40', in Cosgrove and McCartney (eds), *Studies in Irish History Presented to R. Dudley Edwards*, pp 150–63.

Daly, Mary, and David Dickson (eds), *The Origins of Popular Literacy in Ireland: Language Change and Educational Development 1700–1920* (Dublin: Department of Modern History, Trinity College Dublin and Department of Modern Irish History, University College Dublin, 1990).

Daly, Mary E., 'Literacy and language change in the late nineteenth and early twentieth centuries', in Daly and Dickson (eds), *Origins of Popular Literacy*, pp 153–66.

Daniel, J. 'Édouard Cadic ... un "enfant de Locmaria"', in *Terre et Mer / An Douar Hag ar Mor, Bulletin Municipal de la ville de Guidel*, 61, January 2010, p. 2.

Davis, Thomas, 'The young Irishman of the middle classes' (1848), in Deane (ed.), *Field Day Anthology*, vol. 1, pp 1269–86.

Dawe, Gerald, *My Mother-City* (Belfast: Lagan Press, 2007).

de Blaghd, Earnán, 'Hyde in conflict', in Ó Tuama (ed.), *The Gaelic League Idea*, pp 31–40.

de Fréine, Seán, *The Great Silence* (Dublin: Foilseacháin Náisiúnta Teoranta, 1965).

de Gasperin, Vilma, 'Giuseppe Baretti's multifarious approach to learning Italian in eighteenth-century Britain', in McLelland and Smith (eds), *The History of Language Learning and Teaching*, vol. 1, pp 156–72.

de Lacey, Karen, '"A rich and gentle mind" – Maud Joynt and the 1911 Census', blog post, RIA website, https://www.ria.ie/news/library-blog-library/rich-and-gentle-mind-maud-joynt-and-1911-census [accessed 2 September 2023].

de Véricour, Louis-Raymond, *Modern French Literature* (Boston: Gould, Kendall and Lincoln, 1848).

de Véricour, Louis-Raymond, *Historical Analysis of Christian Civilisation* (London: J. Chapman, 1850).

Deacy, Mary Regina, 'Continental organists and Catholic church music in Ireland, 1860–1960', MLitt dissertation, NUIM, 2005.

Deane, Seamus (ed.), *The Field Day Anthology of Irish Writing*, 3 vols (Derry: Field Day, 1991).

Deane, Seamus, 'General introduction', in Deane (ed.), *Field Day Anthology*, vol. 1, pp xix–xxvi.

Deane, Seamus, 'Thomas Moore (1779–1852)', in Deane (ed.), *Field Day Anthology*, vol. 1, pp 1053–6.

Dermody, Merike, and Tania Daly, 'Attitudes towards the Irish language on the island of Ireland' (Dublin: ESRI and Foras na Gaeilge, 2015), https://www.esri.ie/publications/attitudes-towards-the-irish-language-on-the-island-of-ireland [accessed 16 October 2023].

Devlin, Shannon, 'Queen's First Women', https://www.qub.ac.uk/research-centres/CentreforPublicHistory/Blog/ShannonDevlinBlog/

Dewey, C. J., 'The education of a ruling caste: The Indian Civil Service in the era of competitive examination', in *English Historical Review*, 88, 1973, pp 262–85.

Dickson, David, 'Preface', in Daly and Dickson (eds), *Origins of Popular Literacy*, pp ix–xii.

Dillon, Charles, '"Ability and industry scarcely credible": Johann Kaspar Zeuss and *Grammatica Celtica*', blog post, RIA website https://www.ria.ie/news/library-library-blog-focloir-stairiuil-na-gaeilge/ability-and-industry-scarcely-credible-johann, 3 April 2017 [accessed 27 March 2021].

Dillon, Eilís, *Inside Ireland* (London: Hodder and Stoughton, 1982).

Dillon, Eilís, *Citizen Burke* (London: Hodder and Stoughton, 1984).

Dillon, John, 'Some reflections on the Irish classical tradition', in *The Crane Bag*, 3 (2) [*Anglo-Irish Literature: Perspectives*] (1979; 1982 reprint), pp 448–52.

Dillon, John, 'The classics in Trinity', in Holland (ed.), *Trinity College Dublin*, pp 239–54.

Dillon, John Blake, 'Continental literature', *The Nation*, 22 October 1842.

Dillon, Myles, 'Irish in the universities', in *Studies: An Irish Quarterly Review*, 18, 1929, pp 124–30.

Do Céu Fonseca, Maria, 'Londres et les britanniques dans l'ancienne grammaticographie du portugais langue étrangère (XVIIe–XIXe siècles)', in McLelland and Smith (eds), *The History of Language Learning and Teaching*, vol. 1, pp 173–91.

Dockray-Miller, Mary, 'Mary Bateson (1865–1906): Scholar and suffragist', in Chance (ed.), *Women Medievalists and the Academy*, pp 67–78.

Doff, Sabine, '"Let girls chat about the weather and walks": English language education at girls' secondary schools in nineteenth-century Germany', in McLelland and Smith (eds), *The History of Language Learning and Teaching*, vol. 2, pp 87–97.

Dolan, Terence P., 'Translating Irelands: The English language in the Irish context', in Cronin and Ó Cuilleanáin (eds), *The Languages of Ireland*, pp 78–92.

Dolan, Terence P., *A Dictionary of Hiberno-English: The Irish Use of English* (Dublin: Gill, 1998; 3rd edn, 2020).

Doolin, William, 'The Catholic University School of Medicine (1855–1909)', in Tierney (ed.), *Struggle with Fortune*, pp 61–81.

Dowling, P. J., *The Hedge Schools of Ireland* (London: Longman's Green, 1935; revised pb edn, Cork: Mercier Press, 1968).

Downey, Declan M., '*Wild Geese and the double-headed eagle: Irish integration in Austria c.1630–c.1918*', in Leifer and Sagarra (eds), *Austro-Irish Links Through the Centuries, pp 41–57.*

Doyle, Aidan, *A History of the Irish Language: From the Norman Invasion to Independence* (Oxford: Oxford University Press, 2015).

Dudley Edwards, Ruth, *Patrick Pearse: The Triumph of Failure* (London: Faber and Faber, 1977; pb edn, 1979).

Dudley Edwards, R. (ed.), *Ireland and the Italian Risorgimento: Three Lectures by Kevin B. Nowlan, R. Dudley Edwards, T. Desmond Williams* (Dublin: Cultural Relations Committee of the Irish Department of Foreign Affairs and the Italian Institute, n.d., *c.*1958).

Duffy, Eamon, *A People's Tragedy: Studies in Reformation* (London: Bloomsbury, 2020).

Duffy, Seán, 'Antiquarianism and Gaelic revival in County Louth in the pre-Famine era', in *Journal of the County Louth Archaeological and Historical Society*, 21, 1988, pp 343–68.

Dunlop, Dorothy, *1916 and Beyond the Pale* (Croydon: Motelands Publishing, 2016).

Dunne, Tom, John Coolahan, Maurice Manning and Gearóid Ó Tuathaigh (eds), *The National University of Ireland 1908–2008: Centenary Essays* (Dublin: UCD Press, 2008).

Dunne, Tom, 'Coming to terms with the 1997 Act: The National University of Ireland Senate, 1997–2007', in Dunne et al. (eds), *The National University of Ireland 1908–2008*, pp 280–7.

Edgeworth, Richard Lovell, *Essays on Professional Education* (London: J. Johnson, 1809).

Eighth Report of All Hallows College, Drumcondra, Dublin (Dublin: John F. Fowler, 1856).

Einhorn, E., *Old French: A Concise Handbook* (Cambridge: Cambridge University Press, 1974).

Eliot, George [Mary Ann Evans], *The Mill on the Floss* (1860).

Eliot, George [Mary Ann Evans], *Middlemarch* (1871).

Ellmann, Richard, *James Joyce* (New York: Oxford University Press, 1959).

Enright, Anne, 'Censorship in Ireland', *London Review of Books*, 35:6, 21 March 2013.

Evans, D. Ellis, 'The heroic age of Celtic philology', in *Zeitschrift für Celtische Philologie*, 54, 2005, pp 1–30.

Extermann, Blaise, 'L'allemand scolaire en Suisse romande entre langues nationales, langues internationales et dialectes (XIXe–XXIe siècles)', in McLelland and Smith (eds), *The History of Language Learning and Teaching*, vol. 2, pp 98–112.

Fahey, Tony, 'Nuns in the Catholic Church in Ireland in the nineteenth century', in Cullen (ed.), *Girls Don't Do Honours*, pp 7–30.

Fahey, Tony, 'State, family and compulsory schooling in Ireland', in *The Economic and Social Review*, 23, 1992, pp 369–95.

Fanning, Martin, and Raymond Gillespie (eds), *Print Culture and Intellectual Life in Ireland, 1660–1941* (Dublin: The Woodfield Press, 2006).

Fanning, Ronan, 'De Valera, Éamon ("Dev")', DIB.

Fanning, Ronan, 'T. K. Whitaker, 1976–96', in Dunne et al. (eds), *The National University of Ireland 1908–2008*, pp 146–62.

Färber, Beatrix, 'Life and work of Winifred Wulff', CELT, Corpus of Electronic Texts (University College Cork), https://www.ucc.ie/en/research-sites/celt/resources/scholars/wulff/ [accessed 18 September 2023].

Färber, Beatrix 'Life and works of Käte Müller-Lisowski', CELT, Corpus of Electronic Texts (University College Cork), https://www.ucc.ie/en/research-sites/celt/resources/scholars/muellerlisowski/ [accessed 18 September 2023].

Farmar, Tony, *The History of Irish Book Publishing* (Stroud: The History Press, 2018).

Farragher, Seán P., CSSp, and Annraoi Wyer, *Blackrock College 1860–1995* (Dublin: Paraclete Press, 1995).

Farragher, Seán P., CSSp, *The French College Blackrock 1860–1896* (Dublin: Paraclete Press, 2011).

Farragher, S., CSSp, and C. de Mare, 'Le Père Jules Leman et la fondation du collège de Blackrock, en Irlande,' in *Mémoire Spiritaine*, 5:5, 2019, pp 37–62.

Father Stanislas, OSFC, 'An Irish Capuchin pioneer', in *The Capuchin Annual*, 1930, pp 71–84.

Finn, Clodagh, *A Time to Risk All* (Dublin: Gill Books, 2017).

First Annual Report of the Missionary College of All Hallows, Drumcondra, Dublin (1848) (Dublin: Fowler, 1849).

Fischer, Joachim, *Das Deutschlandbild der Iren, 1890–1939: Geschichte – Form – Funktion* (Heidelberg: Winter, 2000).

Fischer, Joachim, 'The eagle that never landed: uses and abuses of the German language in Ireland', in Cronin and Ó Cuilleanáin (eds), *The Languages of Ireland*, pp 93–111.

Fisher, Anthony, OP, '"A glorious future for the infant diocese of Armidale": The emerging church in New England', in *Australasian Catholic Record*, 99:1, 2022, pp 86–95.

Fisher, Samuel K., and Brian Ó Conchubhair (eds), *Bone and Marrow / Cnámh Agus Smior: An Anthology of Irish Poetry From Medieval to Modern* (Winston-Salem: Wake Forest University Press, 2022).

FitzGerald, Garret, 'The decline of the Irish language, 1771–1871', in Daly and Dickson (eds), *Origins of Popular Literacy*, pp 59–72.

FitzGerald, Garret, *Reflections on the Irish State* (Dublin: Irish Academic Press, 2003).

FitzGerald, Garret, 'Foreword', in Dunne et al. (eds), *The National University of Ireland 1908–2008*, pp xiii–xx.

FitzGerald, Garret, *Irish Primary Education in the Early Nineteenth Century: An Analysis of the First and Second Reports of the Commissioners of Irish Education Inquiry, 1825–6* [with contributions by John FitzGerald, Gillian O'Brien and Cormac Ó Gráda] (Dublin: RIA, 2013).

FitzGerald, Jennifer, 'Helen Waddell (1889–1965): The scholar-poet', in Chance (ed.), *Women Medievalists and the Academy*, pp 322–38.

FitzGerald, Jennifer, '"The Queen's girl": Helen Waddell and women at Queen's University Belfast, 1908–1920', in Harford and Rush (eds), *Have Women Made a Difference?*, pp 77–104.

Fitzpatrick, David, '"A share of the honeycomb": Education, emigration and Irishwomen', in Daly and Dickson (eds), *Origins of Popular Literacy*, pp 167–87.

Fitzpatrick, Maurice, *The Boys of St Columb's* (Dublin: The Liffey Press, 2010).

Flegg, Jennifer, *The French School, Bray, Remembered: A History of The French School, Bray 1864–1966* (Dublin: A&A Farmar, 2006).

Fleischmann, Ruth, 'Aloys Fleischmann: Bavarian musician and civilian prisoner of war, 1916–1919', in French (ed.), *Oldcastle Camp 1914–1918*, pp 125–66.

Foerster, Martin, '"The best teachers in the world": Jesuit schooling in Ireland, 1660–90', in Lyons and Mac Cuarta (eds), *The Jesuit Mission*, pp 208–26.

Fogarty, Anne, and Fran O'Rourke (eds), *Voices on Joyce* (Dublin: UCD Press, 2015).

Foley, Tadhg (ed.), *From Queen's College to National University: Essays on the Academic History of QCG / UCG / NUI, Galway* (Dublin: Four Courts Press, 1999).

Foley, Tadhg, and Fiona Bateman, 'English, History, and Philosophy', in Foley (ed.), *From Queen's College to National University*, pp 384–420.

Foley, Timothy P., '"A nest of scholars": Biographical material on some early professors at Queen's College Galway', in *Journal of the Galway Archaeological and Historical Society*, 42, 1989–90, pp 72–86.

Foster, R. F., *Vivid Faces: The Revolutionary Generation in Ireland 1890–1923* (London: Allen Lane, 2014).

Francia, Enrico, 'Radice, Evasio', *Dizionario Biografico degli Italiani*, 86, 2017.

French, Tom (ed.), *Oldcastle Camp 1914–1918: An Illustrated History* (Navan: Meath Co Council Library Service, 2018).

French Diplomatic Archives, Nantes, Œuvres françaises à l'étranger, no. 33, CADN C22/7, Alfred Blanche, 'Enseignement du français dans les écoles de l'Irlande', 21 October 1921.

Friel, Brian, *Translations* (London: Faber and Faber, 1981; reprint 2000).

Froggatt, Richard, 'David Manson (1726–1792): Teacher', DUB.

Frost, Ann, 'The emergence and growth of Hispanic Studies in British and Irish universities', AHGBI [Association of Hispanists of Great Britain and Ireland] online report, 2019, https://www.hispanists.org.uk/news/ahgbi-publication-the-emergence-and-growth-of-hispanic-studies-in-british-and-irish-universities/ [accessed 28 April 2021].

Furlong, William R., *Report of the case of Angeli v. Galbraith, as Tried Before the Lord Chief Justice at the Kildare Summer Assizes, 1856; and Before the Lord Chief Baron in the Court of Exchequer, at the After-Sittings, Michaelmas Term, 1856* (Dublin: Hodges, Smith, and Co., 1857; reprinted from microfilm, New Haven: Yale Law Library, 2021).

Gaffney, Phyllis, '*When we were very young*: University College Dublin's French Department and the fight for Irish freedom', in Maher and Neville (eds), *France-Ireland*, pp 203–23.

Gaffney, Phyllis, Michael Brophy and Mary Gallagher (eds), *Reverberations: Staging Relations in French since 1500. A Festschrift in Honour of C.E.J. Caldicott* (Dublin: UCD Press, 2008).

Gaffney, Phyllis, '*Une certaine idée de l'Irlande*, or the professor as propagandist: Roger Chauviré's Irish fictions', in Gaffney, Brophy and Gallagher (eds), *Reverberations*, pp 390–403.

Gaffney, Phyllis, '"Assistant something-or-other in the new university": life and letters of Mary Kate O'Kelly (1878–1934)', in Harford and Rush (eds), *Have Women Made a Difference?*, pp 105–26.

Gaffney, Phyllis, 'Roger Chauviré's perspective on 1916 and its aftermath', in Joannon and Whelan (eds), *Paris Capital of Irish Culture*, pp 215–26.

Gaffney, Phyllis, and Jean-Michel Picard (eds), *The Medieval Imagination: Mirabile Dictu. Essays in honour of Yolande de Pontfarcy Sexton* (Dublin: Four Courts Press, 2012).

Gaidoz, Henri, review of Eugene O'Curry's *On the Manners and Customs of the Ancient Irish* [*Des Mœurs et des Coutumes des Anciens Irlandais*], in *Revue Celtique*, 2, 1873–5, pp 260–64.

Gallagher, John, *Learning Languages in Early Modern England* (Oxford: Oxford University Press, 2019).

Gannon, Seán William, 'The green frame of British rule? – Irish in the Indian Civil Service', https://www.theirishstory.com/2020/11/27/the-green-frame-of-british-rule-irish-in-the-indian-civil-service/ [accessed 28 September 2023].

Geoghegan, Patrick M., 'Lanigan, John', DIB.

Gerber, Adolph, 'Modern languages in the University of France', in *Modern Language Notes*, 3, 1888, pp 1–5.

Gillard, Derek, *Education in England: A History* (1998; online publication, 2018), http://www.educationengland.org.uk/history [accessed 26 March 2022].

Gillespie, Paul, 'Lessons from history – the Wild Geese and the Irish in Europe', *Irish Times*, 2 November 2002.

Gillespie, Raymond, 'The Ó Cléirigh manuscripts in context', in Bhreathnach and Cunnningham (eds), *Writing Irish History*, pp 42–51.

Gouault, Thierry, 'L'enseignement des langues anciennes au collège de l'Oratoire du Mans au XVIIIe siècle: une remise en cause du latin et du grec?', in *Annales de Bretagne et des Pays de l'Ouest*, 124, 2017, pp 57–73, online edn, 2019, http://journals.openedition.org/abpro/3666 [accessed 7 October 2023].

Greene, David, 'Robert Atkinson and Irish studies', in *Hermathena*, 102, 1966, pp 6–15.

Gwynn, Aubrey, 'The Jesuit Fathers and University College', in Tierney (ed.), *Struggle with Fortune*, pp 19–50.

Gwynn, Denis, 'The origins and growth of University College Cork', in *University Review*, 2, 1960, pp 33–47.

Haas, Renate, 'Caroline F. E. Spurgeon (1869–1942)', in Chance (ed.), *Women Medievalists and the Academy*, pp 99–109.

Haliday, William, *Úraicecht na Gaedhilge: A Grammar of the Celtic Language* (Dublin: John Barlow, 1808).

Hall, Edith, 'Sinn Féin and *Ulysses*: Between Professor Robert Mitchell Henry and James Joyce', in Torrance and O'Rourke (eds), *Classics and Irish Politics*, pp 193–217.

Halpin, Attracta, 'The role of the National University of Ireland in language learning and language research and scholarship', in Maguire (ed.), *Foreign Language Learning and Ireland's Languages Connect Strategy*, pp 4–6.

Hamilton, Hugo, *The Speckled People* (London: Fourth Estate, 2003).

Harford, Judith, *The Opening of University Education to Women in Ireland* (Dublin: Irish Academic Press, 2008).

Harford, Judith, and Claire Rush (eds), *Have Women Made a Difference? Women in Irish Universities, 1850–2010* (Bern: Peter Lang, 2010).

Harford, Judith, 'Women and the Irish university question', in Harford and Rush (eds), *Have Women Made a Difference?*, pp 7–28.

Harris, Jason, and Keith Sidwell (eds), *Making Ireland Roman: Irish Neo-Latin Writers and the Republic of Letters* (Cork: Cork University Press, 2009).

Harris, Jason, and Keith Sidwell, 'Introduction: Ireland and *Romanitas*', in Harris and Sidwell (eds), *Making Ireland Roman*, pp 1–13.

Harris, Jason, 'A case study in rhetorical composition: Stephen White's two *Apologiae* for Ireland', in Harris and Sidwell (eds), *Making Ireland Roman*, pp 126–53.

Harris, Jason, 'The Latin style of the Irish *Litterae Annuae Societatis Jesu*', in Lyons and MacCuarta (eds), *The Jesuit Mission*, pp 63–81.

Harris, John, and Denise O'Leary, 'A third language at primary level in Ireland: An independent evaluation of the Modern Languages in Primary Schools Initiative', in Nikolov (ed.), *Early Learning of Modern Foreign Languages*, pp 1–14.

Harvey, Anthony, *How Linguistics Can Help the Historian* (Dublin: RIA, 2021).

Hatfield, Mary, *Growing Up in Nineteenth-Century Ireland: A Cultural History of Middle-Class Childhood and Gender* (Oxford: Oxford University Press, 2019).

Hattersley, Roy, 'Had there been no Reformation would England have been spared Brexit?', *Irish Times*, 25 February 2017.

Haywood, Eric, *Fabulous Ireland / Ibernia Fabulosa: Imagining Ireland in Renaissance Italy* (Bern: Peter Lang, 2014).

Healy, Roisin, 'The lives of Emily Anderson: Galway professor, music historian, and British intelligence officer', https://mooreinstitute.ie/2017/03/20/lives-emily-anderson-galway-professor-music-historian-british-intelligence-officer/ [accessed 25 October 2022].

Hederman, M. P., and R. Kearney (eds), *The Crane Bag Book of Irish Studies* (Dublin: Blackwater, 1982).

Hélias, Pierre-Jakez, *Le Cheval d'Orgueil* (Paris: Plon, 1975).

Henebry, Richard, 'A plea for prose', in *The Gaelic Journal*, 4:41, June 1892, pp 141–4.

Henebry, Richard, 'Whitley Stokes', in *The Celtic Review*, 6, 1909, pp 65–85.

Hickey, Tina M. (ed.), *Literacy and Language Learning: Reading in a First or Second Language* (Dublin: Reading Association of Ireland, 2006).

Higgins, Michael D., Speech at a state ceremonial event in honour of Patrick Pearse and the Irish language, Pearse Museum, St Enda's Park, Rathfarnham, Co. Dublin, 7 July 2016, https://president.ie/en/media-library/speeches/speech-at-a-state-ceremonial-event-in-honour-of-patrick-pearse-and-the-iris [accessed 26 December 2020].

Higman, Francis M., 'Modern languages in Trinity College, Dublin 1776–1976', in *Hermathena*, 121, 1976, pp 12–17.

Hill, Jacqueline, 'Whitley Stokes senior (1763–1845) and his political, religious and cultural milieux', in Boyle and Russell (eds), *Tripartite Life of Whitley Stokes*, pp 14–28.

Hobsbawm, E. J., *Nations and Nationalism Since 1780: Programme, Myth, Reality* (Cambridge: Cambridge University Press, 1990; reprint 1993).

Hochschild, Arlie Russell, *Strangers in Their Own Land: Anger and Mourning on the American Right* (New York: The New Press, 2016).

Hogan, J. J., 'Mary M. Macken: An appreciation', in *Studies*, 39, 1950, pp 315–18.

Hogan, J. J., 'The Newman heritage: the Catholic University of Ireland, 1854–1883' [Radio broadcast, aired on Radio Éireann, 25 April 1954], in Tierney (ed.), *Struggle with Fortune*, pp 213–21.

Holfter, Gisela, 'Lewy, Ernst', DIB.

Holfter, Gisela, 'Ernst Scheyer', in Holfter (ed.), *German-speaking Exiles*, pp 149–69.

Holfter, Gisela, 'Akademiker im irischen Exil: Ernst Lewy (1881–1966)', in *German Life and Letters*, 61, 2008, pp 363–87.

Holfter, Gisela (ed.), *German-speaking Exiles in Ireland 1933–1945* (Leiden: Brill, 2006).

Holfter, Gisela (and Horst Dickel), *An Irish Sanctuary: German-speaking Refugees in Ireland 1933–1945* (Berlin: De Gruyter Oldenbourg, 2017).

Holfter, Gisela (ed.), *Rückblicke und Reflexionen: A History of German Studies in Ireland* (Trier: WVT Wissenschaftlicher Verlag, 2023).

Holland, C. H. (ed.), *Trinity College Dublin and the Idea of a University* (Dublin: Trinity College Press, 1991).

Holmes, George, *Sketches of Some of the Southern Counties of Ireland* (London: Longman and Rees, 1801).

Hond, Paul, 'How Mozart's librettist became the father of Italian Studies at Columbia: The curious cross-continental tale of Lorenzo da Ponte', *Columbia Magazine*, winter 2020–1.

Horgan, John, 'Strong language', *Irish Times*, 9 January 2022.

Huarte, Amalio, 'El. P. Paulo Sherlock: Una Autobiografía Inédita', in *Archivium Hibernicum*, 6, 1917, pp 156–74.

Hughes, Thomas, *Tom Brown's School Days* (1857).

Husbands, Christopher T., 'German-/Austrian-origin professors of German in British universities during the First World War: the lessons of four case studies', *LSE Research Online*, 2013, pp 1–61, http://eprints.lse.ac.uk/49797 [accessed 28 November 2020].

Hutchinson, Wesley, and Clíona Ní Ríordáin (eds), *Language Issues: Ireland, France, Spain* (Brussels: Peter Lang, 2010).

Hüther, Andreas, 'A transnational nation-building process: philologists and universities in nineteenth-century Ireland and Germany', in Litvack and Graham (eds), *Ireland and Europe in the Nineteenth Century*, pp 101–11.

Hyde, Douglas, 'The necessity for de-anglicising Ireland' (lecture delivered before the Irish National Literary Society in Dublin, 25 November 1892), extract in Deane (ed.), *Field Day Anthology*, vol. 2, pp 527–33.

Hyland, Áine, 'The Investment in Education Report 1965 – recollections and reminiscences', in *Irish Educational Studies*, 33, 2014, pp 123–39.

Hyland, Áine, and Kenneth Milne (eds), *Irish Educational Documents*, vol. 1 (Dublin: Church of Ireland College of Education, 1987).

Hyland, Áine, and Kenneth Milne (eds), *Irish Educational Documents*, vol. 2 (Dublin: Church of Ireland College of Education, 1992).

Istituto Italiano di Cultura, *Italian Presence in Ireland: A Contribution to Irish-Italian Relations*, edited and published on the occasion of the tenth anniversary of the foundation of the Istituto Italiano di Cultura (Dublin: Istituto Italiano di Cultura, 1964).

'Janet Hunter Perry, 1884–1958', obituary, in *Bulletin of Hispanic Studies*, 35, 1958, pp 177–8.

Janson, Tore, *Speak: A Short History of Languages* (Oxford: Oxford University Press, 2002).

J. C., 'Notes and queries: Two Franco-Cork professors', in *Journal of the Cork Historical and Archaeological Society*, 15, 1909, pp 99–100.

Joannon, Pierre, and Kevin Whelan (eds), *Paris Capital of Irish Culture: France, Ireland and the Republic, 1798–1916* (Dublin: Four Courts Press, 2017).

Joannon, Pierre, 'Paris: the promised land?', in Joannon and Whelan (eds), *Paris Capital of Irish Culture*, pp 13–32.

Joyce, James, *Dubliners* (Harmondsworth: Penguin, 1914; 1956 reprint).

Judt, Tony, *Postwar: A History of Europe since 1945* (New York: The Penguin Press, 2005; London: Random House Vintage edn, 2010).

Kang, Minsoo, and Amy Woodson-Boulton (eds), *Visions of the Industrial Age, 1830–1914: Modernity and the Anxiety of Representation in Europe* (Burlington: Ashgate, 2008).

Keaveney, Arthur, 'Classics in Victorian Galway', in Foley (ed.), *From Queen's College to National University*, pp 326–43.

Kelleher, Margaret, *The Maamtrasna Murders: Language, Life and Death in Nineteenth-Century Ireland* (Dublin: UCD Press, 2018).

Kelly, James, and Ciarán Mac Murchaidh (eds), *Irish and English: Essays on the Irish Linguistic and Cultural Frontier, 1600–1900* (Dublin: Four Courts Press, 2012).

Kelly, James, 'Irish Protestants and the Irish language in the eighteenth century', in Kelly and Mac Murchaidh (eds), *Irish and English*, pp 189–217.

Kemmler, Rolf, and María José Corvo Sánchez, 'The importance of the "method Gaspey-Otto-Sauer" amongst the earliest Portuguese textbooks of the German language', in *Language & History*, 63, 2020, pp 120–38.

Kennedy, Máire, 'Antoine D'Esca: first professor of French and German at Trinity College Dublin (1775–1784)', in *Long Room*, 38, 1993, pp 18–19.

Kennedy, Máire, *French books in eighteenth-century Ireland* (Oxford: Voltaire Foundation, 2001).

Kennedy, Michael, 'Power, Ann ("Nancy") Wyse', DIB.

Kiberd, Declan, Editorial, in *The Crane Bag*, 5 (2) [*The Irish Language and Culture*] (1981; 1982 reprint), pp 835–7.

Kirk, Sonya, 'Grammar–translation: Tradition or innovation?', in McLelland and Smith (eds), *The History of Language Learning and Teaching*, vol. 2, pp 21–33.

Kirkham, Graeme, 'Literacy in North-West Ulster, 1680–1860', in Daly and Dickson (eds), *Origins of Popular Literacy*, pp 73–96.

Klapp, Stephanie, 'Death by wrongful humiliation – the story of Valentine Steinberger', *Galway Advertiser*, 4 February 2021.

Knott, Eleanor, 'Ernst Windisch, 1844–1918', in *Studies*, 8, 1919, pp 264–7.

Kuper, Simon, 'The problem with English', *Financial Times*, 12 January 2017.

Kuper, Simon, 'Globish just doesn't cut it any more', *Financial Times*, 11 January 2018.

Kuper, Simon, 'The best place to build a life in English? The Netherlands', *Financial Times*, 25 April 2019.

Kuper, Simon, 'The case for diving into another language', *Financial Times*, 21 April 2021.

Kuper, Simon, *Chums: How a Tiny Caste of Oxford Tories Took Over the UK* (London: Profile Books, 2022).

Lambert, Kevin, 'Victorian stained glass as memorial: an image of George Boole', in Kang and Woodson-Boulton (eds), *Visions of the Industrial Age, 1830–1914*, pp 205–26.

Languages Connect: Ireland's Strategy for Foreign Languages in Education 2017–2026 (Dublin: Irish Government Department of Education and Skills, 2017).

'La Sorbonne au XIXe siècle: le temps des grands travaux sous la Troisième République', https://www.sorbonne.fr/la-sorbonne/histoire-de-la-sorbonne/la-sorbonne-au-xixe-siecle-le-temps-des-grands-travaux-sous-la-troisieme-republique/ [accessed 11 November 2023].

Leathes Report: 'Modern Studies, Being the Report of the Committee on the Position of Modern Languages in the Educational system of Great Britain' (London: His Majesty's Stationery Office, 1918).

Le Cam, Jean-Luc, 'Le parcours de Pierre-Jakez Hélias vu par l'historien de l'éducation ou La mythologie de l'école républicaine', in *Hélias et les siens. Helias hag e dud*, Colloque inaugural du Pôle universitaire Pierre-Jakez Hélias (sep 2000), Centre de Recherche Bretonne et Celtique, Quimper, 1, 2001, pp 87–113.

Le Carré, John, *A Perfect Spy* (London: Hodder and Stoughton, 1986).

Lee, J. J., *Ireland, 1912–1985: Politics and Society* (Cambridge: Cambridge University Press, 1989).

Lee, J. J. (ed.), *Ireland: 1945–1970* (Dublin: Gill & Macmillan, 1979).

Leen, Edward, CSSp, '*Fides et Robur*', *Blackrock College Annual*, 1930, pp 11–20, http://www.blackrockcollege.com/wp-content/uploads/2019/09/Blackrock-College-Annual-1930.pdf [accessed 28 October 2020].

Leflon, Jean, 'Les petits séminaires de France au XIXe siècle', in *Revue d'Histoire de l'Église de France*, 61, 1975, pp 25–35.

Lehmacher, Gustav, SJ, 'Some thoughts on an Irish literary language', in *Studies: an Irish Quarterly Review*, 12, 1923, pp 26–32, followed by a discussion, pp 32–44.

Leifer, Paul, and Eda Sagarra (eds), Austro-Irish Links Through the Centuries [Favorita Papers, special edn] (Vienna: Diplomatic Academy, 2002).

Lepschy, Anna Laura, and Giulio Lepschy, *The Italian Language Today* (London: Hutchinson, 1977).

'Life of David Manson', *The Belfast Monthly Magazine*, 6, 1811, pp 126–32.

Linn, Andrew R., 'Modern foreign languages get a voice: The role of journals in the reform movement', in McLelland and Smith (eds), *The History of Language Learning and Teaching*, vol. 2, pp 145–60.

'List of professors recently appointed in the Queen's Colleges, Ireland', *The Anglo-Celt*, Cavan, 10 August 1849.

Little, David, Bebhinn O Meadhra and David Singleton (eds), *New Approaches in the Language Classroom: Coping with Change*, Proceedings of the Second National Modern Languages Convention, 31 January–1 February 1986 (Dublin: CLCS TCD, 1986).

Little, David, 'Concluding remarks', in Little, O Meadhra and Singleton (eds), *New Approaches in the Language Classroom*, p. 114.

Little, David, and Eugene Davis, 'Facing the challenge of new technologies: interactive video and the AUTOTUTOR project', in Little, O Meadhra and Singleton (eds), *New Approaches in the Language Classroom*, pp 26–33.

Little, George A., 'The Jesuit University of Dublin, *c*.1627', in *Dublin Historical Record*, 13, 1952, pp 34–47.

Little, Roger, 'Beckett's mentor, Rudmose-Brown: Sketch for a portrait', in *Irish University Review*, 14, 1984, pp 34–41.

Litvack, Leon, and Colin Graham (eds), *Ireland and Europe in the Nineteenth Century* (Dublin: Four Courts Press, 2006).

Lloyd, J. H., 'Mid-eighteenth century conversation', in *Gadelica: A Journal of Modern Irish Studies*, 1, 1912, pp 19–31.

Logan, John, 'Sufficient to their needs: Literacy and elementary schooling in the nineteenth century', in Daly and Dickson (eds), *Origins of Popular Literacy*, pp 113–37.

Long, Patrick, 'Roche, James', DIB.

Lowe, Robert, *Primary and Classical Education: An Address Delivered Before the Philosophical Institution of Edinburgh* (Edinburgh: Edmonston and Douglas, 1867).

Luce, J. V., *Trinity College Dublin: The First 400 Years* (Dublin: Trinity College Press [Quatercentenary Series], 1992).

Lunney, Linde, 'Corlett, (Ada) Barbara', DIB.

Lunney, Linde, 'Henry, Robert Mitchell', DIB.

Lunney, Linde, 'Manson, David', DIB.

Lunny, Linda [*sic*], 'Knowledge and Enlightenment: Attitudes to education in early nineteenth-century East Ulster', in Daly and Dickson (eds), *Origins of Popular Literacy*, pp 97–111.

Lydon, James, 'The silent sister: Trinity College and Catholic Ireland', in Holland (ed.), *Trinity College Dublin*, pp 29–53.

Lyons, F. S. L., 'George Moore and Edward Martyn', in *Hermathena: a Dublin University Review*, 98, 1964, pp 9–29.

Lyons, Paddy, 'Ireland, Britain, and mass literacy in nineteenth-century Europe', in Litvack and Graham (eds), *Ireland and Europe in the Nineteenth Century*, pp 89–100.

Lyons, Mary Ann, and Brian MacCuarta, SJ (eds), *The Jesuit Mission in Early Modern Ireland, 1560–1760* (Dublin: Four Courts Press, 2022).

Lyons, Mary Ann, and Brian MacCuarta, SJ, 'Introduction', in Lyons and MacCuarta (eds), *The Jesuit Mission*, pp 15–28.

Lysaght, Charles, 'Leslie, John Randolph ('Shane')', DIB.

McCafferty, John, 'Leuven as a Centre for Irish Religious, Academic and Political Thought', Embassy of Ireland to the Kingdom of Belgium, 2014 (UCD, Research Repository [http://hdl.handle.net//10197/7178].

Mac Cárthaigh, Eoin, 'Dineen, Patrick Stephen', DIB.

McCarthy, Patrick J., 'Lydgate, "the new, young surgeon" of *Middlemarch*', in *Studies in English Literature, 1500–1900*, 10:4 [The Nineteenth Century], 1970, pp 805–16.

McCartney, Donal, *UCD A National Idea: The History of University College, Dublin* (Dublin: Gill & Macmillan, 1999).

McCartney, Donal, 'University College Dublin', in Dunne et al. (eds), *The National University of Ireland 1908–2008*, pp 87–99.

McCartney, Donal, 'Joyce's UCD', in Fogarty and O'Rourke (eds), *Voices on Joyce*, pp 65–75.

Mac Cóil, Liam, 'Irish – one of the languages of the world' ['An Ghaeilge: Ceann de theangacha an domhain', translated by Michael Cronin], in Cronin and Ó Cuilleanáin (eds), *The Languages of Ireland*, pp 127–47.

Mac Craith, Mícheál, review of *Aisling Ghéar Na Stíobhartaigh agus an tAos Léinn 1603–1788* by Breandán Ó Buachalla, in *Eighteenth-Century Ireland / Iris an dá chultúr*, 13, 1998, pp 166–71.

Mac Craith, Mícheál, '"Dochum glóire Dé agus an mhaitheas phuiblidhe so / For the glory of God and this public good": the Reformation and the Irish language', in *Studies*, 106:424, 2017–18, pp 476–87.

Mac Craith, Mícheál, review of three books by Ailbhe Ó Corráin, *The Pearl of the Kingdom: A study of 'A fhir légtha an leabhráin bhig' by Giolla Brighde Ó hEódhasa* (Novus Press, 2013); *The Light of the Universe: Poems of Friendship and Consolation by Giolla Brighde Ó hEódhasa* (Novus Press, 2014); and *The Dark Cave and the Divine Light: Verses on the Human Condition by Giolla Brighde Ó hEódhasa* (Novus Press, 2016), in *ComharTaighde*, 30 November 2018.

McCrea, Barry, *Languages of the Night: Minor Languages and the Literary Imagination in Twentieth-Century Ireland and Europe* (New Haven and London: Yale University Press, 2015).

Mac Curtain, Margaret, 'O'Daly, Daniel (Dominic; Domingos do Rosario)', DIB.

Mac Curtain, Margaret [Sister Benevenuta], 'St Mary's University College', in *University Review*, 3, 1964, pp 33–47.

Mac Curtain, Margaret, 'The 1940s: Women academics at University College Cork', in Harford and Rush (eds), *Have Women Made a Difference?*, pp 127–37.

MacDermott, Martin (ed.), *The New Spirit of the Nation* (London: T. Fisher Unwin, 1894).

MacDevitt, Revd John, *Father Hand: Founder of All Hallows Catholic College for the Foreign Missions* (Dublin: M. H. Gill & Son, 1885).

McDiarmid, Lucy, *The Irish Art of Controversy* (Dublin: The Lilliput Press, 2005).

McDonald, Walter, *Reminiscences of a Maynooth Professor*, edited with a memoir by Denis Gwynn (Cork: Mercier Press, 1967).

McDonough, Ciaran, 'Learning Irish in late-eighteenth- and nineteenth-century Belfast: The antiquarian influence', in *Studia Celtica Fennica*, 10, 2013, pp 39–47.

McDowell, R. B., and D. A. Webb, 'Trinity College in 1830 (part I)', in *Hermathena*, 75, 1950, pp 1–23.

McDowell, R. B., and D. A. Webb, *Trinity College Dublin 1592–1952: An Academic History* (Cambridge: Cambridge University Press, 1982).

McGimpsey, Christopher D., lecture to the seminar on 'The Irish Language and the Unionist Tradition', Ulster People's College, Belfast, 9 May 1992, in Mistéil (ed.), *The Irish Language and the Unionist Tradition*, pp 7–16.

Mac Giolla Chríost, Diarmait, *The Irish Language in Ireland: From Goídel to Globalisation* (Abingdon: Routledge, 2005).

McGrath, Fergal, SJ, *Newman's University: Idea and Reality* (Dublin: Browne & Nolan, 1951).

McGrath, Thomas, 'Doyle, James ("J. K. L.")', DIB.

McGuire, Peter, 'Killing off the classics: "elite" subjects fall from prominence', *Irish Times*, 19 September 2016.

MacHale, Des, *The Life and Work of George Boole: A Prelude to the Digital Age* (Cork: Cork University Press, 2014).

MacHale, Des, and Yvonne Cohen, *New Light on George Boole* (Cork: Cork University Press, 2018).

McKay, Susan, 'The DUP has a new leader, but language is still Northern Ireland's sticking point', *Guardian*, 24 June 2021.

McKay, Susan, 'The Irish language can give us all a sense of home – if we save it from sectarianism', *Guardian*, 10 August 2021.

MacKendrick, Paul, 'Kipling and the nature of the Classical', in *The Classical Journal*, 52, 1956, pp 67–76.

McKnight, Martina, and Myrtle Hill, '"Doing academia" in Queen's University Belfast: Gendered experiences, perceptions and strategies', in Harford and Rush (eds), *Have Women Made a Difference?*, pp 189–217.

McLelland, Nicola, 'French and German in British schools (1850–1945)', in *Documents pour l'Histoire du Français Langue Étrangère ou Seconde*, 53, 2014, pp 109–24.

McLelland, Nicola, *German Through English Eyes: A History of Language Teaching and Learning in Britain, 1500–2000* (Wiesbaden: Harrassowitz Verlag, 2015).

McLelland, Nicola, 'Ripman [*formerly* Rippmann], Walter (1869–1947)', ODNB.

McLelland, Nicola, *Teaching and Learning Foreign Languages: A History of Language Education, Assessment and Policy in Britain* (London and New York: Routledge, 2017; pb edn, 2018).

McLelland, Nicola, 'The history of language learning and teaching in Britain', in *The Language Learning Journal*, 46, 2018, pp 6–16.

McLelland, Nicola, and Richard Smith (eds), *The History of Language Learning and Teaching*, 3 vols (Cambridge: Legenda (Modern Humanities Research Association), 2018).

McManus, Antonia, *The Irish Hedge School and Its Books, 1695–1831* (Dublin: Four Courts Press, 2002).

Mac Mathúna, Liam, 'Verisimilitude or subversion? Probing the interaction of English and Irish in selected warrants and macaronic verse in the eighteenth century', in Kelly and Mac Murchaidh (eds), *Irish and English*, pp 116–40.

Mac Mathúna, Liam, *The Ó Neachtain Window on Gaelic Dublin, 1700–1750*, Cork Studies in Celtic Literatures 4 (Cork: University College Cork, 2021).

Mac Mathúna, Liam, and Máire Nic an Bhaird (eds), *Douglas Hyde: Irish Ideology and International Impact* [*Éigse: A Journal of Irish Studies*, Occasional Publications 3] (Dublin: National University of Ireland, 2023).

Mac Mathúna, Liam, 'Douglas Hyde's intellectual links with John Quinn, Lady Gregory and W. B. Yeats', in Mac Mathúna and Nic an Bhaird (eds), *Douglas Hyde*, pp 51–78.

McMillan, Norman (ed.), *Prometheus's Fire: A History of Scientific and Technical Education in Ireland* (Kilkenny: Tyndall Publications, 1995).

Mac Murchaidh, Ciarán, 'The Catholic Church, the Irish mission and the Irish language in the eighteenth century', in Kelly and Murchaidh (eds), *Irish and English*, pp 162–88.

MacNeill, Eoin, *Irish in the National University of Ireland: A Plea for Irish Education* (Dublin: M. H. Gill & Son Ltd, 1909).

Macaulay, Ambrose, 'Crolly, William', DIB.

Macaulay Report on the Indian Civil Service (1854), included as Appendix B to the Fulton Report (1968), pp 119–28, https://www.civilservant.org.uk/library/1854-Macaulay_Report.pdf [accessed 4 September 2023].

Mack Smith, Denis, *Mazzini* (New Haven: Yale University Press, 1994).

Macken, Mary M., 'Nazism and the Church', in *Studies*, 28, 1939, pp 505–8.

Macken, Mary M., 'Women in the university and the college: a struggle within a struggle', in Tierney (ed.), *Struggle with Fortune*, pp 142–65.

Magan, Manchán, 'The hundreds of Irish words for sea and sea life', *Irish Times*, 9 January 2021.

Magan, Manchán, *Listen to the Land Speak: A Journey Into the Wisdom of What Lies Beneath Us* (Dublin: M. H. Gill and Co., 2022).

Maher, Éamon, and Grace Neville (eds), *France–Ireland: Anatomy of a Relationship. Studies in History, Literature and Politics* (Bern: Peter Lang, 2004).

Maguire, Patricia (ed.) *Foreign Language Learning and Ireland's Languages Connect Strategy: Reflections Following a Symposium Organised by the National University of Ireland with University College Cork*, NUI Education and Society Occasional Papers 1 (Dublin: NUI, 2019).

Malouf, Michael G., *Making World English: Literature, Late Empire, and English Language Teaching, 1919–1939* (London: Bloomsbury, 2022).

Marizzi, Bernd, 'An overview of the history of German language learning and teaching in the Iberian Peninsula, with a particular focus on textbooks for German as a Language for Special Purposes (LSP) in Spain', in McLelland and Smith (eds), *The History of Language Learning and Teaching*, vol. 2, pp 113–26.

Marlowe, Lara, 'Académie Française sounds alarm about the increasing use of English', *Irish Times*, 21 February 2022.

Martínez del Campo, Luis G., 'A utilitarian subject: The introduction of Spanish language in British schools in the early twentieth century', in McLelland and Smith (eds), *The History of Language Learning and Teaching*, vol. 2, pp 179–95.

Mathews, P. J., 'Hyde's first stand: The Irish language controversy of 1899', in *Éire/Ireland*, 35, 2000, pp 173–87.

Maume, Patrick, 'Ryan, Mary Kate ('Kit', 'Cáit')', DIB.

Maume, Patrick, and Thomas Charles-Edwards, 'MacNeill, Eoin (John)', DIB.

Maye, Brian, 'Fit to print – Brian Maye on pioneering publisher James Duffy' [An Irishman's Diary], *Irish Times*, 21 June 2021.

Meaney, Gerardine, Mary O'Dowd and Bernadette Whelan, *Reading the Irish Woman: Studies in Cultural Encounter and Exchange, 1714–1960* (Liverpool: University Press, 2013).

Meek, Donald E., 'Beachdan Ura à Inbhir Nis / New opinions from Inverness: Alexander Mac Bain (1855–1907) and the foundation of Celtic Studies in Scotland', in *Proceedings of the Society of Antiquaries in Scotland*, 131, 2001, pp 23–39.

Meenan, James (ed.), *Centenary History of the Literary and Historical Society of University College Dublin 1855–1955* (Tralee: Kerryman, 1955).

Mercier, Vivian, *Beckett / Beckett* (Oxford: Oxford University Press, 1977; pb edn 1979).

Mercier, Vivian, *Modern Irish Literature: Sources and Founders*, edited and presented by Eilís Dillon (Oxford: Clarendon, 1994).

Migliorini, Bruno, and T. Gwynfor Griffith, *The Italian Language* (London: Faber and Faber, 1966).

Mihas, Elena, Bernard Perley, Gabriel Rei-Doval and Kathleen Wheatley (eds), *Responses to Language Endangerment* [Studies in Language Companion Series 142] (Amsterdam: John Benjamins, 2013).

Millett, Benignus, 'Irish literature in Latin, 1550–1700', in Moody, Martin and Byrne (eds), *New History of Ireland, vol. 3*, pp 561–86.

Minuto, Emanuela, 'The reception of Thomas Moore in Italy in the nineteenth century', in Barr, Finelli and O'Connor (eds), *Nation / Nazione*, pp 193–205.

Mistéil, Pilib (ed.), *The Irish Language and the Unionist Tradition* (Belfast: Ulster People's College and Ultach Trust, 1994).

Modern Language Association, *Report on Higher School Certificate Examinations* (London: Modern Language Association, 1926).

Monck Mason, Henry Joseph, *History of the Origin and Progress of the Irish Society, Established for Promoting the Education of the Native Irish, Through the Medium of Their Own Language*, 2nd edn (Dublin: Goodwin, Son and Nethercott, 1846).

Montesquieu, *Lettres persanes* (1721), edited by Paul Vernière (Paris: Garnier, 1960).

Montgomery, Ian, 'Savory, Sir Douglas Lloyd', DIB.

Moody, T. W., 'Thomas Davis and the Irish nation', in *Hermathena*, 103, 1966, pp 5–31.

Moody, T. W., and J. C. Beckett, *Queen's, Belfast 1845–1949: The History of a University* (2 vols, London: Faber & Faber, 1959).

Moody, T. W., F. X. Martin and F. J. Byrne (eds), *A New History of Ireland, vol. 3: Early Modern Ireland, 1534–1691* (Oxford: Oxford University Press, 1976).

Moody, T. W., and W. E. Vaughan (eds), *A New History of Ireland, vol 4: Eighteenth-Century Ireland, 1691–1800* (Oxford: Oxford University Press, 1986).

Moriarty, Jim, 'Carlow College adapts to changing times', *Irish Times*, 4 Aug. 2003.

Moriarty, L. M., 'Some notes on methods and aims of modern language teaching in public schools', in *The Modern Quarterly of Language and Literature*, 1, 1899, pp 326–30.

Morley, Vincent, 'Ó Coileáin, Seán "Máistir" (O'Collins, John)', DIB.

Morley, Vincent, 'The popular influence of *Foras feasa ar Éirinn* from the seventeenth to the nineteenth century', in Kelly and Mac Murchaidh (eds), *Irish and English*, pp 96–115.

Morpurgo Davies, Anna, *History of Linguistics, vol. 4, Nineteenth-Century Linguistics* (London: Longman, 1998).

Morray, David, 'Ryan, Sir Andrew', DIB.

Morrissey, Thomas J., SJ, *Irish Jesuits in Penal Times 1695–1811: Thomas Betagh and his Companions* (Dublin: Messenger, 2020).

Moynihan, Nóirín, 'The archives held in the National University of Ireland', in Dunne et al. (eds), *The National University of Ireland 1908–2008*, pp 246–56.

Mulcahy, Catriona, 'This week Queen Elizabeth II will visit the Tyndall National Institute at University College Cork' [An Irishwoman's Diary], *Irish Times*, 17 May 2011.

Müller, Friedrich Max, *Lectures on The Science of Language* (London: Green, Longman, and Roberts, 1861).

Mulloy, Sheila, 'Memories of a Connemara man', in *Journal of the Clifden & Connemara Heritage Group*, 2, 1995, pp 33–46.

Murphy, Alison, *When Dublin was the Capital: Northern Life Remembered* (Portaferry and Vancouver: Belcouver Press, 2000).

Murphy, David, 'Neilson, William (Mac Néill, Uilliam)', DIB.

Murphy, David and Linde Lunney, 'Bergin, Osborn Joseph', DIB.

Murphy, Gerard, 'Celtic Studies in the university and the college', in Tierney (ed.), *Struggle with Fortune*, pp 121–41.

Murphy, John A., 'Ó Laoghaire, Peadar (An tAthair Peadar; O'Leary, Peter)', DIB.

Murphy, John A., *The College: A History of Queen's / University College Cork, 1845–1895* (Cork: Cork University Press, 1995).

Murphy, Maureen, 'Colum, Mary Catherine ('Molly')', DIB.

Murphy, William, 'Ryan, Finbar', DIB.

Murray, Charles H., 'The founding of a university', in *University Review*, 2, 1960, pp 10–22.

Murray, Raymond, 'Plunkett, St Oliver', DIB.

Murtagh, Peter, 'Irish woman honoured for wartime work at Bletchley Park', *Irish Times*, 19 January 2016.

Neilson, William, *An Introduction to the Irish Language* (Dublin: Wogan, 1808).

Nelson, Joseph, 'William Neilson, D.D., M.R.I.A.', in *Belfast Literary Society 1801–1901: Historical Sketch with Memoirs of some Distinguished Members* [Centenary volume] (Belfast: The Linenhall Press, 1902), pp 53–59.

Neville, Grace, '"I got second in Latin, Greek, and English, and eleventh in French": Attitudes to language(s) in the correspondence of Daniel O'Connell (1775–1847)', in Hutchinson and Ní Ríordáin (eds), *Language Issues*, pp 77–90.

Newmann, Kate, 'William Neilson (1774–1821): Teacher and writer', DUB.

Ní Bhrolcháin, Muireann, *An Introduction to Early Irish Literature* (Dublin: Four Courts Press, 2009; reprinted 2011).

Ní Chuilleanáin, Órla, *Tiortha na hÓige: Litríocht Ghaeilge na nÓg agus Ceisteanna an Aistriúcháin* (Dublin: Leabhair Comhar, 2014).

Ní Fhaircheallaigh, Úna [Agnes O'Farrelly], *Smaointe ar Árainn* [Thoughts on Aran], ed. Ríona Nic Congáil (Dublin: Arlen House, 2010).

Ní Mhunghaile, Lesa, 'Bilingualism, print culture in Irish and the public sphere, 1700–*c.*1830', in Kelly and Mac Murchaidh (eds), *Irish and English*, pp 218–42.

Ní Mhunghaile, Lesa, 'O'Connell, Frederick William', DIB.

Ní Mhunghaile, Lesa, 'O'Growney, Eugene (Eoghan Ó Gramhnaigh)', DIB.

Ní Mhunghaile, Lesa, 'Ó Luanaigh (O'Looney), Brian', DIB.

Ní Mhunghaile, Lesa, 'Ó Máille, Tomás', DIB.

Nic Congáil, Ríona, *Úna Ní Fhaircheallaigh agus an Fhís Útóipeach Ghaelach* (Dublin: Arlen House, 2010).

Nic Craith, Máiréad, 'Legacy and loss: the Great Silence and its aftermath', in Crowley, Smyth and Murphy (eds), *Atlas of the Great Irish Famine*, pp 580–7.

Nic Dhonnchadha, Aoibheann, 'Medical writing in Irish, 1400–1700', https://www.dias.ie/celt/celt-staff-and-scholars/celt-dr-aoibheann-nic-dhonnchadha/medical-writing-in-irish-1400-1700/ [accessed 7 January 2023].

Ninth Report of All Hallows College, Drumcondra (Dublin: John F. Fowler, 1858).

Ní Nuadháin, Nóirín, 'Putting a bit of spice into reading of Irish in the primary school', in Hickey (ed.), *Literacy and Language Learning*, pp 1–22.

Ní Úrdail, Meidhbhín, *The Scribe in Eighteenth- and Nineteenth-Century Ireland: Motivations and Milieu* (Münster: Nodus, 2000).

Ní Úrdail, Meidhbhín, 'Patrick Ferriter (1856–1924): An Irish scholar at home and abroad', in *American Journal of Irish Studies*, 15, 2019, pp 164–94.

Nikolov, Marianne (ed.), *Early Learning of Modern Foreign Languages: Processes and Outcomes* (Bristol: Multilingual Matters, 2009).

Nolan, Willie, 'Land reform in post-Famine Ireland', in Crowley, Smyth and Murphy (eds), *Atlas of the Great Irish Famine*, pp 570–9.

Northern Ireland Census 1991 Summary Report (Belfast: HMSO, 1992).

Oakes, Leigh, and Martin Howard, 'Foreign language motivation in a globalised world: The case of languages other than English (LOTEs)', in Maguire (ed.), *Foreign Language Learning and Ireland's Languages Connect Strategy*, pp 26–34.

O'Beirne Crowe, John, 'The Catholic University and the Irish language', [pamphlet, dated Belfast, 1854] (Dublin: James Duffy, 1865).

O'Brien, Gillian, 'The 1825–6 Commissioners of Irish Education reports: Background and context', in FitzGerald, *Irish Primary Education*, pp 1–43.

O'Brien, Gillian, *The Darkness Echoing: Ireland's Places of Famine, Death and Rebellion* (Dublin: Doubleday Ireland, 2020; London: Penguin, 2023).

O'Brien, Jennifer, 'Irish public opinion and the Risorgimento, 1859–60', in Barr, Finelli and O'Connor (eds), *Nation / Nazione*, pp 110–30.

O'Brien, Marie Ann, 'A century of change: The (in)visibility of women in the Irish Foreign Service, 1919–1929', in *Irish Studies in International Affairs*, 30, 2019, pp 73–92.

O'Brien, Paul, *A Practical Grammar of the Irish Language* (Dublin: H. Fitzpatrick, 1809).

Ó Broin, Leon, 'The Gaelic League and the Chair of Irish in Maynooth', in *Studies: An Irish Quarterly Review*, 52, 1963, pp 348–62.

O Brolchain, Honor, *Joseph Plunkett* (Dublin: O'Brien Press, 2012).

Ó Buachalla, Breandán, *I mBéal Feirste Cois Cuain* (Dublin: An Clóchomhar Teoranta, 1968).

Ó Buachalla, Séamas, 'Educational policy and the role of the Irish language from 1831 to 1981', in *European Journal of Education*, 19, 1984, pp 75–92.

Ó Buachalla, Séamas (ed.) *A Significant Irish Educationalist: The Educational Writings of P.H. Pearse* (Cork: Mercier, 1980).

Ó Cadhain, Máirtín, 'Conradh na Gaeilge agus an litríocht', in Ó Tuama (ed.), *The Gaelic League Idea*, pp 52–62.

Ó Caollaí, Éanna, 'Uimhir a 6 Sráid Fhearchair: finné ar stair na hÉireann', *Irish Times*, 12 April 2021.

O'Carroll, Ciarán, 'The Irish Papal Brigade: Origins, objectives and fortunes', in Barr, Finelli and O'Connor (eds), *Nation / Nazione*, pp 73–95.

Ó Catháin, Diarmuid, 'O'Curry (Curry, Ó Comhraí), Eugene (Eoghan)', DIB.

Ó Ciosáin, Éamon, 'Le merveilleux et l'espace européen: l'Irlande et les Irlandais dans la littérature médiévale française (XIIe–XVe siècles)', in Gaffney and Picard (eds), *The Medieval Imagination*, pp 158–92.

Ó Ciosáin, Niall, 'Printed popular literature in Irish 1750–1850: Presence and absence', in Daly and Dickson (eds), *Origins of Popular Literacy*, pp 45–57.

Ó Ciosáin, Niall, 'Pious miscellanies and spiritual songs: devotional publishing and reading in Irish and Scottish Gaelic, 1760–1900', in Kelly and Mac Murchaidh (eds), *Irish and English*, pp 267–82.

Ó Cofaigh, Éamon, 'Learning French through Irish: the impact of bilingualism on the acquisition of French as a third language (L3)', in Maguire (ed.), *Foreign Language Learning and Ireland's Languages Connect Strategy*, pp 39–46.

O'Connell, Frederick William, *The Writings on the Walls* (Dublin: M. H. Gill & Sons, 1915).

O'Connell, Frederick William, *Old Wine and New Wine* (Dublin: M. H. Gill & Son, 1922).

O'Connell, Frederick William [Conall Cearnach], *The Fatal Move and Other Stories* (Dublin: Michael Gill, 1924; new edn ed. Reggie Chamberlain-King, Dublin: Swan River Press, 2021).

O'Connell, Patricia, *The Irish College at Alcalà de Henares, 1649–1785* (Dublin: Four Courts Press, 1997).

O'Connell, Patricia, *The Irish College at Lisbon, 1590–1834* (Dublin: Four Courts Press, 2001).

O'Connell, Patricia, *The Irish College at Santiago de Compostela, 1605–1769* (Dublin: Four Courts Press, 2007).

O'Connor, Anne, 'Translating the Vatican: Paul Cullen, power and language in nineteenth-century Ireland', in *Irish Studies Review*, 22:4, 2014, pp 450–65.

O'Connor, Anne, 'The languages of transnationalism: translation, training, and transfer', in *Éire–Ireland*, 51, 2016, pp 14–33.

O'Connor, Anne, *Translation and Language in Nineteenth-Century Ireland: A European Perspective* (London: Palgrave Macmillan, 2017).

O'Connor, Anne V., and Susan M. Parkes, *Gladly Learn and Gladly Teach: Alexandra College and School 1866–1966* (Dublin: Blackwater Press, 1984)

O'Connor, Anne V., 'The revolution in girls' secondary education in Ireland, 1860–1910', in Cullen (ed.), *Girls Don't Do Honours*, pp 31–54.

O'Connor, Thomas, 'Irish Colleges abroad until the French Revolution', in *Encyclopedia of Irish History and Culture*, https://www.encyclopedia.com/international/encyclopedias-almanacs-transcripts-and-maps/irish-colleges-abroad-until-french-revolution [accessed 16 November 2020].

O'Connor, Timothy, 'Remembering one of the trailblazers of our education system', *Irish Examiner*, 7 March 2020.

O'Connor, T. P., 'D'Arcy W. Thompson. An old schoolmaster and a new system', in *UCG: A College Annual*, 1, 1913, pp 9–15.

Ó Corráin, Ailbhe, '*Slán agaibh a fhir chumtha*, a poem by Giolla Brighde Ó hEódhasa', paper read at a study day to mark the retirement of Damian McManus, TCD, 21 May 2021 [Zoom transmission].

Ó Cróinín, Dáibhí, 'Johann Caspar Zeuss (1806–56)' [An Irishman's Diary], *Irish Times*, 7 August 2006.

Ó Cuilleanáin, Cormac, Corinna Salvadori and John Scattergood (eds), *Italian Culture: Interactions, Transpositions, Translations* (Dublin: Four Courts Press, 2006).

Ó Cuilleanáin, Cormac, 'Dante's adventures in Ireland, 1785–2021', in Bacigalupo (ed.), *Dante nel Mondo*, pp 152–80.

Ó Cuív, Brian, 'The Irish language in the early modern period', in T. W. Moody, F. X. Martin and F. J. Byrne (eds), *New History of Ireland, vol. 3*, pp 509–45.

Ó Cuív, Brian, 'Irish language and literature, 1691–1845', in Moody and Vaughan (eds), *New History of Ireland, vol. 4*, pp 374–419.

Ó Cuív, Brian (1996), 'Irish language and literature, 1845–1921', in Vaughan (ed.), *New History of Ireland, vol. 6*, pp 385–435.

Ó Dochartaigh, Pól, '"A shadowy but important figure": Rudolf Thomas Siegfried', in Boyle and Russell (eds), *Tripartite Life of Whitley Stokes*, pp 29–43.

O'Donnell, Frank Hugh, *Mixed Education in Ireland: The Confessions of a Queen's Collegian*, 2 vols, vol. 1: *The Faculty of Arts* (London: Longmans, Green, 1870).

O'Donnell, Frank Hugh, *The Ruin of Education in Ireland and the Irish Fanar* (London: David Nutt, 1902).

O'Donovan, John, *A Grammar of the Irish Language* (Dublin: Hodges and Smith, 1845).

O'Donovan, John, and Jakob Grimm, 'Zeuss's *Grammatica Celtica*', in *Ulster Journal of Archaeology*, 7, 1859, pp 11–32.

O Duibhir, Padraig, 'Gaeilge labhartha na bpáistí i scoileanna lán-Ghaeilge i dTuaisceart na hÉireann: The spoken Irish of pupils in Irish-medium schools in Northern Ireland', in SCoTENS [Standing Conference on Teacher Education, North and South]-funded report (2010).

O'Faolain, Sean, *Newman's Way: The Odyssey of John Henry Newman* (New York: Devin Adair, 1952).

O'Faolain, Sean, *Vive Moi! An Autobiography* (London: Rupert Hart-Davis, 1965).

O'Farrelly, Agnes, 'The reign of humbug' [Gaelic League pamphlet no. 10] (Dublin: The Gaelic League, 1901).

O'Farrelly, Agnes [Ní Fhaircheallaigh, Úna], *Leabhar an Athar Eoghan: The O'Growney Memorial Volume* (Dublin: M. H. Gill, 1904).

Ó Fiaich, Tomás, 'The great controversy', in Ó Tuama (ed.), *The Gaelic League Idea*, pp 63–75.

O'Flaherty, K., 'The teaching of modern languages', in *Cork University Record*, 2, 1944, pp 41–3.

O'Flaherty, K., 'Random notes on QCC in the Fifties', in *Cork University Record*, 10, 1947, pp 26–8.

O'Flynn, Patrick, *A Question of Identity: The Great Trinity & UCD Merger Plan of the 1960s* (Dublin: A&A Farmar, 2012).

Ó Háinle, Cathal, 'Ó Neachtain, Tadhg', DIB.

O'Higgins, Laurie, *The Irish Classical Self: Poets and Poor Scholars in the Eighteenth and Nineteenth Centuries* (Oxford: OUP, 2017).

Ó hÓgáin, Dáithí, 'Folklore and literature in Ireland: 1700–1850', in Daly and Dickson (eds), *Origins of Popular Literacy*, pp 1–13.

Ó hÓgartaigh, Margaret, 'A quiet revolution: Women and second-level education in Ireland, 1878–1930', in *New Hibernia Review / Iris Éireannach Nua*, 13, 2009, pp 36–51.

Ó hUiginn, Ruairí (ed.), *Scoláirí Gaeilge* [Léachtaí Cholm Cille 27] (Maynooth: Maynooth University, 1997).

Ó hUiginn, Ruairí, 'Tomás Ó Máille', in Ó hUiginn (ed.), *Scoláirí Gaeilge*, pp 83–122.

Oireachtas Library and Research Service, 'The Irish language – a linguistic crisis?' [L&RS note], September 2016.

O'Leary, Denis, 'The first professor of Irish in QCC', in *Cork University Review*, 8, 1947, pp 37–44.

O'Leary, Philip, '*Seanchuidhthe, Séadna*, Sheehan, and the "Zeitgeist": Folklore and folklife in Gaelic fiction of the early Revival', in *Proceedings of the Harvard Celtic Colloquium*, 9, 1989, pp 43–99.

O'Leary, Philip, *Gaelic Prose in the Irish Free State, 1922–1939* (Dublin: UCD Press, 2004).

O'Leary, Philip, *Writing beyond the revival: Facing the Future in Gaelic prose, 1940–1951* (Dublin: UCD Press, 2011).

Ó Madagáin, Breandán, 'Irish: A difficult birth', in Foley (ed.), *From Queen's College to National University*, pp 344–59.

O'Malley, Liam, 'Law', in Foley (ed.), *From Queen's College to National University*, pp 16–124.

Ó Mathúna, Seán P., *William Bathe, SJ, 1564–1614: A Pioneer in Linguistics* [Amsterdam Studies in the Theory and History of Linguistic Science, vol. 37] (Amsterdam and Philadelphia: John Benjamins, 1986).

Ó Meadhra, Bebhinn, Bill Richardson and Cormac Ó Cuilleanáin (eds), *Languages in the 1990s* [Proceedings of the Third National Modern Languages Convention, 29–30 January 1989] (Dublin: MLTA/DCU, 1989).

O'Meara, John, 'Augustine versus the love of women', radio talk, Radio 3, 24 January 1972 [typescript, TLN04/RG108B].

O'Meara, John, *The Singing-Masters* (Dublin: Lilliput Press, 1990).

O'Meara, John, 'Remembering Archbishop McQuaid, UCD and reform of Irish education', in *Studies*, 92, 2003, pp 340–8.

Ó Murchú, Máirtín, 'Irish language studies in Trinity College Dublin', in *Hermathena (Quatercentenary Papers)*, 1992, pp 43–68.

Ó Neachtain, Tadhg , 'Ochlán Thaidhg Uí Neachtain' / 'Tadhg Ó Neachtain's Lament', edited and translated by Liam MacMathúna, in Fisher and Ó Conchubhair (eds), *Bone and Marrow / Cnámh agus Smior*, pp 520–31.

O'Neill, Ciaran, *Catholics of Consequence: Transnational Education, Social Mobility, and the Irish Catholic Elite 1850–1900* (Oxford: Oxford University Press, 2014).

O'Neill, Ciaran, 'Jesuit education and the Irish Catholic elite', in *Espacio, Tiempo y Educación*, 6, 2019, pp 99–120.

O'Neill, Rosaleen, 'Modern languages', in Foley (ed.), *From Queen's College to National University*, pp 360–83.

Ó Raghallaigh, Eoghan, 'Haliday, William', DIB.

Ó Raghallaigh, Eoghan, 'Henebry, Richard (de Hindeberg, Risteard)', DIB.

Ó Raghallaigh, Eoghan, 'Hogan, Edmund Ignatius', DIB.

O'Rourke, Fran, 'Joyce's early aesthetic', in *Journal of Modern Literature*, 34, 2011, pp 97–120.

O'Rourke, Malachy, 'Writing the wrongs', *Irish Times*, 26 September 1998.

O'Ryan, Owen, 'Giacomo Leopardi', lecture to the Cork Literary and Scientific Society, 16 February 1882 (Dublin: Hodges, Figgis & Co., 1883); reprinted in Sonzogni (ed.), *Or Volge l'Anno / At The Year's Turning*, pp 259–86.

Ó Saothraí, Séamas, 'William Neilson DD MRIA (1774–1821)', in *Journal of the County Louth Archaeological and Historical Society*, 22, 1989, pp 20–8.

O'Shea Farren, Linda, 'The role of Convocation', in Dunne et al. (eds), *The National University of Ireland 1908–2008*, pp 228–45.

Ó Siadhail, Mícheál, 'Standard Irish orthography: An assessment', in *The Crane Bag*, 5 (2) [*The Irish Language and Culture*] (1981; 1982 reprint), pp 903–7.

Ó Snodaigh, Pádraig, 'Hidden Ulster revisited', in *The Crane Bag*, 5 (2) [*The Irish Language and Culture*] (1981; 1982 reprint), pp 876–8.

O'Sullivan, Patricia A., 'The "Wild Geese": Irish soldiers in Italy, 1702–1733', in Istituto Italiano di Cultura, *Italian Presence in Ireland*, pp 79–114.

O'Toole, Fintan, 'Fashioning the airs that we breathe', *Irish Times*, 24 December 2005.

O'Toole, Fintan, *We Don't Know Ourselves: A Personal History of Ireland Since 1958* (London: Head of Zeus, 2021).

Ó Tuama, Seán (ed.), *The Gaelic League Idea* [RTÉ Thomas Davis Lectures 1968–9] (Cork: Mercier, 1972).

Ó Tuathaigh, Gearóid, 'The decline of the Irish language,' in Lee (ed.), *Ireland: 1945–1970*, pp 111–23; extract reprinted in Bowman (ed.), *Ireland: The Autobiography*, pp 312–13.

Ó Tuathaigh, Gearóid, 'The establishment of the Queen's Colleges: Ideological and political background', in Foley (ed.), *From Queen's College to National University*, pp 1–15.

Ó Tuathaigh, Gearóid, 'The position of the Irish language', in Dunne et al. (eds), *The National University of Ireland 1908–2008*, pp 33–43.

Padbury, Joyce, *Mary Hayden, Irish Historian and Feminist 1862–1942* (Dublin: Arlen House, 2021).

Palmer, Harold E., *The Principles of Language-Study* (London: Harrap, 1922; revised edn, ed. R. Mackin, London: Oxford University Press, 1964).

Parker, William Riley, 'Where do English departments come from?', in *College English*, 28, 1967, pp 339–51.

Parkes, Susan M. (1996), 'Higher education, 1793–1908', in Vaughan (ed.), *New History of Ireland*, vol. 6, pp 539–70.

Parkes, Susan M. (ed.), *A Danger to the Men? A History of Women in Trinity College Dublin 1904–2004* (Dublin: Lilliput Press, 2004).

Parkes, Susan M., 'The first decade, 1904–14: A quiet revolution', in Parkes (ed.), *A Danger to the Men?*, pp 55–86.

Parkes, Susan M., 'The "steamboat ladies", the First World War and after', in Parkes (ed.), *A Danger to the Men?*, pp 87–112.

Parkes, Susan M., 'A danger to the men? Women in Trinity College Dublin in the first decade, 1904–1914', in Harford and Rush (eds), *Have Women Made a Difference?*, pp 55–75.

Paseta, Senia, 'Achieving equality: women and the foundation of the university', in Dunne et al. (eds), *The National University of Ireland 1908–2008*, pp 19–32.

Paulin, Roger, 'Breul, Karl Hermann (1860–1932),' ODNB.

Pearse, P. H., 'Bilingual Education', in *An Claidheamh Soluis*, 23 January 1904, reprinted in Ó Buachalla, Séamas (ed.), *A Significant Irish Educationalist*, pp 31–34.

Pearse, P. H., 'Belgium and its Schools', in *An Claidheamh Soluis*, 5 August 1905–9 March 1907, reprinted in Ó Buachalla, Séamas (ed.), *A Significant Irish Educationalist*, pp 254–310.

Pearse, P. H. [MacPiarais, Pádraic], '"Education" in the West of Ireland', *Guth na Bliadhna* (Edinburgh), 11 April 1905, reprinted in Ó Buachalla (ed.), *A Significant Irish Educationalist*, pp 313–16.

Pearse, P. H., 'By Way of Comment', *An Macaomh*, June 1909, reprinted in Ó Buachalla (ed.), *A Significant Irish Educationalist*, pp 322–8.

Penet, Jean-Christophe, 'Thomas Davis, "The Nation" and the Irish language', in *Studies: An Irish Quarterly Review*, 96, 2007, pp 433–43.

Perlman Lorch, Marjorie, 'Investigating the biographical sources of Thomas Prendergast's (1807–1886) innovation in language learning', in McLelland and Smith (eds), *The History of Language Learning and Teaching*, vol. 2, pp 127–44.

Pettit, Seán F., 'The Queen's College, Cork: Its origins and early history, 1803–1858', PhD dissertation, University College Cork, 1973.

Phelan, Mary, *Irish Speakers, Interpreters and the Courts, 1754–1921* (Dublin: Four Courts Press, 2019).

Phillips, Patricia, *The Scientific Lady: A Social History of Woman's Scientific Interests 1520–1918* (London: Weidenfeld and Nicolson, 1990).

Phillips, Patricia, 'The Queen's Institute, Dublin (1861–1881): The first technical college for women in the British Isles', in McMillan (ed.), *Prometheus's Fire*, Chapter 19. Online http://www.rjtechne.org/tyndall/tyndall_books/prometheus/abstracts/abs19.htm

Picard, Jean-Michel, 'The Latin language in early medieval Ireland', in Cronin and Ó Cuilleanáin (eds), *The Languages of Ireland*, pp 44–56.

Plumb, J. H., *The First Four Georges* (London: Batsford, 1956).

Potter, Matthew, 'William Monsell: a Roman Catholic francophile Anglo-Irishman', in Litvack and Graham (eds), *Ireland and Europe in the Nineteenth Century*, pp 77–88.

'Professor Mary Ryan, D.Litt.', in *U.C.C. Record*, 37, Easter 1962, pp 21–5.

'Publication of early 19th-century architectural albums online', Church of Ireland Historical Society website, http://churchofirelandhist.org/the-weekend-read-publication-of-early-19th-century-architectural-albums-online/ [accessed 10 September 2023].

Pye, Michael, *Antwerp: The Glory Years* (London: Allen Lane, 2021).

Quane, Michael, 'Cavan Royal School', in *The Journal of the Royal Society of Antiquaries in Ireland*, 100, 1970, pp 39–66.

Rafter, Kevin (ed.), *Irish Journalism Before Independence: More a Disease Than a Profession* (Manchester: Manchester University Press, 2011).

Raftery, Deirdre, and Catherine Kilbride, *The Benedictine Nuns and Kylemore Abbey: A History* (Newbridge: Irish Academic Press, 2020).

Raftery, Deirdre, 'The higher education of Women in Ireland, c.1860–1904', in Parkes (ed.), *A Danger to the Men?*, pp 5–18.

Raftery, Deirdre, 'Farewell to the Terrace: the long and hard road to acceptance', *Irish Times*, Supplement, 15 May 2007, p. 6.

Raftery, Deirdre, 'The "mission" of nuns in female education in Ireland, *c*.1850–1950', in *Paedagogica Historica*, 48, 2012, pp 299–313.

Raftery, Deirdre, '"*Je suis d'aucune Nation*": the recruitment and identity of Irish women religious in the international mission field, *c*.1840–1940', in *Paedagogica Historica*, 49, 2013, pp 513–30.

Raftery, Deirdre, *Teresa Ball and Loreto Education: Convents and the Colonial World, 1794–1875* (Dublin: Four Courts, 2022).

Raidió Fáilte, 'An Úcráin – Ag caint le Nadia Dobrianska' (radio interview, 13 May 2022), https://soundcloud.com/raidio-f/an-ucrain-ag-caint-le-nadia-dobrianska-1352022 [accessed 4 September 2022].

Raraty, M. M., 'The chair of German, Trinity College, Dublin 1775–1866', in *Hermathena*, 102, 1966, pp 53–72.

Report of the Queen's Colleges Commission (Dublin: Her Majesty's Stationery Office, 1858).

Reville, William, 'Callan, Nicholas Joseph', DIB.

Rickard, Peter, *A History of the French Language* (London: Hutchinson, 1974).

Rigney, Liam, 'Woodlock, Bartholomew', DIB.

'Roamer: disturbing story from a hundred years ago resonates disquietingly today', *Belfast Newsletter*, 25 August 2016.

Roberts, Stuart, 'The rising tide: Women at Cambridge', on University of Cambridge website, https://www.cam.ac.uk/stories/the-rising-tide [accessed 15 April 2023].

Robertson, Ritchie, 'Tides of Germany', review of *The German Genius: Europe's Third Renaissance* by Peter Watson (New York: Simon and Schuster, 2010), *Times Literary Supplement*, 1 October 2010, pp 7–8.

Robins, R. H., *A Short History of Linguistics* (London: Longman, 1967; 4th edn, 1997).

Robinson, Mary, 'Douglas Hyde (1860–1949): The Trinity connection', in *Hermathena (Quatercentenary Papers)*, 1992, pp 17–26.

Robinson-Hammerstein, Helga, and Charles Benson, *A Bohemian Refuge: Irish Students in Prague in the Eighteenth Century* [exhibition catalogue, Long Room, Trinity College, December 1997–May 1998] (Dublin: The Library, Trinity College Dublin, 1997).

Rodgers, John, *Old Public Schools of England* (London: Batsford, 1938).

Rouse, Paul, 'Connellan, Owen (1800–1869)', DIB.

Rouse, Paul, 'Ó Briain, Liam', DIB.

Rouse, Paul, 'William, Francis Thomas', DIB.

Rudmose-Brown, T. B., *French Literary Studies* (Dublin: The Talbot Press, and London: T. Fisher Unwin, 1917).

Rulhière, Claude Carloman de, 'Sur les disputes', in *Oeuvres de Rulhière*, vol. 6 (Paris: Ménard et Désenne, 1819), pp 332–8.

Rush, Claire, 'Women who made a difference: The Belfast Ladies' Institute, 1867–1897', in Harford and Rush (eds), *Have Women Made a Difference?*, pp 29–53.

Ryan, (Sir) Andrew, *The Last of the Dragomans* (London: Geoffrey Bles, 1951).

Ryan, Mary, 'A Dante discovery', in *Studies: An Irish Quarterly Review*, 10, 1921, pp 425–36.

Ryan, Mary, 'Alfred Noyes on Voltaire', in *Studies: An Irish Quarterly Review*, 26, 1937, pp 281–95.

Sagarra, Eda, 'From the pistol to the petticoat? The changing student body 1592–1992', in Holland (ed.), *Trinity College Dublin*, pp 107–27.

Sagarra, Eda, 'The centenary of the Henry Simon Chair of German at the University of Manchester (1996): Commemorative address', in *German Life and Letters*, 51, 1998, pp 509–24.

Sagarra, Eda, 'Austrian literature in Ireland', in Leifer and Sagarra (eds), *Austro-Irish Links through the Centuries*, pp 143–61.

Sagarra, Eda, 'Waterhouse, Gilbert', DIB.

Sagarra, Eda, *Living with My Century* (Dublin: Lilliput, 2022).

Said, Edward W., *Orientalism: Western Conceptions of the Orient* (New York: Pantheon Books, 1978; Harmondsworth: Penguin, 1991).

Salvadori, Corinna, '*Dove 'l sì sona*: two hundred and thirty years of Italian in Trinity College Dublin', in Ó Cuilleanáin, Salvadori and Scattergood (eds), *Italian Culture*, pp 13–28.

Sandbach, F. E., 'German Studies in the British Isles since 1914', in *Monatshefte für Deutsche Sprache und Pädagogik [Jahrbuch 1927]* (Madison: University of Wisconsin Press, 1926), pp 22–37.

Sanderson, Michael (ed.), *The Universities in the Nineteenth Century* (London: Routledge & Kegan Paul, 1975).

Sargent, Clare, 'The Fellows of St. Columba's College, Stackallan', on The Victorian Web website, https://victorianweb.org/history/education/stcolumba/1.html [accessed 31 March 2021].

Sargent, Clare, 'Singleton, Sewell and the ideal of a school: St Columba's College, Stackallan and St Peter's College, Radley', on The Victorian Web website, https://victorianweb.org/history/education/radley/ideals.html [accessed 31 March 2021].

Satherly, Zoe, 'History under the hammer', *Daily Telegraph* (Australia), 8 July 2005, https://www.dailytelegraph.com.au/news/nsw/lismore/history-under-the-hammer/news-story/c0a99443fe7b2da8087e6f4c026e9c1a [accessed 18 August 2021].

Saunders, Anne Leslie, 'The value of Latin prose composition', in *The Classical Journal*, 88, 1993, pp 385–92.

Savić, V. R., 'The problem of the Adriatic', in *The North American Review*, 206, 1917, pp 885–93.

Schofield, Fr Nicholas, 'The last days of the English College in Douai', on Diocese of Westminster website, https://rcdow.org.uk/news/the-last-days-of-the-english-college-in-douai-/ [accessed 9 May 2021].

Second Annual Report of The Missionary College of All Hallows, Drumcondra, Dublin (1849) (Dublin: Fowler, 1850).

Semple, Patrick, 'The Royal University', in Tierney (ed.), *Struggle with Fortune*, pp 51–60.

Seventh Report of All Hallows College, Drumcondra, Dublin (Dublin: John F. Fowler, 1855).

'Sgoil Árd-Leighinn na Gaedhilge / School of Irish Learning: Report of First Session, 1903', in *Ériu*, 1, 1904, pp 9–12.

Sgoil Éanna, Ráth Fearnáin / St Enda's School, Rathfarnham: Prospectus, 1910–11, http://pearsemuseum.ie/wp-content/uploads/2014/11/Scoil-%C3%89anna-Prospectus-1910-11.pdf [accessed 27 December 2020]

Sheehy, Jeanne, *The Rediscovery of Ireland's Past: The Celtic Revival 1830–1930* (London: Thames and Hudson, 1980).

Shields, Andrew, '"That noble struggle": Irish conservative attitudes towards the Risorgimento, *c*.1848–70', in Barr, Finelli and O'Connor (eds), *Nation / Nazione*, pp 157–75.

Silke, John J., 'Irish scholarship and the Renaissance, 1580–1673', in *Studies in the Renaissance*, 20, 1973, pp 169–206.

Silke, John J., 'The Irish abroad in the age of the Counter-Reformation, 1534–1691', in Moody, Martin and Byrne (eds), *New History of Ireland, vol. 3*, pp 587–633.

Simms, J. G., 'The Irish on the Continent, 1691–1800', in Moody and Vaughan (eds), *New History of Ireland, vol. 4*, pp 629–56.

Simons, Gary F., and Melvyn Paul Lewis, 'The world's languages in crisis: a 20-year update', in Mihas et al. (eds), *Responses to Language Endangerment*, pp 3–20.

Smith, Elisabeth Margaret, 'To walk upon the grass: The impact of the University of St Andrews' Lady Literate in Arts, 1877–1892', PhD thesis, University of St Andrews, 2014.

Smith, Richard, 'Claude Marcel (1793–1876): A neglected applied linguist?', in *Language and History*, 52, 2009, pp 171–81.

Smith, Richard, 'Harold E. Palmer, IRLT and "historical sense" in ELT', in *IRLT Journal*, 12 [Journal of the Institute for Research in Language Teaching, Tokyo: special issue to celebrate the Institute's 90th anniversary], 2013, pp 1–8, pre-publication version, https://warwick.ac.uk/fac/soc/al/people/smith/smith_r/harold_e__palmer_irlt_and_historical_sense_in_elt.pdf [accessed 28 September 2023].

Smith, Richard, and Nicola McLelland, 'An interview with John Trim (1924–2013) on the history of modern language learning and teaching', in *Language & History*, 57, 2014, pp 10–25.

Smith, William, lecture to the seminar on 'The Irish Language and the Unionist Tradition', Ulster People's College, Belfast, 9 May 1992, in Mistéil (ed.), *The Irish Language and the Unionist Tradition*, pp 17–23.

Smith, William L., 'Euntes docete omnes gentes', in *History Ireland*, 3, Autumn 2000, https://www.historyireland.com/euntes-docete-omnes-gentes/ [accessed 23 November 2020].

Smithers, Rebecca, and Ben Whitford, '"Free fall" fears as pupils abandon languages', *Guardian*, 25 August 2006.

Sonzogni, Marco (ed.), *Or Volge l'Anno / At The Year's Turning: An Anthology of Irish Poets Responding to Leopardi* (Dublin: Dedalus, 1998).

Stanford, W. B., *Ireland and the Classical Tradition* (Dublin: Allen Figgis & Co., 1976).

Stanford, W. B., and R. B. McDowell, *Mahaffy: A Biography of an Anglo-Irishman* (London: Routledge and Kegan Paul, 1971).

Stewart, Bruce, 'On the necessity of de-Hydifying Irish cultural criticism', in *New Hibernia Review / Iris Éireannach Nua*, 4, 2000, pp 23–44.

Stieglitz, Gerhard J., 'The Berlitz method', in *The Modern Language Journal*, 6, 1955, pp 300–10.

Stocks Powell, John, *Schooling in Ireland: A Clustered History 1695–1912* (Tullamore: Esker Press (Offaly Historical and Archaeological Society), 2020).

Stocks Powell, John, *Carson's School, Portarlington: Edward Carson and His Headmaster, Francis Hewson Wall* (York: Frenchchurch Press, 2018).

Stray, Christopher, *Classics Transformed: Schools, Universities, and Society in England, 1830–1960* (Oxford: Clarendon, 1998).

Stray, Christopher, 'The shift from oral to written examination: Cambridge and Oxford 1700–1900', in *Assessment in Education: Principles, Policy & Practice*, 8, 2001, pp 33–50.

Swords, Liam, 'History of the Irish College, Paris, 1578–1800: Calendar of the papers of the Irish College, Paris', in *Archivium Hibernicum*, 35, 1980, pp 3–233.

Synge, J. M., *The Aran Islands*, ed. Tim Robinson (London: Penguin, 1992).

Teehan, Virginia, 'Mary Ryan takes central place in the ranks of achieving Irish women' [An Irishwoman's Diary], *Irish Times*, 28 June 2010.

Teichfischer, Philipp, 'Transnational entanglements in colonial medicine: German medical practitioners as members of the health service in the Dutch East Indies (1816–1884)', in *Revue d'Histoire Sociale et Culturelle de la Médecine, de la Santé et du Corps*, 10, 2016 [*Guerre, Maladie, Empire*], pp 63–78.

The Book of Trinity College Dublin, 1591–1891: Tercentenary Celebration presented by the Provost and Senior Fellows of Trinity College, Dublin, July 1892 (Dublin: Hodges Figgis & Co., 1892).

'The Gaelic story at the University of Glasgow', https://sgeulnagaidhlig.ac.uk/20th-c-department-of-celtic/?lang=en# [accessed 5 September 2023].

'The Irish language and Irish intermediate education' [Gaelic League pamphlets 13, 15 and 16] (Dublin: Gaelic League, Browne & Nolan, 1901).

'The late Father O'Carroll SJ', in *The Irish Monthly*, 17, 1889, pp 209–15.

The Nation, 1842–4, viewed on *Irish Newspaper Archives*, https://irishnewsarchive.com [last accessed September 2023].

'The University of Cambridge: The age of reforms (1800–82)', in J. P. C. Roach (ed.), *A History of the County of Cambridge and the Isle of Ely: Volume 3, the City and University of Cambridge* (London: Victoria County History, 1959), pp 235–65, available at *British History Online*, british-history.ac.uk/vch/cambs/vol3 [accessed 2 December 2020].

Thompson, Lucinda, 'The campaign for admission, 1870–1904', in Parkes (ed.), *A Danger to the Men?*, pp 19–54.

Tidman, Gemma, *The Emergence of Literature in Eighteenth-Century France: The Battle of the Schoolbooks* [Oxford Studies in the Enlightenment] (Liverpool: Liverpool University Press, 2023).

Tierney, Michael (ed.), *Struggle with Fortune: A Miscellany for the Centenary of the Catholic University of Ireland, 1854–1954* (Dublin: Browne and Nolan, 1954).

Tissier-Moston, Adeline, 'The campaign for the recognition of the Irish language in national schools (1878–1904)', in Hutchinson and Ní Ríordáin (eds), *Language Issues*, pp 91–103.

Tomamichel, Serge, 'Le latin dans l'enseignement secondaire français: formes et légitimités sociales d'une discipline scolaire entre monopole et déclin (xvie–xxe siècles)', in *Espacio, Tiempo y Educación*, 4:2, 2017, pp 209–26.

Torrance, Isabelle, and Donncha O'Rourke (eds), *Classics and Irish Politics, 1916–2016* (Oxford: Oxford University Press, 2020).

Trevor-Roper, Hugh, *The Rise of Christian Europe* (London: Thames and Hudson, 2nd edn 1966).

Trinity News editorial, 23 March 2010, 'Old Trinity: A 90-degree university': http://trinitynews.ie/2010/03/old-trinity-a-90-degree-university/ [accessed 3 March 2023].

Trove (Australian cultural database), 'The unusual story of a pioneer priest', *Catholic Weekly* (Sydney), 6 August 1942: https://trove.nla.gov.au/newspaper/article/146500583/17325443 [accessed 18 August 2021].

Trove, 'Death of Abbé Schurr, V.G.', *Freeman's Journal* (Sydney), 21 July 1900, p. 15: https://trove.nla.gov.au/newspaper/page/12419798 [accessed 20 November 2020].

Trove, 'Death of the Venerable Abbé Schurr: The apostle of the North Coast', *The Catholic Press* (Sydney), 21 July 1900, p. 11: https://trove.nla.gov.au/newspaper/article/104660994/11826035 [accessed 30 January 2024].

Trove, 'Diocese of Lismore: Historical sketch', *The Catholic Press* (Sydney), 9 September 1937: https://trove.nla.gov.au/newspaper/article/106334704 [accessed 18 August 2021].

Turner, Michael, 'The French connection with Maynooth College, 1795–1855', in *Studies*, 70:277, 1981, pp 77–87.

Tymoczko, Maria, 'Language interface in early Irish culture', in Cronin and Ó Cuilleanáin (eds), *The Languages of Ireland*, pp 25–43.

Uí Chionna, Jackie, *An Oral History of University College Galway, 1930–1980: A University in Living Memory* (Dublin: Four Courts Press, 2019).

Uí Chionna, Jackie, *Queen of Codes: The Secret Life of Emily Anderson, Britain's Greatest Female Codebreaker* (London: Headline, 2023).

Uí Chollatáin, Regina, 'Newspapers, journals and the Irish revival', in Rafter (ed.), *Irish Journalism before Independence*, pp 160–73.

Uí Chollatáin, Regina, 'A new Gaelic League idea? The global context', in Mac Mathúna and Nic an Bhaird (eds), *Douglas Hyde*, pp 15–49.

Unsworth, Monika, 'Epic battle to save classical studies at Queen's', *Irish Times*, 29 August 2002.

Vaughan, W. E. (ed.), *A New History of Ireland, vol. 6: Ireland Under the Union, II, 1870–1921* (Oxford: Oxford University Press, 1996).

Vigner, Gérard, 'Depuis quand enseigne-t-on le français en France? Du *sermo vulgaris* à l'enseignement du français langue maternelle', in *Études de Linguistique Appliquée*, 123–4, 2001, pp 425–44.

Walsh, Brendan, '"Frankly and robustly national": Padraig Pearse, the Gaelic League and the campaign for Irish at the National University', in *Studies*, 103, 2014, pp 318–30.

Walsh, Brendan (ed.), *Essays in the History of Irish Education* (London: Palgrave Macmillan, 2016).

Walsh, John, 'Eamon de Valera, 1921–75', in Dunne et al. (eds), *The National University of Ireland 1908–2008*, pp 135–45.

Walsh, John, *One Hundred Years of Irish Language Policy, 1922–2022* (Oxford: Peter Lang, 2022).

Walsh, T. J., *Nano Nagle and the Presentation Sisters* (Monasterevin: Presentation Generalate, 1959; reprinted 1980).

Walsh, Tom, 'The national system of education, 1831–2000', in Brendan Walsh (ed.), *Essays in the History of Irish Education*, pp 7–43.

Whelan, Aoife, '*Irish Independent* coverage of Douglas Hyde's vision for a de-anglicised Ireland', in Mac Mathúna and Nic an Bhaird (eds), *Douglas Hyde*, pp 79–97.

Whelan, Kevin, 'The memories of "The Dead"', in *The Yale Journal of Criticism*, 15, 2002, pp 59–97.

Whelan, Kevin, 'Between: The politics of culture in Friel's *Translations*', in *Field Day Review*, 6, 2010, pp 7–27.

Whelan, Kevin, 'Paris: capital of Irish culture', in Joannon and Whelan (eds), *Paris Capital of Irish Culture*, pp 33–76.

Whelan, Kevin, *Religion, Landscape and Settlement in Ireland: From Patrick to the Present* (Dublin: Four Courts Press, 2018).

Whitaker, T. K., 'Shut the door on the past', extract from 'Economic development' (Irish Government Publications, 1958), reprinted in Bowman (ed.), *Ireland: The Autobiography*, pp 237–9.

White, Harry, 'The sovereign ghosts of Thomas Moore', in Fanning and Gillespie (eds), *Print Culture and Intellectual Life in Ireland, 1660–1941*, pp 164–85.

White, Lawrence William, 'De Brún, Pádraig (Browne, Paddy)', DIB.

White, Lawrence William, 'MacDonagh, Thomas', DIB.

White, Lawrence William, 'Ó hUallacháin, Colmán', DIB.

Wicks, Margaret C. W., *The Italian Exiles in London 1816–1848* (Manchester: Manchester University Press, 1937; reprinted Freeport, NY: Books for Libraries Press, 1968).

WiSER – All Changed, Changed Utterly, documentary film produced by Angie Mezzetti for TCD Centre for Gender Equality and Leadership, https://www.tcd.ie/tcgel/resources/multimedia.php [accessed 20 May 2023].

Wolf, Nicholas M., 'The Irish-speaking clergy in the nineteenth century: Education, trends, and timing', in *New Hibernia Review / Iris Éireannach Nua*, 12, 2008, pp 62–83.

Woodhouse, J. R., 'Serena, Arthur (1852/3–1922)', ODNB.

Woods, C. J., 'Duffy, James', DIB.

Woods, C. J. 'Madgett, Nicholas', DIB.

Additional online sources, mostly biographical or institutional:

ADB – Australian Dictionary of Biography: https://adb.anu.edu.au/ [accessed 4 November 2020].

ainm.ie – An Bunachar Náisiúnta Beathaisnéisí Gaeilge [The National Database of Irish-Language Biographies]: https://www.ainm.ie/ [accessed on various dates].

All Hallows Missionary College, Publications page: https://allhallows.ie/missionary-college/publications/ [accessed 23 November 2020].

Ambassade de France en Irlande, 'Qu'est-ce que le Lycée français international Samuel Beckett?': https://ie.ambafrance.org/Qu-est-ce-que-le-LFI [accessed 7 March 2023].

Blackrock College Archives: https://www.blackrockcollege.com/about/archives [accessed on various dates].

Britannica, 'Indo-European languages' – 'Establishment of the family' – 'Sanskrit studies and their impact': https://www.britannica.com/topic/Indo-European-languages/Establishment-of-the-family#ref603272 [accessed 22 November 2021].

Britannica, 'Sir William Jones: British orientalist and jurist': https://www.britannica.com/biography/William-Jones-British-orientalist-and-jurist [accessed 22 November 2021].

British Academy, 'Humanities scholars who worked in military intelligence in the Second World War': https://www.thebritishacademy.ac.uk/publishing/memoirs/humanities-scholars-who-worked-military-intelligence-second-world-war/ [accessed 21 September 2023].

Central Statistics Office, 'Life in 1916 Ireland: Stories from statistics', Seán T. O'Kelly: https://www.cso.ie/en/releasesandpublications/ep/p-1916/1916irl/cpr/coir/stk/ [accessed 18 August 2023].

Church of Ireland Historical Society, 'Publication of early 19th-century architectural albums online': http://churchofirelandhist.org/the-weekend-read-publication-of-early-19th-century-architectural-albums-online/ [accessed 10 September 2023].

Cork City and County Archives, *Register of Interments at St Finbarr's Cemetery, Glasheen Road, Cork, Cemetery Burial Register 1867–1896* (Cork City Council, 2017)

Department of Education, State Examinations Commission, State Examinations Statistics: https://www.examinations.ie/statistics/ [accessed 27 November 2023].

Department of Education Statistical Reports (Dublin: Stationery Office) [accessed 27 November 2023].

DIB – Dictionary of Irish Biography: https://www.dib.ie/ [accessed on various dates].

Dictionary of National Biography 1885–1900, 'Haliday, William': https://en.m.wikisource.org/wiki/Dictionary_of_National_Biography,_1885-1900/Haliday,_William [accessed 3 April 2021].

DUB – Dictionary of Ulster Biography: https://www.newulsterbiography.co.uk/ [accessed on various dates].

Durham University Library, Archives and Special Collections, subject guide for Modern Languages and Cultures: https://libguides.durham.ac.uk/mlac/asc [accessed 20 August 2023].

Encyclopaedia Brittanica 1911, 'Renouf, Sir Peter le Page': https://en.wikisource.org/wiki/1911_Encyclop%C3%A6dia_Britannica/Renouf,_Sirh_Peter_le_Page [accessed 2 November 2020].

EUR-Lex.europa.eu, 'European Year of Languages 2001': https://eur-lex.europa.eu/legal-content/EN/TXT/HTML/?uri=LEGISSUM:c11044&from=PT [accessed 24 October 2023].

Gaeltacht UCD, UCD's Global Centre for Irish Language and Culture, video interview with Junhan Zhang: https://www.ucd.ie/irish/en/global/ [accessed June 2022].

Glens of Antrim Historical Society, 'Lament for Seamus "Bhriain" Mac Amhlaigh', 12 February 2006: https://antrimhistory.net/lament-for-seamus-bhriain-mac-amhlaigh/ [accessed 18 October 2023].

Hamilton Memoirs, Chapter 20: https://www.stirnet.com/articles/selectfams/HamiltonMemoirs/CH20.html [accessed 18 August 2021].

Irish Jesuit Archives, 'Delany, William, 1835–1924, Jesuit priest': https://www.jesuitarchives.ie/delany-william-1835-1924-jesuit-priest [accessed 3 December 2020].

Irish Jesuit Archives, 'Ó Neachtain, Peadar, 1709–1756, Jesuit priest': https://www.jesuitarchives.ie/o-neachtain-peadar-1709-1756-jesuit-priest [accessed 27 October 2022].

King's College London, description of the History & Modern Languages with a year abroad BA: https://www.kcl.ac.uk/study/undergraduate/courses/history-and-modern-languages-with-a-year-abroad-ba [accessed 12 November 2020].

Marchivium (archive of the city of Mannheim), 'Bensbach, August Dr./Isaak': https://www.marchivum.de/de/juedischer-friedhof/a2-08-04-bensbach-august-drisaak [accessed 8 March 2023].

Maynooth College Cemetery Documentation & Enhancement Project, 'Burial of presidents, vice-presidents, professors and deans 1817–79': https://avergeen9.wixsite.com/maynoothcemetery/lists-c1pd6 [accessed 4 November 2020].

Maynooth University, About section, 'University history': https://www.maynoothuniversity.ie/about-us/university-history [accessed 12 September 2023].

Maynooth University, French Studies main page: https://www.maynoothuniversity.ie/french [accessed 4 November 2020].

Mercator European Research Centre on Multilingualism and Language Learning (Regional Dossiers series), compiled by Aodán Mac Póilin and Adalgard Willemsma: *Irish: The Irish Language in Education in Northern Ireland*, (Leeuwarden (Netherlands): Mercator-Education, 1997; 2nd edn 2004; 3rd edn 2019), with financial support from the Fryske Akademy and the European Commission (DGXXII: Education, Training and Youth).

National Archives (France), Légion d'Honneur dossier, 19800035/231/30555, 'CADIC Edouard Marie', available on the Léonore database, https://www.leonore.archives-nationales.culture.gouv.fr/ui/notice/62164 [accessed 17 January 2023].

National Library of Scotland, '1808 – Uraicecht na Gaedhilge = A grammar of the Gaelic language': https://digital.nls.uk/108990860 [accessed 2 April 2021].

ODNB – Oxford Dictionary of National Biography: https://www.oxforddnb.com/ [accessed on various dates].

Pontifical Irish College, Rome, Archival list of the Kirby Collection Catalogue, Part 4, Years 1867–1873: http://www.irishcollege.org/wp-content/uploads/2011/02/Kirby-Catalogue-Part-4-1867-1873.pdf [accessed 22 November 2020].

Rice History Corner, 'Prize will honor late Rice professor emeritus, Freund': https://ricehistorycorner.com/wp-content/uploads/2018/04/max-freund-article-1980126.jpg [accessed 13 February 2022].

Rice University Research Repository, 'Dr Freund wins Order of Merit': https://scholarship.rice.edu/bitstream/handle/1911/34769/37.pdf [accessed 13 February 2022].

Rice University Research Repository: https://scholarship.rice.edu [accessed 27 September 2023].

Royal Asiatic Society, 'Sir William Jones (1746–1794)': https://royalasiaticsociety.org/sir-william-jones-1746-1794/ [accessed 22 November 2021].

Scoilnet (Department of Education portal site), 'Discovering Women in Irish History', 'The Intermediate Education Act (1878)': http://womeninhistory.scoilnet.ie/content/unit4/exhibpast.html [accessed 7 March 2023].

Second Wiki, 'Max Freund': https://second.wiki/wiki/max_freund [accessed 27 September 2023].

Sorbonne, 'La Sorbonne au XIXe siècle: le temps des grands travaux sous la Troisième République': https://www.sorbonne.fr/la-sorbonne/histoire-de-la-sorbonne/la-sorbonne-au-xixe-siecle-le-temps-des-grands-travaux-sous-la-troisieme-republique/ [accessed 11 November 2023].

St Mary's University College Belfast, BEd Hons (Bilingual) course description: https://www.stmarys-belfast.ac.uk/academic/education/courses/bed/ime_english.asp [accessed 17 October 2023].

The Gaelic Story at the University of Glasgow, '20th century: The Department of Celtic': https://sgeulnagaidhlig.ac.uk/20th-c-department-of-celtic/?lang=en# [accessed 5 September 2023].

University College Cork Heritage Services, 'Professor Mary Ryan': https://www.ucc.ie/en/heritage/history/people/ucc-staff/prof-mary-ryan/ [accessed 22 August 2023)].

University College Dublin Digital Library, Papers of Eugene O'Curry (1796–1862): https://digital.ucd.ie/view/ivrla:2620 [accessed 5 April 2021].

University College Dublin, news and opinion blog, 'Newman's vision of a liberal education today': https://www.ucd.ie/newsandopinion/news/2019/october/10/newmansvisionofaliberaleducationtoday/ [accessed 11 August 2023].

University of Bologna, terminologia.it, 'La lingua dell'Europa è la traduzione [Umberto Eco]': https://www.terminologia.it/index.php/2016/11/25/translation-is-the-language-of-europe-umberto-eco/?lang=it [accessed 11 February 2023].

University of Edinburgh, Our History, Faculty of Arts: http://ourhistory.is.ed.ac.uk/index.php/Faculty_of_Arts [accessed 12 November 2020].

University of Manchester, Department of German Archives: https://archiveshub.jisc.ac.uk/search/archives/7d53bb62-3b7b-3754-9b8f-ff388bd6d7c7 [accessed 19 October 2023].

University of Oxford, Faculty of History, 'A short history of women's education at the University of Oxford': https://www.history.ox.ac.uk/article/a-short-history-of-womens-education-at-the-university-of-oxford [accessed 15 April 2023].

University of St Andrews, About page for the School of Modern Languages: https://www.st-andrews.ac.uk/modern-languages/about/ [accessed 12 November 2020].

Wikipedia, 'Faculty of Medieval and Modern Languages, University of Oxford': https://en.wikipedia.org/wiki/Faculty_of_Medieval_and_Modern_Languages,_University_of_Oxford [accessed 12 November 2020].

Wikipedia, 'François Gouin': https://fr.wikipedia.org/wiki/Fran%C3%A7ois_Gouin [accessed 2 August 2023].

Wikipedia, 'Irish College': https://en.wikipedia.org/wiki/Irish_College [accessed 3 August 2023].

Wikipedia, 'James Warren Doyle': https://en.wikipedia.org/wiki/James_Warren_Doyle [accessed 19 November 2020].

Wikipedia, 'List of English and Welsh endowed schools (19th century)': https://en.wikipedia.org/wiki/List_of_English_and_Welsh_endowed_schools_(19th_century) [accessed 3 February 2023].

Wikipedia, 'List of modern universities in Europe (1801–1945)': https://en.wikipedia.org/wiki/List_of_modern_universities_in_Europe_(1801–1945) [accessed October 2023].

Wikipedia, 'List of professorships at the University of Cambridge': https://en.wikipedia.org/wiki/List_of_professorships_at_the_University_of_Cambridge [accessed 20 November 2020].

Wikipedia, 'List of universities in the United Kingdom by date of foundation': https://en.wikipedia.org/wiki/List_of_UK_universities_by_date_of_foundation [accessed 12 November 2020].

Wikipedia, 'Maltese language': https://en.wikipedia.org/wiki/Maltese_language [accessed 17 August 2023].

Wikipedia, 'Matthew Kelly (historian)': https://en.wikipedia.org/wiki/Matthew_Kelly_(historian) [accessed 24 November 2020].

Wikipedia, 'Maximilian Berlitz': https://en.wikipedia.org/wiki/Maximilian_Berlitz [accessed 2 August 2023].

Wikipedia, 'St Kilian's German School': https://en.wikipedia.org/wiki/St_Kilian%27s_German_School [accessed 7 March 2023].

Wikipedia, 'St Patrick's, Carlow College': https://en.wikipedia.org/wiki/St._Patrick%27s,_Carlow_College [accessed 19 November 2020].

Wikipedia, 'Thomas Arnold': https://en.wikipedia.org/wiki/Thomas_Arnold [accessed 15 February 2021].

Wikipedia, 'Victor Bayda': https://en.wikipedia.org/wiki/Victor_Bayda [accessed 3 October 2023].

Wikipedia, 'Victoria University of Manchester': https://en.wikipedia.org/wiki/Victoria_University_of_Manchester [accessed 22 November 2020].

Worldometer, world population data: https://www.worldometers.info/world-population/ [accessed 17 August 2023].

Archival collections consulted:

Blackrock College Archives, Blackrock College, Co Dublin
Dublin Diocesan Archives, Drumcondra, Dublin 9
Loreto Irish Province [IBVM] Archives, St Stephen's Green, Dublin 2
Mannheim Municipal Archives, Archivplatz 1, Mannheim
National Archives of Ireland, 8 Bishop St, Dublin 2

National Library of Ireland [NLI], Kildare St, Dublin 2
National University of Ireland [NUI] Archives, Merrion Square, Dublin 2
Trinity College Dublin Library, Early Printed Books Reading Room
University College Cork, Boole Library Special Collections and Archives
University of Galway, James Hardiman Library Special Collections and Archives
University College Dublin, James Joyce Library Archives and Special Collections

Index

2RN radio station 168, 211

Abbott, Revd R.K. 82
Abeltshauser, Ignatius Georg 61, 132, 137–8, 147, 151
academies, private 22, 49–50
Act of Union (1801) 6, 43
Æ (George Russell) 112
Aimers, Margaret 182
Alcalá Galiano, Antonio 84, 132–3
Alexandra College, Dublin 60, 71, 76
An Claidheamh Soluis (ACS) 106, 110, 114, 116
An Foras Teanga 207
An Gúm 196, 206
An Teanglann 203
ancient languages *see* classical languages
Anderson, Alexander 177
Anderson, Benedict 25
Anderson, Emily 170, 173–5, 177–8
Angeli, Basilio 134–8, 142, 223
Angeli v. Galbraith 134–7
Anglicanism 5–6, 8, 24, 26, 38, 69, 138–9, 190
anglicisation 25, 39, 84, 86, 88, 95, 107, 193–4, 217, 219 *see also* de-anglicisation
Anglo-Irish 41, 43
Anglo-Irish literature 219
Anglo-Irish Treaty 111, 180
anglophobia 109 *see also* de-anglicisation
Annals of the Four Masters (Annálacha Ríoghachta Éireann) 28, 98
antiquarianism 4, 66, 83, 87, 89, 91–2, 96–101, 110, 145
Antwerp 14
Arabic 143, 146, 148, 208
Aran Islands 109–10, 181
Arnold, Matthew 15, 88, 102, 107
Arnold, Thomas (father) 3, 11–12, 63–4
Arnold, Thomas (son) 125
Atkinson, Robert 74, 106–8, 131, 143, 147, 150, 188
Austen, Jane 10
Austin, Fr John 32

Ball, Mother Teresa 53–4
Ballinaboy School 48

bardic tradition 27, 86–7, 96, 119
Baretti, Giuseppe 12–13
Barr, Colin 38
Barry, Fr Nicholas 35
Bathe, Fr William 32
Beale, Dorothea 70
Beckett, J.C. 19, 206
Beckett, Samuel 188
Belfast Agreement (1998) 207
Belfast Ladies' Institute 60
Belgium, education in 116–17
Bell, Robert 67
Benedictines 50–1
Bensbach, Augustus 51, 131–2, 139, 141, 149, 153–4, 157
Bergin, Osborn 160, 164, 167
Berlitz Method 116
Bessonnet, Revd Francis 138
Best, David 216
Betagh, Fr Thomas 32
bilingualism 87, 110, 113, 115–17, 132, 219
     see also multilingualism
Blackrock College (French College, Blackrock) 51, 56–9, 62–3, 76, 103, 126, 203
     Civil Service College/Department 58–9, 61, 62
Blake Dillon, John 40, 43
Blanche, Alfred 202
Blaney, Roger 205
Blindboy Boatclub 193
Bliss, Alan 200
Blythe, Ernest 206
Boden, Lt Col. Joseph 145
Bohemian Court 33
Boole, George 132, 142–3
Bowman, John 205
Boyle, Mary (née Curran) 170, 173
Brentano (Renouf), Ludovica 125
Breton 88, 95
Breul, Karl 173
Brexit 223–4, 227
Brontë, Emily 47
Browne, Monsignor Paddy (Pádraig de Brún) 163, 201
Bruford, Walter Horace 146–7

Brumfit, Christopher 214
Burke, Edmund 67
Busby, Keith 25
Butler, Revd H.M. 64
Butler, William F.T. 139, 156–7
Butt, Isaac 135
Buttimer, Cornelius 89, 165
Byers, Margaret 60
Byrne, Peter 130

Cadic, Édouard 127–30, 132, 189
Caldwell, Sir James 26
Callan, Nicholas Joseph 64
Cambridge, University of 4, 16–17, 21, 69, 88, 147, 153 see also Oxbridge
Campbell, Flann 64–6
Carleton, William 68, 87
Carlow College see St Patrick's College, Carlow
Carroll, Lewis 47
Carson, Edward 50
Castleknock College 51
Castilian 30
Cathcart, Kevin 124
Catholic Church, in Ireland 23, 25, 39, 95, 212
Catholic clergy 27–39, 83 see also Irish language
Catholic Emancipation 39–40
Catholic liturgy 25–6, 81
Catholic missionary colleges 35–6
    All Hallows, Drumcondra 35–7
Catholic schools 51, 150
    English 50–1
Catholic University of Ireland (CUI, CU) 6–10, 20, 37, 44, 52, 58, 61, 68, 91–2, 123–30, 138, 14
    see also University College Dublin
    The Atlantis 141
    examinations 148
Catholicism 24–5, 43–4, 212
Catholics 22, 27–8
Céitinn, Seathrún (Geoffrey Keating) 28, 165
Celtic languages 83–4, 88–90, 93, 103, 119, 129, 164, 168–9, 205 see also Irish language; philology
Celtic Society 89
Champollion, Jean-François 143
Charles (Carolinum) University, Prague 33
Chauviré, Roger 188–9
Cheltenham Ladies' College 70
Christian Brothers 49, 103, 162, 204
Church of England see Anglicanism
Church of Ireland 43, 52, 99, 107, 206
    disestablishment 39, 103, 138

civil service 51, 220
    examinations 58, 60, 63, 119, 126, 149, 196, 210, 220 see also Indian Civil Service
Civil War 180
Clancy, George 128
Clarendon Commission (1864) 63–5
classical languages 4, 11, 13–16, 19–20, 55–6, 59–66, 80–1, 88, 101, 105–6, 118–19, 195 see also Greek, ancient; Latin; modern–classical languages debate
Clongowes Wood College 51, 56, 63
Coffey, Denis J. 155
Colbeck, Charles 3–4
Colum, Mary (née Maguire) 54, 148–9, 154, 182
Colum, Padraic 182
Common Market 204
community schools 204
comprehensive schools 204
Conan Doyle, Arthur 37
Connellan, Owen 83–4, 88, 92, 98–9, 101
Conolly, Lady Louisa 23
Convent of Mercy, Ardee 72
convent schools 51–5, 60, 69–74, 78, 104
Cooke, W.C. 134
Coolahan, John 202
Copyright Act (1709) 85
Corish, Patrick 34, 161
Council of Trent (1564) 27
Counter-Reformation 4, 27–30, 39, 223
Crolly, Archbishop William 64
Cruise O'Brien, Máire 201
Cullen, Louis 88
Cullen, Cardinal Paul 20, 37–8, 52, 72, 124–6, 140–1
cultural nationalism 39–42, 105, 107–8, 159
    see also nationalism
Cumann na mBan 111
Cunningham, Elizabeth Margaret (Margery) 112

Daly, Mary 85
Davis, Thomas 39, 41, 68–9
Dawe, Gerald 207
de-anglicisation 93, 102, 105, 108–10, 112, 169, 179, 196 see also anglicisation; anglophobia
de Leusse, Guy 126
de Mailly, Héloïse 55
de Mare, C. 47
de Mauro, Tullio 197
de Valera, Éamon 103, 195, 204–5
de Vaulchier, Louis 125
de Véricour, Louis-Raymond 131–2, 137, 139–43, 147, 149, 157, 189, 223

Deane, Seamus 219
Degani, Maria 170, 173, 178–9
Delaney, Edward 41
Delany, Fr William 63
D'Esca, Antoine 18, 132
Dillon, Eilís 47
Dillon, John 65, 67–8, 213
Dillon, Myles 200
Dineen, Patrick 163
Ditter, Mlle 48
Doff, Sabine 13
Dominicans 52–3, 55, 76, 206
Donovan, Mary Josephine 170
Doolin, William 154–5
Douai Bible 29, 95
Dowling, P.J. 66
Doyle, Aidan 97–8, 104, 114, 193, 198
Doyle, James Warren 34, 36–7
Drennan, William 100
Dublin University *see* Trinity College Dublin
Dublin University Commission 136
Duby, Georges 227
Duffy, Eamon 29
Duffy, James 39
Duke family, Ballymote, County Sligo 48
Dundalk Classical and Mercantile Academy 64, 96
Durham University 17

East India Company 65, 145
Eco, Umberto 216
Edgeworth, Richard Lovell 22
Education Act (1831) 36–7
Edwards, Hilton 188
elementary education 25, 37, 49, 72, 84, 106
    see also hedge schools; national schools;
    primary schools
Eliot, George 14–15, 17, 43
Elizabeth I, Queen 27
Elizabeth II, Queen 193
Ellmann, Richard 128
emigration 20–1, 72, 85–6, 159, 199, 204, 211, 224
Emmet, Robert 87
English College, Douai 50
English language 10–11, 36, 40, 91, 102, 107, 203, 216
    global 5, 74, 154, 190, 194, 197–8, 200, 217–20, 224
    in Ireland 24–6, 84–8, 94–6, 100–1, 109–10, 116, 215
    at universities 21, 88
English literature 16, 88
English public schools 62–4, 80, 166
English universities 10, 15–18, 84
Enright, Anne 201

Ériu, 164
Eton College 62–4
European Economic Community 215
European Union 215–17
    official languages 216, 223–4
    Year of Languages (2001) 217
evangelism 25, 83, 94–5
examination boards 52
examinations 16, 69, 198–9, 202
    university 152 *see also* oral examinations;
    and specific universities

Fahey, Tony 104
Fahy, Fr Anthony 35
Fanning, Ronan 195
Färber, Beatrix 183
Farragher, S.P. 47
Fianna Fáil 205
Fischer, Joachim 171
Fitzgerald, Andrew 34
FitzGerald, Lady Emily 23
FitzGerald, Garret 219
Flanagan, Thomas 67
Fleischmann, Aloys 39, 174
Foras na Gaeilge 207
Foster, Roy 109
Foxcroft School, Portarlington 56
Frädersdorff, Johann Wilhelm 131–2, 139, 143
Franco-German War (1870–1) 126
Freeman's Journal 144
French College, Blackrock *see* Blackrock College
French education system 64
French language 3, 16–19, 22–3, 30, 33–4, 47, 55–9, 71, 189, 195, 197, 202–3, 216, 220, 226 *see also* modern languages
French-language books 22
French literature 40, 88, 149, 203
French Protestant School for Girls, Bray 10, 55
French religious congregations 52–4, 60, 81
French Revolution 34, 43, 50, 149
Freund, Max 42, 186
Friel, Brian 24
Frings, Matthias Joseph 51, 131–2, 139, 141, 143, 149, 151
Frost, Ann 21, 133–4
Fry Commission (1906–7) 77, 181

Gael Linn 210
Gaelic Athletic Association 106
Gaelic Journal (*Irisleabhar na Gaedhilge*) 104
Gaelic League 4, 25, 41, 93, 101, 102–20, 129, 159–69, 179, 181, 194–8, 203, 205–6
Gaelic revival 28, 112, 158–68, 179–80, 183, 194–200

Gaelic Society of Ireland 89
Gaelic Union 144, 158
Gaeltacht 109–10, 116, 166, 199, 206, 208, 210–11, 216
Gaidoz, Henri 91, 93
Galbraith, Joseph Allen 134–8
Gavan Duffy, Louise 118
Geisler, Charles (Karl) 131–2, 137–9, 143–4, 149–50, 157, 189
German immigrants, in Manchester 21
German language 17–18, 21–2, 42, 69, 71, 101, 146–7, 154, 189, 201, 203, 214, 219, 226 *see also* modern languages
German Romantics 39–40
German schools 14, 113, 115
German universities 17, 89
Giraldus Cambrensis 28
girls' education 51–5, 59–60, 69–74, 104, 116
    in England 60, 69–70
Gladstone, William 11
Glasgow, University of 88
Good Friday agreement 207
Goodford, Revd C.O. 65
Gormanston College, Co. Meath 203
Gouin, François 116
Graham, Sir James 19
grammar 11, 13–15, 29, 58, 83, 88, 114–15, 118, 149, 189, 209, 214
grammar schools 47, 63
grand tour 23, 100, 150
Great Famine 20–1, 25, 85, 159
Greek, ancient 19–20, 55, 63, 145, 163 *see also* classical languages
Greene, David 143
Greer, Germaine 73–4
Gregory, Lady Augusta 113

Haliday, William 97
Halpin, Attracta 217
Hamilton, Revd Thomas 160
Hattersley, Roy 227
Haughton, Samuel 134–5
Hayden, Mary 170, 181
Hayes, Edmund 123, 135–6
Hayes, Michael 196
Heaney, Seamus 204, 206
Hebrew 17, 20, 62, 68–9, 71, 96, 145, 148, 150
hedge schools 26, 48–9, 66–9, 80, 85
Hélias, Pierre-Jakez 25
Hely-Hutchinson, John 18
Henebry, Revd Richard 165–6
Henry, Robert Mitchell 206
Hofwyl, Switzerland 142
Hogan, Fr Edmund 160
Hogan, J.J. 174, 176

Hogan, Fr John Francis 157
Holmes, George 67
Holy Ghost Fathers (Spiritans) 51, 56, 203
Home Rule 105, 112, 187
Home Rule Party 103
Hopkins, Gerard Manley 127
Huguenots 22, 50, 139
Hyde, Douglas 49, 93, 101, 102, 104–8, 110, 112–13, 120, 167, 169, 173, 183, 199, 211

Iberno-Celtic Society 89
Identity and Language (Northern Ireland) Act (2022) 207
immigration 21, 194, 211
imperialism 5, 11, 25, 36, 40, 43, 50–1, 66, 129, 145–6, 188, 223
Index of Prohibited Books 140–1
Indian Civil Service examinations 61, 65, 136, 145–6, 150, 215, 222, 226
Indo-European languages 89–91, 93, 144–5
Ingram, John Kells 134–5
Institute for Research in English Teaching (IRET) 200–1
institutes of technology 204, 215
interlanguage 209
Intermediate Certificate Act (1878) 119
Intermediate (Certificate) examination 55, 58–60, 69–71, 83, 103–4, 108, 214
Intermediate Education, Vice-Regal Inquiry into (1899) 106
Intermediate Education (Ireland) Act (1878) 49, 52, 54, 59–60, 170
intermediate schools 56, 103
International Phonetic Association 116
Investment in Education (1965) 65, 204
Irish-Americans 159
Irish Archaeological Society 89
Irish Archaeological and Celtic Society 89
Irish Association of Women Graduates and Candidate Graduates (IAWGCG) 181
Irish colleges 114
    continental 4 27–34
Irish Constitution 196
Irish Free State 168
Irish language 24–5, 41, 94–101, 195, 205, 220, 222 *see also* Celtic languages; language teaching methodologies; Middle Irish; Old Irish
    Caighdeán Oifigiúil (Official Standard) 196, 200
    and the clergy 29, 83, 94–5, 100, 107
    contemporary 4, 92–4, 160, 164, 166–7
    evening classes 108
    grammars 96–101, 104–5, 165, 168, 196
    in Northern Ireland 205–9

policies 210
politicisation 108
revival 196–201, 225
in schools 103–8
spoken 164, 166–7, 169, 197–8, 207, 221
teacher training 103, 108, 114–15, 119, 196
in universities 83–9, 159–69, 189, 199
variations in 198–200, 208
Irish literature 86–7
Irish-medium education 106, 113, 196–7, 206–7, 211
Irish Papal Brigade 43
Irish placenames 160, 196
Irish Society for Promoting the Education of the Native Irish 95–6
Irish studies 108, 184, 195, 225
Irish Theatre, Dublin 111
Irish universities, generally 18–23
Irish Universities Act (1908) 77, 181
Irish Universities Act (1997) 220
Irisleabhar na Gaedhilge (*Gaelic Journal*) 104, 158
Italian 12, 18, 36, 38, 40–1, 71, 100, 136, 150, 161, 197 *see also* modern languages
Italian unification 42–3, 157

Jellicoe, Anne 60
Jesuits 7–9, 29, 31–3, 50–1, 63, 75, 95, 124, 127, 158, 160, 175
Jones, Sir William 145
Joyce, James 109–10, 128
Joynt, Maud 183

Kane, Sir Robert 135
Kavanagh, Rose 181
Keating, Geoffrey (Seathrún Céitinn) 28, 165
Kelly, James 87
Kelly, Matthew 34
Kennedy, Máire 22–3
Kiberd, Declan 198–200
King's College London 6, 16, 19, 21, 84, 88, 138–40
Kirby, Tobias 38
Kirwan, Fr James 89
Kirwan, Richard 33
Knott, Eleanor 183
Kuper, Simon 193
kymograph 152
Ladies' Collegiate School (Victoria College), Belfast 60
land acts 103

Land League 103, 159
land redistribution 103
language diversity 225–6

language education, post-independence 193–221
Language Freedom Movement 199
language laboratories 203
language teaching/learning methodologies 32, 87–8, 92, 104, 114–19, 197–8, 203, 209–20
academic 147–55, 165–6
in Britain 203–4
Common European Framework of Reference 216
direct method (*modh díreach*) 115–18, 164, 198
Languages Connect strategy (2017) 217
languages other than English (LOTES) 226
Lanigan, Revd John 36
Larcom, Thomas 89
Latin 13–15, 17, 22, 25–6, 28–30, 32, 60, 66–71, 90, 115, 143, 145, 150, 161, 163, 194, 212–15, 217, 219, 226 *see also* classical languages
ecclesiastical 26, 81
Latin schools 13, 47, 68
le Carré, John 203–4, 222
Leader, The 42
Leathes, Stanley 18
Leathes Committee/Report on Modern Languages (1918) 18, 80, 154, 187, 193, 201, 203, 208, 220
Leaving Certificate 196, 199, 201–2, 208, 210, 214, 220
Lee, J.J. 193, 218
Leeds, University of 18
Lehmacher, Gustav 200
Leman, Fr Jules 56, 61, 126
Lemass, Seán 204
Leslie, Shane 179
Libermann, Fr Francis 126
linguistics 199, 209–10, 223 *see also* sociolinguistics
applied 115, 194, 201, 209, 220
comparative 89, 143, 145–6
descriptive/synchronic 209
historical 143, 146
literacy 32, 47, 72–3, 84–8, 95, 181, 197, 202, 210, 214
Liverpool, University of 18
Locke, John 22
London, University of 5–6, 19, 75
Longfellow, Henry F. 142
Loreto Abbey, Rathfarnham 53
Loreto order 52, 55, 76–7
Lottner, Carl Friedrich 146
Louvain 27–8, 32, 34
Lowe, Robert 72, 151
Lucena, Revd Lorenzo 133

Lyndsay, Bridget (née Danaher) 170
Lyons, F.S.L. 102

MacAdam, Robert 96
McAleese, Mary 222
Macaulay Report (1854) 65, 123, 145–6
McCallum, Elsie 171
McCarthy, Denis 75
McCartney, Donal 184
Mac Curtain, Margaret 111–12
MacDonagh, Thomas 111
McDowell, R.B. 69, 135, 146
McGavock, Máirín 111
MacHale, Archbishop John 34, 37, 39
McLelland, Nicola 3, 209
Mac Liammóir, Micheál 188
McManus, Antonia 66, 85
Mac Mathúna, Liam 86, 113
Mac Murchaidh, Ciarán 38
MacNeill, Eoin 103, 105, 108, 160, 164, 195
Mac Réamoinn, Seán 188
McWeeney, Edmond J. 155
Macken, Mary (née Bowler) 77–8, 156,
    172–6, 179, 183
Maffei, Andrea 42
Maguire, Mary see Colum, Mary
Mahaffy, John Pentland 49, 69, 72, 102,
    106–8, 112–13, 132
Mahony, Cornelius 83–4, 89
Manchester, Victoria University of 21
Manchester Grammar School 21
Marani, Augusto Cesare 125, 134, 138, 145–6,
    150
Marcel, Claude 50
Marists 48, 52
Martello towers 43
Martin, Gregory 29–30
Martyn, Edward 111
Maxwell, Constantia 171
Maynooth see Royal College of St Patrick,
    Maynooth
Mazzini, Giuseppe 40–1, 133
medieval period 13, 17, 21, 25, 28, 80, 86–7,
    90, 93, 107
Meissner, Albert Ludwig 131–2, 137, 139,
    143, 147, 150–2
Mercier, Vivian 87
Meyer, Kuno 93, 164
Middle Irish 89, 144, 164–5
military cadetship examinations 60–1
Millett, Benignus 28–9
Milligan, Alice 114
missionary colleges see Catholic missionary
    colleges
modern–classical languages debate 11–12,
    22–3, 44, 82, 212–14

in England and Ireland 62–9, 80
Modern Language Teachers' Association
    (MLTA) 16, 214
modern languages 3–5, 7, 10, 16–23, 24,
    35, 39–40, 51–5, 59–74, 77–81, 83–5,
    109, 123–55, 156–9, 170–89, 193,
    201–4, 207, 216, 220–3 see also language
    teaching/learning methodologies
marketplace 12–15, 33
monastic 12–15, 33, 225
in Northern Ireland 208–9
policies on 201
rationale for learning 10–15, 42
monasticism 13–14, 25, 90, 93, 219
Monck Mason, Henry Joseph 82, 95–6
Montesquieu 30
Moody, T.W. 19, 41, 205–6
Moore, Thomas 41–2
Moran, D.P. 42
Moriarty, L.M. 102, 115
Morrissey, Thomas 32
Mulally, Teresa 73
Mulcaile, Fr James Philip 32, 73
Müller, Max 123, 143, 158
Müller-Lisowski, Käte 183
multilingualism 25, 35–7, 43, 90, 111, 145,
    215–19 see also bilingualism
Murphy, James E. 169
Murphy, John A. 175

Nagle, Nano 49
Napoleon Bonaparte 43
Nation, The 40–1, 43, 69
national institutes of higher education 204–5
National Literary Society 105
national schools 25, 49, 66, 68, 72, 84–5, 94,
    103–4, 106, 110, 113–14, 119, 196–7
National University of Ireland (NUI) 7, 77,
    164, 168–70, 171–2, 179, 185, 190, 212
    matriculation 65, 108, 113, 119, 162,
    194–6, 217, 220
nationalism 40–1, 43, 112, 161 see also cultural
    nationalism
Neilson, Revd William 64, 82, 96–100, 105
New York 35, 182
Newman, Cardinal John Henry 7–8, 10, 20,
    37, 44, 52, 68, 75, 91, 124, 138, 140–1
Nic Congáil, Ríona 180–1
Nic Dhonnchadha, Aoibheann 183
Nolan, Willie 85
Northcote-Trevelyan Report (1854) 60
Northern Ireland 169, 194, 205–9, 212, 221

O'Beirne Crowe, John 82, 92–3
Ó Briain, Liam 187–8, 196, 201
O'Brien, Paul 83, 98

Ó Buachalla, Séamas 110, 210
O'Carroll, Fr John James 158–9
O'Casey, Seán 162
Ó Ciosáin, Niall 39
Ó Cléirigh, Mícheál 28
Ó Coileáin, Seán 32
Ó Conaire, Pádraic 166
O'Connell, Daniel 50, 85
O'Connell, Revd Frederick William
        (Feardorcha Ó Conaill) 167–9, 205,
        217–18
O'Connor, Anne 38–40
O'Connor, Anne V. 52–3
O'Connor, Thomas 34
Ó Corráin, Ailbhe 27
O'Curry, Eugene 90–2
Ó Cuiv, Brian 94, 105–6
O'Daly, Daniel 27
O'Daly, Revd Richard 115
O'Donnell, Frank Hugh 73
Ó Donnchadha, Tadhg ('Torna') 166
O'Donovan, John 83, 85, 90–2, 98–9
O'Dwyer, Bishop Edward 8–9
O'Faolain, Sean 174
O'Farrelly, Agnes (Úna Ní Fhaircheallaigh)
        110, 112, 170, 173, 175, 180–2, 190,
        198
Ó Fiaich, Tomás 206
O'Flaherty, Kathleen 140, 202
O'Growney, Eugene (Eoghan) 104, 130, 161,
        175
Ó hEódhasa, Giolla Brighde 27
Ó hÓgartaigh, Margaret 74
Ó hUallacháin, Colmán 203
O'Hickey, Fr Michael 160–2, 223
O'Higgins, Laurie 66
O'Kelly, Mary Kate see Ryan (O'Kelly), Mary
        Kate
O'Kelly, Seán T. 112–13, 180
O'Kelly, Seumas 128
Old Irish 89–94, 99, 118–19, 146–7, 160–1,
        164–5, 167, 225
O'Leary, Peter (Peadar Ó Laoghaire) 163, 168
O'Leary, Philip 166
O'Looney, Brian 160
Ó Madagáin, Breandán 83, 89
O'Mahony, Bishop Timothy 126
Ó Máille, Peaitsín Pheige 49
Ó Máille, Tomás 49, 164, 167
Ó Máille family, Connemara 49
O'Meara, John 197, 204, 213
Ó Neachtain, Fr Peadar 31–2
Ó Neachtain, Tadhg 31–2
Ó Neachtains 86
O'Neill, Ciaran 50–1, 53, 73
O'Neill, Rosaleen 144, 151, 153, 177, 182

O'Rahilly, Thomas F. 169
oral examinations 152–3, 198–9, 202–4, 215
Ordnance Survey 25, 91
O'Ryan, Owen 131, 139, 141, 150–1, 156–7
O'Shea Farren, Linda 195
Ó Siadhail, Micheál 200
Ossianic Society 89
O'Toole, Fr Hugh 61–2
Ó Tuathaigh, Gearóid 156, 205
Owens College Manchester 21
Oxbridge 5, 16–18, 21, 52, 69, 80–1, 152, 212
    scholarships 63
    women's colleges 55, 75
Oxford, University of 16–17, 20–1, 69, 84

Palmer, Harold 200
Panizzi, Antonio 135
Parkes, Susan 222
Parnell, Charles Stewart 105
partition 193, 205–6, 208
Passy, Paul 116
Pearse, Patrick 106, 108, 110, 116–18, 129,
        162, 165–6
Peel, Sir Robert 6, 66
penal laws 4, 27, 32–3, 48, 77, 195
    relaxation of 33–4, 50
Perry, Janet Hunter 182
Petrarch 40
Petrie, George 91
Phillips, Patricia 70
philology 15, 39, 88–9, 91, 101, 102, 141, 144,
        147–8, 151, 164, 175, 178, 203–4, 214,
        220, 223
    Celtic 89–93, 119, 143–4, 146, 164–5,
        167–8
    comparative 5, 17, 21, 90, 93, 123, 146,
        149
phonetics 115–16, 152, 164, 177, 187, 202,
        220
Pius X, Pope 112–13
Plumb, J.H. 43
Plunkett, Joseph 48, 110–11, 128
Plunkett, Oliver 30
Plunkett, Bishop Patrick Joseph 33
Plunkett family 48
Polin, Abbé Georges 59, 126–7, 132
Portarlington, County Offaly 22
Portarlington School 50
Portora Royal School, Enniskillen 56
Portuguese 16, 18, 36, 42
Potter, Matthew 43
Powis Commission 72
Prendergast, Thomas 145
Presbyterianism 85, 89, 100, 205
Presentation Sisters 49, 73

primary schools 114, 225 *see also* elementary education; national schools
printing 86–8, 91
pronunciation 30, 34, 134, 151–2, 197–8
Propaganda Fide, College of 37–8
Protestantism/Protestants 6, 29, 43–4, 50–1, 54–5, 60, 64–5, 71, 86, 95, 138, 141–2, 160, 201, 205, 212 *see also* Church of Ireland; reformed churches
Pye, Michael 14

Queen's College Belfast 9, 132, 160, 168, 171, 221
    Gaelic Society 160
Queen's College Cork 9, 139–41, 156, 160
Queen's College Galway 10, 61, 138, 152–3, 157
Queen's Colleges 5–6, 8–9, 19–23, 51–2, 75, 80, 83–5, 88–9, 131, 139, 141, 146, 149, 154
Queen's Colleges Board 119
Queen's Colleges Commission (1857–8) 51, 88, 151
Queen's University Belfast (QUB) 8, 42, 168, 185–6, 190, 205, 208, 212

Radice, Evasio Antonio 133, 138, 153
radio 168–9, 207, 211
Raftery, Deirdre 52–3
Raidió Fáilte 207
railways 16, 84, 218
Raraty, M.M. 61, 147
Reffé, Fr Édouard 61
Reformation 13, 24, 30, 86
reformed churches 25–6, 83, 95
refugees 18, 22, 34, 126, 132–3, 138, 176, 211
Relief Acts 49
Renouf, Ludovica (née Brentano) 125
Renouf, Peter Le Page 124–5, 132, 141, 143, 150
research 17, 21, 89–90, 141–5, 164, 174–6, 184, 201, 203, 209, 219–20, 223
Rigal, Jean-Louis 201
Rippmann (Ripman), Walter 116
Risorgimento 42–3, 157
Robertson, J.B. 125
Robertson Commission (1901–3) 8, 77, 181
Robinson, Mary 104
Roche, James 33
Ross, Revd Alexander 67
Royal Academical Institution, Belfast 89, 100
Royal College of St Patrick, Maynooth (Maynooth College) 6, 8, 34, 43, 64, 83, 94, 161–3, 201
    Cuallacht Chuilm Cille (League of St Columba) 161

Royal Free Schools, Ulster 64
Royal Irish Academy (RIA) 33, 89, 164
Royal Military Academy, Woolwich 60–1
Royal Society of Antiquaries of Ireland 89
Royal University of Ireland (RUI) 4, 7–8, 20, .52, 55, 59–61, 70–1, 74–6, 150, 156–8, 160, 163, 170–1, 195, 222
    matriculation 119
    University College 124
Rudmose-Brown, Thomas Brown 187–8
Rugby School 63–4
Rulhière, Claude Carloman de 30
Russell, George (Æ) 112
Russian Revolution 42
Ryan, Agnes 111
Ryan, Mary 170, 172–3, 175, 190
Ryan (O'Kelly), Mary Kate (Cáit Bean Uí Cheallaigh) 77–8, 170, 172–5, 179–80, 190
Ryan sisters, Tomcoole, Wexford 78–81, 111

St Alphonsus Liguori 39
St Andrews, University of 10–11, 16
St Angela's College, Cork 76
St Columba's College, Stackallan 56, 99, 103
St Enda's school 111, 117–18
St Joseph of Cluny, Sisters of 52
St Kieran's College, Kilkenny 49, 55–6
St Louis, Sisters of 52, 103
St Louis school, Monaghan 53–5, 70
St Malachy's College Belfast 64
St Mary's Dominican College, Dublin 76, 111–12
St Mary's University College Belfast 207
St Patrick's College, Carlow 34, 38
St Patrick's College, Drumcondra 103
Sacred Heart Convent, Dublin 52, 71
Sagarra, Eda 176, 204
Said, Edward 144
Salvadori, Corinna 136, 150
Sanskrit 143–6, 148, 150
Saul's Court school, Dublin 32
Savory, Douglas Lloyd 187
School of Irish Learning, Dublin 164
Schürr, Abbé Félix 36, 125–6, 132
Scoil Bhríde, Dublin 118
Scoil Íde, Ranelagh 118
Scott, William Alphonsus 130
Scottish universities 15–19
Second Vatican Council 212
Selss, Albert Maximilian 61, 74, 131–2, 143
Series Method 116
Sharkey, James 206
Shea, Margaret (née Cooke) 170, 173
Sheehan, Michael 163
Sherlock, Fr Paul 32

Siegfried, Rudolf Thomas 146
Sigerson, Hester 181
Sisters of Mercy 73
Smith, William 207–8
Smith (MacGowan), Jacobus 33
social class 4, 12, 71–2, 74, 80–1, 84
sociolinguistics 26, 209 *see also* linguistics
Society for the Preservation of the Irish
    Language (SPIL) 103, 106, 159–60
Sorbonne 30, 88
Spanish language 18, 30, 32, 35, 42, 133–4,
    150–1, 220, 224 *see also* modern
    languages
Spellissy, Fr Denis 35
Spiritans *see* Holy Ghost Fathers
spoken language 12–15, 22–3, 26, 33, 53, 58,
    98, 100–2, 106–7, 114–16, 119–20,
    151–5, 172, 193, 198, 203–5, 208, 212,
    216 *see also* Irish language
Stanford, W.B. 212–13
Starkie, Walter 134
Starkie, William Joseph Myles, 106
Staunton, Henry 34
Steinberger, Cécile 182
Steinberger, Valentine 42, 131–2, 138, 143,
    150–2, 177, 182
Stern, Ludwig 93
Stokes, Whitley 94, 146
Strachan, John 164
Strasbourg Oaths (842) 226
Stray, Christopher 66
Sunday schools 72
Sutherland, Peter 215
Sweet, Henry 164
Swertz, Hans Conrad 39
Swertz, Waltraut ('Wally') 170
Synge, J.M. 181
Synod of Thurles (1850) 8, 140

Taunton Commission (1864–8) 69–70
Taylor, J.B. 38
Taylor, Sir Robert 16
teacher training 75, 79, 184, 196 *see also*
    Irish language; language teaching
    methodologies
teachers, travelling 114
Téarmaí Dlí 196
technological universities 215
Tod, Isabella 60
Toynbee, Arnold 171
translation 11, 13–14, 39–42, 58, 86–93, 119,
    148–9, 151–4, 163, 177–8, 182–4, 196,
    216, 222, 225–6
    of religious texts 29–30, 83, 95–6, 168,
    212
transport, international 218

Trend, J.B. 133–4
Trevor-Roper, Hugh 24
Tridentine English College, Douai 29
Trinity College Dublin (Dublin University)
    (TCD, DU) 6, 8, 18, 21, 27, 52, 55,
    60–1, 68–9, 74–6, 83, 88, 107, 131,
    143, 146–7, 150, 169, 171, 185–6, 190,
    212–13
    Board 134–7
    Cumann Gaelach 160
    examinations 69
    Trinity Hall 112
Tullabeg College 51, 63
Tully, James 83
tutors, private 49–50

Uí Chionna, Jackie 177
Ulster Gaelic Society 96
Ulster University 208–9
'Uncle Remus' 181
United Irishmen 87, 100
university chairs 16–18
University College Blackrock 59
University College Cork (UCC) 134, 165–6,
    174–5, 217
University College Dublin (UCD) 7–8, 20,
    77, 167, 170
University College Galway (UCG) 167, 170
University College London (UCL) 5–6, 21, 84
University Education (Ireland) Act (1879) 60
university fellows, religious affiliation 137–41
university matriculation 65, 69, 71 *see also*
    National University of Ireland; Royal
    University of Ireland
Ursuline schools 53
Ursulines 55
Ussher, James 29

Vice-Regal Inquiry into Intermediate
    Education (1899) 106
Victoria College (Ladies' Collegiate School),
    Belfast 60, 71, 76
Viëtor, Wilhelm 115
Vieyra, Antonio 18, 143
Vincentians 51
Virgil 68
von Fellenberg, Philipp Emmanuel 142
von Siebold, Agathe 48

Walsh, John 212
Walsh, Archbishop William 55, 195
Ware, James 29
Waterhouse, Gilbert 186, 193
Webb, D.A. 69, 135, 146
Weekly Freeman, 'Irish Fireside Club' 180–1
Welsh language 88, 107, 207

Whelan, Fr Charles (Maurice) 35–6
Whelan, Kevin 24
White, Stephen 28
White Paper on the Restoration of the Irish
    Language (1965) 210
Whitaker, T.K. 204, 225
Wilde, Oscar 56
Williams, Robert Alan 186
Wilson, Horace 145
Windich, Ernst 164
women academics 156, 170–85
women graduates 74
women students 4, 10–12, 14–15, 21, 52, 59,
    62, 70, 74–80, 184–5, 222 *see also* girls'
    education
        restrictions 75–6

travel abroad 77–80, 172
women's colleges 55, 111, 172
Woodlock, Bishop Bartholomew 37, 58, 127
World War I 18, 42, 169, 171, 186
World War II 187–8, 194, 209, 217
Wright, William 146
written language 12–13
Wulff, Winifred 183–4
Wyse, Thomas 63
Wyse Power, Áine (Neans/Nancy) 182–3

Yeats, W.B. 112–13
Young Ireland 39–42, 69

Zeuss, Johann Kaspar 90
Zimmer, Heinrich 164